AdI
Annali d'Italianistica
The University of North Carolina at Chapel Hill
Chapel Hill, NC 27599-3170
http://www.ibiblio.org/annali   e-mail: annali@unc.edu

Annali d'italianistica, Inc., was founded at the University of Notre Dame in 1983. In 1989 it moved to the Department of Romance Studies at the University of North Carolina at Chapel Hill.

FOUNDER & EDITOR IN CHIEF
Dino S. Cervigni
The University of North Carolina at Chapel Hill, Professor Emeritus
ASSOCIATE EDITOR
Anne Tordi, PhD, *The University of North Carolina at Chapel Hill*
CO-EDITORS
Norma Bouchard, *San Diego State University*
Alessandro Carrera, *University of Houston*
Jo Ann Cavallo, *Columbia University*
Carmine Di Biase, *Jacksonville University*
Valerio Ferme, *University of Colorado at Boulder*
Massimo Lollini, *Oregon University*
Dennis Looney, *The University of Pittsburgh*
Carlo Lottieri, *Università degli Studi di Siena*
Federico Luisetti, *The University of North Carolina at Chapel Hill*
Gaetana Marrone, *Princeton University*
Cristina Mazzoni, *The University of Vermont*
Luca Somigli, *The University of Toronto*
John Welle, *The University of Notre Dame*

© 2016 by Annali d'Italianistica, Inc.
ISSN 0741-7527
ISBN-13: 978-0692794135
ISBN-10: 0692794131

ADVISORY BOARD

Andrea Battistini, *Università degli Studi di Bologna*
Francesco Bruni, *Università di Venezia*
Giuseppe A. Camerino, *Università del Salento*
Paolo Cherchi, *University of Chicago*
Louise George Clubb, *University of California, Berkeley*
Vincenzo De Caprio, *Università della Tuscia, Viterbo*
Giulio Ferroni, *Università della Sapienza, Roma*
Valeria Finucci, *Duke University*
John Gatt-Rutter, *La Trobe University (Melbourne)*
Walter Geerts, *Universiteit Antwerpen*
Antonio Lucio Giannone, *Università del Salento*
Willi Hirdt, *Universität Bonn*
Christopher Kleinhenz, *University of Wisconsin, Madison*
Edoardo A. Lèbano, *Indiana University*
Alfredo Luzi, *Università di Macerata*
Albert N. Mancini, *The Ohio State University*
Olimpia Pelosi, *SUNY-Albany*
Ennio Rao, *The University of North Carolina, Chapel Hill*
Paolo Valesio, *Columbia University*
Rebecca West, *The University of Chicago*
Antonio Vitti, *Indiana University, Bloomington*

Annali d'Italianistica
Volumes 1-21 are available for free consultation:
www.archive.org/details/annaliditalianis212003univ

Editorial Policy
Annali d'Italianistica seeks to promote the study of Italian literature in its cultural context, to foster scholarly excellence, and to select topics of interest to a large number of Italianists. Monographic in nature, the journal is receptive to a variety of topics, critical approaches, and theoretical perspectives. Each year's topic is announced ahead of time, and contributions are welcome. The journal is published in the fall of each year. Manuscripts should be submitted electronically as attachments in Word. Authors should follow the MLA style for articles in English; articles in Italian should conform to the *AdI* editorial style. Visit the journal's website (www.ibiblio.org/annali) for further information. For all communications concerning contributions, address the Editor, *Annali d'Italianistica*, The University of North Carolina at Chapel Hill, Chapel Hill, NC 27599-3170, or email: annali@unc.edu.

Notes & Reviews
This section occasionally publishes essays and review articles on topics treated in previous volumes of *Annali d'Italianistica*.

Italian Bookshelf
Italian Bookshelf is edited by Dino S. Cervigni and Anne Tordi. The purpose of *Italian Bookshelf* is to identify, review, and bring to the attention of Italianists recent studies on Italian literature and culture. *Italian Bookshelf* covers the entire history of Italian literature and reviews books exclusively on the basis of their scholarly worth. To this purpose, junior and senior colleagues will be invited to collaborate without any consideration to academic affiliation and with an open attitude toward critical approaches. Contributions to this section are solicited. Scholars who intend to contribute are encouraged to contact the editors. Book reviews, to be submitted electronically, should be sent to the Editor. For inquiries, post <annali@unc.edu>.

The Journal's Website: www.ibiblio.org/annali
The tables of contents of all issues are available online. As of volume 16 (1998), each issue's introductory essay and all book reviews are available online with their full texts. As of the 2008 issue, book reviews are published exclusively online.

The New Italy and the Jews:
From Massimo D'Azeglio to Primo Levi

L. Scott Lerner and Jonathan Druker
Guest Editors

On the eve of the Revolution of 1848, Massimo D'Azeglio, calling on Pope Pius IX to abolish the Jewish ghetto of Rome and emancipate the Jews, explicitly connected the status of Italian Jewry to the project of Italian unification and nationhood: "The cause of Jewish regeneration," he declared, was "strictly united with that of Italian Regeneration." D'Azeglio's dual campaign on behalf of Italian Jewry and Italian unification stands as the point of departure for this volume.

Did the project of Italian nationhood depend on a symbolic union of Italian Jews, who sought full participation in the new state, with those non-Jewish Italians who viewed the abolition of the ghettos as a *sine qua non* of the "New Italy"? In other words, was modern Italy founded on a true universality — which was only made meaningful by embracing the Jews as the bearers of difference? Or was it founded on difference *and* exclusion? Subsequently, did the New Italy of the Risorgimento and Unification betray itself when it gave way to Fascism, the Lateran Pacts, the Racial Laws and the roundups? Or did the liberal patriotism of the earlier period evolve inexorably into these forms?

Among historians, this question has recently given rise to sharply divergent interpretations. We welcome contributions that stake out a position in this debate by exploring the relationship between the new state and its Jews. Essays could focus either on the significance of Jews in relation to the evolution of Italian national identity or on Jewish experience per se. The conceptual point of arrival for the volume is the placement of an excerpt from Primo Levi's essay, "La ricerca delle radici," on the *maturità* exam in 2010. Has Levi's unique moral voice helped to return Italy to the (secular) project of the liberal state? One image for consideration could be that of Levi and recent popes as separate, though perhaps no longer antagonistic voices, of the conscience of the nation. In this section, "Levi" will serve as an organizing principle but will allow for a broad range of essays on the post-war state in relation to Italian Jews, for not all of the essays would address Levi or his work centrally.

Between these two poles, D'Azeglio and Levi, the volume will examine the itinerary of union and disunion between modern Italy and its Jews with a focus on self-understanding.

We aim to strike a balance between contributions in history and literary/cultural studies. Contributions should be between 6,000 and 9,000 words and may be written in English or Italian. They should be conceived for inclusion in one of the following sections:

    I. *Amor di patria,* 1846-1890
    II. Fulfillment or Betrayal? 1890-1945
    III. Primo Levi Comes Home, 1945-2010

Deadline for submission: September 1, 2017.

Scholars are encouraged to contact the guest editors to express interest in contributing to the volume and to discuss contributions in advance.

    Scott Lerner: slerner@fandm.edu
    Jonathan Druker: j.druker@ilstu.edu

ANNALI D'ITALIANISTICA
volume 34   year 2016

Speaking Truth to Power from Medieval to Modern Italy

Guest Editors:
Jo Ann Cavallo and Carlo Lottieri

---

17   Jo Ann Cavallo and Carlo Lottieri,
Introduction: Speaking Truth to Power from Medieval to Modern Italy

1. The Three Florentine Crowns Politicized

31   **Zane D. R. Mackin**, *Dante, the Rhetoric of Crisis, and Vigilante Preaching*

57   **Steven Baker**, *Writing the Revolution: Petrarch and the Tribunate of Cola di Rienzo*

79   **Karina F. Attar**, *Speaking Truth to Powerful Friends and Foes: Genoese Merchants and the Mamluks in* Decameron *2.9*

2. Fifteenth-Century Humanists and their Discontents

97   **Alessandra Mantovani**, Speculum veritatis: *Giovanni Garzoni e la tradizione dell'*institutio principis *nella Bologna dei Bentivoglio*

121   **Matteo Bosisio**, *"Fuggendo da lui fuggo la morte": libertà, vendetta, polemica anti-cortigiana nella* Panfila *di Antonio Cammelli*

3. Performative Personas across Genres in Renaissance Italy

141   **Jo Ann Cavallo**, *Contracts, Surveillance, and Censure of State Power in Arienti's* Triunfo da Camarino *novella (*Le porretane *1.1)*

163   **Laurie Shepard**, *Petrus Aretinus* acerrimus virtutum ac vitiorum demonstrator

179   **Linda L. Carroll**, *Ruzante Speaks Truth to Venetian Power: Some Hows, Whys, Whens, and Wherefores*

199 **Diletta Gamberini**, *Benvenuto Cellini e il problema di sapere "pur troppo dire il fatto suo" a Cosimo de' Medici*

4. Counter-Reformation Negotiations

219 **Sandra Clerc**, *Verità e potere, ubbidienza e menzogna nella tragedia italiana del Cinquecento (1550-1565)*

243 **Laura Benedetti**, *Le ragioni della poesia: Torquato Tasso e Silvio Antoniano*

261 **Francesco Sberlati**, *"Il buon poeta è il più bugiardo": Adulazione e falsità nella letteratura barocca*

5. Against Paternal and Political Tyranny from the Seventeenth to Nineteenth Centuries

281 **Elissa Weaver**, *"With Truthful Tongue and Faithful Pen": Arcangela Tarabotti Against Paternal Tyranny*

297 **Nicla Riverso**, *Paolo Sarpi: The Hunted Friar and his Popularity in England*

319 **Marco Codebò**, *Potere, dissimulazione e verità nei* Promessi sposi *(1840) e nella* Storia della colonna infame

6. Twentieth-Century Choral and Individual Voices

339 **Valentina Nocentini**, *L'Italia della guerra di Libia (1911-1912): un burattinaio contro il potere*

357 **Quinto Antonelli**, *Una rivolta morale: lettere e diari di soldati italiani dai fronti della Grande Guerra (1915-1918)*

373 **Diana Garvin**, *Singing Truth to Power: Melodic Resistance and Bodily Revolt in Italy's Rice Fields*

401 **Alan Perry**, *Giovannino's "Libertà": Guareschi's Personal Freedom in Opposition to Power*

425 **Maria Giménez Cavallo**, *Elsa Morante's* La storia: *A Posthumanist, Feminist, Anarchist Response to Power*

Italian Bookshelf
Edited by
Dino S. Cervigni and Anne Tordi

As of the 2008 issue, book reviews are published exclusively online. Please visit the journal's website for the complete text: www.ibiblo.org/annali

Review Article

458 *Vita nuova* ⸱ *Rime.* A cura di Donato Pirovano e Marco Grimaldi. Premessa (XIII-XVII) e Introduzione di Enrico Malato (XIX-XXXI). Bibliografia citata in forma abbreviata (XXXII-LXXIV). Volume 1, tomo 1 delle *Opere di Dante.* 8 volumi. Roma: Salerno Editrice, 2015. Pp. 804. (**Dino S. Cervigni**, Professor Emeritus, University of North Carolina, Chapel Hill)

GENERAL & MISCELLANEOUS STUDIES

469 **Bartolo Calderone.** *Funzione-Petrarca. Figure e concordanze del Canzoniere da Leopardi al Novecento.* Leo S. Olschki Editore. 2014. Pp. 130. (**Federica Conselvan**, Università "La Sapienza" di Roma)

472 *Esperienze letterarie. Rivista trimestrale di critica e di cultura* 50.2 (2015). Pp. 158. (**Stefano Evangelista**, University of Durham)

475 *Forum italicum. A Journal of Italian Studies.* Special issue. *Music and Society in Italy* 49.2 (August 2015). Ed. **Alessandro Carrera**. Pp. 273-680. (**Rachel Haworth**, University of Hull)

478 *Forum italicum. A Journal of Italian Studies* 47.2 (August 2013). Special issue: "Italy From Without." Ed. **Giuseppe Gazzola**. Pp. 471. (**Marianna Deganutti**, University of Oxford)

481 **Rosa Giulio.** *"L'azzurro color di lontananza." Infinità dello spazio e sublimità del pensiero nelle letterature moderne.* Stony Brook: Forum Italicum, 2014. Pp. 361. (**Simona Wright**, The College of New Jersey)

485 **Gabriella Guarino.** *Sul Bestiario di Esopo e di Fedro. Lettere greche A-K.* Introduzione a cura di **Pietro Pelosi**. Bibliografia a cura di **Antonio Elefante**. Roma: Aracne, 2014. Pp. 290. (**Olimpia Pelosi**, State University of New York at Albany)

487 **Guy Lanoue.** *Rome Eternal: The City as Fatherland.* London: Legenda, 2015. Pp. 261. (**Francesco Ricatti**, University of the Sunshine Coast, Queensland, Australia)

489 **Joseph Luzzi.** *In a Dark Wood: What Dante Taught Me About Grief, Healing, and the Mysteries of Love.* New York: Harper Collins, 2015. Pp. 297. (**Fabian Alfie**, University of Arizona)

491 Chiara Mazzucchelli. *The Heart and the Island: A Critical Study of Sicilian American Literature.* Albany: State University of New York Press, 2015. Pp. 197. (**Amy Boylan**, *University of New Hampshire*)

494 Rosa Mucignat, ed. *The Friulian Language, Identity, Migration, Culture.* Newcastle upon Tyne: Cambridge Scholars Publishing, 2014. Pp. 197. (**Gabriella Colussi Arthur**, *York University*)

497 *Poesia e preghiera.* A cura di **Erminia Ardissino e Francesca Parmeggiani**. In *Testo. Studi di teoria e storia della letteratura e della critica* 26. 70 (2015). Pp. 164. (**Alberto Comparini**, *Stanford University*)

500 Silvia Tatti. *Classico: storia di una parola.* Roma: Carocci, 2015. Pp. 105. (**Stefano Nicosia**, *Università di Sfax*)

502 Matteo Terzaghi and Matteo Campagnoli, eds. *Negli immediati dintorni: guida letteraria tra Lombardia e Canton Ticino.* Bellinzona: Casagrande and Doppiozero, 2015. Pp. 166. (**Patrick Barron**, *University of Massachusetts, Boston*)

505 **Michael Vena**, trans. and ed. *Modern Italian Theatre: From Praga to Sciascia (Text and Context).* N. p.: Xlibris LLC, 2014. Pp. 499. (**Daniela Cavallaro**, *University of Auckland*)

507 **Antonio C. Vitti and Anthony Julian Tamburri**, eds. *Mare nostrum: prospettive di un dialogo tra alterità e mediterraneità.* New York, NY: Bordighera Press, 2015. Pp. 324. (**Giovanna Summerfield**, *Auburn University*)

MIDDLE AGES & RENAISSANCE

509 Erin E. Benay and Lisa M. Rafanelli. *Faith, Gender and the Senses in Italian Renaissance and Baroque Art: Interpreting the* Noli me tangere *and* Doubting Thomas. Dorchester: Ashgate 2015. Pp. 282. (**Alexandra R. A. Lee**, Phd Candidate, *University College London*)

512 Vittore Branca, ed. *Merchant Writers. Florentine Memoirs from the Middle Ages and the Renaissance.* Trans. Murtha Baca. Toronto: Toronto University Press, 2015. Pp. 424. (**Nina Lamal**, *University of St Andrews*)

515 Alessandra Buccheri. *The Spectacle of Clouds, 1439-1650. Italian Art and Theatre.* Farnham Surrey: Ashgate, 2014. Pp. 216. (**Mara Nerbano**, *Accademia di Belle Artie di Firenze*)

518 Genevieve Carlton. *Worldly Consumers: The Demand for Maps in Renaissance Italy.* Chicago: University of Chicago Press, 2015. Pp. 237. (**Daniel Brownstein**, *UC Davis, Center for Innovation Studies*)

521 Jo Ann Cavallo. *The World beyond Europe in the Romance Epics of Boiardo and Ariosto.* Toronto: University of Toronto Press, 2013. Pp. 337. (**Juliann Vitullo**, *Arizona State University*)

524 Dante Alighieri. *Dante's Lyric Poetry. Poems of Youth and of the* Vita Nuova. Edited with a general introduction and introductory essays to the lyrics by

Teodolinda Barolini; with new verse translations of Dante's lyric poetry by **Richard Lansing**; commentary translated into English by **Andrew Frisardi**. Toronto: University of Toronto Press, 2014. Pp. 344. (**Gandolfo Cascio**, *University of Utrecht*)

527 **Lodovico Dolce.** *Dialogo della instituzion delle donne, secondo li tre stati che cadono nella vita umana.* Ed. **Helena Sanson.** Cambridge (UK): The Modern Humanities Research Association, 2015. Pp. 178. (**Luisanna Sardu**, *The Graduate Center, CUNY*

530 **Elio Durante e Anna Martellotti,** a cura di. *Amorosa fenice. La vita, le rime e la fortuna in musica di Girolamo Casone da Oderzo (c. 1528-1592).* Biblioteca dell'«Archivum Romanicum». Serie I: Storia, Letteratura, Paleografia, vol. 433. 2015. Pp. vi-482 con 4 figg. n.t. (**Sebastiano Bazzichetto**, *University of Toronto*)

532 **Martin Eisner.** *Boccaccio and the Invention of Italian Literature. Dante, Petrarch, Cavalcanti, and the Authority of the Vernacular.* New York: Cambridge University Press, 2013. Pp. 243. (**Michael J. Maher**, *College of Charleston*)

535 **Unn Falkeid and Aileen A. Feng,** eds. *Rethinking Gaspara Stampa in the Canon of Renaissance Poetry.* Farnham: Ashgate, 2015. Pp. 222. (**Clara Stella**, PhD candidate, *University of Leeds*)

538 **Paolo Falzone.** *Desiderio della scienza e desiderio di Dio nel "Convivio" di Dante.* Bologna: Il Mulino, 2010. Pp. 286. (**Paolo Rigo**, *Università degli Studi Roma Tre*)

540 **John Freccero.** *In Dante's Wake: Readings from Medieval to Modern in the Augustinian Tradition.* Ed. **Danielle Callegari and Melissa Swain.** New York: Fordham University Press, 2015. Pp. 268. (**Michael Sherberg**, *Washington University in St. Louis*)

542 **Christopher Kleinhenz and Andrea Dini**, eds. *Approaches to Teaching Petrarch's Canzoniere and the Petrarchan Tradition.* New York: MLA Press, 2014. Pp 312. (**Brandon Essary**, *Elon University*)

544 **Christopher Kleinhenz.** *Dante intertestuale e interdisciplinare. Saggi sulla Commedia.* Ariccia (RM): Aracne Editrice, 2015. Pp. 492. (**Diego Parisi**, *Instituto Storico Italiano per il Medioevo (Roma)*

547 **Marilyn Migiel.** *The Ethical Dimension of the* Decameron. Toronto: University of Toronto Press (Toronto Italian Studies), 2015. Pp. 197. (**Johnny L. Bertolio**, PhD Candidate, *University of Toronto*)

549 **Emily O'Brien.** *The* Commentaries *of Pope Pius II (1458-1464) and the Crisis of the Fifteenth-Century Papacy.* Toronto: University of Toronto Press, 2015. Pp. 335. (**Francesca Facchi**, *University of Toronto*)

552 **Kristina M. Olsen.** *Courtesy Lost: Dante, Boccaccio, and the Literature of History.* Toronto: University of Toronto Press, 2014. Pp. 248. (**Alfred R. Crudale**, *University of Rhode Island*)

554 **Franco Pierno,** ed. *The Church and the Languages of Italy Before the Council of Trent.* Toronto: Pontifical Institute of Mediaeval Studies, 2015. Pp. 319. (**Mary Migliozzi**, *Indiana University*)

557 Christian Rivoletti. *Ariosto e l'ironia della finzione. La recezione letteraria e figurativa dell'"Orlando furioso" in Francia, Germania e Italia.* Venezia: Marsilio Editori, 2014. Pp. 433. (**Christen Picicci**, *Colorado State University*)
560 Sherry Roush. *Speaking Spirits: Ventriloquizing the Dead in Renaissance Italy.* Toronto: University of Toronto Press, 2015. Pp. 263. (**Carlo Annelli**, PhD candidate, *University of Wisconsin-Madison*)
563 Rocco Rubini. *The Other Renaissance: Italian Humanism Between Hegel and Heidegger.* Chicago: University of Chicago Press, 2014. Pp. 408. (**Dylan J. Montanari**, PhD candidate, *Stanford University*)
566 Agostino Valier. *Instituzione d'ogni stato lodevole delle donne cristiane* e *Ricordi di Monsignor Agostino Valier Vescovo di Verona lasciati alle monache nella sua visitazione fatta l'anno del santissimo Giubileo 1575.* A cura di **Francesco Lucioli**. Cambridge: Modern Humanities Research Association, 2015. Pp. 171. (**Marianna Orsi**, *Indiana University, Bloomington*)
568 *Vies d'écrivains, vies d'artistes. Espagne, France, Italie. XVIe-XVIIIe siècles.* Ed. **Matteo Residori, Hélène Tropé, Danielle Boillet et Marie-Madeleine Fragonard.** Paris: Presses Sorbonne Nouvelle, 2014. Pp. 345. (**Olimpia Pelosi**, *State University of New York at Albany*)
571 *War and Peace in Dante: Essays Literary, Historical, and Theological.* Ed. **John C. Barnes and Daragh O'Connell.** Dublin: Four Courts Press, 2015. Pp. 264. (**Fabian Alfie**, *University of Arizona*)

SEVENTEENTH, EIGHTEENTH, & NINETEENTH CENTURIES

574 Davide Colombo, *Foscolo e i commentatori danteschi.* Milano: Ledizioni, 2015. Pp. 217. DIGITAL. (**Diego Parisi**, *Istituto Storico Italiano per il Medioevo (Roma)*
577 Natalia Costa-Zalessow, ed. *Voice of a Virtuosa and Courtesan: Selected Poems of Margherita Costa.* New York: Bordighera Press, 2015. Pp. 270. (**Aria Zan Cabot**, PhD candidate, *University of Wisconsin-Madison*)
580 Giovan Battista Marino. *Dicerie sacre.* Introduzione, commento e testo critico a cura di **Erminia Ardissino**. Roma: Edizioni di Storia e Letteratura, 2014. Pp. 393. (**Olimpia Pelosi**, *State University of New York at Albany*)
583 Lara Michelacci. *Il microscopio e l'allucinazione: Luigi Capuana tra letteratura, scienza e anomalia.* Bologna: Pendragon, 2015. Pp. 175. (**Stefano Serafini**, *Università di Bologna*)
586 Katharine Mitchell. *Italian Women Writers: Gender and Everyday Life in Fiction and Journalism, 1870-1910.* Toronto: Toronto University Press, 2014. Pp. 250. (**James Michael Fortney**, *University of Southern California*)
588 Charlotte Ross. *Sameness and Eccentricity. Discourse on Lesbianism and Desire between Women in Italy, 1860s-1930s.* Oxford: Peter Lang, 2015. Pp. 308. (**Elena Porciani**, *Seconda Università di Napoli*)

591 Cosetta Veronese and Pamela Williams. *The Atheism of Giacomo Leopardi*. Troubador: Leicester, 2013. Pp. 233. (**Simona Wright**, *The College of New Jersey*)

TWENTIETH & TWENTY-FIRST CENTURIES: LITERATURE, FILM, THEORY, CULTURE

595 Giorgia Alù and Nancy Pedri, eds. *Enlightening Encounters: Photography in Italian Literature*. Toronto Italian Studies. Toronto: University of Toronto Press, 2015. Pp. 328. (**Valentina Abbatelli**, PhD candidate, *University of Warwick*)

598 Joseph A. Amato. *My Three Sicilies*. New York: Bordighera, 2016. Pp. 177. (**Giusy Di Filippo**, *University of New Hampshire*)

601 Sean Anderson. *Modern Architecture and its Representation in Colonial Eritrea. An In-visible Colony, 1890-1941*. Farnham (UK): Ashgate, 2015. Pp. XXI + 288. (**Roberto Risso**, *Clemson University*)

603 Paolo Bartoloni. *Sapere di scrivere. Svevo e gli ordigni di* La coscienza di Zeno. Catania: Il Carrubo, 2015. Pp. 190. (**Salvatore Pappalardo**, *Towson University*)

606 Marco Bellardi, *Uno smisurato equilibrio. La narrativa sperimentale di Giuseppe Pontiggia*, Firenze, Franco Cesati editore, 2014. Pp.198. (**Cinzia Gallo**, *Università di Catania*

609 Stefania Benini. *Pasolini: The Sacred Flesh*. Toronto: University of Toronto Press, 2015. Pp. 336. (**Daniela Bini**, *University of Texas, Austin*)

611 Luigi Bonaffini and Joseph Perricone, eds. *Poets of the Italian Diaspora: A Bilingual Anthology*. New York: Fordham University Press, 2014. Pp. 1115. (**Ryan Calabretta-Sajder**, *University of Arkansas*)

614 Emma Bond, Guido Bonsaver and Federico Faloppa, eds. *Destination Italy. Representing Migration in Contemporary Media and Narrative*. Oxford: Peter Lang, 2015. Pp. 467. (**Giacomo Tagliani**, *University of Siena*)

617 Simona Bondavalli. *Fictions of Youth: Pier Paolo Pasolini, Adolescence, Fascism*. Toronto: University of Toronto Press, 2015. Pp. 275. (**Emanuele Occhipinti**, *Drew University*)

620 Bernard J. Bruno. *A Tear and A Tear in My Heart*. Introd. **Fred Gardaphé**. New York: Bordighera Press, 2014. Pp. 243. (**Katja Liimatta**, *The University of Iowa*)

622 Massimo Cacciari. *Europe and Empire: On the Political Forms of Globalization*. Ed. **Alessandro Carrera**. Trans. **Massimo Verdicchio**. New York: Fordham University Press, 2016. Pp. 216. (**Stefano Bellin**, PhD candidate, *University College London*)

624 Giuseppe Antonio Camerino. *Primo Novecento. Con analisi specifiche su Pascoli, D'Annunzio, Saba e Montale*. Avellino: Edizioni Sinestesie, 2015. Pp. 188. (**Charles Klopp**, *The Ohio State University*)

627 Rosetta Giuliani Caponetto. *Fascist Hybridities: Representations of Racial Mixing and Diaspora Cultures under Mussolini.* New York, NY: Palgrave Macmillan, 2015. Pp. 199. (**Kathleen Gaudet**, *University of Toronto*)
630 Mary Ann McDonald Carolan. *The Transatlantic Gaze: Italian Cinema. American Film.* Albany: State University of New York Press, 2014. Pp. 172. (**Giuseppe Faustini**, *Skidmore College*)
633 Leonardo Casalino, Andrea Cedola, and Ugo Perolino. *Il caso Moro: memorie e narrazioni.* Massa: Transeuropa, 2016. Pp. 286. (**Massimiliano L. Delfino**, *PhD Student, Columbia University*)
636 Natasha V. Chang. *The Crisis-Woman: Body Politics and the Modern Woman in Fascist Italy.* Toronto: University of Toronto Press, 2015. Pp. 166. (**Cristina Mazzoni**, *University of Vermont*)
639 Federica Colleoni, Elena Dalla Torre, and Inge Lanslots, eds. *Il cinema di Marco Tullio Giordana: interventi critici.* Roma: Vecchiarelli, 2015. Pp 315. (**Catherine O'Rawe**, *University of Bristol*)
642 Alberto Comparini. *Iride. L'Alcesti di Montale.* Borgomanero: Giuliano Landolfi Editore, 2014. Pp. 152. (**Andrea Matucci**,*Università di Siena*)
644 Claudia Crocco. *La poesia italiana del Novecento. Il canone e le interpretazioni.* Roma: Carocci editore. Pp. 222. (**Anna Maria Cantore**, *Università degli studi di Bari*)
647 Robert Dainotto. *The Mafia: A Cultural History.* London: Reaktion Books, 2015. Pp. 239. (**Nicholas Albanese**, *Texas Christian University*)
649 Matteo Di Gesù. *L'invenzione della Sicilia. Letteratura, mafia, modernità.* Roma: Carocci, 2015. Pp. 159. (**Diego Stefanelli**, *Università di Pavia*)
652 Simone Dubrovic. *Le pagine sfogliate.* Con disegni di Valeriano Trubbiani. Rimini: Raffaelli, 2015. Pp. 61. (**Sara Bonfili**, *Università degli studi di Macerata*)
653 Enrica Maria Ferrara. *Il realismo teatrale nella narrativa del Novecento: Vittorini, Pasolini, Calvino.* Studi e saggi 128. Firenze: Firenze University Press, 2015. Pp. 212. (**Inge Lanslots**, *KU Leuven, (University of Leuven)*)
655 Natalie Fullwood. *Cinema, Gender, and Everyday Space: Comedy, Italian Style.* New York: Palgrave Macmillan, 2015. Pp. 260. (**Meriel Tulante**, *Philadelphia University*)
658 Douglas J. Gladstone. *Carving a Niche for Himself : The Untold Story of Luigi Del Bianco and Mount Rushmore.* VIA Folios 95. New York, NY: Bordighera Press, 2014. Pp. 115. (**Ilona Klein**, *Brigham Young University*)
660 George Guida. *Spectacles of Themselves: Essays in Italian American Popular Culture and Literature.* New York: Bordighera Press, 2015. Pp. 186. (**Lidia Ciccone**, *Italian and English Freelance Teacher/Trainer and Independent Scholar*)
662 Carolyn Mary Kleefeld. *Simenzi di l'arma. Rivelazzioni e disegni / Soul Seeds. Revelations and Drawings / Semi dell'anima. Rivelazioni e disegni.* Translation into Sicilian and Italian by Gaetano Cipolla. Foreword by

Laura Archera Huxley. Mineola (NY): Legas, 2014. Pp. 173. (Marcello Messina, *Universidade Federal do Acre; Macquarie University*)
665 **Giuseppe Leonelli.** *Commentario penniano – Storia di una poesia.* Torino: Nino Aragno Editore, 2015. Pp. 513. (**Simone Dubrovic**, *Kenyon College*)
668 **Dacia Maraini.** *Extravagance and Three Other Plays.* Trans. **James R. Schwarten.** London: John Cabot University Press, 2015. Pp. 313. (**Monica Streifer**, *University of California, Los Angeles*)
671 **Mario Mignone.** *The Story of My People. From Rural Southern Italy to Mainstream America.* New York: Bordighera Press, 2015. Pp. 216. (**Lidia Ciccone**, *Italian and English Freelance Teacher/Trainer and Independent Scholar*)
674 **Fulvio Orsitto and Simona Wright** (a cura di). *Contaminazioni culturali: musica, teatro, cinema e letteratura nell'Italia contemporanea.* Da lontano: Studi e Testi 5. Manziana (Roma): Vecchiarelli Editore, 2014. Pp. 264. (**Inge Lanslots**, *KU Leuven (University of Leuven)*)
677 **Tullio Pagano.** *The Making and Unmaking of Mediterranean Landscape in Italian Literature. The Case of Liguria.* Madison, NJ: The Fairleigh Dickinson University Press. Series in Italian Studies, 2015. Pp. 238. (**Giorgia Alù**, *University of Sydney*)
680 **Nicholas Patruno and Roberta Ricci**, eds. *Approaches to Teaching the Works of Primo Levi.* New York: MLA, 2014. Pp.175. (**Giovanni Miglianti**, PhD student, *Yale University*)
683 *Piccolo mondo antico. Il film di Mario Soldati dalla sceneggiatura allo schermo.* A cura di **Alberto Buscaglia e Tiziana Piras.** Cermenate: New Press Edizioni, 2014. Pp. 301.
Malombra. Il film di Mario Soldati dalla sceneggiatura allo schermo. A cura di **Alberto Buscaglia e Tiziana Piras.** Con un saggio di **Luciano De Giusti.** Cermenate: New Press Edizioni, 2015. Pp. 427. (**Milena Contini**, *Università degli Studi di Torino*)
686 **Robin Pickering-Iazzi.** *The Mafia in Italian Lives and Literature. Life Sentences and their Geographies.* Toronto: Toronto University Press, 2015. Pp. 288. (**Inge Lanslots**, *KU Leuven (University of Leuven)*)
688 **Nicoletta Pireddu.** *The Works of Claudio Magris. Temporary Homes, Mobile Identities, European Borders.* New York: Palgrave Macmillan, 2015. Pp. 138. (**Anna Chiafele**, *Auburn University*)
691 **Andrea Righi.** *Italian Reactionary Thought and Critical Theory: An Inquiry into Savage Modernities.* New York: Palgrave Macmillan, 2015. Pp. 223. (**Nicole Gounalis**, PhD candidate, *Stanford University*)
693 **Roberto Roversi - Leonardo Sciascia.** *Dalla Noce alla Palmaverde. Lettere di utopisti 1953-1972.* A cura di **Antonio Motta.** Bologna: Pendragon, 2015. Pp. 303. (**Diego Vanni**, *Università di Parma*)
696 **Roberto Salsano.** *Pirandello in chiave esistenzialista.* Roma: Bulzoni Editore, 2015. Pp. 115. (**Andrea Sartori**, *Brown University*)

699 Giani Stuparich. *Racconti*. A cura di **Cinzia Gallo**. Roma: Aracne, 2015. Pp. 264. (**Sara Bonfili**, *Università degli Studi di Macerata*)
701 **Anthony Julian Tamburri and Fred L. Gardaphé**, eds. *Transcending Borders, Bridging Gaps: Italian Americana, Diasporic Studies, and the University Curriculum*. Studies in Italian Americana. Vol. 10. New York: John D. Calandra Italian American Institute, 2015. Pp. 168. (**Chiara De Santi**, *State University of New York at Fredonia*)

POETRY & FICTION

704 Laura Benedetti. *Un paese di carta*. Pisa: Pacini Editore, 2015. Pp. 237. (**Damiano Acciarino**, *Università Ca' Foscari*)
706 Laura Benedetti. *Un Paese di carta*. Ospedaletto-Pisa: Pacini Editore, 2015. Pp. 237. (**Serena Alessi**, *Royal Holloway University of London*)
708 **Amedeo Giacomini**. *Presumût Unviâr / It Looks Like Winter / Presunto inverno*. Poesie friulane / Poems in the Friulian Dialect (1984-1986). Trans. **Dino Fabris**. Preface **Francesca Cadel**. Mineola, NY: Legas, 2015. Pp. 63. (**Enrico Minardi**, *Arizona State University*)
711 **Maurizio Landini**. *Àndito*. Massa: Transeuropa, 2015. Pp. 50. (**Simone Dubrovic**, *Kenyon College*)
712 **Guido Mattioni**. *Conoscevo un angelo*. Milano: Ink, 2015. Pp. 166. (**Olimpia Pelosi**, *State University of New York at Albany*)
714 **Joey Nicoletti**. *Reverse Graffiti*. New York: Bordighera Press, 2015. Pp. 69. (**Giuseppe Sorrentino**, *Wagner College*)
716 **Pier Paolo Pasolini**. *The Selected Poetry of Pier Paolo Pasolini: A Bilingual Edition*. Ed. and trans. **Stephen Sartarelli**. Chicago: University of Chicago Press, 2014. Pp. 494. (**Ryan Calabretta-Sajder**, *University of Arkansas*)
718 **Amelia Rosselli**. *Hospital Series*. Trans. **Deborah Woodard, Roberta Antognini, and Giuseppe Leporace**. New Directions Poetry Pamphlet #19. New York: New Directions, 2015. Pp. 80. (**Thomas Simpson**, *Northwestern University*)
720 **Giuseppe Sgarbi**. *Non chiedere cosa sarà il futuro*. Prefazione di **Claudio Magris**. Milano: Skira, 2015. Pp. 137. (**Olimpia Pelosi**, *State University of New York at Albany*)

722 BRIEF NOTICES

Cultura e prospettive 26 (gennaio-marzo 2015). Pp. 112.
Cultura e prospettive 27 (aprile-giugno 2015). Pp. 192.
Esperienze letterarie 39.4 (2014). Pp. 159.

Esperienze letterarie 40.1 (2015). Pp. 164.
Journal of Medieval and Early Modern Studies 44.1 (Winter 2014). Pp. 239.
Misure critiche. Rivista semestrale di letteratura e cultura varia. Nuova serie. Anno 12.2 (luglio-dicembre 2013)-13.1 (gennaio-giugno 2014). Pp. 330.
Renaissance Quarterly 68.2 (Summer 2015). Pp. 419-802.
Renaissance Quarterly 68.3 (Fall 2015). Pp. 803-1160.
Renaissance Quarterly 68.4 (Winter 2015). Pp. 1161-549.

Jo Ann Cavallo and Carlo Lottieri

Introduction: Speaking Truth to Power from Medieval to Modern Italy

> "Non resta che perdere a chi ha perduto la libertà."
> (Once you have lost liberty, there remains nothing else to lose.)
> Arcangela Tarabotti, *Inferno monacale* (translated as *Paternal Tyranny*)

Centuries before Lord Acton coined his famous phrase that "Power tends to corrupt and absolute power corrupts absolutely," the humanist scholar Poggio Bracciolini argued in his *De infelicitate principum* (1440) that one of the four reasons for the general unhappiness of princes is precisely corruption — not as part of human nature, but as a particular vice of rulers ("Neque tantum hoc natura hominum, quantum ipsius evenit vitio principatus" 18).[1] Later in the century the humanist poet Matteo Maria Boiardo would open his *Orlando Innamorato* with the reflection that those in power have the tendency to crave what they cannot have, often putting their realms in danger in a vain attempt to secure something beyond their reach:

> E sì como egli advien a' gran signori
> Che pur quel voglion che non pòno avere,
> E quanto son difficultà magiori
> La disiata cosa ad otenere,
> Pongono il regno spesso in grandi erori,
> Né posson quel che voglion possedere.
>
> (1.1.5)
>
> (And as it happens to great lords
> who only want what they can't have,
> the greater obstacles there are
> to reaching what they would obtain
> the more they jeopardize their realms,
> and what they want, they cannot gain.)

The humanist chancellor of Florence Coluccio Salutati legitimitized every

---

[1] According to Bracciolini princes are also unhappy because of their little interest in culture, their tendency to surround themselves with flatterers rather than men of real intellect, and their lack of virtue. See Loscalzo for a reading of this text as "una polemica di vasti contorni sul disinteresse del potere nei confronti della letteratura e sul rifiuto di ogni compromesso con la politica da parte dell'intellettuale" (388).

Annali d'italianistica 34 (2016). *Speaking Truth to Power from Medieval to Modern Italy*

form of resistance, including tyrannicide, as a response against a ruler whose excessive ambitions had led him to disregard justice and the laws (*De tyranno*).[2] Indeed, the protagonists of Italian Renaissance humanism all underscored, albeit with different emphases, the immorality of power that some men exerted over others and, consequently, the need for an opposition capable of manifesting itself through words, ideas, and testimony.

Yet not all humanists belonged to what Eugenio Garin referred to as the movement's "età eroica in cui la riconquista dell'antico era stata una bella avventura, un'impresa eroica e solitaria da cavalieri erranti, senza maestri che non fossero i libri medesimi"(10). On the contrary, humanists dependent upon ruling elites, whether elective or hereditary regimes, often found themselves obliged to unconditionally support and celebrate their patrons through their writing. Lauro Martines describes these establishment intellectuals as propagandists of the state, rewarded with financial gain and social prestige for manufacturing consent among the populace rather than pursuing truth.[3]

The poet Lodovico Ariosto had so little faith in the integrity of his fellow writers serving patrons that in the *Orlando furioso* he has San Giovanni explain to the knight Astolfo that to arrive at the truth it would be necessary to convert every written statement into its exact opposite: "E se tu vuoi che 'l ver non ti sia ascoso, tutta al contrario l'istoria converti" ("But if you want to know what really happened, invert the story" 35.27). In *Il libro del cortegiano,* Ariosto's contemporary Baldassare Castiglione elaborately crafts three evenings of dialogue before broaching the subject of how a courtier might gain the prince's confidence sufficiently to tell him "la verità d'ogni cosa che ad esso convenga sapere, senza timor o periculo di despiacergli" ("the truth about everything he needs to know without fear or risk of displeasing him" 4.5). Even so, the speaker Ottaviano Fregoso comments: "S'io avessi la grazia di qualche principe ch'io conosco e gli dicessi liberamente il parer mio, dubito che presto la perderei" ("If I had the favor of some of the princes I know, and if I were to tell them freely what I think, I fear I should soon lose that favor" 4.26).

After all, considerations of the political-institutional sphere of society have always shown how every political power structure is based not only on force, but also on ideological mechanisms designed to confer legitimacy upon the use and threat of such violence. The close tie between the power elite and intellectuals at their service has its justification in the necessity for all rulers to provide themselves with instruments to manipulate public opinion. Herein lies the difficulty — across a range of contexts — for individuals to freely voice

---

[2] Sozzi sees Salutati's treatise as a forerunner of Estienne de la Boétie's *De la servitude volontaire,* the quintessential Renaissance treatise on the population's right to refuse to obey an unjust sovereign (17).

[3] His more cynical view of the humanists' affiliation with power can be found in the chapter "Humanism: A Program for Ruling Classes" (191-217).

their thoughts with regard to those in power, especially if their intention is correctional or contestatory.

It is understandable that openly censuring the political class should be deemed a virtually impossible undertaking when any critique could mean the loss not only of one's livelihood, but of one's very life as well. Massimo Rospocher, for example, documents how during the Renaissance perceived verbal or written affronts to the Venetian state by its residents, even statements pronounced outside the borders of its territory, could come under the juridical category of *crimen lesae maiestatis* and result in fines, imprisonment, banishment, or even more extreme physical punishments, such as the cutting out of the offender's tongue (354-55).[4] As readers of Ovid's *Metamorphoses* are shown through the example of the Thracian king Tereus cutting out his sister-in-law Philomela's tongue to prevent her from disclosing his violent rape, this particular form of punishment would additionally aim to prevent further verbal pronouncements by silencing the speaker forever.

Although the penalty is not so gruesome, today one still risks punishment for even verbal offenses to Italy's head of state through the so-called "legge contro il vilipendio." Alan Perry's essay in this volume dealing with Giovannino Guareschi's trial and imprisonment shows that this law, codified under Mussolini, could be applied in the post-war republic even when a citizen aimed not to gratuitiously offend, but to arrive at the truth concerning the possibly illicit activities of a powerful political figure.

Given the difficulty and danger of critiquing those in power across time periods — as well as the advantages to be accrued from actively promoting and supporting their rule — we might not expect to find many willing to openly speak their mind. Nevertheless, history is full of examples, some famous but countless others little-known or still untold, of individuals who have voiced dissent or exposed the misdeeds of the powerful by means of speech, song, performance, art and writing, both directly and through fictional characters. One may recall that even deprived of her tongue a determined Philomela was able to narrate the tale of Tereus's vile act.

Perhaps an even more archetypical representation of the act of speaking truth to power involves another Ovidian character who, like Philomela, communicated through images: Ovid's Arachne used the art of weaving to disclose the abuses of the gods in a contest against Minerva, the goddess of needlework, wisdom, and warfare. In Giovanni Andrea dell'Anguillara's sixteenth-century Italian verse translation of the *Metamorphoses*, the contest between the all-powerful goddess and the defiant female weaver is staged in the

---

[4] Noting that Venice was not unique in this regard, Rospocher provides examples of punishments for dissident voices in other Italian states, not only hanging, beating, whipping, or chaining the perceived offender, but also piercing his (or her) tongue with a nail or impaling it with a poker (355).

epic form of the *ottava rima*. Whereas Minerva's depiction of Jove reinforces his unmovable position as king of the gods — "Giove nel mezzo imperioso siede, / Gli altri sedono bassi, egli eminente" ("Imperious Jove sits in the middle / The others are seated low, he (is) elevated" 84 *verso*) — Arachne (Aranne) strives to reveal his abuses against humankind and in particular against young females: "E con queste lascivie, e questi inganni / Nota i pensier di Giove empi, e tiranni" ("And through these lustful acts and deceptions / She denotes the impious and tyrannical thoughts of Giove" 85 *verso*).[5] Despite the excellence of Arachne's tapestry, the angry goddess rips her artwork to shreds and then takes vengeance upon her body by striking her face and chest (see cover image). The translation makes clear that Minerva's violent reaction is not due to Arachne's immoderate pride in her art, but rather to her censorious depiction of the gods:

> Quanto lodò la Dea d'Aranne l'arte,
> Tanto dannò la sua profana Historia,
> Che senza offender la celeste parte,
> Ben acquistar potea la stessa gloria.
> Tutto straccia quel panno à parte, à parte,
> De celesti peccati empia memoria,
> Per non mostrare à secoli novelli
> Gli eccessi de gli zii, padre, e fratelli.
>
> (86 *verso*)[6]
>
> (As much as the goddess praised Arachne's art,
> That much she condemned the profane history,
> Since without offending the celestial lot,
> She could have acquired the same glory.
> She rips up that cloth piece by piece,
> The impious record of celestial sins,
> In order not to show to future generations
> The excesses of her uncles, father, and brothers.)

Dell'Anguillara's translation first appeared in 1561, two years before the conclusion of the Council of Trent, whose decrees led to a period of censureship in the Italian peninsula that made the previous centuries appear quite mild by comparison.[7]

Although the expression "speaking truth to power" is frequently linked to the American Quakers who used it in the title of their 1955 booklet on

---

[5] Nor does Arachne keep silent about the abuses on the part of other gods, namely Pluto, Neptune, and Apollo.

[6] In Ovid's original, moreover, gods and rulers are connected, for example, through the deification of Julius Caesar and Caesar Augustus (the ruler who later exiled him to Thrace on the Black Sea, where he died). The political implications of an original work by Giovanni Andrea dell'Anguillara, his tragedy *Edippo*, are discussed in the present volume by Sandra Clerc.

[7] For the history of censorship in Italy following the Council of Trent, see Frajese.

international conflict and approaches to peacemaking, the paradigm itself is timeless.[8] Given that the question of speaking truth to power is not limited to either a specific historical period or particular form of government, the guest editors invited scholars to submit essays exploring instances in which literary characters and historical figures ranging from the medieval to the modern period articulated personal, political, economic, or religious freedoms or otherwise challenged the established power of the state. We welcomed attention to all levels of political power, from centralized to local, including the political power of the Church to the extent that it could take preventive or punitive action against individuals even outside the Papal States. While the papacy could — and often did — play a role in countering and limiting the power of contending sovereigns within territories of mutual influence,[9] in many instances the Church was also intertwined with secular politics for a variety of reasons, including the fact that for centuries government representatives were involved in the offices and tribunals of the curia, which itself was often comprised of family members from the ranks of the ruling elite.

Before we move to an overview of the individual essays, it may be useful to further explain the theoretical position underpinning the guest editors' conception of the volume. Simply put, our goal has been to offer essays that shed new light or offer a fresh perspective on a range of individual and group efforts to stand up to power. Power, however, comes in different forms and the term has been used with different meanings. Many authors have grouped together under the same umbrella *political* power (which compels compliance through the use or threat of physical force), *cultural* power (activated through the spread of certain ideas), and *economic* power (which coincides with the possession and use of resources). Against this all-inclusive definition of power, we maintain that culture and wealth do not represent, in themselves, instruments of violence, and therefore can only be appropriately subsumed into the general category when they are in collusion with and backed by the power of the state. For this reason we have chosen to focus critical attention specifically on opposition to political power — for us, the distinctively agressive form of power — because the state, regardless of the structure it assumes, is the only entity that claims a legal monopoly on the use of violence within a given territory and thereby compels compliance through physical aggression.

The conception of state power outlined above is shared by the Austrian School of economics and by libertarian philosophy. Although the Austrian School has roots dating back to the sixteenth-century School of Salamanca and

---

[8] The booklet, whose full title is *Speak Truth to Power: A Quaker Search for an Alternative to Violence*, critiques the United States' aggressive military policy during the Cold War, contending that "military power in today's world is incompatible with freedom, incapable of providing security, and ineffective in dealing with evil" (online).
[9] For historical examples, see Lottieri, *Credere nello Stato?*

even before, its core ideas were advanced by economists working in the nineteenth-century Austro-Hungarian Empire and further developed by twentieth-century Austrian economists. The commonly recognized founder of the Austrian School is Carl Menger (1840-1921), to whom are owed the theory of subjective value (based on the radical irreducibility of personal preference) and a groundbreaking reflection on the spontaneous origin and evolutionary development of human practices such as the use of money, language, and law. Menger, moreover, provided a crucial contribution to the elaboration of methodological individualism, a mode of reasoning that underscores the choices and actions of single individuals and thereby refuses to imagine collective entities (nations, classes, states, etc.) capable of acting subjectively and expressing a will.

In the course of the twentieth century both Ludwig von Mises (1881-1973) and Friedrich von Hayek (1899-1992) drew on Menger's insights to develop a critical position toward state intervention and central planning in economic matters, starting from the centrality of individual human action and underlining the fact that, given the dispersed and limited nature of knowledge and expertise, no political authority could possibly substitute for the free play of social interaction. One of Mises's students, Murray Rothbard (1926-1995), further elaborated these theses in an original way by bringing libertarian philosophy — with its system of ethics based on the principle of non-aggression — to bear on the economic theories of the Austrian School.[10] Rothbard, moreover, connected the subjectivity of individual preference, which is at the heart of the free market, and the objectivity of natural law, which prohibits the acceptance of power exerted over others by force or threat of violence. An important contribution in this latter area of thought comes to us from an Italian author, Bruno Leoni (1913-1967), whose writings articulate how rules that permit social life to operate are the product of social negotiation (the exchange of claims). This perspective gives rise to a focus on alternatives to legislation in the formation of laws, from Roman law (elaborated by jurisconsultants) to common law (which emerges from judgments ruled in the courts).

From the beginning and throughout its development, the Austrian School has confronted Marxism, criticizing the reductionism of a line of thought that ignores the fundamental character of political power, always a superstructure in the interactions among classes. One of the consequences of this perspective in Marx, as well as in those influenced by him in various ways, is the condemnation of "capitalist acts between consenting adults" (to use Robert

---

[10] Rothbard's libertarianism draws largely from classical liberal philosophers such as John Locke (1632-1704) and Thomas Jefferson (1743-1826), who linked their conception of liberty to a strong defense of private property rights, and from the nineteenth-century individualist anarchists Lysander Spooner (1808-1887) and Benjamin Tucker (1854-1939).

Nozick's phrase), without an understanding of the authoritatian, oppressive, and definitive character of force monopolitized by a small group. While the Austrian School shares with Marxism a conception of power as exploitative, it makes an essential distinction between power held and enforced by the state or other coercive institutions (bands of brigands, mafias, terroristic groups, etc.) and other uses of the term. In "Marxist and Austrian Class Analysis," Hans-Hermann Hoppe faults Marxism for "muddling things up" with its "fallacious model of the wage earner versus the capitalist" when in fact the real distinction is between those who acquire and increase their wealth by homesteading, producing, saving and contracting, and those who exploit the homesteaders, producers, savers, and contractors through non-productive and non-contractual acquisitions (84).[11]

The focus on power elite analysis rather than class analysis invites researchers to recognize and investigate the form and effect of political power structures at work in any time period and at any point on the globe. Some of the proponents of this approach have occasionally delved into the interpretation of literature and other forms of cultural expression — for example, J. A. Nock's *Francis Rabelais the Man and his Work* (1929), Henry Hazlitt's *The Anatomy of Criticism* (1933), and Murray Rothbard's film reviews [12] — but it is only recently that scholars in the humanities have begun to ground their critical work directly in the Austrian School and libertarian philosophy. Paul Cantor's pioneering research in this interdisciplinary method has ranged from major English authors the likes of Shakespeare and Shelley to popular American television series such as *Gilligan's Island* and *South Park*. In the volume *Literature and the Economics of Liberty: Spontaneous Order in Culture* (2009), Cantor and his coeditor Stephen Cox present what they believe to be "the first collection of essays that accepts the idea that economics is relevant to the study of literature, but offers free market principles, rather than Marxist, as the means of relating the two fields" (x), with contributions on canonical European and American authors (including Cervantes, Jonson, Shelley, Whitman, H. G. Wells, and Cather) as well as the contemporary Nigerian novelist Ben Okri. Noting that "Marxist literary theory has only deepened what was originally an aristocratic contempt for and distrust of market principles and practices" (ix), the coeditors

---

[11] For further discussions of the economic principles of the Austrian School in relation to Marxism, see especially Osterfeld and Raico. Although Marxism has been largely discredited as economic theory and practice, Marxist criticism nevertheless remains widely known and used in academic literary criticism. See Dario Fernández-Morera's *American Academia and the Survival of Marxist Ideas* (1996) for an account of its origins and stronghold in academic literary and cultural studies.

[12] A selection of the latter, including pieces on *The Godfather* and *Cinema Paradiso*, have recently been collected in the section "Movie Reviews" in *The Rothbard Reader* (293-303). These and many other reviews can be found dispersed throughout *The Complete Libertarian Forum 1969-1984* under the rubric "Mr First Nighter."

argue that Austrian economics, "which focuses on the freedom of the individual actor and the subjectivity of values, is more suited to the study of literature and artistic creativity than a materialist, determinist, and collectivist doctrine such as Marxism" (12).

Austro-libertarian literary criticism has recently yielded new insights in a range of areas, from ancient Chinese moral philosophy (Long 2003) to American cowboy movies (McMaken 2012).[13] Allen Mendenhall's *Literature and Liberty: Essays in Libertarian Literary Criticism* (2014), which likewise argues from a theoretical standpoint for the privileging of methodological individualism over collectivism in the interpretation of texts, focuses on authors as diverse as Geoffrey of Monmouth, Shakespeare, Emerson, Mark Twain, and E. M. Forster. The current volume's guest coeditors have also contributed to this interdisciplinary approach, albeit from different starting points. Carlo Lottieri is a political philosopher of libertarian orientation, who is interested in the historical and ideological roots of contemporary institutions.[14] Jo Ann Cavallo is an Italianist who has looked increasingly to Austrian economics and libertarian philosophy in her interpretation of literary and historical texts.[15]

Readers need not be versed in Austro-libertarian theory, however, in order to appreciate the essays that follow. Indeed, although the contributions to this volume accord well with the Austro-libertarian framework briefly sketched above, most do not refer explicitly to this methology. Some of the contributors have drawn from a range of contemporary theoreticians of power, such as Michel Foucault, Hannah Arendt, and Judith Butler.[16] Others look to cultural anthropology, posthumanism, feminism, and Bakuninian anarchism. Still others eschew theory and base their arguments on a close analysis of the literary text in conjunction with careful attention to the historical context. The guest coeditors were gratified by the fact that a Call for Papers so expressly focused in a radical critique of political power drew the interest of scholars grounded in a variety of

---

[13] More generally, see *Journal of Libertarian Studies* (1977-2008) and *Libertarian Papers* (2009-).

[14] His endeavor to rethink "modernity" is most evident in *Denaro e comunità*, *Credere nello Stato?* and *Un'idea elvetica di libertà*.

[15] This approach is used implicitly in *The Romance Epics of Boiardo, Ariosto, and Tasso: From Public Duty to Private Pleasure*, *The World beyond Europe in the Romance Epics of Boiardo and Ariosto*, and "Purgatory 17: On Revenge," and expressly in "On Political Power and Personal Liberty in *The Prince* and *The Discourses*" and "Marco Polo on the Mongol State: Taxation, Predation, and Monopolization."

[16] We might add that there are nonetheless some convergences between the first two of these critics and the Austrian School. Citing James Miller's biography on Foucault, Cantor notes that Foucault's opening lecture at the Collège de France for 1970 encouraged students to read precisely Ludwig von Mises and Friedrich Hayek ("The Poetics of Spontaneous Order" 11). David Gordon points out that Arendt "owned a large number of books by Mises, even more by Hayek, and two by Rothbard" ("Arendt and the Austrians").

different traditions and methodologies.

Although a volume of this nature cannot aim to be comprehensive, the essays focus on distinct moments across a history of lived experience and fictional literature that stretches from Dante Alighieri to Elsa Morante. In some instances, contributors have revisited the writings of very well-known figures, while in other cases they have shed light on lesser-known writers as well as anonymous pronouncements such as the Pasquinades, private testimonials such as the personal letters of World War I soldiers, and choral voices such as the protest songs of female rice-workers, the *mondine*.

The volume opens with essays on the three Florentine crowns. Zane Mackin argues for the political relevance of Dante's varied and complex uses of preaching in the *Commedia* and elsewhere, exploring in particular the conditions that motivated Dante to assume the preacher's voice and his justifications of his right to preach despite ecclesiastical proclamations prohibiting laypersons from engaging in the practice ("Dante, the Rhetoric of Crisis, and Vigilante Preaching").

Steve Baker goes against the stereotypical portrait of Petrarch as a forlorn unrequited lover or a solitary figure writing letters to ancient figures of antiquity or to posterity in order to examine his involvement in the messy business of trying to improve the political reality of his day, in particular, his active support for the popular leader Cola di Rienzo in his insurrection against the aristocratic rulers of Rome ("Writing the Revolution: Petrarch and the Tribunate of Cola di Rienzo").

Boccaccio's *Decameron*, dubbed a "merchant epic" by Vittore Branca for its vast fresco of human interactions in the marketplace, also includes its share of characters who speak truth to power. Madonna Filippa, for example, in a court trial in which she faces a death sentence for adultery, wittily defends herself by refuting the legitimacy of a law made without her consent, proclaiming self-ownership of her body and evoking free market principles (*Decameron* 6.7). She thereby not only successfully regains her freedom but also succeeds in overturning an unjust law. Karina Attar focuses on another *Decameron* wife who is accused by her husband of adultery — this time wrongly so, despite the literary connotations of her name, Ginevra — and who is eventually able to disclose the truth through her entrepreneurial ingenuity ("Speaking Truth to Powerful Friends and Foes: Genoese Merchants and the Mamluks in *Decameron* 2.9").

One of the fundamental commonalities in speaking out against the power elite regardless of time period and geographical location is the sheer difficulty of the enterprise. Coming through in various essays included in the volume, this theme is at the center of Alessandra Mantovani's discussion of Giovanni Garzoni's *Speculum veritatis*, a work that aims to balance discretion with honest advice ("*Speculum veritatis*: Giovanni Garzoni e la tradizione dell'*institutio principis* nella Bologna dei Bentivoglio").

Matteo Bosisio draws our attention to Antonio Cammelli, another fifteenth-century humanist, whose tragedy *Panfila* lays bare the dark side of courtly politics ("Fuggendo da lui fuggo la morte": libertà, vendetta, polemica anti-cortigiana nella *Panfila* di Antonio Cammelli). Based on Boccaccio's novella of Ghismonda speaking truth to her father, Prince Tancredi of Salerno (*Decameron* 4.1), *Panfila* further develops the themes of corruption, injustice, betrayal, and oppression through both the plot and inserted invectives that echo Cammelli's own poetic output.

Jo Ann Cavallo maintains that the opening novella of Giovanni Sabadino degli Arienti's *Porretane* not only harbors a thinly veiled critique of the military adventurism and rhetorical manipulation of those wielding political power, namely, the pope and the emperor, but also subtly pits the free movement inherent in a market economy against the coercive violence of the political state ("Contracts, Surveillance, and Censure of State Power in Arienti's Triunfo da Camarino novella [*Le porretane* 1.1]").

Laurie Shepard examines the development of Pietro Aretino's vituperative writings over the course of two decades, exploring the Venetian context of his increasingly agressive assertions of his right to act as the scourge of princes. She also situates his satirical works in relation to the genre of pasquinades, witty sayings and poems lampooning mostly prominent figures in the Roman Curia that since the early sixteenth century were customarily displayed on a certain particular in Rome ("*Petrus Aretinus acerrimus virtutum ac vitiorum demonstrator*").

Linda L. Carroll places into historical context the literary and theatrical career of Angelo Beolco, usually referred to by the name of the peasant character Ruzante that he created and played on the stage, in order to help account for both his extraordinary outspokenness and the (temporary) patrician acceptance of his biting critiques ("Ruzante Speaks Truth to Venetian Power: Some Hows, Whys, Whens, and Wherefores"). Her essay includes close analyses that highlight his serious concern for the rights of peasants on the mainland and his various comedic strategies.

Diletta Gamberini takes into consideration Benvenuto Cellini's literary works, in particular his autobiography and *Trattati dell'Oreficeria e della Scultura*. Her analysis demonstrates that even though Cellini is known for his boisterous outspoken character, he was compelled to revise and temper his words against Cosimo de' Medici in a process of self-censorship in order for the latter work to see the light during his lifetime ("Benvenuto Cellini e il problema di sapere 'pur troppo dire il fatto suo' a Cosimo de' Medici"). Her essay also devotes attention to contentious legal petitions that Cellini addressed to the Florentine magistrate — and thus indirectly to Cosimo — shortly before his death.

Noting that in the course of the sixteenth century the genre of tragedy became a privileged space in which to shine a critical spotlight on political

Introduction: Speaking Truth to Power from Medieval to Modern Italy 27

power, Sandra Clerc analyzes the figure of the ruler in four tragedies published between 1550 and 1565: Alessandro Spinelli's *Cleopatra*, Lodovico Dolce's *Ifigenia* and *Marianna*, and Giovan Andrea dell'Anguillara's *Edippo* ("Verità e potere, ubbidienza e menzogna nella tragedia italiana del Cinquecento [1550-1565]"). She finds that while all four tragedies present variations on the theme of speaking truth to a tyrant, it is generally the female protagonist, when present, who most openly challenges an unjust ruler.

Laura Benedetti focuses on Torquato Tasso's epistolary regarding his *Gerusalemme liberata* prior to its publication, chiefly his lengthy letter to Silvio Antoniano of the Roman Curia, highlighting his mode of reasoning and some of his rhetorical strategies ("*Le ragioni della poesia: Torquato Tasso e Silvio Antoniano*"). According to Benedetti, the poet strove to preserve as much personal and artistic liberty as possible in an increasingly restrictive cultural environment.

Francesco Sberlati analyzes the relation beween political power and literary production in the Seicento, focusing especially on the genre of political oratory. He thereby lays bare the reality of court life in which the courtier who serves the ruling elite through encomiastic writing has little scope to speak his mind ("'Il buon poeta è il più bugiardo': adulazione e falsità nella letteratura barocca").

Elissa Weaver's essay is dedicated to the Venetian writer and Benedictine nun Arcangela Tarabotti whose *La semplicità ingannata* (known in English as *Paternal Tyranny*) condemned the unfair treatment of women and especially the practice of forced monasticism, indicting fathers, the State, and the Church for their complicity in denying women the exercise of their free will ("With Truthful Tongue and Faithful Pen": Arcangela Tarabotti Against Paternal Tyranny").

It may also happen that one's protest against the abuses of the political elite, while suppressed or ignored in one's own milieu, will instead be positively received and even used as propaganda by rival or enemy nations. Nicla Riverso demonstrates how this occurred in the case of the polemical Catholic theologian Paolo Sarpi, whose criticisms of papal politics offered Protestant writers in England the means to support their arguments against the pope and the Church of Rome ("Paolo Sarpi: The Hunted Friar and his Popularity in England").

Marco Codebò's "Potere, dissimulazione e verità nei *Promessi sposi* (1840) e nella *Storia della colonna infame*" investigates the lack of truthfulness prevalent among characters at all levels of society in Manzoni's opus before focusing on two important exceptions in which a powerless individual in both *I promessi sposi* (1840) and *La storia della colonna infame* nevertheless finds the courage to speak truth to power.

Valentina Nocentini examines the massive propaganda campaign preceding and surrounding the 1911-1912 War in Libya, noting the complicity of the state apparatus, the banking cartels, and the military-industrial complex, as well as many Italian journalists and authors, before analyzing a short story by the little-known writer Arturo Rossato whose puppeteer protagonist refuses to comply with the war machine via an unforgettable gesture ("L'Italia della guerra di Libia (1911-1912): un burattinaio contro il potere").

Quinto Antonelli offers us a glimpse into the roughly four billion postcards and letters penned by Italian peasant soldiers during World War I, underscoring those that protested not only against the brutal conditions facing them, but also against the dubious premises under which they were sent to the front to kill or be killed ("Una rivolta morale: lettere e diari di soldati italiani dai fronti della Grande Guerra [1915-1918]").

Diana Garvin's "Singing Truth to Power: Melodic Resistance and Bodily Revolt in Italy's Rice Fields" uses work songs and testimonials to investigate how the *mondine* challenged and rebelled against the Fascist propaganda that attempted to cast them as a symbol of productive womanhood as they worked in the rice paddies.

Alan Perry traces Giovannino Guareschi's resistance to Nazi brutality as a prisoner of war, his opposition to the Communist party in the post-war period, and his accusation against the Christian Democrat Alcide De Gasperi in a consistent non-violent condemnation of the abuses of those who wielded power ("Giovannino's 'Libertà': Guareschi's Personal Freedom in Opposition to Power").

In the volume's final essay Maria Giménez Cavallo uses posthumanism, feminism, and anarchism as a lens to show how the characters in *La storia* give bodily form to Morante's passionate denunciation of all institutionalized systems of control ("Elsa Morante's *La storia*: A Posthumanist, Feminist, Anarchist Response to Power").

We chose to arrange the twenty selected essays in chronological order not to impose a teleological vision, but to help contextualize occurrences in which writers dared to confront power structures across the centuries, allowing similarities and differences to emerge naturally across the peninsula's shifting social, economic, and political configurations. As Clifford Geertz remarked when referring to the general concept of culture, "we need to look for systematic relationships among diverse phenomena, not for substantive identities among similar ones" (44). Readers will undoubtedly encounter both commonalities and differences in the manner of speech employed, the nature of the truth expounded, and the form of political power addressed and opposed among the many thought-provoking contributions contained in this volume.

Columbia University
Università degli Studi di Siena

Works Cited

Ariosto, Ludovico. *Orlando furioso*. Trans. Guido Waldman. New York: Oxford UP, 1983.

———. *Orlando furioso*. Ed. Lanfranco Caretti. 2 vols. 1966. Torino: Einaudi, 1992.

Boiardo, Matteo Maria. *Orlando in Love*. Trans. Charles S. Ross. West Lafayette, IN: Parlor Press, 2004.

———. *Orlando Innamorato. L'Inamoramento de Orlando*. Ed. Andrea Canova. 2 vols. Milano: BUR, 2011.

Bracciolini, Poggio. *De infelicitate principum*. Ed. Davide Canfora. Roma: Edizioni di storia e letteratura, 1998.

———. *Facezie*. Ed. Marcello Ciccuto. Milano: Rizzoli, 1983.

Cantor, Paul. *Gilligan Unbound: Pop Culture in the Age of Globalization*. Lanham, MD: Rowman and Littlefield, 2003.

———. "The Poetics of Spontaneous Order: Austrian Economics and Literary Criticism." *Literature and the Economics of Liberty: Spontaneous Order in Culture*. Ed. Paul Cantor and Stephen Cox. Auburn, AL: Ludwig von Mises Intitute, 2009. 1-98.

———. *The Invisible Hand in Popular Culture: Liberty vs. Authority in American Film and TV*. Lexington, KY: UP of Kentucky, 2012.

Cantor, Paul, and Stephen Cox, eds. *Literature and the Economics of Liberty: Spontaneous Order in Culture*. Auburn, AL: Ludwig von Mises Intitute, 2009.

Castiglione, Baldassare. *The Book of the Courtier*. Trans. Charles S. Singleton. New York: Doubleday, 1959.

———. *Il libro del cortegiano*. Ed. Walter Barberis. Torino: Einaudi, 1998.

Cavallo, Jo Ann. "Marco Polo on the Mongol State: Taxation, Predation, and Monopolization." *Libertarian Papers* 7.2 (2015): 157-68.

———. "On Political Power and Personal Liberty in *The Prince* and *The Discourses*." *Machiavelli's* The Prince *at 500*. Ed. John McCormick. *Social Research: An International Quarterly* 81.1 (Spring 2014): 107-32.

———. "Purgatory 17: On Revenge." *Purgatory: Lectura Dantis*. Ed. A. Mandelbaum, A. Oldcorn, C. Ross. Berkeley: U of California P, 2008. 178-90.

———. *The Romance Epics of Boiardo, Ariosto, and Tasso: From Public Duty to Private Pleasure*. Toronto: U of Toronto P, 2004.

———. *The World beyond Europe in the Romance Epics of Boiardo and Ariosto*. Toronto: U of Toronto P, 2013.

Cultura e potere nel Rinascimento. Ed. Luisa Secchi Tarugi. Firenze: Cesati, 1999.

Dell'Anguillara, Giovanni Andrea. *Le Metamorfosi d'Ovidio*. Venezia: Giovanni Griffio, 1561.

Fernández-Morera, Darío. *American Academia and the Survival of Marxist Ideas*. Westport, CT: Praeger, 1996.

Frajese, Vittorio. *La censura in Italia: dall'Inquisizione alla Polizia*. Roma: Laterza, 2014.

Garin, Eugenio. "Ritratto di Poggio." Bracciolini. *Facezie* 5-24.

Geertz, Clifford. "The Impact of the Concept of Culture on the Concept of Man." *The Interpretation of Cultures. Selected Essays*. New York: Basic Books, 1973. 33-54.

Gordon, David. "Arendt and the Austrians." November 15, 2006. https://mises.org/blog/arendt-and-austrians. Online.

Hoppe, Hans-Hermann. "Marxist and Austrian Class Analysis." *Journal of Libertarian Studies* 9.2 (fall 1990): 79-93. Reprinted in Maltsev, ed. *Requiem for Marx* 51-73.

Long, Roderick T. "Austro-Libertarian Themes in Early Confucianism." *Journal of Libertarian Studies* 17.3 (2003): 35-62.

Loscalzo, Donato. "L'infelicità dei principi e la felicità dei letterati in Poggio Bracciolini."

Cultura e potere nel Rinascimento 379-88.
Lottieri, Carlo. *Credere nello Stato? Teologia politica e dissimulazione da Filippo il Bello a WikiLeaks*. Soveria Mannelli: Rubbettino, 2011.
———. *Denaro e comunità. Relazioni di mercato e ordinamenti giuridici nella società liberale*. Napoli: Guida, 2000.
———. *Un'idea elvetica di libertà. Dopo lo Stato moderno*. Brescia: La Scuola, 2016.
McMaken, Ryan. *Commie Cowboys: The Bourgeoisie and the Nation-State in the Western Genre*. Creative Commons. 2012.
Maltsev, Yuri N., ed. *Requiem for Marx*. Auburn, AL: Ludwig von Mises Institute, 1993.
Martines, Lauro. *Power and Imagination: City-States in Renaissance Italy*. New York: Alfred A. Knopf, 1979.
Mendenhall, Allen. *Literature and Liberty: Essays in Libertarian Literary Criticism*. Lanham, MD: Lexington Books, 2014.
Nock, Albert Jay, and C. R. Wilson. *Francis Rabelais, the Man and his Work*. London: Harper, 1929.
Ovidius Naso, Publius. *Metamorphoses*. Trans. David Raeburn. Intro. Denis Feeney. New York: Penguin, 2004.
Rospocher, Massimo. "'In vituperium status Veneti': The Case of Niccolò Zoppino." *The Italianist* 34.3 (October 2014): 349-61.
Rothbard, Murray N. *The Complete Libertarian Forum 1969-1984*. Auburn, AL: Mises Institute, 2012.
———. *The Rothbard Reader*. Ed. Joseph T. Salerno and Matthew McCaffrey. Auburn, AL: Mises Institute, 2016.
Salutati, Coluccio. *De tyranno. Political Writings*. Ed. Stefano U. Baldassarri. Trans. Rolf Bagemihl. Latin and English. Cambridge, MA: Harvard UP, 2014. 64-143.
Sozzi, Leonello. "Cultura e potere nel Rinascimento." *Cultura e potere nel Rinascimento* 9-18.
Speak Truth to Power: A Quaker Search for an Alternative to Violence. Originally published 1955. http://www.quaker.org/sttp.html. Online.
Tarabotti, Arcangela. *Inferno monacale*. Ed. Francesca Medioli. Torino: Rosenberg & Sellier, 1990.
———. *Paternal Tyranny*. Ed. Letizia Panizza. Chicago: U of Chicago P, 2004.

Zane D. R. Mackin

Dante, the Rhetoric of Crisis, and Vigilante Preaching

Abstract: In order to secure the right to speak authoritatively on issues ranging from theology, to politics, to morality, Dante claims that the official source of moral and spiritual instruction, the Church, has fallen short in its duties. This "rhetoric of crisis" that Dante devises is part of the rhetorical apparatus of preachers in his time, and had been theorized in preaching manuals. This is one of many tools that Dante borrows from preaching in his construction of an identity (applicable to both the Poet and the Pilgrim) as a divinely-sanctioned preacher and prophet. This paper examines the particulars of Dante's "rhetoric of crisis" and shows how it can affect our reading of scenes in the *Commedia*, particularly *Inferno* 23 and 28, in which Dante highlights the pastoral failure of official ecclesiastics and downplays the perils of unsanctioned preaching.

Key Words: Dante Alighieri, Preaching, Giordano da Pisa, Thomas of Chobham, Epistle to the Cardinals, Letter to the Cardinals, Inferno 23, Inferno 28, Fourth Lateran Council, Jovial Friars, Fratres Gaudentes, Salimbene, fra Dolcino

Introduction

Dante's interest in sermons and preaching is evident across the span of his writing, starting with his *Vita nuova* setting of an encounter with Beatrice in a religious context, arguably in church while words are spoken about Mary ("ove s'udivano parole della Regina della gloria" 5.1), and ending with Beatrice's diatribe against bad preachers in *Paradiso* 29.103-26). Instances of Dante's reporting on preaching as some social phenomenon external to him, something done by others, are dwarfed, however, by the many occasions he uses sermonic techniques as part of his rhetorical apparatus. Across his oeuvre Dante employs the rhetorical structures, cadences and key vocabulary frequently found in sermons of his time. Indeed because of their frequent recourse to the language of sermons, the *Commedia* and some of Dante's other writing can themselves be considered, after a fashion, preaching texts.

Dante's varied and complex uses of preaching in the *Commedia* and elsewhere is extensive enough to merit a full monographical treatment. This study's limited aim is to explore what motivates Dante to assume the preacher's voice in the first place, and to outline how Dante consolidates his claim to the right to preach.

Preaching in Dante's time was an activity under Church jurisdiction. Without official ecclesiastical authorization, one could not simply preach without encountering immediate anathemas and prohibitions. In response to this, Dante uses what I call a "rhetoric of crisis." Such rhetoric outlines a situation in which the Church has lost sight of its pastoral obligation and the populace is starving for guidance; in consequence a self-appointed "preacher of justice" must rise up and fill the pastoral void. For the first part of this essay, I will rely largely on Dante's epistle to the Cardinals of 1315, while making occasional comparisons to contemporary accounts of preaching, and referring to the theoretical treatises on preaching, primarily Thomas of Chobham's *Summa de arte praedicandi*. In the second part of this paper, I will explore two textual loci in the *Commedia* — the encounter with the Jovial Friars in *Inferno* 23 and the discussion of fra Dolcino in *Inferno* 28 — to illustrate how a knowledge of the importance of preaching both in Dante's thought and his historical period might contribute to a better understanding of these passages.

Until recently few scholars examined the issue of preaching in the *Commedia*, aside from Carlo Delcorno, who studied the possible echoes of Giordano da Pisa's sermons in Dante's language.[1] Delcorno did not aim to prove that Dante witnessed the sermons of Giordano and was directly influenced by them, so much as he meant to illustrate how typical features of medieval preaching cadences and exclamations, so familiar to an average lay listener, find echo in Dante's writings.[2] The emphatic apostrophe, "O Simon mago, o miseri seguaci" initiating *Inferno* 19, for example, echoes a commonplace rhetorical fillip used in preaching for emphasis (302-03).[3] There are also traces of the formulas used in catechistic preaching in *Inferno* 19, which Dante deploys with utmost irony in the pilgrim's

---

[1] "Dante e l'exemplum medievale," "Cadenze e figure della predicazione nel viaggio dantesco," "Schede su Dante e la retorica della predicazione," "Dante e il linguaggio dei predicatori." More recently, Nicolò Maldina has been exploring Dante and preaching: "Dante e l'immagine del buon predicatore nel Paradiso," "Tra predicazione e liturgia. Modelli e fortuna del 'Pater noster' di Purgatorio XI 1-21." Maldina is working on a book on the topic, hopefully to be published later this year.

[2] "Nel sistema retorico della *Commedia* agiscono i modelli retorici della predicazione," Delcorno says, and later adds that these are are "i moduli sintattici volgari resi familiari all'orecchio dei fiorentini dalla martellante pastorale degli ordini Mendicanti" ("Schede su Dante e la retorica della predicazione" 301).

[3] Here, Delcorno also claims that the *exclamatio* of *Par.* 11 (1-12), beginning, "O insensata cura de' mortali," likewise intends to recall the emphatic exhortations heard from the pulpit. Delcorno admits that some of these apostrophes could be credited to Classical influence such as the satires of Persius, but he adds that this would not justify the complex of phrases following Aquinas's initial exclamation ("chi dietro a *iura* e chi ad amforismi / sen giva, e chi seguendo sacerdozio [...]"), which he argues are more common to preaching: "All'esclamazione segue un ampio gioco di correlazioni 'a effetto descrittivo,' secondo un uso frequentissimo dell'oratoria sacra" (302). For an alternate opinion, see Luciano Rossi, who claims instead that "una simile *deploratio* fa parte della tradizione satirica medievale," using *Carmina Burana* and *Roman de la Rose* as examples (1775). Also, see Lucia Battaglia Ricci, who in turn identifies traces of Persius and Boethius in Dante's exclamation (137).

conversation with Pope Nicholas III.[4] The poet's assumption of the preaching voice here highlights a crisis in pastoral care, which is one of his main concerns in this canto, especially regarding the failings of the pope, the *servus servorum Dei*. Dante front-loads *Inferno* 19 with nuances of the confessional long before the condemned pope is identified, and in so doing he sets the stage — or pulpit, rather — from which the pilgrim issues his long invective against papal corruption, and which likewise shows the bold colors of a heated sermon.[5]

The pilgrim's deployment of the preacher's language in his dialogue with Nicholas III illustrates an ironic role reversal between the quondam pope and Dante the layman, suggesting a harsh critique of those who preach by profession. Dante here uses the structures of preaching to "authorize" his critical voice, while at the same time questioning the authority of the Church, the very entity that officially legitimizes preachers. The daring of this move is amplified when it is recognized that the privilege to preach was always conferred by religious authorities, and was never extended to laypersons. What does it mean, then, when a layperson deliberately reverses the roles between preacher and preached-to?[6] While it is clear that Dante uses preaching to give a certain credibility and heft to his own voice, he does so in open breach of canon law governing these matters.

Dante breaks with customary practices regarding preaching as part of his articulation of the Church's negligence of pastoral care, which he considers a serious social emergency. Emphasis on this state of emergency is not limited to the encounter with Pope Nicholas III here, but is actually sustained throughout the entirety of *Commedia*. For, in fact, across the poem are situations in which an official exponent of the Church is either silent or silencing another, and as a result an underdog is pushed into the spotlight as the preacher of truth. With rare exception, those who preach in the *Commedia* are never sanctioned, and their

---

[4] Delcorno calls the pilgrim's screed against Nicholas III "ironicamente modulato sulle formule catechistiche della predicazione" ("Schede su Dante e la retorica della predicazione" 304). Benedetto Croce also recognizes the "oratoria" in this canto. While Croce does not claim that Dante's speech is that of a preacher here, he does concede that the pilgrim functions as a proxy for divine justice, speaking "non solo da pubblico accusatore, ma da esecutore e giustiziere" (91). As a temporary human representative of divine justice, Dante, at least for this moment, appears to take on the role of pope.

[5] "Tutto il canto XIX può essere studiato come stilizzazione e a tratti parodia delle modalità di enunciazione del discorso dei predicatori, soprattutto i vv. 90-117, dove il poeta lancia la sua invettiva contro il papa simoniaco, che, confitto in uno dei fori della terza bolgia, può rispondere solo con i movimenti convulsi delle 'piote'" ("Schede su Dante e la retorica della predicazione" 303).

[6] It also bears mention that Nicholas III was especially concerned with preaching and its authorization. His 1279 bull *Exiit qui seminat*, which, as Dameron says, "redefined papal ownership of the ideal of apostolic poverty" also energetically reaffirms papal authority to determine where, when and how Franciscans may preach (214, *Les Registres de Nicolas III* 239).

sermons are a product of deep spiritual inspiration, supplemented by Scriptural allusions and references. Against these impromptu preachers Dante contrasts those designated to preach by ecclesiastical mandate, but who neither speak nor allow others to do so.[7] This dynamic is central to Dante's "rhetoric of crisis," which he uses to ultimately authorize himself as the speaker of truth *par excellence*.

Medieval Preaching: A Brief Historical Background
The history of preaching and its legislation in Dante's time dates back to the very end of the twelfth century and beginning of the thirteenth century, when preachers were deployed in the southern Languedoc to combat heretical preaching by the Cathars. Although from its inception the Church always delivered sermons, from roughly 1050 its dedication to pastoral care had declined and become so scarce that until the thirteenth century some members of the laity infrequently heard sermons (Vauchez 97; Roberts 152; Delcorno, "Medieval Preaching in Italy" 450). This is noted in a 1305 sermon by Giordano da Pisa, which describes an Italy completely barren of sermons until St. Dominic begs permission to preach from an astonished Innocent III:

[...] perocché a quel tempo non facean prediche se non i Vescovi; i monaci, i preti, i remiti non predicavano; non piaccia a Dio, ma i Vescovi. Questo era loro proprio officio; e questi erano già a tanto venuti, che non predicavano quasi di niuno tempo. Leggesi bene di Santo Augustino, e di Santo Jeronimo, che diceano alcun'otta al popolo certe omelìe, e questo fecero rade volte; gli altri non si trova che quasi predicassero se non rade volte; quasi nella città in tutto l'anno facea una predica il Vescovo, sicchè non si sapea che si fosse predicare.
(*Prediche del Beato fra Giordano da Rivalto* 1: 235)

---

[7] The issue of speech and silencing is itself a subcomponent of a general principle that underlies the entirety of Dante's *Commedia*: absence vs. presence; vacancies vs. occupation, the void vs. fullness. These are often cast in an ethical key. We see this dynamic at work in Dante's harsh treatment of Rudolph of Habsburg (*Purg.* 7.94-96), who is explicitly called out (along with his son, Albert) earlier in *Purg.* 6 for not assuming his role as emperor, thereby leaving Italy without leadership, keeling like an unhelmed ship in a storm ("nave sanza nocchiere in gran tempesta") and going wild ("indomita e selvaggia") like a horse without a rider ("la sella è vota") (*Purg* 6.77, 98, 89). To illustrate the delinquent state of monastic orders, St. Benedict uses the language of concavity: "Le mura che solieno esser badia / fatte son spelonche" ("the walls that used to be abbeys / have been made caves" *Par.* 22.76-77). St. Peter calls the Papal Seat ("il luogo mio") vacant in the eyes of Jesus ("che vaca / ne la presenza del Figliuol di Dio" *Par.* 27.23-24).The poet's world view is literally one of holes, negative spaces, that need to be re-filled, replenished. Most obvious is Hell itself, a concave space created when Lucifer was cast out of heaven, and Mount Purgatory, the convex mound that redeems the vacancy of Hell by means of a literal stairway to Heaven, replenishing the promise of eternal life. Spiritual knowledge is often compared to food, of which the Pilgrim is "digiuno," hungry, fasting, barren. (*Par.* 15.49, 19.25, to name two occasions). And finally, in *Paradiso*, are the vacant seats in the rose of the Empyrean (*Par* 32.25-27), which will be entirely filled at the day of Judgment.

([…] seeing that at that time no one gave sermons except Bishops; monks, priests, hermits did not preach. This did not please God, but it pleased the bishops. This was their specific duty, and even these had come to such that they gave sermons hardly at all. One reads indeed of Saint Augustine, and Saint Jerome, that they delivered homilies to the people sometimes, but this they only did rarely; one finds that the rest almost did not preach at all if not rarely; in the city the Bishop maybe gave a sermon once in a year, such that nobody knew what preaching was.)

Until that point, the Church had assumed that the laity did not need sermons and could be kept within the fold through the sacraments alone (Rouse and Rouse 43-44). Instead, distracting new ideologies began to sprout up here and there, especially in the Languedoc and in northern Italy. By propagating new theological ideas through preaching, these sects — the Cathars, Waldensians and others — were met with enthusiastic public response, and over time their increasing popularity began to challenge the Church's previously absolute control over faith and its expression. By 1200, Jacques de Vitry expresses concern about such "pseudo or false preachers," highlighting a new point of stress between popular religious expression and the institutional Church (d'Avray 25). Eventually the Church would have to respond to these challenges or otherwise suffer ideological adulteration of the integrity of the body of Christ by new theologies.[8]

Like any hegemon seeking to establish and maintain its authority, the Church needed to curtail those movements seeking to challenge it: leaders of heresy must be suppressed and those at risk of switching sides must be kept within the fold. Dual goals require dual tactics. To control those already organized in opposition against it, the Church worked aggressively to extirpate entrenched heresy through various repressive measures: prohibitions, anathemas, inquisitorial processes, and the Albigensian Crusade, all aiming to strike at these resilient new sects.[9] Those who had not yet abandoned the fold but could potentially stray required more gentle shepherding.[10] For these, persuasion would work better than pyres, hence

---

[8] "The progress of Catharism and other heterodox religious movements forced the clergy and the papacy to react promptly, before the entire edifice was undermined" (Vauchez 99).
[9] While sometimes repression of heresy was extreme, as is the case for the Albigensian Crusade, some scholars say that much anti-heretical legislation was mostly bluster, at least until the end of the thirteenth century: "Extant communal legislation against heretics often looks pro forma. Cities inserted Frederick II's antiheresy decree into their statutes verbatim or pledged to obey it without any provisions for enforcement" (Thompson 139-40). For more on inquisitorial aims and processes in the Middle Ages, and especially in the 13th century, see Cardini and Montesanto, and Merlo. Moore has recently published a volume, *The War on Heresy*, in which one of the main arguments is that the "heretic" was often merely a person or group of people who could "frustrate the ideals or obstruct the ambitions of secular or ecclesiastical power" (330). Thus inquisitions and wars against heresy were really only a way to consolidate power, and to "extend the reach of governmental intrusions" (329).
[10] This concern for reconciliation is clear in Innocent's emphasis on assimilating these new

the Church began to deploy preachers into zones troubled by heresy. These first sallies, however, revealed insufficient preparation compared to the superior preaching of the heretics, as the case with Cathar preachers in the Languedoc shows (Rouse and Rouse 52-55). These initial efforts in the last quarter of the twelfth century were halting and sporadic, and preachers struggled under their meager training. In response, Church thinkers proposed various vetting apparatuses to raise standards and to keep preaching orthodox.[11]

This trend towards greater quality and control eventually led to the Fourth Lateran Council in November 1215, and its resultant legislation was the first universal attempt to address preaching and preachers seriously and systematically through prescription and proscription (Rouse and Rouse 53). One of the canons from this council ordered that Bishops appoint properly trained men to preach to the laity:

Inter cetera quae ad salutem spectant populi Christiani, pabulum verbi Dei permaxime noscitur sibi esse necessarium, quia sicut corpus materiali, sic anima spirituali cibo nutritur, eo quod *non in solo panem vivit homo, sed in omni verbo quod procedit de ore Dei*. Unde cum saepe contingat, quod episcopi [...] per se ipsos non sufficiunt ministrare populo verbum Dei, maxime per amplas dioeceses et diffusas, generali constitutione sancimus, ut episcopi viros idoneos ad sanctae praedicationis officium salubriter exequendum assumant, potentes in opere et sermone, qui plebes sibi commissas vice ipsorum cum per se idem nequiverint sollicite visitantes, eas verbo aedificent et exemplo.
(Among the various things that are conducive to the salvation of the Christian people, the nourishment of God's word is recognized to be especially necessary, since just as the body is fed with material food so the soul is fed with spiritual food, according to the words, *man lives not by bread alone but by every word that proceeds from the mouth of God*. It often happens that bishops by themselves are not sufficient to minister the word of God to the people, especially in large and scattered dioceses [...]. We therefore decree by this general constitution that bishops are to appoint suitable men to carry out with profit this duty of sacred preaching, men who are powerful in word and deed and who will visit with care the people entrusted to them in place of the bishops, since these by themselves are unable to do it, and will build them up by word and example.)
(*Decrees of the Ecumenical Councils* 239-40)

---

unorthodox groups popping up, like the Humiliati and the Waldensians. In 1199, he orders that laymen may read the Scripture in the vernacular, as it is better for them to know the true Scriptures "lest these simple people should be forced into heresy" (qtd. in d'Avray 26). For Innocent's view on vernacularized Scripture, see Boyle 97-107. And yet, history proves that access to Scripture does not keep heresy at bay. For example the Cathars had a strong book culture, and Scripture figured very strongly in their preaching practice. They often had the New Testament or the gospel of John to expound from, which one Cathar would read in Latin while a *perfectus* would expound on it in the common tongue (Arnold 186-87).

[11] Odo of Sully, bishop of Paris from 1197-1208, was especially vocal about this, as was Robert Courson, who expressed his opinions in the councils of Paris in 1213 and Rouen in 1214 (Baldwin 110).

Simply put, bishops, previously the only ones authorized to preach, were required to devolve their authority to preach upon others, to ensure that all people would have the chance to hear the word of God. This proposal for increased recruitment of suitable preachers was essentially a move to insure quality control; the Church would multiply its number of preachers, train them rigorously, and then deploy them across Europe, enough that the entire continent echoed with the official theology of the Church and replaced the many heretical voices that before drowned out the official message.[12] The canon elsewhere addresses these heretics more directly and sternly: anyone attempting to preach without episcopal permission would be outside of the protection of the Church, and any rebel who persisted would likely find himself before the inquisitor, maybe tortured, and even lashed to the stake and burnt.[13]

Thus preaching in Dante's time was both facilitated and controlled through the absolute juridical power of the Holy See, and the only legitimate preachers were those vetted by the ecclesiastical hierarchy. And yet, medieval theoreticians of preaching, who knew their history, understood that the religion had suffered crises in the past, and could potentially suffer one in the future. Such a crisis could be exacerbated — and perhaps even caused by — a lack of properly trained preachers willing to execute their function as spiritual leaders, leaving the collective soul of Christendom hanging in the balance. In his *Summa de arte praedicandi* Thomas of Chobham allows for the possibility of preaching without certification in times of acute need:

Adiciendum est ad predicta, quod in tempore necessitatis, scilicet cum inminet periculum fidei, potest et debet quilibet predicare, sine exceptione et conditionis et etatis et sexus.
(It should be added to the aforementioned that in a time of need, for example in the threat of immediate peril to faith, that anyone can and ought to preach, with no exception to condition or age or sex.)

(Chobham 71)

Thus, when the true faith is in some way under threat and there are no qualified clergy to defend it, others may step into the breach. Chobham enumerates historical cases in which "unauthorized" preaching saved the faith: he notes St. Catherine's resolution to preach against paganism at the palace of Emperor Maxentius, even though she was called and driven to do so by no church authority ("non vocata, non compulsa venit ad palatium propter defensione fidei

---

[12] For more on the religious training of preachers, at least among Franciscans, see Roest's two very comprehensive works: *A History of Franciscan Education*, and *Franciscan Literature of Religious Instruction before the Council of Trent.*

[13] The Church's stance is uncompromising on permission. Not only are unauthorized preachers categorically criminalized, even those who merely provided places for preachers to stay or deliver sermons could have their houses destroyed (Arnold 185). The torture and execution of preachers was a real threat, as the fate of fra Dolcino, whom we discuss later in this paper, will show.

christianae"). He also mentions Paul the Hermit, who had neither erudition nor literary skill ("rusticus et fere illitteratus") but still preached, when Arians threatened Christian orthodoxy. Thus, even though the official stance on lay preaching by Dante's time is one of total prohibition, Chobham's words demonstrate that views on lay preaching were not always in lockstep with Papal decisions, and that some people were still haunted by the specter of pastoral collapse and ensuing spiritual crisis.

Dante's Letter to the Cardinals and His Claim to the Right to Preach
Dante exploits that fear of emergency, attributable to the scarcity of qualified preachers, by announcing a real crisis in his letter to the Cardinals in the Spring of 1315. Here he describes the clergy not in terms of their competence but in terms of their failure. Their rejection of pastoral care suggests a situation of grave "periculum fidei" in his time, a void in leadership that begs for someone, neither "vocatus" nor "compulsus," to step into the figurative pulpit.

The letter is itself rather a fiery sermon of rebuke in response to the deadlock and crisis of leadership among the Cardinals in conclave at Carpentras. The Holy See, transferred to Avignon since 1309, had undergone a year of *sede vacante* following the death of Clement V. The Cardinals were split into factions and were thus unable to decide a successor — a situation that would last for over another year. Probably pessimistic about the immediate future of the Church after the death of the pope whom he called a "pastor sanza legge" (*Inf.* 19.83), Dante likely wavered between hope and dread as the Cardinals deliberated over the selection of the next pope. That they finally settled on John XXII in August 1316, the pope whom Dante in *Par* 18.130-36 deemed so greedy for gold ("colui che volle viver solo / e che per salti fu tratto al martiro" indicates John the Baptist, whose face adorned the florin) that he no longer recognized the apostles Peter or Paul ("il pescator né Polo"), likely confirmed the worst of fears Dante might have nurtured during the conclave process. Dante's epistle urges the Cardinals at Carpentras to resolve this crisis of authority. Who, Dante asks, will lead the people? It is in this particular context that he writes the following words regarding speech and pastoral care:

Quippe de ovibus in pascuis Iesu Christi minima una sum; quippe nulla pastorali auctoritate abutens, quoniam divitie mecum non sunt.
(*Opere Minori*, tome 2, *Epist.* 11.9, p. 584)
(I am certainly the least of the sheep in Christ's fields; certainly in no way do I abuse the authority of a pastor, for I have no riches.)

With these words, Dante seeks to stake his claim as one with both the right and the obligation to speak his mind. The humility expressed in the words "minima una [ovis] sum" is certainly disingenuous, for they draw directly from the words of the apostle Paul, who in his letter to the Corinthians calls himself the least of the apostles ("minimus apostolorum" 1 Cor. 15. 9). Even though he was not one of the twelve apostles who knew Jesus while alive, Paul emphasizes that his vision of the risen Christ (a vision that occurred when he was traveling on the road to Damascus to persecute Christians, Acts 9]) qualifies him too as an apostle: "novissime autem omnium tanquam abortivo, visus est et mihi" ("and last of all, he was seen by me, as by one born out of due time" 1 Cor. 15. 8). As Paul leverages mystical vision to claim the status of an Apostle, Dante hitchhikes onto Paul's now canonical status to validate his own claim to authority. In this way, the man Dante earlier in this letter called preacher to the gentiles ("Paulus gentium predicator") thus validates Dante as a preacher to the Cardinals (580).

Dante was not the first after Paul to claim to be "minimus," for the term was already employed in medieval preaching when the speaker either needed to communicate an urgent message or to sway a crowd not normally disposed to listening. In the *De eruditione praedicatorum,* Humbert of Romans explains that preachers can use the exordium of their sermons to call attention to their inexperience or insufficiency in order to gain the sympathy of their listeners.[14] An anecdote recorded by Rangerius, the late eleventh-century bishop of Lucca, demonstrates this practice in action when an anonymous monk gives teeth to a sermon against a simonist by downplaying his own rhetorical skill: "Non sum doctus homo," the monk says, "sed fretus simplicitate / Atque fide sana, si placet aspicere. / Ecce probo, non ambiguis, non arte dolosa, / sed rebus certis te male desipere" ("I am not a learned man, but rely on my guilelessness and pure faith, if it should please you to look. See here, I demonstrate — not with ambiguities, not with deceptive artifices, but rather with certain facts — that you act foolishly and wrongly") (1264). Like this unnamed monk, Dante engineers a theatrical presentation of himself as a humble preacher of truth, one who is driven, almost spontaneously, to speak words against figures more powerful than himself.

This profession of humility followed by denunciation is but one of the strategies that Dante employs to give heft to his voice while simultaneously neutralizing the risk of preaching without authorization. In the second part of this

---

[14] "Notandum vero quod prothema quandoque sumitur a persona praedicantis, ut quando aliquis ignotus praedicator de ordine Fratrum Praedicatorum, vel Minorum, vult praedicare in aliqua parochia, in qua est ignotus ipse et status ordinis sui, exponit in principio statum suum et ordinis sui, ne forte credatur esse quaestuarius praedicator, dicens illud Pauli, 2 *Cor.* 12: Non quaerimus quae vestra sunt, sed vos; vel quod insufficientiam suam cognoscens, ipsam praetendit exemplo Hieremiae, *Hier.* 1: A, a, a, Domine, quia puer ego sum, et ecce nescio loqui" ("The theme of the exordium may refer to the person of the preacher, for instance when the preacher is a religious of the Order of Friars Preachers or Friars Minor visiting a parish, where both he and his Order are unknown. He will make known, therefore, at the beginning, the spirit and the mission of his order, so that it will not be thought that he is preaching in order to collect money. He should therefore say with St. Paul: 'I do not seek yours but you' [II Cor. 12:14]. And when he feels his own insufficiency, he shall say with Jeremias: 'Ah, ah, ah, Lord God, behold I cannot speak, for I am a child' [Jer 1:6]") (*Opera de vita regulari* 481-82; *Treatise on Preaching* 119-20).

phrase, "nulla pastorali auctoritate abutens," Dante introduces his rhetoric of crisis, an alert that something has gone wrong within the traditional ecclesiastical hierarchy. As in the case of the anonymous preacher in the above example, Dante projects humility while simultaneously denouncing his addressee. And with deft use of Scripture, he links himself to a Pauline tradition of self-validation by acknowledging a higher authority than terrestrial representatives of the faith.

The Cardinals have shirked their duties. They have abandoned their flocks. Indeed they have done even worse through silencing those summoned on Divine command to suture this breach in pastoral leadership. Dante calls attention to these latter figures, and aligns himself with them:

Nam etiam "in ore lactentium et infantium" sonuit iam Deo placita veritas, et cecus natus veritatem confessus est, quam Pharisei non modo tacebant, sed et maligne reflectere conabuntur. Hiis habeo persuasum quod audio."
(Opere Minori, tome 2, *Epist.* 11.10, p. 584)
(For even "in the mouth of the suckling and the infant" has the truth pleasing to God resounded, and a blind newborn has confessed the truth which the Pharisees not only were silent about, but evilly tried to turn away. I am persuaded to dare on account of these examples.)

The passage is calculated to criticize and perhaps even to offend. The Cardinals, who in the Pope's absence are the Church's most elite representatives of the faith, are compared to Pharisees, whose silence ("non modo tacebant") was overshadowed by their attempt to thwart the speech of others ("maligne reflectere conabuntur"); the reference to Pharisees intends to recall Jesus's ongoing struggle against the Pharisees in the Gospels. In spite of — indeed because of — an oppressive atmosphere of censorship that Dante describes, truth must be spoken; but who is left to speak when the priests have abdicated their roles? Dante suggests that in times of crisis, new speakers are designated by miraculous action: the "infans," by definition without language, speaks by Divine fiat. As for the infant, so too for the suckling. Milk often represents both poetic and theological knowledge in Dante's symbolic economy.[15] A baby still at its mother's teat, still

---

[15] Dante consistently associates milk with both poetic and divine speech in the *Commedia*. Here are a few examples: Homer is called the one "che le Muse lattar più ch'altri mai" ("whom the Muses suckled more than any other" *Purg.* 22.101-02); In *Paradiso* 11, Thomas Aquinas remarks on those Dominican preachers who, not following the mandates of their order's founder, return to the sheepfold with no milk to give to the rest of the flock ("e vagabunde più da esso vanno / più tornano a l'ovil di latte vòte" ("and the farther his sheep go wandering / from him, the emptier of milk / do they at last come back into the fold" *Par.* 11.128-29); Dante narrates something of an apotheosis of this symbolic relationship of milk to truth, when he compares the angelic host extending its flames upwards towards Mary to an infant extending its arms to its mother after suckling ("E come fantolin ch'nver' la mamma / tende le braccia, poi che 'l latte prese, / per l'animo che 'nfin

ingesting milk, is not yet capable of delivering it to others, and yet from its mouth issues truth pleasing to God. Likewise, the "cecus natus" ("someone born blind") is suddenly endowed with sufficient vision to know and profess truth. According to this logic, to speak truth does not require ecclesiastical status, university training or natural skill; instead, a miracle occurs in the mouth of a baby, and vision is instilled in the mind of the blind. In the context of *impossibilia* miraculously overcome, Dante finds the courage and claims the right to speak ("his habeo persuasum quod audeo").

The Silent Preachers of Inferno *23*
While the Church's attitude to preaching primarily regards authorization and control, Dante's *Commedia* proposes a different stance, at once stricter and more tolerant. Dante emphasizes far more than does the Church that its representatives are duty-bound to preach and must not sway from that obligation. An exploration of the Jovial Friars Catalano dei Malavolti and Loderingo degli Andalò of *Inferno* 23 will illustrate how Dante's emphasis on silence means to highlight his intolerance of religious figures who do not preach. As we see also in the Letter to the Cardinals, in these circumstances silence is truly an abomination.

The Ordo Militiae Beatae Mariae Virginis Gloriosae, popularly and derisively called the Fratres Gaudentes or Jovial Friars, was founded in Bologna around 1260.[16] Its rule, which followed the Augustinian model, was approved by Urban IV on December 23, 1261 (De Stefano 2229; Meersseman 304). Although the order was founded by several people working together, sources confirm that Loderingo degli Andalò was its principal founder and first prior (De Stefano 228). The ostensible reason for this order's existence was to defend those who could not defend themselves, as Jacopo della Lana puts it: "[...] il quale ordine sarebbe ad aiutare in ditto e in fatto, con arme e con cavalli, mettendo la vita per ogni vedova e ogni pupillo, ogni pellegrino e ogni povero etc." ("[...] the order would be to help in word and in deed, with arms and with horses, risking one's life for every widow and little child, every pilgrim and every pauper etc.").[17] Although

---

di fuor s'infiamma; ciascun di quei candori in sù si stese / con la sua cima, sì che l'alto affetto / ch'elli avieno a Maria mi fu palese" ("And, like a baby reaching out its arms / to mamma after it has drunk her milk, / its inner impulse kindled into outward flame, / all these white splendors were reaching upward / with their fiery tips, so that their deep affection / for Mary was made clear to me" *Par.* 23.121-25).

[16] Salimbene introduces them thus: "Isti a rusticis truffatorie et derisive appellantur Gaudentes, quasi dicant: ideo facti sunt fratres, quia nolunt communicare aliis bona sua, sed volunt tantummodo sibi habere" ("These men were jokingly and derisively called Godenti by the populace, as if to say: they have become brothers [friars] simply because they do not wish to share their goods with others but to have them wholly to themselves") (*Salimbene de Adam Cronica* 678; *The Chronicle of Salimbene de Adam* 477).

[17] All early commentaries to Dante's *Commedia* were retrieved according to canto and verse from the Dartmouth Dante Project (http://dante.dartmouth.edu).

42 Zane D. R. Mackin

the order officially operated to pursue these noble goals, the Jovials were in effect little more than the police wing of the church, enforcing papal interests wherever their muscle was needed (De Stefano 226). Hence the ruin that the shade of the friar Catalano de' Malavolti describes in the following lines:

> Frati godenti fummo, e bolognesi;
> io Catalano e questi Loderingo
> nomati, e da tua terra insieme presi
>   come suole esser tolto un uom solingo,
> per conservar sua pace; e fummo tali,
> ch'ancor si pare intorno dal Gardingo
> (We were Jovial Friars, born in Bologna.
> My name was Catalano, his Loderingo.
> Your city made the two of us a pair,
>   where usually a single man was chosen,
> to keep the peace within, and we were such
> that all around Gardingo the ruins can be seen.)
>   (*Inf.* 23.105-08).[18]

Central to Catalano's confession is the joint taking of the podestà (at the Pope's behest) of Florence in conjunction with Loderingo ("da tua terra insieme presi"), a position originally meant to go to "un uom solingo." This led to social and political unrest, and finally internecine local violence. Under pressure from Clement IV, Catalano and Loderingo allowed the Guelphs to return to the city, and this in turn led to the ouster of Guido Novello, head of the Ghibellines, from the city. A popular uprising followed, in which Ghibelline properties were destroyed, including the houses of the Uberti family, which Catalano obliquely mentions in "intorno dal Guardigno," as the houses were located there.[19]

From its beginning, the canto is filled with suggestions of monasticism, as many scholars have noted, which highlights the fact that the sinners named here are all designated religious leaders.[20] The Pilgrim and Vergil too are absorbed into

---

[18] Citations of the *Commedia* are from *La commedia secondo l'antica vulgata*, edited by Giorgio Petrocchi. Translations are from Robert and Jean Hollander's edition of *The Divine Comedy*.

[19] For more on the political involvement of the Gaudentes and their two founders, see: De Stefano, *Riformatori ed eretici del Medioevo* 228-69; Meersseman, *Dossier de l'ordre de la pénitence au XIIIe siècle* 304-05. For a more specific examination of their involvement in the political situation of Florence that Dante describes here, see Maggini 14-16 and Giannantonio 223-26. For general information on the Gaudentes, see Federici's classic study, and Meersseman 295-307. Regarding Catalano and Loderingo as represented in Dante's *Inferno*, see Raimondi 229-49.

[20] Raimondi sees in the opening tercet a "grigia atmosfera ecclesiastica" and an "aria claustrale" that "si stende cauta ma prepotente dietro la trama di parole chiave quali 'monaci, Clugnì, manto, stola, collegio, cappe, frati'"(239-40). Russo, more synthetically

this monastic atmosphere, as they enter the space "taciti, soli, sanza compagnia," plodding in single file in the customary manner of traveling Franciscans ("come frati minor vanno per via" 23.1-3). On first seeing the sinners in this bolgia, Dante again uses monastic language:

> Là giù trovammo una gente dipinta
> che giva intorno assai con lenti passi,
> piangendo e nel sembiante stanca e vinta.
>   Elli avean cappe con cappucci bassi
> dinanzi a li occhi, fatte de la taglia
> che in Clugnì per li monaci fassi.
>   Di fuor dorate son, sì ch'elli abbaglia;
> ma dentro tutte piombo, e gravi tanto,
> che Federigo le mettea di paglia.
>   Oh in etterno faticoso manto!
>
> (*Inf.* 23.58-67)
>
> (Down there we came upon a lacquered people
> who made their round, in tears, with listless steps.
> They seemed both weary and defeated.
>   The cloaks they wore, cut like the capes
> sewn for the monks at Cluny,
> had cowls that hung down past their eyes.
>   Gilded and dazzling on the outside,
> within they are of lead, so ponderous
> that those imposed by Frederick would seem but straw.
>   Oh what a toilsome cloak to wear forever!)

---

than most before and after him, notes the accumulation of different terms and adjectives to "rendere quell'atmosfera greve e conventuale che sembra incombere su questa bolgia" (37). Giannantonio confirms the emphasis Dante intends in these lines, noting the many instances in Franciscan literature that describe the silence and walking in pairs that Dante here highlights. This emphasis, Giannantonio says, means to direct us towards a certain interpretation for the whole canto, which "ci induce a riflettere anche sulla commessa ispirazione claustrale dell'intera bolgia, ossia del 'collegio de l'ipocriti tristi' (vv. 91-92) che evoca cappe e stole, linguaggio biblico e casta sacerdotale, colpa clericale come l'ipocrisia e pena ricalcata su abiti conventuali" (212). Giannantonio reaffirms the importance of the monastic element in this canto when discussing the Jovial Friar's great lead capes (221-22). Keen also notes the monastic atmosphere of this canto, although her interpretation overlooks Dante's intended irony: for her, the "collegio / de l'ipocriti tristi" (*Inf.* 23.91-92) is not an opportunity to meditate on the obvious problem of Catalano and Loderingo's monastic fraudulence, but rather "an attempt to lend an air of familiarity, even dignity, to this assembly dressed in monastic style" (183). Some studies pay little to no attention to the patently monastic elements in this canto, notably: Bonora, Maggini, di Pino, Hollander, and Kleinhenz.

Later, one of these "gente dipinta," Catalano de' Malavolti, refers to this bolgia, to which he too belongs, as a "collegio," another term for "monastero" or "convento," to which he immediately adds in a bitterly ironic turn "de l'ipocriti tristi" ("of sad hypocrites" 23.91-92).[21] If this place is a monastery, it is an infernal one.[22] To add to this claustral atmosphere, the poet never refers to any figure here simply as "ombra" or "anima" as is his custom, but instead calls them "frati." The pilgrim calls out "O frati" (23.109), Catalano specifies himself and Loderingo as "frati godenti" (23.103), and Dante repeatedly refers to Catalano as "frate" in the narration (23.114, 127, 142).

The early commentary to this passage suggests that hypocrisy is a sin very closely related to speech. For example, Benvenuto da Imola highlights the performative and rhetorical aspects of hypocrisy by noting as example a colorful story about a church pastor who "potavit se multa malvasia" ("got drunk on much malvasia"), passed off his drunken weeping during his sermon as pious sorrow, and thus moved his audience to weeping and emptying their purses into the alms box.[23] Pietro Alighieri recalls the Scriptural foundation for Dante's representation of hypocrisy, Matthew 23.27, in which Jesus compares the Pharisees and scribes to whited sepulchers, which are beautiful on the outside, but contain nothing but death within ("sepulchris dealbatis quae a foris parent hominibus speciosa intus vero plena sunt ossibus mortuorum et omni spurcitia"). Guido da Pisa and Pietro Alighieri find echoes of Matthew 7.15 in Dante's gold-plated capes. In the gospel

---

[21] When referred to in the singular, "collegio" in Dante is almost always colored by monasticism. In *Purgatorio*, the spirit of Guido Guinizzelli refers to heaven as a monastery where Christ is abbot: "Or se tu hai sì ampio privilegio, / che licito ti sia l'andare al chiostro / nel quale è Cristo abate del collegio, / falli per me un dir d'un paternostro [...]" ("Now, if you possess such ample privilege / that you are allowed into the cloister / where Christ is abbot of the brothers, / say a Paternoster there for me [...]" *Purg.* 26.127-30). In *Paradiso*, after his speech to Dante, St. Benedict, founder of cenobitic monasticism in the western church, rejoins the other contemplative spirits, his "collegio" ("Così mi disse, e indi si raccolse / al suo collegio, e 'l collegio si strinse"; "Thus he spoke, and then returned himself / to his cloister, and the cloister gathered itself together" *Par.* 22.97-98; my transl.). In his prose works, Dante is less rigorous, using "collegio" also in a secular sense, for example: "lo collegio delli rettori fu detto Senato" (*Convivio* 4.27.10). It is also no accident that Catalano calls this place both a monastery and the domain of the "tristi." It was commonplace knowledge in the Middle Ages that acedia was endemic to monasteries, a "species tristitiae" to which monks were extremely susceptible (Aquinas, *ST* II, II, 35, 1-3).

[22] Such an absurd contradiction has not escaped the notice of critics. Raimondi calls it a "convento paradossale," noting the strangeness of a monastery "proprio nel mezzo di Malebolge e sotto il controllo dei 'neri cherubini'" (40).

[23] Later, the preacher used these funds to buy himself an episcopate. And thus, Benvenuto concludes, money turns hypocrisy into simony ("ita quod lucrum hypocrisis convertit in simoniam").

passage, Jesus warns his followers of false prophets, who are wolves in sheep's clothing: "Attendite, inquit a falsis prophetis, qui veniunt ad vos in vestimentis ovium, intrinsecus autem sunt lupi rapaces" ("Beware of false prophets, who come to you in the clothing of sheep, but inwardly they are ravening wolves"). Guido da Pisa goes on to contrast these wolves with the good "pastor," who caringly guides his flock. The "false prophet," used frequently in polemics against heretics, is a familiar bugbear for a period so concerned with orthodoxy and correct preaching. In his sermon "Attendite a falsis prophetis," based on the above cited passage from Matt 7.15, Thomas Aquinas associates hypocrisy with heresy. In that same sermon's *collatio* he ties false prophets and ravenous wolves directly to the hypocrite, identifying Pharisees as supreme among these ("Attendite a falsis prophetis").[24]

Dante's description of hypocrisy might also intend to obliquely suggest heresy, evident in his reference to Frederick II's punishment for lèse-majesté in line 66. Here, Dante compares the hypocrites' "faticoso manto" to the leaden tunics that Frederick designed for condemned men, who were then tossed into a furnace, the metal melting to their bare skin. Lèse-majesté finds parallels in ecclesiastical legal theory. Starting with Innocent III's bull *Vergentis in Senium* (1199), the Church begins to describe heresy as a kind of lèse-majesté against the Divine (Ames 184). As lèse-majesté was punished by fire in the secular sphere, so too would fire be used against heretics offending divine rule, as the canonist Enrico da Susa clarifies in his gloss on Lucius III's bull *Ad Abolendam* (Ames 184). Hypocrisy, Dante seems to suggest, is a lèse-majesté against the Divine, and by implication, heresy.

As a matter of historical fact, Christian thinkers of this era did criticize the Jovials precisely for their lack of any discernible Christian service, preaching, or pastoral care. Salimbene of Parma, for instance, who expresses continued interest in the preaching of his confrères and other religious figures, sees no reason for the existence the Jovials, an order that in his eyes does no useful pastoral service (D'Alatri 64).[25] This opinion is in keeping with the instructions of Thomas of

---

[24] "Quatuor modis contingit esse falsam prophetiam. Primo ex falsitate doctrinae. Secundo ex falsitate inspirationis. Tertio ex falsitate intentionis. Et quarto ex falsitate vitae. Primo dicuntur aliqui falsi prophetae ex falsitate doctrinae, ut quando falsa annunciant et docent" ("there are four ways to be considered a false prophet. The first is through false teaching. The second by false inspiration, the third by false intention and the fourth is by false living").

[25] While Salimbene does not directly address preaching in his critique of the Jovials, he clearly and exhaustively criticizes their neglect of pastoral duties, in which preaching is always fundamental. The first four of his criticisms regard their lack of charity, their luxury and their greed, typical sins of bad clerics. The last more specifically addresses their shortcomings as spiritual "pastors": "Quinto et ultimo, quia non video ad quid deserviant in Ecclesia Dei, id est ad quid utiles sint, nisi forte quia salvos faciunt semet ipsos; que a

Chobham, who in his *Summa de arte praedicandi* declares prelates who refuse to preach "diabolical," since they would reap the substantial material rewards of their position without sowing the spiritual seeds ("Sed hoc diabolicum est: carnalia metere et spiritualia non seminare").[26] Chobham later specifies the base motivations keeping preachers out of the pulpit, principally luxury, striving for power, and simple cowardice:

[...] scilicet propter explendas uoluptates uel propter ambitionem honorum uel maioris dignitiatis, ut illi qui militant in curiis magnatum, uel forsitan quia nolunt sustinere timorem defendendi gregem suum, omnes tales inexcusabiles sunt.

(56)

([...] whether because of pleasures they want to fulfill or because of ambition for honors or greater office, like those who are active in the court of nobles, or perhaps because they do not want to withstand the fear of defending their flock, all such reasons are inexcusable.)

Ieronimo 'sancta rusticitas' appellatur, que 'solummodo sibi prodest, et quantum edificat ex vite merito Ecclesiam Christi, tantum nocet, si destruentibus non resistat.' Sed longe melius valet ille cui dici potest, Luc. XXIII: *Salvum fac temet ipsum et nos*. Ita dumtaxat, quod ipse obtemperanter respondeat: 'Domine si adhuc populo tuo sum necessarius, non recuso laborem. *Fiat voluntas tua!*'" ("Fifth and last, I do not see what use they can be to the Church of God - save perhaps to save their own souls. And Jerome has commented on this: 'The holy solitary life is indeed profitable to a particular person alone, and insofar as the merit of his life helps to strengthen the Church it is a good, but where it fails to resist those bent on the Church's destruction, it is an evil.' But that man is worth much more to whom it can be said, Luke 23 [.39]: 'Save thyself and us.' Thus let the man answer obediently, 'Lord if I am necessary to your people, I will not refuse the labor. Thy will be done!'" *Salimbene de Adam Cronica* 2. 680; *The Chronicle of Salimbene de Adam* 478).

[26] Chobham clearly states that the preacher who fails to preach takes advantage of his church, and falls far short of his pastoral duties. "Sed hoc diabolicum est: carnalia metere et spiritualia non seminare, ecclesias parochiales habere et numquam in eis predicare, nec exemplo bone vite informare nec in necessariis pro posse subuenire. Vnde horrendum est quod quidam clerici multas ecclesias habent quas numquam uel raro uiderunt, nec umquam in eis predicauerunt, nec umquam elemosinas ibi dederunt, nec aliquod exemplum nisi malum per absentia suam ibi ostenderunt. Vnde potest ibi dicere populus gemens et plorans: *cur nos pastor deseris, aut cur nos desolatos relinquis? Inuadent gregem tuum lupi rapaces*. Quomodo possunt tales dicere quod dicit Dominus: *cognosco oves meas et cognoscunt me mee*? Et Gregorius ait: *nulla est excusatio pastoris si lupus deuorat gregem et pastor ignorat.*" ("But this is diabolical: to reap the carnal but not sow the spiritual, to have parochial churches and never preach in them, nor to inform with an example of good living nor to be able to assist them in their necessity. Thus, it is horrendous that certain clerics have many churches which they never or rarely see, nor ever preach in them, nor ever give alms there, nor do they show there any example except as an evil one by their absence. Therefore can the people say there with groans and weeping: 'Why do you desert us, shepherd, and why do you leave us desolate? The rapacious wolves invade your flock.' In what way can such (pastors) say what the Lord says: 'I know my sheep and they know me'? For Gregory says: 'There is no excuse for a shepherd if the wolf devours the flock and the shepherd does not notice'" 55).

Whereas in the above passage Chobham notes only the negligence of the prelate who does not defend his flock, he later goes one step further by calling that figure a wolf rather than a pastor/shepherd ("lupus potius quam pastor").[27] In *De eruditione praedicatorum,* Humbert of Romans equates the silent preacher with the Pharisee, which tellingly dovetails not only with the appearance of Caiaphas in this canto (23.115-17), but also with Dante's letter to the Cardinals; in fact, like Dante in his letter Humbert details not only the Pharisee's silence, but also his efforts to silence others:

Alii sunt quos retrahit perversitas Ecclesiae rectorum, qui frequenter impediunt praedicationem, quam promovere deberent, similes Scribis et Pharisaeis inter Judaeos, et pontificibus templorum inter gentiles, qui semper studuerunt impedire praedicationem Christi: immo summe persecuti sunt praedicatores Christi, sicut patet ex *Actibus Apostolorum,* et *Legendis Sanctorum.*
(*Opera de vita regulari,* vol. 2. 419)
(Others, again, are rebuffed by the unpleasant dispositions of certain pastors of the Church, who hinder rather than foster preaching. They are like the Scribes and Pharisees of the Jews, and the priests of the pagans, who sought to prevent Christ from preaching and violently persecuted those who proclaimed the Gospel, as we see in the Acts of the Apostles and the stories of the Saints.)
(*Treatise on Preaching* 51)

Dante's inclusion of all these referents shared by these texts — the hypocrite/heretic, the refusal to preach, the silencing of others, the wolf, the Pharisee — suggests not only that he draws from the same rhetorical commons as did preachers and theoreticians of preaching, but that he includes figures like the Jovial Friars in his general condemnation of those who do not preach the Gospel even though they are ordered to do so — not by the Pope, but by Christ himself.

The Vigilante Preacher fra Dolcino

While Dante's condemnation of a non-preaching order like the Jovials is absolute and severe, he will, in contrast, prove far more tolerant in his dealing with vigilante preachers, those who take it upon themselves to preach in times of pastoral crisis. In *Inferno* 28, the poet carefully articulates a condemnation of fra Dolcino, the leader of a renegade religious sect called the *Apostolics,* while studiously avoiding a condemnation of his preaching or even his controversial doctrinal claims. Dante's treatment of Dolcino — whom the Church tarred as a heresiarch and burned at the stake — shows that the poet resists immediately labeling as "heresy" any expression of faith that falls outside the Church's narrow

---

[27] "Et Gregorius ait: nonne lupus est, potius quam pastor, qui ouiculam ecclesiastici pastoris tondet per rapinam, polluit per ebrietatem, rapit per fornicationem, deuorat per adulterium?" ("And Gregory says: is he not a wolf, rather than a shepherd, who shears the lamb of the Church's shepherd through plunder, who defiles it through drunkenness, who violates it through fornication, who devours it through adultery?")

definition of orthodoxy. Instead, Dante's careful and precise condemnation of Dolcino as a schismatic demonstrates the poet's concern with him specifically as a political actor who threatened social stability. In sum, it is not Dolcino's doctrine but his actions that award him punishment in Hell. Indeed, since Dante and Dolcino share more ideological common ground than would be convenient to note explicitly in this canto, Dante does well to leave the theology of a condemned heretic in the background. However, by this omission he tacitly defends the freedom to speak for those outside of the Church's ordainment.

Dante's treatment of Dolcino demonstrates how far the poet is willing to go to avoid the easy equation of difficult figures with heresy, but this does not mean that Dante treats him in any way favorably. In *Inferno* 28, the pilgrim and Vergil encounter the schismatics and sowers of discord, whose bodies are mutilated in various ways. One of these, Muhammad, mentions Dolcino by name:

"Or di a fra Dolcin dunque che s'armi
tu che forse vedra' il sole in breve,
s'ello non vuol qui tosto seguitarmi,
sì di vivanda, che stretta di neve
non rechi la vittoria al Noarese,
ch'altrimenti acquistar non saria leve."

(*Inf.* 28.55-60)

("You, who perhaps will shortly see the sun,
warn fra Dolcino to provide himself —
unless he'd like to join me here quite soon —
with stocks of victuals, lest the siege of snow
hand the Novarese the victory
not otherwise easy to attain.")

In 1300, in Parma, fra Dolcino assumed leadership of an independent sect of Christian religious called the Apostolics. The order, which was never approved or sanctioned by the Church, and which persisted in its practices long after it was given orders to cease and desist, found itself in continuous conflict with the authorities. Driven out of Parma, Dolcino and the Apostolics eventually settled in the hills of Piedmont, where they made new converts and forged alliances with local populations in opposition to the Pope (Orioli, *Venit perfidus heresiarcha* 222, 242). Dante's Muhammad prophesies the ultimate defeat of Dolcino's Apostolics in the Val Sesia region between Novara and Vercelli. The Pope's armies laid siege to mount Rubello, where Dolcino and about a thousand followers were hiding. Over time many of the Apostolics died or deserted; by 1307, exhausted by the winter and continual lack of resources, the remaining few submitted to defeat (253-54, 257, 272-74). Dolcino was tortured and burnt at the stake in Vercelli, in punishment for his resistance. Muhammad's speech above alludes to the siege and final defeat in his sympathetic advice that Dolcino stock up on resources in order to withstand the long winter atop the mountain where he and his followers were destined for great suffering and ultimate defeat at the hands of a crusading papal army.

Dante's early commentators mostly agree about the basics of Dolcino's biography and history, but they differ on what exactly Dolcino's heresy was, or if he even was a heretic. Some of the commentaries to the *Commedia* accuse Dolcino of being a Patarine (Codice Cassinese, Pietro Alighieri), but Patarines were not heretics. Patarines were primarily a reform movement combating simony, concubinage, and marriage by priests, but they did not seriously challenge key doctrinal issues, as did Cathars.[28]

Neither does Dolcino's history strike us as all bad, even though he ultimately took up arms against the papacy as a schismatic. Benvenuto da Imola seems to admire and even romanticize some of Dolcino's outlaw traits in his commentary on these lines in *Inferno*. Perhaps this attitude provides an interpretive key for the attenuated condemnation that Dolcino receives at Dante's hand. In an extended comment, which not once mentions heresy (though the word "scisma" is certainly present), Benvenuto recounts Dolcino's entire biography, beginning with his childhood in Prato and later Vercelli (Piedmont), continuing through his precipitous rise as the leader of the Apostolic sect, and finally concluding with a long and gruesomely detailed account of his capture, torture and final execution. Benvenuto emphasizes Dolcino's brilliance and irresistible speaking skills: "Dulcinus erat intelligens et eloquentissimus, adeo quod suavissima facundia sua ita ligabat auditores, quod nullus accedens ad eum semel, poterat unquam recedere" ("Dolcino was intelligent and wonderfully eloquent, of such delightful fluency that he bound his listeners so that no one upon hearing him once, could ever escape"). Benvenuto's treatment of Dolcino's torture and ultimate execution similarly shows a degree of sympathy for his stoic resilience. Benvenuto even goes so far as to state that Dolcino's execution could be considered a martyrdom if it were not for his clear intentions against the Church ("Poterat martyr dici, si poena faceret martyrium, non voluntas").[29]

---

[28] Even *The Catholic Encyclopedia* does not label Patarines as heretics.

[29] He dramatizes Dolcino's bloody end at the hands of the secular arm, such that his execution seems more a martyrdom than a justifiable consequence to heresy. Benvenuto details Dolcino's resistance to torture minutely, perhaps even enthusiastically: while his flesh is torn from his body, Dolcino never changes expression ("numquam mutasse faciem"); when his nose is lopped off, he only shrugs ("strinxit parum spatulas"); and even when his penis is cut off, he does not cry out but only sighs through the mutilated remains of his nose ("ubi traxit magnum suspirium contractione narium"). Finally, in a touch of splendid melodrama, Benvenuto heralds the fidelity of Dolcino's consort Margherita. Even after his death she remains "constans," refusing offers of marriage from many nobles who could save her life ("numquam potuit flecti"). She finally meets her own bloody and fiery end, but even then she follows her Dolcino "courageously," to Hell, according to the writer ("illum audacter sequuta est ad inferos"). While Benvenuto carefully emphasizes that Dolcino and Margherita were enemies of the Church, it is impossible to miss his clear

If the evidence from the Dante commentaries alone provides little to qualify Dolcino as a heretic in the true and proper sense, neither does a persuasive case materialize in the opinions on him expressed by ecclesiastics. From the Church's perspective Dolcino is a heretic simply because of his rebellion — to disobey the church is a de facto heresy — but Dolcino's theology in itself is not extraordinarily unusual, especially when compared to real doctrinal innovators like the Cathars. Salimbene's chronicle presents valuable information about the birth and development of the Apostolic order in the period pre-dating Dolcino's involvement. Originating in Parma in the 1260s, the Apostolics were not initially a militant sect. Nevertheless, Salimbene views them and their founder, Gerardo Segarelli, with severe disapproval.[30] It is hard to understand Salimbene's opprobrium, since under Segarelli's guiding hand the Apostolics were no more a threat to the Church than were any other assortment of passionate lay converts practicing piety and poverty, inspired by the model of the early Franciscans (Orioli, *Venit perfidus heresiarcha* 51).[31] Decades later, the inquisitor Bernard Gui identifies the group as heretically preaching against the Church ("dogmatizans contra communem statum sancte romane ecclesie") and introducing a "novam doctrinam" into the faith, but he does not identify that doctrine, nor does Salimbene's testimony provide any earlier evidence of it (*De secta illorum* in Segarizzi 17).[32] What Salimbene does provide is a slew of unfavorable and hyperbolic descriptions, referring to the Apostolics as "congregationem illorum ribaldorum et porcariorum et stultorum et ignobilium qui se dicunt Apostolos esse et non sunt, sed sunt synagoga Sathane" ("that group of rascally and swinish men, those fools and base creatures who say they are Apostles and are not, but are the synagogue of Satan" *Salimbene de Adam Cronica* 2:369; *The Chronicle of Salimbene de Adam* 249). Harsh words, but they do not constitute an accusation of heresy. Instead, Salimbene continues with *ad hominem* attacks, identifying Segarelli as a poor preacher of pitiful intellectual and rhetorical skills.[33] Despite Salimbene's efforts, support for Segarelli only

---

attraction to these two figures, his admiration for their tenacious fidelity to their beliefs in spite of the cruelest torture, and his romantic coloring of their mutual love and devotion.

[30] Salimbene's discussion of Segarelli is largely limited to pages 250-92.

[31] For more on Segarelli, Dolcino, and the Apostolics, see also the study edited by Mornese and Buratti; Mornese, *Eresia dolciniana*; Anagnine; and the volume edited by Orioli, *Nascita, vita e morte di un'eresia medievale*.

[32] Orioli does not find any credible accusation of heresy in Salimbene's account (*Venit perfidus heresiarcha* 25).

[33] When Salimbene's criticism is specific, it hinges largely on matters of intellectual ability rather than issues of orthodoxy or heterodoxy. A notable example is Salimbene's mention of Segarelli's somewhat macaronic rendering of familiar Latin phrases: "Verumtamen verbum Domini frequenter dicebat 'Penitençagite!' - nesciebat enim exprimere ut diceret: 'Penitentiam agite'" ("And he frequently repeated the words of the Lord, 'Doyepenance!'

increased among the Parma locals. Eventually his popularity grew enough to persuade the Franciscans to lobby for drastic measures to suppress him and his followers. In 1300, the local episcopate turned against Segarelli and his followers and had him burnt at the stake by the grand inquisitor of Parma. But Segarelli's execution could not stop the movement; it only increased in popularity and militancy when fra Dolcino took leadership that same year, setting in motion the seven-year journey towards their eventual grisly end at the hand of the pope's armies.

Noting the difficulty in identifying any doctrinal heresy in Dolcino's opinions, historians generally agree that his persecution was politically motivated, therefore furthering the belief that Dante's punishment for Dolcino primarily (perhaps even exclusively) regards his violent rebellion rather than theological difference.[34] Dolcino's equation of Boniface VIII with the Antichrist could hardly have won them many friends in Rome, nor would have his claims that no pope could absolve anyone from sin unless he lived in perfect poverty, waged no wars, and allowed people to practice their own faith in peace and freedom.[35] While accepting Dante's clear condemnation of Dolcino, we must register that the anti-papal language that Dolcino issues finds echo in Dante's own withering criticism of popes and other church figures whom he finds failing in their sacred mission.[36] Thus, in *Inferno* 27, Dante, like Dolcino, challenges papal absolution, at least in certain cases. Here, the Franciscan Guido da Montefeltro recounts Pope Boniface VIII's claim to clear him of his sin ("tuo cuor non sospetti; / finor t'assolvo" ("Let

---

For he was ignorant of the proper words, 'Do ye penance.'") (*Salimbene De Adam Cronica* 2:372; *The Chronicle of Salimbene de Adam* 252).

[34] Carniello dismantles Salimbene's accusations of Apostolic heresy by exposing the rivalry going on between orders in Parma at the time. Drawing from documentary evidence, Carniello shows that Segarelli had the ear of many prelates and bishops in Parma and in the Emilia-Romagna region and was gaining popularity, while the Franciscans were losing followers as they gradually strayed from their founder's austere practices. Carniello concludes that the reason for Salimbene's harsh invective "was mendicant rivalry, and not any heretical tendencies inherent in Segarelli's religious enthusiasm" (237). Orioli likewise has little to say about Apostolic heterodoxy, instead identifying the Apostolics' rebellion as the driving force behind their persecution (*Venit perfidus heresiarcha* 119-20).

[35] These claims come from Bernard Gui's account of Dolcino's heresy: "[...] nullus papa romane ecclesie potest aliquem absolvere vere a peccatis nisi esset ita sanctus sicut fuit beatus Petrus apostolus vivendo in omnimoda paupertate sine proprio et in humilitate, non faciendo guerras, nec aliquem persequendo, set permittendo vivere quemlibet in sua libertate" (*De secta illorum* in Segarizzi 24).

[36] Unlike Dolcino, however, Dante does not go so far as to criticize Ecclesiastical institutions themselves, only their corrupt ministers, as St. Peter makes clear in *Paradiso*: "[...] la sedia che fu già benigna / più a' poveri giusti, non per lei, / ma per colui che siede, che traligna [...]" ("[...] the papal seat, not now as benevolent / to the upright poor as it was once - not flawed in itself, / but degenerate in its occupant [...]" *Par.* 12.88-90).

not your heart mistrust / I absolve you here and now" *Inf.* 27.100-01]). In a debate over Guido's soul, right after his death, between St. Francis and a demon claiming to be a logician ("löico"), the latter argues that papal absolutions are meaningless if the sinner does not repent, as is the case with Guido, deceivingly absolved by the pope even before Guido offers his fraudulent advice (27.112-23). The poet's other famous challenges to papal supremacy are manifold and well documented.[37] In addition to their common claims against papal infallibility, both Dante and fra Dolcino share similar eschatological visions. According to Dolcino, a new Holy Roman emperor would arise and eliminate the pope, strip the Church of its wealth and temporal power, and instate a "holy Pope," ushering in a new era and a return to the virtues of the Early Church (Orioli, *Nascita, vita e morte di un'eresia medievale* 98-99; *Venit perfidus heresiarcha* 119-20). Dolcino's apocalyptic prophecy of a secular leader (not a divine pope, as Joachim of Fiore prophesies) recalls Dante's own prophecy of the "veltro" of *Inferno* 1 and the secular leader identified only as "DXV" in *Purgatorio* 33.43-44. Thus, in both their general disdain for the state of the contemporary church as well as a few particulars regarding papal authority, Dante and fra Dolcino share more ideological common ground than one might imagine.

Tellingly, Dante's judgment of fra Dolcino has nothing to do with his theology or his preaching. Dante could have simply repeated the Church's official judgment on fra Dolcino, including its claim to his heresy, but here the poet consistently refuses to do that. This decision does not mean that the poet is insensitive to heresy when he sees it. Note for example his praise of St. Dominic's preaching against the Cathar "heretical brambles" ("sterpi eretici" *Par.* 12.100), or his decision to assign Folquet de Marselha, who waged combat against the Albigensians, in the Sphere of Venus in Heaven (*Par.* 9.94).

However, it is important to remember that what the Church considers heresy and what Dante considers heresy can be two different things. Dante clearly opposes attempts by the Church to leverage its moral authority in the pursuit of political gain, especially when those pursuits include military operation. This stance is apparent in his opposition to Boniface VIII's war against the Colonna family, which challenged the abdication of Celestine V (*Inf.* 27.85-93), as well as in St. Peter's broad condemnation of any combat against the baptized ("che contra battezzati combattesse") (*Par.* 27.51). In fact, the impetus behind his opposition to papal armies also lies behind his condemnation of the schismatics in *Inferno* 28: a concern for social peace, stability and unity. All the other figures in this canto — Pier da Medicina, Gaius Scribonius Curio, Mosca de' Lamberti, and Bertran de Born, even Muhammad to a major degree— are here not because they

---

[37] For a summary review of Dante's progressively antagonistic relationship to the papacy, see Holmes 18-43. Dante's challenge of papal right to govern secular politics, outlined in *Monarchia,* met energetic ecclesiastical opposition, which Cassell studies in depth in his book *The* Monarchia *Controversy.*

believed different faiths, but because they tore apart societies previously unified. The focus on the schismatics here in *Inferno* 28, in keeping with Dante's ethics across the rest of this canticle, regards the political and social consequences of their actions above everything else (Barolini 400).

Conclusion
In *Paradiso* 11, St. Thomas Aquinas condemns those Dominicans that fall short in their ministry to others, criticizing them for returning to the fold with no milk to offer the flock ("tornano a l'ovil di latte vòte" 11.129). The crime here, as it is everywhere else, is ultimately social: letting starve those who are famished for sound doctrine. In this way we see that the reluctant preacher is no less guilty than the schismatic of contributing to the collapse of society. Aware of the importance of spiritual ministry, Dante takes an uncompromising stance towards those designated to preach, and time and again he emphasizes the Church's failure to adequately serve its pastoral obligation, as has been shown in the discussion of the Jovial Friars of *Inferno* 23. On the other hand, Dante articulates the danger posed by those opposed to the Church, as in the case of fra Dolcino, while simultaneously steering clear of any blanket condemnation of unauthorized doctrinal preaching. All of these occasions, however, are motivated by a much larger strategic goal. Dante uses such cases as the Jovials and fra Dolcino to describe a situation of pastoral crisis, in which those called to preach are silent or silencing others, while the noisiest preachers are calling for violent insurrection against the Church. This ultimately untenable predicament calls for a voice ordained not by man but by the Divine, who will invigorate the complacent, calm the overly-passionate, and direct the misguided flocks. Dante in his letter to the Cardinals announces his readiness to take on that role in his words "hiis habeo persuasum quod audeo": I am convinced that I must speak!

By 1314, the year of this letter's composition, much of the *Commedia* was already finished: the *Inferno* was circulating, and the *Purgatorio* was complete or nearing completion. Dante's unflinching claim in this letter for the right to speak suggests that his most passionate preaching is yet to come. *Paradiso* — with its extended discussion of preaching in canto 29, speeches on pastoral care by Aquinas and Bonaventure in cantos 10-13, and the larger discussion of doctrine and theology across all cantos, studded everywhere with appearances by apostles, theologians and saints — may prove to be, ultimately, that fiery sermon that Dante dares to preach at last.

Tokyo University of Foreign Studies

Works Cited

Alighieri, Dante. *Convivio*. Ed. Franca Brambilla Ageno. Le Lettere, 1995.
——. *La commedia secondo l'antica vulgata*. Ed. Giorgio Petrocchi. 3 vols. Milano: Mondadori, 1967.
——. *Opere Minori. Convivio*. Ed. Cesare Vasoli and Domenico De Robertis. Tome 1, part 2. Milano: Ricciardi, 1988.
Opere minori. Vita nuova. Rime. Tome 1, part 1. Ed. Domenico De Robertis and Gianfranco Contini. Milano: Ricciardi, 1995.
Ames, Christine Caldwell. *Righteous Persecution: Inquisition, Dominicans, and Christianity in the Middle Ages*. Philadelphia: U of Pennsylvania P, 2009.
Anagnine, Eugenio. *Dolcino e il movimento ereticale all'inizio del Trecento*. Firenze: La Nuova Italia, 1965.
Arnold, John. "The Preaching of the Cathars." *Medieval Monastic Preaching*. Ed. Carolyn Muessig. Leiden: Brill, 1998. 183-205.
Baldwin, John. *Masters, Princes and Merchants: The Social Views of Peter the Chanter and His Circle*. 2 vols. Princeton: Princeton UP, 1970.
Barolini, Teodolinda. "Bertran De Born and Sordello: The Poetry of Politics in Dante's Comedy." *PMLA* 94 (1979): 395-405.
Battaglia Ricci, Lucia. "Nel cielo del Sole - *Paradiso* X-XI-XII." *Esperimenti danteschi: Paradiso 2010*. Ed. Tommaso Montorfano. Genova: Marietti, 2010. 113-55.
Benvenuto da Imola. *Benvenuti da Rambaldis de Imola comentum super Dantis Aldigherij Comoediam, nunc primum integre in lucem editum*. Ed. Jacobo Philippo Lacaita. Firenze: G. Barbèra, 1887. (Dartmouth Dante Project, http://dante.dartmouth.edu/.)
Bonora, Ettore. *Gli ipocriti di Malebolge, e altri saggi di letteratura italiana e francese*. Milano: Riccardo Ricciardi, 1953.
Boyle, Leonard. "Innocent III and Vernacular Versions of Scripture." *The Bible in the Medieval World: Essays in Memory of Beryl Smalley*. Ed. Katherine Walsh and Diana Wood. Studies in Church History 4. Oxford: Blackwell, 1985. 97-107.
Cardini, Franco, and Marina Montesanto. *La lunga storia dell'Inquisizione: luci e ombre della "leggenda nera."* Roma: Città Nuova, 2005.
Carniello, Brian R. "Gerardo Segarelli as the Anti-Francis: Mendicant Rivalry and Heresy in Medieval Italy, 1260-1300." *Journal of Ecclesiastical History* 57.2 (2006): 226-51.
Cassell, Anthony Kimber. *The Monarchia Controversy: An Historical Study with Accompanying Translations of Dante Alighieri's Monarchia, Guido Vernani's Refutation of the Monarchia Composed by Dante and Pope John XXII's Bull, Si Fratrum*. Washington D. C.: CUA Press, 2004.
Croce, Benedetto. *La poesia di Dante*. Scritti di storia letteraria e politica. Bari: Laterza, 1921.
D'Alatri, Mariano. "Predicazione e predicatori francescani nella cronica di fra Salimbene." *Collectanea Franciscana* 46 (1976): 63-91.
Dameron, George W. *Florence and Its Church in the Age of Dante*. Philadelphia: U of Pennsylvania P, 2005.

d'Avray, D. L. *The Preaching of the Friars: Sermons Diffused from Paris before 1300*. Oxford: Clarendon Press, 1985.
Delcorno, Carlo. "Cadenze e figure della predicazione nel viaggio dantesco." *Letture classensi* 15 (1985): 41-60.
——. "Dante e il linguaggio dei predicatori." *Letture classensi* 25 (1995): 51-75.
——. "Dante e l'exemplum medievale." *Letture Classensi* 12 (1982): 113-38.

———. "Medieval Preaching in Italy (1200-1500)." *The Sermon.* Ed. Beverly Mayne Kienzle. Typologie des sources du Moyen Age Occidental 81-83. Turnhout: Brepols, 2000. 449-559.

———. "Schede su Dante e la retorica della predicazione." *Miscellanea di studi Danteschi in memoria di Silvio Pasquazi.* Vol. 1. Napoli: Federico & Ardia, 1993. 301-12.

De Stefano, Antonino. *Riformatori ed eretici del Medioevo.* Palermo: F. Ciuni, 1938.

Di Pino, Guido. "Il canto XXIII." *Italianistica* 8.3 (1979): 499-513.

Federici, Domenico Maria. *Istoria de' Cavalieri Gaudenti.* 2 vols. Venezia: Coleti, 1787.

Francesco da Buti. *Commento di Francesco da Buti sopra La Divina Commedia di Dante Allighieri.* Ed. Crescentino Giannini. Pisa: Fratelli Nistri, 1858. (Dartmouth Dante Project, http://dante.dartmouth.edu/.)

Gay, M. Jules, ed. *Les Registres de Nicolas III.* Vol. 14.3. 2 564. Paris: Bibliothèque des Écoles Françaises d'Athènes et de Rome, 1916.

Giannantonio, Pompeo. "Il canto XXIII dell'Inferno." *Critica Letteraria* 7.23 (1979): 211-34.

Giordano da Pisa. *Prediche del Beato fra Giordano da Rivalto dell'ordine dei Predicatori, recitate in Firenze dal MCCCIII al MCCCVI, ed ora per la prima volta pubblicate.* 2 vols. Firenze: Magheri, 1831.

Guido da Pisa. *Expositiones et Glose super Comediam Dantis, or Commentary on Dante's Inferno.* Ed. Vincenzo Cioffari. Albany, NY: State U of New York P, 1974. (Dartmouth Dante Project, http://dante.dartmouth.edu/.)

Hollander, Robert. "Virgil and Dante as Mind-Readers (Inferno XXI and XXIII)." *Medioevo romanzo* 9 (1984): 85-100.

Holmes, George. "Dante and the Popes." *The World of Dante: Essays on Dante and His Times.* Ed. Cecil Grayson Oxford: Clarendon Press, 1980. 18-43.

Humbert of Romans. "De eruditione praedicatorum." *Opera de vita regulari 2. Expositio in constitutiones. Instructiones de officiis ordinis. De eruditione praedicatorum. Epistolae encyclicae.* Ed. Joachim Joseph Berthier. Torino: Marietti, 1956.

———. *Treatise on Preaching.* Ed. Walter M. Conlon, O. P. Trans. Dominican Students Province of St. Joseph. Westminster, Maryland: Newman Press, 1951.

Jacopo della Lana. *Comedia di Dante degli Allaghieri col Commento di Jacopo della Lana bolognese.* Ed. Luciano Scarabelli. Bologna: Tipografia Regia, 1866. (Dartmouth Dante Project, http://dante.dartmouth.edu/.)

Keen, Catherine. "Fathers of Lies: (Mis)readings of Clerical and Civic Duty in Inferno XXIII." *Dante and the Church: Literary and Historical Essays.* Ed. Paolo Acquaviva and Jennifere Petrie. Dublin: Four Courts Press, 2007.

Kleinhenz, Christopher. "Deceivers Deceived: Devilish Doubletalk in Inferno 21-23." Ed. Amilcare A. Iannucci. *Quaderni d'italianistica* 10.1-2 (1989): 133-56.

Maggini, Francesco. *Due letture dantesche inedite (Inf. XXIII e XXXII) e altri scritti poco noti.* Ed. Antonio di Preta. Firenze: Le Monnier, 1965.

Maldina, Nicolò. "Dante e l'immagine del buon predicatore nel Paradiso." *L'Alighieri* 43 (June 2014): 41-64.

———. "Tra predicazione e liturgia. Modelli e fortuna del 'Pater noster' di Purgatorio XI 1-21." *Le teologie di Dante. Atti del Convegno internazionale di Studi Ravenna, 9 novembre 2013.* Ravenna: Centro dantesco dei frati minori conventuali, 2015. 201-33.

Meersseman, G. G. *Dossier de l'ordre de la pénitence au XIIIe siècle.* Fribourg: Editions Universitaires, 1961.

Merlo, Grado Giovanni. *Inquisitori e inquisizione del medioevo.* Bologna: Il Mulino, 2008.

Moore, R. I. *The War on Heresy.* Cambridge: Belknap Press, 2012.

Mornese, Corrado. *Eresia dolciniana e resistenza montanara*. Roma: DeriveApprodi, 2002.

———, and Gustavo Buratti, eds. *Fra Dolcino e gli apostolici tra eresia, rivolta e roghi*. Roma: DeriveApprodi, 2000.

Orioli, Raniero, ed. *Nascita, vita e morte di un'eresia medievale*. Milano: Jaca Book, 1983.

———. *Venit perfidus heresiarcha: il movimento apostolico-dolciniano dal 1260 al 1307*. Studi storici (Istituto storico italiano per il Medio Evo), fasc. 193-196. Roma: Istituto Storico Italiano per il Medio Evo, 1988.

Raimondi, Ezio. "I canti bolognesi dell'Inferno dantesco." *Dante e Bologna nei tempi di Dante*. Ed. Università di Bologna. Facoltà di lettere e filosofia. VII centenario della nascita di Dante 11. Bologna: Commissione per i Testi di Lingua, 1967. 229-49.

———. *Metafora e storia: studi su Dante e Petrarca*. Torino: Einaudi, 1970.

Rangerius. *Vita Anselmi Episcopi Lucensis*. Monumenta Germaniae Historica: Scriptores 30, 2. Hanover, 1934.

Roberts, P. B. "Preaching In/and the Medieval City." *Medieval Sermons and Society: Cloister, City, University*. Louvain-la-Neuve: Fédéracion Internationale des Instituts d'Études Médiévales, 1998. 151-64.

Roest, Bert. *Franciscan Literature of Religious Instruction before the Council of Trent*. Leiden: Brill, 2004.

———. *A History of Franciscan Education (c. 1210-1517)*. Leiden: Brill, 2000.

Rossi, Luciano. "Canto XI." *Paradiso*. Ed. Georges Güntert and Michelangelo Picone. Lectura Dantis Turicensis. Firenze: Cesati, 2000. 167-79.

Rouse, Richard H, and Mary A. *Preachers, Florilegia and Sermons: Studies on the Manipulus Florum of Thomas of Ireland*. Studies and Texts - Pontifical Institute of Mediaeval Studies 47. Toronto: Pontifical Institute of Mediaeval Studies, 1979.

Russo, Vittorio. *Esperienze e/di letture dantesche: tra il 1966 e il 1970*. Napoli: Liguori, 1971.

Salimbene de Adam. *The Chronicle of Salimbene de Adam*. Binghamton, N.Y.: Medieval & Renaissance Texts & Studies, 1986.

———. *Salimbene De Adam Cronica*. Ed. Giuseppe Scalia. Corpus Christianorum Continuatio Mediaevalis. 2 vols. Turnhout: Brepols, 1998.

Segarizzi, Arnaldo, ed. *Historia fratris Dulcini heresiarche di anonimo sincrono: e, De secta illorum qui se dicunt esse de ordine Apostolorum di Bernardo Gui*. Rerum Italicarum Scriptores 9.5. Città di Castello: Lapi, 1907.

Tanner, Norman P., ed. *Decrees of the Ecumenical Councils*. Washington D.C.: Georgetown UP, 1990.

Thomas, Aquinas. "Attendite a falsis prophetis," (Corpus Tomisticum, www.corpusthomisticum.org/haf.html)

———. *Summa Theologiae*. New York: McGraw-Hill, 1964.

Thomas of Chobham. *Summa de arte praedicandi*. Corpus Christianorum Continuatio Medieualis. 82. Turnhout: Brepols, 1988.

Thompson, Augustine. *Cities of God: The Religion of the Italian Communes 1125-1325*. University Park, Pennsylvania: Pennsylvania State UP, 2005.

Vauchez, André. *The Laity in the Middle Ages: Religious Beliefs and Devotional Practices*. Notre Dame: U of Notre Dame P, 1993.

Steven Baker

Writing the Revolution: Petrarch and the Tribunate of Cola di Rienzo

Abstract: On the occasion of Cola di Rienzo's ascension to power in Rome at the end of May 1347, Petrarch composed a letter in which he likens the self-styled "liberator of the holy Roman republic" to a new Romulus, a second Camillus, and a third Brutus. In his usual pedagogical mode of teaching by *exemplaritas*, Petrarch even holds him up to the model of Augustus Caesar, the revered author of the period of peace to which he longed to return. The superlative tone of these historical analogues reflects the fact that Petrarch did indeed have high hopes for the initiative of his quixotic friend. Following the trajectory of Cola's brief tenure as Roman Tribune, this paper is a study of Petrarch's attempt to mold after his own image the opportune revolution of Cola di Rienzo in Rome in 1347, and surveys the ways in which he continued to write the Roman revolution long after the tribune himself was out of the picture.
Key words: Petrarch, Cola di Rienzo, Familiar Letters, Charles IV, 14th-century Rome, Petrarchan humanism

Introduction
"I shall not stop writing to you daily" (*Disp.* 9), writes Francesco Petrarca in a letter from July 1347 to Cola di Rienzo, who had proclaimed himself Roman tribune just two months prior. If Petrarch did continue to write the tribune with such frequency, with very few exceptions any trace of such voluminous correspondence is lost to us now.[1] Considering the momentousness of his involvement with the upstart populist leader in Rome, this absence is particularly glaring in the context of the *Familiares*, the humanist's first collection of familiar letters that chronicles this period. Only one of the purported myriad letters he addressed to Cola di Rienzo is to be found there, although it happens to be a very telling one.

Written on November 29, 1347, from Genoa, *Familiares* VII 7 is a letter of reproach, through which transpires Petrarch's palpable sense of disappointment. Petrarch himself gave the letter a subtitle — a framing device he employs throughout the carefully curated collection — that designates it as a letter of "indignation mixed with entreaties regarding the Tribune's changed reputation."

---

[1] Eight of Petrarch's letters to Cola survive: *Fam.* VII 7, *Sine nom.* II-IV, and *Disp.* 8-11. Other writings that address Cola's controversial rise and fall include: *Eclogue* 5: "The Shepherds' Affection"; *Sine nom.* VIII-IX; *Fam.* VII 1; VII 4-5; XI 16-17; XIII 6-7; *Sen.* I 4; *Fam.* XV 1; XVIII 1; *De remediis* I 89; and *Invectiva in Gallum*. For Cola's acknowledgment of their friendship, and recognition of Petrarch's reverence for Rome, see Di Rienzo, *Epistolario*, XV, *Cola di Rienzo a Francesco Petrarca*, July 27, 1347.

News of the collapse of Cola's government had reached Petrarch in Genoa where he found himself in transit on his way to join the tribune in Rome.[2] He had gambled a good deal on the sudden glimmer of hope that Cola represented, and now that hope was suddenly lost. In Avignon, he was in the process of negotiating a separation from his long time patron, the Colonna family, in order to dedicate himself to the Roman cause. He found himself in a bind and his reputation was on the line. His ties to Cola di Rienzo, a *persona non grata* in the eyes of both the Colonna family and the papal court at large, had to be reckoned with somehow. Whitewashing his involvement with the tribune is one of the ways he went about reconciling the situation.

Apart from *Familiares* VII 7, the rest of Petrarch's correspondence with the Roman tribune has been relegated to less prominent places in his oeuvre. A handful of the other extant letters addressed to Cola, as well as those in which he discussed matters pertaining to the Cola debacle, come down to us in ancillary collections. These are the secretive *Liber sine nomine* (letters 2-4), which Petrarch intentionally kept out of circulation during his lifetime because of its controversial politics, and the *Lettere disperse* (letters 8-11), a posthumous repository for all other extant letters that Petrarch choose to exclude from all three of his personally curated epistolary collections but that have come down to us through other means despite his efforts to silence them.

Petrarch may have largely edited Cola out of the primary body of work that he intended to leave to posterity, in which we encounter a carefully constructed account of his life, but the Roman tribune and the movement that he stood for nevertheless appear on numerous occasions in his activities as public intellectual over the next two decades. The humanist's late career is punctuated by a variety of attempts to promote the values of Cola di Rienzo's tribunate, often more in spirit than by name, in a number of other arenas of power, from the papal court in Avignon to the imperial court in Prague. With increasing conviction from 1347 to the end of his life, Petrarch will continue to write the revolution that Cola started as though his legacy as a public intellectual and the brand of humanism he tirelessly worked to propagate depended on it. After a brief overview of Cola's rise and fall, what follows is a survey of several textual moments in the years between 1347 and 1355 in which the goals boldly put forth by the Roman tribune remained among Petrarch's abiding concerns long after his quixotic friend exited the picture.[3]

---

[2] Cola di Rienzo was chased from the city, which left Petrarch's dreams of a renewal of the imperial splendor in shambles. Petrarch had already expressed his intentions to leave his outpost in the south of France before his departure, and he would make his break definitive upon his return a few years later.

[3] Petrarch's obsession with the notion of a *renovatio* or *translatio imperii* is a recurring theme in his correspondence with the Imperial Court in Prague. See, for example, *Fam.* X 1; X 6; XII 1; XVIII 1; XXI 1; XXIII 2; XXIII 9; XXIII 12; XXIII 15-16. His fervent support of Cola in

Cola di Rienzo and the Roman Revolution

The son of a Roman innkeeper and a washerwoman, Cola di Rienzo (1313-1354) was an autodidact and self-made man in every sense when it came to both his intellectual development and his political aspirations.[4] He was indeed a product of the same early humanistic ferment that Petrarch's career would spearhead, earning the latter a great many emulators throughout Italy and Europe.[5] Following the example of Petrarch's revival of the coronation ceremony with all of its classical poet laureate pomp, Cola staged a series of ceremonial spectacles to legitimize the position he fashioned for himself as Roman "tribune" — just one of many titles he quixotically recovers from the annals of Roman history.[6] Cola's antiquarian eccentricity is apparent in the colorful nomenclature he adopted for himself from his reading of classical Roman historians, which he injected into the political discourse of the time.[7] He sourced other archaizing terminology from the various ancient inscriptions found all over his native city that he attempted to reintroduce into current usage.

In late May 1347, Cola led a popular uprising that would serve as a wake up call to the noble families of Rome and send ripples through the political world in places as far as Avignon and Prague. Within the first few weeks of his short seven-month tenure as self-appointed leader of the city (May 19 to December 15, 1347), Cola di Rienzo sent variations of the same letter to the major city-states of central and northern Italy — including neighboring Viterbo, Florence, Lucca, Mantua, Modena and Perugia — in which he invites each to contribute arms and men to the cause of freedom not only for Rome but also for the Italian peninsula as a whole.[8] Calling himself the "*libertatis, pacis iustitieque tribunus et sacre Romane*

---

general also attests to his particular fervor for Rome's revival. For a more philosophical exposition of his ideas on a united Italy, see *Sine nom.* IX.

[4] For a biographical sketch, see Collins, *Greater Than Emperor* 15-26; Di Carpegna Falconieri, *Cola di Rienzo*; and Musto, *Apocalypse in Rome*. For more than fifty of Cola's letters, some familiar but most official-political in nature, see *Epistolario di Cola di Rienzo*.

[5] For Petrarch's intention to influence and initiate a movement in his own humanistic image, see his *Coronation Oration*. For an expression of Petrarch's retrospective self-satisfaction late in life regarding his legacy in the form of the intellectual cultural movement he was leaving behind, see *Sen.* XVII, 2.

[6] In the first two months of his tribunate he officially referred to himself in the *salutatio* of his letters as: "Nicholaus severus et clemens, libertatis, pacis iustitieque tribunus et sacre Romane reipubblice liberator" ("Severe and clement Nicholaus, tribune of liberty, peace and justice and liberator of the holy Roman republic"). After the christening ceremony he staged on August 1 before an audience of ambassadors from the major city-states of central and northern Italy, he changed his title to: "miles Nicolaus severus et clemens, liberator Urbis, zelator Ytalie, amator orbis et tribunus augustus" ("Severe and clement, Sir Nicolaus, liberator of Rome, zealot of Italy, lover of the world and august tribune").

[7] In *Disp.* 8, Petrarch gives Cola some stern instructions, including a very specific definition of the role and responsibilities that come along with the title "tribunus" he adopted, rather than, say, "consul." For a further discussion, see below.

[8] The purpose of his epistolary campaign was to restore liberty (*libertas*), peace (*pax*) and justice (*iustitia*) to the Roman people and their provinces, as well as to renew the ancient friendship

reipubblice liberator," or the "tribune of liberty, peace and justice, and liberator of the Holy Roman Republic," Cola lays the blame outright on the noble families of Rome for the state of lawlessness and decay in which the once great capital has come to find itself. He makes clear what he intends to do as long as he can lay claim to his newfound status as plebeian "tribune" and Roman "liberator" (*Al Comune di Lucca* 16-17). The goals he explicitly states are to reform and renew justice, liberty, peace and security, according to the ancient model, in order to establish a *status pacificus* in Rome (*Al Comune di Lucca* 17). The picture he paints of the great city in his letters is not a pretty one. He describes the wretched conditions to which Rome had been reduced: peace expelled, liberty prostrate, security robbed, love damned, truth oppressed, compassion and devotion profaned (*Al Comune di Viterbo*, May 24, 1347, 6).

Abandoned by both the emperor and the pope, Rome had objectively fallen into the hands of two powerful baronial clans, the Colonna and the Orsini, who plundered the city for their own profit and left its inhabitants to their own devices. The corruption and negligence of the nobles hastened the decline in population since they allowed the city to descend into a permanent state of lawlessness causing many to flee to the surrounding countryside.[9] Rome was in desperate need of some form of local authority to reintroduce basic law and order to the most rudimentary level of civic life.[10] This was the void that Cola di Rienzo groomed

---

(*amicitia*) that had once united Italy as a whole. *Cola di Rienzo al Comune di Firenze*, late June 1347, *Epistolario* VII (19-20): "Ad salutatem, libertatem, pacem et iustitiam sacri Romani populi et Romane provincie, ad reconciliationem totius sacre Ytalie et antique amicitie renovationem inter sacrum Romanum populum, vos et ipsam sacram Ytaliam universam [...]" ("For the welfare, liberty, peace and justice of the sacred people of Rome and of the Roman provinces, for the reconciliation of every corner of sacred Italy and for the renewal of ancient friendship among the sacred Roman peoples, you and all of sacred Italy [...]"). Translation mine. See also, Cola di Rienzo, *Epistolario*, V, *Al Comune di Lucca*, June 7, 1347 (17).

[9] For a description of the state of the city prior to Cola's restoration of order, see *Al Comune di Lucca* 16: "[...] nec mirandum erat, cum ipsa sacra civitas, que ad consolationem animarum constructa fuit et que fidelium omnium debet esse refugium, facta erat offensionis silva; et spelunca latronum, potius quam civitas, apparebat" ("It was not surprising, then, when this very holy city, which was built for the consolation of souls and which should be a refuge for all the faithful, had become a forest of crime; and it seemed to be more a den of thieves, than a city"; translation mine). For an indication of the chaos of the situation in and around Rome at the time from Petrarch's own experience, see *Fam*. IV 8: "But so that I might learn from fresh experience how sad things always accompany joyful things, we had scarcely left the walls of the city when I, together with those who had followed me on land and sea, fell into the hands of an armed band of thieves. How we were freed from them and were forced to return to Rome, how upset the people were because of this, how we left on the following day supported by an escort of armed men, and the other events on our trip would make too long a story for me to recount here" (Bernardo 196).

[10] For the reconstruction of the socio-political climate of fourteenth-century Rome, see Miglio, *Scritture, scrittori e storia*; Maire-Vigueur, "Il comune romano"; and Modigliani, *L'eredità di Cola di Rienzo*.

himself to fill.[11]

Within less than a month, news of Cola's initiative reached Petrarch, who was still residing in the South of France. In an open letter (*Disp.* 8) addressed to both Cola and the Roman people, a sort of panegyric composed for the occasion of Cola's ascension to power, often called either his *Hortatoria* or his "hymn to freedom," Petrarch takes up the cause of the Roman revolution with great fervor and proceeds to recast it in his own terms, rhetorically shaping it to his own desires.

In his open letter, Petrarch likens the self-styled "liberator of the Roman people" to a new Camillus, a new Romulus, and a third Brutus. "Hail then our Camillus, our Brutus, our Romulus! Or — if you prefer to be addressed by some other name — hail author of Roman liberty, of Roman peace, of Roman tranquility. The present age owes you the fact that it will die in liberty; posterity will owe you the fact that it is conceived in liberty" (*Disp.* 8).[12] In his usual pedagogical mode of teaching by *exemplaritas*, Petrarch presents three exemplary models for his advisee to aspire to and other corresponding glorious titles. Later in the letter, he will again hold him up to the example of Caesar Augustus, revered author of the *pax Romana* — the esteemed period of peace to which he longed to return.[13] The superlative tone of these classical analogues accurately reflects the fact that Petrarch did indeed have high hopes for the initiative of his quixotic friend. In his only extant epistolary response to Petrarch, Cola expresses his gratitude to the humanist for calling to mind such inspirational models to emulate.[14]

Petrarch's enthusiasm for the cause does not stop at dubbing Cola the "author of Roman liberty, Roman peace, Roman tranquility."[15] He goes on to invoke more specific details from those same classical models for him to follow.

I do not desire to goad you further, nor to reproach you with bygones. I wish, rather, to offer you a way to hide your embarrassment. Even your ancestors were ruled by kings —

---

[11] His ambitions from the very beginning were not limited to Rome alone. Petrarch and Cola also longed for a united Italy, and the fact that Rome would assume a role of central importance in such a project was obvious to both of them at the time. In the mid-fourteenth century, however, there was a vacuum of power in the great *Urbs* of antiquity.

[12] In his third letter to Charles IV of Bohemia, which is discussed below, Petrarch will again fashion Cola in the image and likeness of Brutus, calling him this time the "vindex libertatis," the "avenger of liberty," the same epithet that Brutus bears in Livy.

[13] See Petrarch, *Disp.* 8. The coordinates of the prince or statesman and the poet-teacher are players in the Cola-Petrarch dynamic.

[14] For Cola's embrace of Petrarch as teacher, see *Cola di Rienzo a Francesco Petrarca*, July 27, 1347, *Epistolario* XV (37-8): "[I]n gratissimo exhortamine vestro, per exempla laudabilia bonorum veterum, per eccitationes ad virtutum amplexus, nos sumus et fuimus plurimum recreati" ("In your very gratifying letter of exhortation, you have summoned the praiseworthy examples of the heroes of old to spur us on to emulate their virtuous deeds, whereby our spirits are and have been thoroughly revived").

[15] *Disp.* 8 325-27: "Romane libertatis, Romane pacis, Romane tranquillitatis auctor."

and by kings who were not always of Roman origin but also, at one time, of Sabine, at another of Corinthian, and — if we are to believe tradition — of servile origin. But evil fortune must come to an end as well as good fortune. The restorer of the early Romans' liberty and the restorer of your liberty were both unexpected. Each age produced its Brutus. There are now three named Brutus celebrated in history. The first exiled the proud Tarquin; the second slew Julius Caesar; the third has brought exile and death to the tyrants of our own age. Our third Brutus, then, equals both the others because in his own person he has united the causes of the double glory that the other two divided between them. He is, however, more like the earlier Brutus in disguising his nature and in concealing his purpose. Like him he is young but of a far different temperament; and if he assumed the false exterior of that other Brutus, it was so that, biding his time beneath this false veil, he might at last reveal himself in his true character — the liberator of the Roman people.

(Disp. 8 112-31; Cosenza 13-14)

Petrarch lavishes many titles and honors on Cola, including placing him third in a line of legendary over-throwers of tyrants, of the caliber of the Tarquin kings and Julius Caesar. He squarely likens the Colonna and the other noble families of Rome to the tyrants of their age. There is a pronounced anti-noble sentiment underlying the way both men frame their efforts to restore peace and security to Rome. An anti-baronial movement is afoot and Petrarch is unambiguously ready to get behind it.

Freedom from "Barbarians"
When Cola took office, Petrarch offered to serve as poet to Cola's prince in the capacity of official mouthpiece and chronicler of the movement: "And since you are occupied in performing noble deeds, until you find a genius capable of recounting your deeds in worthy language, I promise you the service of my feeble intellect and of my pen — if God permits me to live. In this way I shall — to borrow Livy's words — perform my part in enhancing the memory of the most noble people in the world. Nor will my Africanus mind yielding to you for a short while" (*Disp.* 8; Cosenza 41). Petrarch offers his services as scribe to the cause, as the poet to his prince, the Ennius to his Scipio. His offer to set aside his labors on the *Africa* suggests that, for the time being, he sees Cola's new undertaking as being of greater importance.[16]

In the only letter in the *Familiares* addressed to Cola, Petrarch in fact makes reference to Scipio Africanus in the context of the great joy he felt for the Tribune's accomplishments: "I confess that you have caused me recently to repeat often and with great pleasure the words that Cicero has Africanus speak: 'What is this that fills my ears, so great and so sweet a sound it is?'" (*Fam.* VII 7; Bernardo 349). Comparisons to Scipio appear throughout his treatment of Cola, Petrarch's *Scipio redivivus*. Idealistic but also at turns practical, the open letter encourages

---

[16] On July 28, 1347, Cola responds to Petrarch — the only surviving letter Cola wrote to his friend, see *Epistolario* XV 38: "Et utinam persone vestre presentia Rome foret!" ("If only you were present at Rome in person!" Cosenza 38).

the newly minted tribune to begin the morning by hearing mass and advises him to pray fervently.

> I hear the following reports about you: that it is customary for you to receive the sacrament of Our Lord's body with sincerest devotion and after a most searching examination of conscience. This is doubtless as it should be for the wise man who regards the frailty of the flesh and the brevity of life and who beholds the manifold dangers that threaten on all sides. That most illustrious of Rome's generals [Scipio] would have followed the same course, I believe, had he lived in these days.
>
> (*Disp.* 8; Cosenza 19-20)

Petrarch envisions Cola as the reincarnation of his beloved Scipio Africanus, the great liberator of Italy from Hannibal's invasion, "who first freed Italian soil from the foot of the barbarian, or as the embodiment of Dante's Greyhound, who was to be the savior of that low Italy 'on whose account the maid Camilla died'" (Cosenza 3).

Of course, the threat on their contemporary Rome came from the local nobility and not from barbarians, at least not at first glance. But a closer look reveals that Petrarch did indeed configure the noble Colonna and Orsini families as invading barbarians: the former reputedly of German descent; the latter from Spoleto in nearby Umbria, though his designations are not strictly reliable.[17]

> Let those who desire to establish hair-splitting definitions of terms decide whether these lords, who are entirely devoid of reason, are worthy of the name men. Whether they are to be your masters, since it is your interests that are at stake, I leave you to decide yourselves, Romans, provided that you keep clearly in mind that they cannot be lords and you free men at the same time and in the same city. The one fact, however, that I can decide is that they surely are not Romans. All these, as you remember, were so fastidious about their empty titles of nobility, no matter where they came from, no matter what ill wind blew them here, or what barbarian country turned them loose, even though they roamed about in your Forum, though they ascended the Capitol attended by hordes of armed retainers, and though they trod haughtily on the ashes of illustrious Romans. I say there was not one of them who was not an alien.
>
> (*Disp.* 8 88-101; Cosenza 12-13)

Here he goes so far as to make a philosophical argument against the very claim that the nobles of Rome are even human. Their lack of adherence to the human faculty of reason seems to disqualify them from being considered men. He then proceeds to assure the true born Roman citizens that their noble class are definitely not Romans, in the strict sense, because of the foreign origins of their blood lines. Cola may make a case against the noble families of Rome in his epistolary

---

[17] See *Disp.* 8: "But what makes the cup of grief and shame overflow is the thought that you have had as tyrants strangers and lords of foreign birth. Enumerate the ravishers of your honor, the plunderers of your fortunes, the destroyers of your liberty. Think of their separate origins. The valley of Spoleto claims this one; the Rhine, or the Rhone, or some obscure corner of the world has sent us the next" (Cosenza 11).

campaign to take power in the city from which vantage point he also intends to unify all of Italy, but Petrarch goes a couple of steps beyond Cola in terms of the sheer spleen he unleashes against the prior ruling class.

Petrarch picks up on Cola's anti-baronial project and skews it even further by likening them to greedy tyrants, rapacious wolves and cruel slave drivers. This is all the more shocking since one of the objects of his attack just also happens to be a branch of the very same Colonna family whose patronage Petrarch had enjoyed for nearly two decades in Avignon. His fervent backing of the Roman tribune was the beginning of the end for his life in the Avignonese court.

On the ideal bonds between *podestà* and the citizens of the commune, Petrarch follows with several paragraphs that are both descriptive and advisory. In a passage of central importance, Petrarch discusses the *gravitas* of the undertaking:

But you, most brave man, you who have buttressed the immense weight of the tottering state with your patriotic shoulders, gird yourself and watch with equal vigilance against such citizens as against the most bitter enemy. You, younger Brutus, always keep the example of the first Brutus before you. He was Consul, you are Tribune. If we compared the two offices we would find that the consuls performed many acts hostile to the welfare of the Roman plebs; indeed — and I will speak out bravely — they often treated it harshly and cruelly. But the tribunes were always and constantly the defenders of the people. If then that consul slew his own sons because of his love of liberty, realize what is expected in all circumstances from you as a tribune.

(*Disp.* 8; Cosenza 17)

When Petrarch joins the movement, he commits and takes Cola at his word. He unpacks in great detail the implications of the title the tribune has chosen for himself, and seizes upon it as an opportunity to implant the proper ends and responsibilities such pretensions bring with them. The responsibilities of a tribune differ from those of a consul. Whereas the latter is known for acting often against the interests of the common people, the former is their champion.

At the center of both Cola's and Petrarch's vision for the revolution is the concept of *libertas*, which is primarily cast as freedom from the oppression of the nobles. Petrarch goes to some length throughout the letter to emphasize the fact that freedom comes with responsibilities and often paradoxically requires control and certain sacrifices. But those challenges should not delude the people into thinking that the cup of the slave is more appealing than the abstinence of the freeman. In the concluding passage of his letter, Petrarch takes pains to lay out some of what the citizens might now be free to do:

Erase every vestige of civil fury from your midst, I beseech you. Let the flames that had been fanned among us by the breath of tyrants be extinguished by the warnings and the guarded kindness of your deliverer. Take this friendly rivalry upon yourselves: not who is to be the more powerful, but who is to be the better and more patient citizen, who is to reveal the deeper love of country, the greater humility toward his neighbors and the more implacable hatred for the tyrants. Enter this contest with your tribune: as to whether he will show greater foresight in the honest administration of government than your readiness in obeying.

(Disp. 8; Cosenza 23)

Petrarch reconfigures the social sphere of Cola's post-baronial reality in terms of a new challenge that he puts forth. He attempts to rewrite the rules of the game in terms of a "friendly rivalry" that poses new objectives for daily civic competition and proposes new bonds of love and common interest that he hopes will transcend the old craving for power and bind the new society together. At least, this is the vision conjured up in Petrarch's rhetoric, which, as history tells us, was as vain an attempt as any to write a revolution in the key of utopian optimism: "And if, perhaps, love — than which there is nothing stronger — proves insufficient to bring your hearts into harmony, then may considerations of common interest persuade you. At least be united by this bond."

In the last lines of the *Hortatoria*, however, Petrarch acknowledges the fact that he is only capable of accomplishing so much with words alone and that there is now need for decisive action in order to achieve his objectives. Despite this final admission of the limits to what rhetoric can attain on its own, the giving of sound advice as a public intellectual or poet to the prince — while looking to the illustrious Roman past for modes of thinking and models of exemplary behavior — remains at the heart of Petrarch's humanistic project.

Risk-Taking and Regret
For the next several months, Petrarch will risk everything to place all of his hopes in the cause of the Roman tribune. Sheer optimism and enthusiasm will carry him through much of this period. Book VII of the *Familiares* is a turning point in this regard. In it Petrarch maps out the high point of his faith in a new dawn for Italy.[18] He will leave the familiar haunts of his beloved Valchiusa in the fall of 1347 and will spend all of the following year in Italy, between Verona and Parma. His departure from Avignon for Italy is the initial cause of his break from the Colonnas, the family that had treated him as their adoptive son for most of his formative years.[19]

Familiares VII 1 was written on September 11, 1347, on the eve of his departure for Italy, and is addressed to Barbato da Sulmona. In the context of the first of his officially sanctioned letter collections, *Familiares* VII 1 gives us our first glimpse into the Cola di Rienzo affair and the turbulent state of Italian

---

[18] *Fam.* VII 1-4 were written in Provence, while letters VII 7-18 (with the exception of 8 and 9) were written in this period in Italy.

[19] Petrarch would subsequently try to right himself with members of the Colonna family, even while standing up against their influence in the city (Rome) that he loved equally, if not more. When Stefano Colonna is killed in one of the battles that ensues after Cola releases the nobles he had imprisoned, Petrarch writes a heartfelt letter of consolation to his father even though he had openly supported Cola's side of the affair.

politics.

> See how now the Italian dust is flying because of the advance of the barbarians, and where we were once conquerors of peoples, we are now, alas, the prey of conquerors. Either our sins have deserved that punishment or some evil and gloomy constellation harasses us with its baleful light, or else (as I believe to be the case) with the virtuous being confused with the wicked, we are being punished for the crimes of others. But let it not be said that I fear all of Italy from which, rather, the rebels will have something to fear as long as the tribunal power, which has recently returned to the city, flourishes, and our capital, Rome, is not ill.
> (Bernardo 331)

Italy as a whole may be in dire straits but Rome is a beacon of light. Petrarch is on board with the fresh start that the advent of Cola's "tribunal power" seems to portend. So, in this first letter, Book VII of the *Familiares* is off on an optimistic start regarding the state of affairs at least in Rome, where a glimmer of hope shines in the form of Cola di Rienzo, the still newly minted tribune of Rome. "I confess that I enjoy substantial favor with the tribune," he remarks, "a man of humble background but of lofty mind and purpose, and I also enjoy the favor of the Roman people" (Bernardo 332). His boasting of being in Cola's good graces, whom he takes to be one of the enlightened rulers of the peninsula, leads him to optimistically put forth the hope that the tribune will likewise transform Rome into an island of peace on the peninsula, a refuge for those who, like Barbato, are in search of solace from the turbulent storm of Italian politics elsewhere on the peninsula. In that same vein, *Familiares* VII 2 is an extended letter to a friend that delivers up a long lesson on the values of humility, the very virtues that he perceives Cola to possess.

The tune suddenly changes, however, just a few letters later. In *Familiares* VII 5, written on November 22, 1347, in transit on his way to Italy, we discover that Petrarch has received word of Cola's demise.

> The copy of the letter of the Tribune which was sent me I have seen, read, and been amazed by; I know not what to answer. I recognize the fate of the fatherland, for wherever I turn I find reason and occasion for grief. Once Rome is torn to pieces what will happen to Italy? Once Italy is disfigured what would my life be? In this sorrow, which is both public and private, some will contribute wealth, others bodily strength, and still others power and advice. I see nothing that I can contribute except tears.
> (Bernardo 345-46)

The humanist is distraught. His journey to Rome was only meant to be one facet of his trip south of the Alps, but the news was devastating. The dream of Roman *libertas* and a united Italy would last all of six months, during which time Petrarch would risk every semblance of security in his life: patronage, home, livelihood. This is where the letter of rebuke mentioned in the opening of this essay comes into play. The fallout that ensued would come to constitute a major transition in the development of the public intellectual and European humanist that Petrarch would go on to become. His abiding concerns for the values that Cola injected into the political discourse of the time will, nevertheless, continue to inform the persona that Petrarch will assume.

Petrarch's Thwarted Hope for "Italica libertas"
Petrarch's resentment towards the tribune lasts for several years. In late July 1352, roughly five years after the collapse of his initial contested tribunate in Rome, Cola di Rienzo was sent as a prisoner by Charles IV of Bohemia to the Papal court in Avignon.[20] The pope assembled three princes of the Church who were charged with the task of deciding "the appropriate punishment for a man who wished the republic to be free" (*Fam.* XIII 6 10; Bernardo 194). Cola stood accused not of having favored evil men or forsaking the freedom of his people, but of having dared to grant security and freedom to Rome, a city that knew neither of these civic virtues, and of wanting all matters dealing with Rome to be dealt with in Rome and not elsewhere.[21]

The nobility of Cola's aims was not missed by Petrarch. The absurdity of the situation did not escape him either, even if he felt that Cola deserved his fate. To Petrarch, Cola acted foolishly in the declining moments of his tribunate. Had he behaved with conviction, he would have gone down with the ship of state he had helmed, rather than abandon it, if that is what circumstance dictated, dying gloriously where he belonged, on the Capitoline. Instead, at the end of 1347, Cola was chased out of the city and had spent the intervening years in exile. In Petrarch's ruthless estimation of the situation, Cola marred his dignity through idleness and change of purpose, which is one thing that cannot be said about Petrarch during this period or in the years to come.[22]

Written on August 10, 1352, to Francesco Nelli, one of his dearest friends and closest confidants, *Familiares* XIII 6 is a remarkable document on a number

---

[20] *Familiares* VII 7 is not the only time in the collection that Petrarch makes his position clear with respect to his controversial ties to the Cola di Rienzo debacle. In *Familiares* XIII 6, he recapitulates the situation to his regular interlocutor, Francesco Nelli.

[21] *Fam.* XIII 6 19-21: "He is not being blamed for what good men dislike in him; and he is considered guilty not for the outcome of his endeavors but for their initiation. Nor is he accused of favoring evildoers, or forsaking liberty, of fleeing the Capitoline when nowhere else could he have lived more nobly or have died more gloriously. What is it then? Only one charge is directed against him, and if he is condemned for it, he will, at least for me, be not infamous but worthy of eternal glory. *The crime is that he dared to have wanted the republic safe and free, and to have all matters dealing with the Roman Empire and Roman power dealt with in Rome.* O crime worthy of the cross and of vultures, that a Roman citizen should grieve to see his land, the rightful mistress of all others, enslaved to the basest of men! This indeed is the nature of his crime, this is why his punishment is sought" (Bernardo 196; emphasis added).

[22] For an impassioned outpouring of Petrarch's dream to reform the state of things in Rome, see *Sine nom.*, VII. For analysis of this tendency in his work, see Foresti, "Sognando la riforma del governo di Roma" 263-67; Wilkins, *Studies in the Life and Works of Petrarch* 179-81, 186-92; Pastore Stocchi, "Petrarca e i potenti della terra" 39-42. For two thematically related letters, also discussed below, see *Fam.* XI, 16 (November 18, 1351) and *Fam.* XI, 17 (November 24, 1351).

of levels. The setting is the return of Cola to the papal court in Avignon in 1352 where he is due to await the aforementioned trial. Petrarch is particularly ruthless in his reassessment of the legacy of what he would have liked to see Cola accomplish.

I admit that he is indeed worthy of every kind of punishment, because what he wished he did not wish with as much persistence as he should have and as circumstances and necessity required. After his self-proclamation as the champion of freedom, he released all the enemies of liberty, still armed, when he might have crushed them — an opportunity fortune rarely grants to any commander. O fearful and hideous mist that veils the eyes of mortals in the midst of their greatest undertakings! Had he decided to exercise only one of his surnames and not the one necessary for the well-being of the republic (he wished to be called both Severe and Clement), if then he had exercised only his clemency against the country's murderers, he could have kept them alive, after having deprived them of all their instruments for doing harm, and, above all, disarmed them of their arrogant skills. Thus they would either have become citizens of the city of Rome instead of its enemies, or despicable enemies to be scorned rather than feared.

(*Fam.* XIII 6 10-12; Bernardo 194-45)

The letter is of interest not least of all for the glimpse it affords into the proto-Machiavellian mind of the father of Renaissance humanism. Cola had the opportunity to crush the enemies of freedom, which he did not take. Petrarch's biggest regrets were that Cola sent mixed signals by being both severe and clement. Petrarch chides him for not having dealt with his enemies more forcefully. Once he had the foremost members of the opposition imprisoned, he should have disposed of them when he had the chance, rather than free them shortly after capture, which is what spelled the beginning of the end for the unsuspecting tribune. The advice is not unlike that of the author of *The Prince* years later.

Cola's return to the court at Avignon gave Petrarch pause to think about their shared past. In *Familiares* XIII 6, Petrarch reflects on the perils and the pitfalls of his all too hasty and overzealous involvement in the Cola debacle from the beginning.[23]

But enough of this, for I speak too passionately, interrupting the separate stages of my

---

[23] *Fam.* XIII 6 10-11: "Upon his arrival, then, the pontiff immediately assigned three princes of the church to hear his case. Their assignment was 'to decide the appropriate punishment for a man who wished the republic to be free.' *O tempora, o mores* — as I am compelled to exclaim again and again! I admit that he is indeed worthy of every kind of punishment, because what he wished he did not wish with as much persistence as he should have and as circumstances and necessity required" (Bernardo 194). See also, *Fam.* XIII 6 9: "He who filled evil men throughout the world with terror and fear, he who gave good men the most joyful hope and expectation, entered the Curia humble and despised. He who was once accompanied by the entire Roman populace and by the foremost citizens of Italian cities was unhappily walking hither and yon, accompanied by two guards, through a crowd eager to see the face of the man whose name was recently so celebrated" (194).

account and saddened, as you see, to have placed my last hope for Italian liberty in that man whom I had long known and loved. Once he had dedicated himself to such an undertaking, I had allowed myself to cherish and admire him above all others. Therefore the more I had hoped in him, the more I now grieve for my last hope, and I confess that, however this may all end, I cannot but marvel at the way it began.

(*Fam.* XIII 6 15; Bernardo 195)

The solitary singer of Laura is not usually conceived of as an impulsive political player; however, in *Familiares* XIII 6 he confesses to having allowed his enthusiasm to get the best of him.

Recently there came to the Curia Nicola di Lorenzo — I should not say that he came but that he was led there captive — once a truly feared tribune of the city of Rome yet now the most miserable of men. What is even worse, miserable though he is, I know not whether he is worthy of pity. While he might have died with great glory on the Capitoline, he instead suffered imprisonment in Bohemia and shortly afterward in Limoges, to his shame and that of the Roman name, and even to that of the republic. How involved my pen was in praising and advising him is better known than I would perhaps wish. I loved his virtue, I praised his aims, I admired his spirit. I rejoiced with Italy, and I foresaw the sovereignty of the Holy City and peace throughout the entire world. I was unable to conceal my joy that sprang from so many sources. I seemed a participant in all this glory by sending him words of encouragement in his endeavors, words that he felt very strongly, according to the reports of his messengers and indications in his letters.

(*Fam.* XIII 6 5-6; Bernardo 193-94)

Once again, the feeling of disappointment is palpable in the humanist's words. Petrarch admits to having been swept away by his frenzy for the promise Cola di Rienzo showed in the early stages of his time in office, but all that hope was misplaced and his praise was premature. Petrarch was spurred on by the joy of the tribune's initial triumphs and by the fact that he was so warmly received in so many corners of the peninsula. The humanist dispatched letters, made moves, even sought to join the revolution in Rome and cut ties with longtime friends and patrons in Avignon in order to realign himself with the dream of Roman liberty and Italian unification. Now at a distance of roughly five years since Cola's tribunate had run its course, the humanist seizes the opportunity to reassess what made that brief moment in time so special. Petrarch recounts the motivations that drove him to join the movement in Rome so fervently from so early on.

All the more eagerly I tried to think of ideas to enkindle his fervent spirit. Since I knew very well that nothing fires a noble heart more than glory and praise, I would include praises, perhaps overdone in the minds of many but truly warranted in my opinion; commending him on his accomplishments I would encourage him to other endeavors.

(*Fam.* XIII 6 7; Bernardo 194)

The humanist saw the value in what Cola was doing and claims that he rose to the occasion and did everything he could to advise him — the way a courtier would goad a prince to proceed in the right direction. Petrarch tried to speak truth to power the best he could, but his advocacy and advice were not enough to cure his fearless demagogue of the demons of his own personality.

> I still have a number of my letters to him for which I feel no regrets; unaccustomed as I am to being a prophet, I indeed wish that he had not tried to be one! In any event, what he was doing and seemed about to do at the time I was writing him certainly deserved, not only my praise and admiration, but that of all mankind. I know not whether these letters merit destruction simply because he preferred to live shamefully than to die honorably; but one ought not to deliberate on impossible things. Although I would very much like to destroy the letters, I shall be unable to do so; once in the public domain, they are no longer within my control.
>
> (*Fam*. XIII 6 8; Bernardo 194)

Some of his letters, Petrarch admits, are cause for a certain amount of embarrassment for him, which as we have seen was the cause for silencing most all of them in his official letter collections. Despite this epistolary self-censorship, he nevertheless remains proud of the values behind what they set out to achieve, despite the fact that the quixotic populist leader he was betting on ultimately failed. Reliving the humiliation of the defeat of his idealistic fool's errand of ever supporting Cola so wholeheartedly, he is reminded of how much he risked at the time to go to Rome to take his place alongside his latter-day Brutus, his Scipio *redivivus*. In the process, he ended up putting a lot of strain on his relationship with the Colonna family, as noted above, especially Giovanni Colonna, of whom he continues to speak with great familial fondness right up to the end of his life in his letter to posterity, the *Posteritati*, found at the end of the *Seniles*.[24]

In the spring of 1353, he will leave his life and his ties in Provence definitively in order to dedicate himself to the cause of Italy in a variety of capacities. No one would consider Petrarch to be a systematic political thinker; however, the abiding concerns that are apparent in every aspect of his involvement in Italian and European politics remain consistent throughout his opus. For much of the rest of his life, Petrarch will continue to lobby on behalf of the same core values that drove Cola di Rienzo's meteoric flash across the Roman night sky.

Papal Mission to Reform the Government in Rome

During the time of Cola's exile, between the end of 1347 and 1352, Petrarch continued to rally on behalf of the liberation of the Roman people. His letters to the council of four cardinals who were commissioned in 1351 by the Pope with the task of reforming the government in Rome attest to this commitment.[25] In two

---

[24] Petrarch, *Sen*. XVIII 1: "Returning from there, for many years I was under his brother, Giovanni Cardinal Colonna, not as under a master but under a father, or rather, not even that, but with a most loving brother or with myself in my own home" (Bernardo 675).

[25] See *Fam*. XI 16 9-10: "It must occur to reasonable men that it was neither by chance nor without reason, but by divine decree that the Roman pontiff assigned to you from among the cardinals of the Sacred College this glorious and meritorious burden, although in balance not too weighty. In addition to your profound wisdom and abundant learning, experience has taught

consecutive letters (*Fam.* XI 16 and 17), both addressed to all four men collectively, bearing the dates November 18, 1351, and November 24, 1351, Petrarch adapts the arguments he employed in the context of Cola's campaign to his new addressees, who represent a renewed hope as well as another chance to "champion suppressed liberties" and bring political change to Rome and Italy. This time the intervention is to be carried out under the authority of the Pope, but Petrarch's ultimate goals remain the same: assure security, justice and peace for the people of Rome so that the city might rise again to attain its former glory.

In the first of the two letters, Petrarch even continues his invective against the nobles. He lists the transgressions of the tyrannical Colonna and Orsini clans as follows:

> I would think considerable progress had been made, had I persuaded those proud spirits to be citizens and not oppressors of citizens, nor would I then expel them from the ranks of office with the rigor of a Manlius. But in the name of God who has compassion for human affairs, O most gentle fathers, if you have any feeling for the Roman name, I ask you to consider whether they have seized the Roman Republic for the sake of giving succor with their own wealth to public poverty. Would that they had this in mind! I could then grant pardon to their bountiful ambition and admit them to candidacy regardless of their place of origin. But believe me, they are contemplating the opposite course; they doubtless enkindle, more than they appease, the insatiable hunger of their avarice with the remains of a devastated city. But they will perhaps try to deny this and conceal with the impudence of a single word the vicissitudes of an entire life, which are known to all, wishing to appear as Roman citizens and lovers of their native land. It is not so. Indeed it is a capital offense for them to be called citizens or men rather than princes or lords.
> (*Fam.* XI 16; Bernardo 123)

The letter contains a sustained tirade against the Colonna and the Orsini families in Rome, whom he does not call "spirto gentil" in the mode of one of his political ideals, but rather "proud spirits."[26] As he makes explicit in the letter, they are non-citizen outsiders, which is a trope we encountered above in the *Hortatoria*. The mission is to free the Roman people from the "foreign" domination of the nobles, who hail either from the Rhine, in the case of the Colonna, or from Spoleto, in the case of the Orsini. His desire is to free the Roman people in order to facilitate self-government, or Roman *libertas*, which should also sound familiar. The general thrust of his mission remains anti-baronial.

In *Familiares* XI 16 and 17, Petrarch expresses many of the same sentiments we encountered in his correspondence with the Roman tribune, only now his scope has shifted from the local and the secular to the spiritually mandated power

---

three of you knowledge of Roman affairs. The fourth is indeed not only of Roman origin but, as some believe, a descendent of the noble and ancient family Cornelia, and yet — O genuine piety, O sweet love of the fatherland! — also a powerful defender of the common people against the proud nobility and a champion of suppressed liberties" (Bernardo 121).

[26] The letter then moves into a brief excursus on the nature of true nobility (Bernardo 122-23). For the political ideal of the *spirto gentil*, see *Rvf.* 53.

of the Church operating more broadly on the European stage.[27] Despite the difference in the arena of power, his appeal, nevertheless, remains strikingly similar, despite the new tone compromise that underlies it. He proceeds to solicit the same kind of assistance in order to achieve many of the very same goals. This time around, however, he gives the cardinals some very specific political advice, which he couches in an anecdote borrowed from Livy (Livy 9 46):

Here reference should be made to what seems a small item related by Titus Livy, but it provides clear evidence of the nobility's arrogance and the people's independence. Gneus Flavius, a scribe's son, very humble in origin but otherwise sagacious and eloquent, was made curule aedile. That so upset the horrified nobility because of its novelty that, for the occasion, many of them removed their gold rings and other ornaments as though in mourning. Unperturbed, he calmly opposed his unshakable perseverance to their arrogance. Thus, during his visit to a sick colleague, some young nobles who happened to be present when he entered the bedroom did not stand, out of contempt. He had his curule chair brought at once, and having thereby become a more noble despiser than his despising young nobles, he disdainfully looked down upon them in their envy from the seat of public office and not from an ordinary chair. This single act of independence indeed makes him for me most worthy not only of the aedileship but even of the consulship. I have purposely left this discussion to the end because the two senators who still remain from the great number of conscript fathers can surely be viewed as successors to the two consuls.[28] Just as that magistracy had a limited term, so does this one, whereas the senatorial office did not. If I were to begin narrating how often men ruthlessly struggled for this consulship, I would stray from the central purpose of my letter, to which I now hasten. Let it suffice to say that, when the common people of Rome demanded a share even in the highest office, the nobility considered it a terrible disgrace and resisted them with all its strength.[29] In this area as well it finally had to succumb to defeat. Following much violent struggle, they first arrived at the compromise to create four military tribunes with consular powers rather than additional consuls. Not even this satisfied the wishes of the common people, and what they had long been denied because of puffed-up arrogance was obtained through the power of justice. Thus, a plebeian consul sat next to a patrician one; and both ruled a single fatherland, and the empire acquired through their common effort an equal majesty.[30]

(*Fam.* XI 16 28-32; Bernardo 125-26)

Petrarch's advice in the immediate aftermath of Cola's failure now swings toward compromise. What is needed is a mixed government in which the interests of both the plebs and the patricians are represented. Most remarkable of all is that the anecdote from Livy recalls the recent efforts of his disgraced friend and man

---

[27] *Fam.* XI 16: "Thus, having been chosen by God as judges in this sacred cause, leave no room for indolence, for human requests or favors. But to summarize briefly the heart of my doubts and thought, I believe that an ancient controversy is being repeated, and I pray that none of the ancient arrogance will be added to the new tyranny" (Bernardo 121).

[28] After Cola's fall, when Betrand de Déaulx occupied the city in the name of the Church in 1348, the senatorial regime was reinstated with Bertoldo Orsini and Luca Savelli. Petrarch rightly places these two men in roles that are descended of the two ancient consuls.

[29] See Livy 4 6 8.

[30] The first plebeian consul was Lucius Sextius in 366 BCE. See Livy 6 42 9.

of similarly humble origins, Cola di Rienzo, who bore the same resentments against the noble class. Similarly, it was the noble class — backed by the pope — that ran him out of town much like the trials and tribulations of Livy's Gneus Flavius. The specter of the Roman tribune haunts Petrarch's further interventions in the politics of the city he loves.

In the same way the pope will assemble a committee of judges to sentence Cola to the punishment he deserves not even a year later, Petrarch here breeches the subject of punishment for the nobles who have been the root cause of the problems Rome faces:

Thus the mistress of peoples, fallen into all kinds of wretchedness and mourned by no one, torn not by her own hands, as was once the case, but by foreigners, has lost the ancient solace for her misfortunes: "To admit no kings but to serve its subjects." And yet one hesitates to oppose this kind of harm, and overlooks a question worthy of consideration before all others, namely, what types of appropriate punishments should be used against such public plunderers, or at least how distant from public office in a free state should these enemies of freedom be kept? Surprisingly this alone is the question to be resolved: whether the Roman people, once rulers of all peoples, ought to reacquire as much liberty as will allow it today to participate with local tyrants in its own governance on its own Capitoline."
(Bernardo 122)

For Petrarch, it is not right that the enemies of freedom escape the reach of justice, whether they are baronial families or not. Exacting just punishment on the nobles who abused the situation to their own benefit is foremost among his concerns in righting the wrongs that were committed against the city in order to ensure that they will not occur again in the future:

Cowardly and self-indulgent without reason and scornful of all things, the nobility abusing the excessive submissiveness of the Roman commoners, shamefully dragging them in a triumph as if they were captured Carthaginians or Cimbrians condemned to the yoke. And yet, no law prescribes, no custom allows, and no words have ever proclaimed that one may triumph over conquered fellow citizens. At this point, so that not even a single doubt interfere and so that no suspicion arise that my words be touched with even the slightest animosity, let me say that of the two families involved in controversy I have never disliked the one; as for the other, as everyone knows, not only do I love it, but I have always cherished it with intimate devotion, for no princely family is dearer to me, as is Rome, Italy, and the peace and security of good citizens.
(Bernardo 121)

Petrarch turns the question of punishment into a problem of legality, of custom. What are the rules of engagement that dictate the way we treat our fellow citizens in the civic space? In his *Hortatoria* to Cola and the People of Rome he had attempted, as we saw above, to institute an ethos of friendly rivalry and love, which are not the modes of conduct that have informed the behavior of the two noble families whom he blames for creating the situation. Of course, it is also here at the end of this passage that Petrarch makes explicit his highly affective relationship to the Colonna family. In case it was not clear that he is acting selflessly in the interest of what is best for Rome, Petrarch is even going against his adoptive family.[31] It is a question of principle. He is anti-noble on pure principle, even though it cuts close to home. When it comes to prioritizing the peace and security of ordinary citizens, he refuses to let cronyism, familial privilege, and affective bonds get in the way. The abiding concerns of Petrarch's political intervention remain consistent.

From the Pontiff's Men to the Holy Roman Emperor
Throughout this period, Petrarch went on to expand the scope of his plea for a renewal not only of pontifical but also of imperial interest in a peaceful Rome as well as in the unification of Italy. His first attempt to reach out to the uppermost echelon of European power dates to February 24, 1351. Written from Padua, *Familiares* X 1 is the first in a long series of letters addressed to Charles IV of Bohemia.[32] In the Holy Roman Emperor, ever the idealist, Petrarch seeks "a resolute defender of our freedom" ("libertatis nostre promptissimum assertorem").[33] For the next fifteen years, the Italian humanist will indefatigably continue to shower the Emperor with exhortations to descend into Italy to restore the empire with Rome as its head — *Roma caput mundi* being its famous motto.[34]

In *Familiares* X 1, Petrarch calls upon the supreme ruler of earthly things, the Holy Roman Emperor in Prague, to perform his Christian role for mankind: that is, to take his place in Rome where he can whip the rest of Italy back into shape, restore the serenity of peace to the peninsula. His is a Dantesque dream of a universal monarchy, the paragon of law and order in human affairs across

---

[31] *Fam.* XI 17: "I shall therefore speak out of sincerity, serving my conscience rather than glory, not from the desire that my words be praised buy that my silence not be blamed. Nor will it greatly matter whom my words offend as long as they do not offend justice. It is certainly difficult to attack the powerful, particularly if they are dear friends, but that man is a friend of truth who places it before friends and all other matters. Therefore, I lay aside my feelings to question these foreign tyrants, though they be very dear to me and close friends of long standing" (Bernardo 128).

[32] After Fam. X 1, see also, *Fam.* XII 1; XVIII 1; XIX 1 and 12; XXIII 2, 15 and 21; not to mention all of the letters he began to exchange with other members of the imperial court in Prague. See Dotti, *Lettere all'imperatore*.

[33] Using language that recalls political canzoni of the *Canzoniere*, like *Spirto gentil*, *Rvf* 53, Petrarch appeals to the gentle heavenly spirit in the Emperor. See *Fam.* X 1 2: "Nos equidem sperabamus te, celitus nobis missum, libertatis nostre promptissimum assertorem; tu refugis et ubi facto opus est, longissimis consultationibus tempus trahis" ("We truly hoped that you, like a messenger from heaven, would be a resolute defender of our freedom. You flee instead; when there is need for action, you waste time in tedious deliberations" Bernardo 49).

[34] Charles IV of Bohemia was not officially crowned Emperor until 1355, although he had been proclaimed king of the Romans in Avignon in 1346 upon his father's abdication. Petrarch's first letter to Charles IV (*Fam.* X 1) was written February 24, 1351, but the Emperor's response did not reach Petrarch until 1353, following his second appeal in *Fam.* XII 1 (written February 1352). Both appeals were written prior to Petrarch's personal acquaintance with the Emperor in 1354.

Christendom. What Henry VII, also known as "alto Arrigo" in *Paradiso* XXX 137, was to Dante's dream of a universal monarchy, Charles IV was to Petrarch's analogous aspiration.[35] Of course, the coincidence is not casual. Charles is, after all, Henry VII's grandson. To fill the shoes of Cola in the previous incarnation of his quixotic dream to restore the seat of empire to Rome, in *Familiares* X 1, Petrarch casts the emperor in the role of the ardent defender of Italian liberty. The liberator of Italy this time is Charles IV of Bohemia.

Because of his newfound itinerant lifestyle after breaking with the Colonna family in Avignon in the wake of the Cola di Rienzo debacle, Petrarch only received Charles IV of Bohemia's response (*Laureata tui*) to his initial missive (*Fam.* X 1) two years later, even though he responded to the original in a matter of months. The emperor's response all but outright dismisses the first of Petrarch's calls for an imperial intervention in Italy. In closing, the Holy Roman Emperor echoes a sentiment found also in the opening of the letter. He suggests that Petrarch need not be too overzealous about his cult of antiquity. "You must, therefore, my friend, know how to compare the past with the present in such a way that the moral integrity of the prior is restored, and the disgraceful iniquity of the latter is repelled, which without a whirlwind is a very difficult thing to do" (*Laureata tui* 8 588). Drawing on the past for models of excellence and political virtue to follow, in the opinion of the emperor, has its limits and can only get us so far, the Emperor gently chides.

Charles IV's subtle critique of Petrarch's mode of thinking about real political questions through the lens of the past, especially Livy, touches on what will go on to become one of the cornerstones of humanistic political thought through the Renaissance and beyond. His political theory is largely based on a poetics of *exemplaritas*, or drawing on illustrious examples from the past in order to hold them up to models of excellence for the present. This practice will become a norm of sorts for authors up through Machiavelli's *Discorsi sulla Prima Deca di Tito Livio* and beyond, without forgetting Hobbes's notable translation of Thucydides. Petrarch's abiding concerns remain consistent throughout the rest of his career.

Starting in Book X of the *Familiares*, he presents himself as an engaged public intellectual who continuously strives to make the ancient myth of Rome a living reality, and he manages to turn heads elsewhere in the court of Prague by means of his humanistic agenda. Correspondence with the imperial chancellor Jan ze Středa (also known as Johann von Neumarkt) will come to dominate the next several years of Petrarch's epistolary output, jettisoning the Italian humanist to European respectability and prominence.

---

[35] See *Fam.* X 1 13: "[…] Iuventus labori apta, otio senectus; profecto autem ex omnibus optimis ac sanctissimis curis tuis nulla gravior quam ut italicum orbem tranquilla pace componas" ("Youth is more suited to toil, old age to repose. There is little question that, of all your most worthy and holy cares, none is more important than restoring a tranquil peace to Italy" Bernardo 51).

When Petrarch finally receives the Emperor's response two years later, he responds, on December 23, 1353, to each of his points one by one in *Familiares* XVIII 1. The same message continues — fight the nobles, free the people, in the background anyway — in the letters he addresses to Charles IV. Petrarch is still in search of someone capable of freeing the people from the corrupting influence of the careless, self-interested nobles in Rome and the rest of Italy. He is still looking for the catalyst for unification.

The emperor's dignified response can be broken down into three main points. Petrarch addresses them each, one by one. The emperor advises Petrarch that Italy is not what it was in antiquity. Petrarch responds with: "Your first excuse for the delay is the changing times, which you exaggerate with so many words that I am compelled to admire and praise the writer's skill rather than the Emperor's spirit. What is there at present, I ask, that did not previously exist?" (Bernardo 37). It is easy to say that the present is not like the past, but this is not an excuse in Petrarch's mind, but rather a rhetorical flourish.

The emperor's second point is even more cowardly. He claims that it is difficult to govern an empire. After giving the emperor a brief history lesson, in which he corrects his mistaken attribution of a quote about wild "belva" to Augustus, Petrarch launches into more political optimism: "[The empire] is an extremely powerful monster, but one that a skilled hand may control; it is an enormous but manageable monster, untamed only if not handled with care. Be bold, act, seize the reins in your hands and ascend the throne that is yours; if you are fearful, it will find other occupants" (Bernardo 39). This is his opportunity to elevate the political discourse of his time, and to raise the emperor's awareness of what needs to happen in his beloved Italy. If the emperor is worthy of his title, then he will rise to the occasion and shape the world in those ways that he sees fit. Petrarch is unbridled in his advocacy for an imperial intervention from a restored seat of power in Rome.

Finally, Charles IV warns that the use of force should be avoided except as a last resort. Petrarch can do nothing but agree with the emperor's sentiments regarding the judicious use of hegemonic violence and he invokes the great Roman humanist playwright Terence to justify the point. Despite agreeing with him that violence is not necessary, Petrarch does everything but accuse the emperor in any case of being all too rooted in cowardice:

For upon whose honor do the kingdom's misfortunes weigh, if not its ruler's? You say that the empire's freedom has been destroyed: you, as father of the empire, will restore it; that the Romans have been subjected to the yoke of slavery: you will remove it from their backs; that justice has been prostituted in the brothel of greed: you will restore it to its sacred chambers; that peace has fled the minds of mortals: you will return it to its proper abode. For you have been born to it, destined to this office, so that you might do away with the republic's ugliness and restore its pristine face to the world.

(*Fam.* XVIII 1 35-36; Bernardo 41)

The language here is redolent of that of Cola di Rienzo in his assessment of the situation in Rome when he stepped up as tribune: "the empire's freedom has been destroyed" ("dirupta est imperii libertas"), "the Romans have been subjected to the yoke of slavery" ("sumpta Latinis servitus"), "justice has been prostituted in the brothel of greed" ("ad avaritie lupanar prostituta iustitia"), and "peace has fled the minds of mortals" ("pax e mentibus lapsa mortalium"). These are all the same symptoms of decay and decline that Cola had set out to remedy in his good intentioned campaign to restore order to Rome, no matter how quixotic his attempt might have been.

In fact, Petrarch then goes on to conclude the letter with a nod to a special someone. He puts forth the familiar example of Cola di Rienzo. If someone of such humble origins as Cola managed to accomplish so much, it is fair to assume that someone with the stature of the emperor could take it to the next level. He remarks:

A few days ago, a man of low station rose above all others. He was not a Roman king, not a consul or patrician, but a Roman citizen of little fame, having no titles of his own and no statues of his ancestors, in short, not exemplary at that time for any virtue, and yet he declared himself *the avenger of Roman liberty*! A splendid declaration of an obscure man! At once, as you know, Tuscany eagerly offered him her hand and recognized his rule; gradually all of Italy, and then Europe, were following suit, and the entire world was on the move. What need is there for more? This we did not read but saw, and already justice seemed to be making its return together with peace and their companions, cherished faith, peaceful security, and finally traces of the golden age. Yet in the very flowering of events, he withered. Do not blame him or anyone else; I do not condemn the man nor do I absolve him; I am not his judge but I do know what I believe. He had assumed the title of tribune, the most humble of Roman honorary titles; if the title of tribune could achieve so much, what might the title of Caesar accomplish?

(*Fam.* XVIII 1; Bernardo, 38. Emphasis added)

In this letter Petrarch gives Cola the acknowledgement he deserves. Here he points out the extent to which the humble tribune's initiative was warmly received by neighbors in Tuscany and even in the rest of Europe. The tides were turning in his favor and so the pump may just be primed to bring change to the political economy of Rome and Italy as a whole. If Cola was able to do what he did, he says, just think of what the imperial court could do. Cola was merely a plebeian tribune; Charles IV is emperor.

Though he enlarges the scope of his political aspirations, his abiding concerns remain the same: *libertas* and *tranquilla pax*. Time passes, prior projects fail, but Petrarch's message endures. From the short-lived tribunate of Cola di Rienzo that got the ball rolling in real, though rather quixotic political ways, Petrarch adapted his goals to the diplomatic council he lavished on the four cardinals who were sent to Rome in the aftermath of Cola's campaign to straighten things out again and reform the local government in the capital. At the same time, Petrarch also engaged in correspondence with the Holy Roman Emperor in Prague which led him to be taken seriously in new ways on the international stage and in turn resulted in the forging of a new identity, namely that of public intellectual, arguably making him the first European humanist. Through it all, Petrarch never changes his song. No one would credit Petrarch for being a systematic political thinker *per se*, but what emerges in this survey of his personal letters is a portrait of the father of Renaissance humanism speaking the same truth to power throughout the period that spans from the rise of Cola di Rienzo in 1347 to the crowning of Charles IV in 1355. Though he enlarges the scope of his vision, the same enduring concerns can be found at the heart of his political and humanistic project.

Columbia University

Works Cited

Di Rienzo, Cola. *Epistolario di Cola di Rienzo*. Ed. Annibale Gabrielli. Roma: Forzani e C. Tipografi del Senato, 1890.

Dotti, Ugo. *Petrarca civile. Alle orgini dell'intellettuale moderno*. Roma: Donzelli, 2001.

Foresti, Arnaldo. "Sognando la riforma del governo di Roma." *Aneddoti della vita di Francesco Petrarca*. Ed. Antonia Tissoni Benvenuti. Padova: Antenore, 1977. 263-67.

Maire-Vigueur, Jean-Claude. "Il comune romano." *Storia di Roma dall'antichità a oggi*. Roma medievale. Roma: RR inedita, 2004. 117-58.

Miglio, Massimo. *Scritture, scrittori e storia*. Roma: Vecchiarelli, 1991.

Modigliani, Anna. *L'eredità di Cola di Rienzo: Gli statuti del Comune di popolo e la riforma di Paolo II*. Roma: RR inedita, 2004.

Pastore Stocchi, Manlio. "Petrarca e i potenti della terra." *Francesco Petrarca: da Padova all'Europa*. 2 vols. Padova: Antenore, 2007. 37-50.

Petrarca, Francesco. *Le familiari* (Libri XI-XV). Ed. and trans. Vittorio Rossi, Umberto Bosco, and Ugo Dotti. Torino: Aragno, 2007.

———. *Lettere a Petrarca*. Ed. Ugo Dotti. Torino: Nino Aragno Editore, 2012.

———. *Lettere all'imperatore. Carteggio con la corte imperiale di Praga (1351-1364)*. Reggio Emilia: Diabasis, 2008.

———. *Lettere disperse*. Ed. Alessandro Pancheri. Parma: Fondazione Pietro Bembo, 1994.

———. *Letters of Old Age*. Trans. Aldo S. Bernardo et al. New York: Italica Press, 2005.

———. *Letters on Familiar Matters*. 3 vols. Trans. Aldo S. Bernardo. New York: Italica Press, 2005.

———. "Petrarch's Coronation Oration." *Studies in the Life and Work of Petrarch*. Ed. Ernest Hatch Wilkins. Cambridge: Mediaeval Academy of America, 1955.

———. *The Revolution of Cola di Rienzo*. Ed. Mario Cosenza. New York: Italica Press, 1996.

———. *Le senili* (Libri XIII-XVIII). Ed. Elvira Nota and Ugo Dotti. Torino: Aragno, 2010.

Wilkins, Ernest Hatch. *Studies in the Life and Work of Petrarch*. Cambridge: Mediaeval Academy of America, 1955.

Karina F. Attar

Speaking Truth to Powerful Friends and Foes: Genoese Merchants and the Mamluks in *Decameron* 2.9[1]

Abstract: This article investigates the documented commercial and diplomatic activities of the Genoese Segurano Salvaygo as a possible additional source for *Decameron* 2.9, the tale of Zinevra. Extant evidence about Segurano Salvaygo is limited but compelling for Boccaccio's formulation of Zinevra's alter-ego, Sicurano. Moreover, contextualizing the tale highlights the resilience and ingenuity of historical figures and fictional characters who challenge church, state, and patriarchy in order to survive, make a living, and reclaim their honor in the fourteenth-century Mediterranean.
Key Words: Christian-Muslim relations; Mamluk sultanate; Decameron; Boccaccio; Trade; Genoa.

Giovanni Boccaccio's *Decameron* (c. 1349-51) speaks many truths to many powers. In the introduction to Day 4 and in the author's conclusion, for instance, Boccaccio challenges the potential and actual charges brought by critics against his collection, calling attention — amongst other things — to the double standards by which his work had been evaluated and defiantly adding that readers are free to skip those novellas "che pungono" and read only "quelle che dilettano" ("Conclusione dell'autore" 19).[2] In the opening prologue, moreover, he offers his collection in aid of a group he views as particularly disenfranchised, namely women in love who might otherwise be "ristrette da' voleri, da' piaceri, da' comandamenti de' padri, delle madri, de' fratelli e de' mariti" to spend their days "nel piccolo circuito delle loro camere racchiuse" with nothing to do but lament their circumstances ("Proemio" 10). The subsequent declaration that men can instead resort to numerous distracting activities when emotionally burdened ("l'andare a torno, udire e veder molte cose, uccellare, cacciare, pescare, cavalcare, giucare o mercatare" 12) reinforces Boccaccio's ostensible critique of the gender inequalities at work in the patriarchal social order of his day. The conceit of a mixed-gender *brigata* that asserts its right to flee plague-ridden Florence and grants equal authority to both

---

[1] This essay develops research presented in 2014 at the Annual Meeting of the Renaissance Society of America and at Columbia University's Department of Italian. I thank the organizers at both venues, as well as audience members, for their valuable comments, particularly Teodolinda Barolini, Jo Ann Cavallo, and Janet Levarie Smarr. Thanks also to Hannah Barker for her helpful feedback on this essay.
[2] All citations from the *Decameron* are from Vittore Branca's edition.

Annali d'italianistica 34 (2016). *Speaking Truth to Power from Medieval to Modern Italy*

its male and female members further shows, as Teodolinda Barolini argues, that there "is power in the text's ability to imagine a different social order from that which it can ultimately predict or endorse" ("Sociology of the *Brigata*" 6). In fact, as many of the essays in *Boccaccio's* Decameron: *Rewriting the Christian Middle Ages* implicitly suggest, and as Dino S. Cervigni explicitly argues in his contributions to the volume, the entire *Decameron* could be read as a critique of the Christian world view prevailing in the Middle Ages.

Turning to the hundred novellas themselves, we find myriad instances of marginalized or downtrodden protagonists who make good of bad situations by taking powerful figures down a peg or two. Examples include tales wherein socio-economically subordinate (male) figures call their (male) superiors out (through words or deeds) on their moral shortcomings, sometimes even for the very same misdemeanors of which they stand accused (e.g., 1.4, 1.6, 1.7, 1.8, and 6.2). Female protagonists who put their honor, livelihood, and/or lives on the line by speaking truth to (almost invariably male and sometimes political) power and taking destiny into their own hands include the Marchioness of Montferrat (1.5), a lady from Gascony (1.9), the daughter of the King of England (2.3), Zinevra (2.9), Bartolomea (2.10), the wife of Messer Francesco Vergellesi (3.5), Ghismonda (4.1), Andreuola (4.6), the wife of Pietro di Vinciolo (5.10), Monna Nonna de' Pulci (6.3), Madonna Filippa (6.7), and the nun Isabetta (9.2). While all these women advocate for their personal rights thanks to their intelligence, quick wit, eloquence, and (at times) serendipitous circumstances, the heroine of 2.9, Zinevra, distinguishes herself by exploring the transcultural, interfaith, male-dominated world of Mediterranean travel, trade, and diplomacy disguised as a man. In addition, while all the other heroines listed above must contend with a single threat to their honor and/or life (be it from an institution or an individual), Zinevra successfully overcomes dangers from multiple sources of authority in both Christian and Muslim realms.

Critics have approached 2.9 from various related formal and gendered perspectives, including as a variant of wager narratives and as an example of the *Decameron*'s discursive strategies concerning women's agency and the power of storytelling, while taking also into consideration Boccaccio's sexual poetics and intratextual self-referentiality.[3] In this essay, I propose a historicized reading of Zinevra's novella by considering the context of Genoese-Mamluk relations and in particular the singular travels of a Genoese merchant, Segurano Salvaygo, who was active in the Mamluk sultanate in the early 1300s. As I will show, the available evidence about Segurano Salvaygo is germane to a reading of 2.9 that attends to the overarching theme of this volume. Both the fictional Zinevra, who impersonates a man, and the real-life Salvaygo, prosper in potentially hostile

---

[3] See, for example, Barolini, "'Le parole son femmine e i fatti son maschi'"; Cavallero; Migiel, especially chapter 4: "To Transvest not to Transgress" (83-108); Paris; and Wayne.

domains, successfully (albeit temporarily) speak truth to power, and realize their ideological, economic, and personal imperatives thanks to their influential positions within the Mamluk court, their ability to inhabit different identities, and their pragmatism, ingenuity, and fearlessness in the face of peril at home and abroad.

Segurano Salvaygo (c. 1300-1323)
Three kinds of sources document the activities of Segurano Salvaygo: (1) late 13th- and early 14th-century Genoese notarial records related to trade in Caffa (present-day Feodosia) on the Black Sea, (2) 14th- and 15th-century Mamluk chronicles, and (3) the Dominican bishop William of Adam's crusade treatise *Tractatus quomodo Sarraceni sunt expugnandi* (*How to Defeat the Saracens*, c. 1317), which condemns Christian slave traders, the Genoese in particular, and Segurano above all, for trafficking with the Mamluks. The first two sets of sources help offset Adam's ideologically skewed and at times misleading portrait of Segurano. In "Segurano-Sakrān Salvaygo: un mercante genovese al servizio dei sultani mamalucchi, c. 1303- 1322," Benjamin Kedar provides a meticulous study of these documents and convincingly identifies a Christian merchant named Sakrān in the Arabic texts with the Segurano Salvaygo who appears in European records. Most recently, Hannah Barker's *Egyptian and Italian Merchants in the Black Sea Slave Trade, 1260-1500* further contextualizes Segurano's activities and contributes an important corrective to earlier studies of his role in Mediterranean trade.

By all accounts operating one of the most successful international trading businesses of the time, the Salvaygos established bases in Genoa, Caffa, and Alexandria, as well as networks across continental Europe, including Bruges and several French cities. Genoese sources related to Caffa record the presence of Salvaygo family members in this important Black Sea colony since its creation in the 1260s. Segurano Salvaygo first appears in notarial records for having made a loan in Caffa in 1300, and his brother Ambrogio is recorded for buying and renting ships, making loans, and nominating attorneys (Kedar 77-78).

From Mamluk chronicles, we learn instead about Segurano's relations with two Mamluk sultans and two khans of the Golden Horde. An anonymous fourteenth-century chronicle records the arrival of a Christian merchant named Sakrān at the Mamluk court of sultan al-Nāṣir Muhammad in 1303 or 1304. Sakrān, aka Segurano, brought the sultan many gifts, including wool, precious textiles, atlases, and birds. Over the course of the next twenty years, Segurano was granted increasing privileges and responsibilities in Mamluk Egypt. By around 1307, for instance, it seems that Segurano and his brother Ambrogio had gained the favor of al-Nāṣir's amirs, Salār and Baybars. When the sultan released the Genoese Matteo Zaccaria after many years of captivity, Zaccaria asked the Salvaygo brothers, on behalf of several Aragonese prisoners, to facilitate peace between the sultan and James II of Aragon. The Salvaygos reportedly petitioned the amirs, who in turn successfully interceded with the sultan, and Zaccaria left for the Aragonese court with conciliatory letters from al-Nāṣir (Kedar 79).

A few years later, Segurano acted on the sultan's behalf in another thorny diplomatic affair. Around 1311 or 1312, the Genoese of Chios kidnapped Tokhta Khan's ambassadors to Egypt and their Mamluk escort as they sailed back to Alexandria after visiting the court of the Golden Horde. When al-Nāṣir received this news, he retaliated by imprisoning all Christian merchants (or perhaps only the Genoese) residing in Alexandria and Damietta, and confiscated their goods. According to a contemporaneous Mamluk chronicler, Segurano traveled to Chios and secured the freedom of the captured ambassadors, a move that in turn ensured the release of the Christian merchants in Egypt (Kedar 84; Barker 391). Since at the time members of the Zaccaria family governed Chios, one might ponder whether the fact that Segurano had assisted Matteo Zaccaria a few years earlier eased his negotiations on the island.

Another chronicle, composed by Mamluk historian Ibn al-Dawādārī in the fourteenth century, documents Segurano's participation in the retinue transporting Uzbak Khan's niece (the daughter of Tokhta Khan) to Alexandria in 1320, as Barker reports:

[Segurano] and an unnamed companion [...] accompanied the representative of Uzbak Khan to deliver Uzbak's niece as a bride for al-Nāṣir Muḥammad, cementing the Mamluk-Golden Horde alliance. [...] a single ship carried the ambassadors, the bride, Segurano, and numerous male and female slaves to Egypt. Of the 2,400 people who came, 400 died at sea and 440 mamluks arrived. Al-Nāṣir Muḥammad bought 240 of them for himself, and the others were purchased by amirs. Segurano was said to be accompanying (ṣuḥbah) the ambassadors and the bridal party in his capacity as a Frankish trader (tājir al-ifranjī).

(392)

An Egyptian chronicler writing in c. 1451 notes that Baybars II (al-Nāṣir's former amir) called Segurano his brother. According to this fifteenth-century historian, after Baybars II's death in 1310, the Mamluk Royal Treasurer, whose duties included investing the sultan's capital for a profit and trading on his behalf, gave Segurano 60 thousand dinars, as well as sugar and other goods valued at 40 thousand dinars, for use in trade (Kedar 80-81). At the time, Segurano was known as "'the important Frankish merchant' (tājiran kabīran min al-afranj)" (Barker 391).

The portions of William of Adam's *Tractatus quomodo Sarraceni sunt expugnandi* that catalog Segurano Salvaygo's affronts to Christianity are worth citing in full:

Behold, father and lord, how great are the evils done by these our sellers of the souls of men [...]. The above-mentioned merchants do not commonly perpetrate this outrage, but most greatly the Genoese, nor all the Genoese but particularly Seguranus Salvago, the fount of sin, and the members of his house and family, whom he has attracted to serve with him the enemy Satan and whom he dedicated with himself so greatly to the service of the Devil that Seguranus and the members of his family who agree with him seem to devote themselves only to how, by these works, contrary to God, they can confound the church and strengthen the Saracens, the enemies of the cross and persecutors of our faith. Seguranus is called the brother of the sultan, is believed to be a Saracen, and as an enemy is said to be a supporter, promoter, and defender of the faith of the Mohammedans. He is so closely allied with the sultan that the sultan himself in his letters calls him his brother and friend. He is a Saracen to such an extent that he allows the aforesaid sins against nature to be perpetrated in his ships. He himself and some members of his family have also carried the banner of Mohammed and of the sultan of Babylon in their ships and galleys, as I have seen with my own eyes with horror and detestation. That he supports the Saracens is clearly shown by the fact that when the sultan wanted to send a legation or messengers to the emperor of the northern Tartars in order to propagate the cult of the Saracens they were carried by him [...]. He has shown himself a greater supporter of these people than any predecessor who was not himself a Saracen, and he has greatly assisted and promoted that pestiferous sect by bringing them many thousands of Christian and other boys to engage in evil and the other illicit activities mentioned above and by transporting a great supply of iron, wood, and other things forbidden by the church. Not only have he and his brothers, grandsons, and relatives, however, provided such power to the Saracens in this way, but also many other Genoese, whom he has attracted by his example to do similar things, when he himself precedes and excels as the leader in this iniquity and teacher of evil against God. As a result it is truthfully proven that there is almost no noble family of Genoa or common family of some standing of which some members have not sent to Alexandria, some carrying boys and some other forbidden goods. And since Seguranus alone is said to have carried ten thousand boys to the Saracens, neither the multitude nor the number of those carried by others can be known.

(Adam 33-35)

The details corroborated by the Mamluk sources are that Segurano was called the sultan's brother, escorted Tatar ambassadors, and acted as a merchant for the Mamluks. Barker crucially notes that most secondary sources present Segurano "as the face of Genoese slaving" (390) because they accept as fact Adam's contention that Segurano was responsible for selling thousands of male Christian children to the Mamluks.[4] As Barker explains, while Adam's "accusations against Segurano seem to hold up in most cases" and he "was probably right to identify Segurano Salvaygo as a mamluk trader, his description of Segurano's activities misled readers by greatly exaggerating his role in the slave trade" (390, 393). In fact, only the 1320 journey to deliver a bride to al-Nāṣir Muḥammad "strongly implicate[s] Segurano himself in the slave trade" (392).

While Adam's claim that Segurano flew the sultan's flag on his shipments of merchandise is not confirmed in the Mamluk chronicles, in a 1317 letter

---

[4] See, for instance, Epstein: "Supplying slaves was clearly part of Segurano's purpose as far as the Mamluks were concerned, and he was quite successful" (164). Adam's claim is also misleading because the most prominent traders of Mamluk slaves were Mamluk subjects and not Italians (Barker 215-18).

addressed to the Genoese Republic Pope John XXII condemns Genoese merchants for trading with the Mamluks and sailing with "i vessilli dell'abominevole Maometto" (Kedar 81-82). This measure would have secured Segurano's passage across and trade within locations from which Genoese merchants were periodically banned. For instance, in 1307 Tokhta Khan ordered the destruction of Caffa ostensibly to prevent Genoese merchants from kidnapping and enslaving children from the Black Sea region. Despite subsequent prohibitions against the slave trade by Christian authorities (such as Clement V at the Council of Vienna in 1312), the Genoese returned to Caffa in 1313 with the permission of Uzbak Khan (Barker 162). By flying the Mamluk flag where Genoese merchants were banned from trade, whether by the khan or the pope, Segurano and his cargoes could travel incognito. Even if we set aside the specious details of Segurano's activities that issue from William of Adam's treatise, it is clear that he gradually earned both al-Nāṣir's and Baybars II's trust sufficiently to achieve a privileged position during their reigns, managing vast sums of money and serving as Mamluk trader, shipment escort, and political negotiator — a position that could only be seen as treacherous by Christian authorities.

Segurano's close association with Mamluk rulers, however, also resulted in his untimely death. In the early 1320s, the Golden Horde and Persian Ilkhanate were at war, but Mamluk relations with Persia had considerably improved (a peace treaty was signed in 1323), and al-Nāṣir refused to aid Uzbak Khan in the conflict. When, around 1322-23, Uzbak received notice from his returning ambassador that he had been offended at the Mamluk court, Segurano happened to be in the khan's territory with a shipment of merchandise. Uzbak retaliated by confiscating Segurano's goods and having him killed (Barker 391-92). Uzbak later disclaimed responsibility and accused an unspecified "king of the islands" of this murder, possibly a reference to the Zaccaria in Chios or the rulers of another Aegean island, according to Kedar (86).

The Decameron, *Genoa, the Mamluks, and the Golden Horde*
As is well known, Boccaccio was intimately familiar with mercantile spheres (especially Genoese): his father was an independent merchant, who joined the Florentine Compagnia de' Bardi as its principal agent at the Neapolitan court of King Robert of Anjou, and Boccaccio spent his early years in this multicultural center of trade and learning (1327-41). Given the periodic references to Genoa and Genoese merchants, Muslim sultans in Egypt, and Uzbak Khan of the Golden Horde (which Boccaccio identifies as Turkish) across the *Decameron*, there is no doubt he would have been aware of the broader political and commercial contexts outlined above.[5]

---

[5] While Boccaccio does not explicitly reference Mamluks in the *Decameron*, and the Saladin of 1.3 and 10.9 is usually identified in commentaries as Salah ad-Din (1137-

Genoa and the Genoese are referenced in more than ten novellas, usually in the context of travel for commerce or crusade (1.5; 1.8; 2.4; 2.6; 2.9; 3.3; 4.3; 5.7; 8.1; 10.3; and 10.9). Passages in three of these tales are particularly relevant to my analysis of Zinevra's tale in light of Segurano Salvaygo's (alleged) activities. The novella of Teodoro and Violante (5.7), set in the reign of King Guglielmo of Sicily, indicates that Boccaccio was aware of Genoese involvement in the enslavement of children from Western Asia, albeit in this case of Christian Armenians: "Amerigo Abbate da Trapani […] avendo di servidori bisogno e venendo galee di corsari genovesi di Levante, li quali corseggiando l'Erminia molti fanciulli avevan presi, di quegli, credendogli turchi, alcuni comperò" (5.7.3-4), including Teodoro, whom he has baptized and christened ("credendo che turchio fosse, il fé battezzare e chiamar Pietro" 5.7.5).[6]

In 10.3, the Genoese act as conduits for information about notable personages all the way from China to Europe: "Certissima cosa è, se fede si può dare alle parole d'alcuni genovesi e d'altri uomini che in quelle contrade stati sono, che nelle parti del Cattaio fu già uno uomo di legnaggio nobile e ricco senza comparazione, per nome chiamato Natan" (10.3.4).[7] Similarly, 10.9 features the arrival of "certi genovesi per ambasciadori al Saladino per la ricompera di certi lor cittadini" (10.9.52), thanks to whom Messer Torello attempts to send word that he is alive back to his wife Adalieta in Italy. In this tale, however, the transmission of overseas news is twice thwarted: the ambassadors, and Torello's missive, are shipwrecked on their way to Genoa, and in the meantime the death of another Messer Torello (of France) is inaccurately announced to Adalieta as her husband's. The narrative suggests that this report

---

1193), as I observe below the Muslim ruler who features in 2.9 should be identified as Mamluk because the novella is set after the 1291 fall of Acre to Mamluk forces. See Kinoshita and Jacobs for a historicized reading of *Decameron* 2.7 that accounts for its "dense network of Mediterranean politics and exchange" (165) and construes Alatiel as the daughter of a (fictional) Mamluk sultan. See also Kirkham and Menocal as well as Smarr for readings that consider the incidence and significance of Arabic culture in the *Decameron*.

[6] It is also of interest to recall Dante's reference to trade in Mamluk territory and condemnation of the Genoese in *Inferno*, the work in which Boccaccio was most engrossed (aside from revising the *Decameron*) in the final years of his life through a series of public lectures, his *Esposizioni sopra la "Comedia"* (1373): "Lo principe d'i novi Farisei, / avendo guerra presso a Laterano, / e non con Saracin né con Giudei, / ché ciascun suo nimico era cristiano, / e nessun era stato a vincer Acri / né mercatante in terra di Soldano" (27.85-90); and "Ahi Genovesi, uomini diversi / d'ogne costume e pien d'ogne magagna, / perché non siete voi del mondo spersi?" (33.151-3). On Boccaccio's reading of *Inferno* 1-17, see Hollander 884-933.

[7] Marco Polo's *Il Milione* was of course already circulating in the early fourteenth century, and may have been one of Boccaccio's sources on the East, though it is never explicitly mentioned in the *Decameron*.

is credited "per che molti italici tornarono con questa novella, tra' quali furon de' sí presuntuosi che ardiron di dire sé averlo veduto morto e essere stati alla sepoltura" (10.9.62). The *Decameron* thus dramatizes the role played by the Genoese in disseminating news across borders as well as the unreliability of such news.

In Naples, where he arrived in 1327, Boccaccio may have come into contact with Genoese and other merchants who had been personally acquainted with Segurano, his brother Ambrogio, and other members of the Salvaygo family. Perhaps, likewise, Boccaccio heard reports about Segurano's death, which took place four or five years earlier, on the order of Uzbak Khan of the Golden Horde, the same "Osbech [...] re de' turchi" who features as one of Alatiel's many abductors and lovers (2.7.76) and whose "Empress" is among Bruno's tongue-in-cheek list of women in 8.9.23: "'Voi vedreste quivi la donna de' barbanicchi, la reina de' baschi, la moglie del soldano, la 'mperadrice d'Osbech, la ciancianfera di Norrueca, la semistante di Berlinzone e la scalpedera di Narsia.'"[8]

Zinevra, Sicurano, and the Mamluks

Decameron 2.9 opens in Paris, as a group of wealthy Italian merchants lodging in the same inn chat about their sexual exploits abroad and assert that their wives back in Italy must be engaging in similar trysts. Only one merchant, Bernabò Lomellin of Genoa, speaks up in defense of his wife's loyalty and honor. In a passage often cited in studies of the *Decameron*'s representation of gender, Bernabò further praises his wife in the following terms:

Oltre a questo, niuno scudiere, o famigliare che dir vogliamo, diceva trovarsi il quale meglio né più accortamente servisse a una tavola d'un signore, che serviva ella, sí come colei che era costumatissima, savia e discreta molto. Appresso questo la commendò meglio saper cavalcare un cavallo, tenere uno uccello, leggere e scrivere e fare una ragione che se un mercatante fosse [...].

(2.9.9-10)

When fellow-merchant Ambrogiuolo challenges him to wager on his wife's faithfulness and then deceitfully tricks him into believing he successfully seduced her, Bernabò accepts defeat and sentences his wife to death. The wife, Zinevra, successfully pleads for her life with her executioner, disguises herself as a sailor, adopts the name Sicuran da Finale, escapes aboard a Catalan ship, and finally lands in the service of the Mamluk sultan in Alexandria. In Acre on business for the sultan, Sicurano happens to meet Ambrogiuolo, discovers why

---

[8] While here I follow Branca (2.7.76n6) in identifying Boccaccio's Osbech with Uzbak Khan, Kinoshita and Jacobs argue that his actions in 2.7 more closely evoke Umur Bey of Aydin (180-81). It is of course also possible that Boccaccio intended to evoke both rulers in his readers' imagination: Uzbak through the protagonist's name and Umur through his deeds.

Bernabò ordered Zinevra's murder, and begins to orchestrate a public revelation of the truth thanks to a close network of mercantile connections in Alexandria and Genoa, a great deal of ingenuity, and his influential position with the sultan.

The first name of Zinevra's male persona, "*Sicuran* da Finale" (2.9.43; emphasis added), is typically viewed as Boccaccio's creative allusion to the protagonist's steadfastness, courage and aplomb. It is also symbolically related to Bernabò's claim, during the merchants' Parisian debate, that "'quelle che savie sono hanno tanta sollecitudine dello onor loro, che elle diventan forti piú che gli uomini, che di ciò non *si curano*, a guardarlo; e di queste cosí fatte è la mia'" (2.9.18; emphasis added). The second half of her name, "da Finale," may refer to a town on the Ligurian coastline west of Genoa and may also allude to the propitious conclusion of Zinevra's adventures. Sara Alloati and Barbara Käppeli, for instance, read "Sicurano da Finale" as suggestive of *sicuro del finale*, thus linking Zinevra's male cover with the "onomastica fiabesca, in cui i nomi dei personaggi possono contenere informazioni o anticipazioni sul loro destino o sull'agire futuro" (see "Personaggi" in Alloati and Käppeli). These interpretations notwithstanding, I propose that Boccaccio may also have fashioned the name Sicurano after hearing of Segurano Salvaygo, and then worked a phonetically cognate reflexive verb (*si curano*) into Bernabò's speech and a geographically realistic provenance (*da Finale*) into his narrative in order to add to the novella's allusive layers.

With respect to Boccaccio's naming of protagonists in *Decameron* 2.9, it is notable that an anonymous thirteenth- or fourteenth-century novella identified by some scholars as the probable direct source for 2.9, and certainly as its closest analog, calls one of its characters simply "un Mercatante, molto bellissimo giovane, che aveva a nome Cherico, ed era d'Alessandria" (Ambrogiuolo da Piagenza in Boccaccio's novella). Boccaccio's Bernabò is only identified as "uno giovane di Genova," while Zinevra is "la donna" and does not adopt a male name when she dons a male servant's garments as a disguise (Lami 41).[9] Similarly, the "gentile uomo catalano, il cui nome era segner En Cararh" in whose service Sicurano first escapes Italy (2.9.42), is in the anonymous tale an unnamed "Gentiluomo di Catalogna" at the helm of a "Nave di Corsali" (Lami 46). Vittore Branca notes that "segner En Cararh" is meant to sound Catalan (2.9.42n10); thus, if the anonymous tale indeed served as the direct source for 2.9, it is interesting to consider the phonetically kindred Catalan verb *encarar* (to face, handle, cope with; to confront, challenge, defy; to bring face to face). The chance encounters with the nameless Catalan and En Cararh function, respectively, as the woman's and Zinevra's gateway to a new identity that will allow them to challenge structures of power in each variant of this story. In view of the *Decameron*'s other symbolically coded names —

---

[9] Branca notes this antecedent, among others, describing it as "un racconto forse trecentesco molto simile citato dal Lami" (*Dec.* 2.9.1n2).

arguably, for instance, those of the frame characters and Alatiel ("la lieta" of 2.9) — one cannot totally exclude that Boccaccio may have also intended to evoke *encarar* with "En Cararh." Likewise, just as Boccaccio explicitly identifies Bernabò as a member of the noble Genoese Lomellini family, which acquired fame and riches thanks to its seafaring and mercantile activities, so too could he have named Sicurano and Ambrogiuolo after the historically documented figures of Segurano and Ambrogio Salvaygo.

Another detail of Sicurano's journey for which readers find meaning elsewhere in the *Decameron* is that he sails with En Cararh on a ship bringing "certi falconi pellegrini al soldano" (2.9.44).[10] The passage is usually linked to Bernabò's declaration that his wife is exceptionally skilled at "tenere uno uccello" (2.9.10) as well as to the inclusion of "uccellare" among the list of male occupations which Boccaccio enumerates in the prologue ("Proemio" 12). These earlier mentions of falconry certainly guide readers to reflect more critically on the agency Zinevra acquires as Sicurano on the way to, and in, Alexandria.

To be sure, the four other *Decameron* tales illustrating the predilection for and practice of falconry among medieval Christian and Muslim nobles characterize it as an exclusively masculine pursuit (4.4, 5.9, 6.4, and 10.9). In the collection's penultimate tale of mutual magnanimity, Messer Torello first meets Saladin near Pavia as he rides to his country estate "con suoi famigliari e con cani e con falconi" (10.9.7), then, on the following morning, invites Saladin to observe how his falcons fly (10.9.21), and later becomes Saladin's personal falconer (10.9.50).

Unlike Messer Torello, however, Sicurano never actually works as a falconer for either the Catalan or the sultan. He comes to the sultan's notice because of his manners and service: "[...] veduti i costumi di Sicurano, che sempre a servir l'andava, e piaciutigli, [il soldano] al catalano il dimandò" (2.9.44). Barker notes that in Mamluk Egypt "free people who wanted to wield political power had to become slaves first" and cites the "classic example" of Qawṣūn, "an amir who came to Egypt from the Golden Horde as a merchant in the retinue accompanying the daughter of Uzbak Khan" (the same retinue that included Segurano Salvaygo; 95). The Mamluk historian Ibn Taghrī Birdī (1410-1470) describes how Qawṣūn made such an impression on the sultan while "selling leather blade strops and embroidered leather items in the citadel of Cairo" that he sold himself as a slave and was then rapidly promoted to amir (Barker 95). Similarly, Baybars was first the slave of a goldsmith and

---

[10] The anonymous 13th-century French prose romance *La Fille du Comte de Pontieu*, another close antecedent for Boccaccio's tale listed by Branca (2.9.1n2), also figures Catalan merchants gifting falcons — along with the heroine — to the sultan. The anonymous Italian novella cited above simply narrates that the woman, disguised as a male servant, arrives in "Saracinia a uno porto della terra, dove abitava il Grande Cane" (Lami 47).

"Ashiqtamur al-Mardinī al-Nāṣirī was a successful amir, but gained his first promotion through his skill at playing the oud" (Barker 114).

There was a certain cachet, in both Christian and Muslim spheres, associated with the ability to attract the attention of dignitaries through one's deportment, skills, and/or material goods. The Mamluk chronicle that reports Segurano Salvaygo's arrival in Alexandria leaves unspecified the type of birds he brought to sultan al-Nāṣir along with wool, precious textiles, and atlases, but it is likely that they were also birds of prey. Mamluk sultans in this period, and al-Nāṣir in particular, frequently received hawks and falcons as gifts from loyal subjects and allies, and spent huge fortunes buying hunting birds from foreign merchants, often gifting the birds to high-ranking members of the Mamluk military in recognition of service and as gestures of affection.[11]

Boccaccio's representation of Sicurano aboard a ship carrying peregrine falcons and description of his pleasing "costumi" while serving the Catalan could, *at once*, refashion earlier variants, exemplify the general culture of and prestige associated with falconry in his day, recall other references to falconry in the collection, *and* be calculated to evoke the particular figure of Segurano Salvaygo. The historical Segurano and fictitious Sicurano did not become slaves first but, like Qawṣūn, they both drew the attention of reigning Mamluks through their accomplishments and were promoted to power-wielding positions.

Notably, Sicurano "la grazia e l'amor del soldano acquistò col suo bene adoperare" to such a degree that he is deemed qualified to *supervise* the sultan's merchants and merchandise at a major annual trade fair in Acre:

[...] in processo di tempo avvenne che, dovendosi in un certo tempo dell'anno a guisa d'una fiera fare una gran ragunanza di mercatanti e cristiani e saracini in Acri (la quale sotto la signoria del soldano era), acciò che i mercatanti e le mercatantie sicure stessero, era il soldano sempre usato di mandarvi, oltre agli altri suoi uficiali, alcuno de' suoi grandi uomini con gente che alla guardia attendesse. Nella quale bisogna, sopravegnendo il tempo, diliberò di mandare Sicurano, il quale già ottimamente la lingua sapeva; e così fece.

(2.9.45-46)

The favor and esteem Sicurano acquires from the sultan offers another tantalizing consonance with Segurano Salvaygo, the Genoese merchant who according to William of Adam became "so closely allied with the sultan that the sultan himself in his letters calls him his brother and friend" (Adam 33). The yearly fair referenced by Boccaccio could have been the annual spice market in Acre. In the early thirteenth century, "convoys for Acre and Alexandria left Venice in August for the yearly spice fair"; these triangulated coordinates, Venice-Acre-Alexandria, would shift in the second half of the thirteenth century, and especially after the 1291 fall of Acre to the Mamluks, to Genoa-Acre-

---

[11] For birds of prey as gifts in Mamluk Egypt, see Shehada 68-72.

Alexandria, when "supremacy in European trade with the Moslem Levant was in the hands of the Genoese" (Ashtor 10). Boccaccio situates his tale precisely in the period when Acre "sotto la signoria del soldano era" (2.9.45).

It is in the description of the events unfolding in Acre that two more of the verbs occurring in the *Decameron*'s "Proemio" reappear:

> Venuto adunque Sicurano in Acri signore e capitano della guardia de' mercatanti e della mercatantia, e quivi bene e sollecitamente faccendo ciò che al suo uficio appartenea e andando da torno veggendo, e molti mercatanti e ciciliani e pisani e genovesi e viniziani e altri italiani vedendovi, con loro volentieri si dimesticava per rimembranza della contrada sua.
>
> (2.9.47)

The description of Sicurano "andando da torno veggendo" relates back to the freedom of mobility and experience traditionally accorded to men and withheld from women as Boccaccio outlines in his prologue. From this perspective, it is noteworthy that employment in the sultan's service affords Sicurano a greater degree of agency in the world of commerce than was the case for Bernabò's Zinevra, who was said to be adept at domestic service, horse-riding, falconry, reading, writing, and accounting. The latter three activities accord with Italian notarial records documenting the active participation of many noble Genoese (and other Italian) women in the administrative and economic aspects of travel and commerce, whether on behalf of absent husbands, as a result of widowhood, or independently of male relatives.[12] In Acre, however, Sicurano goes beyond this range of activity since he is charged with inspecting the marketplace and ensuring the safety of the sultan's interests. This high level of engagement in economic and political affairs recalls Segurano Salvaygo in his capacity as Mamluk trader and escort when he accompanied a bride and cargo of slaves from the Golden Horde to al-Nāṣir Muḥammad in 1320.

It is while serving the sultan as his head patrol in the market at Acre that Sicurano comes across a bag and a belt he recognizes as having belonged to Zinevra. Inquiring about their owner and sale, Sicurano comes, unwittingly at first, face to face with the party guilty of stealing the items and causing Zinevra's trials and tribulations. When Ambrogiuolo hears that the inquiry comes from the sultan's "capitano della guardia" (2.9.49), he replies that they are not for sale, declares his willingness to gift them to Sicurano, and falsely boasts that Zinevra gifted them to him after they spent the night together. Such a response could only be occasioned by Ambrogiuolo's implied desire to ingratiate himself with and show off to an individual who holds a particularly powerful position in Mamluk Acre, the sort of position that seems to have been enjoyed by Segurano Salvaygo, for instance, when in 1307 Matteo Zaccaria

---

[12] On women's involvement in trade in medieval Italy, see Crabb 558-59 and Angelos 407-08.

asked him to intercede with the sultan to broker peace with Jayme II of Aragon.

In the final portion of the novella, Sicurano's efforts to bring about a public revelation of Ambrogiuolo's crime and restore Zinevra's honor underline Zinevra's ability, *qua* Sicurano, to navigate the male-dominated world of commerce, diplomacy, and justice by exercising all the know-how of a first-rate merchant. Indeed, his actions bear witness to an exceptional degree of ingenuity, a trusted network of connections, copious funds, powerful allies, and an almost sultan-like status. We first read that Sicurano succeeds in entering into such confidence with Ambrogiuolo in Acre that he convinces him to travel to Egypt, sets him up with a warehouse, and puts a large sum of money at his disposal:

[...] artatamente prese con costui una stretta dimestichezza, tanto che per gli suoi conforti Ambruogiuolo, finita la fiera, con essolui e con ogni sua cosa se n'andò in Alessandria, dove Sicurano gli fece fare un fondaco e misegli in mano de' suoi denari assai: per che egli, util grande veggendosi, vi dimorava volentieri.

(2.9.56)

With the assistance of influential Genoese trading acquaintances and several clever pretexts, Sicurano then contrives to have Bernabò, now impoverished as a result of losing his wager with Ambrogiuolo, also brought to Alexandria and secretly housed with some of his friends:

Sicurano, sollecito a voler della sua innocenzia far chiaro Bernabò, mai non riposò infino a tanto che con opera d'alcuni gran mercatanti genovesi che in Alessandria erano, nuove cagioni trovando, non l'ebbe fatto venire: il quale, in assai povero stato essendo, a alcun suo amico tacitamente fece ricevere, infino che tempo gli paresse a quel fare che di fare intendea.

(2.9.57)

Might Sicurano's ushering of Ambrogiuolo and Bernabò to Alexandria not recall, in an imaginatively divergent context, William of Adam's condemnation of Segurano Salvaygo for having encouraged his own family members and countless other Genoese traders to traffic in forbidden goods with the Mamluks? Might the authority and ease with which Sicurano first grants Ambrogiuolo a warehouse and gives him some of his own money, and then brings Bernabò to Alexandria with the help of important Genoese merchants, not also evoke the rapport that Segurano Salvaygo must have had with other Genoese merchants in the Mamluk sultanate, as well as the fact that he was seen as "the important Frankish merchant" by the sultan's inner circle?

Having prepped and entertained the sultan by inviting Ambrogiuolo to narrate his fabricated story of Zinevra's seduction at court, Sicurano begs the Mamluk ruler to have Ambrogiuolo and Bernabò brought before him and to extract the truth from the former, with harsh measures if necessary:

[...] dal soldano impetrò che davanti venir si facesse Ambruogiuolo e Bernabò, e in presenzia di Bernabò, se agevolmente fare non si potesse, con severità da Ambruogiuolo si traesse il vero come stato fosse quello di che egli della moglie di Bernabò si vantava.

(2.9.58)

While the sultan, following Sicurano's instructions, "con rigido viso" commands Ambrogiuolo to speak the truth, Sicurano nevertheless takes the leading role in the affair: "[...] con viso troppo piú turbato gli minacciava gravissimi tormenti se nol dicesse" (2.9.59). What is more, as soon as Ambrogiuolo "chiaramente, come stato era il fatto, narrò ogni cosa" (2.9.60), Sicurano, acting as though he were the sultan's public prosecutor — "quasi essecutore del soldano" (2.9.61) — demands that Bernabò reveal how he punished his wife for this falsehood.

Sicurano is not the only Christian protagonist who rises to this degree of (potential) power within the Muslim world of the *Decameron*. In 10.9, the only other novella featuring Acre, Alexandria, and Genoa together, Saladin even invites Messer Torello to be co-regent of his territory:

"Messer Torello, poi che Idio qui mandato mi v'ha, pensate che non io oramai, ma voi qui siate il signore." [...] "Sarebbemi stato carissimo, poi che la fortuna qui v'aveva mandato, che quel tempo, che voi e io viver dobbiamo, nel governo del regno che io tengo parimente signori vivuti fossimo insieme [...]."

(10.9.58, 73)[13]

The overarching theme of mutual magnanimity that governs Day 10, the context of the Third Crusade (1189-1192) that frames this novella, and Messer Torello's gender and noble social rank provide the narrative grounds for Saladin's remarkable invitation. Anticipating Saladin's more expansive entreaty, for instance, earlier in the tale Torello's wife Adalieta presents Saladin and his companions (who are posing as merchants) with her husband's robes "non miga cittadine né da mercatanti ma da signore" (10.9.31), while Torello and Saladin are as reluctant to part ways in Italy (10.9.36) as they are later in Alexandria. Conversely, in 2.9 the unjustly accused Zinevra, in the guise of Sicurano, acquires the means to punish Ambrogiuolo and vindicate her honor by provisionally taking on the sultan's legislative power.

Remarkably, Sicurano demands and obtains the sultan's blind faith in his words: first, that there is a truth to be extracted from Ambrogiuolo's tale of Zinevra's seduction, and, second, that there is a valid motive for doing so, since the sultan does not know "ancora a che Sicurano, che questo ordinato avea e domandato, volesse riuscire" (2.9.63). Sicurano subsequently strikes a deal with the sultan: he will have Zinevra brought before them if the sultan promises "di spezial grazia fare di punire lo 'ngannatore e perdonare allo 'ngannato" (2.9.65).

---

[13] For another Christian protagonist who ingratiates himself with a Muslim ruler, see *Decameron* 5.2, in which Martuccio Gomito is freed from captivity by the King of Tunis to help him strategize a successful defense against a Granadan would-be invader and receives the king's leave to marry his long-lost beloved Gostanza.

The sultan is "disposto in questa cosa di volere in tutto compiacere a Sicurano" and makes "la concessione" (2.9.66-67). Once again, it is worth noting the parallel between Sicurano's position in the sultan's court and Segurano Salvayo's seemingly privileged patronage in Mamluk Egypt.

In the tale's dramatic conclusion, Sicurano reveals himself to be Zinevra in disguise by falling on his knees in tears, abandoning his "maschil voce" (2.9.67), tearing open his shirt, and declaring to the sultan:

"Signor mio, io sono la misera sventurata Zinevra, sei anni andata tapinando in forma d'uom per lo mondo, da questo traditor d'Ambruogiuolo falsamente e reamente vituperata, e da questo crudele e iniquo uomo data a uccidere a un suo fante e a mangiare a' lupi."

(2.9.68)

The sultan, stunned by this revelation of Sicurano's true identity, keeps his word: he forgives Bernabò, sends him and Zinevra back to Genoa laden with gifts and money, and punishes Ambrogiuolo by having him tied to a post, smeared with honey, and devoured by insects down to the bone.[14]

While Madonna Filippa (6.7) — who stands (accurately) accused of adultery — successfully argues for her right to a lover and even rescinds the unjust law governing the women of Prato, Zinevra — whose honor is falsely tarnished — has no recourse in Genoa and is pronounced guilty by hearsay. It is only after she has spent six years "tapinando in forma d'uom per lo mondo" and is firmly installed in the faraway Muslim court of the sultan that she can finally not only reveal her identity but also extract a confession from her accuser.[15]

---

[14] To my knowledge, it has not been previously pointed out that Ambrogiuolo's punishment replicates a form of torture attributed to ancient Greece, described in St Jerome's *Life of St Paul the Hermit*, and recorded in Jacobus de Voragine's *Legenda Aurea* (c. 1260), a medieval bestseller with which Boccaccio was certainly familiar. In Voragine's hagiography of St. Paul, we read that the hermit witnessed the tortures inflicted on Christians by the emperor Decius, including that of a man who "had his whole body coated with honey and was exposed under a blazing sun to be stung to death by flies, hornets, and wasps" (Voragine 84). In precisely the same manner, Boccaccio's "Ambrogiuolo il dì medesimo che legato fu al palo e unto di mele, con sua grandissima angoscia dalle mosche e dalle vespe e da' tafani, de' quali quel paese è copioso molto, fu non solamente ucciso ma infino all'ossa divorato [...]" (2.9.75). More intriguing still, vis-à-vis Boccaccio's tale of the cross-dressing Zinevra, is the description of this form of torture that appears in *Lectionum antiquarum libri XXX* (1516) by the humanist Lodovico Ricchieri, better known as Caelius Rhodiginus. According to Ricchieri, the punishment named "cyphonismus" in antiquity consisted of fastening anyone who had scorned the law to a public pillory and leaving them naked and covered with milk or honey for twenty days to be bitten by flies and bees before being dressed in women's clothes and thrown off a cliff (Ricchieri 362).

[15] For another novella in which a protagonist in disguise travels abroad to redeem his (economic and romantic) fortune, and condemns the double standards and injustices of

Conclusion

As I hope to have shown, the complementary journeys and exploits of Sicurano and Segurano merit comparison. The Dominican bishop William of Adam, who singled out Segurano as the "head of all vice," wrote his crusade treatise while serving as papal missionary in Persia, perhaps as early as 1314 or as late as 1323. Boccaccio may have gotten wind of this text from clerical and noble circles in Naples, or he may have heard reports about Adam's views and/or about Segurano's activities from Genoese merchants and other European travelers returning from Persia, the Near East, and North Africa to Italy. The presence of analogous narrative details in the anonymous novella that may antedate the *Decameron* complicates, but does not undermine, the possible correlation between Segurano Salvaygo and Sicuran da Finale, given that the names are aligned and the setting is in Mamluk Egypt only in Boccaccio's novella.[16]

Even when the correspondence between fact (or legend, or anecdote) and fiction remains more suggestive than definitive, pursuing such trails enriches our discussion and enjoyment of the *Decameron* and its Mediterranean settings. Boccaccio himself invites readers to find connections among his "cento novelle, o favole o parabole o istorie che dire le vogliamo" ("Proemio" 13). Like Zinevra, albeit for different reasons, Segurano Salvaygo was denounced as a traitor to social order and morality. Did Boccaccio deliberately transform Segurano into Sicurano, himself a cover for Zinevra? If so, it is possible that Boccaccio intended to redeem the actions of this legendary, infamous merchant by recasting the controversial matter of Christian-Muslim, Genoese-Mamluk

---

his own milieu, see 3.7: Tedaldo degli Elisei takes on a new identity, departs from Italy, and returns (rich and famous) to claim his beloved. At this point in the narrative, Tedaldo denounces the hypocrisy of those who "sgridano contra gli uomini la lussuria, acciò che, rimovendosene gli sgridati, agli sgridatori rimangano le femine; essi dannan l'usura e i malvagi guadagni, acciò che, fatti restitutori di quegli, si possan fare le cappe piú larghe, procacciare i vescovadi e l'altre prelature maggiori di ciò che mostrato hanno dovere menare a perdizion chi l'avesse" (3.7.38). See also 2.3, in which the daughter of the king of England travels disguised as an abbot.

[16] Other details in the anonymous tale analogous with passages in *Decameron* 2.9 include: 1) the disguised woman tells the Catalan merchant, "'io sono buono Ragioniere, e buono Scrittore, e ben so servire a tavola'"; 2) the Catalan "invaghì sì di costui pegli suoi begli costumi"; 3) Gran Cane is impressed by his "begli reggimenti" and forces the Catalan to leave him behind; 4) Gran Cane is so pleased by his table service that "parvegli sì savissimo, che pensò di fargli onore, e feciolo Maliscalco d'una buona Cittade"; 5) during a great "fiera" in that city, the Maliscalco comes across Cherico and the stolen items; and 6) in the final scene "el detto Maliscalco si spogliò ignudato, e mostrò com'ella era femina." Different from Boccaccio's novella is the fact that the Maliscalco obtains from Gran Cane permission to travel to Genoa, presents himself to the impoverished husband as "barone del Gran Cane," and brings him back to "Saracinia" himself (Lami 47-50).

relations in a more positive light. After all, the *Decameron* is packed with narratives that imaginatively rework historical realities and favorably portray figures viewed as anathema in more orthodox Christian texts. William of Adam condemns the sultan of Egypt as "the enemy Satan" and Muslims as "the enemies of the cross and persecutors of our faith." As in *Decameron* 1.3 (Melchisedek and Saladin) and 10.9 (Torello and Saladin), in Zinevra's novella Boccaccio follows the lead of more flattering reports about Muslims circulating in his day and may similarly have gone against the grain of disparaging notions about Segurano Salvaygo. If *Decameron* 2.9 shows the upside of consorting with the enemy abroad, it is also in order to underline homegrown social and moral shortcomings. Indeed, both Segurano and Sicurano found powerful allies, agency, and a voice, among the same ostensible foes, and similarly tenacious enemies in their very own Christian world.

As is the case for many narrative components of the *Decameron* and the novella tradition in general, it is often difficult to make categorical claims about source material for a genre so profoundly permeated with the cross-cultural oral transmission of information. Whether Zinevra's tale more generally illustrates the medieval Mediterranean's varied historical contexts or validates the specific historical figure of Segurano Salvaygo, it clearly invites its most immediate readers, fourteenth-century nobles, merchants, and women, to challenge vicarious reports of misdeeds and to contemplate a case in which the truth can only be spoken to power after travel beyond the borders of one's country and even beyond the limits of one's gender.

Queens College, CUNY

Works Cited

Adam, William of. *How to Defeat the Saracens. Guillelmus Ade. Tractatus quomodo Sarraceni sunt expugnandi.* Ed. and trans. Giles Constable. Washington: Dumbarton Oaks Research Library and Collection, 2012.

Angelos, Mark. "Investment and Credit." *Women and Gender in Medieval Europe: An Encyclopedia.* Ed. Margaret Schaus. New York: Routledge, 2006. 407-08.

Alloati, Sara, and Barbara Käppeli. http://www.rose.uzh.ch/static/decameron/seminario/II_09.

Ashtor, Eliyahu. *Levant Trade in the Middle Ages.* Princeton: Princeton UP, 2014.

Barker, Hannah. *Egyptian and Italian Merchants in the Black Sea Slave Trade, 1260-1500.* Diss. Columbia University, 2014.

Barolini, Teodolinda. "'Le parole son femmine e i fatti son maschi': Toward a Sexual Poetics of the *Decameron (Decameron* II, 10)." *Studi sul Boccaccio* 21 (1993): 175-97.

_____. "Sociology of the *Brigata*: Gendered Groups in Dante, Forese, Folgore, Boccaccio – From 'Guido, i' vorrei' to Griselda." *Italian Studies* 67.1 (March 2012): 4-22.

Boccaccio, Giovanni. *Decameron.* Ed. Vittore Branca. Torino: Einaudi, 1992.
Cavallero, Daniela. "Alatiel e Zinevra: Il 'peso' di silenzio, la leggerezza dei 'vestiti.'" *Romance Languages Annual* 9 (1998): 165-70.
Cervigni, Dino S., ed. *Boccaccio's* Decameron: *Rewriting the Christian Middle Ages. Annali d'Italianistica* 31 (2013).
Crabb, Ann. "Women of Merchant Families." *Women and Gender in Medieval Europe: An Encyclopedia.* Ed. Margaret Schaus. New York: Routledge, 2006. 558-59.
Dante, Alighieri. *The Divine Comedy of Dante Alighieri.* Ed. and trans. Robert M. Durling. Vol. 1. *Inferno.* Oxford: Oxford UP, 1996.
Epstein, Steven. *Purity Lost: Transgressing Boundaries in the Eastern Mediterranean, 1000- 1400.* Baltimore: Johns Hopkins UP, 2006.
La Fille du comte de Ponthieu, nouvelle du XIIIe siècle, "roman" du XVe siècle. Trans. Roger Dubuis. Paris: Champion, 2010.
Hollander, Robert. "Boccaccio's Divided Allegiance (*Esposizioni sopra la* Comedia)." *Boccaccio: A Critical Guide to the Complete Works.* Ed. Victoria Kirkham, Michael Sherberg, and Janet Levarie Smarr. Chicago: The U of Chicago P, 2013. 884-933.
Kedar, Benjamin. "Segurano-Sakrān Salvaygo: un mercante genovese al servizio dei sultani mamalucchi, c. 1303-1322." *Franks in the Levant, 11th to 14th Centuries.* Aldershot: Variorum, 1993. 75-87.
Kinoshita, Sharon, and Jason Jacobs. "Ports of Call: Boccaccio's Alatiel in the Medieval Mediterranean." *Journal of Medieval and Early Modern Studies* 37.1 (2007): 163-95.
Kirkham, Victoria, and María Rosa Menocal. "Reflections on the Arabic World: Boccaccio's Ninth Stories." *Stanford Italian Review* 7 (1987): 95-110.
Lami, Giovanni. *Appendice all'illustrazione storica del Boccaccio scritta da Domenico Maria Manni.* Milano: Pirotta, 1820.
Migiel, Marilyn. *A Rhetoric of the* Decameron. Toronto: U of Toronto P, 2003.
Paris, Gaston. "Le Cycle de la gageure." *Romania* 32 (1903): 481-551.
Polo, Marco. *Il Milione.* Trans. Maria Vittoria Malvano. Ed. Daniele Ponchiroli. Torino: Einaudi, 2005.
Ricchieri, Lodovico. *Lodovici Caelii Rhodigini lectionum antiquarum libri XXX.* Basileae: per Ambrosium et Aurelium Frobenios fratres, 1566.
Shehada, Housni Alkhateeb. *Mamluks and Animals: Veterinary Medicine in Medieval Islam.* Leiden: Brill, 2013.
Smarr, Janet Levarie. "Other Races and Other Places in the *Decameron.*" *Studi sul Boccaccio* 27 (1999): 113-136.
Voragine, Jacobus de. *The Golden Legend: Readings on the Saints.* Trans. William Granger Ryan. Princeton: Princeton UP, 2012.
Wayne, Valerie. "Romancing the Wager: *Cymbeline's* Intertexts." *Staging Early Modern Romance: Prose Fiction, Dramatic Romance, and Shakespeare.* Ed. Mary Ellen Lamb and Valerie Wayne. New York: Routledge, 2009. 163-87.

Alessandra Mantovani

Speculum veritatis: Giovanni Garzoni e la tradizione dell'*institutio principis* nella Bologna dei Bentivoglio

Sinossi: Il *De eruditione principum* di Giovanni Garzoni, medico umanista vissuto nella Bologna di Giovanni II Bentivoglio, rappresenta un *unicum* nel panorama dell'Umanesimo bolognese poiché ripropone, adattandolo all'orizzonte cittadino, il genere dello *speculum principis*. Dialogando con i testi paradigmatici della teoria politica classica, medievale e umanistica, da Aristotele a Egidio Romano a Pontano, in una *institutio* conciliante e per nulla eversiva, il Garzoni si impegna a persuadere il Signore della necessità di un governo "misto", che contemperi tradizioni repubblicane, istanze oligarchiche e ambizioni signorili e sappia far coincidere il nome dei Bentivoglio con la stessa identità politica e culturale della città.
Parole chiave: Giovanni Garzoni, *speculum principis*, Bologna, Bentivoglio, buon governo, tirannide, oligarchia, tradizioni repubblicane.

Tiranni e Signori nella città della libertas
Alle carte 182*v*-190*v* del manoscritto Latino 741 della Biblioteca Universitaria di Bologna, uno dei codici miscellanei che ci tramandano le opere di Giovanni Garzoni, medico e umanista bolognese, agiografo e storico, poligrafo tra i più versatili e fecondi dell'età aurea di Giovanni II Bentivoglio, troviamo, tra una composita serie di opere — orazioni, epistole, saggi eruditi e testi agiografici — due scritti, identificati nei cataloghi (Manfré 37) con i titoli di *Declamatio in tyrannos* e *Pro libertate*, difficili da contestualizzare e ancora più da interpretare, se non in via di ipotesi. In essi, evidentemente frammenti contigui di un testo più ampio per noi perduto, si inneggia alla morte di un tiranno che ha vessato per ben venticinque anni, con la crudeltà efferata dei comportamenti e la depravazione dei costumi, una città in cui il regime di terrore ha a lungo impedito ogni tentativo di affrancamento e ribellione. Ora, morto il tiranno, è finalmente possibile celebrare l'elezione dei "tribuni plebis", la magistratura che è, di per sé, segno tangibile della recuperata "libertas".[1]

Nessun elemento del testo consente, in modo inequivoco, l'identificazione della città a cui il testo allude con la città di Bologna, né d'altro canto queste pagine sembrano appartenere a nessuna delle opere storiche del Garzoni, prima fra tutte quelle *Historiae Bononienses* in cui Garzoni, intorno al 1494, aveva riassemblato e opportunamente aggregato, con una complessa operazione di

---

[1] Per il testo completo della *Declamatio in tyrannos* e della orazione *Pro libertate*, contenuti alle cc. 182*v*-190*v* del manoscritto Latino 741 della Biblioteca Universitaria di Bologna, si rimanda all'*Appendice* del presente saggio.

montaggio, vari degli opuscoli dedicati alla storia della città nel corso di un trentennio. In quell'opera, la vicenda travagliata del *populus bononiensis* alla conquista dell'agognata *libertas*, che gli appartiene come un destino con il quale coincide la sua identità (Mantovani, *Giovanni Garzoni* 33-34), appare caratterizzata da una estrema instabilità e nessuno dei governi "tirannici" che si sono succeduti è mai stato così duraturo. È vero d'altro canto che, proprio nelle *Historiae*, Garzoni più volte rimarcava come i *tribuni plebis* — la magistratura popolare dei gonfalonieri del popolo più profondamente rappresentativa del "governo del popolo e delle arti" — fossero un elemento caratterizzante della struttura istituzionale che legittimamente rappresentava Bologna e ne incarnava il buon governo o, più precisamente, lo "stato di libertà" (De Benedictis, *Identità politica* 13-83).

Questa ricorrenza terminologica, all'interno di un lessico politico del tutto istituzionalizzato, non può non far pensare; allo stesso modo i venticinque anni di malgoverno, in un computo che rimane un'ipotesi euristica, ma che pure stranamente sembra creare una curiosa coincidenza, sono gli stessi che intercorrono tra l'ascesa di Giovanni II al governo di Bologna nel 1463, dopo la morte di Sante Bentivoglio, e la congiura dei Malvezzi nel 1488, l'evento più traumatico di un *principatus* che a tutti gli effetti si presenta come tale, nei riconoscimenti e nei successi internazionali, oltre che nella realtà quotidiana di una vita cittadina e di corte pienamente signorile, senza che chi lo detiene ne abbia giuridicamente il titolo.

Siamo di fronte ad un nodo istituzionale che mette conto illustrare preliminarmente, giacché proprio all'interno di quell'orizzonte cittadino si colloca la riflessione politica del Garzoni, che non si limita certo a questo enigmatico *j'accuse*, affidato a prove di scrittura frammentarie, destinate, per quanto ne sappiamo, a rimanere inedite. Si tratta infatti di pagine che possono fungere poco più che da mero spunto introduttivo, per quanto non manchino di stupire se le rapportiamo al profilo di uno scrittore che è, senza alcun dubbio, un uomo d'ordine, figura di spicco dell'*entourage* filobentivolesco, impegnato apparentemente senza riserve in un'azione di persuaso fiancheggiamento intellettuale e propaganda legittimistica (Raimondi, *Politica* 45-48). Converrà piuttosto prendere in esame la sua opera didascalico-pedagogica più ambiziosa, quel trattato *De eruditione principum* destinato — come avremo modo di vedere — a una ricezione pubblica e ufficiale e che costituisce il *focus* di questa riflessione.

*Giovanni Garzoni e l'*institutio principis
All'interno del *regimen politicum et regale*, istituito e regolato dalla sottoscrizione dei Capitoli del 1447, con cui si definisce la complessa identità di Bologna, città libera e nel contempo suddita del sovrano pontefice e se ne affidano le prerogative ad una prassi di controversa e sempre ardua rinegoziazione, il governo della città è affidato all'ufficio dei Riformatori dello

Stato di Libertà (De Benedictis, *Repubblica* 148-50). La riforma di questa suprema magistratura, introdotta da papa Paolo II nel 1466, ne promuove la trasformazione in senso compiutamente aristocratico e conferisce validità giuridica, all'interno di essa, al primato di Giovanni II Bentivoglio, a cui si riconosce quel ruolo di *primus inter pares* che costituisce la forma e il limite del suo essere di fatto, ma senza mai averne il titolo, il signore di Bologna (Robertson 223).

Questo è il quadro politico in cui, proprio alla fine degli anni Ottanta, all'indomani della congiura dei Malvezzi che di quell'equilibrio istituzionale rappresenta un drammatico punto di crisi, Giovanni Garzoni decide di cimentarsi, nelle forme di una compostezza cortigiana ossequiosa e piena di cautele, nella composizione di un'ampia e impegnativa *institutio principis*, un vero e proprio trattato *De eruditione principum*.

Ciceroniano fervente e appassionato lettore di classici, abile divulgatore di quegli *studia humanitatis* a cui si accosta senza sperimentalismi, ma con intelligenza sicura del nuovo ed inesausta curiosità intellettuale, Garzoni di certo non ci stupisce scegliendo di scrivere uno *speculum principis*, la forma più retoricamente formalizzata e vincolata dall'appartenenza ad una definita tradizione di genere della letteratura politica tra Medioevo ed età moderna (Skinner 115-40), nella quale il carattere topico e ripetitivo dell'argomentazione deve però, alla fine, poter esprimere la specificità dei problemi, la diversità degli orizzonti temporali, la concretezza variabile delle situazioni.

Anche nel caso di Garzoni si dovrà quindi porre il problema della relazione dinamica che sempre si crea, nella letteratura degli *specula*, fra contesto e riproposizione di un modello: se la retorica coincide con la forma stessa della riflessione politica, viene da chiedersi, al di là della logica cortigiana — pure determinante — del discorso epidittico, quali siano le ragioni del recupero del problema teorico e pratico della formazione del principe nella Bologna dei Bentivoglio. In altre parole, non pare fuorviante, almeno in via di ipotesi, interrogare e leggere il testo di Garzoni, proprio nel momento in cui lo scrittore sembra ambire al ruolo di araldo entusiasta delle fortune del Signore di Bologna, come un modo per "dire la verità al principe": definire l'immagine del principe ideale può infatti diventare una via programmaticamente non eversiva, per quanto affatto acritica, per verificare se esista un equilibrio possibile tra *principatus*, oligarchia e tradizioni repubblicane, governo dei molti e potere individuale, nel contesto di un'area come quella bolognese e padana dove, come è stato detto, la legittimazione dei signori appare spesso subordinata al loro ruolo di garanti dell'identità storica, culturale e politica della città (Anselmi 37-65).

Il dialogo con i maestri: Egidio Romano
L'ambizione dottrinale e l'impegno speculativo con cui Garzoni affronta il problema della formazione del principe e dell'ottimo governo si esprimono

attraverso una precisa modalità operativa che lo porta a organizzare i tre libri del *De eruditione principum* come riscrittura ed epitome ragionata del *De regimine principum* di Egidio Romano, lo *speculum* più autorevole, commentato e discusso dalla trattatistica politica e giuridica tra XIV secolo e Umanesimo (Lambertini, *Philosophus videtur* 277-326; Quaglioni, *Il modello* 103-22).

Il riferimento al pensiero e all'opera di Egidio Romano, fondativa dell'identità culturale stessa dell'ordine agostiniano (Pini 81-113), appare ben giustificato per chi, come il Garzoni, ha fatto non solo della frequentazione professionale, ma dell'amicizia e del sodalizio intellettuale con i Padri Eremitani del convento bolognese di San Giacomo un punto fermo della propria esperienza di umanista e letterato. Uno dei più assidui destinatari delle sue lettere è infatti padre Giovanni Paci da Ripatransone, teologo ed editore a Bologna di Egidio Romano, a lungo priore del convento e confessore di Giovanni II, a cui Garzoni si rivolge proprio per ottenere che il *De eruditione principum* sia presentato degnamente al Signore della città (Lind 271). Ma più ancora del Paci, appaiono coinvolti nella discussione sui nodi concettuali della teoria politica esposta nel *De eruditione* i frati predicatori dello Studio Domenicano di Bologna (D'Amato 465-70; Banfi 365-78), protagonisti di primo piano della fervida attività culturale che, dal convento di San Domenico e dalla sua biblioteca, si intreccia a più livelli con il mondo dell'Università e dei suoi maestri: non ultimo il Garzoni, promotore fervido e appassionato, fra coloro che spesso gli sono stati anche scolari, di un Umanesimo cristiano culturalmente vivificato dalla lezione dell'eloquenza ciceroniana (Raimondi, *Codro* 69-71; Knowles Frazier 182-87).

Questo rapporto privilegiato di amicizia, magistero e discepolato con Domenicani e Agostiniani illustri rappresenta sicuramente per Garzoni una motivazione forte — e forse decisiva — a calare la propria riflessione politica negli schemi di riferimento del trattato egidiano, paradigma autorevolissimo di quell'attenzione degli Ordini Mendicanti alle dinamiche politiche e governative e ai loro lessici descrittivi che ha coinciso largamente, tra XIII e XIV secolo, con la ricezione e l'interpretazione critica della filosofia morale di Aristotele (Lambertini, *Governo ideale* 231-77).

Garzoni trova nel *De regimine principum*, in primo luogo, un modello plurale per temi e prospettive d'indagine: il principe come soggetto e personalità da plasmare e il principato come istituzione; l'ordinamento pratico della casa e, di conseguenza, della corte e del regno; i diversi modelli politici e le loro dinamiche di funzionamento, in pace e in guerra. Queste macrosezioni corrispondono puntualmente ai tre libri del *De eruditione* garzoniano, dedicati nell'ordine alle virtù del principe e ai suoi *mores*; alla cura della *res familiaris* in rapporto alla composita comunità domestica; al governo dello stato e all'arte della guerra. Senza che vi sia mai, da parte dell'interprete, alcun riferimento diretto all'archetipo egidiano, se non forse allusivamente nella scelta del titolo, questo funge di fatto non da semplice fonte, ma da vero e proprio palinsesto della versione moderna, nella dinamica di un rapporto di intertestualità complessa e, come si vedrà, perfino tendenziosa. Con un'esplicita presa di posizione iniziale, Garzoni esibisce la propria adesione a quella teologia politica di cui Egidio Romano è riconosciuto maestro, secondo la quale dell'ordine sacro di questo mondo il principe è parte attiva, custode e segno vivente; ma nello stesso tempo mostra anche di voler realizzare uno *speculum principis* aggiornato e moderno. Per questo motivo rimane ben poco della struttura argomentativa rigorosamente deduttiva del modello: il discorso si semplifica dal punto di vista concettuale e contemporaneamente si arricchisce di un ricco repertorio di esempi tratti dalle letterature antiche, soprattutto quella latina, che trovano nella ricontestualizzazione umanistica la loro specifica funzionalità comunicativa e pragmatica. Si tratta di una vasta antologia di luoghi topici della trattatistica umanistica sul principe, ricavati da Cicerone, Livio, Seneca, Valerio Massimo che, mentre collocano il testo in un preciso orizzonte di genere (Orvieto 153-80), confermano la piena appartenenza del Garzoni all'ambiente universitario bolognese, quello dei più grandi *commentatores* — dal Beroaldo allo stesso Codro — per i quali il testo antico è il punto di partenza di un discorso in cui l'esegesi linguistica si dilata in enciclopedia, *silva* di richiami eruditi e l'universo dei classici è messo interamente a disposizione dell'interprete e del lettore (Raimondi, *Politica* 36-45; Chines 17-32).

Intertestualità "tendenziosa": la lezione di Aristotele
Dove invece appare più evidente l'autonomia del commentatore, ed insieme la sua ambiguità ideologica, è soprattutto nella selezione dei temi oltre che nei riferimenti in presa diretta alla *Politica* e all'*Etica Nicomachea*, in un dialogo recuperato con il testo aristotelico che si pone accanto e oltre la lettura egidiana, secondo una prassi operativa che pluralizza la parola nel gioco stratificato dei rimandi, amplificati dall'esegeta moderno tramite il corollario degli *exempla* latini. Ed è logico che il lavoro di filtraggio selettivo dell'autore moderno si attivi soprattutto nel terzo libro, il più ideologicamente sensibile, dove si confrontano diverse concezioni politiche e soprattutto si discute di quale sia la migliore forma di governo.

Non stupisce da parte del Garzoni, animato indubbiamente da ragioni di opportunità cortigiana, la scelta di assumere come referente principale del *De eruditione* l'opera di Egidio Romano: coerente con i modi della lunga ricezione della *Politica* e dell'*Etica Nicomachea* da parte degli Ordini Mendicanti, Egidio ha infatti depurato la riflessione di Aristotele sulla definizione dell'ottima forma di governo della sua natura "aporetica", optando in modo inequivoco per la superiorità del *regimen unius*. Questa semplificazione funzionale, giustificata da una coerente visione teologico-politica, si ripropone come paradigma di riferimento e autorevole giustificazione ideologica in tutta la trattatistica quattrocentesca sul principe, rispetto alla quale i testi elaborati dall'Umanesimo bolognese non fanno eccezione; basti pensare, oltre al Garzoni, a Filippo

Beroaldo seniore con il suo *De optimo statu et de Principe*. Ma ciò che distingue il Garzoni anche dal suo più illustre concittadino è la singolare e disinvolta operazione riassuntiva rispetto all'avantesto egidiano, in una pagina che conviene a questo punto richiamare in parte:

> Si igitur civitatis gubernatio penes unum sit aut penes paucos aut penes multos sequanturque communem utilitatem, erunt haec rerum publicarum species. Quod si ad propriam utilitatem gubernatio fit, labem dicemus quae suis nominibus distinguntur. [...] Est autem non parva dubietas nunquid unus, qui optimus sit, civitati dominari debeat, an plures, qui optimi sint. Nam si plures sint qui virtute praestent et prudentia, id civitati conducibilius dixerim. Etenim in unum collati fiunt, quasi homo unus multos habens pedes, multas manus, multos oculos multosque sensus. Melius ergo iudicabunt. Facilius praeterea unus quam plures gratia flectitur aut precio corrumpitur. Haec quamquam ita sint, laudabilior tamen et dignior est unius quam multorum gubernatio. Si enim qui civitati praeest sapientes et experientia doctos in consilium adhibeat, in unum evadet quasi hominem multos pedes, multas manus, multosque oculos habentem. Quod si ei recte dominari optabile est, nec precio corrumpetur nec gratia flectetur.
>
> (III 24-25)[2]

Quello che colpisce della sintesi garzoniana è che, se nessuna delle argomentazioni può dirsi in alcun modo originale, il senso complessivo vira in conseguenza della loro *dispositio* e della selezione che su di esse viene operata e finisce per riportare in evidenza, al di là delle intenzioni forse più pragmatiche che ideologiche dell'autore, la complessità dell'archetipo aristotelico: la tesi della superiorità del governo di uno solo, ampiamente sviluppata nel testo di Egidio,[3] si riduce così per Garzoni ad un'affermazione apodittica e isolata —

---

[2] "Se dunque il governo della città è nelle mani di uno solo o di pochi o di molti e i vari regimi perseguono l'utilità comune, queste forme di governo saranno delle repubbliche. Se invece il governo persegue un'utilità privata, sarà una rovina che ha i suoi nomi specifici. [...] Vi è d'altronde non poca incertezza se debba dominare la città un solo uomo, che sia il migliore, o più uomini che siano i migliori. Se quelli che si distinguono per virtù e prudenza sono più di uno, direi che questa è la soluzione più conveniente per la città. Si fondono infatti insieme come un solo uomo che ha molti piedi, molte mani, molti occhi, molti sensi e quindi potranno giudicare meglio. Inoltre è più facile per uno solo piuttosto che per molti cedere alla parzialità o lasciarsi corrompere. Ma per quanto le cose stiano così, il governo di uno solo è più pregevole e conveniente che quello di molti. Se infatti chi è a capo della città si consulterà con chi ha saggezza ed esperienza riuscirà — per così dire — a diventare un uomo con molti piedi, molte mani e molti occhi. E se è suo desiderio governare secondo giustizia, non si lascerà corrompere né cederà alla parzialità."
[3] Aegidii Romani *De regimine principum* III 2 3-4. Il capitolo 3, *Quod melius est civitatem et regnum regi uno quam pluribus et quod regnum est optimus principatus*, elenca tutte le argomentazioni canoniche a favore del *regimen unius*: "[...] Nam pax et unitas civium debent esse finaliter intenta a legislatore, sicut sanitas et aequalitas humorum est finaliter intenta a medico: hanc autem unitatem et concordiam magis efficere potest quod est per se unum; magis autem per se unitas reperitur in uno

"Haec quamquam ita sint laudabilior tamen et dignior est unius quam multorum gubernatio" —, mentre le ragioni a favore di un governo dei molti, poste in risalto anche dall'ordine dell'esposizione, finiscono per assumere un rilievo preponderante: contestualmente alla tesi della superiorità del governo monarchico si propone, nel momento stesso in cui essa viene rapidamente enunciata e senza apparente contraddizione, quella di una sovranità suffragata e in qualche modo corretta da un'efficace dimensione collegiale, quella dei "sapientes et experientia doctos" su cui di fatto converge l'attenzione di chi legge.

L'ambiguità evidente della riscrittura garzoniana trae origine e ispirazione dagli stessi equilibri ancipiti della politica bolognese alla fine degli anni '80: le insofferenze e il risentimento nei confronti dell'egemonia bentivolesca da parte di molte tra le famiglie più illustri dell'oligarchia cittadina, appartenenti alla magistratura dei Riformatori, hanno già mostrato di poter essere incanalate verso la strada eversiva della congiura. Riconoscere il ruolo di Giovanni come primo cittadino di Bologna può convenientemente e prudentemente lasciare spazio, nei termini di una *institutio* in tutto e per tutto conciliante, al richiamo ad un modello politico che è sotteso alla struttura istituzionale della città: quel governo "misto", che è tale non soltanto in virtù della compresenza dell'oligarchia patrizia e del legato papale, ma soprattutto per la natura condivisa di un potere da gestire collegialmente da parte dei Riformatori e del *dominus* Giovanni (De Benedictis, *Quale Corte* 13-33), pena gravi squilibri e drammatiche perdite di consenso.

Il primato della legge
Questa posizione, ispirata ad una cautela non priva di opportunismo, si conferma nel modo in cui Garzoni affronta, attraverso il filtro esegetico della *Politica* aristotelica, il tema della "gubernatio civitatis", mettendo in primo piano il ruolo e il primato della legge: un'esposizione che, di nuovo, riassembla e riassume il

---

principatu, si dominatur unus princeps, quam si dominabitur plures. [...] Secunda via ad investigandum hoc idem sumitur ex civili potentia quae requiritur in regimine civitatis. Nam quanto virtus est magis unita, fortior est seipsa dispersa [...] quae si tota civilis potentia quae est in pluribus principantibus congregatur in uno principe efficacior esset. [...] Tertia via sumitur ex his quae videmus in natura. Ubicumque est regnum naturale semper totum illud regnum reducitur in aliquod unum principans. Ut si in eodem corpore ubi sunt diversa membra ordinata ad diversa officia et diversos motus, est dare aliquod unum membrum ut cor, ex cuius motu sumit originem omnis motus animalis factu in toto corpore. [...] Quarta via sumitur ex his quae experimento videmus in regimine civitatum. Experti enim sumus civitates et provincias non existentes sub uno rege esse in penuria, non gaudere in pace, molestari dissensionibus et guerris; existentes vero sub rege, e contrario, guerras nesciunt, pacem sectantur, abundantia florent." Il capitolo 4, *Quibus rationibus ostendi potest quod appareat melius esse civitatem aut provinciam regi pluribus quam uno et quomodo solvi possunt rationes illae*, è interamente dedicato alla confutazione della tesi della superiorità del governo dei molti.

testo di Egidio[4] in un florilegio di citazioni, in cui ciò che conta a riorientare la lettura sono di fatto le vistose ellissi:

Leges memoria repetat, quod hae sunt quarum praesidio civitates regnaque conservantur. Ad has si iudex sententias ferendas rettulerit, nullius in se concitabit odium. Nec a recto declinet quod alter ei sit odio, in alterum summo sit amore, quamquam minime negaverim ei non nihil in reum adhibendum esse misericordiae et quae a iure civili proficiscuntur, ea ad facilitatem et aequitatem referre. Controversias tollat nec litium actiones constituat. In ferendis autem sententijs haec illi consideranda erunt, iudicandi ut insit auctoritas, leges calleat, iusticiae inhereat, experientia doctus existat. Non enim Aristoteles minus tribuit expertis quam scientibus. Quod vero iudicem misericordia commoveri oporteat, cui dubium est, cum fragilitas humana facile labatur? Non quid lex iubeat sed qua fuerit mente legis lator consideret. Moderetur legibus, quas in mitiorem partem accipiat. [...] Satis superque est ut a principe, vel ab eo qui in eius locum suffectus fuerit, hae leges condantur quae a iusticia minime abhorreant, quae utilitatem communem explicent, quarum mandata quivis possit exequi. Sunt autem promulgandae ne qui excusatione adducti, se se flagicijs contaminent, quae delinquentem quas emeritus est poenas cogant luere, probos vero ac studiosos muneribus complectantur. [...] Sed ut ad id redeamus unde digressi sumus, civibus bene feliciterque eveniet si legibus parebunt, quod et studiosi et probi habebuntur. Insuper civitatis saluti consulitur, vitia exterminantur, libertas confirmatur. Hos enimvero liberos dicimus, qui legibus parent: pax, ocium, tranquillitas augetur.

[III 38-43][5]

---

[4] Aegidii Romani *De regimine principum* III 2 1-35.
[5] "Il principe citi a memoria le leggi perché è grazie alla loro tutela che si conservano repubbliche e regni. Se un giudice si richiamerà ad esse nel pronunciare le proprie sentenze, non si attirerà l'odio di nessuno. E non si discosti da ciò che è giusto perché ha in odio uno e invece ama un altro, per quanto mi senta di dire che dovrebbe mostrare misericordia verso l'imputato e riportare i princípi che nascono dal diritto civile a ragioni di indulgenza ed equità. Elimini le controversie e non intenti azioni giudiziarie per dirimere le liti. Nel pronunciare le sentenze, affinché vi sia in lui l'autorità per ben giudicare, dovrà invece basarsi su queste regole: conoscere le leggi, attenersi alla giustizia, avere un'esperienza consolidata. Aristotele infatti non attribuisce meno valore agli esperti che agli studiosi della materia. E chi può dubitare che il giudice debba essere misericordioso dal momento che la fragilità umana cade facilmente nell'errore? Tenga conto non di che cosa prescrive la legge, ma di quale sia stata l'intenzione di chi l'ha promulgata. Stabilisca un limite alle leggi interpretandole in senso più mite. [...] Basterà che un principe, o chi su sua nomina lo sostituisce in quella funzione, promulghi leggi che non si discostino dalla giustizia, rappresentino l'utilità comune e le cui prescrizioni possano essere messe in atto da chiunque. D'altro canto le leggi vanno promulgate affinché nessuno si macchi di delitti e si possa giustificare; per costringere chi delinque a pagare la giusta pena e premiare invece gli onesti e i meritevoli. [...] Ma per tornare al punto da cui abbiamo preso le mosse, i cittadini vivranno bene e felicemente se ubbidiranno alle leggi, così saranno giudicati onesti e probi. Oltre a ciò si salvaguarda la prosperità della città, i vizi vengono banditi, la libertà consolidata. Diciamo infatti che sono liberi quelli che ubbidiscono alle leggi: la pace, la tranquillità civile, la quiete ne risultano rafforzate."

Scompare, nella redazione garzoniana, il tema cardine della regalità giuricentrica (Kantorowicz 130-35) che tanto spazio occupa nel *De regimine*: se il principe si identifica con la *lex animata*, in quanto mediatore tra diritto naturale e legge positiva, è di conseguenza ontologicamente superiore ad essa, in una visione che oppone alla imperfezione generalizzante di una norma in sé inerte la superiorità vivente di chi governa. Al contrario e in alternativa ai modi con cui Egidio rielabora il grande tema aristotelico se sia preferibile essere governati dalle leggi migliori o dall'uomo migliore,[6] Garzoni recupera la plurivocità dell'*auctoritas* antica, insieme ai suoi corollari canonici che meglio si prestano a sottendere il difficile equilibrio cittadino tra governo signorile ed istituzioni oligarchiche: la sovranità delle leggi e la loro insufficienza rispetto alla molteplice realtà, il ruolo del magistrato e la sua corruttibilità in una dialettica di rischi che oppone il governo del singolo a quello dei molti.[7]

Attraverso la mediazione della cultura legalistica latina, assimilata all'interno di quella *scientia iuris* che è tutt'uno con l'identità medievale e moderna di una città universitaria come Bologna (Greci 537-63), Garzoni pone l'accento sulla centralità della legge, riproponendo, nella canonica formulazione ciceroniana,[8] il motivo della coincidenza tra obbedienza alle leggi — "si legibus parebunt" — e la "libertas" che è tutt'uno con la "salus civitatis". In questo modo, attraverso una vera e propria decostruzione del testo egidiano, il discorso dell'esegeta moderno recupera obliquamente la dimensione legalitaria e condivisa del governo cittadino, in cui il ruolo di Giovanni II Bentivoglio non può essere *legibus solutus*.

---

[6] Aegidii Romani *De regimine principum* III 2 29: *Qualiter melius regitur civitas aut regnum, utrum melius regatur optimo rege quam optima lege*. "Philosophus III Polit. Inquirit utrum regnum aut civitas sit melius regi optimo rege aut optima lege. Adducit autem rationes duas quod melius sit politiam regni regi optima lege quam optimo rege. Prima sumitur ex eo quod rex debet esse quasi organum et instrumentum legis. Secunda ex eo quod facilius est corrumpi regem quam legem. [...] Nam (ut ait) lex universaliter dicit quod non est universaliter; oportet enim humanas leges quantumque sint exquisitae in aliquo casu deficere: melius est igitur regnum regi rege quam lege ut per regem corrigi possunt legales defectus. [...] Sciendum est regem et quemlibet principantem esse medium inter legem naturalem et positivam; nam nullus recte principatur nisi agat ut recta ratio dictat; nam ratio debet esse regula humanorum operum. Quae si nomen regis a regendo sumptum est et decet regem regere alios et esse regulam aliorum, oportet regem in regendo alios sequi rectam rationem et per consequens sequi naturalem legem, quia in tantum recte regit in quantum a lege naturali non deviat; est tamen super legem positivam, quia illa sua auctoritate constituit [...] ; quare positiva lex est infra principantem sicut lex naturalis est supra."
[7] Arist. *Pol.* III 15-16, 1285b-1287b.
[8] Cic. *Cluent.* 146: "Hoc enim vinculum est huius dignitatis qua fruamur in re publica, hoc fundamentum libertatis, hic fons aequitatis: mens et animus et consilium et sententia civitatis posita est in legibus"; Arist. *Pol.* IV 4, 1292a: "[...] dove le leggi non imperano non c'è costituzione."

L'insistenza sul tema tradizionale dell'"aequitas", per cui l'autorevolezza della legge non viene mai meno pur nel suo declinarsi e adeguarsi alla molteplicità del reale, in un processo affidato alla "mens" competente del legislatore, porta in primo piano, oltre alle competenze tecniche — che il principe "leges calleat" — le doti del "iudex", sia quelle professionali dell'"auctoritas" e dell'"experientia", che quelle morali della clemenza e della giustizia. E non è un caso che il discorso si rivolga simultaneamente al *princeps* e al *iudex* e ne sovrapponga le immagini: non solo perché, come è stato autorevolmente detto, il giudice è la figura simbolo su cui convergono "il linguaggio politico medievale e una precisa idea di legittimità" (Costa 284); ma anche perché il tema del governo dei giudici appartiene a una tradizione secolare al centro della quale sta la definizione stessa del concetto di regalità, che oppone la figura del "rex" a quella del "tyrannus" (Quaglioni, *L'iniquo diritto* 209-29).

Gli optima fundamenta regni*: i rischi della tirannide*
Universale polemico della letteratura politica antica e medievale, il tema della tirannide, inteso nello specifico come degenerazione patologica del *regimen unius* e prevaricazione soggettiva del bene comune, si colloca al centro di quella trattatistica umanistica sul principe, da Bracciolini a Pontano, di cui Garzoni mostra di condividere temi, ragioni e *loci communes*. Rispetto a questo argomento cruciale, tuttavia, il tessuto argomentativo generale del trattato garzoniano non riproduce, se non desultoriamente, il testo di Egidio Romano, ma recupera direttamente l'*auctoritas* aristotelica. In questo caso — e si tratta di un *unicum* rispetto alla struttura complessiva del testo — Garzoni si discosta dall'organizzazione tematica dell'archetipo medievale, anticipando in parte il discorso sulla tirannide già alla fine del II libro, dedicato al governo della casa e della famiglia.

Il richiamo agli "optima fundamenta regni", da affrontare sistematicamente nel III libro, rispetto al quale questo inserto funge da premessa generale, coincide con la riproposizione del capitolo V 11 della *Politica* di Aristotele, nella sezione che tratta dei modi con cui si conserva la tirannide.[9] Un luogo su cui Garzoni si è interrogato a lungo, come possiamo constatare dall'epistolario in cui ritroviamo tracce di una discussione specifica sul tema, probabilmente risalente agli ultimi anni '90, che Garzoni intrattiene con il domenicano Bartolomeo Manzoli.[10] Lettore attento e compiacente dell'opera storica garzoniana e anche dei libri del *De eruditione principum*, di cui elogia la sapienza erudita e retorica applicata all'esposizione ornata di "tota moralis

---
[9] Arist. *Pol.* V 11, 1313a-1314a.
[10] Fra Bartolomeo Manzoli O. P., figlio di Filippo Manzoli e Violante Lambertini, fu discepolo di Antonio Urceo Codro negli anni '90 del XV secolo. Detto "il Diogene" per la sua acclarata competenza filosofica, fu autore di varie opere ispirate al pensiero tomistico tra cui *Tractatus de formalitatibus*, *De definitionibus* e *Quaestiones logicales*.

philosophia" (Lind 105), il Manzoli, in virtù della sua acclarata competenza in campo filosofico, viene più volte interpellato dal nostro, proprio su un problema esegetico posto dalla nota pagina aristotelica sulle "cautelae tyrannicae" (Lind 191-92; 161-62), che a Garzoni pare un atto di connivenza complice, inqualificabile e soprattutto inspiegabile da parte del grande filosofo.

La risposta del Manzoli rettifica il fraintendimento di una lettura moralistica ingiustificata del testo di Aristotele, che attribuisce valore di imbarazzante prescrizione, lesiva della "libertas", a considerazioni che invece sono neutre, puramente descrittive delle ragioni e dei processi per cui i diversi ordinamenti politici si conservano e, alternativamente, si corrompono (Lind 193-94). Ma negli anni della composizione del *De eruditione*, di certo antecedenti a questo carteggio, scrupoli evidentemente insormontabili o nuove cautele, dettate dai tempi corruschi e disameni, hanno suggerito a Garzoni addirittura una parafrasi *e contrario* del testo aristotelico:

Accedamus ad alias praeceptiones quas, si exequetur, imperij sui optima — ut inquit eximius orator — iacta erunt fundamenta. Cavendum est igitur ne viris doctrina praestantibus atque disciplina praeditis vim afferat. Hoc enim populum in ipsum concitat. Multos extitisse legimus qui, ut imperare possent, non modo viros graves et sapientes ex civitate exturbarunt, sed cognatos quoque atque amicos ferro venenoque petierunt. Quorum qui fuerit exitus, historici litteris prodiderunt. Utilitati communi studebit si ut in civitate litterarum studia vigeant, omni curabit diligentia. Huic sententiae minime accedunt tyranni, timore adducti ne existant qui eos obiurgentur. Conetur ut cives se mutua benivolentia prosequantur, amicicias ineant. Delatores, dicaces, detractores exterminet. Nullam eis fidem adhibeat. Id multis obfuit. Si qui inter se cives dissidebunt, componendae pacis confestim curam suscipiat. Subditos nequaquam in paupertatem redigat. Nullas civibus, nisi belli pericula impendeant, pecunias imperet. Si qui supplicio aut morti addicti fuerint, iusticiam consulat ne qui sub eius imperio subijciuntur ipsum iracundia aut odio adductum existiment. Haec si fecerit, nullas populi timebit insidias, quin vitam tranquillam aget et quietam.

(II 49-50)[11]

---

[11] "Passiamo ad altri precetti, seguendo i quali – come dice l'esimio oratore – si porranno ottime fondamenta al regno. Il principe deve pertanto evitare di usare violenza a coloro che eccellono per dottrina e sapere. Questo infatti solleva il popolo contro di lui. Leggiamo di molti che, per poter regnare, non solo hanno esiliato gli uomini più autorevoli e saggi, ma hanno ucciso con il ferro e il veleno perfino i congiunti e gli amici. Quale sia stata la fine di questi individui ce lo raccontano gli storici. Provvederà all'utilità comune se metterà ogni cura a far sì che nel suo regno fioriscano gli studi letterari. I tiranni non vedono questo con favore, perché temono che possa esserci chi li biasima. Faccia in modo che tra i cittadini vi sia reciproca benevolenza e si allaccino rapporti d'amicizia. Allontani da sé delatori, detrattori e mordaci, non presti loro fede. Questo atteggiamento ha già danneggiato molti altri. Se alcuni dei cittadini sono in disaccordo tra loro, provvederà subito a mettere pace. Non riduca mai i sudditi in povertà e non esiga da loro denaro, a meno che non incomba il pericolo di una guerra. Se qualcuno viene condannato al supplizio o a morte, faccia appello alla giustizia, affinché nessuno di coloro che sono sottoposti al suo potere pensi che agisce spinto dall'ira o dall'odio. Se

A queste indicazioni, che traducono in forma esplicitamente antitirannica l'argomentazione aristotelica, segue nel III libro la ripresa della seconda opzione offerta da Aristotele, quella della possibile trasformazione della tirannide in regno.[12] Essa costituisce il canovaccio per la più dettagliata *pars construens* della riflessione garzoniana sul buon governo, a dimostrazione di quanto questo equilibrio, fondato sul compromesso, sia raggiungibile solo percorrendo la strada impervia e insidiosa della educazione del principe. Inquadrandolo nella esemplificazione dei temi canonici della solitudine del tiranno e della "virtus formidulosa"[13], per cui i probi divengono inevitabilmente una minaccia per il tiranno, il commentatore moderno ribadisce il dovere del principe di costruire una socialità produttiva e concorde, rispettosa della persona dei cittadini, delle loro proprietà e della sicurezza complessiva dello stato, del ruolo dell'intelligenza creativa e della cultura, del riconoscimento del merito e di uno stile di vita virile e improntato a sobrietà.

Abile *collage* di citazioni aristoteliche ed egidiane, il testo del Garzoni gravita tuttavia sostanzialmente intorno a due principi fondamentali: da un lato, l'obbedienza alla "utilitas communis", fondata su una concezione dell'"imperare" che "nec quicquam aliud est quam imperium in multos partiri" (III 27); dall'altro, e di conseguenza, la legittimazione del potere attraverso una legalità condivisa, giacché "difficile est profecto pluribus nolentibus imperare et contra legem" (II 56). Si tratta di argomenti indubbiamente comuni alla trattatistica sull'ottimo principe, ma che assumono, in pagine dedicate al Signore di Bologna, un significato che non pare improprio provare a declinare e ricontestualizzare all'interno dell'orizzonte cittadino.

La propaganda legittimistica filobentivolesca, di cui Giovanni Garzoni è voce prestigiosa e autorevole, è solita giustificare il primato politico della famiglia Bentivoglio proprio facendo riferimento ad un suo ruolo decisivo nella lotta contro quei governi "tirannici" che, nel corso del XV secolo, hanno fomentato le fazioni e offeso i cittadini, nella persona e negli averi; ovvero hanno portato la città alla guerra, con la conseguente, continua e rovinosa *status commutatio*, in cui guerra guerreggiata e contesa civile si sono saldate insieme, in un rapporto perverso di causa-effetto (Quaglioni, *Politica e diritto* 39-71).

Da questo punto di vista, il fatto che Garzoni lavori alle *Historiae Bononienses* negli stessi anni in cui si accinge a rielaborare il *De eruditione principum* (Mantovani, *History* 227-33; *Educare il Principe* XI-XV) può rappresentare ben più che una semplice concomitanza cronologica: la parenesi collettiva del discorso storico, che si richiama ai princìpi di un'identità cittadina condivisa di cui i Bentivoglio sono presentati come i difensori, va integrata da

---

farà questo, non dovrà temere nessuna insidia da parte del popolo, anzi vivrà una vita tranquilla e pacifica."
[12] Arist. *Pol.* V 11, 1314b-1315a.
[13] Sall. *Catil.* 7, 2.

un'operazione didascalica individualizzata *a parte subiecti*, rivolta a chi, come Giovanni II Bentivoglio, di quell'ordine complesso non deve dimenticare di essere il garante più che il sovrano.

Se, all'inizio degli anni Settanta, redigendo l'opuscolo epidittico *De regenda civitate*[14] che del III libro del *De eruditione* rappresenta a tutti gli effetti l'archetipo (Mantovani, *Educare il principe* XXII-XXV), Garzoni aveva potuto salutare in Giovanni il difensore della *libertas bononiensis*, assimilandolo alla realtà della *civitas* e del suo *populus*, non v'è dubbio che le pagine seriori dell'opera maggiore riflettano, pur attraverso gli schermi di inevitabili cautele, una verità più inquietante.

Ormai la "tirannide" di Giovanni II Bentivoglio non è solo una condizione politica reale, prodotta dallo sbilanciamento dei poteri all'interno della magistratura dei Riformatori a partire dal 1470, con gli esiti nefasti sul piano degli equilibri interni all'oligarchia, di cui la congiura dei Malvezzi rappresenta l'esito più recente e clamoroso. Nella magnificenza esibita di una vita di corte proiettata su uno spazio cittadino coinvolto in un progetto di grandiosa ridefinizione urbanistica (Terpstra 389-96), la tirannide è anche un'idea o un sospetto, alimentato dall'opinione condivisa del popolo, degli intellettuali, degli osservatori stranieri e degli altri Stati Italiani, che Giovanni sia, a tutti gli effetti, il Signore di Bologna (Robertson 113-16; Sorbelli 65-73). L'educazione del principe, attraverso la mediazione inevitabile dell'ossequio cortigiano, si muove perciò sul crinale periglioso di istanze non facilmente conciliabili, indicando l'orizzonte ideale di un *principari*, ovvero dell'esercizio di un potere che sappia essere governo piuttosto che dominio e a cui, di conseguenza, si possa davvero guardare "tamquam in speculo" (II 23).

Il ruolo dei sapientes: *una prospettiva "bolognese"*
Il significato del messaggio pedagogico del *De eruditione principum*, veicolato da un'operazione retorica in apparenza neutra di riproposizione e commento di modelli illustri, si esplicita con maggiore chiarezza laddove la scrittura garzoniana opera in autonomia rispetto al modello medievale e si presenta, nella solennità celebrativa delle pagine proemiali, come opera di un umanista ambizioso e moderno. Rispondendo alle critiche che qualcuno gli rivolge in merito alla presunta non ortodossia cristiana e aristotelica delle tesi sostenute nella sua *institutio principis*, Garzoni, senza mai citare Egidio Romano, afferma di aver voluto riscrivere ed imitare il "liber magnificus et regius" (Lind 128) del

---

[14] Il *De regenda civitate libellus ad magnificum ac prestantem equitem auratum Johannem Bentivolum* è un opuscolo garzoniano che ci è trasmesso alle cc. 1r-18v del Ms. Latin 6694 della Bibliothèque Nationale de France di Parigi, un manoscritto cartaceo del XV secolo già segnalato dal Fantuzzi (99-100), ma che è rimasto fino ad oggi ignorato negli studi che hanno, in qualche modo, incrociato la figura del Garzoni. Unica eccezione le pagine di Thorndike (277-80).

De officiis di Cicerone e, implicitamente, dichiara di aver sviluppato la propria riflessione situandola entro l'orizzonte teorico dell'*honestum* e della ridefinizione di un'etica per le classi dirigenti, ispirata dalla nuova cultura e dai suoi maestri.

Al centro del proemio al libro I campeggia infatti la definizione ciceroniana della sapienza intesa come cultura funzionale all'azione, in un sostanziale superamento della contrapposizione tra vita attiva e vita contemplativa che avvicina il politico al *sapiens*, in nome di un sapere che, in quanto pienamente umano, è anche condizione imprescindibile per l'esercizio dell'azione politica e di governo (Gilli 425-42). In quest'ottica si spiega la presenza, di per sé indicativa di una precisa genealogia culturale, della figura di Scipione l'Africano, protagonista del proemio al libro II. Eroe della *respublica*, ma anche *exemplum* canonico della riflessione politica di orientamento monarchico, e quindi opportunamente "spendibile" in ambito bolognese, Scipione non evoca solo il paradigma di una virtù eminentemente politica, ma richiama una certa tradizione di principato civile (Rubinstein 212-14), dove il *princeps*, come nel caso del Bentivoglio, è cittadino e "pater patriae" (I 52), se è vero che concepisce la propria azione di governo "pro illius salute" (I 4), come servizio allo stato. D'altro canto, la ragione intimamente politica della pratica delle discipline liberali, raccomandata proprio in questo libro per l'*institutio* dei giovani principi, viene ricondotta alla loro funzione di propedeutica all'esercizio delle virtù morali, che "se offerent et non vocatae respondebunt" (II 26) a chi dovrà assumersi responsabilità di governo.

Non è dunque improprio supporre che anche la paludata retorica del proemio al libro III, di nuovo nella forma di un prevedibile riecheggiamento ciceroniano, sottintenda un messaggio più ampio: il problema del rapporto tra virtù civili e virtù militari, della superiorità dei "sapientum consilia" sulle "res bellicae" (III 3), non va letto semplicemente come richiamo topico ad uno dei temi più frequentati e consunti della "disputa delle arti", risolto per altro dal Garzoni nel consueto tono conciliativo, quasi da esercizio letterario. A Bologna, in quella stessa irrequieta *fin de siècle*, la riproposizione della disputa delle arti, da Sabadino degli Arienti al Beroaldo, dal Magnani al Beccadelli, può infatti assumere — come è stato da tempo autorevolmente dimostrato — il senso di una riflessione mediatamente politica e giuridica sul tema dei rapporti di potere e sui diversi ruoli sociali (De Benedictis, *Retorica e politica* 411-38).

È verosimile allora che anche Garzoni si soffermi a riflettere su quale spazio possa essere riservato ai "sapientum consilia" (Armstrong-Kirshner 16), ovvero di come la cultura sia in grado di condizionare l'azione di governo, se è vero che occorrono determinate qualità, più di altre, per garantire un regime e il suo corretto funzionamento. Così, se all'inizio degli anni Settanta, nel *De regenda civitate* Garzoni si era diffuso in un appassionato elogio delle armi e della virtù militare, di cui il giovane signore di Bologna prometteva di offrire un chiaro esempio[15], il *De eruditione principum* si impegna a confermare, in una stagione ormai molto differente, la funzione complementare e concorde della *sapientia* accanto alle armi:

> Saepe ac multum mecum cogitavi, Joannes Bentivole, maioribus ne laudibus qui se totos in rem publicam conferunt an qui rem bellicam exercent digni censendi sunt. Nam, si quae ex re militari emolumenta reportantur ipse considero, hos amplioribus laudibus collaudem necesse est. Quid enim praestantius inveniri potest quam eos esse a quibus belli pericula repellantur? Quis ignorat quantas calamitates afferat belli suspicio cum pecora — teste Cicerone — relinquantur, agricultura deseratur, mercatorum navigatio conquiescat? Cum bellum imminet, omnia litterarum studia spernuntur: forum castris cedit, ocium militiae, stilus gladio, umbra soli. Res militaris populo Romano aeternam gloriam peperit eique orbem terrarum coegit parere. Haec me in eam sententiam impellunt ut qui se militem profitetur, hunc viro qui consilio polleat ac prudentia praeferendum existimem affirmemque omnes res urbanas in tutela et praesidio bellicae virtutis latere. Nec vero desunt qui primorum sapientum consilia rebus bellicis anteponant. Non enim Themistocles amplissimam illam de Xerse reportasset victoriam ni ipse qui unus sapientum fuisse traditur Solon ei suo consilio suaque sapientia profuisset. Quid Pausanias? Quid Lisander? Quorum alter, quamquam Mardonium ad Plateas proelio fuderit, alter bellum quod annos sex et viginti inter Athenienses et Peloponnesios duraverat confecerit, nequaquam tamen cum Lygurgo conferendi erunt. Nec Scipio Affricanus, excisa Numantia, rei publicae romanae profuisset, ni eodem tempore Publius Nasica Tiberio Graccho legem agrariam ferenti subselliorum fragmentis vitam erripuisset. Nec minus utilitatis urbi attulit Marcus Scaurus cum de sumptibus et suffragijs libertinorum legem tulit, cum viam Aemiliam stravit, cum pontem Aemilium struxit quam Caius Marius, cuius res amplissime gestas multi litteris memoriaeque prodiderunt. Complures his rationibus adducti res urbanas bellicis preferunt. Atqui ut mentem meam quisque teneat, utrasque aequis laudibus prosequendas censeo. Non enim res bellicae sine sapientum consilijs nec sapientum consilia sine rebus bellicis civitatibus multum prodesse possunt.
>
> (III 1-3)[16]

---

[15] G. Garzoni, *De regenda civitate*, c. 2r: "Accedit rei militaris peritia que quantam tibi gloriam pariat quivis optime potest agnoscere. Nulla me hercle scientiarum est que tantum prestet utilitatis quantum est militaris cum teste Cicerone res urbanae in ipsius presidio lateant. Hoc virtutis bellice ne civitates diripiantur, castra incendantur. Ab hac hostium copie arceantur, finis imperij propagatur.".

[16] "Mi sono chiesto spesso, Giovanni Bentivoglio, se siano da ritenere più degni di lode coloro che si dedicano completamente allo stato o quelli che praticano l'arte della guerra. Se infatti considero quali vantaggi si ricavino dall'attività militare, sono coloro che la praticano a meritarsi le lodi maggiori. Chi può essere più nobile di chi allontana i pericoli della guerra? Chi ignora quante calamità porti con sé il timore della guerra, quando — scrive Cicerone — il bestiame viene abbandonato, l'agricoltura trascurata, il commercio sul mare si ferma? Quando la guerra incombe, vengono trascurati gli studi letterari, il foro cede il posto all'accampamento, la quiete all'esercizio delle armi, la penna alla spada, l'ombra al sole. L'arte della guerra ha procurato al popolo romano eterna gloria e il dominio sul mondo intero. Queste considerazioni mi inducono a pensare che chi si dichiara soldato sia da preferire a chi eccelle per saggezza e prudenza; oserei anzi dire che tutte le attività civili sono sotto la tutela e la protezione della virtù guerriera. Ma vi è

Più volte membro della magistratura degli Anziani consoli in qualità di maestro dello Studio,[17] Garzoni sembra ribadire in questo contesto, con l'orgoglio del letterato, la propria appartenenza a quel ceto che aveva svolto un ruolo di primo piano nel "governo del popolo e delle arti" e che, proprio nell'ultimo decennio del Quattrocento, stava sperimentando una progressiva marginalizzazione politica (Roversi Monaco 420-22).

Certo i "sapientum consilia", di cui Garzoni difende qui il valore e l'utilità, sono funzionali al perseguimento di un generale "prodesse", ovvero di un bene comune che riporta il testo entro i confini canonici della riflessione letteraria, affidata agli schemi ripetitivi e ormai un po' usurati dello *speculum principis*. Pure, senza che mai gli si possa attribuire una coerenza di ideologo, non pare improprio riconoscere al Garzoni un'intelligenza avvertita, per quanto non priva di cautele e di ambiguità, delle dinamiche e dei conflitti su cui si fondano gli equilibri politici della *respublica bononiensis*.

Esperto conoscitore dei paradigmi illustri del genere dell'*institutio principis*, lettore curioso e sagace di *auctores* antichi e contemporanei, dall'Isocrate dell'orazione *A Nicocle*, sulle cui tracce compone un agile *De principis officio*, dedicandolo al duca d'Urbino Guidubaldo da Montefeltro (Mantovani, *Educare il Principe* XLI-XLVIII), fino al Pontano del *De principe*, di cui annota e trascrive alcuni estratti,[18] Garzoni ha vivido il senso delle ragioni

---

anche chi antepone all'arte militare la saggezza dei sommi sapienti. Temistocle non avrebbe riportato la famosa vittoria su Serse se il famoso Solone, che si tramanda fosse uno dei Sapienti, non lo avesse sostenuto con il suo consiglio e la sua saggezza. Che dire di Pausania? Che dire di Lisandro? Per quanto l'uno abbia sbaragliato Mardonio presso Platea, l'altro abbia concluso la guerra tra Ateniesi e Spartani che era durata ventisei anni, non possono certo essere paragonati a Licurgo. E nemmeno Scipione Africano avrebbe potuto giovare alla repubblica romana con la distruzione di Numanzia, se nello stesso tempo Publio Nasica non avesse ucciso Tiberio Gracco, promotore della legge agraria, colpendolo con gli scanni. E Marco Scauro che presentò la legge sulle spese e sul diritto di voto per i figli dei liberti, spianò la via Emilia, costruì il ponte Emilio non fu meno utile a Roma di Caio Mario, di cui molti hanno tramandato la storia e le gesta gloriose.Sulla base di queste considerazioni, parecchi antepongono le virtù civili a quelle militari. Ebbene, per dire chiaramente la mia opinione, ritengo che entrambe queste virtù meritino di essere parimente elogiate. Infatti non possono essere di gran giovamento agli stati né le virtù militari senza i consigli dei saggi, né i consigli dei saggi senza le virtù militari."
[17] Garzoni fu tra gli Anziani consoli negli anni 1467 (bimestre Gennaio-Febbraio), 1473 (bimestre Marzo-Aprile), 1483 (bimestre Novembre-Dicembre), secondo le notizie riportate in Pasquali Alidosi.
[18] Nel Ms. Latino 2648 della Biblioteca Universitaria di Bologna, il testimone più recente tra quelli che ci trasmettono, insieme ad altre opere garzoniane, il testo del trattato *De eruditione principum*, troviamo alla carta 206v una serie di appunti, rubricati sotto la voce "Pontanus". Si tratta della trascrizione di alcuni passi del trattato pontaniano *De principe*, un "classico" tra gli specula umanistici, ma nel contempo un testo che non sembra appartenere al circuito culturale bolognese, nemmeno sul versante universitario. Come in

della prudenza reticente e dei limiti entro i quali si può pensare di "dire la verità al principe". Non può stupirci allora che l'appassionata invettiva contro il tiranno che per venticinque anni ha vessato una città che potrebbe essere proprio Bologna, da cui ha preso le mosse il nostro discorso, resti un frammento destinato — per quanto ci è dato sapere — a una fruizione rigorosamente privata; così come analogo destino sembrano aver avuto le pagine di *Heliogalbalus*,[19] un singolare racconto a chiave in cui il protagonista, depravato "princeps lenonum", ha caratteri così simili al tiranno che è al centro della vibrante denuncia *post mortem* contenuta nella *Declamatio in tyrannos*.

Ben diversi sono i toni delle scritture destinate alla ricezione pubblica e al decoro compostamente cortigiano di quella che, non molti anni dopo, sarà la strada obbligata della "dissimulazione onesta": la scelta da parte del Garzoni di scrivere uno *speculum principis* come il *De eruditione* e di concepirlo come una parafrasi ragionata delle *auctoritates* più accreditate, prevedibili e canoniche rientra entro un'opzione di ragionata e opportunistica prudenza.

Se dunque lo si sa intravedere tra gli anfratti di un'argomentazione moderata e spesso reticente nella sua dominante vocazione epidittica, anche nel trattato garzoniano le convenzioni del genere si modulano impercettibilmente fino a farci intravedere un orizzonte cittadino reale. Educare il principe può così essere un modo, forse l'unico che resta all'umanista cortigiano, fedele ai Bentivoglio, per indicare la strada di una conciliazione possibile tra governo signorile, istanze oligarchiche e tradizioni repubblicane, a cui è affidata la tutela, sempre più precaria e contesa, dell'identità di Bologna negli anni drammatici di quelle che saranno di lì a poco definite "le guerre d'Italia".

---

un taccuino o in un prontuario di formule pronte al riuso, l'annotazione garzoniana seleziona alcuni dei motivi canonici della riflessione politica intorno al tema della formazione dell'ottimo governante: il primato dell'educazione e il consiglio dei sapientes; le virtù morali, prime fra tutte la giustizia e la clemenza, che salvaguardano il principe da *inhumanitas* e crudeltà; il monito a trovare in se stessi la norma e il limite della propria volontà, in un mondo dominato dalla volubilità della fortuna, al cui gioco capriccioso i principi sono esposti non meno degli uomini comuni (Mantovani, *Educare il principe* IX-XI).
[19] Bologna, Biblioteca Universitaria, Ms. Latino, 746 cc. 48v-56v. Il protagonista di questo curioso racconto di perversione e sadismo, maestro di depravazione tanto da meritarsi il titolo di "prin*ceps* lenonum" — "Eas preibant lenones duodecim. Uni ex his qui ceteros aetate anteibat Anichino nomen erat, quod eleganti erat lingua atque animi et corpori (*sic*) viribus poterat (etenim omnem aetatem suam in lustris gurgustijsque consumpserat) principatum detulerant" (c. 49*r*) — reclama per sé lo pseudonimo di "Heliogalbalus". Su questo esperimento narrativo e una possibile interpretazione, si rimanda a Knowles Frazier 186.

Opere citate

Aegidii Romani *De regimine principum libri III*, Romae, apud Antonium Bladum, Pont. Max. Excusorem, 1556.

Anselmi Gian Mario. *Il tempo ritrovato. Padania e Umanesimo tra erudizione e storiografia*. Modena: Mucchi, 1992.

Armstrong Lawrin-Kirshner Julius (a c. di). *The politics of law in late Medieval and Renaissance Italy*. Toronto-Buffalo-London: University of Toronto Press, 2011.

Banfi Florio. *Un Umanista bolognese e i Domenicani. A proposito dell'opera inedita su Giovanni Garzoni del P. Vincenzo Domenico Fassini O.P., contenuta nel Codice Vat. Lat. 10686*. "Memorie Domenicane" 52 (1935): 365-78; 53 (1936): 14-25; 69-80.

Chines Loredana. *Valla e la grande pratica del commento a Bologna*. In *Lorenzo Valla e l'Umanesimo bolognese. Atti del Convegno Internazionale Comitato Nazionale VI centenario della nascita di Lorenzo Valla, Bologna 25-26 Gennaio 2008*. A c. di G. M. Anselmi-M. Guerra. Bologna: Bononia University Press, 2009. 17-32.

Costa Pietro. *Iurisdictio. Semantica del potere politico nella pubblicistica medievale (1100-1433)*. Milano: Giuffré, 1969.

D'Amato Alfonso. *I Domenicani a Bologna*. I. *1218-1600*. Bologna: Edizioni Studio Domenicano, 1988.

De Benedictis Angela. *Quale "Corte" per quale "Signoria"? A proposito di organizzazione e immagine del potere durante la preminenza di Giovanni II Bentivoglio*. In *Bentivolorum Magnificentia. Principe e cultura a Bologna nel Rinascimento*. A c. di B. Basile. Roma: Bulzoni, 1984. 13-33.

_____. *Retorica e Politica: dall'"Orator" di Beroaldo all'ambasciatore bolognese nel rapporto tra respublica cittadina e governo pontificio*. In *Sapere e/è potere. Discipline, Dispute e Professioni nell'Università Medievale e Moderna. Il caso bolognese a confronto. Atti del 4° Convegno, Bologna, 13-15 Aprile 1989. Dalle discipline ai ruoli sociali*. Vol. III. A c. di A. De Benedictis. Bologna: Istituto per la Storia di Bologna, 1991. 411-38.

_____. *Repubblica per contratto. Bologna: una città europea nello Stato della Chiesa*. Bologna: Il Mulino, 1995.

_____. *Identità politica di un governo popolare: la memoria (culturale) dei Tribuni della Plebe*, in *Diritti in memoria, carità di patria. Tribuni della plebe e governo popolare a Bologna (XIV-XVIII secolo)*. A c. di A. De Benedictis. Bologna: Clueb, 1999. 13-83.

_____. *Lo "stato popolare di libertà": pratica di governo e cultura di governo (1376-1506)*, in *Storia di Bologna. 2. Bologna nel Medioevo*. A c. di O. Capitani. Bologna: Bononia University Press, 2007. 899-950.

Fantuzzi Giovanni, *Notizie degli Scrittori Bolognesi*, IV, Bologna, Stamperia di San Tommaso d'Aquino, 1784. (Rist. anast. Bologna, Forni, 1965.)

Garzoni Giovanni. *Historiae Bononienses*. Ed. critica a c. di A. Mantovani. Bologna: Bononia University Press, 2010.

_____. *De eruditione principum. De principis officio*. Ed. critica a c. di A. Mantovani. Roma: Edizioni di Storia e Letteratura, 2014.

Gilli Patrick. *Vie active, vie contemplative chez les humanistes italiens du XVe siècle*. In *Vie active et vie contemplative au Moyen Âge et au tournant de la Renaissance*. Ch. Trottman (s.d.). Rome: École française de Rome, 2009. 425-42.

Greci Roberto. *Bologna nel Duecento*. In *Storia di Bologna*. Vol. 2. *Bologna nel Medioevo*. A c. di O. Capitani. Bologna: Bononia University Press, 2007. 537-63.

Kantorowicz Ernst Hartwig. *I due corpi del Re*. Torino: Einaudi, 1989.
Knowles Frazier Alison. *Possible Lives: Authors and Saints in Renaissance Italy*. New York: Columbia UP, 2005.
Lambertini Roberto. *Governo ideale e riflessione politica dei frati mendicanti nella prima metà del Trecento*. In *Etica e politica: le teorie dei Frati Mendicanti nel Due e Trecento. Atti del XXVI Convegno internazionale, Assisi, 15-17 Ottobre 1998*. Spoleto: Centro Studi Italiani sull'Alto Medioevo, 1999. 231-77.
_____. *"Philosophus videtur tangere tres rationes." Egidio Romano lettore e interprete della Politica nel III libro del De regimine principum*. In "Documenti e studi sulla tradizione filosofica medievale" 1 (1990) 1: 277-326.
Lind L. R. *The Letters of Giovanni Garzoni. Bolognese Humanist and Physician (1419-150)*. Atlanta: Scholar Press, 1992.
Manfrè Guglielmo. *La biblioteca dell'umanista bolognese Giovanni Garzoni (1419-1505)*. In "Accademie e Biblioteche d'Italia" 27 (1959), pp. 249-278; 28 (1960), pp. 17-72.
Mantovani Alessandra. *Giovanni Garzoni e le "Historiae Bononienses". Uno storico umanista alla corte dei Bentivoglio*. In G. Garzoni. *Historiae Bononienses*. Ed. critica a c. di A. Mantovani. Bologna. Bononia University Press, 2010. 9-63.
_____. *History as Civic Vocation: Historiae Bononienses by Giovanni Garzoni*, "Storicamente" 8 (2012), art.17, DOI10.1473/stor423, http://www.storicamente.org/01_fonti/mantovani_garzoni.htm.
_____. *Educare il Principe. Giovanni Garzoni e l'"institutio principis" nella Bologna dei Bentivoglio*. In G. Garzoni. *De eruditione principum. De principis offìcio*. Ed. critica a c. di A. Mantovani. Roma: Edizioni di Storia e Letteratura, 2014. VII-LXVIII.
Orvieto Paolo. *Biografia ed aneddotica storica nei trattati umanistici 'De institutione principis' (e nel 'Principe' di Machiavelli)*. In *La Storiografia Umanistica. Atti del Convegno internazionale di studi di Messina, 22-25 Ottobre 1987*. A c. di A. Di Stefano et al.. Messina: Sicania, 1992. 1: 153-80.
Pasquali Alidosi Giovanni Niccolò. *Quinto Libro delli Antiani, Consoli, Confalonieri di Giustizia dal 1456 al 1530*. Bologna: Sebastiano Bonomi, 1621.
Pini Giorgio. *Le letture dei maestri dei frati agostiniani: Egidio Romano e Giacomo da Viterbo*, in *Libri, biblioteche e letture dei frati Mendicanti (XIII-XIV). Atti del XXXII Convegno Internazionale, Assisi, 7-9 Ottobre 2004*. Spoleto: Centro Studi Italiani sull'Alto Medioevo, 2005. 81-113.
Quaglioni Diego. *L'iniquo diritto. 'Regimen regis' e 'ius regis' nell'esegesi di I Sam. 8, 11-17 e negli 'specula principum' del tardo Medioevo*. In *Specula Principum*. A c. di A. De Benedictis con la collaborazione di A. Pisapia. Frankfurt am Mein: Vittorio Klostermann, 1999. 209-41.
_____. *Il modello del principe cristiano. Gli 'specula principum' fra Medio Evo e prima Età Moderna*. In *Modelli nella storia del pensiero politico*. A c. di V.I. Comparato. Firenze: Olschki, 1987.103-22.
_____. *Politica e diritto nel Trecento italiano. Il 'De Tyranno' di Bartolo da Sassoferrato (1314-1357)*. Firenze: Olschki, 1983.
Raimondi Ezio. *Codro e l'Umanesimo a Bologna*. Bologna: Il Mulino,1987.
_____. *olitica e Commedia. Dal Beroaldo al Machiavelli*. Bologna: Il Mulino, 1972.
Robertson Ian. *Tyranny under the Mantle of St Peter. Pope Paul II and Bologna*. Turnhout: Brepols, 2002.
Roversi Monaco Francesca. *Bene comune ed esperienza signorile*. In *Il bene comune: forme di governo e gerarchie sociali nel Basso Medioevo. Atti del XLVIII Convegno Storico Internazionale, Todi 9-12 Ottobre 2011*. Spoleto: Fondazione Centro

Italiano di Studi sull'Alto Medioevo, 2012. 419-45.
Rubinstein Nicolai. *Le dottrine politiche nel Rinascimento.* In AA.VV. *Il Rinascimento. Interpretazioni e problemi.* Roma: Laterza, 1983. 183-237.
Skinner Quentin. *Le origini del pensiero politico moderno.* I. *Il Rinascimento.* Bologna: Il Mulino, 1989.
Sorbelli Albano. *I Bentivoglio Signori di Bologna.* Bologna: Cappelli, 1969.
Terpstra Nicholas. *Civic Self-fashioning in Renaissance Bologna: Historical and Scholarly Contexts.* "Renaissance Studies" 13. 4 (1999): 389-96.
Thorndike Lynn, *Giovanni Garzoni on Ruling a City,* "Political Quarterly Review" 46 (1931), pp. 277-280.

Appendice
Bologna, Biblioteca Universitaria, Ms. Latino 741
Declamatio Johannis Garzonis in tyrannos cc. 182v-186v

Quoniam fato nostro factum dixerim, patres conscripti, ut annos quinque et viginti acerbissimum servitutis iugum subire coacti fuerimus. Eas passi sumus calamitates quas cum mihi in mentem redigo, nullis possum temperare lachrymis. Quotiens mihi fuit in animo moriendi voluntas ne tantas susciperem molestias? Quotiens qui vita cum morte commutassent eos in summa felicitate constitutos existimavi, quod a tantis miserijs alieni existerent? Sit dijs gratia: qui nos calamitosa servitute tenebat oppressos tyrannus humanis rebus excessit. Ad inferos deiectus est et in aeternam damnabitur poenam. Maximo dijs immortalibus obstringimur beneficio, qui admirabili illorum virtute a desperatione ad spem, a morte ad vitam vocati sumus. Erit igitur vestri muneris, Patres conscripti, ne tanti deorum immortalium in nos beneficij memoriam abiecisse videamur ut in triduum supplicationes fiant providere.

 Fortasse ex me quaeritis cur tantum temporis spiritum duxerit, cur defuerint qui ipsum, quando de omnibus civibus male mereretur, de medio sustulerint. Nunquam potuit neque ferro neque veneno neque igne confici. Magnam vim armatorum ad sui corporis custodiam mercede conduxerat. Sive domi sese contineret sive per urbem iter susciperet sive in villam se conijceret, non aberant armati qui, eductis gladijs, eum tuerentur. Semper agmine incedebat quadratus. Qui magnitudine animi et corporis robore praestabant a tergo, a fronte, a latere circumspiciebant. Qui litteras attulisset nequaquam ei, ni ex ipso an ferro succinctus esset, primum percontatio fieret, sui conveniendi potestatem faciebat. Qui ferro accinctus esset, illum ferrum deponere cogebatur. Neque nocte neque interdiu, ni ad cubiculi fores stationes praesidiaque disposuisset, somnum capiebat. Nullis poterat venenis absumi, quod adversus ea multis ante medicaminibus corpus firmarat. Dixisses alterum Mitridatem. Anichina meretrix est quadrantaria. Huius domus patefacta est omnium cupiditati, quod se se palam in meretricia vita collocat. Virorum alienissimorum convivijs utitur; non modo libertatis sermone sed etiam complexu et esculatione ac se homines allicit. Eius amore, quod non sine pudore commemorare possum, deperibat vir bonus et egregius, qui ut vilissimi scorti voluntati morem gereret et crudelissimo desyderio accederet, Anichinam servum in convivium accersiri iussit. Omnibus cenatis multisque verbis ultro citroque habitis ad spectaculum impudentissimi scorti miserum securi percutiendum curavit. Nunquam postea parricidio abstinuit. Nam qui semel gladium tanto scelere imbuunt, nulla res eis nisi defatigatio cedendi finem affert. Ut igitur de eo facinore per urbem habitus est sermo ad Anichinam (sese enim tenebrae intendebant) iter contuli, eam conveni, magnam sum ei, si veveno tyrannum tolleret, vim auri atque argenti pollicitus. Ut mihi assentiretur multis sum verbis hortatus. Nunquam ipsam ad sententiam meam traducere potui, causatam quod amplissima a tyranno praemia reportasset de se; si necasset, confestim actum esse. Quare in alterius rei curam animum meum converterem. Tum ipsam ut hac de re omnes celatos vellet, quibus potui precibus obsecravi. Sic re infecta domum iter retro verti. Abundabat multitudine servorum et eorum praesertim quos ab ineunte adolescentia fidelissimos constantissimosque cognoverat. Nunquam cibum aut potum sumebat quin ex servis quinque illi propinassent. Nam si ei potus, si cibus offerebatur, semper ab illis leniter pregustabatur. Quis tam amens et tam parum consideratur in quibus habitabat edibus ignem iniecisset, cum satellites instructi atque armati die noctuque parietibus obequitarent? Subijsset is dementissimam temeritatem qui nocte pertransiens manu ignem gessisset: omnibus capitis poenam constituerat. Priore anno, id quod memoria teneo, puer nescio quis huius edicti immemor nocte ignem gerens prehensus est; cui iussu tyranni carnifex nulla interiecta mora collum in laqueum inseruit. Nemo fuit quin pueri morte moveretur. Non mihi excidit unumquemque vestrum me vidisse summo dolore affectum.

Quot quanta que ab eo admissa sint scelera meministis vos, patres conscripti. Neque enim oblivisci potestis. Illa a me dedita opera omittuntur. Nos de Dijs, si dicere fas est, queri possumus, qui si erga nos vel minima fuissent misericordia commoti, nequaquam tot annos tam miseram et tam luctuosam servivissemus servitute. Ferenda fuit quam sors dederat conditio.

Tyrannus vita functus est: tanta calamitate liberati sumus. Nos, cladibus nostris docti, in posterum tempus nobis sapientius consulemus. Quod si quis imperium affectaverit nosque in servitutem redigere cogitaverit, is eandem quam Manlius Torquatus subivit fortuna, subire cogendus erit. Adsunt Athenienses, quorum virtutem imitari et possumus et debemus. Nam quanto apud eos in odio essent tyranni, maxima dederunt documenta. Si enim civem aliquem libido capiundae rei publicae invasisset, non solum interfectoribus premia statuebant, sed maximis quoque honoribus afficiendos curabant. Harmodio et Aristogitoni, cum crudelissimos tyrannis cede occidissent, statuam aeneam, quam Praxiteles politissima arte perfecerat, in foro statui iusserunt. Nullam sibi cum tyrannis volenbant esse societatem. Ut ab eis distraherentur summa curabant diligentia. Qui tyrannum exilio mulctasset fortunisque spoliasset ac, si potuisset, necasset, huic amplissimis verbis gratias agebant. Tyberius Gracchus, Spurius Melius, C. Gracchus, L. Saturninus, quod libertatem urbis tyrannide opprimere nitebantur, a nobilissimis fortissimisque civibus cede occisi sunt. Qui rei publicae studiosi erant, hos summis ad celum laudibus efferebant, quippe honestum esse nec contra naturam factum arbitrabantur. Arbitrabantur profecto hoc hominum genus adeo pestiferum et impium ut ex hominum communitate esse propulsandum. Age quanta est illa et Atheniensium et Romanorum sententia laude celebranda, qua optimos cives ut medicos imitentur hortantur? Suadent enim ut membrum, cum putret, ne aliam possit corporis partem labefactare, incidant et penitus eradicent. Sic tantam feritatem atque immanitatem, in qua nequicquam hominis est praeter figuram ac speciem, ab omni humanitate corporis prorsus extirpent.

Nulla nos igitur admiratio teneat si hi de quibus loquor Athenienses Milciadem in custodiam publicam, ubi extremum diem morte confecit, conijci iusserunt. Videbatur equidem trahi ad imperijj cupiditatem. Laudanda nimirum Herculis Thebani sententia cui, apud poetam, nulla maior deferri poterat optio quam ut tyranni, in quem omnes summo exardent odio, libaret cruorem, quod nullus gratior aras tingeret liquor nullaque magis opima victima quam tyrannus Iovi mactari posset.

Quadringentos et eo amplius annos, si historiarum scriptoribus fides habenda est, Roma libertate usa est. Id temporis non defuerunt, ut ante dixi, qui tantae urbi servitutis iugum imponere molirentur pernitiosissimi cives: Tiberius Gracchus, C. Gracchus, L. Saturninus. Alium Scipio Nasica, alium Lucius Opimius, alium C. Marius morte mulctavit. Omnes senatus iure cesos censuit. Haud sane intelligo quid hi viri praestantius efficere potuerint quam ne quid detrimenti res publica caperet providere. Cum igitur deorum immortalium beneficio in libertatem restituti fuerimus, nihil nobis ut eam conservare ac tueri possimus laboris defugiendum est. Nunquam eos qui libertatem contempsissent laude dignos censui. Nihil mea sententia vitae miserius inveniri potest quam eorum qui servitutem serviunt. Non est autem supplicationum memoria dependenda ne, ut ante dixi, ingratitudinis notam subire videamur. Ego tantum beneficium dijs immortalibus acceptum refero. Sed cum vos ad eam rem agendam propensos ferri videam, orationi meae modum statuam atque ne in posterum turpi et ignominiosa premamur servitute enixe opera dabitis.

Bologna, Biblioteca Universitaria, Ms. Latino 741
187r- 190v
Pro libertate

Quod mihi in iucundissimo conspectu vestro oblata sit dicendi facultas, patres conscripti, et gaudeo et vehementer letor, cum praesertim his de rebus sim verba facturus quae ad patriae vestrae libertatem conservandam pertinent.

Fuit haec civitas annos quinque et viginti a crudelissimo tyranno servitute oppressa. Ille caede occisus est. Maximas dijs immortalibus gratias habere et agere debemus, qui suo beneficio libertatem recuperavimus quae ut conservetur omnis a nobis enixe opera danda est. Nam si calamitatis, iatturae, dedecoris quae illo vivente passi sumus nullam abiecimus memoriam, omnes cogitationes vestras eo referetis. Enimvero nihil praestantius, nihil memoratu dignius efficere potestis quam libertatem, vobis a dijs immortalibus tributam, augere, tueri et conservare. Romani atque Athenienses, si historiarum scriptoribus fides habenda est, cum da conservandam patriae libertatem omne ingenium suum contulisset, eam gloriam consecuti sunt quae vix caelo capi posse videtur. Optimos habetis praeceptores, quorum virtutem, cum praecipua sit et singularis, imitari potestis et debetis. Erit hoc, patres conscripti, factu facilimum.

Atrocissimo tyranno ut ante dixi ferro vita erepta est. Qui consilijs vestris occurrat, si qui illi studebant propulsabuntur, erit nemo. Non me fallit ipsos qui ab hac sententia dissident. Hi sunt qui, cum per se hanc urbem lacerare non possent, sub illius scelere delere nitebantur. Quibus iniurijs nos lacessiverint non nescij estis. Illi visceribus vestris magnificas domos extruxerunt. Illi optimos cives excruciatos necarunt. Illi virginibus vestris stupra intulerunt. Exuenda est in eos omnis inhumanitas. Adhibenda omnis crudelitas in sceleratos et crudeles cives. Par pari referendum est. Cogendi sunt dignam suis sceleribus poenam suscipere. Mulctentur vita, exilio, carcere perpetuo, publicentur eorum bona. Quod si eos in urbe retinendos censueritis, magno metu percellor ne quid mali in vos machinentur. Non est his habenda fides qui civium bonis fortunisque oculos semper adijciunt. Ita effrenati et pene dementes sunt ut auctores sint egregij ad animos imperitorum excitandos et ad ineunda evertendae libertatis consilia. Difficile est, ut a philosophis sapientissime traditur, sensum confirmatum deponere. Est igitur periniquum et non ferendum quod urbem colant. Quantum coniectura consequi possum, universus populus, sua calamitate doctus, ad libertatem exardet. Nihil iocundius sibi accidere arbitratur quam si servitutis iugum deponat. Adeo dulcis est libertas. Videmus feras bestas, cum vinciuntur aut clauduntur, refringere claustra cupientes. Miramini, patres conscripti, illa Romana prodigia atque miracula, Horatium, Mutium, Cloeliam? Omnes pro tuenda libertate nullum mortis genus recusandum duxerunt. Potuit Brutus liberos, cum de revocandis in urbem regibus inivisse consilia comperisset, occidere: liberi populi maiestatem quam liberorum vitam potiorem habuit. Potuerunt Decij se dijs manibus devovere et in confertissima se hostium tela conijcere, tanta libertatem patriae benivolentia complectebantur. Athenienses, quae pro tuenda libertate gesserint, sapientissimi veterum memoriae prodiderunt, ut constet eos Romanorum nequaquam fuisse dissimiles. His ex rebus intellegi datur eum non solum bonum verum et optimum civem qui se ab omnibus caeteris actionibus et cogitationibus ad defendendam conservandamque libertatem contulisset.

Danda igitur erit opera ut discordiae discidiaeque tollantur cum saepenumero incidant. Nulla inter nos sit disceptatio. Omnia cum summa concordia a vobis gerantur. De his quae ad conservandam libertatem pertinent inter vos conveniat. Si quae a Micipsa animam extremam, ut aiunt, labijs tenente tradita sunt praecepta Iugurtha memoria tenuisset, nunquam Hiempsalem, nunquam Adherbalem necandos curasset, nunquam ipsum populus Romanus in triumpho cathenis opertum aspexisset. Suadebat Micipsa, ut liberi Iugurtham, quod eos aetate anteibat, colerent, venerarentur, diligerent. Nullae essent inter ipsos diversae sententiae nec distinctae. Omnes mutuo se amore complecterentur, quod res maximas discordia in perniciem duceret.

Nulla potest urbibus maior clades inferri quam si a civibus inter se discidentibus teneatur. Romani quadrigentos prope annos, teste M. Tullio, libertate usi sunt. Tantam felicitatem, tot triumphos, tot victorias de atrocissimis hostibus reportatas, uni acceptas concordiae referant. Ubi enim inter eos qui rei publicae praeerant discordia nata est, confestim Romanum imperium corruit. Hinc Syllanae, illinc Marianae, hinc Pompeianae, illinc Cesarianae factiones. Quo res Romana deducta sit eventus docet. Quid loquar de Atheniensibus qui, post maximos hostiles exercitus proelio superatos, discordia civium eo calamitatis devenerunt ut Athenae funditus eversae sint.

Quae cum ita sint, patres conscripti, etsi supervacaneum sit ad libertatem concordiamque servandam hortor. Vos ad caelum posteri summi laudibus efferent. Omnes vobis cum si urbi nostrae cui a crudelissimo tyranno et ea quidem molesta acciderunt benigne factum fuerit, bene actum existimabunt. Reliquum est, quoniam cadaver nullis - ut meritum erat - imaginibus, nullis exequiis, nulla pompa, nulla laudatione in sepulchro constitutum est, ut consules et tribuni plebis creerentur. Ipsorum omnis ratio et cogitatio nihil aliud sit quam constans, perpetua, fortis, invicta libertatis defensio. Plura non dicam cum unumquenque videam id effecturum quod quivis spectatae virtutis civis urbi nostrae conducibile iudicabit.

Matteo Bosisio

"Fuggendo da lui fuggo la morte": libertà, vendetta, polemica anti-cortigiana nella *Panfila* di Antonio Cammelli

Sinossi: L'articolo prende in esame la tragedia *Panfila* di Antonio Cammelli, esemplata secondo il modello di *Decameron* 4.1. L'opera, dedicata a Isabella d'Este nel 1499, si configura quale accusa diretta contro il potere cortigiano. Il contributo si sofferma sulle caratteristiche formali e contenutistiche della tragedia; in particolare, l'analisi si incentra sui conflitti che animano i personaggi e sui concetti di libertà e vendetta da loro incarnati ed espressi. Al termine dell'opera è possibile rinvenire in Tindaro — il cortigiano che determina la morte dei giovani protagonisti per rivalersi dell'anziano re Demetrio — un *alter ego* ideale di Cammelli, che ne proietta le spinte iconoclaste e ne concretizza le denunce alla società del tempo.
Parole chiave: Antonio Cammelli, Tragedia, *Panfila*, *Decameron*, Isabella d'Este, Rinascimento.

I. Introduzione: la *Panfila* di Cammelli e la polemica anti-cortigiana
1. Nella civiltà letteraria di corte del XV secolo non è raro rinvenire testi che denunciano l'opacità del potere politico, la rigidità di certe regole produttive e comportamentali, le ingiustizie perpetrate da iniqui meccanismi di selezione della classe dirigente.[1] Nondimeno, gli scrittori affidano sovente la ricerca di autonomia dal sistema di committenza cortigiano a una protesta endogena e non ostile alla corte stessa e alla sua cultura. Le rivendicazioni più forti e drammatiche si verificano allorché gli scrittori vivono una situazione di carcerazione e di restringimento delle proprie libertà individuali.

È il caso, ad esempio, di Pandolfo Collenuccio, il quale nel 1488 viene imprigionato a causa di gravi contrasti sorti con Giovanni Sforza, signore di Pesaro. Ai giorni della detenzione, durata sedici mesi, viene dedicata la famosa canzone *Alla morte*. Essa si configura quale mesta resa del poeta, che non manca certo di riferire i soprusi sofferti, ma può solo invocare l'intervento della Morte quale soluzione per porre fine a ogni dolore.[2]

---

[1] Sulla questione e, più in generale, sulla letteratura di corte del Quattrocento, si vedano Gaeta 149-255; Esposito; Tissoni Benvenuti 435-46; Meneghetti 185-99; Rinaldi 1993 e 2010; Malato; Cavallo 297-321; Montagnani; Cappelli 73-91.
[2] Collenuccio 117.65-68 e 76-80: "questa c'ha nome vita falso in terra, / ch'altro è che fatica, affanno e stento, / sospir, pianto e lamento, / dolore, infermità, terrore e guerra?"

Parimenti, Giovanni Antonio De Petruciis — ritenuto uno dei responsabili dell'organizzazione della congiura dei baroni a danno di Ferdinando I d'Aragona e perciò recluso nella Torre di San Vincenzo per quattro mesi sino alla condanna capitale (1486)[3] — scrive un esile canzoniere che consta di settantasette sonetti e un sirventese. I testi accolgono le riflessioni di un intellettuale che medita sulla natura umana, sulle ipocrisie della corte e sul fato; la sorte non lascia spazio ad alcuna istanza di autodeterminazione, tanto che la raccolta si apre con un sonetto volto a dimostrare la mancanza di libertà del genere umano. Il rapporto con la corte risulta ambiguo, poiché alle ripetute critiche, velate o esplicite, indirizzate al sovrano aragonese e ai suoi collaboratori[4] si accompagnano componimenti in cui prevale la nostalgia per una realtà ormai perduta.[5]

2. Un'accusa diretta verso il potere cortigiano e i regnanti sembra provenire, invece, dalla tragedia *Panfila* di Antonio Cammelli.[6] Informazioni preziose circa le origini dell'opera vengono fornite dall'autore in una lettera del 18 giugno

---

[…] Tu sei quella, tu sei quella benigna / madre, che i vil pensier dai petti sgombri / e' nostri mali adombri / di lunga oblivion d'immortal scorte: / soccorrimi adunque, o graziosa Morte". Sullo scrittore si vedano Tanda e Bertini.

[3] In merito rinviamo a Tateo 111-28 e Caliri 149-75.

[4] De Petruciis 44.3-8: "dove è fuggita la piacevolecza, / dove li lodi che dalo suo core / parevan che venissero, et con amore? / O re Ferrante, con quanta prestecza / li hai voltati in una gran fierezza / contra de me innocente de omne errore!".

[5] La vita di corte è contraddistinta da "li nostri risi con li iochi e feste, / tante allegricze con mutar de veste, / tante diverse e varie canzone, / el docto disputar le questione / de omne doctrina, e mai de cose meste" (25.2-6). Si veda anche 37.1-4: "pompusi fausti con diverse gale, / lieti triumphi con polite feste, / varïe insegne de oro et supra veste, / superbi nomi de case reale".

[6] Antonio Cammelli, detto il Pistoia dalla città d'origine, nasce nel 1436. Il padre era stato un politico locale di una certa rilevanza. Nel 1479 si trova alla corte di Niccolò da Correggio, in cui spicca per la qualità delle sue poesie comiche e burlesche; risulta a Ferrara prima della guerra tra il ducato estense e Venezia (1482-1484). Nel 1485 viene nominato contestabile con funzione di gabellino, ovvero di esattore delle tasse, presso la porta di Santa Croce di Reggio. Nel 1497 viene esautorato da tale incarico, che otterrà di nuovo due anni dopo. Le difficoltà incontrate presso la corte estense, la scarsa considerazione goduta, l'impossibilità di emergere, la diffidenza manifestata dagli altri cortigiani nei suoi confronti danno materia per numerosi testi poetici. Nel 1490 trascorre un breve soggiorno a Roma, in cui scrive componimenti contro i vizi e l'immoralità del clero nonché i famosi cinque sonetti a Djem, figlio di Maometto II, imprigionato dal papa Innocenzo VIII. I testi encomiastici rivolti a Ludovico il Moro e la conoscenza di personaggi dell'*entourage* ludoviciano fanno sospettare qualche possibile collaborazione occasionale con la corte sforzesca. Sono più saldi i legami con Mantova, segnatamente con Isabella d'Este, cui dedica vari sonetti. Sullo scrittore, che morirà a Ferrara nel 1502, rinviamo a Clarizia; De Robertis 277-86; Pallone; Olivastri; Rossi 2005, 43-61 e 2008 e Cammelli 2006.

Libertà, vendetta, polemica anti-cortigiana nella *Panfila* di A. Cammelli   123

1499 a Isabella d'Este.[7] Cammelli comunica l'invio di un "libretto della Tragedia nominata *Pamphila*" — finita di comporre nel corso della "quaresima passata" — e un "nuntio delli Sonetti faceti" (D'Ancona 375-76). Le indicazioni aggiunte in seguito escludono una rappresentazione sulla scena, in quanto sembrano chiari gli inviti a leggere il testo durante l'estate e a farlo rilegare in modo appropriato.[8] È probabile che l'opera fosse stata dedicata in precedenza a un altro signore, forse a Ercole I d'Este, come si può desumere dal sottotitolo riportato nella *princeps*: "tragedia de Antonio da Pistoia a lo ill.mo et excell.mo duca Ercule de Ferrara" (Cammelli 1508).

Il consiglio di leggere il testo e di non rappresentarlo — suggerimento comune a quello che fornirà nel 1502 Galeotto Del Carretto con un'altra tragedia, la *Sofonisba* — viene giustificato dall'eccezionalità dell'opera, che si incarica di rendere lo schema, la struttura, le forme della tragedia classica. Se nel teatro volgare del tardo Quattrocento molti miti caratterizzati da una conclusione luttuosa vengono proposti al fine di ribaltarne l'esito mediante un sorprendente lieto fine, nella *Panfila*, per converso, Cammelli non lascia spazio ad alcuna redenzione palingenetica o a miracolose resurrezioni.[9]

3. La trama e l'ambientazione dell'opera sono riprese dalla celebre novella 4.1 del *Decameron*:[10] l'azione si trasferisce dalla Salerno medievale alla Tebe antica (città simbolo della tragedia greca); Tancredi diventa Demetrio,[11] mentre i due amanti sono chiamati Panfila e Filostrato.[12] Vengono poi aggiunti altri personaggi: spiccano, oltre a servitori e damigelle minori, le figure di Tindaro (domestico di Filostrato nel *Decameron*) — che personifica un anziano funzionario di corte, il cui alacre servigio non ha avuto alcun riconoscimento — e del consigliere del re Pandero.

Se nel Cinquecento gli scrittori attingeranno dal *Decameron* soprattutto quale modello comico ai fini della caratterizzazione dei personaggi, della

---

[7] Sulla marchesa mantovana e i suoi rapporti mecenatistici con letterati e artisti si rimanda a Luzio e Renier. Si precisa che il volume raccoglie alcuni articoli pubblicati dai due studiosi negli anni 1899-1903.
[8] D'Ancona 376: "[...] questa basti per legierla talvolta la Excell.ia Vostra in villa per fuggire, o per il troppo caldo o per le noiose piogge, lo otio: e se la opera fosse per più degno poeta di me composta, la averìa in carta membrana con maiuscole d'oro fatta scrivere e pingere: ma tale qual è l'opera, tal vesta porta".
[9] Sul teatro nel Quattrocento, segnaliamo da ultimo Bosisio 2016 (in corso di stampa, in cds o in press).
[10] Sulla fortuna della novella nella letteratura e nell'iconografia quattrocentesca, si fa riferimento a Poletti 2004, 101-39 e 2007, 239-302.
[11] Il nome ricorda quello di Demetrio Poliorcete, le cui feroci imprese sono descritte nel *De casibus*, 4.14.
[12] Nel *Decameron* troviamo Panfilo, re dell'ultima giornata e narratore sovente di novelle dal contenuto amoroso (es. 2.7; 5.1; 7.9; 8.2 e 9.6), e Filostrato (il cui nome significa "vinto da amore"), che proprio nella IV giornata diviene il re della brigata.

mimesi stilistico-linguistica e della rielaborazione dei temi del gioco delle parti, della beffa, della contrapposizione ironica tra sacro e profano, Cammelli ne sfrutta la valenza tragica.[13]

II. La *Panfila* e la "tragedia delle corti"
1. La tragedia si discosta dalla novella soprattutto per l'inserimento di una tematica inedita, che riguarda la vita cortigiana. Essa è contrassegnata quale inautentica, frutto di ipocrisie, sopraffazioni, invidie. L'amore, a differenza di quanto sostengono i drammaturghi milanesi coevi come Baldassar Taccone e Gaspare Visconti (Bosisio 2012, 11-52), non può essere coltivato a corte né si possono manifestare atti di lealtà, di giustizia, di saggezza. Il ruolo del cortigiano è inutile, perché i consigli ragionevoli di Pandero non verranno ascoltati dal sovrano; Tindaro, invece, palesa come la frustrazione e il risentimento possano scatenare pericolose idee di vendetta. Sarà quest'ultimo a riferire a Demetrio la storia d'amore tra la figlia e il servo Filostrato per assecondare il suo desiderio di rivalsa sulla casata regnante. Ciò che nel *Decameron* Tancredi scopre per puro caso, nella tragedia è determinato dal raggiro di Tindaro.

Già il discorso del re in apertura di tragedia introduce gli argomenti principali dell'opera:[14] Demetrio confessa alla figlia la fatica e la pena provate a governare (1.1-6). La paura per i tradimenti, le congiure e le guerre fanno rimpiangere a Demetrio di non essere stato un privato cittadino. Dopo le parole di Panfila di conforto al sovrano, segue un elogio del servo ideale, incarnato da Filostrato (1.105-41). La descrizione delle virtù del giovane viene accompagnata per analogia dalla lode della primavera (1.142-75). Le immagini di rinascita e rigogliosità aumentano in Panfila l'amore per Filostrato (1.180-221).

Nel secondo atto compare sulla scena Tindaro, il quale espone le sue osservazioni circa l'inadeguatezza dei regnanti (2.89-242). Il discorso affronta anche la questione della sfortuna dei servi e dell'ingiustizia della vita di corte, in cui si sperimentano l'odio, le invidie, le adulazioni, la superbia (2.104-33). Lo scrittore si serve di questa figura per palesare al lettore una realtà evidente, ammissibile a corte grazie alla marginalità del personaggio rispetto ai protagonisti della vicenda e al suo ruolo di antagonista.

Il terzo atto è formato da due scene speculari: nella prima Filostrato riferisce a Tindaro, che si servirà del giovane quale mero strumento di rivincita, di essersi innamorato di Panfila (3.1-132); nella seconda Demetrio — che con un veloce passaggio narrativo è stato informato da Tindaro — delibera a Pandero la punizione da infliggere a Filostrato (3.133-223).

Nel quarto atto si giunge allo scontro tra gli amanti e il re, mentre il quinto,

---

[13] Si vedano almeno Borsellino 1-33; Stäuble 1975-1976, 103-17 e 2009, 37-47 e Perocco 23-36.
[14] Si cita da Cammelli 1983, 403-68.

Libertà, vendetta, polemica anti-cortigiana nella *Panfila* di A. Cammelli

che aderisce in parte alle ultime sequenze della vicenda raccontata nel *Decameron*, si distingue per le esitazioni di Pandero; il servo, fedele confidente del padrone, non si esime dal criticare il re, non più capace di governare a causa dell'età avanzata (5.1-45). Tuttavia, la ritrattazione è parziale, giacché alla fine del discorso e nell'ultima scena il servitore tornerà a giurare devozione eterna nei confronti di Demetrio (5.363-68).

I poli antitetici in conflitto non risultano solo due, come in Boccaccio: alla contrapposizione che separa amore e giovinezza da onore e vecchiaia si aggiunge la prospettiva di Tindaro. Sicché viene messo in scena uno scontro fatale, una "tragedia delle corti" (Aurigemma 17): l'amore dei due giovani viene osteggiato dal re, il quale è a sua volta avversato da Tindaro; egli concretizza la propria vendetta rendendo esplicita la relazione della figlia del sovrano con il servo Filostrato. Alla fine, Tindaro — unico personaggio a portare a termine i propri propositi — scapperà dalla corte, Filostrato verrà ucciso, Panfila si suiciderà, mentre un resipiscente Demetrio si assumerà la colpa dell'accaduto.[15]

2. I temi espressi intorno alla corruzione e alle ingiustizie che albergano presso le corti e l'incapacità delle classi dirigenti di governare in modo retto affiorano pure nella raccolta delle rime dello scrittore, dedicata a Isabella d'Este (Biblioteca Ambrosiana, Milano, H 223 inf.). La silloge — che comprende più di cinquecento sonetti, un capitolo ternario in morte di Beatrice d'Este e un testo in prosa esemplato sulla scorta dei dialoghi dei morti di Luciano[16] — risulta attraversata da diverse tematiche (es. vita familiare, caricature di donne e di personaggi singolari, argomenti moralistici, satira anticlericale, polemiche e invettive, corrispondenza con amici, sonetti "alla burchia").[17] Uno spazio di

---

[15] Una ricognizione intorno ai vocaboli più frequenti del testo aiuta a comprendere l'insistenza di Cammelli su tali concetti. Su 2789 forme registrate, possiamo ripartire il lessico impiegato in tre macro-ambiti: *a)* amore e gioventù ("amor": 33; "amore": 25; "cuore": 17; "cor": 15; "giovene" e "gioveni": 5 ciascuna; "amato": 4; "amoroso": 3; "giovanetto" e "gioventute": 3); *b) forma mentis* dell'anziano regnante, basata su un'etica 'dell'onore e della vergogna' ("vergogna": 15; "vecchio": 12; "età": 10; "onor" e "punito": 7; "errore": 6; "vecchi": 6; "crudeltà": 5; "colpa", "sdegno" e "vecchiezza": 4; "vecchia": 3): *c)* mentalità di Tindaro ("servi" e "vendetta": 10; "servo": 8; "corte": 7; "regno": 5; "invidia": 4). Tutto ciò viene inserito entro uno sfondo in cui dominano un destino inviolabile e acute sofferenze ("morte": 31; "fortuna": 18; "morire": 13; "morir" e "morto": 11; "crudeltà": 5; "pianti" e "pianto": 5).

[16] Nel *Dialogo* si finge che l'anima del poeta, una volta deceduto, raggiunga le porte dell'Inferno, dinanzi alle quali incontra Caronte. I due parlano di diversi argomenti: astrologia, alchimia, medicina, religione e clero. Proseguendo il viaggio, viene mostrata allo scrittore la geografia ultramondana: la valle dello Stige, l'albero Vanegio, il Lethe, il Flegetonte, il Cocito, il recinto dei sapienti, i Campi Elisi. Alla fine, egli giunge al cospetto di Plutone, il quale, in segno di stima, gli permette di fare ritorno sulla terra. Sull'opera rimandiamo a Rozzoni 74-93.

[17] Rimane fondamentale lo studio complessivo di Percopo. Si citerà da Cammelli 1908.

rilievo viene conferito a testi di interesse storico-politico e di critica verso le corti, di cui forniamo di seguito un breve prospetto.

Nel sonetto 369 il poeta si duole perché un signore, la cui identità non viene rivelata, dà credito alle maldicenze di "qualche arpia", che gli consiglia di non fare accedere il poeta alla propria cerchia (v. 7); la forte concorrenza tra i cortigiani costringe l'io poetico a vivere di stenti (44), a guisa di un "frate osservante" (45.11). Del resto, egli viene sovente superato da altri concorrenti (50-51). Il motivo è rintracciato nella "troppa fede" e "nell'esser leale" (49.10-11); questi valori sono dannosi se praticati a corte, in cui per fare carriera bisogna "simular parole", "sapere il gusto e quel ch'uom più desia" (379.2 e 4). L'unica consolazione risiede nella possibilità di "veder la vendetta in poco e in breve" (49.19).[18]

Gli uomini che compongono le corti si distinguono per una serie di vizi e di azioni disoneste: presso i signori dominano le false promesse, le vane "parole", le continue "bugie", l'"invidia", gli "adulator", il "Dispetto", la "Ingiuria", il "Tradimento", l'"Avaritia" (233.2, 6, 8, 10, 12, 13 e 14). I superbi e i detrattori formano una categoria alquanto rappresentata: tra questi, Timoteo Bendedei pare sempre "di rabbia pien", "in odio ha il viver suo vicioso e scelo / la terra e 'l mare, e chi l'ode e chi 'l vede" (281.7 e 13-14). A corte non si possono stringere amicizie: ad esempio, l'io poetico stimava degne di rispetto tre persone, che, dopo aver ottenuto incarichi importanti, si erano comportate in modo sleale nei suoi confronti (283). Ciò nonostante, il successo non costituisce un parametro affidabile per giudicare l'operato degli uomini, poiché è facile cadere in disgrazia (72; 184; 302; 357-58).

Non mancano frequenti attacchi rivolti ai sovrani, complici inermi della *finis Italiae*, della perdita di indipendenza a seguito delle spedizioni di Carlo VIII e Luigi XII:[19] le divisioni tra gli stati italiani, l'inconsapevolezza della gravità della situazione, le diffidenze reciproche incoraggiano le strategie dei francesi.[20] Gli "italici mastin", i "crudi tyranni" si affrontano per aggiungere territori irrilevanti ai loro regni e non capiscono che, invece, occorre allearsi e

---

[18] Il termine "vendetta" ricorre con insistenza (28 volte): 41.16; 72.5; 115.13; 146.17; 185.5; 283.11; 306.13; 335.4; 354.8 e 17; 372.3; 382.2 e 19; 394.6; 410.17; 415.8; 421.14; 425.19; 431.12; 452.14; 462.17; 472.18; 484.20; 485.16; 492.2; 514.4; 515.4; 523.6.

[19] 529.1-4: "io ti mando un capitol fatto adesso / de Italia, ove i pensier tuo' exaltar possi: / udiralla smembrata insino a gli ossi / col capo chino e 'l corpo genuflesso". Si vedano, inoltre, le seguenti battute contenute nel *Dialogo* (19-20) "*A*: [...] 'dim[m]i come vivon quelli tuoi Signori hora'. *S*: 'male, perché l'uno aita a far cader l'altro, né si accorgono che 'l primo non gionge al fondo, che 'l secondo trabocca'. *A*: 'così va chi non mira se non quello che ha denanti alli piedi, et così andranno tutti li altri, fin che Italia sia ben disolata'".

[20] 452.12-13: "molti occhi stanno aperti ad un tagliere, / pochi son che cognoscano i lor guai".

difendersi dagli stranieri (461.2).
Ludovico il Moro, elogiato lungo numerosi sonetti (es. 70, 371, 378, 383, 391-392, 395-399, 413, 417-423), diviene poi il bersaglio polemico dello scrittore, in quanto la figura del duca esprime la tracotanza, l'insipienza dei regnanti italiani. Lo Sforza viene raffigurato altresì quale personaggio superbo, "pusillo", "tiranno vil", che ha conquistato il potere solo grazie a un colpo di stato ed è ora pronto a fuggire (497.11 e 16).[21]

III. Portare la tragedia a corte
1. L'inserimento di questioni impegnative e attuali nella *Panfila*, l'ambientazione di corte, la vicenda funesta, la sostanziale vittoria impunita del servitore Tindaro sulla tirannia del re Demetrio nonché il genere stesso praticato da Cammelli dovevano trovare alcune giustificazioni, tali da consentire un'operazione ardita e sperimentale. Alcuni temi sono resi ammissibili per un pubblico cortigiano grazie a calibrati accorgimenti: le responsabilità del sovrano vengono attenuate dalla sua vecchiaia e dall'intervento della Fortuna nella storia;[22] all'infedeltà di Tindaro si contrappone l'atteggiamento leale di Pandero e Tinolo; alle rivendicazioni di Panfila sull'autenticità dei propri sentimenti fanno da contraltare i dubbi sull'Amore, enunciati in punto di morte da Filostrato.

In aggiunta, lo scrittore — che, come ricordato, non concepisce la *Panfila* quale opera rappresentabile — legittima il proprio testo grazie all'elaborazione dell'ipotesto boccacciano e all'inserimento di un "argumento" pronunciato da Seneca. Il filosofo, che collega *lato sensu* la storia della tragedia alla propria esperienza vissuta presso la corte neroniana,[23] dichiara di aver scritto la tragedia da giovane e sostiene di essere tornato sulla terra in virtù di un permesso accordatogli da Plutone.

L'espediente della comparsa di Seneca e la finzione della composizione dell'opera sotto sua ispirazione permettono a Cammelli di cautelarsi, di motivare le scelte diegetiche e strutturali del testo. La presenza del tragediografo, infatti, non è dettata da una reale imitazione, da un'ispirazione diretta alle sue opere, ma soltanto da una necessità di nobilitazione.[24] Inoltre, la dichiarazione esplicita

---

[21] I lessemi "tiranno" e suoi derivati risultano attestati nella silloge in undici occasioni (399.7; 454.7; 457.7; 458.8; 461.2; 476.16; 497.16; 499.1²; 514.13²).
[22] Invece, in Boccaccio Tancredi si macchia di un'azione sanguinosa nella vecchiaia, ma la sua mente non si indebolisce a causa dell'età avanzata. Cfr. 4.1, 3: "Tancredi, prencipe di Salerno, fu signore assai umano e di benigno ingegno, se egli nell'amoroso sangue nella sua vecchiezza non s'avesse le mani bruttate".
[23] vv. 4-6: "io son di quel Morale / el spirto, a cui el corpo fe' Nerone / morire inanzi il corso naturale".
[24] L'unico legame potrebbe essere istituito con l'*Octavia*, tragedia che mette in scena la feroce tirannia di Nerone; la paternità senecana dell'opera, negata dalla maggior parte della critica recente, non veniva messa in discussione ai tempi di Cammelli.

della fonte serve a mettere in luce l'originalità della *Panfila*, ad affermare un primato: le tragedie dello scrittore latino, a differenza dei commediografi Plauto e Terenzio e di quanto avverrà nel pieno Cinquecento (Jacquot), non avevano ancora goduto di grande fortuna.[25]

Le parole di Seneca e l'episodio stesso del ritorno sulla terra al fine di recare una nuova tragedia sembrano ricalcare, oltre al *Dialogo*, il prologo del *Timone* di Boiardo, recitato da Luciano di Samosata, e quello della *Pasitea*, in cui Cecilio Stazio lascia i Campi Elisi per suggerire a Gaspare Visconti il tema dell'opera (Visconti 342-96). Il tentativo di competere con il modello della *Pasitea*, che si era in parte posta il compito di restituire i caratteri regolari della commedia antica, si spiega con il progetto conforme della *Panfila*, nella quale Cammelli cerca di imitare le forme e la struttura della tragedia classica.

2. Ci soffermiamo ora sui passaggi del testo in cui risalta il conflitto tra amore-onore-vendetta e vengono espresse diverse richieste di libertà (morale e personale) per mostrare le implicazioni ideologiche più significative e le scelte stilistiche di maggior rilievo. Il primo atto, che non deriva dalla novella del *Decameron*, viene interamente occupato dal confronto tra re Demetrio e la figlia Panfila. Il sovrano, che afferma di avere "septanta anni" (v. 25), sviluppa un ragionamento circa la condizione delle persone di elevata classe sociale. In particolare "gli alti gradi de la signoria / fan molte fiate ai prìncipi parere / la morte assai più aspra" (vv. 1-3); invece, chi versa in umili condizioni interpreta la morte come la fine "d'ogni dispiacere" (v. 6).

La premessa viene confutata da Demetrio stesso, in quanto la vita di un re risulta contrassegnata da "affanni" e da un continuo "dubio" (vv. 23 e 26). Egli sospetta spesso che insorga qualche "ascoso inganno" e teme che i servitori siano corrotti (v. 30). Il re si dice pronto ad abdicare, in quanto considera la vita un "lutto" (v. 43); soltanto l'"onor" (v. 45), come abbiamo visto termine chiave che marca la caratterizzazione del personaggio e le sue azioni, lo trattiene dalle intenzioni espresse.[26]

---

[25] Nel secolo XV si conoscono quattro edizioni collettive delle tragedie (Ferrara, Belforti 1478; Venezia, De Suardi, 1492; Venezia, Capcasa, 1493; Venezia, Tacuino, 1498) e tre volgarizzamenti, probabilmente mai messi in scena: il primo, in terza rima dell'*Agamennone*, viene realizzato da Evangelista Fossa e stampato nel 1497 (Venezia, Monferà); il secondo, sempre in terzine dell'*Ippolito*, risulta approntato da Pizio da Montevarchi (Venezia, Pensa da Mandello, 1497); il terzo, dell'*Hercules furens*, è messo a punto dal medesimo autore e conservato in forma manoscritta presso la Biblioteca Classense di Ravenna (ms. 106). Una disamina puntuale si trova in Rossetto 24-42.

[26] Le considerazioni citate potrebbero derivare dal *De infelicitate principum* di Poggio Bracciolini (1440). Il dialogo tra Cosimo de' Medici e gli umanisti Niccolò Niccoli, Carlo Marsuppini e Poggio stesso parte dalla questione della condizione dei funzionari della corte papale, ma presto vira sulla felicità dei regnanti. Costoro, secondo Niccoli, non possono aspirare a tale condizione, poiché il potere da essi esercitato rappresenta uno

Libertà, vendetta, polemica anti-cortigiana nella *Panfila* di A. Cammelli   129

Segue una considerazione, che chiama in causa direttamente Panfila, di inaudita contravvenzione alle leggi della società cortigiana (vv. 52-57):

> E creder dèi che una maritata
> stia molto peggio, figliola, di te,
> la quale è serva e tu sei liberata.
> O quante già ne furno e quante ne è
> che vivon serve, e 'l marito hanno seco
> qual non gli observan né patto né fé!

L'affermazione pare una sorta di controcanto della morale ufficiale di corte, di indiretta conferma delle tesi anti-matrimoniali di cui Orfeo si fa portatore nella "fabula" di Poliziano (vv. 261-92). La risposta di Panfila, per stessa ammissione della giovane,[27] non può proporre una visione alternativa, una soluzione forte alle preoccupazioni del padre. Ella si limita ad augurare al re di vivere ancora a lungo, di cercare conforto nel "piacere" e di dilettarsi con "canti suoni balli feste e giochi" (vv. 73 e 75).

Demetrio, a seguito del confronto, inizia a elogiare le virtù eccelse del suo miglior servitore, ossia Filostrato. Questi, che presto tradirà la fiducia del re, si dimostra sempre "fidele e obediente", "prudente", "gentile" (vv. 109, 111, 130); in aggiunta, le numerose qualità intellettuali ed etiche sono specchio della sua bellezza. Il discorso presenta poi un brusco cambiamento, in quanto Demetrio svolge un inno alla primavera intessuto di *topoi*, di richiami mitologici, di immagini petrarchesche.[28] Tale *excursus* (vv. 142-75) sembra inopportuno, in quanto pronunciato da un personaggio anziano e che, per giunta, pochi versi addietro aveva delineato un bilancio irrimediabile dell'esistenza umana. Non a caso Panfila, una volta uscito il padre di scena, incolpa Demetrio di non essersi accorto dei propri sentimenti. La ragione di questa insensibilità viene rintracciata nella vecchiaia del personaggio, incapace di interpretare i reali desideri della figlia.[29]

3. L'inizio del secondo atto riprende il tema amoroso del precedente, poiché Filostrato confessa di essersi innamorato di Panfila. Le sensazioni ambivalenti del personaggio, che prova nel contempo "vergogna [...] desìo e paura" (v. 4),

---

strumento di corruzione, una fonte di ansie e turbamenti. Il potere, afferma il personaggio, rende malvagi, tanto che non vi sono differenze sostanziali tra sovrani e tiranni. Quindi, l'unica soluzione per gli intellettuali è lasciare la corte e intraprendere una vita appartata, dedita agli studi. Si cita da Bracciolini.

[27] vv. 62-64: "la poca esperienza e 'l manco indizio / e la mia verde età non voglion che io / sappia ancor di tal cose dar iudizio".

[28] I versi 142-44 ("fior frondi arbor frutti e tener erba / Zefir rinova e la sua bella Flora, / e canta el rusignol l'ingiuria acerba") sono eco di *RVF* 305.5 e 310.1-4.

[29] vv. 188-90: "ma gli è de' vecchi un lor commune errore: / crescendo el tempo, el cervel tanto scema / che per loro il tacer seria migliore".

vengono presto sostituite dall'amore incondizionato e assoluto per la principessa, descritta secondo stilemi tradizionali (vv. 28-33). Pur tuttavia, il servo si ripromette di dimostrarsi prudente, perché "bono è guardarse de fugire / la crudeltà dei patron che son vecchi" (vv. 40-41). Sembra che Filostrato, servitore fedele e integerrimo per ammissione di Demetrio, si comporti in modo corretto esclusivamente per evitare di subire le punizioni del re; quest'ultimo non gode del favore dei sudditi, ma viene rispettato per la paura che incute.

Nella scena successiva compare Tindaro, contrassegnato da un linguaggio sentenzioso e apodittico. La caratterizzazione formale e ideologica del personaggio risente in modo tangibile dei sonetti "cortigiani" di Cammelli. Tindaro, accumunabile al re per l'età avanzata, si dispera per la propria condizione (v. 92): "o vecchio disgraziato, che farai?".

L'afflizione del personaggio viene spiegata nelle terzine successive, in cui è offerto uno spregiudicato ritratto dell'indole dei sovrani (vv. 98-99): "tra' grandi è morta la discrezione: / non cognosce un signore amore o fede". In aggiunta, Demetrio gratifica soltanto i cortigiani "adulatori" che "ben san simular mal del compagno" (vv. 105-06). L'amore dei servi non viene ricompensato e la virtù risulta ormai un valore "stracciato e vilipeso" (v. 108), giacché la giustizia e l'attività di governo sono gestite da "ignoranti" (v. 110).

La descrizione dell'*entourage* di Demetrio viene approfondita mediante un elenco di vizi, che sembrano costituire le vere basi su cui si fondano la vita e la morale cortigiana (vv. 113-20): "nequizia... odio extremo... certa perfidia... invidia... adulazione... accidia... ambizïon, nemica del diletto... superbia". Viene così delineato un mondo alla rovescia, iniquo, paradossale, che "i più tristi alcia, e i magior precipizia" (v. 115). Inoltre, i cortigiani si rallegrano per le disgrazie altrui e si macchiano di vili complotti; perciò Tindaro — che si sente "tradito" da Demetrio, "re aspro e crudele" — è pronto a vendicarsi per il dolore provato (vv. 131 e 132).

Dopo un breve ingresso di Filostrato, che ha ricevuto da Panfila una lettera in cui ella confessa di ricambiare i sentimenti del servo (vv. 134-60), compare di nuovo Tindaro. Egli è intento a valutare ogni ingiustizia patita e a giustificare, quindi, il suo prossimo tradimento. La condotta del personaggio viene sigillata da una terzina icastica, secondo cui uno "iusto sdegno" porta naturalmente a "divenir crudeli" (vv. 173-74).

L'ulteriore ingresso in scena di Filostrato permette a Tindaro di confrontarsi con il servo e di venire a conoscenza della storia d'amore tra i due protagonisti. Alla fine Tindaro — che finge di interessarsi al giovane e promette di non riportare a nessuno la confidenza ricevuta[30] — si comporta alla stessa stregua dei cortigiani simulatori e sleali da lui disprezzati. Filostrato, di contro, non sembra un personaggio tragico, bensì è portatore dell'evanescenza e delle

---

[30] vv. 191-93: "tu sei palido fatto, che vuol dire? / Hai tu nulla egritudine o dolore? / Dìl, che agli amici è buon di conferire".

Libertà, vendetta, polemica anti-cortigiana nella *Panfila* di A. Cammelli 131

ingenuità tipiche dell'innamorato della commedia classica.

Dopo che Filostrato legge ad alta voce una lettera vergata da Panfila, nella quale si consiglia all'amato di utilizzare quale punto di ritrovo una "grotta antica" non lontana dal palazzo reale (v. 277), Tindaro sprona l'interlocutore ad accettare. Inoltre, spiega al personaggio dove si trovi il luogo indicato. Il servo, una volta rimasto solo, chiarisce il suo piano (vv. 322-25): "or vedi che è venuto il tempo mio; / se 'l re la mia fatica pur me invola, / de far vendetta spero ancor per Dio, / e mezzo mi serà la sua figliola".

Il coro delle sirene chiude il secondo atto: esso espone i contrasti ineludibili tra destino e libero arbitrio, tra Fortuna e influssi astrali.

4. L'atto seguente si apre con un monologo di Tindaro, perplesso se realizzare sino in fondo il proprio piano. Espressioni alquanto efficaci, che si rifanno a un linguaggio quotidiano e gergale (es. v. 3: "cossì vedess'io el re 'n mezzo d'un foco!"), si alternano ai ripensamenti per aver posto gli amanti in "gran pericol" (v. 7). Il desiderio di vendetta risulta, però, superiore e spinto dal bisogno di riscattarsi e di punire il re (vv. 13-22):

> Perché gli è bono a far patir chi erra;
> e bono è a tempo far la sua vendetta;
> et a quel che vòl guerra, dargli guerra.
> L'offeso che ha l'ingiuria in petto stretta,
> non se la scorda mai; e lo offensore
> ne porta pena el dì che non l'expetta.
> Or così gli avess'io cavato il core,
> come io l'ho questo giorno vergognato,
> che ancor gli parerà morte l'errore!
> Trionfa alle sue spese Filostrato.

L'ultimo verso, contraddistinto da bramosia di rivalsa, viene preceduto da un lessico preciso, a volte persino crudo ("patir; erra; vendetta; guerra; ingiuria; pena; cavato il core; vergognato; morte; errore") e da frequenti *geminationes* e figure etimologiche ("è bono [...] bono è; guerra [...] guerra; offeso [...] offensore").

All'improvviso riappare Filostrato, di ritorno dalla grotta, che esprime la propria soddisfazione per i "tempi [...] felici" e i "diletti senza guai" trascorsi (vv. 74-75). L'ironia tragica della scena viene avvalorata dalla risposta di Tindaro, il quale suggerisce all'interlocutore di "parlar poco", di guardarsi dall'"invidia cortigiana" (vv. 95 e 99). Il personaggio, che si staglia con nettezza rispetto alla figura tanto entusiasta quanto inconsapevole di Filostrato, si esprime mediante un linguaggio basso e formule proverbiali.[31]

---

[31] vv. 130-132: "oggi è quel dì che abandono la corte / lassando al re per vendetta un capello; / ché fuggendo da lui fuggo la morte".

La scena successiva presuppone un brusco salto narrativo, poiché Demetrio è già stato informato da Tindaro circa la storia d'amore tra la figlia e il servo.[32] Il re si trova a colloquio con il segretario Pandero al fine di prendere un adeguato provvedimento nei confronti dei due protagonisti. Lo sdegno del personaggio per l'oltraggio subito viene condensato da numerose frasi esclamative e interrogative retoriche. Il sovrano sembra in questo frangente un corrispettivo di Tindaro, poiché invoca a sua volta il bisogno di ottenere "vendetta" (vv. 169 e 183). Il lessico impiegato mostra con nitore i pensieri del personaggio, che indica la figlia quale "iniqua" e "disleale", mentre la "macchia" sarà punita con la morte, evocata in ben cinque occasioni nell'arco di pochi versi (vv. 160-77).

La risposta di Pandero mira a confortare il re, a consigliarlo con distacco e saggezza. Il servitore appare antitetico a Tindaro: egli afferma di essere riconoscente nei confronti del suo signore,[33] che lo ha gratificato creandolo "viceré" (v. 205); tuttavia tale devozione non impedisce di riconoscere nell'età avanzata del re il motivo delle sciagure che hanno colpito il regno.

Nella scena successiva Tindaro fugge, prendendo congedo dalla corte: questi saluta ironicamente la "morte" e l'"insidia" che albergano a palazzo nonché l'"onor" del re che condannerà gli amanti (vv. 225 e 226). Il servo, in accordo con l'atto precedente, descrive la corte con una serie di anafore, di costrutti simmetrici, di parallelismi, di aggettivi e di sostantivi elencati per accumulo e accostati secondo un ordine asindetico e paratattico.[34] La caratura tragica del personaggio viene amplificata dal cinismo che traspare dalle sue affermazioni: ad esempio ai versi 239-41 egli augura sarcasticamente a Filostrato, che ancora non è "stracco", di giovarsi del "bel de la sua etade" e d'"amor empirsi el sacco". (Per la rima molto espressiva e connotata in –acco Cammelli potrebbe essersi ispirato al celebre sonetto petrarchesco *L'avara Babilonia ha colmo il sacco*.)

Il coro finale dell'atto ha per protagoniste le tre parche, le quali anticipano gli sviluppi futuri della tragedia. A seguito di un ragionamento di carattere generale intorno all'ineluttabile destino degli uomini, vengono sintetizzati gli avvenimenti che presto si verificheranno a corte (vv. 283-91).

5. Il quarto atto inizia con un discorso di Pandero affine a quello che verrà

---

[32] Di fatto Tindaro e il re, i due veri antagonisti dell'opera, non si incontrano mai in scena.

[33] Vv. 202-04: "el tempo che ho con epso mai no' l persi. / El m'ha donato, el m'ha pur fatto grande, / lui mi è reffugio ne' mei controversi".

[34] Vv. 227-38: "réstati tra costor, perfida invidia; / resta, impeto del re; resta, nequizia; / sta' tra lo odio e 'l dispetto, cruda accidia. // Tu, fra' tiranni te riman, giustizia; / fede, dai detrattor rimanti presa; / virtù, trionfa pur fra la avarizia. // Servitù, resta tra gli ingrati offesa; / speranza, va' te impica per la gola; tu, carità, rimanti vilipesa. // Rimanti tra costor, lascivia, sola; / sta' tra' crapulator, re, Mida e Bacco: nelle braccie a Cupido è tua figliola".

pronunciato al termine della tragedia. La costatazione dell'"infamia", dell'"ira" sproposistata del re viene accompagnata da un'apostrofe contro la "Fortuna crudel" che si è abbattuta sul giovane (vv. 2, 4, 23). Il personaggio — nonostante queste convinzioni, ribadite poi di seguito (es. v. 7: "tanto el comandamento me dispiacque") — ammette di non poter intervenire, di non essere in grado di soccorrere il protagonista. Il tono sommesso e l'atmosfera lugubre sono accompagnati da uno stile eterogeneo, che comprende ora battute consone alla situazione e al genere letterario tragico,[35] ora locuzioni proverbiali e appartenenti a un registro diafasico quotidiano.

La scena successiva è dedicata al dialogo tra Pandero e Demetrio, che si incardina su alcune parole d'ordine e concetti precisi: Demetrio afferma di voler fornire un "exemplo" tangibile attraverso la punizione dell'"excesso", del "grave errore" compiuto dai due amanti (vv. 34, 38, 39). Il desiderio di "vendetta" è motivato dalla "pena crudele", dal "gran martoro" patito dal sovrano, che prova "vergogna" a causa della perdita dell'"onor" (vv. 45-49).[36] Pandero, sebbene riconosca la serietà della situazione, tenta di placare l'ira del re, ricordandogli le possibili conseguenze che l'uccisione di Filostrato arrecherà alla famiglia reale.

Demetrio si dimostra, però, irremovibile dalle proprie posizioni e ordina di condurre la figlia al proprio cospetto. Il dialogo tra i due personaggi risulta esemplato con fedeltà sulla scorta dell'omologo boccacciano tra Ghismonda e Tancredi. Si confrontino, per esempio, le prime battute del sovrano:

"Ghismonda, parendomi conoscere la tua vertù e la tua onestà. [...] Di che io, in questo poco di rimanente di vita che la mia vecchiezza mi serba, sempre sarò dolente di ciò ricordandomi. E or volesse Idio che, poi che a tanta disonestà conducer ti dovevi, avessi preso uomo che alla tua nobiltà decevole fosse stato; ma tra tanti che nella mia corte n'usano eleggesti Guiscardo, giovane di vilissima condizione, nella nostra corte quasi come per Dio da piccol fanciullo infino a questo dì allevato. [...] Di Guiscardo, il quale io feci stanotte prendere quando dello spiraglio usciva, e hollo in prigione, ho io già meco preso partito che farne; ma di te sallo Idio che io non so che farmi."

(*Decameron* 4.1.26-28)

"Panfila, a me cognoscer parse già / esser in te non pur sola virtù, / ma prudenzia infinita et onestà [...] / Deh! che in questo poco rimanente / che vecchiezza mi serba, a tanto male / pensando ognora viverò dolente. / Almen volesse Idio, doppoi che a tale / disonestà giongesti, avesti preso / un ch'al tuo sangue fusse stato equale. / Ma in fra tanti qui de nobil peso, / un tolto n'hai de più vil condizione, / come n'hai sempre pel passato inteso: / alevato da noi picol garzone / in fino a questo dì, come quel angue [...] / Di te non so che partito pigliare; / de Filostrato ho già partito a pieno / qual feci questa notte impregionare."

(*Panfila* 4.90-122)

---

[35] Vv. 25-27: "così il mondo pasce / sempre l'uom de fatiche, e ben si po' / chiamar felice quel che more in fasce".
[36] Sul binomio "onore – vergogna" si veda Heller.

Cammelli tende a preservare il ritmo vivo e dialogato del racconto mediante esclamazioni e interrogative retoriche, ma senza perdere la tensione della novella.[37] Il rispetto sostanziale del testo del *Decameron*, dilatato e accresciuto (vv. 90-239), viene trasgredito in due passaggi, che evidenziano le ragioni di Panfila: nel primo viene marcata la polemica anti-nobiliare già *in nuce* in Boccaccio;[38] nel secondo Demetrio non rifiuta a priori la validità delle tesi della giovane.[39]

Al termine del confronto subentra il coro di Atropos, la quale sembra sostenere la decisione del re. La convinzione secondo cui "ciascun mal sempre è punito" viene collegata alla storia di Panfila e Filostrato (v. 240).

IV. Conclusione: dire la verità al principe
1. L'ultimo atto recupera l'inizio del precedente, poiché Pandero svolge un nuovo monologo, che commenta l'"accerba pena" prevista da Demetrio (v. 2). Questi si comporta con tanta "crudeltà" a causa della "vecchiezza" da non comprendere gli atteggiamenti dei giovani (vv. 4, 5); una naturale distanza dalle loro problematiche, l'invidia per la "gioventute", da tempo trascorsa e dimenticata (v. 8), motivano il risentimento e l'ostinazione del sovrano. Pandero, nonostante la critica al re sia profonda, non sceglie di ribellarsi al pari di Tindaro, anzi proclama la necessità di assecondare, anche contro ogni evidenza e opportunità, le indicazioni dei regnanti (vv. 22-27):

> Ma perché pur lo obedire è virtute
> agli servi i patron, mal son contento
> che l'ore di costui siano compiute.
> Non conviene a bon servo esser mai lento
> di quanto gli è dal signor comandato,
> ché altro facendo, gli serìa tormento.

---

[37] Non mancano, però, alcune cadute di stile, ricorsive nel testo (vv. 155: "se di carne sei"). Ciò ha spinto Aurigemma a parlare di un "tono da lite casalinga" (31).
[38] vv. 187-95 ("nobile è quel che alla virtute attende: / benché a pochi oggi tocchi questa sorte; / di lei sol conto Filostrato rende. // E se riguardi ben per la tua corte, / non è nesun de toi qual più gentile / che questo nobil peso in spalla porte. // Ciascuno appresso lui troverai vile: / e chi 'l dice villano, o invitto re, / villano è lui, e de stirpe più umile") con *Dec* 4.1.40-41 ("e per ciò colui che virtuosamente adopera, apertamente sé mostra gentile, e chi altramenti il chiama, non colui che è chiamato ma colui che chiama commette difetto. Raguarda tra tutti i tuoi nobili uomini e essamina la lor vita, i lor costumi e le loro maniere, e d'altra parte quelle di Guiscardo raguarda: se tu vorrai senza animosità giudicare, tu dirai lui nobilissimo e questi tuoi nobili tutti esser villani").
[39] La glossa del *Decameron* inserita dal narratore (4.1.46: "conobbe il prenze la grandezza dell'animo della sua figliuola") viene messa in bocca direttamente a Demetrio (vv. 230-35: "io penso poi quanta fortezza d'animo / ha la mia figlia in le pronte risposte / che fan che manco contra lei me inanimo. // E a tutte le ragion ch'io gli ho proposte, / tanto ben giunte v'ha le sue parole / che par che un anno fa l'abbia composte").

L'ingresso in scena di Tinolo e Pinzia interrompe il ragionamento del personaggio, il quale dispensa istruzioni ai servi su come uccidere Filostrato. Anche i sicari si mostrano contrari a portare a termine un tal "mallefizio", pur tuttavia non possono esimersi, giacché pensano sia sempre bene ascoltare le disposizioni dei padroni (v. 46).[40] Inoltre, essi riducono le responsabilità del proprio signore, poiché la colpa di quanto accaduto sarà da addebitare soprattutto alla "Fortuna [...] invidiosa" (vv. 185 e 186).[41]

I servi, terminato il proprio compito, recano a Demetrio il cuore di Filostrato, di cui descrivono l'uccisione. Il racconto accurato dell'episodio — contraddistinto da particolari macabri e patetici (es. v. 84: "ecco, o re, il cor del tuo servo caldissimo" e v. 107: "a trargli el cor non femmo altro che piangere") — viene completato dalle ultime parole dell'amante, messaggio postremo che, come da tradizione, sintetizza la morale del personaggio e ne spiega il ruolo (vv. 99-101): "e quando mai d'alcuna inamoratevi, / abbiate a mente a me che a questo termine / condutto sono e per me experti fatevi". L'invito a prestare attenzione alle insidie provocate dall'amore sembra allontanare Filostrato dalla morale del *Decameron* e dal pensiero medesimo di Panfila, che interpreta il sentimento quale forza naturale e invincibile.

In seguito i due servitori esibiscono, secondo le richieste dal re, il cuore di Filostrato all'amata. Ella reagisce in modo opposto rispetto al giovane, perché rivendica le proprie scelte e decide di suicidarsi giusto in nome dell'amore eterno che la lega al protagonista.[42] La tenacia di Panfila viene condensata nella scena successiva, in cui definisce il padre "causa" di quanto accaduto (v. 305).

Pandero, a seguito della morte di Panfila, cerca di consolare Demetrio ricordandogli che la scomparsa della figlia assomiglia a quella di Tisbe, di Didone, di Filide, di Ero. L'amore accomuna "giovani e vecchi" e, pertanto, non deve essere oggetto di "vergogna o vituperio" (vv. 337 e 339). Il re si addossa ogni colpa per l'accaduto e ordina di seppellire Panfila accanto a Filostrato. Però, il commento finale — affidato a Pandero e che sostituisce il compito del coro di esporre il messaggio della tragedia — presenta una versione edulcorata, tendenziosa: il dolore provato dal padrone cancella ogni responsabilità; infatti, vengono individuati nell'"Amor" e nel "mondan piacere" i motivi per cui si è "dismembrata" la casata regia (vv. 372, 373 e 375).

---

[40] La questione se sia sempre giusto obbedire agli ordini di un principe informerà il secondo libro del *Cortigiano* di Castiglione (2.22-24).

[41] L'attenuante era stata smentita con forza da Panfila (4.181-83): "tu [Demetrio] in questo segui la gente vulgare / la Fortuna incolpando quale abassa / gli iusti, e gli iniusti fa regnare".

[42] Vv. 219-25: "o molto amato core, ogni mio offizio / fatto ho, qual ho a far teco; né mi resta / se non di morte l'ultimo supplizio, // e che l'anima mia sì afflitta e mesta / con la tua si congionga; e così passo / lieta questo amplo mar pien de tempesta. // O mondo traditore, adio, ti lasso!".

2. La "tragedia scura", come è definita al penultimo verso, si chiude non senza alcune apparenti contraddizioni, motivate dalla novità stilistica e teorica dell'operazione di Cammelli, dalla difficoltà di proporre un testo simile a un pubblico di corte e di attenuare possibili riferimenti troppo radicali e severi: il lessico non si mantiene sempre uniforme, ma ricorre non di rado a proverbi, frasi gnomiche, espressioni quotidiane tipiche della commedia;[43] invece, dall'impianto diegetico e ideologico emergono personaggi ora colpevoli e negativi, ora riabilitati tramite rettifiche e correzioni. La vecchiaia di Demetrio si configura in modo intermittente quale colpa e aggravante o possibile giustificazione. Dell'amore, forza positiva e legittima nei primi atti, si evidenziano anche gli aspetti pericolosi, da evitare laddove il peso della Fortuna giunge a ricoprire un ruolo pressoché pervasivo.

L'unica figura coerente — a differenza di Filostrato che sembrerà pentirsi della sua mancata avvedutezza — sembra Panfila, la quale difenderà sino alla fine le proprie posizioni; il suicidio, come quello di Ghismonda in Boccaccio, appare un estremo sacrificio teso ad affermare i valori in cui ella crede in opposizione alla crudeltà paterna. Le ricorsive precisazioni non celano, però, un dato di fondo palmare con cui misurare l'esito complessivo dell'opera di Cammelli: per quanto la causa sia attribuita alla Fortuna, all'Amore, all'impeto giovanile di Filostrato o alla condotta del vecchio sovrano, Tindaro, il vero colpevole, non solo risulta impunito, felice e vittorioso, ma non verrà nemmeno sospettato dagli altri personaggi.

3. Tindaro rimane nascosto per buona parte dell'opera e fugge prima che il meccanismo tragico si avvii; egli, proprio per la posizione defilata ricoperta, può essere indicato nel personaggio che palesa al lettore i significati più reconditi e inquietanti del testo. Cammelli, per mezzo di una figura minore come Tindaro, diffonde un messaggio permesso a corte solo se veicolato da toni velati e criptici:[44] ogni alibi costruito artatamente dai fedeli servitori del re — faziosi, eppure mai coerenti o convinti del tutto nel difendere il proprio signore — viene smentito dall'analisi impietosa e lucida sulla vita di corte prospettata da Tindaro. Non occorre proteggere Demetrio attraverso scuse apologetiche o spiegare quanto successo sulla base di fenomeni e decisioni preternaturali. Il sovrano risulta colpevole quanto il Tancredi del *Decameron*, nonostante le frequenti giustificazioni. Esse non sono convincenti perché ciò che viene dichiarato da Tindaro, e in parte pure da Panfila, basta ad attribuire e segnalare le autentiche

---

[43] Si vedano "argumento", v. 3 ("la ragion dice e tace l'appetito"); 1.39 ("dove è più roba son più guai"); 1.173-174 ("vattene, fia, a cibarte, perch'io / conosco, essendo l'ora, el tuo appetito"); 2.103 ("sempre pensa mal un che mal sède"); 2.125 ("piccoli solfanelli accendon foco"); 4.19-21 ("sta male al pedestro / a cui doce l'artefice, s'el vole / lavorar poi coi ferri del maestro").
[44] Un espediente conforme verrà seguito da Torquato Tasso con il monologo del satiro dell'*Aminta*, collocato all'inizio del II atto.

responsabilità del personaggio.

Del resto, l'immagine di una corte corrotta e ingiusta trova fondamento nel comportamento stesso di Tindaro, che si serve dell'amore e dell'ingenuità dei giovani nonché dell'orgoglio del re al fine di ordire un progetto di vendetta spregiudicato. Egli non si colloca su un piano superiore, non è incorruttibile, non si mostra estraneo ai giochi di potere e agli intrighi di palazzo; il suo unico obiettivo sembra affrancarsi da una situazione opprimente e iniqua, contro la quale è pronto a utilizzare ogni mezzo.

Benché si debba accostare con estrema cautela un personaggio storico a uno di finzione, pare possibile rinvenire in Tindaro un *alter ego* ideale di Cammelli, che ne proietta le spinte iconoclaste: il servo, che si allontana dalla corte ponendola in serio pericolo e si libera per sempre da un giogo non più sostenibile, esprime ciò che lo scrittore — profondamente turbato dalla *finis Italiae*, dalla corruzione dei ceti dirigenti e della Chiesa, dall'insicurezza della vita cortigiana, dalla caduta di Ludovico il Moro — non avrebbe potuto compiere in vita, ma denunciare mediante la sublimazione letteraria. I fruitori della tragedia non devono certo aderire alle scelte di Tindaro, bensì riflettere alla luce dei suoi comportamenti.

Cammelli non indirizza la *Panfila* contro un sovrano in particolare né tale scelta sarebbe stata possibile in modo esplicito;[45] ciò non attenua certo la portata corrosiva della sua opera, che si rivolge all'intero panorama delle corti italiane. L'esigenza catartica ed etica insieme di "dire la verità al principe" e ai propri lettori, come ha osservato Alessandra Rozzoni per il *Dialogo*, si mantiene anche nella *Panfila* su un piano generale e si esplica in un'osservazione del mondo — come scrive la studiosa — "intelligente, acuta e pure mordace senza avere né l'intenzione né la necessita di andare oltre, nella consapevolezza che, se fatta con sincerità e buon senso, essa è operazione sufficiente a incidere sulla realtà" (89).

Università degli Studi di Milano

---

[45] Orvieto: "[...] il suo è uno dei più sconfortanti quadri d'insieme [...] di degradazione morale e politica delle signorie italiane di fine secolo. Il Pistoia, e questo sta a suo merito, ha un rapporto difficile con i vari signori, li adula, certo, ma non si umilia in servili encomi o in roboanti panegirici" (XIX).

Regesto bibliografico

Aurigemma, Marcello. La *"Panfila" di Antonio Cammelli e la posizione storica del teatro dell'ultimo Quattrocento*. In *Studi sulla letteratura teatrale ed eroica del Rinascimento*. Roma: Signorelli, 1968. 11-68.

Bertini, Ferruccio (a c. di). *Pandolfo Collenuccio: atti del Congresso tenuto in occasione del V centenario della morte (1504-2004)*. Sassoferrato-Pesaro: Istituto internazionale di studi piceni — Società pesarese di studi storici, 2005.

Boccaccio, Giovanni. *Decameron*. A c. di Amedeo Quondam, Maurizio Fiorilla e Giancarlo Alfano. Milano: Rizzoli, 2013.

Boiardo, Matteo Maria. *Timone* e *Orphei tragoedia*. A c. di Maria Antonietta Acocella e Antonia Tissoni Benvenuti. Novara: Interlinea, 2009.

Borsellino, Nino. *"Decameron" come teatro*. "Biblioteca teatrale" 9 (1974): 1-33.

Bosisio, Matteo. *Ludovico il Moro come personaggio teatrale nelle rappresentazioni milanesi del XV secolo*. "Stratagemmi" 23 (2012): 11-52.

_____. *Il teatro "pre-classicista" nelle corti padane: geografia, storia e forme*. Torino: Accademia University Press, 2016 (in corso di stampa, in cds o in press).

Bracciolini, Poggio. *De infelicitate principum*. A c. di Davide Canfora. Roma: Edizioni di Storia e Letteratura, 1998.

Caliri, Francesco. *Aspetti del volgare napoletano nel de Petruciis*. "Magisterium" 1 (1997): 149-75.

Cammelli, Antonio (detto il Pistoia). *Panfila*. In *Teatro del Quattrocento*. A c. di Antonia Tissoni Benvenuti e Maria Pia Mussini Sacchi. Torino: UTET, 1983. 399-468.

_____. *Sonetti contro l'Ariosto*. A c. di Carla Rossi. Alessandria: Edizioni dell'Orso, 2006.

_____. *Sonetti faceti secondo l'autografo ambrosiano*. A c. di Erasmo Percopo. Napoli: Jovene, 1908.

_____. *Tragedia de Antonio da Pistoia novamente impressa*. Venezia: Bonelli, 1508.

Cappelli, Guido. *Sapere e potere. L'umanista e il Principe nell'Italia del Quattrocento*. "Cuadernos de Filología italiana" 15 (2008): 73-91.

Cavallo, Jo Ann. *L'"Orlando Innamorato" come speculum principis*. In *Il Boiardo e il mondo estense nel Quattrocento. Atti del convegno internazionale di studi (Scandiano-Modena-Reggio Emilia-Ferrara, 13-17 settembre 1994)*. A c. di Giuseppe Anceschi e Tina Matarrese. Padova: Antenore, 1998. 297-321.

Clarizia, Domenico. *Un poeta giocoso del Rinascimento: il Pistoia*. Salerno: Beraglia Editore, 1929.

Collenuccio, Pandolfo. *Opere*. A c. di Alfredo Saviotti. Bari: Laterza, 1929.

D'Ancona, Alessandro. *Origini del teatro italiano*. Torino: Loescher, 1891.

De Petruciis, Giovanni Antonio. *Sonetti*. A c. di Emiliano Picchiorri. Roma: Salerno editrice, 2013.

De Robertis, Domenico. *Antonio Cammelli*. In *Dizionario biografico degli italiani*. Vol. 17. Roma: Istituto della Enciclopedia italiana, 1974. 277-86.

Esposito, Roberto. *Ordine e conflitto. Machiavelli e la letteratura politica del Rinascimento italiano*. Napoli: Liguori, 1984.

Gaeta, Franco. *Letteratura e potere. Dal comune alla corte rinascimentale*. In *Letteratura italiana*, I. A c. di Alberto Asor Rosa. Torino: Einaudi. 149-255.

Heller, Agnes. *Il potere della vergogna*. Roma: Editori Riuniti, 1985.

Jacquot, Jean. *Les Tragédies de Sénèque et le théâtre de la Renaissance*. Paris: CNRS,

1964.

Luzio, Alessandro e Rodolfo Renier. *La coltura e le relazioni letterarie di Isabella d'Este Gonzaga.* A c. di Simone Albonico. Milano: Sylvestre Bonnard, 2006.

Malato, Enrico (a c. di). *Il Quattrocento.* In *Storia della letteratura italiana.* Roma: Salerno editrice, 1996.

Meneghetti, Maria Luisa. *Scrivere in carcere nel Medioevo.* In *Studi di Filologia e Letteratura italiana in onore di Maria Picchio Simonelli.* A c. di Pietro Frassica. Alessandria: Edizioni dell'Orso, 1992. 185-199.

Montagnani, Cristina. *"Andando con lor dame in aventura": percorsi estensi.* Galatina: Congedo, 2004.

Olivastri, Valentina. *Antonio Pistoia: The Poetic World of a Customs Collector.* PhD Thesis. London: University of London, 1999.

Orvieto, Paolo. *Introduzione.* In *Antonio Cammelli. Sonetti faceti secondo l'autografo ambrosiano.* Pistoia: Libreria dell'Orso, 2005. (Ristampa anastatica dell'edizione Napoli: Jovene, 1908).

Pallone, Rocco. *Anticlericalismo e giustizie sociali nell'Italia del '400: l'opera poetica e satirica di Antonio Cammelli detto il Pistoia.* Roma: Trevi, 1975.

Percopo, Erasmo. *Antonio Cammelli e i suoi sonetti faceti.* Roma: Giannini, 1913.

Perocco, Daria. *Boccaccio (comico) nel teatro (comico) di Machiavelli.* "Quaderns d'Italià" 14 (2009): 23-36.

Petrarca, Francesco. *Canzoniere.* A c. di Marco Santagata. Milano: Mondadori, 1996.

Poletti, Federico. *Fortuna letteraria e figurativa della Ghismonda (Dec. IV, 1) fra Umanesimo e Rinascimento.* "Studi sul Boccaccio" 32 (2004): 101-39.

———. *Fortuna letteraria e figurativa della Ghismonda (Dec. IV 1).* "Studi sul Boccaccio" 35 (2007): 239-302.

Poliziano, Angelo. *L'"Orfeo" del Poliziano.* A c. di Antonia Tissoni Benvenuti. Padova: Antenore, 1986.

Rinaldi, Rinaldo. *Rinascimenti: immagini e modelli dall'"Arcadia" al Tassoni.* Milano: FrancoAngeli, 2010.

———. *Umanesimo e Rinascimento.* In *Storia della civiltà letteraria italiana,* vol. 2, 1. A c. di Giorgio Barberi Squarotti. Torino: UTET, 1993.

Rossetto, Laura. *Un capitolo della fortuna di Seneca nel '400, l'"Hyppolitus" e l'"Hercules furens" nella traduzione di Phytio da Montevarchi.* In *Tra commediografi e letterati. Rinascimento e Settecento veneziano.* A c. di Tiziana Agostini ed Emilio Lippi. Ravenna: Longo editore, 1997. 25-42.

Rossi, Carla. *La Disperata, capitolo conclusivo dei Sonetti faceti del Pistoia.* "Letteratura italiana antica" 6 (2005): 43-61.

——— *Il Pistoia, spirito bizzarro del Quattrocento.* Alessandria: Edizioni dell'Orso, 2008.

Rozzoni, Alessandra. *Satira politica e anticlericale nel "Dialogo" di Antonio Cammelli detto il Pistoia.* "Annali On-Line di Ferrara. Lettere" 7 (2012): 74-93.

Stäuble, Antonio. *La brigata del "Decameron" come pubblico teatrale.* "Studi sul Boccaccio" 9 (1975-1976): 103-17.

——— *Antecedenti boccacciani in alcuni personaggi della commedia rinascimentale.* "Quaderns d'Italià" 14 (2009): 37-47.

Tanda, Nicola. *Pandolfo Collenuccio e il dramma della saviezza.* Roma: Bulzoni, 1988.

Tateo, Francesco. *Giannantonio de Petruciis e l'umanesimo napoletano.* In *Tradizione e realtà nell'Umanesimo italiano.* Bari: Dedalo, 1967. 111-28.

Tissoni Benvenuti, Antonia. *Le armi e le lettere nell'educazione del Signore nelle corti padane del Quattrocento.* "Mélanges de l'Ecole française de Rome" 99 (1987): 435-

46.
Visconti, Gaspare Ambrogio, *Pasitea*. In *Teatro del Quattrocento*. A c. di Antonia Tissoni Benvenuti e Maria Pia Mussini Sacchi. Torino: UTET, 1983. 342-96.

Jo Ann Cavallo

Contracts, Surveillance, and Censure of Political Power in Sabadino degli Arienti's "Triunfo da Camarino" Novella (*Le porretane* 1.1)

Abstract: This essay argues that the first novella of Giovanni Sabadino degli Arienti's *Porretane* asserts the individual's right to privacy and underscores the importance of contractual obligations regardless of social status. It offers, moreover, a thinly veiled critique of the military adventurism and rhetorical manipulation of those wielding political power, specifically the pope and the emperor, implicitly pitting the free movement inherent in a market economy against the coercive violence of the political state.

Key words: Sabadino degli Arienti, *Porretane*, Triunfo da Camarino, novella, Renaissance, Cockaigne, Bentivoglio, contracts, surveillance, Ercole d'Este.

In the opening tale of his sixty-one novella collection entitled *Le porretane*, Giovanni Sabadino degli Arienti (1443/5-1510) tells the story of a servant named Triunfo da Camarino, who regularly stages a dialogue between the emperor and the pope during his daily hour of privacy and who abruptly leaves his aristocratic employer after the latter spies on him and discovers his secret pastime.[1] The introductory summary announces that the tale will end with the "shaming" of Triunfo and at the conclusion of the story the fictional listeners gathered in Porretta all laugh at the servant and comment on his apparent folly.[2] Arienti's actual narrative, however, suggests quite opposite meanings to those explicitly offered to us in the frame. Through a close reading of the novella, with particular attention to its economic and political aspects, this essay aims to tease out the more radical implications of Triunfo's words and actions that could have been discerned by an attentive late fifteenth-century reader.

---

[1] I would like to thank Carolyn James for her feedback on an earlier draft of this essay. For more on Sabadino's literary career, see James's *Giovanni Sabadino degli Arienti* as well as her edition of his letters, *The Letters of Giovanni Sabadino degli Arienti: 1481-1510*.

[2] Taking the introductory announcement at face value, Bruno Basile adds his own note asserting that "the novella is dedicated to the popular theme of the dream as a possible evasion of a very modest social condition" (12n).

Annali d'italianistica 34 (2016). *Speaking Truth to Power from Medieval to Modern Italy*

A Labor Contract

The novella opens as Piero delli Ubaldini hires Triunfo as a stable boy for his horses ("uno famiglio per il bisogno delli suoi cavagli" 12). The description of the labor agreement highlights the agency of the latter through the specific conditions that he sets: "He stipulated that he wanted every day to have an hour for himself" ("pattegiò seco che ogni giorno voleva una ora di tempo per lui"). Triunfo's one free hour per day may seem exceedingly meager to us, but the reference to Triunfo's negotiation ("pattegiò") draws attention to the contractual nature of the employment. Although not usually the focal point of fiction, contracts were in fact a common facet of life in fifteenth-century Italy, regularly used to establish relationships of all kinds, from marriage to military service to artistic commissions, and including, as in the case of the present novella, domestic employment.[3] As defined by Stephen Kinsella, "a contract is a non-coerced mutual agreement between two or more parties [...] usually used to make long-term commitments structured and clearly defined" (12).[4] In distinguishing contractual bonds from hegemonic bonds, Ludwig von Mises contrasts the symmetrical nature of voluntary interpersonal exchange contracts with the asymmetrical nature of relations based on coercion (196).[5] Thus, despite Triunfo's lesser economic means and lower social status, the voluntary nature of the contract renders him an equal party exercising his individual preference and acknowledges his right to self-ownership.[6]

Piero delli Ubaldini accepts Triunfo's terms without further ado because he finds him "of good appearance and seeming to be in accordance with his name"

---

[3] In a practice continued today, marriage contracts were read aloud so that everyone present would be a witness to the agreement. The military title of "condottiere" is actually derived from the "condotta" or contract for raising and leading troops. For contracts in commissioning art, see O'Malley. For domestic labor, see Romano, who points out that there was actually a sellers' market for domestic labor in the fifteenth and early sixteenth century, partially due to severe outbreaks of plague which reduced the numbers of men available for such service. Consequently, wage rates for male servants increased during this period.

[4] Historians of contract law credit the nineteenth-century legal scholar Henry Sumner Maine for outlining the opposition between relationships based on contracts, or voluntary stipulations, and those based on hereditary status, or ascribed positions within a society along a hierarchically ordered social scale. According to Maine, societies of contract, based on the principle of the free exchange of goods and services on the marketplace, have clear advantages over societies of status since the former entail a more efficient distribution of rights and duties, leading to increased economic productivity as well as greater personal liberty.

[5] For the equilibrium between both parties in a labor contract — against the Marxist view that workers are necessarily at a disadvantage with respect to their employer — see Mises 196-69 ("Contractual Bonds and Hegemonic Bonds") and Leoni 105-26.

[6] For the universal right of self-ownership, see Rothbard 33-36.

("de bono aspecto e parendoli quello consequente al nome" 12). This linking of Triunfo's pleasing demeanor to his given name, reminiscent of the Latin dictum "nomina sunt consequentia rerum," invites us to reflect on the name's connotations. The usage of the term *triumph* ranges from the glory of military victory to the literary genre immortalized by Petrarch in *I trionfi*, a moral poem describing the triumphs of love, chastity, death, fame, time, and eternity, in successive visions. Arienti, using *triumph* in the latter sense, would later make prominent use of the term in his *De triumphis religionis* (1497), a treatise celebrating the "triumphs of the many virtues" ("triumphi de tante virtute" 30) of Duke Ercole d'Este of Ferrara (r. 1471-1505). Indeed, Arienti reaffirms the centrality of the triumph conceit in the headings of each of the ten books of that work, including the "triumpho" of magnanimity (37), of the dignity of munificence (50), and of faith (79).[7] For Piero delli Ubaldini to immediately conclude that Triunfo's appearance matched such an illustrious name, the latter must have made quite a first impression.

And yet, while taking the time to describe Piero delli Ubaldini's rank, provenance, personal habits, reputation, and wealth (i.e., he was a gentleman and knight from the city of Urbino, of excellent habits, with a good reputation and very abundantly endowed with the goods of fortune), Arienti does not divulge any information whatsoever about Triunfo's identity beyond his appellation "da Camarino," alternately written "da Camerino.") One might initially wonder whether this surname could suggest his possible geographical origin just as Piero's designation "delli Ulbaldini" points to his family's hereditary nobility.[8] Camerino, a town in the Marche region located about 120 kilometers from Urbino, the novella's location, does not, however, provide any immediate keys to further understanding the character. Although this small mountain town had its own ducal court, a thriving economy, and a university offering degrees in civil law, canonical law, medicine, and literary studies, there are no textual clues regarding Triunfo's own prior activities.[9] All one can really

---

[7] The heading to Book 7 uses both the noun and verb form: "Dela conditione, dignitate et excellentia della iustitia e suo triumpho, le virtù dela quale se intender à con illustri exempli l'huomo farsi citadino del cielo et Ferrara de felicità triumphare" (82). In the same work, Arienti explicitly links names to their referents, maintaining that the Belfiore palace should be called "Iocundo Sole" because of its "magnifice opere" (72).

[8] Although Piero has not been identified with a historical personage, "Degli Ubaldini" was a noble family name. The Archbishop Ruggieri degli Ubaldini, condemned to suffer within the jaws of Count Ugolino in Dante's *Inferno*, is just one of many notables with that family name. The preposition "di" indicates his family nobility whereas "da" indicates simply one's provenance.

[9] The connotation, in any event, would have been positive. De Marchi calls Camerino a "vital link in the traffic between the Adriatic and the hinterland," where "opposing tendencies and worlds crossed paths" (25). Di Stefano specifies that during the

know about Triunfo is in the here and now of the novella, in which he carries out his duties so marvelously ("che era una maraviglia") that Piero "would not want him to leave for anything in the world" ("per cosa del mondo non l'averebbe lassato da sé partire"). Indeed, whereas Triunfo had originally been hired simply as a groom for the horses, it appears that before long he was in charge of the entire household, including his patron: "Using his condition of a servant with discretion, he served and governed his patron, the house, and the horses with much faithfulness and diligence" ("usando cum discrezione la sua servitù, il patrone, la casa e li cavagli cum tanta fede e diligenzia serviva e governava").

More precise information about Triunfo is only offered to the reader when it comes to describing his daily hour of leisure. The narrator envisions him as he enters his room ("camera") and locks the door so that nobody can enter without his permission ("senza sua licenzia"). This precaution underscores the fact that the daily hour owned by Triunfo must be free not only from interference and interruption, but also from surveillance. Speaking of privacy as the condition of personal autonomy, Carlo Lottieri remarks that as political states become absolute powers in the course of history, "it is only by hiding that a subject can succeed in preserving his own privacy" (Lottieri 105). In the domestic space evoked at the onset of the novella, however, Triunfo's right to privacy is a mutually agreed-upon condition of his employment.

This action of carving out an impenetrable, private space might thus suggest another connotation of "Camerino," which in Italian means "a small room." This was a common noun in late fifteenth-century Italy, used not only in a generic sense, but also to connote a private, intimate chamber valued precisely for its strictly personal nature and often richly decorated. In his *De triumphis religionis*, Arienti describes numerous "stantie e camarini et lochi" adorned with imaginative mural paintings in the Estense country residences (72).[10] The Castello Estense's "Camerini del principe" are considered to have been "il luogo più fastoso e segreto" of the castle.[11] A century later Torquato Tasso (1544-1595) would complain about not having any "camera" or "camerino" of his own as a courtier in Ferrara.[12]

Quattrocento the town witnessed a significant rise in "entrepreneurial and merchant activities at all levels of society" (48).

[10] The images in these rooms evoked both real and imagined spaces, from commemorations of recent events involving the Estense (61), to mythological scenes (64), to "camerin[i] a leoni" (70) and other exotic animals.

[11] Castello Estense di Ferrara: http://www.castelloestense.it/it/il-castello/alla-scoperta-del-castello/primo-piano/i-camerini-del-principe/

[12] Tasso's usage is cited in the *Grande dizionario della lingua italiana* under "camerino."

A Staged Scene

When Triunfo withdraws into the confines of his "camera" to engage in an activity beyond the gaze of his aristocratic employer or anyone else within the fictional space of the story, Arienti nevertheless allows the reader to witness the extraordinary scene that ensues.[13] Setting up along the wall "a curtain of black cloth, in which was depicted the pope with the cardinals, in the manner of an assembly, along with many kings, princes, lords, and Christian dukes" ("una cortina di tela nera, in la quale era dipincto il papa cum li cardinali, in modo quando fanno concistoro, e multi re, principi, signori e duci cristiani" 13), Triunfo takes on the role of emperor by placing a diadem on his head and scepter in his hand. Nevertheless, he begins by giving voice not to the emperor, but to the pope, who proposes certain measures "for the health of the common Christian states" ("in salute de li communi Stati cristiani"). Reported in direct discourse, the "pope" exhorts those present to love one another and to "leave aside your weapons and warfare amongst yourselves and take up arms in defense of the Christian faith, which is still being afflicted and tormented by those Infidels and rabied Turks" ("lassare le arme e guerre fra voi e quelle prendere solamente in defensione della cristiana fede, che da quilli infideli e rabidi turchi è tuttavia afflicta e cruciata" 13). He goes on to threaten them with both earthly destruction and eternal damnation if they do not heed his call to institute a Crusade: "If this proposal of mine is not embraced by you with high spirits, in the end you will lose grace in this world and glory in heaven and you will go to the infernal realms, where you will be eternally tormented" ("Questo mio proponimento non essendo da voi cum alto animo abrazzato, perdereti alfin la grazia de questo mondo e la gloria del cielo e andarete a l'infernali regni, dove eternamente sareti tormentati" 13-14).[14] Although it is not directly stated here, popes routinely used the threat of excommunication to instill fear and force obedience.

After being told that the pope said many other things that are not reported or even summarized, the reader gets to hear the emperor's reply in first-person discourse. Accusing the pope of not practicing what he preaches, the "emperor" proclaims his intention to govern his realm as he pleases: "But you want your speeches to be believed? Begin first, like a good shepherd, to give an example to us! And if you won't give this example, I intend, as far as I'm concerned, to enjoy my realm without fear of the Turks or of Hell" ("Ma voleti voi che a le vostre persuasione si creda? Cominciate prima, come bon pastore, dare exemplo

---

[13] It was apparently not unusual for a servant to have his own private chamber.

[14] In remarking that "the poor *famiglio* does not do anything other than evoke a widespread outlook in this period" (13n), Basile fails to note that Triunfo critiques the hypocrisy of this viewpoint immediately after evoking it.

a nui! E se questo exemplo non darete, io intendo, quanto per me, goldere il mio reame senza paura de turchi né de inferno" 14).

The most striking part of the emperor's speech, however, is the vision from the previous night that he goes on to relate as evidence of the emptiness of the pope's threats. After recounting some preliminaries, the "emperor" recalls how he found himself in a fantastic landscape in which a long-toothed Lucifer appeared exiting a sumptuous palace and mounting a horse. Although the emperor was warned by someone present that the devil would devour him, he had no qualms about running over to Lucifer in order to pay his respects ("volendo per reverenzia correre a tenere la staffa" 14-15). As if to prove the falseness of the warning, the emperor claims that Lucifer was overjoyed to see him and welcomed him warmly, saying: "My son, you are now and always welcome here!" ("Figliuol mio, tu sii adesso e per sempre el benvenuto!" 15).

As the vision continues, the reader learns that the dominion of the devil is not the place of torment conjured up by the pope, but rather a realm of plenty filled with an infinite multitude of souls where "one drinks and eats in abundance" ("Se beve e mangia alla gagliarda!" 15). Such gastronomical havens, often referred to as the "land of Cockaigne" or "paese di Cuccagna" in medieval and Renaissance popular literature, are generally situated in a remote time and place or even in a heavenly afterlife (Rossi 402-08).[15] Whereas such imagined sites free from the scarcity of resources conditioning life on earth generally counter the realities of poverty and death, especially for the disadvantaged, in this case the vision is evoked to refute the pope's threat of the hellish torments for those who refuse to embark on a new crusade. The emperor demonstrates a mocking, irreverent attitude toward orthodox belief, moreover, when he states that he is not simply uninterested in battling the Turks and unconcerned with Hell, but he would actually prefer to remain in Lucifer's realm where he can indulge his senses.

Not only is the emperor attracted to the pleasures available in Hell, but he also seeks to secure for himself the power that the pope commands on earth: "I intend that the absolute power that you normally have, Holy Father, more than all the others with your cardinal sons of the Church, be granted to me."[16] The phrase "figliuoli cardini della Chiesia" is especially ambiguous since the term

---

[15] Among the renditions of the "paese di Cuccagna" in Italian Renaissance literature, Rossi lists a sixteenth-century *Trionfo dei poltroni* (399) and early seventeenth-century *Trionfo della Cuccagna* (400). See also Boiteux 36-45. Basile refers to this segment as simply reflecting a "carnevalesque code in decline" ("codice carnascialesco in declino") and "the myth of the 'saturnali'" (12n).

[16] Of course, the emperor exaggerates since the pope never had absolute power. See Lottieri for how the power struggles between the pope and various secular authorities played out over time, actually allowing for greater autonomy of Italy's smaller political units.

"sons" could be read in a biological rather than spiritual sense to indicate papal nepotism.[17] After all, Pope Innocent VIII (1484–92) had two illegitimate children before he entered the clergy. When his eldest son married Lorenzo de' Medici's daughter, he granted the cardinal's hat to Lorenzo's son Giovanni (later Pope Leo X). Pope Alexander VI (1492–1503) was particularly notorious for conferring church benefices upon his illegitimate sons, most famously Cesare Borgia upon whom he bestowed the cardinalate in 1493 (Gervaso 102-13).[18]

As the narrative moves back to third person discourse, the reader learns that the emperor went on to speak "of arms and great deeds of war and, taking the currycomb in his hand, made fencing motions in front of those kings, princes, and lords, and then in their name responded with the most inane speeches in the world" ("de opera d'arme e de gran facti de guerra e, prendendo la striglia in mano, scrimiva denanti a quilli re, principi e signori, e poi in nome de loro respondeva le magior papolate del mondo" 15-16). The scene concludes as the emperor, "creating mayhem in the world through his weapons" ("ponendo il mondo sottosopra in arme" 16), counters the pope's initial speech with an exhortation to take up arms on his behalf. And while the emperor's vision of a diabolical paradise may have vividly opposed the pope's threats, in his own desire to rule the earth he simply replaces the pope's spiritual threats and incentives with material ones: "Brothers of mine, if you will not follow my will and counsel for love of fava-bean polenta and soup, you will fall into my disfavor" ("Fratelli miei, se non sequireti il mio volere e consiglio per amore del maco e della suppa, cadereti nella mia disgrazia" 16). Indeed, his reference to purely culinary incentives dispenses with the pretense that he is concerned with the fate of humankind or Christendom when inciting others to wage war. His choice, moreover, of dishes that were staples of peasant cooking rather than exquisite or exotic delicacies apt to entice royalty, while comically deflating the figure of the emperor, may also remind readers of the humble social origins of the actor behind the imperial persona he is portraying.

---

[17] I thank one of my readers for noting further that the syntagm "figliuoli cardini" contains an additional ironic, parodic, and satirical tone in that several of the prelates' biological sons also became cardinals, a term derived from *cardine* (hinge, pivot), in this case of the church.

[18] "All [popes ruling from the 1450s on] exploited the papacy to promote their families' political and economic interests. The horror provoked by the cardinalates and bishoprics that Sixtus IV [1471-84] showered on his licentious and bloodthirsty Riario nephews (six bishoprics to Pietro) was exceeded only (perhaps) by Alexander VI's favours to his son Cesare Borgia, Captain General of the papal armies" (Peterson 74).

148   Jo Ann Cavallo

The Drama's Political Implications
In his classic *Popular Culture in Early Modern Europe*, Peter Burke asks: "How can we tell whether ordinary people were politically conscious or not?" (259). Studying popular movements and literature from western Europe between 1500 and 1800, Burke finds, in fact, that "craftsmen and peasants were taking an increasing interest in the actions of governments and feeling a greater sense of involvement with politics than before" (259).[19] Their attention, moreover, tended to be focused on rulers of states rather than local affairs.[20] It may therefore not be so incongruous that Arienti's stable boy spends his only free hour each day elaborately staging a diatribe between the pope and emperor. This provocative criticism of papal and imperial authority would have resonated, moreover, with contemporary readers, who routinely witnessed popes engaging in secular politics to increase their temporal power as well as potentates warmongering to extend their wealth and territory.

Yet, rather than comment on Triunfo's blatantly irreverent treatment of the pope and emperor, the narrator intervenes at this point to draw attention to the protagonist's state of mind: "And in this way, sweetly fantasizing, he persuaded himself during that time that he was the emperor" ("e a questo modo, beccandose dolcemente il cerveletto, se persuadeva per quel tempo essere imperatore" 16). Bruno Basile, editor of the novella collection's most recent edition (1981), instructs the reader to view Triunfo's actions in equally disparaging terms, replacing the narrator's allusion to a purportedly mental feat of persuasion with a reference to Triunfo's emotional state of "hopefulness" and, subsequently, to his "sweet madness" (12n). Nothing in the narrative itself, however, would lead us to surmise either that Triunfo had persuaded himself he was actually an emperor, as the narrator would have it, or that in his craziness he hoped to rule the world, as Basile would seem to suggest. At no point during the scene does Arienti allow us to ascertain what Triunfo is harboring within his heart and soul as he gives voice to the pope and emperor. On the contrary, by directly reporting the dialogue and action, the author compels us to experience the scene as a performance.[21]

---

[19] Although *Le porretane* fall outside Burke's range of dates by a decade, his study still offers invaluable insights into the daily reality of working classes in Renaissance Italy relevant to this novella.

[20] "For the early modern period it may be appropriate to define as 'affairs of state,' not local issues but the concerns of rulers, in other words the succession, war, taxation, and economic and religious problems in so far as they forced themselves on the attention of governments. Political consciousness might be defined as awareness of these problems and their possible solutions, involving a 'public opinion', and a critical (though not necessarily hostile) attitude to the government" (Burke, *Popular Culture* 259).

[21] The novella genre allows for a split between the events related and the storyteller's commentary on those events. Since the judgment expressed in this instance is contrary to

Indeed, Triunfo's contrast between the pope and emperor has all the trappings of an outright theatrical spectacle. Through the backdrop, props, and various characters impersonated in the dialogue, Triunfo has brought an imaginary setting to life, even enacting a play within a play by relating the emperor's visit to Lucifer's realm in first-person discourse. What is particular to this novella is that the protagonist is staging a daily performance, not for an audience of spectators, but for his own private pleasure. Triunfo has intentionally kept his show beyond the gaze of his employer — and everyone else, for that matter. At the end of his allotted hour, he returns to his customary duties in the house and stables "with the greatest diligence" ("cum summa diligenzia").

In this light, the dramatic space may evoke yet another connotation of "Camerino," pertaining specifically to theater, since the "camerino" is the dressing room in which an actor sheds his everyday identity and takes on the guise of the character he will be portraying. At the outset, in fact, the reader witnesses Triunfo changing into the personage of the emperor by donning a crown and taking hold of a scepter, two symbols of his power. At the conclusion of the emperor's dialogue, moreover, he refers to his power metonymically as "this crown of mine" ("questa mia corona") while putting "his hand over the round gilded white paper on his head" ("la mano sopra una carta tonda dorata avea in capo" 16). By simultaneously picturing both the "emperor" speaking within the play and the actor Triunfo making use of his props, Arienti comically draws our attention from the scene represented to the act of representation itself.[22]

Interestingly, Italian folk theater that has survived into the present shares some of the same characteristics as Triunfo's one-man show. Traditional puppet theater, currently confined to Sicily but once popular in parts of the Italian peninsula as well, often begins with a council scene in which the emperor Charlemagne is surrounded by his knights and the Bishop Turpin, with the puppeteer giving voice to the various characters in turn.[23] Storytellers and

---

the details of the plot, I treat it as the view not of the author himself but of the storyteller, who later explains his personal relation to the events described.

[22] In this context, the repeated references to the "camera" in this scene may be deliberately evocative of Triunfo's theatrical vocation: he is depicted entering his "camera," extending the backdrop along the wall of this same "camera," and exiting the "camera" to go back to his daily business; moreover, when Piero later takes on the guise of spectator, he is said to be looking through a hole in the wall of the "camera."

[23] As McCormick notes, "passing references reveal much puppet activity in the sixteenth century, but the concrete documents out of which a history might be written are all but non-existent" (9). He goes on to cite a 1552 description in which glove-puppets "catch each other, play, joke, kill one another and take castles from each other" (10). On this matter see also Calì 21-34.

singers (*cuntisti* and *contastorie*) have also traditionally adopted the voices of their different characters, using rudimentary, symbolic props, such as a sword and a crown, as needed. And like Triunfo's play, the chivalric narratives in folk representations are noted to have sometimes staged politically charged critiques of those in power (Pasqualino 115-19).

Surveillance
All is well until Piero delli Ubaldini, "unable to ascertain or even imagine how Triunfo was spending [his free time]" ("né potendo pensare né imaginare in che cosa Triunfo el spendesse" 16), decides to find out for himself and "secretly" ("secretamente") watches Triunfo through a crack in the wall of the room. Surveillance was certainly not unknown in Renaissance Italy. On the contrary, it was customary for a ruler to spy on political rivals and allies as well as those under his control. Noting that "the use of secret viewing and listening devices was common in the palaces of rulers," Randall Albury cites Paolo Cortesi's recommendation of this practice in the residences of cardinals, the architect Francesco di Giorgio's design of a listening tube for use in the palaces of princes, and Pope Julius II's peephole in the wall of the Sistine Chapel (330). Piero, however, is not a suspicious ruler spying on subordinates to discover machinations against him or surreptitiously supervising the output of his workers. He is more akin to a *voyeur* eager to catch a glimpse of actions that are outside his jurisdiction. Additionally, given that the detailed description of the scene is recounted prior to the act of surveillance, readers are not made to look through the peephole along with Piero, as it were, and are thus distanced from his questionable action.

Yet in his obsession to discover Triunfo's personal business, Piero does more than display unruly curiosity. Using Henry Sumner Maine's distinction between a "society of contract" — where free agreements made between individuals are to be respected — and a "society of status" — where a hereditary position grants one a privilege over the lives of those beneath one's social rank — one could say that Piero here illicitly steps from the former to the latter.[24] His infringement of the contract is a denial of Triunfo's negotiated right to privacy, even a negation of his personhood. Indeed, it seems to be the very fact of his servant's privacy that is so disturbing to him.

It may therefore not be a coincidence that at the moment in which the

---

[24] Or perhaps, using Kant's distinction between "*citizen* (*citoyen*)" and "servant," we might say that Triunfo considers himself the former, being "*his own master* (*sui iuris*)" in that "he own[s] some sort of property — among which may be counted any skill, craft, fine art, or science that supports him," whereas Piero here reveals that he treats his domestic employees as the latter, "mere *operarii*" or providers of "services (*operam*)" (emphasis in the original, 63).

nobleman spies on the stable boy, the latter is referred to as *his* ("il suo") Triunfo for the first time in the novella. The confirmation that Piero views the groom as his possession comes with the first words that he speaks after witnessing the spectacle: "O Triunfo mio" (16).[25] In addition, while Piero is still looking through the peephole, he calls "some of his familiars" ("alcuni suoi domestici") to share the vision. And although the tale's narrator had hitherto not indicated any personal relation to Piero, he now discloses that his own father was among those called to witness the scene. This would make his father a subordinate within Piero's intimate circle, asked to share his point of view while joining in the fun at Triunfo's expense. This stated personal connection may also alert the reader to a possible bias in the storyteller's opinions or judgments regarding the action.

When Piero has "taken enough pleasure" ("preso assai piacere" 16) from Triunfo, his interruption of the play confirms that he is laughing at his servant rather than appreciating his biting wit. The only aspect of the performance that Piero perceived, it seems, was Triunfo's transformation from his everyday domestic role in the household to that of his stage character in the privacy of his chamber. He subsequently ridicules the notion of social mobility — the very possibility that a groom could rise to the rank of a ruler, even in his imagination — by mockingly declaring his great happiness ("io me alegro summamente" 16) over Triunfo's advancement from stable boy to the emperor of Christendom. Perhaps Piero's skewered interpretation of the performance implies a latent insecurity. Although in a society of status such social ascension would in fact be inconceivable, it was perhaps not theoretically impossible at the time if one recalls Machiavelli's attention in *Il principe* to the ways in which private citizens (*privati*) could become rulers (*principi*) (especially chapters 6-8).[26]

The Voided Contract
Piero delli Ubaldini reveals that he does not think of Triunfo as an individual, moreover, but rather as part of a category when he comments that the servant's ascent from stable boy to emperor has brought about not his own personal happiness, but rather the "consolation of your family and your homeland" ("consolazione di tuoi e della tua patria" 16). In attempting to spread the taint of Triunfo's supposed folly to his relatives and birthplace, the aristocratic employer

---

[25] Although the possessive adjective in these cases may also denote familiarity or affection, the possessive quality nevertheless fits well with Piero's invasion of Triunfo's privacy.
[26] In *Discorsi* 2.2, moreover, Machiavelli muses that in a society in which "a man has children in the confidence that he can rear them and feels sure that his patrimony will not be taken away" (280; "ciascuno procrea volentieri quegli figliuoli che crede potere nutrire, non dubitando che il patrimonio gli sia tolto" 1: 750), his children could even become rulers (*principi*) through their virtue (*virtù*).

apparently cannot go beyond a collectivist mindset which groups people according to their circumstances of birth rather than their individual identity and merit. Triunfo does not even deign to reply to this jibe on social mobility. What he does instead is to immediately demonstrate his *physical* mobility: "[...] having quickly taken his curtain from the wall and folded it, without taking leave he departs from the house and the territory" ("[...] tolto prestamente la sua cortina dal muro e quella piegata, senza prendere licenzia se partì de casa e della terra" 17).

Although the summary introducing the novella anticipated that Triunfo "in the end would be shamed" ("alfin se trova vergognato"), the narrative at this point does not depict him as experiencing any shame at all. The only reference to his state of mind is his utter bewilderment ("se smaritte oltra modo" 17). By underscoring the immediacy of Triunfo's departure, Arienti highlights above all his decisiveness in asserting his rights even in a state of shock. A crucial phrase in the account of his departure is "without taking leave" ("senza prendere licenzia"), which echoes the earlier statement that nobody was authorized to enter his room "without his permission" ("senza sua licenzia"). Indeed, as Triunfo was earlier free to establish a relationship with his employer by mutual consent, he is now free to depart when the latter has broken his side of the agreement. Through this demonstration of unobstructed autonomy, Triunfo acts out — indeed, for real this time — the concept of self-ownership.

Even though Piero makes fun of Triunfo for impersonating the emperor, it is he who loses out in the end. His unauthorized surveillance violates the only condition that Triunfo had imposed upon him, thus rendering the contract null and void. His punishment is to be deprived of a marvelously capable employee, one that, as noted earlier, he would not have wanted to lose for the whole world ("che per cosa del mondo non l'averebbe lassato da sé partire" 13). And just as no information is provided about Triunfo's activities before he establishes an employment contract with Messer Piero, neither the reader nor the nobleman shall ever know what becomes of him after his exit: "And where he may have gone it seems that nobody ever knew" ("e dove s'andasse pare non se sapesse mai" 17). If knowledge is power, Arienti does not allow anyone to gain even this kind of implicit power over his protagonist. This refusal to indulge the reader's potential curiosity at the novella's conclusion reaffirms Triunfo's absolute right to privacy.

If Dennis Romano's study of household contracts in Venetian account book entries is any indication, Triunfo's early departure would not have been that unusual. On average men servants stayed only 1.5 years of the contracted period of 5.4 years, while women remained 3.5 years of a stipulated 7.6 years.[27]

---

[27] The contracts examined were numerically very few (eighteen in the course of two centuries), but the results are telling as a point of comparison for Arienti's novella. La

Moreover, servants moved back and forth between service and other occupations. Romano further points out that servitude as a contractual relationship was at odds with the paternalistic standards of loyalty and obedience masters expected. In Arienti's novella, the nobleman forgets that their relationship is a contractual one and behaves as though he had ownership over his employee's privacy. Triunfo's instantaneous departure exposes Piero's error.

Triunfo's freedom of movement is not only in opposition to servitude, which binds individuals to the land and to others without their consent, but is also beyond the mobility allowed within the courtier system that pertained in Renaissance Italian courts. Indeed, Triunfo's utter autonomy would have been the envy of many of the author's contemporaries of higher social standing. A few decades later Baldassare Castiglione risked being seized by agents of the Marquis Francesco Gonzaga of Mantova, incensed that the courtier had left his entourage to serve Guidobaldo da Montefeltro in Urbino.[28] The Estense in nearby Ferrara had instituted laws prohibiting those in their service from seeking employment elsewhere without their permission. From his prison cell, where he was detained indefinitely, Torquato Tasso compared the Estense ruler to Nero, complaining that his fault was simply to have made statements that courtiers make when they aim to seek employment elsewhere (*Prose* 852 and 846).

The Fictional Frame

The terms for pleasure (*piacere*) and fun (*solazzo*) are used in conjunction with both Triunfo's daily performances in themselves and the experience of the frame's viewers — even if the nature of the pleasure and the fun differs significantly in each case. Initially, Triunfo is said to spend his customary hour "in this pleasure" ("in questo piacere"), signalling the performance as an enjoyable activity associated with leisure.[29] At the moment of Piero's eavesdropping, the scene he witnesses is initially referred to as "this amusement" ("questo solazzo"), and the nobleman subsequently calls his familiars to share with him "so much pleasure" ("tanto piacere"). At this point the storyteller's own father also hears and sees Triunfo "to his very great amusement" ("cum suo grandissimo solazzo" 16). In this final instance, with the

---

Roncière also notes the frequency with which masters changed servants (and vice versa): "Of thirty engagements mentioned in the fifteenth-century memoirs of three Florentine families, only four were for more than one year" (232).

[28] For references to Castiglione's letters regarding this incident and further reading on the character of Francesco II Gonzaga, see Barberis xxixn65.

[29] Pleasure takes on a different connotation in the scene reported to the reader when the emperor's summary of the hedonistic life-style he seeks includes "triumph" in the impersonal usage of the verb ("se li triunfa" "one triumphs there") along with the phrase "dasse piacere, buon tempo e chiara vita" ("one enjoys pleasure, a good time, and a happy life" 15).

shift from a single spectator to additional privileged onlookers, the magnitude of the enjoyment reaches the absolute superlative. Yet the delight associated with Triunfo's performance is quite distinct from the kind of satisfaction the aristocratic employer and his immediate subordinates derive from their prying.

Those comprising the *nobile brigata* also clearly derive pleasure from the tale since they are said to have been listening with "festive laughter" ("festevol riso"). Is theirs the complicit enjoyment of an ideal audience or the derogatory amusement shown by the frame's eavesdroppers? Arienti does not make this immediately apparent; indeed, the group's reaction offers two very different ways of reading the novella. Claiming without any basis that Triunfo was a crazy person who lacked self-understanding, their first *sententia* is that the "defect of the madman is that he believes himself wise (whereas, were he to recognize his madness, he would commit suicide)" ("defecto del pazzo sì è ch'el crede essere savio ove, se la sua pacia [pazzia] cognoscesse, se occidirebbe" 17). The second moral expounds the exact opposite, i.e., that Triunfo was indeed happy with his status:

In this world there is no greater repose than to be content with one's own state, as was Triunfo, who according to his empty pumpkin-head led himself to believe he was the emperor, not worrying any further about himself, since to him it was as though this was his own status.

In questo mondo non è magior riposo che contentarse del stato suo, come faceva Triunfo, il quale secundo la sua zuca vota se dava a intendere essere imperatore, non più oltra curandose, ché tanto a lui valeva come proprio fusse stato.

(17)

Yet even a mildly attentive reader could notice the contradiction between first praising Triunfo as an illustration of the peace of mind derived from accepting one's station in life and then immediately afterward deriding him for believing he was an emperor. With his role-playing dubbed as subjective illusion, Triunfo is thus transformed into a Don Quixote *avant la lettre*, a predecessor of the poor *hidalgo* who fancied himself a great knight, forsaking reality to live within his own fantasy world. In addition to not corresponding to the actual details related in the story, this conclusion is a clear example of double-talk.

The fictional frame thus provides Arienti with the cover for speaking against the power elite in a way that would not otherwise be permitted in polite discourse. Triunfo's brazen condemnation of the pope (and, to a lesser extent, the emperor) can be registered by the reader, while the fictitious inner circle of listeners, both within the novella and in the frame story, shift the focus back onto the protagonist.[30] Given the danger of openly critiquing the pope and other powerful figures, the brigata's off-the-cuff comments following the novella may not indicate their incapacity for understanding, but rather offer a way to draw attention away from the provocative content of Triunfo's discourse by alleging his insanity.[31] The claim of insanity, after all, was a strategy contemplated by Torquato Tasso to protect himself from the Inquisition, although it was subsequently used against him by the Estense state to keep him confined to prison (Gigante).

We may recall that the first novella of the *Decameron* likewise involves multiple audiences whose understanding depends upon their greater or lesser knowledge of the protagonist. Ser Ciappelletto's deathbed performance — in which he retroactively refashions his life from the most sinful to the most saintly — holds a different meaning for the unwary priest who hears his confession, the two brothers who host Ciappelletto, the credulous people of the village, and ultimately those in the frame story and beyond. Although we know that the unscrupulous notary was sent to collect unpaid debts in Burgundy, Boccaccio's narrator refuses to tell us his whereabouts after his departure from the world, i.e., whether he ended up in heaven or hell. Even if the two *novelle* are dissimilar in fundamental ways, they both point to issues involving contractual relationships, the withholding of knowledge regarding the protagonist's ultimate destination, and varying degrees of readerly competence. What is most relevant for Arienti's first novella is how Boccaccio devised diametrically opposed interpretations of Ciappelletto's staged confession based on differing knowledge of the situation.

Historical Context
Regarding specifically the political content in Triunfo's staged scene, historians point out that throughout this period the European sovereigns, including the popes, tended to pay lip service to combating the Turks while they were mostly intent on aggressing against each other (Housley 124–25). It would be difficult,

---

[30] Such prohibition did not completely stop writers from voicing critiques of papal abuses, from Dante's and Boccaccio's condemnation of the popes and the Roman curia to Castiglione's jokes about the violence and ineptitude of previous popes and the general state of corruption in Rome.

[31] Using the same words to convey a range of meanings to distinct members of an audience was a skill expected of the diplomat and courtier. A few decades later Castiglione would assert that at the court of Urbino "fine questions would sometimes be proposed, and sometimes ingenious games [...] in which, under various concealments, those present revealed their thoughts allegorically to whomever they chose" ("talor si proponeano belle questioni, talor si faceano alcuni giochi ingeniosi [...] ne' quali sotto varii velami spesso scoprivano i circonstanti allegoricamente i pensier sui a chi più loro piaceva" *Book of the Courtier* 1.5).

however, to find any writings openly speaking against the crusades because of the possible repercussions. As James Hankins notes, "The arguments in favor of a policy of crusade could be stated, the arguments against it could not. Nevertheless," as he goes on to point out, "there are numerous hints and indirect evidence that many humanists, like other members of the public, had deep reservations about the feasibility and utility of crusading" ("Renaissance Crusaders" 124). It would be more likely to encounter critiques voiced through dissimulation, the technique that Baldassar Castiglione (1478-1529) defines as saying one thing and tacitly meaning another (*Book of the Courtier* 2.72).

Directly condemning a current pope or ruler for any reason, moreover, could have been deemed "verbal violence," a crime sometimes punished with gruesome measures. In noting that, "generally speaking, insults by inferiors to superiors were taken very seriously," Peter Burke relates that "in fourteenth-century Venice, 'verbal violence' against the doge or lesser officials of the commune was severely punished (sometimes by cutting off the offender's tongue)" (*Historical Anthropology of Early Modern Italy* 99). Unofficial forms of censorship were also at work well before the first Index of Prohibited Books was put into place in 1557. Ludovico Ariosto (1473-1533), for example, wrote his comedy *Il Negromante* at the invitation of Leo X, to be performed in Rome during the carnival of 1520. But it was not staged at that time, Dennis Looney notes, most likely because comments in the prologue about ecclesiastical abuses upset the pope so much that he blocked its performance. When it was finally staged for the carnival in Ferrara in 1529, it had been substantially rewritten with a new prologue in which the offensive comments about the papacy had been removed (Looney 33-34).

There was also a series of conflictual relations between the Papal See and the Bentivoglio rulership that forms a specific historical background to the play within the novella. During the 1460s, Pope Paul II engaged in a power struggle to "secure more revenue from Bologna and to impose more control by the Apostolic Camera" (Robertson 206). It was generally believed that the pope's goal in his dealings with Bologna "was to establish there direct Papal rule" (Robertson 207). Although, ironically, Paul II's interference in Bolognese affairs actually enabled the tyrant Giovanni Bentivoglio to gain greater political power over the city, a later pope, Pope Julius II, would succeed in overthrowing Bentivoglio's regime militarily in 1506, an occasion commemorated at the opening of Castiglione's *Cortegiano*.[32] Papal pressure on Bologna, moreover,

---

[32] Robertson notes: "Although there are ways in which Julius II can be seen as thereby carrying further the programme of Paul II for Bologna, it needs to be remembered that the 'tyranny' from which Julius liberated Bologna was not so much the one that Paul II had in his sights from the beginning of the pontificate, as the new 'tyranny' which Paul II himself, probably inadvertently, created through his intervention in Bolognese affairs"

was not an isolated case. As David S. Peterson writes, "Renaissance popes became obsessed with creating a temporal state in central Italy that drew them ever deeper into secular politics, thereby diminishing their spiritual credibility" (60).[33]

Giovanni Sabadino degli Arienti's Life and Other Works
Arienti's own personal history, moreover, suggests an affinity with Triunfo's situation. The son of a barber and student of contract law ("notaria") at the University of Bologna, he was employed as secretary to Andrea Bentivoglio, the central figure in *Le porretane*'s frame story, until the latter's death in 1491. When Bologna's despot Giovanni Bentivoglio refused to renew his position in 1495, Arienti sought and obtained for a couple of years the patronage of Ercole I d'Este, at whose court he had been temporarily employed as "cameriero secondo" during the festivities accompanying Alfonso d'Este and Anna Sforza's 1491 wedding (James, *Giovanni Sabadino degli Arienti* 35). It is during this latter period that Arienti published *Le porretane*, dedicating the volume to Ercole d'Este. If Triunfo seems to have been a voluntary free-lance stable boy, Arienti was forced by circumstances to become a free-lance courtier.

Throughout his career as a courtier serving different patrons, in fact, Arienti directed his attention to the uses (and obliquely, abuses) of political power. In an early work meant for very limited circulation, the warm praise of Andrea Bentivoglio's father Ludovico implicitly harbored strong criticism of the current ruler Giovanni Bentivoglio (*De civica salute*).[34] In his *Vita del conte e senatore Andrea Bentivoglio*, Sabadino degli Arienti maintains that although Andrea could have become a *condottiere*, Ludovico explicitly wanted to keep his son away from a position of power ("volle lui urbanamente vivesse senza mormorazione di alcuno; conciofossecché sempre egli aveva fuggito tale stato e quello gli andava dietro" 13). A later encomiastic work commissioned by Giovanni Bentivoglio, the description of the wedding celebration of Giovanni's son Annibale to Ercole d'Este's daughter Lucrezia, may denote an implicit critique of the ruler's politically motivated courtly display through its dry, unenthusiastic rendering (*Hymeneo Bentivoglio*). Characterizing the work as a "modulated and rather impassive, if faithfully observed, account of the wedding," James wonders whether Giovanni's dissatisfaction with it may have

---

(225). See Robertson for a detailed history of the vicissitudes between Pope Paul II and Bologna, especially the chapter "The Impact of Paul II's Intervention in Bolognese Affairs" (205-25). See Ady for the Bentivoglio's regime in Bologna.

[33] On the political power of popes during the Renaissance, see also Jong and Prodi.

[34] James finds Arienti's early tributes to Ludovico and Andrea Bentivoglio to be, like those in the contemporary *Le porretane*, "a regretful and nostalgic acknowledgement of the greater wisdom of their political values" (*Giovanni Sabadino degli Arienti* 51). For the *De civica salute*, see also Robertson 118-20.

influenced his refusal to reverse the decision to discontinue Arienti's stipend (*Giovanni Sabadino degli Arienti* 50). And even Arienti's volume of women's biographies, *Gynevera de le clare donne*, often expresses "concern that power be exercised within a moral context," clearly acknowledging that his powerful female addressees "could be instruments of more positive political values" (James, *Giovanni Sabadino degli Arienti* 79).

Yet the writing by Arienti that might have resonated most for Ercole d'Este and his entourage is the above-mentioned *De triumphis religionis*.[35] Likewise dedicated to Ercole, this treatise opens reflecting on the praise that would be due humankind if humans could only live by the following divine commandment of nature: "Let us not do to others that which we would not want done to us" ("Non faciamo noi ad altri quello che non vorebbeno fusse facto a noi" 29). Adherence to this commandment — which readers can recognize as the Golden Rule that reverberates across centuries and cultures, from the *Analects* of Confucius to all major religions to the non-aggression principle at the basis of contemporary libertarian philosophy — is said to be especially important for "the princes of the earth, who, as is rightful and reasonable, must give a good example to others" ("li principi dela tera, li quali debeno dare non meno per debito che per rasone, felice examplo al proximo" 29). In a panegyric that could also serve as positive reinforcement, Arienti celebrates Ercole precisely in this regard "for the excellent example that you give to your illustrious and distinguished progeny and to those who rule and govern realms, states, and empires, and to any mortal whether of noble or humble birth" ("per lo optimo exemplo che duoni al tuo illustre e preclaro sangue et a chi rege et guberna regni, stati et imperi e a qualuncha mortale de alta e humile fortuna" 29). If in the encomiastic *De triumphis religionis* the Estense duke serves as a model for the kind of behavior to follow, in the novella the lowly stable boy Triunfo stages and critiques instead the kind of behavior to avoid.

Conclusion
Regarding the staged scene, then, one might say that Triunfo da Camarino enacts a "Triumph from the Little Room" since it is within his small chamber that he stages a memorable drama that successfully speaks truth to power. Whereas the power structure of *raison d'état* requires absolute secrecy regarding a ruler's machinations but transparency regarding the most mundane activities of the subjects, Triunfo enacts a reversal in which he uses his right to privacy to lay

---

[35] The *De triumphis religionis* was written in 1495. The dating of *Le porretane* is more problematic: although Arienti claimed to have completed *Le porretane* in 1478 and the incunabulum bears the fictitious date of 1483, James posits that some parts were written as late as 1489 and 1492, with its final completion dating between 1492 and 1495 (*Giovanni Sabadino degli Arienti* 26).

bare the machinations of the pope, one of Europe's most powerful rulers. Assuming the guise of the emperor, the pope's secular counterpart, Triunfo soundly refutes the pope's argument and exposes his hypocrisy, exercising a freedom to chastise that would be dangerous if expressed by someone with less power than that of the emperor, whom he pretends to personify. At the same time, despite the verve with which Triunfo plays the part of the emperor, he nevertheless reveals a figure who similarly resorts to threats to coerce others to carry out his military aggression. As Mises writes with regard to "the Reich of the Nazis and the commonwealth of the Marxians," the emperor's plan requires nothing less than "the violent subjection of all those not ready to yield without resistance" (199).

In the end, Triunfo opposes the pope's and the emperor's coercive *modus operandi* not only through the scene he stages in his small room (his "triunfo da camerino"), but also through his own actions in the course of the novella. Whereas his performance draws attention to the *political means* used by those in power, his interactions with his employer illustrate instead the *economic means* underlying consensual exchange in the marketplace. According to sociologist Franz Oppenheimer, who coined the terms, there is a fundamental opposition between these two means of seeking to attain one's desires: the first, epitomized by the state, entails the dominion of a victorious group over the vanquished and the forced appropriation of the labor of others; the second, at work in society at large, rests on the voluntary exchange of goods and services among groups and individuals (24-27). In the first case, the pope and emperor resort to coercion and threats — concerning both this world and the next — in order to wage war and increase their power. By contrast, in the private space of Piero's household, the contractual parties freely negotiate mutually acceptable conditions. When the aristocratic employer violates the contract by invading the servant's privacy, the latter responds by exercising his unquestioned right to depart as a sovereign individual. His spontaneous and wordless action underscores the fact that his employer, despite his superior social status, does not hold any power over him. Whereas Piero had initially noted that Triunfo's *appearance* corresponded to his illustrious name, by the end of the tale one realizes that his *behavior* does so even more strikingly since he could be said to exemplify the triumph of self-ownership, complete with a lesson in consensual contracts, personal privacy, and the indisputable freedom of movement.

Columbia University

Works Cited

Ady, Cecilia M. *The Bentivoglio of Bologna: A Study in Despotism*. London: Oxford UP, 1937.

Albury, William Randall. "Castiglione's *Francescopaedia*: Pope Julius II and Francesco Maria della Rovere in *The Book of the Courtier*." *Sixteenth Century Journal* 42.2 (2011): 323–47.

Arienti, Giovanni Sabadino degli. [*De triumphis religionis*] *Art and Life at the Court of Ercole I d'Este: The* De triumphis religionis *of Giovanni Sabadino degli Arienti*. Ed. with an introduction and notes by Werner L. Gundersheimer. Geneva: Libraries Droz, 1972.

———. *Le porretane*. Ed. Bruno Basile. Roma: Salerno Editrice, 1981.

———. *Vita del conte e senatore Andrea Bentivoglio*. Ed. Gaetano Giordani. Bologna: Tipi della Volpe, 1840.

Barberis, Walter, "Introduction." *Il libro del Cortegiano*. By Baldesar Castiglione. Ed. Walter Barberis. Torino: Einaudi, 1998. VII-LXV.

Basile, Bruno, "Introduction." Arienti. *Le porretane* ix-lii.

Boccaccio, Giovanni. *The Decameron*. Trans. G. H. McWilliam. 1972. New York: Penguin, 1995.

———. *Decameron*. Ed. Amedeo Quondam, Maurizio Fiorilla, and Giancarlo Alfano. Milano: BUR Classici, 2013.

Boiteux, Martine. "L'immaginario dell'abbondanza alimentare. Il paese di Cuccagna nel Rinascimento." http://digidownload.libero.it/aisea/atti_2006/saggio%20BOITEUX.pdf.36-45. Updated version of essay originally in *Strategie del cibo: simboli, saperi, pratiche*. Ed. Ernesto Di Renzo. Roma: Bulzoni, 2005. 23-40.

Burke, Peter. *Historical Anthropology of Early Modern Italy: Essays on Perception and Communication*. Cambridge: Cambridge UP, 1987.

———. *Popular Culture in Early Modern Europe*. c1978. Burlington, VT: Ashgate, 2009.

Calì, Massimo. *Burattini e marionette tra Cinque e Seicento in Italia*. Azzano San Paolo (BG): Associazione Peppino Sarina, 2002.

Castiglione, Baldassare. *The Book of the Courtier*. Trans. Charles S. Singleton. New York: Doubleday, 1959.

———. *Il libro del Cortegiano*. Ed. Walter Barberis. Torino: Einaudi, 1998.

De Marchi, Andrea. "Pittori a Camerino nel Quattrocento: le ombre di Gentile e la luce di Piero." In *Pittori a Camerino nel Quattrocento*. Ed. Andrea de Marchi. Milano: Federico Motta, 2002. 24-99.

Di Stefano, Emanuela. "Un profilo economico: i mercanti e le arti." *Il Quattrocento a Camerino: luce e prospettiva nel cuore della Marca*. Ed. Andrea De Marchi and Maria Giannatiempo López. Milano: Federico Motta, 2002. 46-50.

Gervaso, Roberto. *I Borgia*. Milano: Rizzoli, 1976.

Gigante, Claudio. *Tasso*. Roma: Salerno, 2007.

Hankins, James. "Renaissance Crusaders: Humanist Crusade Literature in the Age of Mehmed II." *Dumbarton Oaks Papers* 49 (1995): 111–207.

Housley, Norman. *The Later Crusades, 1274–1580: From Lyons to Alcazar*. Oxford: Oxford UP, 1992.

James, Carolyn. *Giovanni Sabadino degli Arienti: A Literary Career*. Firenze: Olschki, 1996.

———, ed. *The Letters of Giovanni Sabadino degli Arienti: 1481-1510*. Firenze: Olschki, 2002.

Jong, Jan L. de. *The Power and the Glorification: Papal Pretensions and the Art of Propaganda in the Fifteenth and Sixteenth Centuries*. University Park, PA: Pennsylvania State UP, 2013.

Kant, Immanuel. *On the Old Saw; That May Be Right in Theory but it Won't Work in Practice*. Trans. E. B. Ashton. Intro. George Miller. Philadelphia, U of Pennsylvania P, 1974.

Kinsella, Stephan. "A Libertarian Theory of Contract: Title Transfer, Binding Promises, and Inalienability." *Journal of Libertarian Studies* 17.2 (2003) 11-37. http://mises.org/journals/jls/17_2/17_2_2.pdf

La Roncière, Charles de. "Tuscan Notables on the Eve of the Renaissance." *A History of Private Life*. Vol. II. *Revelations of the Medieval World*. Ed. Georges Duby. Trans. Arthur Goldhammer. Cambridge, MA: The Belknap Press of Harvard UP, 1988. 157-310.

Leoni, Bruno. "About Strikes and Lockouts." *Law, Liberty, and the Competitive Market*. Ed. Carlo Lottieri. With a foreword by Richard A. Epstein. Trans. Gian Turci and Anne MacDiarmid. New Brunswick, NJ: Transaction Publishers, 2009. 105-26.

Looney, Dennis. "Ariosto's Dialogue with Authority in the *Erbolato*." *Modern Language Notes* 128 (2013): 20-39.

Lottieri, Carlo. *Credere nello Stato? Teologia politica e dissimulazione da Filippo il Bello a WikiLeaks*. Soveria Mannelli: Rubbettino, 2011.

McCormick, John, with Alfonso Cipolla and Alessandro Napoli. *The Italian Puppet Theater: A History*. Jefferson, NC: McFarland, 2011.

Machiavelli, Niccolò. *Discorsi sopra la prima deca di Tito Livio, Dell'arte della guerra e altre opere*. 2 vols. Ed. Rinaldo Rinaldi. Torino: UTET, 2006.

———. *The Discourses*. Ed. Bernard Crick. Trans. Leslie J. Walker, S.J. New York: Penguin, 2003.

———. *The Prince*. Intro. Anthony Grafton. Trans. George Bull. New York: Penguin, 2003.

———. *Il principe*. Ed. Giorgio Inglese. Torino: Einaudi, 1995.

Maine, Henry Sumner. *Ancient Law; in Connection with the Early History of Society, and its Relation to Modern Ideas*. Kitchener, Ont.: Batoche, 1999.

Mises, Ludwig von. *Human Action: A Treatise on Economics*. Auburn, AL: Ludwig von Mises Institute, 1998.

O'Malley, Michelle. *The Business of Art: Contracts and the Commissioning Process in Renaissance Italy*. New Haven: Yale UP, 2005.

Oppenheimer, Franz. *The State: Its History and Development Viewed Sociologically*. Trans. John M. Gitterman. Indianapolis: Forgotton Books, 2012.

Pasqualino, Antonio. *L'opera dei pupi*. Palermo: Sellerio, 1977.

Peterson, David S. "Religion and the Church." *Italy in the Age of the Renaissance*. Ed. John M. Najemy. Oxford: Oxford UP, 2004. 59-81.

Prodi, Paolo. *The Papal Prince: One Body and Two Souls: The Papal Monarchy in Early Modern Europe*. Trans. Susan Haskins. Cambridge, MA: Harvard UP 1987.

———. *Il sovrano pontefice. Un corpo e due anime: la monarchia papale nella prima età moderna*. Bologna: Il Mulino, 1982.

Robertson, Ian. *Tyranny under the Mantle of St Peter: Pope Paul II and Bologna*. Turnhout, Belgium: Brepols, 2002.

Romano, Dennis. *Housecraft and Statecraft: Domestic Service in Renaissance Venice, 1400-1600*. Baltimore: Johns Hopkins UP, 1996.

Rossi, Vittorio. "Il paese di Cuccagna nella letteratura italiana." *Le lettere di messer Andrea Calmo*. Ed Vittorio Rossi. Torino: Ermanno Loescher, 1888. 398-410.

Rothbard, Murray. *For a New Liberty: The Libertarian Manifesto*. 1973. Auburn, AL: The Ludwig von Mises Institute, 2011.
Tasso, Torquato. *Prose*. Ed. Ettore Mazzali. Milano: Ricciardi, 1959.

Laurie Shepard

Petrus Aretinus
Acerrimus Virtutum ac Vitiorum Demonstrator[1]

Abstract: Although Pietro Aretino is closely associated with the vituperative pasquinades attacking prelates at the Roman Curia, the paper argues that Aretino emerges as a satirist who claims the right to speak truth to power only after he settles in the Venetian Republic. The second *Cortigiana,* prepared for publication in 1534, reveals the limits of the pasquinade genre, and in the voice of the courtier Flamminio, Aretino expresses the right to transcend those limits and to speak freely, with the more coherent arguments that would later characterize him as *il Veritiero.*
Key Words: Rome, Venice, Aretino, Leo X, Hadrian VI, Clement VII, Giovanni dalle Bande Nere, Pasquino, pasquinades, comedy, vituperation, satire, courtier.

Aretino as the Voice of Pasquino
Pietro Aretino, a young man of humble birth, limited formal education, quick wit and boundless ambition, arrived in Rome in 1517. Later, Aretino would refer to himself as the Scourge of Princes, *il Flagello dei Principi,* but it is unlikely that his arrival in the papal city caused much of a stir. In 1517, the Medici Pope Leo X was facing multiple crises: an expensive battle to secure the dukedom of Urbino for his nephew Lorenzo, a suspected conspiracy among the cardinals, and empty Church coffers. In the same year and ultimately of far greater consequence was a challenge by an Augustinian friar, Martin Luther, who posted ninety-five theses protesting papal abuse of ecclesiastical power in Wittenberg. The public voice of dissent in Rome was a statue — a limbless torso with a featureless head that had been set outside the Palazzo Braschi in Parione by Cardinal Oliviero Carafa in 1501. Known as Pasquillo or Pasquino, the statue was the physical *locus* for displaying epigrams and poems of protest — for the most part witty and vituperative attacks on prominent figures in the Roman Curia.[2] Pietro Aretino neither invented the pasquinade genre, nor was the most ferocious of its practitioners, but he claimed Pasquino's voice as his own, and

---
[1] "Pietro Aretino Keenest Voice of Virtue and Vice." The epithet is inscribed in Marcantonio Raimondi's engraving of the writer as a young courtier in Rome, and later portraits. It recurs in the Marcolini editions of Aretino's *Lettere* in 1538 (Waddington 273n17).
[2] Cesareo identifies "Pasquillo" as the more archaic form (169).

the fearless persona of Pasquino became a means to express his vision of life in the Eternal City and beyond.

This paper explores several episodes in the development of Pietro Aretino as a writer and satirist that take place over almost twenty years from the time of his arrival in Rome in 1517 as a court poet, to propagandist and author of pasquinades advocating the elevation of Giulio de' Medici to the papal throne; to playwright of the first draft of the *Cortigiana*, a comedy hastily sketched in 1525 and in his pack when he fled the city after an attempted assassination; to the satirical voice that claims the freedom to speak the truth to power in the revised *Cortigiana*, published in Venice in 1534.[3] Castiglione, in *Il Cortigiano*, establishes the freedom to speak truth to power as the pinnacle of a courtier's achievements, the reward for meticulously nurturing the trust of the prince.[4] Aretino claims it not as a courtier, but as a citizen of the Republic of Venice where he established himself in 1527. He claims it as an author when he absorbs the voice of Pasquino into the voice of *Monna Comedia*.

What role did the featureless statue in autocratic Rome play in the evolution of the satirist? To argue that the witty dissent of Pasquino allowed the young man to become *Petrus Aretinus acerrimus virtutum ac vitiorum demonstrator,* or later *il Veritiero* as the mature satirist, would be reductive. In fact, by tracing Aretino's increasingly militant assertions of the right to speak his mind, the constraints on the "voice" of the statue become apparent. Aretino's claim to speak the truth as he saw it was achieved through the assiduous cultivation of relationships with the powerful, and the energetic use of the press to disseminate his work to an ever larger and more widely dispersed public.[5] It was achieved in

---

[3] The importance of Aretino's comedies in the maturation of the writer is emphasized by Baratto: "In conclusione, *La Cortigiana* e il *Marescalco* sono le sole opere che esprimano un'esperienza viva e autentica; lontane ugualmente da un impiego strumentale della parola e da una vacua velleità letteraria. Lo scrittore nasce con le due commedie" (*Tre* 85).

[4] In Book IV of *Il Cortigiano,* Ottaviano Fregoso argues that the many years of training and self-denial endured by the courtier have a single proper end: "Il fine, adunque, del perfetto cortigiano, del quale insino a qui non si è parlato, estimo io che sia il guadagnarsi, per mezzo delle condizioni attribuitegli da questi signori, talmente la benevolenza e l'animo di quel principe a cui serve, che possa dirgli, e sempre gli dica, la verità di ogni cosa che a esso convenga sapere, senza timore o pericolo di dispiacergli" (IV.2.15).

[5] Della Corte, editor of an on-line version of the 1534 *Cortigiana,* makes an unambiguous connection between Aretino's exploitation of the press and his appropriation of freedom of speech: "Proprio attraverso questa curvatura sull'impresa editoriale marcoliniana l'argomento si sposta — bruscamente, e però direi seguendo un percorso ancor più profondo — dalla ricchezza di intellettuali a Venezia alla libertà veneziana sub specie di libertà di parola" (208).

the Republic of Venice, where (Dionisotti writes) he lived "libero [...] da ogni servitù cortigiana" (239). As Cairns notes, "by 1534 [...] Aretino had acquired security in Venice, the protection of the Doge, respect 'internationally,' and a fruitful network of contacts with the Venetian patriciate [...]" (37). Nevertheless, throughout his life Aretino retained the animus of Pasquino as a lion does his retractable claws, the analogy he makes in a letter to the Duke of Florence in January 1553, only a few years before his death.[6]

The court of Pope Leo X was the epicenter of Italian cultural life.[7] With Giovanni de' Medici's elevation to the papal throne in 1513 a host of talented Tuscans gathered in Rome. Aretino found a rich stable of wits when he arrived: Cardinal Bernardo Bibbiena; Bernardo Accolti, better known as L'Unico Aretino, poet, playwright and mentor to Aretino; Niccolò Campani (lo Strascino), who became his close friend; Francesco Berni, Aretino's future enemy; Angelo Firenzuola, and Anton Lelio. He befriended artists, most notably Raffael, Titian and Maestro Andrea, another companion. Aretino's activities during his first years in Rome are unknown; he was probably a secretary of the banker Agostino Chigi; then he moved into the circle of Cardinal Giulio de' Medici, the future Pope Clement VII. Aretino received a stipend from Leo on August 21, 1520 (Cesareo 198). Distinguished for his sharp tongue, he is mentioned for the first time in a text entitled *Farza*, a 231-verse conversation in a pastoral setting, in which a young Neapolitan shepherd with ambition to go to court is instructed by a more experienced courtier. Authorship of the *Farza* remains in dispute.[8] It was not written before 1520, and the poem refers to Aretino as a *maldicente,* recommending that the aspiring courtier curry his favor. Although the criticism of life in court is a staple of Aretino's literary production, in the *Farza* the portrait of life there is still entirely enviable.

---

[6] Romei quotes the letter. "Io Signor magnanimo non ho lasciato il Satirico andare di Pasquillo, ma bene, in tenerlo per qualche buon' rispetto da parte, imito i Leoni, i quali, quando caminano, tirano l'vnghie come l'aquile indentro, accio non si logrino, & perche siano tagliente allhora, che gli bisogna preualersene contro le fiere che gli apparisccono innanzi, col veleno, & co i morsi" ("Aretino" 44).

[7] See, for example, Cesareo, Chapter 10, "I letterati" 257-66. Simonetta argues against the reputation of Leo as the patron of artists, citing the fact that the post of "piombatore o sigillatore apostolico" held by the great architect Donato Bramante was given, after Bramante's death, to the buffoon Mariano Fetti. Simonetta observes, "Il grande architetto sostituito dal cortigiano che adulava indiscriminatamente il pontefice per l'uso della sua bocca, che parlasse o mangiasse, rivela senza ombra di dubbio quali fossero le priorità culturali di Leone X" (105).

[8] Larivaille argues that Aretino is not the author (41) — and more recently D'Onghia has published a series of linguistic analyses of the text that prove quite conclusively that this is the case. Faini (ed., 41-48) and Innamorati, *Pietro* (125-30), among others, attribute the work to Aretino.

Following the death of Pope Leo on December 1, 1521, the ensuing period, during which cardinals gathered in conclave to elect a successor, exposed the volatility of papal rule. For the families of cardinals, the *sede vacante* presented the prospect of future prosperity through connections with a newly elected pontiff, but Villard argues that more generally the *sede vacante* aroused a widespread sense regarding the Curia "di frode e di dissimulazione" which was founded "sulla constatazione poco lusinghiera delle transazioni tra i cardinali" (41). Thus the *sede vacante* was open season for pasquinades, the expression of pent-up rage, disappointment, and disdain toward the dead pope and his possible successors, at least anonymously. Composed in Latin in the early decades, the earliest known epigram attacking the Curia dates from the interregnum following the death of Clement IV, which took place in 1268; it was likely the longest conclave in the Catholic Church's history, lasting from the death of Clement IV until 1271, when his successor, Gregory X, was elected. The pasquinades take two forms: the epigram or the metrically loose, extended sonnet, called *sonetti caudati*. Some of the most effective pasquinades are a single verse: *Quod non fecerunt Barbari, Barberini fecerunt* (What the Barbarians didn't do, the Barberini did), following the death of Urban VIII Barberini in 1644.[9] The heterogeneous corpus of pasquinades, which accumulated throughout the centuries, includes accusations of greed, nepotism, simony, lust, sodomy, pederasty, gluttony, vanity, stupidity, and cannibalism. A comprehensive critique of the political system is absent because the pasquinades are *ad hominem* vituperative attacks. Unsuccessful attempts were made to counter the venom of Pasquino with the benign *grillate*.[10] However, the faceless statue played a vital role in the city as an anonymous vehicle to vent rage and envy, while maintaining the status quo.[11]

The quantity and subject of the protests varied with the season. For

---

[9] The text is found at http://www.treccani.it/vocabolario/quod-non-fecerunt-barbari-barbarini-fecerunt/. The translations are mine, with the exception of two pasquinades, translated by Jon Tveit (see note below), and the 1525 *Cortigiana*, translated by Campbell and Sbrocchi. Some scholars view the above-mentioned pasquinade satirizing Urban VIII (Barberini) as apocryphal and unjust: "Barbari e Barberini: una 'pasquinata' ingiusta e apocrifa" (http://www.storiainrete.com/3503/600-e-700/barbari_barberini/).

[10] See, for example, Lastraioli. The *grillate* are the poetic production of a cultural circle patronized by the Roman Curia, which was founded to counter the venom of Paquino. Mostly in vernacular, the *grillate* sing of the glory of Rome, among other more benign topics. The movement was extinguished at the time of the Sack of Rome in 1527. There is another tradition of pasquinades that were essentially associated with scholastic exercises of praise — described by Romei as "rituali, encomiastiche" and "pedantesche" — celebrated on April 25 (feast of Saint Mark the Evangelist), and published intermittently ("Poesia" 2).

[11] I have made these observations in Shepard, "The Power."

example, according to the pope's biographer Giovio, Bishop of Nocera, during the pontificate of Leo X there was a pause in the production of anonymous attacks on the papacy following his brutal suppression of the Petrucci conspiracy in 1517 (Cesareo 109). Over seven hundred pasquinades remain from the decades between 1500 and 1565, and only a dozen from the final decades of the century, when the statue was placed under surveillance (Romei, "Poesia" 2). In 1558, the Roman Inquisition linked the denigration of the faith, Church, and clergy to pasquinades, and harsh penalties were announced for authoring, possessing, or diffusing libelous material in the bull *Romani Pontificis providentia* (1572).[12] Aretino's one-time secretary and protégé, Nicolò Franco, was accused of authoring pasquinades attacking Pope Paul IV and was hanged in Rome in 1570. Nicolò Franco's defense is interesting: he protested that "he had not condemned the Papacy in general," which is in keeping with the limits observed by the authors of pasquinades (Grendler 47-49). In fact, pasquinades attacked individual viciousness but not papal authority.

In 1513, the year of Giovanni de' Medici's election, the Roman treasury was flush with money, but within three years Leo had exhausted the Church's resources. To raise money, Pope Leo created thirty-one new cardinals, as well as 540 new knights, all for a price. He sold the office of cardinal and camerlengo, the administrator who oversees Church revenues, to the powerful merchant Francesco Armellino for the price of 15,000 ducats in cash (Simonetta 195). Pasquino mocked the transaction, suggesting that the Romans themselves be weighed and taxed by the pound:

> Che ogni uomo s'ha giustamente a pesare
> Col manto, con le calze e col brachiero;
> E chi in Roma è stato un giorno intero,
> Un bajocco per libbra ha da pagare.[13]

> (That every man must be properly weighed
> with cloak, stocking and belt;
> And whoever spends a full day in Rome,
> must pay a penny a pound.)

---

[12] Condemned were "Pasquilli omnes, omnesque conscriptiones, in quibus Deo, aut sanctis, aut sacramentis, aut catholicae ecclesiae, et eius cultui, aut Apostolicae Sedi quomodocumque detrahatur" (Fragnito 181-82n1).

[13] Simonetta 195; Romei describes Armellini "dimostrando un'inventiva fiscale e una rapacità fuor del commune" ("Aretino" 31). A *battuta* in the 1534 *Cortigiana* recalls the pasquinade: as Messer Maco prepares to be "moulded" into a courtier, Maestro Andrea quips: "Non ti scordar de la stadera, che subito che l'abbiamo formato bisogna persarlo, e pagar tanto per libbra secondo l'ordine de l'Armellino" (IV.1).

The pope, guided by Armellino, sold or taxed, or attempted to tax whatever was at hand: wine, meat and salt; he tried to sell Lakes Bolsena and Terracina (Cesareo 83). Pasquino quipped that Leo did not receive last rites when he died so suddenly, because he had sold them: "Sacra sub extrema, si forte requiritis, hora / cur Leo non potuit sumere? Vendiderat" (Marucci 87) (If perhaps you ask why Leo was not able / To take the sacraments at his last hour? He had sold them).[14].

Pasquinades that list cardinals and their sins, like "Non ti maravigliar, Roma, se tanto," again from 1521, become typical of the genre in the sixteenth century:

> Non ti maravigliar, Roma, se tanto
> s'indugia a far del papa la elezione,
> perché fra' cardinai Pier, con ragione,
> non truova chi sie degno del suo manto.
> La ragion è che sempre ha moglie acanto
> questo, e quel volentier toca il garzone,
> l'altro a mensa disputa d'un bocone
> e quel di inghiottir pesche si dà il vanto.
> Uno è falsario, l'altro è adulatore
> e questo è ladro e pieno di eresia
> e chi di Giuda è asai piú traditore.
> Chi è di Spagna e chi di Francia spia
> e chi ben mille volte a tute l'ore
> Dio venderebbe per far simonia,
> sí che truovisi via
> di far un buon pastor fuor di conclavi,
> che di san Pietro riscuota le chiavi.
> E quest'uomini pravi,
> che la Chiesa di Dio stiman si poco,
> al ciel per cortesia sbalzi col fuoco.
>
> (Marucci 65-66)

> (Rome, do not marvel if
> it takes so long to elect the pope,
> because among the cardinals, quite rightly, Peter
> does not find one who is worthy of his mantle.
> The reason is that this one always has a wife by his side,
> that one gladly touches his boy,
> another argues over a morsel of food,
> and a fourth boasts he swallows peaches whole.
> One falsifies documents, another is a sycophant
> and this one is a thief full of heresy,

---

[14] Jon Tveit, a 2010 Boston College graduate, translated these pasquinades under the auspices of an undergraduate research fellowship. He is also partially responsible for the translation of *Non ti maravigliar, Roma, se tanto*.

more traitorous than Judas.
One is a spy for Spain, and one for France,
and another would sell God for simony
a thousand times and each hour of the day.
Thus may a way be found
to elect a good pastor outside of conclaves
to redeem the keys of Saint Peter,
and may he, these depraved men
who esteem so little God's Church,
toss up to the sky with fire.)

Romei points to the quantity and quality of writers, especially from Tuscany, attracted to Rome by the court of Leo X as a reason for the rich trove of pasquinades following the pope's death ("Aretino" 27).

In fact, Romei argues, most authors of anonymous pasquinades were easily identified, because they were known to be writing in the service of one or another prominent prelate. Aretino, a polemicist in the camp of Giulio de' Medici, emerged as a voice of Pasquino because he called attention to himself more so than others rather than for the quality of his production. The difficulty of definitively attributing many pasquinades to Aretino on the basis that he was not prolific is countered by the number of times his name is mentioned as practitioner of the genre.[15] Aretino's early contributions, compared to those of a polemicist like Anton Lelio, are not particularly acerbic (Larivaille 40). For example, he amended the final lines of Lelio's "Piàcevi, mona chiesa onesta e buona," in which the Church is asked which cardinal she will accept as spouse. The original reads: "— Medici, uom di valore, / pigliate, adunque. / — E manco questo accetto, / perché in lui solo è acolto ogni difetto, / e per questo rispetto, / per fugir sangue, puzza, ingano e lite, / d'entrar son ferma nelle Convertite" (— Then take Medici, / a man of worth. / — Nor this one do I accept, / because in him alone every defect is collected, / and for this reason / to flee blood, filth, deceit and strife, / I am decided to enter the *Convertite*). Aretino's version reads: "Or non tanto romore: / se con Medici sposa non me unite, / andrò fallita ne le

---

[15] Romei, "Aretino" 38-43. "Allo stato attuale delle conoscenze si possono assegnare con certezza all'Aretino appena cinque pasquinate: 1. 'Piàcevi, mona Chiesa onesta e buona' (1522). 2. 'Dice ognun: Io stupisco che 'l colegio' (1522). 3. 'Savio colegio, miserere mei!' (1522). 4. 'Patafio di maestro Adriano Pecora Campi' (Qui iace Adrian sesto, omo divino) (1523). 5. 'I miracoli al mondo furno sette' (1525). [...] Poi sono possibili attribuzioni in via del tutto ipotetica: pasquinate per il conclave di 1521-22 apertamente filomedice ('A un cardo è Trani e Cesi a una scopetta'; 'Voi che la lunga èta, più che altro, degni'; 'Quanta invidia vi preme e quante pene'; 'Cuoco è san Pier, s'è papa un de' tre frati'; 'Spetate Ivrea, col mal che Dio vi dia' [...] o segnate da considerevoli riferimenti aretiniani ('Or che Cornaro un gaudio ce ha nunziato'; 'O cardinali, avisavi Ceccotto')."

Convertite" (Now, not so much noise: / if you do not give me Medici as spouse, / I will go, a failure, to the *Convertite*).[16]

An example of Aretino's slander is "Or Patafio di Mastro Ardiano Pecora Campi," an "epitaph" for Pope Hadrian VI, who died on September 23, 1523. The accusations are hackneyed, intended for immediate consumption.

> "Patafio di Mastro Adriano Pecora Campi"
> Qui iace Adrian sesto, omo di-vino
> cioè todesco, figlio a un cimatore,
> che 'l fe' far cardinal l'imperatore, [17]
> perché gli insegnò leggere a Tozzino.
> Dico che fu pedante: a ogni facchino
> teneva scola e per un ladro errore,
> pecora essendo, diventò pastore. [...]
>
> (Marucci 90-91)
>
> ("Epitaph of Mastro Adriano the fool.")
> Here lies Hadrian VI, a man of spirits,
> that is, a German, son of a trimmer,
> whom the emperor made cardinal,
> because he taught Tozzino [a buffoon] to read.
> I say he was a pedant: he taught
> every porter and by a thieving error,
> being a sheep, he became shepherd. [...])

The poem continues with a series of banal insults. Just as for many other compositions associated with Pasquino by Aretino, there is no reason to think the epitaph for Hadrian was ever posted on the statue.

When Giulio de' Medici ascended to the papal throne as Pope Clement VII in 1523, he rewarded his polemicist with the title of *Cavaliero di Rodi*. Aretino may, at this point, have aspired to become a counselor in important matters of state at the Roman court.[18] He was given the responsibility of organizing the celebration of Pasquino in 1525, but the event was canceled by Clement, and the poems suppressed. On July 28, 1525, Aretino was the target of an attempted assassination by Achille della Volta; when he recovered, he fled Rome for good.

---

[16] Both versions of "Piàcevi, mona Chiesa onesta e buona" are in Marucci 63-65. The "Convertite" refer to the reformed prostitutes associated with Santa Maria Maddalena, according to Fineschi (322).

[17] Hadrian of Utrecht, tutor of the emperor Charles V, was made cardinal at the emperor's request in 1517.

[18] Several canzoni suggest this, including the "Laude di Clemente VII" and "L'esortazione della pace fra l'Imperatore e il Re di Francia," both urging the pope to launch a new crusade against the infidel. Even after the defeat of the French king in Pavia on February 24, 1525, Aretino wrote in ardent support of the defeated king (Larivaille 60-62).

The motive for the attack continues to be debated.[19] It may have been Aretino's pasquinades directed at the cardinals of the Curia; or his vocal support for the French king even after his defeat at Pavia, when the pope readily made peace with the victor, the emperor Charles V; or the episode of his sixteen "sonetti lussoriosi" published in the final months of 1524 to accompany a set of sexually explicit engravings by Marcantonio Raimondi known as *I modi*.[20] As Romei puts it, Aretino was "non ancora il 'segretario del mondo' sulla scena europea delle *Lettere* (che era ancora da inventare), ma almeno il segretario di Pasquino, il portavoce del 'vero', e cioè il protagonista del 'dir male', che aveva radicalmente messo in crisi il suo ruolo [...] all'interno della corte romana" ("Dalla Toscana" 21-22).

This is a turning point for Aretino. He traveled to the camp of the Medici condottiere, Giovanni dalle Bande Nere, where he did manage to ingratiate himself as an intimate, trusted advisor and fellow reveler before Giovanni died of a wound on November 30, 1526. Aretino then returned to the court of Mantua, then left for Venice in 1527. Giovanni dalle Bande Nere is thought to be the first to call Aretino "il Flagello dei Principi," which occurs in print in the 1532 edition of Ariosto's *Orlando Furioso*, Canto 46 (Larivaille 82 and 437n11).

Aretino as the Voice of "Monna Comedia"
Written in haste, and incomplete, the first *Cortigiana* was nonetheless important enough to Aretino that he took it with him when he fled; then he rewrote it, perhaps intermittently, and published it in 1534 — or rather, he published a comedy with the same title and plot.[21] In the 1525 version, Pasquino's voice establishes the tone of the irreverent comedy. In the 1534 version, Pasquino's role is eclipsed; the satire of Roman society is more mature, presenting coherent

---

[19] Larivaille cites a letter in which Clement accepts the responsibility (436n68): "Due anni dopo il tentato omicidio di Aretino, il Papa, confessando i suoi torti, dichiarerà: 'confessammo il torto fatto a l'Aretino, e il comportammo per importarci più Giammateo [Giberti] ministro dei nostri segreti che lui, che in luogo di amico e non di servitor lo tenevamo'" (436n68).

[20] Larivaille 72. The sonnets are obscene, as the first two quatrains of the first sonnet announce: "Questo è un libro d'altro che sonetti, / Di capitoli, d'egloghe o canzone; / Qui il Sannazaro o il Bembo non compone / Né liquidi cristalli né fioretti; / Qui il Barignan non v'ha madrigaletti, / Ma vi son cazzi senza discrezione / E v'è la potta e il cul, che li ripone, / Appunto come in scatole confetti" (Romei, "Sonetti" 35). Later Aretino would call the poems a "trastullo de l'ingegno."

[21] According to Larivaille, the 1525 version was merely the sketch of a play that Aretino circulated among friends. The manuscript Magliabechiano VII 84 in the Biblioteca Nazionale di Firenze indicates interpolations in the *Prologue* after the death of Armellini in October 1527 (65).

arguments, and this is the development that I will explore in the remainder of this paper.

The work, with respect to the *commedie erudite* being produced in the courts of Italy, is revolutionary.[22] Although Aretino plundered and parodied vernacular comedies like Bibbiena's *Calandria* and Machiavelli's *La mandragola*, the conventions of the genre are missing, including ancient Roman plot antecedents, a struggle between father and offspring, a marriage that promises familial renewal and restores order, and, for that matter, any social order whatsoever. A series of micro-narratives — practical jokes and slapstick pranks, rants, and short-circuited conversations — propels the plots. The recreation of an ideal city in the classic *commedia erudita* — its scenographic symbols of power representing reimposition of order at the conclusion of comic mayhem — is replaced by a vertiginous no-place that is immediately recognizable to both the players and the public (Baratto, *La commedia* 39-45). As the First Histrion states in the Prologue, "e mi vien da ridere perch'io penso che inanzi che questa tela si levassi dal volto di questa città, vi credevate che ci fussi sotto la torre de Babilonia, e sotto ci era Roma. Vedete Palazzo, San Piero, la Piazza, la Guardia, l'Osteria de la Lepre, la Luna, la Fonte, Santa Caterina e ogni cosa." ("It makes me laugh to think about it: before the curtain opened, you probably thought it was the Tower of Babel back there, but instead it was Rome itself. Look: there's the Palace, St. Peters, the piazza, the fortress, a couple of taverns — the Hare and the Luna — the fountain St. Catherine's — the whole thing," 1525; Prolog, Campbell and Sbrocchi 53).

In the first version Aretino claims Pasquino's voice as his own to condemn not merely the prelates of the Curia, but more generally the corruption of the papal city.[23] In the published version of the *Cortigiana* of 1534, the young courtier Flamminio replaces Pasquino as the voice of Aretino,[24] and he demands not the freedom to denounce scandal but to speak truth: "Voglio inanzi che mi nocia il dire il vero che non vo' che mi giovi il dir bugie" ("I wish that before it harms me to speak the truth, it not avail me to tell lies" III.7).

---

[22] Baratto's perspective is instructive: "Nel 1534, ricuperando un'opera scritta dieci anni prima — in modo analogo aveva agito per *Il Marescalco* pubblicato nel 1533 — l'Aretino si prefigge dunque di 'riaprire' quel mondo della commedia che tendeva a chiudersi in un repertorio tanto più fisso e astratto, conservatore, quanto più si aggravava la decadenza dei gruppi sociali (la colta borghesia cittadina, l'aristocrazia di corte) che lo avevano espresso in un fruttoso ricambio di impulsi culturali" (*Tre* 73-74).

[23] In the Prologue, the First Histrion makes the point: "E non è niuno che sappia meglio di Pasquino quello si può usare o no. Egli ha un libro il qual tratta de la sua geneologia e c'è di belle cose, come intenderete, e perché gli è nato di poeta però qui lo faccio autore" (Prologo 1525).

[24] The opinion that Flamminio is the voice of Aretino is widely shared by critics (Baratto, *Tre* 167; Larivaille 55, 69).

The 1525 comedy still has the qualities that define a pasquinade. It offers the audience the opportunity to participate in the pleasure of immediate recognition or comprehension, most especially in the prologue when the First Histrion taunts the public with a harangue that is both insulting and titillating. In the Prolog, he refers to events that must have been vivid in the public memory, such as the public spectacle of execution and quartering of the doctor Battista da Vercelli, accused of plotting to poison the pope in the Sienese Petrucci cardinals' conspiracy in 1517, as well as to scandals like the practices of local sodomites:

Chi cercassi tutta la maremma non che Italia, non saria mai possibile a ragunare tanta turba di sfaccendati, e ognuno è córso al romore e non è niuno che sappia a che proposito. Almen quando quel medico da Verzelli e i compagni si squartorno, e' si sapeva per dua giorni inanzi perché e per come. Sarà qualche satrapo che dirà essere venuto per avere qualche piacere de la comedia, come se la comedia non avesse altra faccenda che farlo ridere... Ma voi non volete star queti; orsù, ch'io vi chiarisco ch'io vi vituperò tutti, per Dio! Per Dio che se non fate silenzio ch'io sciorrò el cane, e dirò: el tal è agens, el tal è patens. ...
(You can look wherever you want — not just in Italy but the whole world — and you'll never find another crowd of loafers like this, all gathered in one place. You all rushed in when you heard the racket, but none of you had any idea what it was all about. At least when they had that doctor from Vercelli and his friends drawn and quartered, people knew the whys and wherefores of it a couple of days beforehand. Now I suppose some wise guy out there's going to say he just came to enjoy the show — as if a play has nothing else to do but make him laugh. You won't shut up, eh? I'm warning you — I wouldn't hesitate to expose every last one of you. By God, if you don't shut up I'll sic the dog on you. I'll tell everyone which of you are doing it, and which of you are having it done.)[25]

The plot of the comedy, divided into two story lines connected by a insignificant link, portrays a young Sienese fool, seeking to become a courtier, who is led through a series of increasingly humiliating practical jokes by a Roman trickster named Mastro Andrea, until the latter tires of the game and

---

[25] Campbell and Sbrocchi, 52. In the version of 1534, some of the same material recurs in Maestro Andrea's description of the qualities and skills required of the courtier. Maestro Andrea: "La principal cosa il cortigiano vuol saper bestemmiare, vuole esser giuocatore, invidioso, puttaniere, eretico, adulatore, maldicente, sconoscente, ignorante, asino; vuol saper frappare, far la nimpha, et essere agente e paziente [...]." Messer Maco: "Adagio, piano, fermo. Che vuol dire *agente e paziente?* Io non intendo questa cifera." Maestro Andrea: "Moglie e marito vuol dire'" (I.22). Simonetti discusses the brutal judicial proceedings of Leo's officials that led to the condemnation of Vercelli and the majordomo of cardinal Alfonso Petrucci, Marco Antonio Nino (161-67).

withdraws: "Zoppino, questa comedia m'è venuta a noia, perché costui è la sciocchezza in carne e in ossa, e non ne piglio piú piacere." ("Zoppino, I'm tired of this joke. This guy is stupidity incarnate, and he's no fun anymore," 1525;V.8, Campbell and Sbrocchi 129). In the second story line, there is a middle-aged courtier, Parabolano, who fancies himself in love and is tricked by his servant Rosso and a ruffian named Alogia into believing that he will have a tryst with his beloved Madonna Laura, impersonated by Togna, the baker's wife. The *Cortigiana* ends in a good laugh when Messer Parabolano recognizes that he is the only one who would suffer were he to call attention to his foolish wooing: "Ah, ah, per Dio, ch'i mi voglio mutare di proposito e ridermi di questa cosí ladra burla e de la mia pazzia!" ("Ha, ha! By God, I've changed my mind — I'm going to laugh at this silly prank and my own stupidity!" 1525; V.20, Campbell and Sbrocchi 136).

A counterpoint to "il nostro cianciar lungo," as Aretino characterizes his comedy, is developed in the 1534 version.[26] In response to the stream of chicanery, hallucinations and blind blunders, two courtiers, Valerio and Flamminio, speak to the folly and madness they perceive on every side. The courtiers replace the aggressive, impulsive and provocative voice of Pasquino in the first *Cortigiana* with a sustained critique of Roman society.[27] Valerio is an older, more traditional courtier in the service of the deluded lover Parabolano, while Flamminio is young and impatient, and has no particular part to play except that of interlocutor for Valerio and commentator. Valerio's role is given slightly more prominence in the 1534 version, while Flamminio's verbal presence in increased by almost 250%.[28] The courtiers speak in full sentences and dominate the stage at the beginning and the end of acts, when they will be remembered. Writing of the first version, Baratto warns that "un'analisi letteraria rischia di disperderne le qualità peculiari, di negare (qualunque sia l'essenza di essa nel nostro accertamento) la loro *teatralità*" (*Tre* 78).

---

[26] The phrase occurs in the parting words of Valerio, in Act V, Scene 24 of the 1534 version.

[27] Pasquino does recur in the 1534 version. In the first act, Messer Andrea defines Pasquino as one who does not bow and scrape for ecclesiasts. Messer Maco: "Chi è maestro Pasquino?" Maestro Andrea: "Uno che ha stoppati dietro signori e monsignori." In Act III, Scene 8, the servant Rosso recites verses from several pasquinades for Messer Parabolano, agreeing with the rogue Barbieraccio that a few should be read at mass in the morning: "Io, quando stava con Antonio Lelio Romano, furava il tempo per leggere le cose che componeva in laude de' cardinali; e ne so a mente una frotta. Oh, son divini, e sono schiavo al Barbieraccio, che disse che non saria errore ignuno a leggerne ogni mattina dui tra la pistola e 'l vangelo." The most significant mention of Pasquino in the 1534 version is discussed below.

[28] Flamminio's word-count of 1282 in the 1525 version is inflated to 3160 words in the 1534 version, in large part because of his paean to Venice (and France) in III.7.

Nevertheless, the theatricality of ephemeral immediacy that characterizes the 1525 version, of which there is no record of a formal performance, is already threatened by a more robust and intrusive presence of Valerio and Flamminio in the 1534 version.

The First Histrion, in the voice of Pasquino in the *Prologue* of the 1525 *Cortigiana,* implicitly establishes that there can be no order, no weight and no conclusion to the "ciancia," that humanist and ecclesiastic pretentions to virtue and exemplarity are nonsense, and that Babel has replaced language. In the published version, the collapse of civilization is explained by recent events: Valerio tells Parabolano that there is no moral order to be protected or restored in Italy because recent disasters have reduced it to a state of decadence: "Perché le guerre, le pesti, le carestie, e i tempi che inclinano al darsi piacere, hanno inputtanita tutta Italia sí, che cugini e cugine, cognati e cognate, fratelli e sorelle si mescolano insieme, senza un riguardo, senza una vergogna, e senza una coscienza al mondo" (II.10) (Because wars, plagues, famines, and present times inclined to pleasure-seeking have prostituted all Italy so much that now cousins with cousins, brother-in-laws and sister-in-laws, brother and sisters all mix together, without a thought, without shame, and without a concern in the world).

The role of the courtier is complex in the published version: he may not wish to delude or speak ill of his lord, as Valerio tells Messer Parabolano in the opening of Act III, "Quanto a me, ho sempre fatto ufficio di buon servidore e d'amatore del vostro onore" 1534; III.1; (For my part, I have always tried to do the office of a good servant and protector of your honor). But there is dystopia for honorable service: "Ma bisogna fare e dire il peggio che si può a questi signori, chi vuol esser favorito loro: che chi colomba si fa, il falcon se lo mangia" (1534; I.8, "But you have to do and say the worst that you can to these lords, if you wish to be their favorite: whoever plays the dove is devoured by the falcon").[29]

The truth that an honest man must lie to serve his lord is applied to the issue of speech in general. At the heart of the comedy, Act III, Scene VII is dedicated to the contrast between corrupt Rome and candid Venice, and the younger courtier's intention to go to Venice where he will enrich himself with its liberty.[30] Flamminio claims the right to speak the truth, the freedom to speak his mind: "Voglio inanzi che mi nocia il dire il vero che non vo' che mi giovi il dir bugie" III.7; ("I wish that before it harms me to speak the truth, it does not avail

---

[29] The same phrase, "il falcon se la mangia," occurs in Act I.2 of the 1525 version as a phrase that is not entirely absorbed into the syntax of a solicitation by Maestro Andrea to be hired by the foolish Messer Maco: "Cercate voi padrone? Il falcon se lo mangia."

[30] Flamminio: "Io me ne andrò forse a Vinegia, ove sono già stato; et arrichirò la povertà mia con la sua libertade." The analogous scene in the 1525 version, III.7 focuses on the role of fortune in the courtier's life.

me to tell lies"). Valerio responds that it is Flamminio's (Aretino's?) outspokeness that has left him penniless and in trouble with the Curia.[31] The truth is the one thing that may never be uttered at court:

> Questo dire il vero è quello che dispiace, e non hanno altro stecco ne gli occhi i signori che 'l tuo dire il vero. De i grandi bisogna dir che 'l male che fanno sia bene, et è tanto pericoloso e dannoso il biasimargli quanto è sicuro et utile il laudargli. A loro è lecito di fare ogni cosa, e a noi non è lecito di dire ogni cosa, e a Dio sta di correggere le sceleraggini loro, e non a noi.
> (1534; III.7)
> (This telling the truth is what they dislike, and there is no poke in the eye more offensive than telling the truth. Of great men you must say that the evil they are doing is good, and it is more dangerous and harmful to blame them than it is safe and useful to praise them. For them everything is permitted, and we are not allowed to say anything, and it's up to God to chastise their bad deeds, not us.)

Flamminio repeats the obvious: "Perché ho io a vergognarmi di dire quello che essi non si vergognano di fare?" ("Why must I be ashamed to say what they are not ashamed to do?"). The older courtier has nothing to offer in response: "Perché i signori son signori" ("Because *signori* are *signori*").

Valerio actually returns to the voice of Pasquino in his admonishment of the younger courtier, reminding him that attacks on the Curia in the voice of the statue are confined to the questions of the court — presumably, to the clerics and their moral failings: "Và pur dietro, ma sarebbe manco male il cianciar che fai della corte, perché sempre Pasquino ne parlò, e sempre ne parlerà" ("Think back, your sharp tongue at the court is less damaging because Pasquino always talked, and always will talk"). But Flamminio did not limit himself to attacks on ecclesiastic viciousness: "Tu sei poi entrato in sul temporale" ("Then you got into politics"), or, more precisely, secular politics, which got him into trouble. It is tempting to refer back to Aretino's own efforts to become a political advisor in the circle of Clement VII, but not necessarily legitimate to do so. Valerio's comment calls to mind Franco's self defense: that his pasquinades had never directly attacked papal rule. The unspoken, circumscribed freedom of Pasquino's voice is articulated only when Flamminio calls for the right to speak out as he chooses. Flamminio, and quite obviously Aretino, wanted more.

In Aretino's *Cortigiana*, *Monna Comedia* is deeply stained by a painful reality of both the tyranny of mendacity that stifles Roman society, and the implosion of Italian institutions. No longer focused on the corruption of the papal city through the voice of Pasquino, as in the 1525 *Cortigiana,* in the published version Aretino claims the freedom to speak truth to power in the

---

[31] Valerio: "Dico, saltando di palo in frasca, che il tuo non aver nulla è proceduto dal poco rispetto che sempre tu avesti alla corte. Il dar menda a ciò ch'ella pensa, et a quel ch'ella adopra ti noce sempre, et sempre nocerà" (III.7).

personage of the young courtier, Flamminio. Although the writer will state repeatedly that the animus of Pasquino still salts his blood, the juxtaposition of the two versions of the comedy suggests that in the later version, revised in Venice, Aretino's satire matures beyond vituperation for immediate consumption, and roots itself in a broader and more coherent judgment of men and their actions, which he claims is his right to voice.

Boston College

Works Cited

Aretino, Pietro. *Cortigiana*. (1525). Ed. Giuliano Innamorati. Torino: Einaudi, 1970.

———. *Cortigiana*. [1525]. Trans. J. Douglas Campbell and Leonard G. Sbrocchi. Ottawa: Dovehouse, 2003.

———. *Cortigiana* (1534). Ed. Guido Davico Bonino. *Il teatro italiano 2. La commedia del Cinquecento*. Torino: Einaudi, 1977. 185-314.

———. *Cortigiana* (1534). Ed. Federico Della Corte. Online.

———. *Operette politiche e satiriche*. Vol. 2. Ed. Marco Faini. Roma: Salerno, 2012.

Ariosto, Ludovico. *Orlando Furioso*. Eds. Marcello Turchi and Edoardo Sanguineti. Milano: Garzanti, 1982.

Baratto, Mario. *La commedia del Cinquecento*: (aspetti e problemi). Vicenza: Neri Pozza, 1977.

———. *Tre studi sul teatro: Ruzante, Aretino, Goldoni*. Vicenza: Neri Pozza, 1964.

Cairns, Christopher. *Pietro Aretino and the Republic of Venice. Researches on Aretino and his Circle in Venice, 1527-1556*. Firenze: Olschki, 1985.

Castiglione, Baldasare. *Il cortigiano*. Ed. Amedeo Quondam. Milano: Mondadori, 2002.

Cesareo, Giovanni Alfredo. *Pasquino e pasquinate nella Roma di Leone X*. Roma: Biblioteca Vallicelliana, 1938.

Dionisotti, Carolo. *Geografia e storia della letteratura italiana*. Torino: Einaudi, 1967.

D'Onghia, Luca. "La 'Farza' è davvero di Pietro Aretino? Note linguistiche su un testo d'incerta attribuzione." *Scaffale aperto* (Dec. 2013): 115-37.

Fineschi, F. Vincenzio. *Memorie i storiche che possono servire alle vite degli uomini del Convento di S. Maria Novella di Firenze dall'anno 1221 al 1320*. Vol. 1. Firenze: Gaetano Cambiagi, 1790.
https://books.google.com/books?id=DcZVLDZGtrkC&pg=PA322&lpg=PA322&dq =Fineschi+%22le+convertite%22&source=bl&ots=CpYPnR2B7Q&sig=cgCjq3KG 75Pho1tprpUYvdqYS-8&hl=en&sa=X&ved=0ahUKEwi59-mZ8JDMAhWDGj4K HSK4BkcQ6AEIHzAA#v=onepage&q=Fineschi%20%22le%20convertite%22&f=f alse

Fragnito, Gigliola. "Censura ecclesiastica e pasquinate." *Ex Marmore. Pasquini, pasquinisti, pasquinate nell'Europa Moderna: Atti del Colloquio Internazionale Lecce-Otranto, 17-19 novembre, 2005*. Ed. Chrysa Damianaki, Paolo Procaccioli

and Angelo Romano. Roma: Vecchiarelli, 2006. 181-86.
Grendler, Paul F. *Critics of the Italian World. 1530-1560. Anton Francesco Doni, Nicolò Franco & Ortensio Lando.* Madison: U of Wisconsin P, 1969.
Innamorati, Giuliano. *Pietro Aretino. Studi e note critiche*. Firenze: G. D'Anna, 1957.
Larivaille, Paul. *Pietro Aretino fra Rinascimento e Manierismo*. Trans. Mariella di Maio and Maria Luisa Rispoli. Roma: Bulzoni, 1980.
Lastraioli, Chiara. *Pasquinate, grillate, pelate e altro Cinquecento librario minore.* Roma: Vecchiarelli, 2012.
Marucci, Valerio, ed. *Pasquinate del Cinque e Seicento.* Roma: Salerno, 1988.
Romei, Danilo. "Aretino e Pasquino." Romei. *Da Leone X a Clemente VII* 23-44.
_____. *Da Leone X a Clemente VII. Scrittori toscani nella Roma dei papati medicei (1513-1534)*. Roma: Vecchiarelli, 2007.
_____. "Poesia satirica e giocosa nell'ultimo trentennio del Cinquecento." "Nuovo Rinascimento, Banca Dati 2, http://www.nuovorinascimento.orgrinasc/saggi/ pdf/ ramei/cinque.pdf.
_____, ed. *Pietro Aretino. Sonetti lussuriosi.* http://www.nuovorinascimento.org/n-rinasc/ testi/pdf/aretino/sonetti.pdf.
Rossi, Vittorio. *Pasquinate di Pietro Aretino ed anonime per il conclave e l'elezione di Adriano VI.* Palermo: Carlo Clausen, 1891.
Shepard, Laurie. "The Power of the Word: Pasquinades and Other Voices of Dissent." *The Pamphilj and the Arts: Patronage and Consumption in Baroque Rome.* Ed. Stephanie C. Leone. Chestnut Hill: McMullen Museum of Art, 2011. 199-209.
Simonetta, Marcello. *Volpi e leoni. I Medici, Machiavelli e la rovina d'Italia.* Milano: Bompiani, 2014.
Villard, Renaud. "Incarnare una voce: il caso della sede vacante (Roma, XVI secolo)." *Quaderni storici* 41.1 (2006) 39-68.
Waddington, Raymond B. "Pietro Aretino: The New Man of Letters." *Pietro Aretino: Subverting the System in Renaissance Italy.* Burlington: Ashgate, 2013. III.2.

Linda L. Carroll

Ruzante Speaks Truth to Venetian Power: Some Hows, Whys, Whens, and Wherefores[1]

Abstract: In his daring utterances about their conduct to the largely patrician audiences of his theatrical works, exemplified in the quotations below, Angelo Beolco, better known by the name of the peasant character Ruzante that he created and played on the stage, reached the zenith of the Renaissance phase of speaking truth to power. The present essay explicates his extraordinary candor and the (temporary) patrician acceptance of it by accounting for factors at the personal and local levels and then at the international level.
Key Words: Angelo Beolco, Ruzante, Venice, Padua, comedy, nature, illegitimacy, Italian Renaissance, patrician, peasant, theater, dialect.

Seconda Oration
And we don't have a law on our side, and no one who speaks for us or who has ever been one of us. I hear talk about the law of Datus, the law of Bartolus, the law of Digestion and talk like that; I never hear no one say Nick's law or Nale's law or Duozo's law. All these laws are for the city people. And if you will call on us, we will make our own laws [...].[2]

Parlamento de Ruzante (Primo dialogo; Reduce)
Ruzante: [...] me, I was at the rear as a squadron leader, as a lance-corporal, and when they started to flee, it was incumbent on me as a gentleman to flee as well.[3]

Ruzante: Now Sir Bortholomew who was such a show-off in Vicenza, didn't he throw

---

[1] Gratitude is expressed to the American Philosophical Society for a grant to transcribe the manuscripts and to Tulane University for the Suzanne and Stephen Weiss Presidential Fellowship, which provided partial support of the research.
[2] "A no Haon leza dal nostro lo, ne digha per nu, ne che ge supia sto negun d'i nuostri. A sento lome dire la leza de Datto, La leza de Bartole, la leza de Gesto dire cosi; a' no sento me dire: la leza de Menego, la leza de Nale, la leza de Duozo. Tutte ste leze e de citaini. Se a ne ciameri an nu, a faron an nu le nuostre [...]." Beolco, *Seconda oratione*, 204r-v shortly before where the manuscript version ends, followed by a blank space where the rest of the speech was to have been transcribed (Beolco, *Teatro* [hereafter *IT*] 1216-19). The quotations will be documented and contextualized below. Translations are by the present author unless otherwise noted.
[3] Ruzante: "[...] mi agiera dadrio de cao de squara, de caporale, e igi muce. A scovini muzar an mi da valenthomo" (Beolco, *Parlamento de Ruzante*, 174r; *RT* 524-25); "Mo el segnor Bortholamio che giera si braoso a vicenza se trasselo mo in laqua per muzare e si vene che gialtri se anegava e corse a pava a imbusarse?" (174v; *RT* 526-29).

Annali d'italianistica 34 (2016). *Speaking Truth to Power from Medieval to Modern Italy*

himself in the water to flee and, as it happened, the others were drowning and he ran to Padua to hole up?

Bilora (*Secondo dialogo*)
Bilora: Oh, let the pox eat you, you broken-down old man. [...] Give me my woman now. You should have let her be. Whoah, wait, I think he's dead, I do. He's not kicking his foot or his leg. [...] Oh, my God, good night! He's crapped his grapestalks, he has. I told you so, didn't I?[4]

Introduction
Angelo Beolco, as the illegitimate (natural) offspring of a branch of an upper-class Milanese family transferred to the Venetian Republic and an anonymous lower-class mother, occupied the nether world between those two distant classes. From the time that Angelo's grandfather Lazaro de Beolco arrived in Padua and Venice, probably around 1460, to the end of the fifteenth century, the family enjoyed great wealth based on international commerce developed by its patriarch in Milan, Lazaro's elder brother Zuan. That wealth made Zuan one of the most important financiers to the Sforza and thus one of the most powerful men in Milan. During the period, the Beolco also provided much-needed financial assistance to Venetian patrician families with whom they conducted business, families whose commercial galley traffic to northern Europe was beset by serious and prolonged problems. By the final years of the fifteenth century, the extent of the loans made to the Sforza had severely depleted Beolco family finances, which could not be replenished because of the decline in the trade on which they were based. It was at this time that Zuan Francesco Beolco, the elder of Lazaro's legitimate sons and destined to a career within the university, fathered Angelo, probably with a domestic servant from a recently-urbanized village family. According to current archival research, Angelo's mother, released from service to the family, may have continued to live nearby.

By the time of Angelo's birth, the options available to illegitimate sons in the Venetian Republic were becoming severely restricted, largely to preserve the patrimony by reducing the number of heirs but justified with a stricter moral stance. Thus Angelo no longer had available to him the civic offices that his illegitimate uncle was able to hold just a generation before, ones that would have given him a civic profile enabling him to earn the kind of living that his uncle could despite not receiving a share of the patrimony. Angelo instead turned to the world of performance, perhaps even before the wars of the League of

---

[4] Bilora: Ah, te magne el morbo, vecio strassinò! [...] Dàme mo la mia femena. Te la divi lagar stare. Poh, moa, a' cherzo che 'l sea morto, mi. Mo no 'l sbate pí né pè né gamba. [...] Miedio, bondì! L'ha cagò le graspe, elo. Te l'hegi dito? Beolco, *Bilora* (*Secondo dialogo*), *RT* 578-79; there are no known manuscripts of this play.

Cambrai and beginning in Pernumia, Reoso, or Motta di Montagnana, where both the Beolco and many of the patrician families later inviting him to Venice to perform had agricultural property. From this property the patricians planned to produce foodstuffs both for personal consumption and to sell to replace income lost with the decline in commerce. His plays center on peasant life in the Paduan countryside, explicating the good and bad conditions that peasants faced with a depth of knowledge and an empathy not found in other contemporary authors.

From 1520 to 1526, Angelo is recorded by Venetian patrician diarist Marin Sanudo as performing in Venice at the invitation of the patrician festive societies known as *compagnie della calza* or of one or more patrician families. During these years as well, patricians tried to restart the interrupted maritime trade with northern Europe on which their fabulous fortunes had been based. That trade by then required the cooperation of the new emperor Charles V, who after his election in 1519 controlled almost the entire litoral of the galleys' route and who was not pleased with Venice for its long-term affiliations with his greatest enemies, France and the Turkish Porte. That they invited Beolco to perform publicly for the first time within months of Charles's election and for the last time months before Venice's public announcement of adherence to the French-led League of Cognac does not seem coincidental, especially given the connections to the empire of Beolco's family members, of members of his Paduan noble acting circle, and of the circle of Alvise Cornaro his patron.

In sum, out of an identification with the peasants' condition, one that was close to that of his mother's family, Angelo Beolco created a peasant character who affirmed the peasants' value and protested the control over their lives by others with more social power, those same others who were inviting Beolco to perform and who sat in his audiences. He was given special leeway to call his Venetian audiences' attention to their exploitative treatment by their awareness that his Milanese family had sustained their power and by their need of the peasants both for agricultural expertise to extract profit from their new endeavors and as defense forces to retain their state. Perhaps the patricians inviting him to perform also wanted to signal to the emperor that they were willing, through Beolco's affiliates, to find a *modus vivendi* with him; and, perhaps, the new, overweening power of the emperor in their lives left them identifying with the subjugated condition of the peasants. However, Venice's definitive declaration of French partisanship through the League of Cognac corresponded to an immediate and complete truncation of his performances in the city. His accusations of Venetian inequity and cowardice quoted above come in works written after this exclusion.[5]

---

[5] Lovarini; Sambin; Menegazzo. For the documentation of points made here and below, see Carroll, *Commerce*; Carroll, *Angelo Beolco*; Carroll, "'(El) ge sa bon laorare'"; and

182   Linda L. Carroll

Background Factors
Over the latter fifteenth century and with increasing speed, population growth reversed the dearth caused by the waves of plague that had struck Italy in the preceding hundred years, as well as the unusually favorable situation that depletion had caused for the survivors. Many more people meant more competition for resources, accelerating the hierarchicalization of society then underway. The trend was compounded in the last few decades of the fifteenth century and the first few of the sixteenth century both by the damage inflicted on Italian states by Turkish aggression, especially on Venice with its maritime empire extending east, and by the three decades of wars among the nation-states — France, Spain, and the Holy Roman Empire with the latter two uniting under Charles V — for control of the Italian peninsula. At first disrupting authority systems, in part by forcing recognition of the importance of peasants to defense and provisioning, the wars ultimately buttressed hierarchical political authority through Charles's victory over the Church and virtually all secular governments except Venice's, which he nonetheless hemmed in. In the cultural sphere, the spread of humanism and Petrarchism provided new, and thus in some senses liberating, but also imitative, and therefore stultifying, paradigms. For the first three decades of the sixteenth century and with continuing echoes beyond, this co-existence of cultural and political forces setting new freedoms and recognition of basic human rights against a vertical organization concentrating authority and resources in a minute group created volcanic pressures. In some individuals particularly subject or sensitive to them, the pressures erupted into new paradigms, often destroying old ones. Chief among these individuals was Angelo Beolco.[6]

The key to Beolco's extraordinary confidence in so audaciously addressing his powerful patrician hosts has remained neglected since the documents containing it were discovered by Emilio Lovarini in 1899. The neglect stems in part from difficulty in tracing the documents caused by the reorganization of Padua's archives and in part from the efficacy of Beolco's own rustic creation. A clearer delineation of the playwright's situation is now made possible by their rediscovery and augmentation with new material from Venetian family archives, which also allows a greater understanding of information gleaned by Paolo Sambin and Emilio Menegazzo.[7]

Belonging to the upper echelon of Milanese society and with roots in the

---

scholarly apparatus in Beolco, *Prima oratione*, especially the bibliography. The present work is based on the entire web of that research; considerations of space have resulted in only the most relevant sources being cited individually here.
[6] For the social dynamic in general, see Herlihy; Vermes 3-8, 169-224; LeRoy Ladurie; Davico Bonino; Rebel.
[7] See note 5 above.

imperial feudal system, the Beolco family was headed in the latter fifteenth century by the wealthy and powerful Zuan de Beolco, a principal financier to the Sforza.[8] His younger brother Lazaro served as the family's agent in the Venetian dominions, expanding their merchant endeavors along the Po after the 1454 Peace of Lodi. In Venice Lazaro developed intense enough relations with the business community that he moved there permanently, leaving his sons in Padua. However, Lazaro died in late 1483 or early 1484. His elder legitimate son Zuan Francesco having been destined to a university medical career, Lazaro's role devolved upon the younger legitimate son, Zuan Jacopo, who moved to Venice.

Being under the legal majority of twenty-five, Zuan Jacopo was assisted by a trusted *fattore* and by his illegitimate half-brother Melchiorre. Events soon tested his talents. In 1485, the cargo of Venice's Flanders galleys — the convoy taking lucrative luxury goods to northern Europe that provided the capital for Venetian banks and much patrician wealth — was seized in France. The leading investors — the Foscari but also the Agostini, Bernardo, Capelo, Contarini, Grimani, Gritti, Lipomano, Loredan, Michiel, Pesaro, Pisani, Soranzo, Trevisan, and Venier — turned to Zuan de Beolco for infusions of capital, probably to pay the crews and release the cargo.[9] Not only did he supply it himself, but the sudden appearance in the lists of backers — previously limited to Venetian patricians and a few faithful Venetian *cittadini* or subjects — of clearly Lombard and Savoiard names hints that he recruited others as well. Additional assistance was provided in 1490 by Lazaro's in-laws, Antonio and Gratiosa da Pernumia, who purchased a large rural holding from the galley investor Antonio Giustinian. The purchase seems to have met the needs of both parties, as the da Pernumia were building up their holdings in their home village and Giustinian received an infusion of cash to offset his losses. When Gratiosa later bought her brother's half, her funds were routed from the bank of Zuan de Beolco (women's legal actions were handled by male agents) through the Garzoni bank in Venice, which the family used on other occasions.[10] Later, during the French campaign for Milan, Zuan de Beolco handled some of Ludovico Sforza's financial transactions with the Venetian government.

Family loyalties were tested in the early sixteenth century when, after

---

[8] See also Del Bo 105-06, 212 (without mention of Ruzante) and bibliography in Carroll, *Commerce*.
[9] Carroll, *Commerce*, esp. chapters 1 and 3; Carroll, "Venetian Attitudes."
[10] Archivio di Stato Padova, *Archivio Notarile*, busta 1756, 246r; busta 1758, 498r-v; Archivio di Stato Venezia, *Archivio Gradenigo Rio Marin*, busta 250, 16r, 27r, 62v, 73r; for other instances of family use of the Garzoni bank, see Archivio di Stato Padova, *Archivio Notarile*, busta 1759, 436r-37r; busta 1760, 21v, 392r-v; and see Gullino, 19 for the Foscaris' need to similarly recoup losses from this round by selling a valuable rural property.

Venice's defeat by the League of Cambrai in 1509, Zuan Jacopo and Melchiorre joined other feudatories in returning Padua to imperial rule while Zuan Francesco, already prominent at the Università di Padova, remained faithful to the Serenissima and even held university office during the war. However, he too may have harbored divided financial loyalties as evidenced in his renewal of the commercial society with the Milanese branch of the family in August of 1513, two months after Louis XII, ignominiously defeated at the hands of Massimiliano Sforza, had left Italy. A second renewal came in 1523, in the midst of the period in which Angelo was regularly invited to perform in Venice (1520 to 1526, with possibly some earlier dates) and shortly before Venice succumbed to pressure from the emperor and the pope to join their alliance.

Obstacles to all three of the western galley routes (to Alexandria, to the Barbary coast, and to Flanders) increased in the postwar years. The Alexandria and Barbary galleys were threatened by the recently achieved Turkish dominion over the eastern Mediterranean shore through north Africa. The Flanders galleys had barely resumed their commerce after the eight-year suspension of the war when, in 1519, Charles was elected Holy Roman Emperor and assumed control or important influence over much of the litoral of both rounds. The leading patricians invested in these routes (there were others to eastern Mediterranean ports and to France) understood that this choice of emperor required them to moderate their support for Francis I over Charles. The moderation resulted in a formal alliance with Charles and Adrian VI in 1523 under Doge Andrea Gritti, whose ardent public pro-French stance was belied by private acknowledgment of the need to make accommodations to the emperor.

Angelo's personal situation too was fraught with difficulties. The eldest and an illegitimate or natural son, he was born about 1494, his mother probably a servant of a recently urbanized family of peasant origin.[11] His birth was almost immediately followed by his father's marriage and the production of legitimate children. The disadvantages of illegitimacy were increasing at this time. Melchiorre, though excluded from a share in the patrimony and unable to attend the university, had been elected to civic office and held other responsible positions; by his nephew's time, these too were barred to illegitimates. As I have long argued, Angelo's status as a natural son was an important source of his emphasis on "nature" and "natural," combined with chosen elements of philosophy (Stoic, especially Aristotelian, of which the Università di Padova was a leader, as well as Epicurean), a view accepted by other scholars.[12]

---

[11] On the date of birth see Piovan; on the mother see, most recently, Calore and Liguori. A mother of humble social origin, perhaps particularly if, as Calore and Liguori hypothesize, she remained nearby, could explain Beolco's sympathy for the poor.

[12] Carroll, *Angelo Beolco*, 30, 69, 82, 97; Carroll, "Ruzante's Early Adaptations"; Carroll, "A Nontheistic Paradise"; Ferguson 193-224.

Angelo's pursuit of a theatrical career offered other financial options: the short-term one of payment for individual performances and the long-term one of patronage. While it is unknown exactly when his career began, its nucleus likely formed before the Cambrai wars and developed during them, when the closure of the university and the confinement caused by the many battles around Padua provided time and incentive for entertainment. Several of the works show signs of having had early versions or segments written in that period. By the time of his first datable complete work, the *Pastoral* of about 1517, Beolco was a fully mature writer and actor. His audience soon extended to Venice, understandably so given his family's deep connections to the patriciate. The rolls of the *compagnie della calza* inviting him — the Immortali, the Ortolani, the Zardinieri, and the Triumphanti — display congruence with a list of the investors in the Flanders and Alexandria galleys: Foscari, Agostini, Bernardo, Capelo, Contarini, Grimani, Gritti, Lipomano, Loredan, Michiel, Pesaro, Pisani, Soranzo, Trevisan, and Venier. Other points of contact were the Università di Padova, the only university at which Venetians were permitted to study, and property in Pernumia or Montagnana, where many of the same patrician families and the Beolco had holdings. These contacts, together with the connections of his incipient patron Alvise Cornaro, resulted in invitations by members of these families or the *compagnie della calza* to which they belonged to perform in Venice at Carnival and on a few other special occasions there and elsewhere.[13] Named by diarist Marin Sanudo (Marino Sanuto) from 1520 to 1526, Beolco may have begun performing in Venice in 1518 or earlier; stagings occurred on the mainland as well, for locals and for patricians who were there for governance, business, or pleasure.

Truth-telling in Beolco's Plays
In his works, Angelo pushed back against exclusion by emphasizing the equality of all human beings, which is based on their common nature and which provides a guide to ethical and efficacious conduct.[14] While serving his interests and those of the rural and working classes, Beolco's philosophy also served various ones of patricians. The patriciate was then stratifying into the very wealthy and everyone else, while inclusion in it was being challenged by multiplying and rigorously applied filters that resulted in the exclusion even of the children of the naval hero Vincenzo Capello.[15] The patricians devalued in these processes

---

[13] On the *compagnie* in general see Casini; on those inviting Ruzante, Carroll, "Venetian Attitudes"; Carroll, "'I have a good set of tools'"; Carroll, *Commerce*, chapter 3.
[14] See note 11 above.
[15] Crescenzi 3, 12, 27, 426-30. For the questionable legitimacy of Stefano Magno, who copied the *Pastoral*, see Carroll, *Commerce*, chapter 2, although he was born slightly before these requirements.

could find comfort in his assertion of equality. In the political sphere, the connections to the empire of his family, of many members of his supporters' and of his circles, and likely of himself meant that his performances gave a public signal of positive interest in the empire for those Venetian patricians wishing to give such a signal without personal involvement.

Beolco's effort, which begins with his creation of the *maschera* of Ruzante and his choice of Paduan rural dialect, is clearly stated already in the *Pastoral*, which probably attracted the attention of Venetian patricians in Padua.[16] Shortly thereafter he was invited to give a comic correlate to the tedious formal speeches celebrating the new bishop of Padua Cardinal Marco Cornaro, perhaps at Cornaro's incognito 1518 appearance and certainly at his formal 1521 entrance. Beolco's oration — the most confident, joyful, and thorough presentation of his literary and social program of the value of all living beings — provides the largest number of his direct efforts to bring the behavior of his audience into line with this program through an unvarnished characterization of their current behavioral defects. Beolco begins with the assumption that on some level, even an inchoate one, his patrician audience has accepted universal human value and only needs his articulation of it and its logical consequences to conform their actions to it. In choosing Paduan rural dialect, Beolco acts on the patrician audience's knowledge of it through frequent contact with their peasant leaseholders, servants, and others. Ruzante's announcement that his village council, the *visinanza* composed of all male heads of families, has elected him as their spokesman puts the peasant community on the same level as the patricians, who govern themselves through their own councils that also elect ambassadors. He is to bring the *visinanza*'s recommendations for new laws favorable to them to Cornaro, empowered by his authority as bishop to implement them throughout the extensive diocese (cfr. Favaretto).

Having established his membership in the peasants' community, Ruzante demonstrates his membership in the patricians' community through his easy intimacy with them, as well as their participation in a common humanity. He cites the cardinal's passage through the birth canal, which also provides the first access to women's genitals with their erotic function that sets in motion the new cycle of reproduction:

Now, the thing that is on the other side, on the front side, between their legs, a little higher, that thinking about it my heart melts and for rebellence of your Spectability, because after all you are a priest, I don't want to name but I am saying what my heart

---

[16] For this duality, see Davico Bonino, esp. "Premessa" 7-11; for the *Pastoral*, see Baratto. Questions of the dating of Beolco's works are complicated by the paucity of manuscript sources and the probability that the plays were reworked, perhaps continually, over years. The *Parlamento* (*Reduce*), for example, may have originated in 1513.

tugs me to say, don't you well know? That thing that even you kissed, when you came into the world — let's leave it alone, because it isn't very safe to talk about it, because even men can go all ropey, like horses do.[17]

What Beolco, Cornaro, and likely much of the audience also knew was that Cornaro was (in)famous for his association with prostitutes. Thus the proclamation of modesty about the topic exemplifies what Salvatore Di Maria has termed "blame-by-praise irony."[18] Ruzante/Beolco then works against the violent domination that is the enemy of commonality by demolishing other orators' praise associating Cornaro with the mercenary soldiers who had devastated the countryside:

On my faith, they gave you a nice bit of praise. Now, there is no worse breed than the Romagnolers. Now aren't they Eezy-beezies or Politans from Robbing? There is very little difference between them and the Spanish. Now haven't they proved that in these wars and shitermishes and routs? There never was a Romagnoler who had either faith or law. Now aren't they all blasphemers when you get down to it? Do they treat God and the saints as if they had carved them with a bowie knife? Do they stab them, the pox on it, as if they were stabbing a willow? Cups and florins! Does it seem to you now that they have given you a nice bit of praise? I tell you now, I who am no sliterato like they are, that you are from the Venetian isles, a Venetian of the good kind and of the most important.

(88-89)[19]

In the identification of the bishop with (peaceful) Venice, blame-by-praise irony is again at work: Venice's mercenaries caused as much damage to Paduan peasants as the enemy, if not more. Beolco's rejection of others' praise of "bad"

---

[17] "Mo quello che è po da l'altro lò dananzo, in fra le gambe, un somesso alto, che pensanto se me desconisse el cuore, e per rebelentia de la vostra Spetabilitè, che pur si un preve, a no'l vuogio dire — a dige mo quello che me tira el cuore de dire, saí ben? Quello don fin vu vegnanto al mondo el basassi. Lagonlo pur stare, che la n'è troppo segura a favelarge, che an l'homo se porae incordare con fa i cavagi." Beolco, *La prima oratione*, 84-87, transcription of Biblioteca Civica Verona, ms. 36 Cl. B. Lett Ubic. 82.1. All quotations will be from this edition.

[18] Carroll, *Commerce*, chapter 3; Marucci, Marzo and Romano, 1: nos 202, 170, 180, 184, 178, 191, 204, 101, 102; Di Maria.

[19] "[C]redanto laldarve, i ve disea contra, per che i dise che a si de schiata vegnua de Romagnolaria da Roma. A la fe i v'a do un bel laldo. Mo no g'è la pezor zenia de romagnaruoli. Mo no ègi sbissigiegi o politani da Robin? Da igi a spagnaruoli e[l] g'è puocha differentia. Mo no ghi haonte provè in ste guerre e scagaruole e muzaruole? No fo mé romagnaruolo che havesse fe né leza. Mo n'ègi tuti a bel fato biastemaore? A fagi de Domene e de santi con se i ghi avesse fatti col cortellazo. A ge tragi el cancaro co si el traesse in un salgaro. Coppe fiorin! Te par mo che i v'habbi dò un bel laldo? A dige mo mi, ch'a no son sletran con giè igi, che a si da le Veniesie, venitian d'i buoni e d'i maore."

characteristics and substitution of it with his praise for characteristics congruent with his program continues in his mockery of other orators' statements that Cornaro is a "big" (great) man (shortness of stature characterized the family). He praises instead Cornaro's greatness of heart that will allow him to identify with the peasants, assuring Cornaro (again ironically) that he, the bishop, is not one of those nasty folks who want to dominate others and use that power to appropriate special privileges.[20]

Beolco then leverages Cornaro's established common humanity to recommend his implementation of the peasant council's laws allowing them pleasures similar to Cornaro's own, such as hunting on Sunday. He next points out to Cornaro the burdens inflicted on peasants by the priests' fragility of the flesh, which results in their producing children with peasant women that the peasant husbands are then obligated to support. He proposes either commonality (that priests be allowed to marry so that their wives will bear peasant men's children) or castration. Examples of ecclesiastics known to the audience for succumbing to the attractions of the flesh include Pietro Bembo, with relatives in the Ortolani and the Triumphanti, and Agostino Barbo, with a relative in the Triumphanti.

Egalitarianism is next applied to the enmity between city folk and country folk engendered by the greater privileges of the former (cfr. Favaretto). Ruzante/Beolco proposes as a counter-measure to give both country men and country women the special privilege of four spouses, so attractive that it will draw masses of city folk to the country. By also increasing the birthrate, given that multiple partners will solve the problem that some men are incapable of impregnating some women, the new norm adds the advantage that there will be more local forces to prevent the anal rape of "us" by the Turks, anal rape being the ultimate symbol of dominance — a dominance that the Turks had recently achieved through their many naval victories over Venetian forces (headed by hosts of Ruzante, including Antonio Grimani) and their raids on Italian soil.[21] To clinch his advice, he buffets the bishop just as bishops buffet confirmands at the end of the sacrament that initiates Catholic adulthood, asserting to Cornaro that without the peasants he is nothing, a declaration that, given the proportion of peasant agricultural rents in the income of the Paduan diocese, was not far off the mark.[22] Alvise Cornaro would later become the administrator of these rents

---

[20] This and the following paragraphs summarize relevant points in Beolco, *Prima oratione* 90-101.
[21] The overt reference to anal rape illuminates a double entendre for the question posed by the old lady in Niccolò Machiavelli's *Mandragola* III, 3: "Credete voi che 'l Turco passi questo anno in Italia?"
[22] For this period, see Padua, Biblioteca capitolare, Archivio della cura vescovile, *Mensa vescovile*, t. 95.

and was likely already expressing interest in the office.

Lengthy and much rewritten over the second and third decades of the century, *Betia* is prefaced by two prologues, one for performances in Venice, one of which is likely to have occurred in 1525, and the other for performances in the Paduan countryside. The Venetian prologue expresses various of Beolco's concerns about the privileges with which his hosts have endowed their city and that have come, it is implied, at the expense of the peasants.

Where is there another town where nothing is born and yet where anything can be found; even if you were called on to use crane's milk by a doctor such as Guoiene da Ropegara, which cannot be found anywhere in the world, you would find it here in Venice.[23]

Hidden beneath the marvel at the rare goods available in a city where nothing is born is criticism not only of the medical quackery indulged in by the rich, but of Venice's requirement that all goods going to and from the mainland pass through its port and pay customs duties, thus taxing the mainland while robbing it of commerce. Ruzante goes on to express gratitude for being born an Italian rather than a German or a Frenchman and under the Venetian state and not another. Here again, the apparently ingenuous praise reveals the threat of conquest of the peninsula and the end of Venetian autonomy, which a growing patriotic unity movement opposed under the byword "Italian."[24] The restriction of "others" to Germans and French rather than also Spanish would appear to be a relic of a draft dating to before the unification of the German and Spanish lines by Charles V, or of a draft made when the imperial ambassador to Venice, who would be likely to attend the performance, was Spanish (often the case after Charles's election).

Bazarelo justifies the characters' concentration on love thus:

[...] because I'll tell you / the entire truth / because love is God and Lord / and because at every moment / he carries a bow and arrow / and all of the arguments / and he will pierce your brain with them / [...] because a great literary man / the greatest on the Pavan / taught this to me / and he had studied it.[25]

---

[23] "Un è deversamen terra che no ghe nasa niente e sí se ghe cata d'ogni cosa; s'te volessi essere chiamà de metre late de grua an al medego, dirè Guoiene da Ropegara, ch'el no s'incata al mondo t'inchaterisi chi a veniexia." Beolco, *Betia*, 1r; Beolco (Ruzante), *Teatro* (*RT* 148-49); note that the Zorzi edition is a diplomatic one whose integration of two different manuscript versions is mostly silent.

[24] See its exemplary use by Niccolò Machiavelli in *Il principe*, including the closing exhortation to free 'Italia' from the barbarians; Headley, *The Emperor* 11-12; Headley, "The Habsburg World Empire"; Zimmermann 11, 35, 55-56, 70, 78, 197, 199.

[25] "ch'a ve dirè / tuta la verità / perque amore è dio e signore / e perque a tute l'ore / el porta l'arco e i bolzon / e tute l[e] raxon / e vele ficharè in lo cervelo / [...] / perque un gran sletran / maor che sea sul Pavan / me l'ha insegnio / che la stuio." Beolco, *Betia*,

Again, the apparently innocuous surface conceals an urgent, practical critique: while foreigners menace, the greatest literary man in the Paduan countryside, conventionally assumed to be the Venetian patrician Pietro Bembo, turns his attention to the frivolous topic of Cupid. While scholarly discussion of the passage usually focuses on the "greatest" (*maor*) and the assumption that it refers to Bembo's large derrière, the critique's emphasis instead, I believe, is on the subjugation of the learned mind to frivolous love, the Phyllis-and-Aristotle topos common in the Middle Ages. Bembo, instead of dedicating his efforts to duty in a time of need, fritters away his time in his villa with artful conversations about unrequited love. And indeed, such self-deluding ignorance was displayed by a group of patricians during the war of the League of Cambrai when they attempted to tour the countryside reciting a pastoral as they had in peacetime until fears of skirmishing soldiers ended the idyll (Padua, Biblioteca del Seminario, Sezione Antica, ms. 568, 69r-v.). By contrast, the hired foreign *condottiero* Bartolomeo d'Alviano, who died in 1515 shortly after his victory at Marignano had salvaged his reputation from the disastrous defeat at La Motta of the preceding year, has gone to heaven because of his loyalty to Venice, saving the devils from his presence in the fiery place and their terror that he would treat them as he had the peasants.

Still conveying the playful spirit of the brief respite from war, the *Lettera giocosa* (c. 1524) continues the *Prima oratione*'s emphasis on fertility. Here Ruzante vaunts his ability, through skillful tending, to bring forth abundant fruit from the "farm" of his lady love (*morosa*), whose chamber he has frequented (Carroll, "'I have a good set of tools'"). Continuing to flaunt intimacy with patricians, this short piece, in its assumption of the better ability of some rough peasant men to succeed in impregnating the women of the upper class, silently proclaims the biological fusing of upper and lower classes and the raising of a peasant man's child to the patriciate, as well as the fecklessness of some patrician men.

The final three plays that articulate egalitarian values in an overt way (*Seconda oratione, Parlamento de Ruzante* and *Bilora*) were all staged outside of Venice. There is no evidence that Beolco returned to Venice after his performance at a scandalous festivity in which the captured Francis I was mocked with a mutilated rooster, shortly before Venice publicly abandoned the empire for France in the League of Cognac (1526). By then a confirmed member of Alvise Cornaro's artistic household, Beolco continued his performances with groups that he organized in Padua, in rural locations, and in Ferrara.

Several years of bad weather preceding the *Seconda oratione* (1528) having spread famine through the countryside, Beolco took advantage of the celebration of the cardinalate of Francesco Cornaro, brother of Marco, to plead with him to

---

12v; *RT* 176-79. For Alviano (below): 99r-v; *RT* 470-71.

help the peasants dying of hunger. Francesco had been among the cardinals created for a high price by Clement VII to procure money for his ransom after his capture by imperial troops in the 1527 Sack of Rome. Though Francesco had been reluctant to accept, he was required to do so by his brother's death several years before, his own unmarried status, and the family's insistence on having a cardinal as an essential actor in acquiring the favor in Rome that would result in the lucrative benefices with which the income lost from commerce was increasingly being substituted (cfr. Hallman). These circumstances reveal the ironic contradiction of Ruzante's proclamation to him that "what is given by nature" must be, even if it is water freezing in August, and explain the reference to his bachelor state and to the Church as his bride (Beolco, *Seconda oratione*, 203r; cfr. *RT*, 1208-13). The comic honorific "Paternité de vu" is here lacking in the playful *s-* prefix sported in the earlier oration ("la vostra Spaternité"), indicating its use in full literal meaning: Francesco had several notorious illegitimate sons active in Padua.

Moving to the substance of his appeal on behalf of the peasants, Beolco becomes more aggressive, his earlier advice about treating the peasants properly not having been heeded and the situation having deteriorated substantially. He abjures Cornaro to do so now to keep the peasants in the Roman church, adding that if he does so, Peter and Paul will no longer fear losing their heads. The threat expressed is not subtle: Peter and Paul had been made to "lose their heads" by the largely Lutheran Austrian-German peasant soldiers sacking Rome the year before when they played soccer with relics claimed to be the skulls of those saints. The soldiers' fury had been set in motion during the 1525 peasant revolt against the greed of the Alpine cardinal bishops (Carroll, "A Newly-Discovered *Charles V*," 47-48). It gathered speed when, recruited by Charles to fight Venice and the other Italian states allied with France and the papacy in the League of Cognac, the soldiers were left without direction or pay.

Again employing a strategy of intimacy, Ruzante first declares Cardinal Cornaro to be his brother, then gives him several pieces of advice to solve both the cardinal's and the peasants' problems. After each, he buffets Francesco with a remark about its smell that typically accompanies a punch in the nose.

And we don't have a law on our side, and no one who speaks for us or who has ever been one of us. I hear talk about the law of Datus, the law of Bartolus, the law of Digestion and talk like that; I never hear no one say Nick's law or Nale's law or Duozo's law. All these laws are for the city people. And if you will call on us, we will make our own laws. And if you make a single law, we will all govern ourselves according to it because I know that you will make it right and just and equal. And that will be great: if you do that, it will be the best way to keep the world in peace that could ever be found because you know that many men are killed because of conflicts and love is lost through them too, for goodness sake. And two. And this one doesn't smell rancid either.

Mister Jesus God said to our father Adam, and to all of us who have come after him, "By the sweat of your brow shall you eat your bread." Now it seems to me that now things are going in a different direction, that we who sweat never have anything and those who don't sweat are eating. Oh, let's let it go, since the pox wants it that way: we sweat but we can never get enough and so it is necessary, if we want to live, for us to always be turning to usury. And because usurious lending is a great sin, you can only find a few who practice it and those few, because it is a great sin, want to make big earnings. And we, because we can't make do with less, harvest those little jujubes and crabapples and are ruined even though we have done nothing wrong. And therefore, I would like, for the good of all men, that whoever had some could lend at interest at an honest rate and not an excessive one and that usury would not be a sin, but meritorious, to help the poor folks. Because once everyone could lend at interest, we would always find someone to do so and we would not get such big crabapples. Because you know that hunger makes people do terrible things. People are doing a lot of bad things now because they can't find anyone to give them bread and if they could, they wouldn't do those things. And this one won't muck up the world either.[26]

The recommendation of providing the peasants with the law that they now lack and that, being one and equal for all, will bring peace again enfolds the threat of peasant violence if such a law is not forthcoming. The citation of the Biblical injunction to eat by the sweat of one's brow, coupled with the reference to the famine killing the peasants who grow food but have nothing to eat, aims at the conscience of patricians who not only do not work to produce food but who as members of governing councils require the appropriation of the food grown by

---

[26] "A no Haon leza dal nostro lo, ne digha per nu, ne che ge supia sto negun d'i nuostri. A sento lome dire la leza de Datto, La leza de Bartole, la leza de Gesto dire cosi; a' no sento me dire: la leza de Menego, la leza de Nale, la leza de Duozo. Tutte ste leze e de citaini. Se a ne ciameri an nu, a faron an nu le nuostre; e se a in fari una sola, a se governeron tutti per quela, che a se che la fari derta e giusta e gualiva. E da bel mo, se a fari questo, el sara el pi bel tegnire el mondo in pase cha se poesse me catare, perche a sai che per le lite a s'amaza purasse uomeni e se perde l'amore, madesi. E do. Gnian questo no sa da granzo. ... El disse Messier Ieson Dio al nostro pare Adamo, e an a nu tuti che a' ghe seón vegnù drio: 'In suore vultu tui te magnerè pane tui'. Mo el me pare mo cha la vaghe a un altro muò, cha nu, che a' se suóm, a' no n'aón me', e gi altri, cha no se sua, el magne. Mo lagónla pur anare, dasche' el cancaro vuole cussì: a' se suóm, e si a' no in possón mai aere tanto che ne faghe, e si a' besogna, s'a' vogiàn vivere, che a' 'l togiom sempre a l'usura. E perché el dare a l'usura e un gran pecò, el s'in cata puochi ch'in daghe, e qui puochi, per el gran pecò, vuole far gran guagno; e nu, perché a' no possón far con manco, a' scapón su quele zuzole e zucole, e sì ne deroinóm senza colpa. E perzontena a' vorae, per ben de agn'om, che chi aesse, poesse dare a l'usura per un priessio onesto, e no miga a pì valere e che el dare a l'usura no foesse pecò, mo mierito, per agiare i poeriti. Perché con tuti poesse dare a l'usura, a' in cateron sempre, e sì no arón sì gran zucole; perché a' saí che la fame fa fare de gran cosse. El se fa purassé male, adesso che 'l no se cata chi daghe pan; che, com s'in catasse, el no s'in farae. Gnan questa no impegherà el mondo." Beolco, *Seconda oratione*, 204r-v through "a farì," where the manuscript version ends, followed by a blank space where the rest of the speech was to have been transcribed; *RT* 1216-19.

the peasants for consumption in Venice to prevent food riots there. The following plea to avoid usury embodies Beolco's solicitation of fairness toward the peasants, bolstered by basic religious norms that the new cardinal is supposed to uphold. It would have reminded locals of the Monte di Pietà, founded by the reforming bishop Pietro Barozzi, that was then languishing (cfr. Gios). It is also spoken from an agonized heart, as Beolco himself served as witness to the deeds by which his wealthy patron Alvise Cornaro and others, including the religious reformer Gaspare Contarini, acquired leases from peasant holders in debt because poor harvests had not yielded sufficient crops for them to pay their portion to the owner. The owners, in turn, required the peasants to pay by relinquishing the value of the leasehold and any improvements (such as buildings, fences, etc.) they had made.

Possibly originally dating to 1513-1514, and rewritten around 1529 when similar disastrous war conditions returned, the *Parlamento de Ruzante* (also known as *Reduce* or *Veteran* and as *Primo dialogo*) bitterly evokes the craven reaction of the Venetian army and its *condottieri* and patrician *proveditori* (civilian overseers) in both wars. The latter in 1509 had included Zorzi Cornaro, father of Marco and Francesco, who had left the field the day before the crucial battle. Ruzante's claim at the play's opening, that he made it from Cremona (the battle front) to Venice in three days, has been dismissed by some as hyperbolic. However, the route he describes in fact tracks the course of Venetian couriers bringing news of Agnadello in less than a day, though on horseback, and then of the Venetian forces as they fled "like whores and women" to the edge of the lagoon.[27] Ruzante does not flinch from citing this cowardice in the army's leaders right up to the *capitano generale* Bartolomeo d'Alviano, whose residence in Pra' da la Valle near the Beolco home made him well known to the playwright:

[...] me, I was at the rear as a squadron leader, as a lance-corporal, and when they started to flee, it was incumbent on me as a gentleman to flee as well [...]
Now Sir Bortholomew who was such a show-off in Vicenza, didn't he throw himself in the water to flee and, as it happened, the others were drowning and he ran to Padua to hole up?[28]

Alviano's reckless impulsivity at La Motta is emphasized here, in contrast to the more charitable characterization of the *Betìa*, a critique made safe by his death and the long failure of the Republic to recognize him. One suspects, however,

---

[27] Sanuto, 8: 231, 243, 246, 247, 248; 16: 343-44; quotation from Priuli, 54.
[28] "[...] mi agiera dadrio de cao de squara, de caporale, e igi muce. A scovini muzar an mi da valenthomo" (Beolco, *Parlamento de Ruzante*, 174r; *RT* 524-25); "Mo el segnor Bortholamio che giera si braoso a vicenza se trasselo mo in laqua per muzare e si vene che gialtri se anegava e corse a pava a imbusarse?" (174v; *RT* 526-29).

that if Emilio Menegazzo was correct in his hypothesis that Beolco joined Venetian forces in 1526, Angelo's real targets may have been closer to hand, as implied by the arrogant treatment of peasant foot soldiers by the French field commanders and the top officers' safe location at the back of the battlefield, details that, again, accurately report the facts.[29] Beolco may have even been criticizing his own failure to remain faithful to his imperial leanings.

Bilora, Beolco's final and most extreme flare of truth-telling — and one that he displaced onto Girolamo Castegnola / Bilora, the character played by the actor in his theatrical company who would later marry Beolco's widow — sums up his entire social program and critique of arrogant entitlement in few and telling words. The rapacious old Venetian, representative of city greed, had taken Bilora's wife; Bilora had given him fair warning of the consequences and asked for her back, but the Venetian refused. Bilora now attacks the Venetian, defending his right as husband, and the Venetian pays the ultimate price for his failure to respect it:

Oh, let the pox eat you, you broken-down old man. [...] Give me my woman now. You should have let her be. Whoah, wait, I think he's dead, I do. He's not kicking his foot or his leg. [...] Oh, my God, good night! He's crapped his grapestalks, he has. I told you so, didn't I?[30]

All of this had been rehearsed in the preceding scene, in which Bilora had also imagined a get-away by horse (*RT* 574-77), truncated in this final scene.

Remaining in the Venetian dominion and under Alvise Cornaro's patronage by a kind of coerced choice (the late plays comment often on avoiding exile because of its sufferings, which Beolco's half-brother endured in Ferrara), Beolco in his final plays limited his truth-telling to much more oblique expressions, closing his literary opus with a version of the *Lettera all'Alvarotto* in which he fantasizes a perfect, happy life on the farm of Lady Mirth.

Conclusion: Beolco's Context and Legacy

During the late period of the Cambrai wars (1509-1517) and the early 1520s, a perfect storm of conditions favored Beolco's audacious expression of his nature-based egalitarianism to Venetian patrician audiences. The mainland peasants had helped Venice regain much of what had been lost in the war and provided a new and accessible source of the food and the raw materials of manufacturing that were no longer being supplied by areas under Turkish control. Prompted by the

---

[29] For the accuracy of the description, see Francesco Maria della Rovere, 8r-9v.
[30] "Ah, te magne el morbo, vecio strassinò! [...] Dàme mo la mia femena. Te la divi lagar stare. Poh, moa, a' cherzo che 'l sea morto, mi. Mo no 'l sbate pí né pè né gamba. [...] Miedio, bondì! L'ha cagò le graspe, elo. Te l'hegi dito?" (Beolco, *Bilora*, *RT* 578-79; there are no known manuscripts of this play).

humiliation of defeat, Venetians undertook a collective examination of conscience and realized that their failings in the administration of justice in their dominions had fostered hostility in the local populations. A new interest in the Gospels inspired a renewal of Christian charity and justice. Charles V had taken over much of the coast along which Venice's most lucrative galleys sailed. Beolco took advantage of these factors to candidly advance a program of egalitarianism, but by 1526 the auspicious conditions were evaporating. *Libido dominandi* was overcoming Christian charity, the 1525 Peasants War left the upper classes feeling terrorized by the peasants, Venice returned to a French alliance, the northern galleys stopped sailing and, after the last blow-out festivity mocking Francis (discussed above), Beolco stopped performing in Venice. Hierarchy took its revenge, aided by the paralysis of straitened circumstances. The old order remained in place until the late eighteenth century; and after the French Revolution swept it away, George Sand (1804-1876) and her son Maurice (1823-1889) staged *Bilora* in their home theater, their revival of Beolco's work consistent with their favoring of the poor and progressive views on various social issues.

Tulane University

Works Cited

Baratto, Mario. "L'esordio del Ruzante." *Tre studi sul teatro*. Vicenza: Neri Pozza, 1968. 11-68.

Beolco, Angelo (Il Ruzante). *Betìa*. 1515-1525. MS. Grimani-Morosini 4. Biblioteca Civica Correr, Venezia.

_____. *Lettera giocosa*. 1524. MS. Ital. cl. XI, 66 [=6730]. Biblioteca Nazionale Marciana, Venezia.

_____. *Parlamento de Ruzante (Primo dialogo, Reduce)*. 1513-1529. MS. Ital. cl. XI, 66 [=6730]. Biblioteca Nazionale Marciana, Venezia.

_____. *La prima oratione*. Ed. and trans. Linda L. Carroll. London: Modern Humanities Research Association, 2009.

_____. *Seconda oratione*. 1528. MS. Ital. cl. XI, 66 [=6730]. Biblioteca Nazionale Marciana, Venezia.

_____. *Teatro*. Ed. Ludovico Zorzi. 2nd ed. Torino: Einaudi, 1967.

Calore, Andrea, and Francesco Liguori. *Le donne del Ruzante*. Padova: Panda Edizioni, 2012.

Carroll, Linda L. *Commerce, Peace, and the Arts in Renaissance Venice. Ruzante and the Empire at Center Stage*, London: Routledge, 2016.

_____. *Angelo Beolco (Il Ruzante)*. Boston: Twayne, 1990.

_____. "'(El) ge sa bon laorare': Female wealth, male competition, musical festivities, and the Venetian patriciate in Ruzante's *pavan*." *Sexualities, Textualities, Art and Music in Early Modern Italy. Playing with Boundaries*. Ed. Melanie L. Marshall, Linda L. Carroll, and Katherine A. McIver. Burlington, VT: Ashgate, 2014. 155-83.

_____. "'I have a good set of tools': The Shared Interests of Peasants and Patricians in

Beolco's *Lettera giocosa.*" *Theatre, Opera and Performance in Italy from the Fifteenth Century to the Present. Essays in Honour of Richard Andrews.* Ed. Brian Richardson, Simon Gilson, and Catherine Keen. Occasional Papers 6. Egham, UK: The Society for Italian Studies, 2004. 83-98.

———. "A Newly-Discovered *Charles V with Dog.*" *Ateneo Veneto,* ser. 3, 4.2 (2005), 43-77.

———. "A Nontheistic Paradise in Renaissance Padua." *Sixteenth Century Journal* 24 (1993): 881-98.

———. "Ruzante's Early Adaptations from More and Erasmus." *Italica* 66 (1989): 29-34.

———. "Venetian Attitudes toward the Young Charles: Carnival, Commerce, and *Compagnie della Calza.*" *Young Charles V 1500-1531.* Ed. Alain Saint-Saëns. New Orleans: UP of the South, 2000. 13-52.

Casini, Matteo. "The 'Company of the Hose': Youth and Courtly Culture in Europe, Italy, and Venice." *Studi veneziani* 63 (2011): 1217-37.

Crescenzi, Victor. "Esse de Maiori Consilio": *Legittimità civile e legittimazione politica nella repubblica di Venezia (Secc. XIII-XVI).* Nuovi Studi Storici. Roma: Istituto Storico Italiano per il Medio Evo, 1996.

Davico Bonino, Guido. *Lo scrittore, il potere, la maschera.* Padova: Liviana, 1979.

Del Bo, Beatrice. *Banca e politica a Milano a metà Quattrocento.* Roma: Viella, 2010.

Della Rovere, Francesco Maria. *Discorsi militari.* MS 99, Biblioteca Universitaria Centrale, Padova.

Di Maria, Salvatore. "Blame-by-praise Irony in the *Ecatommiti* of Giraldi Cinzio." *Quaderni d'italianistica* 6.2 (1985): 178-92.

Favaretto, Lorena. *L'istituzione informale. Il territorio padovano dal Quattrocento al Cinquecento.* Milano: Edizioni Unicopli, 1998.

Ferguson, Ronnie. *The Theatre of Angelo Beolco (Ruzante). Text, Context, and Performance.* Ravenna: Longo, 2000.

Gios, Pierantonio. *L'attività pastorale di Pietro Barozzi a Padova (1487-1507).* Padova: ISEP, 1977.

Gullino, Giuseppe. *Marco Foscari (1477-1551): l'attività politica e diplomatica tra Venezia, Roma, e Firenze.* Milano: Franco Angeli, 2000.

Hallman, Barbara McClung. *Italian Cardinals, Reform, and the Church as Property.* Berkeley: U of California P, 1985.

Headley, John M. *The Emperor and His Chancellor. A Study of the Imperial Chancellery under Gattinara.* Cambridge: Cambridge UP, 1983.

———. "The Habsburg World Empire and the Revival of Ghibellinism." *Medieval and Renaissance Studies,* Proceedings of the Southeastern Institute of Medieval and Renaissance Studies. Summer 1975. Ed. Siegfried Wenzel. Chapel Hill: U of North Carolina P, 1978. 107-14.

Herlihy, David. "Popolazione e strutture sociali dal XV al XVI secolo." *Tiziano e Venezia.* Venezia: Neri Pozza, 1980. 71-74.

LeRoy Ladurie, Emmanuel. *Carnival in Romans.* Trans. Mary Feeney. New York: Braziller, 1979.

Lovarini, Emilio. *Studi sul Ruzzante e sulla letteratura pavana.* Ed. Gianfranco Folena. Padova: Antenore, 1965.

Marucci, Valerio, Antonio Marzo, e Angelo Romano, eds. *Pasquinate romane del Cinquecento.* 2 vols. Roma: Salerno Editore, 1983.

Menegazzo, Emilio. *Colonna, Folengo, Ruzante and Cornaro.* Ricerche, Testi, e Documenti. Ed. Andrea Canova. Medioevo e Umanesimo 93. Padova: Antenore,

2001.
Piovan, Francesco. "Tre schede ruzantiane." *Quaderni veneti* 27-28 (1998): 93-105.
Priuli, Girolamo. *I diarii di Girolamo Priuli*. Ed. Roberto Cessi. Rerum Italicarum Scriptores, Tomo 24, Parte 3, fasc. 310. n.d. Torino: Bottega d'Erasmo, 1968.
Rebel, Hermann. *Peasant Classes. The Bureaucratization of Property and Family Relations Under Early Hapsburg Absolutism 1511-1636*. Princeton: Princeton UP, 1982.
Sambin, Paolo. *Per le biografie di Angelo Beolco, il Ruzante, e di Alvise Cornaro*. Restauri di archivio rivisti e aggiornati da Francesco Piovan. Padova: Esedra, 2002.
Sanuto, Marino (Marin Sanudo). *I diarii*. Ed. Rinaldo Fulin et al. 58 vols. Venezia: Visentini, 1879-1902.
Vermes, Geza. *Post-Biblical Jewish Studies*. Leiden: Brill, 1975.
Zimmermann, T. Price. *Paolo Giovio. The Historian and the Crisis of Sixteenth-Century Italy*. Princeton: Princeton UP, 1995.

Diletta Gamberini

Benvenuto Cellini, o del sapere "pur troppo dire il fatto suo" a Cosimo de' Medici

Sinossi: Il saggio intende analizzare le diverse strategie comunicative adottate da Benvenuto Cellini in merito alla questione di "dire la verità" a Cosimo I de' Medici. Il contributo prende in esame le principali opere letterarie dell'artista, l'autobiografia e i *Trattati dell'Oreficeria e della Scultura*, e alcune petizioni dall'autore indirizzate (nell'ultima parte della sua vita) al signore di Firenze, per sottoporre a verifica l'immagine leggendaria di uno scrittore alieno da ogni scrupolo di prudenza nel rapporto con il potere.
Parole chiave: Benvenuto Cellini, autobiografia, trattati d'arte, Cosimo I de' Medici, Firenze medicea

Introduzione
Nel panorama letterario del Cinquecento italiano, il nome di Benvenuto Cellini potrebbe venire alla mente quale una delle più paradigmatiche personalità di scrittore in grado di "dire la verità al principe". Non poche pagine della *Vita*, in cui l'autore immortalò le proprie schermaglie verbali con i signori che si trovò a servire, da papa Clemente VII a Cosimo I de' Medici, contribuiscono a consolidare quel quasi leggendario alone di spavalda sincerità, difetto di accortezza cortigiana ed arroganza nel rapporto con i potenti che da secoli avvolge l'immagine dell'artista. In effetti, già i contemporanei avevano messo in evidenza l'inusuale grado di libertà che Cellini aveva manifestato nelle sue relazioni con i prìncipi. Allibito dal suo comportamento si era ad esempio dimostrato Annibal Caro quando, nel 1539, raccontava le pericolose intemperanze verbali dell'orefice fiorentino, all'epoca prigioniero di papa Paolo III in Castel Sant'Angelo, con l'accusa di sottrazione indebita ai danni del tesoro pontificio. Il letterato marchigiano rilevava con sconcerto come Cellini non riuscisse proprio a trattenersi dal dire "certe sue cose, a suo modo, le quali [...] turbano la mente del Principe", con tutta evidenza sprezzando le più elementari considerazioni di opportuna prudenza legate alla sua condizione di detenuto.[1]

---

*Il presente contributo mette a frutto uno studio da me condotto grazie a una borsa di ricerca presso l'Italian Academy for Advanced Studies in America, della Columbia University: sono molto grata per l'opportunità che quella magnifica esperienza mi ha offerto di continuare a indagare la produzione letteraria di Benvenuto Cellini. Sono in debito con Jo Ann Cavallo, Dino Cervigni e Carlo Lottieri per una serie di suggerimenti

Famoso, poi, l'icastico ritratto che Giorgio Vasari, nell'edizione giuntina delle *Vite*, aveva fornito dell'artista, definito "in tutte le sue cose animoso, fiero, vivace, prontissimo, e terribilissimo, e persona che ha saputo pur troppo dire il fatto suo con i Principi, non meno che le mani, e l'ingegno adoperare nelle cose dell'arti" (2: 874), con quell'enfasi rilevata proprio sul singolare eccesso di libertà ("pur troppo") nei rapporti col potere.

Lo stesso Cellini, in un importante passaggio dell'autobiografia, aveva dato a intendere che le tribolazioni sofferte alla corte di Firenze fossero il risultato della propria mancanza di piaggeria, attribuendo allo stesso Cosimo de' Medici il riconoscimento che una fondamentale "terribilità" di carattere e un difetto di servilismo cortigiano avevano avuto conseguenze esiziali sulla carriera dell'artista.[2] Riflessione analoga era poi stata affidata dallo scultore a una delle poesie da lui composte durante la prigionia del 1556, quando, a fronte di un'incriminazione per percosse ai danni dell'orefice Giovanni di Lorenzo di Papi, egli prospettava l'eventualità che il reato contestato potesse essere, per le

---

che hanno migliorato il testo.

[1] La citazione è tratta dalla lettera del Caro a Luca Martini, datata 22 novembre 1539, riportata da Tassi: "Benvenuto si sta ancora in Castello, e con tutto che sollecitamente, e con buona speranza si negozi per lui, non mi posso assicurare affatto dell'ira, e della durezza di questo vecchio. Tuttavolta il favore è grande, e 'l fallo non è tanto, che di già non sia stata maggior la pena. Per questo ne spero pur bene, se non gli nuoce la sua natura, che certo è strana. E da che sta prigione, non si è mai potuto contenere di dir certe sue cose, a suo modo, le quali, secondo me, turbano la mente del Principe, più col sospetto di quel che possa fare, o dire per l'avvenire, che la colpa di quel che s'abbia fatto, o detto per lo passato" (2: 93). Importante, da questo punto di vista, anche la missiva che lo stesso letterato marchigiano inviò a Benedetto Varchi il 5 dicembre dello stesso anno, quando Cellini era ormai stato rilasciato dalle segrete di Castel Sant'Angelo ma non sembrava per questo incline a porre un freno alla propria lingua: "Di Benvenuto doverete avere inteso che è fuor di Castello in casa del Cardinale di Ferrara; ora a bell'agio le cose sue s'acconceranno; ma ci fa rinnegare il mondo con quel suo cervello eteroclito. Non si manca di ricordargli il ben suo, ma giova poco, perché per gran cosa che dica, non gli par dir nulla" (Tassi 2: 95-96).

[2] Il passaggio in questione della *Vita* riporta lo scambio di battute fra il signore di Firenze e l'ambasciatore di Lucca (Girolamo Lucchesini), che aveva fatto seguito a un appassionato discorso in cui Cellini aveva esortato il duca a non concedere la commissione per la fontana del Nettuno senza prima far svolgere un concorso fra gli scultori di corte: "Subito che io ebbi ditte queste parole [...], lo inbasciatore di Lucca disse al Duca: 'Signore, questo vostro Benvenuto si è un terribile uomo'. Il Duca disse: 'Gli è molto più terribile che voi non dite, e buon per lui se e' non fussi stato così terribile, perché gli arebbe aùto a quest'ora delle cose che e' non ha aùte'. Queste formate parole me le ridisse il medesimo inbasciatore, quasi riprendendomi che io non dovessi fare così. Al quale io dissi che io volevo bene al mio Signore, come suo amorevol fidel servo, e non sapevo fare lo adulatore" (*Vita* II 100, p. 739). Le citazioni dalla *Vita* sono tratte dall'edizione critica a cura di Lorenzo Bellotto.

autorità fiorentine, soltanto un pretesto per punire chi aveva voluto parlare "troppo aldacie".[3]

A fronte di queste testimonianze, che convergono a tracciare il ritratto di un autore del tutto alieno da ogni considerazione di opportunità in merito al rapporto con il principe, il presente contributo mira a fornire un'immagine più sfumata della sua strategia comunicativa con il potere, e nello specifico con Cosimo de' Medici. Attraverso una ricognizione di campionature testuali tratte dalle sue maggiori opere letterarie, la *Vita* e i *Trattati dell'oreficeria e della scultura*, e da due suppliche risalenti agli ultimi mesi della biografia, il saggio intende avviare un discorso meno impressionistico sulle tattiche da lui adottate per rispondere al cruciale problema di dire la verità al principe. La rassegna permetterà, infatti, di gettare luce sui difficili tentativi celliniani di conquistare, negoziare e difendere, entro le strette maglie della Firenze medicea, uno spazio di libera espressione della propria apologia.

La "Vita"

Ai fini della presente indagine, un primo campo di ricerca è offerto proprio dal capolavoro autobiografico del Cellini, l'opera che più di ogni altra ha dato risalto all'immagine di un autore incapace di limitare le proprie intemperanti rivendicazioni contro signori reputati non all'altezza del proprio talento. In corrispondenza ad alcuni fra i più polemici passaggi del racconto relativi agli anni trascorsi alla corte di Cosimo, il manoscritto originale della *Vita* (oggi codice Med. Palat. 234[2] della Biblioteca Laurenziana di Firenze) permette in effetti di registrare come l'artista avvertisse la necessità di espungere dal testo alcune notazioni particolarmente compromettenti in merito al potere mediceo. Come notava Orazio Bacci nell'introduzione alla sua fondamentale edizione critica del testo, del 1901, il volume Laurenziano, approntato dall'artista nel periodo compreso tra lo scorcio del 1558 o gli inizi del 1559 e i primi mesi del 1567 (LXXVII), presenta sporadiche tracce di cassature a carattere censorio. Se, come riconosceva l'editore, alcune fra queste "non furon certo del Cellini o del copista, ma di possessori e lettori che vollero togliere dal testo alcuni passi di censura a persone potenti o amiche" (XXIII), in altri casi ci troviamo in presenza di eliminazioni e riscritture di mano dello stesso autore o degli scribi che operavano sotto la sua diretta supervisione. Tali interventi, che risultano essere stati apportati in un momento successivo alla prima stesura del testo (si tratta infatti di varianti non inserite nel *continuum* della scrittura, bensì nell'interlinea superiore o a margine della pagina), sono da ricondursi al proposito celliniano di

---

[3] Si veda il sonetto *Già tutti i Santi, ancor Saturno e Giove*, vv. 9-11: "Stentato ò qui [in carcere] duo mesi disperato: / chi dicie ch'io ci son per ganimede [per sodomia], / altri che troppo aldacie i' ò parlato" (Cellini, *Rime* 47).

pubblicare la propria autobiografia.[4] Nel quadro di simile progetto, l'artista dovette reputare opportuno cassare un limitato numero di passaggi in cui la critica al signore di Firenze assumeva toni particolarmente caustici: ma, come si vedrà, simili interventi non erano certo sufficienti a cambiare di segno il messaggio dall'autore affidato agli ultimi capitoli dell'autobiografia, che delineavano un ritratto impietoso della meschinità di Cosimo e delle miserie imperanti alla sua corte.

Istanze autocensorie
L'esempio più significativo, da questo punto di vista, proviene da un celebre brano in cui Cellini rievocava le ingannevoli promesse che il duca gli aveva fatto per indurlo a restare al suo servizio, nel 1545. La narrazione è tutta tendenziosamente costruita in modo da mettere in evidenza l'adescamento congegnato dal signore di Firenze ai danni dell'artista.[5] L'autocensura del Cellini, nondimeno, si appuntò soltanto sulle più compromettenti espressioni in origine utilizzate per commentare il mancato rispetto, da parte di Cosimo, della parola data: una slealtà, a dire dello scultore, ben poco confacente a un sistema di valori principeschi, ma che tradiva invece un approccio grettamente mercantile alla committenza. La redazione originale del brano incriminato (cc. 443v-444r del codice Laurenziano), trascritta da Matteo di Michele di Goro Vestri dalla Pieve a Groppine,[6] recitava così:

Certamente che se io fussi stato astuto a·llegare per contratto tutto quello che io avevo di bisogno in queste mia opere, io non arei aùto e' gran travagli, che per mia causa mi son venuti: perché la voluntà sua [*scil.* del Duca] si vedeva grandissima sì in voler fare delle opere e sì nel dar buon ordine a esse. Però non conoscendo io che questo Signore aveva più modo di mercatante che di duca, liberalissimamente proccedevo con Sua Eccellenzia come duca e non come mercatante.[7]   (Vita II 53, pp. 609-10)

---

[4] Che l'autore avesse in mente di dare alle stampe la *Vita* è dimostrato dalle apostrofi a un generico pubblico che egli inserisce nel testo (vedi II 71, p. 655: "sappiate, benigni lettori" e II 83, p. 684: "Or senti un terribile accidente, piacevolissimo lettore"), che si ritroveranno anche nelle pagine dei *Trattati dell'oreficeria e della scultura*.
[5] Vedi ad esempio: "[...] il mio Duca [...] mi disse: 'Se tu vuoi far qualcosa per me, io ti farò carezze tali, che forse tu resterai maravigliato [...]". Io poverello isventurato [...] risposi al mio Duca che volentieri, o di marmo o di bronzo, io gli farei una statua grande in su quella sua bella piazza" (*Vita* II 53, pp. 607-08).
[6] Sull'identità dell'adolescente estensore della prima parte del codice della *Vita* (cc. 1r-460v), si veda Cellini, *Rime* 126.
[7] Il migliore inquadramento a questo brano e alla contrapposizione istituita tra liberalità principesca e slealtà della classe mercantile è offerto da Tylus (31-53). Sui contrasti tra l'autore e Cosimo I nell'ambito della *Vita*, si veda Cervigni (126-28). Per comprendere la natura delle accuse rivolte a Cosimo, giova ricordare le sarcastiche parole con cui Cellini, nella stessa autobiografia, rievocava l'esito del contratto relativo a un prestito a interesse

Resosi conto della problematicità di quanto affermato nell'ultimo periodo, l'artista dovette a un certo punto reputare opportuno tornare sui propri passi, dettando al copista subentrato (poco dopo la stesura del passaggio in questione) a Matteo Vestri una riscrittura in senso cortigiano dell'arrischiata dichiarazione.[8] Lo sprezzante sintagma "più modo di mercatante che di duca" venne allora vigorosamente cassato, e sostituito sul margine destro della carta dall'ossequioso "gran desiderio di far grandiss.e jmprese"; allo stesso tempo, venne accuratamente depennata la clausola "e non come mercatante". Le cassature e la variante censoria non andavano però a intaccare la sostanza di questa pagina dell'autobiografia, tesa a fornire un'immagine ben poco lusinghiera del duca di Firenze: la minima riscrittura, con quel suo tono riguardoso nei confronti della figura di Cosimo, risultava infatti del tutto incoerente rispetto al contesto entro cui era inserita.

Un fenomeno analogo interviene nel brano che descriveva il duca Cosimo non più nei panni dell'ingannatore, bensì in quelli — non meno negativi — dell'ingenuo ingannato, vittima di un raggiro da parte dell'orefice e "sensale di gioie" Bernardone Baldini (*Vita* II 60, pp. 625-28).[9] In questo passaggio dell'autobiografia, Cellini raccontava come Baldini avesse acquistato a Venezia un diamante di scarsa qualità, nella speranza di poterlo rivendere al signore di Firenze a un prezzo di gran lunga superiore al suo effettivo valore. Cosimo, che secondo l'autore vantava di possedere una grande competenza in materia di pietre preziose "ma però non se ne intendeva", per via della propria presuntuosa ignoranza si era poi dimostrato vittima ideale dell'imbroglio. Nella narrazione, Cellini si compiaceva di mettere in ridicolo la sua sciocca supponenza, tratteggiando con toni caricaturali le reazioni del duca ai propri avvertimenti circa il modesto valore della pietra. Leggiamo così che Cosimo, messo in guardia dall'artista circa i difetti del diamante, una volta resosi conto che Cellini poteva avere ragione "fece un mal grugno", esortando quindi l'interlocutore a fornire una stima dell'oggetto: di fronte alla cifra di diciottomila scudi, prospettata dall'autore, "il Duca levò un rumore, faccendo uno O più grande che una bocca di pozzo", rivelando di avere già sborsato per quell'acquisto oltre venticinquemila scudi. Dopo l'uscita di scena del signore, Cellini narrava di avere spiegato ad alcuni degli altri artisti presenti a palazzo (gli orafi Giovan Paolo e Domenico Poggini, il ricamatore Antonio Bachiacca) come Cosimo

---

da lui stipulato con il banchiere Bindo Altoviti, fuoruscito fiorentino di stanza a Roma, e della commissione relativa al suo busto-ritratto in bronzo, oggi all'Isabella Stewart Gardner Museum di Boston: "Da poi che così male io avevo fatto la mia faccenda con Bindo Altoviti, col perdere la mia testa di bronzo et 'l dargli li mia danari a vita mia, io fui chiaro di che sorte si è la fede dei mercatanti" (II 82, pp. 682-83).

[8] L'intervento è infatti di mano dello scriba che trascrive le cc. 461r-464v del codice.

[9] Come ha dimostrato Cervigni, il personaggio di Bernardone è protagonista di numerose scene a carattere burlesco nell'autobiografia del Cellini (143-44).

avesse pagato una cifra spropositata per l'acquisto, e concludeva il resoconto dell'episodio descrivendo l'irrisione di quei cortigiani nei confronti del gabbato: "ridendo ci passammo quella sinplicità del Duca" (c. 458v del codice). È su quest'ultima, irriverente frase che l'autore concentrò il suo intervento correttorio: il sostantivo "sinplicità", quasi un marchio lessicale del tipo comico del beffato ("semplicità" è, ad esempio, la caratteristica distintiva di Calandrino in *Decameron* VIII 3, 4), con una cassatura parziale venne ridotto alla forma aggettivale "sinplice", integrato dal sintagma "credentia del buon Duca".[10] Ancora una volta, però, la minima riscrittura non cambiava di segno il tono irrispettoso del brano.

Come ultimo esempio, giova riportare quanto riscontriamo in un passaggio dell'autobiografia di poco successivo a quello appena analizzato (c. 459r del manoscritto Laurenziano). Cellini vi rievocava l'irriducibile avversione dimostratagli da Pier Francesco Riccio, l'influente maggiordomo del duca, all'epoca in cui lo scultore andava predisponendo il getto del bronzo del *Perseo*. Per vendicarsi di quel dignitario, a suo dire colpevole di avere concertato contro di lui quella falsa accusa di sodomia che lo aveva costretto a riparare a Venezia nel 1546, l'artista ne tratteggiò un ritratto fulminante che, nel porre l'accento sul nefasto potere del Riccio, metteva in luce la negativa situazione della propria patria, assoggettata all'arbitrio di cortigiani di quella risma:

E perché Sua Eccellenzia parlava [...] delle mie saccenterie [*scilicet* cognizioni tecniche], il suo maiordomo, che continuamente cercava di qualche lacciuolo per farmi rompere il collo, e perché gli aveva l'autorità di comandare a' bargelli e a tutti gli uffizi della povera isventurata città di Firenze, che un pratese, nimico nostro, figliuol d'un bottaio, ignorantissimo, per essere stato pedante fradicio di Cosimo de' Medici innanzi che fussi duca, fussi venuto in tanta grande autorità [...] pensò un modo di far qualcosa.

(*Vita* II 61, p. 629)

L'intervento autoriale, in questo caso, si limitò a prescrivere l'eliminazione della dittologia "povera isventurata", che lasciava trapelare una valutazione integralmente negativa dell'amministrazione del potere nel ducato, senza però riguardare gli altri elementi a disdoro della maestà di Cosimo, come quella considerazione che il signore di Firenze era stato educato da un "pedante fradicio" e "ignorantissimo".

Fra l'interruzione dell'autobiografia e il progetto dei "Trattati"
La rassegna delle poche e circoscritte varianti censorie adottate da Cellini nella *Vita*, non esaustiva ma sintomatica delle tendenze che ispirarono i ripensamenti dell'autore, lascia aperti gli interrogativi che avvolgono i motivi per i quali

---

[10] Anche in questo caso, come pure nel successivo, la stesura originale del passaggio è di mano di Matteo Vestri e la revisione di quella del secondo, anonimo copista del codice.

l'opera, all'inizio del 1567, rimase bruscamente interrotta. Secondo un'ipotesi di Nino Borsellino, l'artista si sarebbe reso conto dell'impossibilità di ottenere l'*imprimatur* per quel materiale così corrosivo nei riguardi del potere cosimiano e avrebbe progressivamente abbandonato il progetto della *Vita* per dedicarsi ai *Trattati dell'oreficeria e della scultura*.[11] Si potrebbe quindi sospettare che egli abbia compreso che gli interventi apportati risultavano del tutto inadeguati a rendere pubblicabile il testo cui andava lavorando da anni.

Tuttavia, simile lettura non dà conto della problematicità dei contenuti e della vicenda editoriale dei *Trattati*, il solo libro celliniano che sia stato stampato vivente l'autore. Sulla base della congettura di Borsellino, ci aspetteremmo infatti di rinvenire in quest'opera una scrittura che, grazie al carattere tecnico-didascalico, avrebbe potuto ottenere senza difficoltà l'avallo alla pubblicazione, e che fosse il risultato di una più prudente strategia nella comunicazione col potere mediceo: attesa smentita dalla lettura del manoscritto approntato e donato da Cellini al principe Francesco de' Medici (primogenito di Cosimo e reggente del ducato fin dal 1564), visto che questo testo era non meno critico della *Vita* nei riguardi del duca suo padre. Al contempo, la storia dei *Trattati* dimostra quale grado di mutilazione e riscrittura delle proprie ragioni contro il signore di Firenze (un grado ben diverso da quello tentato con le minime emendazioni al dettato dell'autobiografia) l'artista abbia dovuto vedere imporsi per riuscire ad approdare alla stampa.

---

[11] Borsellino: "Pur senza pretese ideologiche, la *Vita* tutt'intera, e in particolare l'ultima sezione medicea-fiorentina, era diventata un testo incomodo e sconveniente. L'ottica memorialistica, impudicamente ravvicinata a papi cardinali sovrani principi, sorpresi senza controllo esteriore, dietro le quinte, denudava l'immagine di rito dei potenti: di Cosimo in particolare, monarca instabile e capriccioso, se non addirittura sordido [...]. Di fatto, proprio perché istituiva la possibilità di un discorso sulle corti, memorialistico anziché trattatistico [...], la *Vita* finiva per smentire i modelli storiografici ufficiali e quelli dei trattati cortigiani e accademici [...]. Pur [...] essendo vincolata a esasperate rivendicazioni personali, la *Vita* poteva ricevere dal pubblico, una volta stampata, il crisma di un anticodice della regalità e quindi dei doveri del cortigiano e del suddito. Il C. capì che il libro non avrebbe oltrepassato la soglia dell'*imprimatur* e si autocensurò senza tuttavia distruggere l'opera. Tatticamente anzi ne recuperò le irrinunciabili motivazioni polemiche e difensive nei *Trattati* scritti tra il 1565 e il 1567 e non suscettibili di impedimenti editoriali in ragione della loro più esplicita funzione, quella didattico-professionale" (446-47). Una diversa, suggestiva soluzione al problema dell'interruzione della *Vita* è offerta da Dino Cervigni, secondo cui la sezione finale dell'autobiografia dell'artista, quella che fa seguito al racconto del disvelamento del *Perseo*, dimostrerebbe, con la sua cronaca di piccole magagne private sullo sfondo della Firenze cosimiana, la sostanziale incapacità dell'autore di fornire una coerente e adeguata conclusione alla propria opera apologetica (170).

La revisione dei "Trattati dell'oreficeria e della scultura"
Sebbene a lungo trascurata dagli studi su Cellini scrittore, la ricostruzione della vicenda editoriale dei suoi scritti tecnico-artistici può oggi avvalersi di alcuni contributi mirati.[12] Basterà, quindi, ripercorrerla sommariamente, al fine di sottolineare l'incidenza delle istanze di conversione in senso encomiastico del discorso celliniano sul potere mediceo, e soprattutto di cercare di comprendere se l'autore possa aver dato l'avallo a simile stravolgimento delle proprie verità sul duca Cosimo. Sulla base dei dati in nostro possesso, sappiamo che l'artista lavorò ai *Trattati* dal 1565 al 1567, quando un manoscritto dell'opera — forse lo stesso idiografo a noi pervenuto, il cod. Marc. 5134 della Biblioteca Nazionale Marciana di Venezia — venne dedicato e donato a Francesco de' Medici.[13] Probabilmente l'anno successivo, i *Due Trattati uno intorno alle otto principali arti dell'Oreficeria, l'altro in materia dell'Arte della Scultura* uscivano a stampa per i tipi di Valente Panizzi e Marco Peri, preceduti da un'ossequiosa lettera di dedica al fratello minore del principe, il cardinale Ferdinando. Nella dedicatoria si alludeva all'identità di colui che aveva sollecitato la pubblicazione e che era quasi sicuramente stato il revisore del testo: il giovane, colto e poliedrico segretario del dedicatario, Gherardo Spini.[14] Il tono deferente

---

[12] Per un inquadramento della genesi dell'opera, delle differenze riscontrabili fra manoscritto e stampa e per un sommario ragguaglio sul profilo intellettuale del revisore si rimanda a Milanesi (XIV-XIX e XLV-XLVII), a Trento (80-83), e soprattutto al contributo di Rossi, cui si deve aggiungere il recente saggio di Allen (8-9; 42-61). Per un'analisi specificamente dedicata alla censura ideologica dei *Trattati*, con una nutrita serie di esempi tratti dai testi (qui solo brevemente ripercorsi), si veda Gamberini.
[13] Milanesi (XII-XIII e XLII).
[14] Vedi: "[...] parendomi che perciò mi si porgessi occasione di poterle dimostrare in parte quanto io mi senta obbligato alla sua Illustriss. casa [...] facendole dono d'alcune mie fatiche ch'io già composi intorno alle dett'arti, et altre simili; le quali già furono vedute scritte in penna dall'Illustriss. S. Principe di Fiorenza suo Fratello: col consiglio del detto M. Gherardo [...] mi deliberai ponendole in luce farne humilmente dono a V. S. Illustriss." (*Due Trattati* Aiiv). Su Spini, si vedano almeno, accanto ai contributi citati nella nota 12, gli studi di Acidini (18-30) e Payne (114-68). A correzione di quanto scritto nel mio precedente contributo sul libro, dove avevo datato la stampa dei *Due Trattati* al 1569 (cronologia prospettata anche da Rossi 173), devo riconoscere che l'effettivo anno di pubblicazione del testo dovrebbe essere il 1568. La lettera dedicatoria del volume reca la data del 26 febbraio 1568, il che — considerato il calendario fiorentino, *ab Incarnatione*, che faceva iniziare l'anno il 25 di marzo — indurrebbe a riferire senz'altro la stampa al 1569. Possediamo però dei documenti notarili che indicano come la composizione del volume risultasse giunta a metà del testo alla data del 7 febbraio 1568 (Calamandrei 49), cosa che rende assai inverosimile un completamento nel 1569. D'altronde neppure le *Vite* giuntine del Vasari, precedute da una lettera datata 9 gennaio 1568 (Aiiir) ed effettivamente pubblicate in quell'anno, seguivano, contrariamente all'uso di gran lunga prevalente nelle tipografie fiorentine, lo stile *ab Incarnatione*: vedi Procacci.

dell'epistola compendiava il senso della radicale riscrittura dell'opera che era stata approntata dall'artista. Il libro dedicato al principe di Firenze era infatti intriso di rivendicazioni polemiche contro il duca Cosimo e si appellava alla solidarietà dei lettori contro la denunciata grettezza e volubilità di quel committente che, a dire dell'autore, aveva tradito la luminosa storia di munifico mecenatismo promossa dai suoi predecessori di casa Medici.[15] La stampa dell'opera era caratterizzata, invece, dal dispiegamento di un solenne panegirico di Cosimo, Francesco e Ferdinando de' Medici e della loro magnifica politica delle arti. Nella versione preparata da Gherardo Spini, i *Due Trattati* (45v) potevano ben essere presentati come l'umile e devoto omaggio di un artista "grato, & conoscente degl'infiniti beneficii" ricevuti "dalla real cortesia" del duca e dei suoi figli. L'intervento emendatorio, che incise pesantemente sulla

---

[15] Nell'introduzione alla versione manoscritta dei *Trattati*, Cellini così alludeva alle motivazioni polemiche alla base della stesura dell'opera: "Conosciuto quanto e' sia dilettevole agli uomini il sentire qualche cosa di nuovo, questa è stata la prima causa che mi ha mosso a scrivere. E la seconda causa (forse la più potente) è stata che, sentendomi fortemente molestare lo intelletto per alcune mie fastidiose cause, le quali in questo mio piacevole discorso modestamente io le farò sentire, sono certo che le moveranno i lettori grandemente a compassione, e a sdegno non piccolo" (593; vedi anche Gamberini 56). La spiegazione delle allusioni contenute nella prefazione aveva poi luogo nel dodicesimo capitolo del *Trattato dell'oreficeria*, laddove venivano ripercorse le ragioni dell'autore contro il duca di Firenze e della propria forzata conversione alla scrittura, frutto dell'impossibilità di continuare a operare come artista: "Io promessi innel principio del mio libro di dire parte della causa che mi movea a scrivere questo volume, la qual causa io dissi che moverebbe gli uomini a grande sdegno del caso e compassione di me: avvenga che ora io non lo posso più tener serrato drento al mio petto, io son forzato a dirlo" (677-80). Il brano era premesso al racconto del trionfale disvelamento del *Perseo*, dopo il quale, a dire dell'autore, il duca aveva inopinatamente cambiato il proprio atteggiamento nei riguardi dell'artista: "Passato che fu dua giorni, io viddi turbato il mio signore sanza mai avergline dato causa nessuna; e, se bene io gli ho domandato molte volte licenzia, egli non me l'ha data, né manco m'ha comandato nulla: per la qual cosa io non ho potuto servire né lui né altri, né manco ho saputo mai la causa di questo mio gran male. Se non che, standomi così disperato, ho reputato che questo mio male venissi dagli influssi celesti che ci perdominano, però io mi messi a scrivere tutta la mia vita e l'origine mio e tutte le cose che io avevo fatte al mondo: e così scrissi tutti gli anni che io avevo servito questo mio glorioso signore duca Cosimo. Ma, considerando poi quanto e' principi grandi hanno per male che un lor servo dolendosi dica la verità delle sue ragioni, io rimediai a questo; e tutti gli anni che io avevo servito il mio signore il duca Cosimo, quegli, con gran passione, e non senza lacrime, io gli stracciai e gitta'gli al fuoco con salda intenzione di non mai più scrivergli. Solo per giovare al mondo e per essere lasciato da quello scioperato, veduto che m'è impedito il fare [...], così io mi son messo a dire". Da notare, il fatto che Cellini sostenesse, mentendo, di avere dato alle fiamme i capitoli fiorentini della propria autobiografia, perché consapevole che essi sarebbero risultati inaccettabili per il duca: su questo, si rimanda a Borsellino 446.

veste linguistica del testo e sullo stile della prosa celliniana,[16] si era infatti appuntato con particolare zelo cortigiano sui passaggi del manoscritto in cui l'autore aveva osato dare voce alla "verità delle sue ragioni" contro il signore di Firenze (*Trattati*, 680). Solo in questa forma encomiastica, l'opera visse e circolò per quasi tre secoli.[17]

"Libertà" della riscrittura
La distanza che intercorre fra il manoscritto che lo scultore aveva presentato al principe Francesco e la stampa uscita nel 1568, con tre blasoni medicei sul frontespizio (quasi a ratificare l'avvenuta conversione ideologica dei *Trattati*), induce a guardare con cautela alla tesi di Paolo Rossi, secondo cui Cellini avrebbe fornito il suo pieno sostegno alla riscrittura dello Spini.[18] Tale lettura, infatti, basata su un esame della sola trasformazione stilistica dell'opera, non tiene conto dello stravolgimento dei contenuti fortemente critici verso Cosimo de' Medici che Cellini aveva affidato al codice Marciano: di conseguenza, essa non rileva come, per un simile messaggio, fosse impossibile pervenire alla stampa in ambito fiorentino. Se avallo probabilmente ci fu (come sembrano testimoniare la lettera dedicatoria della stampa, che fa riferimento all'assenso autoriale nei riguardi della proposta di Gherardo Spini di pubblicare i *Due Trattati*, e il fatto che l'edizione del 1568 conservi tracce di quella che parrebbe essere stata una sporadica cooperazione del Cellini alla riscrittura del testo),[19]

---

[16] Su questi aspetti, si veda soprattutto il contributo di Rossi, che riassume in questi termini il senso della revisione stilistica: "The vivid, lively, and entertaining prose of the Marciana manuscript is replaced with a staid, informative, and academic text" (182).

[17] La versione originale dei *Trattati*, secondo la lezione del manoscritto Marciano, venne infatti per la prima volta pubblicata nel 1857, a cura di Carlo Milanesi.

[18] Vedi Rossi: "Anyone who is conversant with Cellini's literary remains, his *Vita*, letters, Ricordi, Suppliche, archival documents, and the accounts by others of his character must find it inconceivable that he did not play a major role in this revision or that he did not give the revision his full support" (187-88).

[19] Induce a ritenere plausibile l'avallo celliniano alla revisione editoriale dell'opera anche il fatto che i libri privati di ricordi dell'artista e i documenti relativi alla lite per il contratto di pubblicazione con i tipografi Panizzi e Peri (vedi Calamandrei 39-52 e 172-75 e Trento 80-83) non registrino alcuna reazione dell'autore alla riscrittura dello Spini. Si devono poi verosimilmente allo stesso Cellini delle informazioni relative alla sua biografia che rinveniamo nella stampa del 1568 e che erano invece assenti nella versione manoscritta dei *Trattati*. Fra queste, il dettaglio relativo all'identità di uno dei suoi collaboratori all'epoca del servizio presso Francesco I Valois, nel codice originale designato semplicemente come "un valente giovane, di chi io facevo assai conto" (*Trattati* 720), divenuto nella stampa "un certo Claudio Fiammingo mio lavorante, giovane molto ingegnoso & sufficiente" (*Due Trattati* 33v). Più significativa, la notizia relativa al progetto celliniano di pubblicare un prezioso apografo di scritti di Leonardo sulle arti e sulla prospettiva, dallo scultore acquistato mentre si trovava in Francia. Nel manoscritto Marciano, nell'ambito del discorso *Sull'Architettura* posto a corredo

esso non fu il risultato di una volontà libera da considerazioni esterne al processo creativo. In effetti, i *Trattati* potrebbero forse rientrare in quella variegata casistica di interventi che Luigi Firpo studiò nel suo magistrale saggio sulle "correzioni d'autore coatte". Quei ripensamenti, cioè, dettati da pressanti ragioni di opportunità, che hanno indotto scrittori antichi e moderni ad accettare radicali mutilazioni a un loro testo pur di sventare il pericolo di una sua distruzione o di un probabile divieto di stampa.[20] Cellini, ormai ai margini della scena artistica fiorentina[21] e alla ricerca di un estremo riscatto attraverso la

---

dell'opera, Cellini faceva riferimento a tale progetto in questi termini: "[...] mi sono messo a scrivere questo poco del discorso di queste arti; in fra le quali spero di questa prospettiva mettere in luce, secondo e' capricci del gran Lionardo da Vinci, pittore eccellentissimo, cosa che sarà utilissima al mondo; ma voglio che sia libro appartato da questo" (*Trattati* 820). Solo con la stampa intervenne l'importante precisazione, attribuibile allo stesso Cellini, che quel codice leonardesco era stato indebitamente sottratto al suo legittimo proprietario, assieme ad altri suoi scritti: "Ma perché io mi riserbo altra volta a parlare di ciò, et particolarmente della prospettiva, dov'io farò palese, oltre a quello ch'io intendo di trattare, infinite osservazioni di Lionardo da Vinci intorno a detta prospettiva, le quali trassi da un suo bellissimo discorso: che poi mi fu tolto insieme con altri miei scritti" (*Due Trattati* 61v, cap. *Breve discorso intorno all'Arte del Disegno*). Sfortunatamente, la stampa del 1568 non precisa le circostanze in cui avvenne la sottrazione dell'apografo leonardesco e degli scritti celliniani, né il contenuto di questi. Ma se questa nota fosse da ricondurre a un evento verificatosi in seguito al completamento del manoscritto dei *Trattati* (1567), essa potrebbe forse prospettare una spiegazione inedita per l'interruzione della *Vita* in quello stesso anno. Seppure questa sia un'ipotesi ad oggi non comprovabile, l'autobiografia avrebbe potuto fare parte di quelle scritture celliniane di cui si lamentava la sottrazione nell'edizione dei *Trattati* del 1568, tanto più che il grosso codice della *Vita* non veniva registrato negli inventari notarili dei beni dell'artista redatti all'indomani della sua morte (Bacci XVIII-XIX).

[20] Firpo: "In tema di violenza occorrerà dunque distinguere anzitutto la mutilazione, l'interpolazione o la manipolazione testuale avvenute all'insaputa dell'autore, non importa se lui vivente e magari consenziente genericamente alla pubblicazione, da quelle avvenute con il suo consenso esplicito o almeno con sua piena cognizione e acquiescenza [...]. Opportunismo politico, conformismo religioso, rispetti mondani, rigorismo moraleggiante hanno indotto in ogni tempo editori intenti a fini pratici a far violenza ai testi, pubblicando edizioni espurgate, classici *ad usum Delphini*, pudiche antologie scolastiche [...]. Per poter configurare un'ipotesi di vera e propria violenza [sui testi] occorre presumere invece un'acquiescenza rassegnata, un consenso coatto: la volontà non deve risultare esclusa, né separata dalla sua determinazione causale (nel nostro caso l'intento di diffondere o pubblicare una data opera), bensì menomata nella propria libertà. La spinta del timore agirà allora come minaccia di un male anche peggiore della mutilazione — ad esempio il divieto di pubblicazione, la distruzione dell'opera, sanzioni penali all'autore — e questi si indurrà ad evitarlo abbracciando di malanimo il danno minore (soppressioni parziali, adattamenti conformistici), esercitando in definitiva una scelta di tipo economico" (152-53).

[21] Sulla fase più crepuscolare della carriera da artista del Cellini, il cui astro era ormai stato eclissato da una generazione di scultori alieni da ogni "terribilità" nei rapporti col

divulgazione di un libro che lo accreditasse quale *auctoritas* nel campo della riflessione tecnico-didascalica sulle arti, potrebbe avere accettato il tradimento del messaggio apologetico e polemico che egli aveva in origine assegnato alla sua opera. Ciò non dimostra un suo tardivo allineamento ai corifei della propaganda medicea: semmai, è la riprova che anche l'uomo la cui mancanza di accortezza nei rapporti con i principi aveva scandalizzato i contemporanei si trovò a dover sottostare alle limitazioni imposte, nella scena del nascente Granducato, alla possibilità di dire pubblicamente una verità difforme dal messaggio dei panegiristi di quel potere.[22]

Il caso dei memoriali ai Soprassindaci
Che il tono encomiastico dei *Trattati* andati a stampa non fosse il frutto di una libera conversione celliniana al partito degli entusiasti sostenitori di casa Medici risulta, peraltro, dimostrato da testimonianze documentarie risalenti all'ultimo scorcio della biografia dell'autore. Nel 1570, Benvenuto Cellini si trovò ancora una volta a tentare di dare voce alle proprie ragioni nel quadro di un impari rapporto con Cosimo de' Medici. Stavolta, il tentativo non riguardava una scrittura pubblica, bensì un messaggio rivolto allo stesso potere responsabile delle ingiustizie di cui l'autore si sentiva vittima, e ai suoi apparati fiorentini: mi riferisco ai lunghi memoriali dall'artista indirizzati, pochi mesi prima della morte (nel febbraio del 1571), a quella magistratura cittadina dei Soprassindaci che doveva effettuare una revisione complessiva dei conti economici in sospeso tra lo scultore e il signore di Firenze.

Genesi e natura dei testi
La rilevanza dei documenti in questione, in apparenza solo un frammento del nutrito *dossier* giudiziario frutto della turbolenta biografia celliniana, è in verità ben diversa da quella delle carte relative alle infinite contese legali che, nei suoi ultimi anni, videro contrapposto il rissoso artista di volta in volta ad editori insolventi, fittavoli morosi e personaggi di dubbio mestiere che operavano nel sottobosco della città toscana.[23] Questa volta, Cellini si trovava coinvolto in una

---

potere (si pensi ai profili di Bartolomeo Ammannati, Vincenzo Danti e Vincenzo de' Rossi), si veda Pope-Hennessy 253-84.
[22] Da questo punto di vista, nel panorama censorio degli anni che seguirono l'Indice dei libri proibiti di Paolo IV (1559) e quello del Concilio di Trento (1564), i *Trattati* costituiscono un interessante caso di espurgazione di un testo dettata da motivi prevalentemente politici e non religiosi (sebbene istanze controriformistiche di moralizzazione non fossero estranee alla riscrittura di Spini).
[23] Come ha ricordato Calamandrei, 11, dopo un'esistenza in cui non aveva esitato a ricorrere alla violenza per risolvere le proprie contese, nei suoi ultimi anni l'autore si convertì in un accanito litigante nelle aule di tribunale: "Così, a quarantatré anni [con riferimento al racconto di *Vita* II 28], egli aveva trovato che 'una gran daga' era il miglior

causa che lo vedeva, nella sostanza, contrapposto allo stesso Granduca: la contesa davanti ai Soprassindaci è la pagina conclusiva di una quasi interminabile serie di recriminazioni economiche dell'artefice in merito al lungo servizio da lui prestato alla corte di Cosimo, a partire dall'estate del 1545.[24]

Nelle sue suppliche ai funzionari della burocrazia medicea, l'artista aveva per anni lamentato di non aver mai ricevuto quei compensi che il signore di Firenze gli aveva promesso, e di aver riscosso soltanto una minima parte di quanto dovuto per la realizzazione di lavori di oreficeria e scultura per il duca. Nel maggio del 1570, l'ennesima petizione era stata accolta con un rescritto che trasferiva gli incartamenti relativi al saldo dei conti del Cellini e l'incarico di chiudere quella vertenza alla magistratura dei Soprassindaci, responsabile dell'amministrazione delle finanze granducali.[25] La causa cominciò ad essere dibattuta a partire dai mesi di settembre e ottobre, quando l'artefice presentò agli ufficiali in quel momento in carica, Carlo de' Medici e Filippo dell'Antella, due dettagliati memoriali in cui rievocava i quasi ventisei anni trascorsi alla corte di Firenze, passava in rassegna le opere d'arte che aveva realizzato in quel periodo ed esponeva le proprie richieste economiche al Granduca in merito a ciascuno di quei lavori.

Questi memoriali, "piati queruli e cavillosi" a dire di Nino Borsellino (446), in virtù dei loro toni effusivi e dei contenuti retrospettivi rappresentano in effetti delle testimonianze di grande interesse per lo studioso che intenda fare luce sulle motivazioni polemiche e autoapologetiche che costituiscono il nucleo generatore dell'intera produzione letteraria dell'artista.[26] Al contempo, essi illuminano

---

modo di porre fine ai giudizi. Ma in vecchiaia, dopo i sessant'anni, abbandonò questi metodi sbrigativi: ed anzi parve prender gusto, da litigante buon intenditore, alla lunghezza e alla complicazione delle liti". In generale, il volume di Calamandrei resta l'insuperato lavoro di riferimento per ricostruire le vicissitudini legali del Cellini.

[24] Una sintetica ricostruzione delle annose vertenze economiche tra l'artista e il signore di Firenze, destinate a restare in sostanza irrisolte (Cellini non riuscì infatti a vedersi pagare i crediti richiesti), è offerta da Camesasca 46-64.

[25] Il rescritto è riportato da Tassi 3: 179.

[26] Secondo Maier, Cellini autobiografo "intende [...] fare una esaltazione di se stesso e difendere la propria posizione umana e la propria arte contro i numerosi oppositori e rivali. La *Vita* nasce [...] da un intendimento [...] polemico; e deve far vedere quale sia l'uomo, cui molti si permettono di mostrarsi avversi; quale tempra abbia l'artista, al quale il duca Cosimo, piccolo principe di un piccolo principato, reca terribili offese, preferendogli l'Ammannati e il Bandinelli e tenendolo a corto di danaro e di materiale" (38). Borsellino ha poi ribadito le motivazioni "polemiche e autoapologetiche" alla base del progetto autobiografico della *Vita* (446), e Gerarda Stimato ha rilevato l'unità di ispirazione che lega le principali opere letterarie del Cellini, scrivendo tra l'altro: "L'*infelicitas* esistenziale di Benvenuto non può che risolversi [...] nell'interruzione della *Vita*; non per questo, però, la vena autoapologetica dello scrittore si esaurisce, anzi, essa continua a fluire copiosamente, anche se in forme e modi diversi di scrittura" (53).

l'estremo tentativo del Cellini di creare e difendere uno spazio di comunicazione privata col potere mediceo in cui fosse possibile sostenere le proprie ragioni.

Doppio registro
Illuminante, da tale punto di vista, è il passaggio che inaugura la seconda petizione ai magistrati fiorentini:

> Magnifici Signori Soprassindachi.
> Con tutto che io abbia fatto un poco di discorso a Vostre Signorie del modo che io mi fermai a servire il Gran Duca nostro; ancora e' m'è di necessità di fare questo altro poco a Vostre Signorie, perché avvenga che il primo Vostre Signorie lo volessino far vedere al Gran Duca, io crederrò che questo Vostre Signorìe non si cureranno di mostrarlo a quella, avvenga che questo sia con qualche poco di dimostrazione di mie vere passioni.
> (Tassi 3: 213).

Il brano costituisce uno snodo di rilievo ai fini della presente indagine: nell'*incipit* della supplica, il mittente si premura infatti di istituire una sorta di "doppio registro" nella propria comunicazione. Cellini, dopo aver inoltrato una prima missiva in cui ripercorreva per sommi capi, con appena "un poco di discorso", il lungo servizio alla corte fiorentina, nella consapevolezza che i magistrati avrebbero potuto condividere i contenuti di quel memoriale con Cosimo de' Medici, rivolgeva ai Soprassindaci la richiesta che il nuovo memoriale, stavolta contenente "qualche poco di dimostrazione" delle "vere passioni" del mittente, non fosse invece mostrato al signore della città.

La lettura sinottica delle due memorie ai Soprassindaci mette dunque a riscontro una comunicazione destinata (sia pure indirettamente) a Cosimo con un'altra, ad essa speculare nei contenuti, che si vuole però confinata a un rapporto riservato tra querelante e magistrati. Il diverso tono dei testi non lascia sussistere dubbi sulle buone ragioni che indussero Cellini a raccomandare riserbo ai suoi destinatari circa lo sfogo delle proprie passioni, sebbene sia lecito dubitare che il suo invito sia poi stato accolto dagli ufficiali fiorentini, che regolarmente mettevano al corrente il signore della città in merito alle loro deliberazioni.[27] Nel primo dei due documenti, rinveniamo infatti un resoconto teso a rivendicare la fondatezza delle proprie ragioni entro un quadro di ossequio alla giustizia e alla magnanimità di Cosimo, designato come "benignissimo Signore, sempre innamorato delle virtù" (Tassi 3: 204), anzi come "benignissimo e santissimo, pieno di cortesia, solo nato per esempio del bene" (3: 205). Il ragguaglio del servizio alla corte di Firenze si avvale di una dicotomia di comodo, che, nel ripercorrere le ingiustizie e le "gran tribulazioni"

---

[27] Litchfield: "Cosimo [...] introduced his own men into the magistracies and the subordinate staff, who gave him cognizance of their deliberations and control over the entire administration" (72).

(3: 206) subìte dall'artista, scagiona il duca da ogni responsabilità. La repentina e immotivata freddezza del committente all'indomani del trionfale disvelamento del *Perseo*, già accoratamente rievocata dall'autore nelle pagine della *Vita* e dei *Trattati dell'oreficeria e della scultura*, viene ad esempio attribuita all'influsso nefasto dell'invidiosa maldicenza di alcuni, innominati cortigiani, di cui il signore di Firenze è presentato come incolpevole vittima.[28] Ancora più significativa, poi, è la conclusione della missiva, laddove Cellini — dopo aver espresso il proprio rimpianto per la condizione di irripetibile felicità vissuta negli anni trascorsi al servizio del re di Francia, Francesco I Valois (1540-1545) — dava voce al rammarico per non essersi visto accordato, nel 1562, il permesso di lasciare Firenze per tornare a Parigi, al servizio di Caterina de' Medici. La rievocazione dell'episodio, che trova puntuale corrispondenza nelle ultime pagine della *Vita* (II 112), offriva all'autore lo spunto per fare un bilancio dei propri travagli, ancora una volta ribadendo che "Sua Altezza" non aveva avuto alcuna colpa. In questo caso, Cosimo era scagionato dal Cellini attraverso l'attribuzione di ogni responsabilità dei propri tormenti e della propria rovina economica a quell'oscura quanto esiziale "mala fortuna" che rivestiva un ruolo di primo piano anche nella mitopoiesi dell'autobiografia:[29]

Questo non piacque al mio Gran Duca, dove che io persi una tanto mirabile occasione [...]; più succintamente che mi sie stato possibile ho fatto a quelle questo poco del discorso, con il quale io solo mi dolgo, non di Sua Altezza, perché in quella ho conosciuto tutte le divinità, che mai sia stato in altro uomo; né manco mi dolgo di nessuna colpa mia, perché, considerato tutte le azioni di questo negozio, conosco espressamente essere stato malignità di mala fortuna. Perché, se io fussi stato fermo in Francia, io sarei oggi uomo di più di 50000 scudi; dove che sendo stato nella mia dolce patria commesso dalla mia mala fortuna in tanto travaglio [...]. Io crederrò sempre, che se Vostre Signorie riducono a quella santissima memoria di Sua Altezza questo mio breve discorso, che quella, insieme con l'altre sue benignissime e sante grazie, darà fine in quel modo che Dio la spirerà [...]. Così prego Vostre Signorie che chiegghino a Sua Altezza grazia che in tutti que' modi che Dio la spira, la determini et ponga silentio a tutti questi mia gravi affanni, che in tutti e' modi che quella dia la fine io ne ringrazierò Dio et Sua Altezza.

(Tassi 3: 211-12)

---

[28] Tassi: "Sua Altezza non si potette difendere dalle velenose invidie, che non gli imbrattassino alquanto que' sua gloriosi e virtuosissimi orecchi" (3: 207).
[29] Vedi Maier: "Il Cellini giunge naturalmente a ritenersi vittima di un'universale congiura e scorge ovunque avversari, tra i quali è da collocare, anzitutto, il medesimo destino. Attraverso quest'ideale prospettiva si matura la *Vita* [...] ed è ovvio ch'essa si configuri come un machiavellico dissidio tra 'fortuna' e 'virtù', tra l'acerbo destino [...], da una parte, e il protagonista, illuminato dalla divina grazia, dall'altra" (42). Sulla sostanziale mancanza di una visione coerente di entità come il destino e la fortuna nell'autobiografia celliniana, si veda Cervigni (32).

Cellini non si peritava di attingere all'armamentario retorico delle iperboli celebrative tipiche delle suppliche del tempo per incensare il signore di Firenze, presentato quale divina incarnazione di ogni virtù: un ritratto che risultava del tutto funzionale a sollecitare dal Granduca una rapida risoluzione alla propria causa, cui l'artista si dichiarava pronto a rimettersi docilmente.

Non sorprende che tutt'altro sia il tono del memoriale "riservato" ai Soprassindaci. Qui, gli accenti si facevano subito più esacerbati rispetto a quelli della precedente missiva. Come in alcuni dei passaggi più polemici dell'autobiografia, lo scultore non esitava ad accusare il signore di Firenze di aver tradito la parola data, non osservando in alcun modo l'accordo economico che era stato pattuito in merito alle condizioni di servizio dell'artista. Le recriminazioni si appuntavano, in particolare, sulle annose dispute scaturite dal dono, da parte del duca, della casa in cui l'artefice viveva e lavorava fin dal 1545, dal momento che quella assegnazione era rimasta per molti anni lettera morta, ed era anzi più volte stata messa in discussione dai funzionari medicei.[30] La missiva proseguiva passando in rassegna altre imputazioni (quali l'impossibilità di avvalersi di aiutanti qualificati nella propria attività lavorativa e lo smacco della commissione all'Ammannati del marmo per realizzare la fontana del Nettuno, lungamente vagheggiata dal Cellini) che avevano già sostanziato gli ultimi capitoli della *Vita*. Il ragguaglio assumeva toni apocalittici nella chiusa, laddove il mittente, obiettando alla scelta dei Soprassindaci di conteggiare minuziosamente i crediti già percepiti dall'artista prima di procedere al saldo dei suoi conti, addensava acri auspici di rivalsa ultraterrena:

Ora voi, Signori Soprassindachi, pare che Vostre Signorie mi voglino computare quel poco delle provvisioni in nelle mie opere, questo non è il dovere, e ne fate dispiacere a Dio e mancamento agli primi patti che io feci con Sua Altezza. Sappiate, Signiori, che a me mi pare trapassare San Bartolommeo di merito di gran martire: lui fu solamente iscorticato, ma io sono stato nella mia gloriosa patria a torto scorticato, e appresso s'è fatto la notomia del resto della mia male avventurata carne [...]. Solo mi conforto che io spero per essere tanto stato marterizzato a torto in questa mia vita, che in quell'altra io sarò franco: solo attendo a pregare Iddio che non mi voglia vendicare, siccome gli ha

---

[30] Tassi: "[...] io dissi, che, se Sua Altezza si contentava che io lavorassi, io ero contento di servirlo, e così mi offerse tutti li medesimi patti che aveva il Bandinello e dissemegli. Al quale io dissi che ero contento, ma che io volevo che Sua Altezza mi promettessi di crescermi quei patti, sicondo il merito delle mie opere. E in questo modo noi convenimmo. Per la qual cosa io ho sopraffatto di gran lunga della promessa che io feci, e a me non m'è stato osservato nulla. Ancora per avere qualche occasione di risolvermi a fermarmi nella mia patria, io dissi a Sua Altezza che quella mi comperassi la detta Casa [...]. I grevi affanni che io ho auto di questo, Iddio n'è testimone, e non s'arebbe a far così veramente" (3: 214-15). Per una ricostruzione dell'intricata vicenda del dono della casa, si vedano i documenti raccolti e ordinati da Rusconi e Valeri (539-51).

fatto per il passato, che io tremo e piango a ricordarmene di quello che ha dimostro Iddio in quelli, che m'hanno fatto male a torto. Or finitela, in nome di Dio.

(Tassi 3: 219)

Alla luce dei contenuti del memoriale "riservato", è chiaro come, agli occhi del Cellini, fra i primi a doversi preoccupare della giusta collera divina dovesse essere proprio il signore di Firenze. Soltanto un residuo margine di ritegno (o, più probabilmente, di ben motivato timore che la supplica venisse mostrata dai Soprassindaci al Granduca) dovette frenare la penna del risentito artefice, trattenendola dall'esplicitare l'identità degli obiettivi della sua apocalittica invettiva: bersagli individuati invece a chiare lettere nelle pagine private dei libri di ricordi.[31] Questa forma di autocensura, però, non andava in sostanza a incidere sulla gravità delle parole del Cellini, né sul peso delle accuse da lui rivolte a Cosimo: essa rappresentava, al massimo, un tentativo di evitare una piena compromissione nel caso in cui i magistrati avessero voluto mettere il Granduca al corrente dei contenuti del memoriale.

Conclusioni

La rassegna delineata nelle pagine precedenti aiuta a fornire, rispetto all'immagine consueta dello scrittore, un quadro più articolato e storicamente attendibile delle scelte operate, e forse talvolta subìte, dal Cellini in merito al decisivo problema di dire la verità al principe. Da un lato, la vicenda redazionale della *Vita* ha rivelato un autore preoccupato di censurare, ma con interventi di entità marginale, le considerazioni più corrosive sul duca di Firenze, verosimilmente nella speranza di poter pubblicare l'opera. D'altro canto, la metamorfosi che i *Trattati* conobbero nel passaggio dal manoscritto approntato da Cellini alla stampa rivista da Gherardo Spini ha illustrato quanto più drastica dovesse essere, per approdare alla stampa, la conversione delle riflessioni

---

[31] Si veda il ricordo relativo alla valutazione monetaria che Cosimo de' Medici aveva nel 1557 spuntato, grazie al ricorso all'intermediazione di Girolamo degli Albizi, per il *Perseo* riportato da Tassi: "Fu giudicata dal detto Ierolimo, tenendo più la parte del Duca che quella della santa iustizia e della ragione, tremila cinquecento scudi [...], io sono stato rubato et assassinato [...]. A questo il Principe, mosso da avarizia, per darmene il meno che lui poteva, così ingiustamente la fecie giudicare dal detto Ierolimo delli Albizzi [...]; così fui assassinato ed ho rimesso in Dio le mie vendette, perché troppo è il male che io ho ricevuto a gran torto" (3: 75-76). Allusivo a Cosimo è anche il passaggio, di tono analogo della *Vita*, laddove la rievocazione della morte violenta dell'antico nemico e persecutore Pierluigi Farnese si prestava a proiettare una nera profezia di sventura sulla corte di Firenze: "[...] la gran virtù de Dio non lascia mai inpunito di qual si voglia sorta di uomini, che fanno torti e ingiustizie agli innocenti [...]; però nessun Signore, per grande che e' sia, non si faccia beffe della giustizia de Dio, sì come fanno alcuni di quei che io cognosco, che sì bruttamente m'ànno assassinato, dove al suo luogo io lo dirò" (II 51, pp. 604-05).

celliniane sugli arbitrî e la grettezza di Cosimo. Con tutta probabilità, la riscrittura encomiastica operata dal giovane segretario di Ferdinando de' Medici fu condotta nel segno di un "consenso coatto" dell'autore (Firpo 153), costretto suo malgrado ad accettare la trasformazione di un'opera profondamente polemica nei riguardi del duca in un magniloquente panegirico della munificenza cosimiana. Tutti i motivi dello scontento dello scultore nei riguardi della committenza del signore di Firenze sono poi in effetti riemersi nel memoriale privato che l'artista indirizzò alla magistratura dei Soprassindaci nel 1570, laddove il memoriale concepito per essere letto dal duca ha proposto un caso di comunicazione debitamente emendata degli strali polemici contro di lui.

Le vicende testuali ripercorse risultano, nel complesso, emblematiche delle insormontabili limitazioni alla libertà di parola con cui, nell'ambito della Firenze di Cosimo I, dovette fare i conti anche un personaggio che già i contemporanei ritenevano inusitatamente e pericolosamente schietto nel suo rapporto coi potenti. I casi richiamati possono essere assunti a documentare la notevole efficacia della politica culturale cosimiana e di quello che Furio Diaz ha definito "un cosciente programma di egemonizzazione da parte del nuovo principato degl'intellettuali fiorentini" (201). L'interruzione del progetto della *Vita*, la circolazione dei *Trattati* in una forma organica agli orientamenti della cultura ufficiale del ducato, i memoriali ai Soprassindaci convergono ad attestare che, in una scena fiorentina che vide la conquista, da parte di Cosimo, dell'agognato titolo di Granduca (1569), nessun circuito comunicativo pubblico era rimasto per una protesta contro i soprusi di quel signore. Il regime cosimiano fu evidentemente in grado di esercitare una rilevante capacità di controllo del dissenso, e se anche Cellini, fino al termine della sua parabola biografica, cercò di rivendicare le proprie ragioni contro quel committente che gli aveva procurato tante amarezze, simili tentativi si trovarono ad essere sempre più circoscritti entro i limiti di un acre sfogo privato.

Diletta Gamberini
Kunsthistorisches Institut in Florenz

Opere citate

Acidini Cristina (a c. di). *"I Tre Primi Libri sopra l'Instituzioni de' Greci et Latini Architettori intorno agl'ornamenti che convengono a tutte le fabbriche che l'architettura compone" di Gherardo Spini*. In *Il disegno interrotto. Trattati medicei d'architettura*. Firenze: Gonnelli, 1980. Vol. 1. A c. di Franco Borsi. 11-201.

Allen Denise. *Crafting a Profession. Cellini's Discussion of Precious Stones & Jewelry in his Treatises*. In *Marks of Identity. New Perspectives on Sixteenth-Century Italian Sculpture*. A c. di Dimitrios Zikos. Boston: Isabella Stewart Gardner Museum, 2012.

Bacci Orazio (a c. Di). *Vita di Benvenuto Cellini*. Firenze: Sansoni, 1901.

Biblioteca Medicea Laurenziana, cod. Med. Palat. 234[2].
Borsellino Nino. *Cellini, Benvenuto*. In *Dizionario Biografico degli Italiani*. Roma: Istituto dell'Enciclopedia Italiana, 1979. Vol. 23. 440-51.
Calamandrei Piero. *Scritti e inediti celliniani*. A c. di Carlo Cordié. Firenze: La Nuova Italia, 1971.
Camesasca Ettore. "Introduzione." *La Vita*. Milano: Rizzoli, 2004[6]. 5-76.
Cellini Benvenuto. *Due Trattati. Uno intorno alle otto principali arti dell'Oreficeria. L'altro in materia dell'Arte della Scultura*. Firenze: Panizzi e Peri, 1568.
____. *La Vita*. A c. di Lorenzo Bellotto. Parma: Guanda / Fondazione Pietro Bembo, 1996.
____. *Rime*. A c. di Diletta Gamberini. Firenze: Sef, 2014.
____. *Trattati dell'Oreficeria e della Scultura* e *Discorsi sull'arte*. In *Opere*. A c. di Giuseppe Guido Ferrero. Torino: UTET, 1980[2]. 591-835.
Cervigni, Dino Sigismondo. *The "Vita" of Benvenuto Cellini: Literary Tradition and Genre*. Ravenna: Longo Editore, 1979.
Diaz, Furio. *Il Granducato di Toscana. I Medici*. Torino: UTET, 1976.
Firpo Luigi. *Correzioni d'autore coatte*. In *Studi e problemi di critica testuale*. Bologna: Commissione per i testi di Lingua, 1961. 143-57.
Gamberini Diletta. *"E' principi grandi hanno per male che un lor servo dolendosi dica la verità delle sue ragioni". La censura dei "Trattati" di Benvenuto Cellini*. "Schifanoia" 44-45 (2013): 47-62.
Litchfield R. Burr. *Emergence of a Bureaucracy: The Florentine Patricians, 1530-1790*. Princeton: Princeton University Press, 1986.
Maier Bruno. *Umanità e stile di Benvenuto Cellini scrittore (studio critico)*. Milano: Trevisini, 1952.
Milanesi Carlo. "Prefazione." *I trattati dell'oreficeria e della scultura di Benvenuto Cellini; nuovamente messi alle stampe secondo la originale dettatura del codice Marciano*. Firenze: Felice Le Monnier, 1857.
Payne Alina. *The Architectural Treatise in the Renaissance: Architectural Invention, Ornament, and Literary Culture*. Cambridge: Cambridge University Press, 1999.
Pope-Hennessy John. *Cellini*. Milano: Mondadori, 1986. (Trad. it. di Elda Negri Monateri di *Cellini*. New York: Abbeville Press, 1985).
Procacci Ugo. *Di un estratto della vita di Michelangiolo dall'edizione Giuntina del 1568 delle "Vite" del Vasari*. "La Bibliofilia" 32, 11-12 (1930): 448-50.
Rossi Paolo. *"Parrem uno, e pur saremo dua". The Genesis and Fate of Benvenuto Cellini's "Trattati"*. In *Benvenuto Cellini. Sculptor, Goldsmith, Writer*. A c. di Margaret Ann Gallucci e Paolo Rossi. Cambridge: Cambridge University Press, 2004. 171-98.
Rusconi Arturo Jahn e Valeri Antonio. Apparati di *La Vita di Benvenuto Cellini seguita dai Trattati dell'oreficeria e della scultura e dagli scritti sull'arte*. Roma: Società Editrice Nazionale, 1901.
Stimato Gerarda. *Autoritratti letterari nella Firenze di Cosimo I: Bandinelli, Vasari, Cellini e Pontormo*. Bologna: Bononia University Press, 2008.
Tassi Francesco. Apparati e note di *Vita di Benvenuto Cellini orefice e scultore fiorentino scritta da lui medesimo restituita alla lezione originale sul manoscritto Poirot ora Laurenziano ed arricchita d'illustrazioni e documenti inediti dal dottor Francesco Tassi*. Firenze: Piatti, 1829. Voll. 2 e 3.
Trento, Dario (a c. di). *Benvenuto Cellini. Opere non esposte e documenti notarili*. Firenze: Museo Nazionale del Bargello, 1984.

Tylus Jane. *Writing and Vulnerability in the Late Renaissance*. Stanford: Stanford University Press, 1993.
Vasari Giorgio. *Le vite de' più eccellenti pittori, scultori, e architettori*. Firenze: Giunti, 1568.

Sandra Clerc

Verità e potere, ubbidienza e menzogna nella tragedia italiana del Cinquecento (1550-65)

Sinossi: Plasmato sui modelli della classicità greca e latina, il genere tragico diventa, nel corso del XVI secolo, uno dei luoghi prediletti per il dibattito politico sul potere e sulla figura del regnante. Attraverso lo studio di quattro tragedie, pubblicate tra il 1550 e il 1565 (la *Cleopatra* di Alessandro Spinelli, l'*Ifigenia* e la *Marianna* di Lodovico Dolce, e l'*Edippo* di Giovan Andrea dell'Anguillara), questo contributo mostra come i tragediografi di metà Cinquecento rispondono all'interrogativo sulla liceità del "dire la verità al tiranno".
Parole chiave: Anguillara, Castiglione, Cinquecento, Cleopatra, Dolce, Edipo, finzione, Ifigenia, Marianna, menzogna, potere, Spinelli, tirannia, tragedia, verità

"Io vi dico e dirò il ver senza spavento": verità e potere in scena
Nella tragedia italiana del Cinquecento lo scontro fra verità e potere, e il coraggio di chi osa opporre la prima al secondo, costituiscono temi di grande importanza declinati in maniere diverse attraverso il secolo. La capacità e il prezzo di "dire la verità senza spavento", come Marianna a Erode nel verso qui citato di Ludovico Dolce, offrono spunti per riflessioni più ampie sui canoni del buon governo e sulle condizioni dell'opposizione alla tirannia. A queste si mescolano altre questioni legate al genere femminile, ai rapporti di parentela, alle relazioni tra religione e governo, o alla capacità dei subalterni di far sentire la propria voce.

Il presente contributo prende in esame quattro opere, pubblicate per la prima volta tra il 1550 e il 1565: la *Cleopatra* di Alessandro Spinelli (1550), l'*Ifigenia* (1551) e la *Marianna* (1565) di Lodovico Dolce, e l'*Edippo* di Giovan Andrea dell'Anguillara (1565).[1] Esso si propone di delineare alcuni aspetti che caratterizzano la produzione tragica di questo periodo, di mettere in risalto i rapporti di potere che intercorrono tra i personaggi e di segnalare i dibattiti circa l'opportunità di dire o meno la verità a chi detiene il potere politico.

Per meglio comprendere la specificità di queste trattazioni, la prima sezione offre un quadro stilistico e storico di riferimento. In un primo tempo è sinteticamente definito il genere tragico nel Cinquecento, ricordando in

---

[1] L'*Edippo* fu forse composto e rappresentato già nel 1556 e pubblicato una prima volta nel 1560 a Padova; è invece certa la rappresentazione della tragedia a Vicenza nel 1560, sulla prima scena lignea costruita da Palladio per l'Accademia Olimpica. Le due stampe della tragedia oggi superstiti sono rispettivamente quella di Padova, per Lorenzo Pasquatto (ma da attribuire probabilmente a Cristoforo Griffio) e quella di Venezia, presso Domenico Farri. Esse si differenziano unicamente per la presenza, nell'edizione padovana, della nota inquisitoriale; si tratta di una delle prime attestazioni della censura applicata a testi tragici.

particolare la funzione politica di queste rappresentazioni; in un secondo momento, si propone di ripensare la periodizzazione della produzione tragica del secolo sottolineando la funzione di cerniera svolta dagli anni tra il 1550 e il 1565. Onde permettere di situare gli esempi analizzati nel loro contesto narrativo, la seconda sezione riassume le trame di queste opere. La parte principale del contributo si concentra su passaggi scelti di ciascuna tragedia. I diversi testi si distinguono per il risalto dato a un aspetto particolare della relazione fra verità e potere. Questo diviene il fulcro dal quale si diramano temi secondari che permettono di ricostruire un insieme di rimandi impliciti fra le tragedie. In due di queste opere — la *Cleopatra* e la *Marianna* — il personaggio femminile si fa portavoce di una ragione legata prima di tutto alla giustizia, e non tanto al dissidio tra Ragione di Stato e ragioni del cuore messo in scena in molte tragedie del Cinquecento (Speroni, *Canace*; Aretino, *Orazia*; Cesare de' Cesari, *Romilda* e *Scilla*, etc.). L'eroina — con l'appoggio di altri personaggi che assumono via via maggiore importanza nell'intreccio, quali consiglieri, servi e sacerdoti — si oppone a un comportamento tirannico teso unicamente all'utile personale, sulla scorta dell'esempio dell'*Antigone* sofoclea, ripreso anche dalla *Sofonisba* di Trissino e dalla *Rosmunda* di Rucellai. L'*Ifigenia* presenta invece un caso particolare di contrasto tra Ragione di Stato e affetti, che è prima di tutto interno ai singoli personaggi; l'*Edipo*, infine, mostra i legami tra Fato, conoscenza e potere. Dalle conclusioni emerge come l'opposizione al potere assuma varie forme all'interno della tragedia cinquecentesca. Tra l'opportunismo di chi decide di non mettere in discussione l'operato del tiranno, i dubbi di chi si interroga sui destinatari della propria fedeltà, le gelosie cortigiane, l'inganno rivolto a sé o agli altri, e il coraggio di chi, nonostante tutto, decide di seguire ciò che ritiene giusto, la parola pronunciata o taciuta avrà un ruolo fondamentale.

La tragedia nel Cinquecento: aspetti ideologici ed evoluzione stilistica
a) *Rappresentazione del potere e dell'opposizione al potere*
La tragedia del Cinquecento è, come noto, una rappresentazione prevalentemente politica: per argomento, ma anche e soprattutto perché diviene ben presto lo spettacolo privilegiato delle corti principesche, in una sorta di catarsi apotropaica. Si mette in scena il potere tirannico, criticandolo; si denuncia l'ipocrisia delle corti, presentate come luogo del complotto; al contempo, si dedicano le tragedie a sovrani "ideali", di cui sono esaltate le numerose virtù. La tragedia, vero e proprio "specchio de' Principi",[2] diviene strumento di edificazione morale e spazio in cui continuare la riflessione aperta, tra gli altri, da Machiavelli e da Castiglione, sul potere e le sue derive, sul

---

[2] Tale è definita, per esempio, nella lettera di dedica dell'*Asdrubale*, tragedia del fiorentino Jacopo Castellini, a Francesco de' Medici (Firenze, Torrentino, 1562); l'espressione, utilizzata anche da Torelli, dà il titolo a un volume di Pietro Montorfani.

delicato equilibrio tra giustizia, moralità e utilità. Gli autori di tragedie — che, in alcuni casi, sono anche teorici del genere: su tutti, valgano gli esempi di Giraldi e Trissino — sono talvolta nobili e cortigiani, spesso letterati legati ad accademie e altri sodalizi. Sono persone che hanno, di norma, un rapporto più o meno stretto con le figure istituzionali del potere (che si tratti, a seconda delle realtà geografiche, del Senato di Venezia oppure dei Signori delle varie corti dell'Italia centro-settentrionale), e hanno un'esperienza diretta delle dinamiche politiche del proprio tempo: sicché è facile comprendere le valenze anche extra-letterarie di questi testi.

Quello rappresentato nella tragedia è, quindi, prima di tutto il potere politico. I vari personaggi, e naturalmente in primo luogo il detentore del potere assoluto, sia egli empio tiranno o — più raramente — re giusto, si muovono attraverso una rete di relazioni nelle quali esercitano la propria autorità e libertà personale, di fare e di far fare. Così, la tragedia si sviluppa attorno all'opposizione, al contrasto tra volontà divergenti e concezioni diverse del potere, che si riflettono nell'interrogativo sulla liceità del "dire la verità al tiranno". Spiccano al riguardo due poli o tipi di antitesi, che trovano nel teatro classico i loro archetipi. Come già anticipato da Bertana, "concepire una tragedia altro non significava allora che gettare una materia qualsiasi negli stampi di Euripide o di Sofocle" (39). Infatti, secondo una dinamica già invalsa nella drammaturgia greca, da una parte troviamo figure, generalmente femminili, che si oppongono alle leggi stabilite dall'uomo (in accordo, invece, con leggi morali e/o divine); è il modello dell'*Antigone* euripidea — ma anche di Elettra, Ecuba, Alcesti e Ifigenia. D'altra parte troviamo figure, generalmente maschili, che cercano di contrastare il Fato (di solito invano), come nel mito di Edipo narrato da Sofocle.

b) *L'evoluzione del genere tragico a metà Cinquecento*
Dal punto di vista della scansione temporale e dello sviluppo del genere, Ferdinando Neri suddivide la produzione del secolo in tre periodi: il primo trentennio, detto dei "grecizzanti fiorentini"; il secondo, caratterizzato dalla "riforma giraldiana", del quale fanno parte anche Speroni, Aretino, Dolce; infine, l'ultimo trentennio del Cinquecento, che vede la nascita e l'evoluzione della tragedia barocca e controriformistica. Come nota Paola Mastrocola, "è anche il periodo dello sfaldamento e della crisi, dove il genere tragico si contamina maggiormente sino a cedere il posto ai generi vincenti del secolo successivo: la pastorale e il melodramma" (11). La studiosa invita inoltre a ridurre la tripartizione di Neri a due soli periodi, facendo cadere il discrimine a metà Cinquecento, anticipando così l'inizio della fine:

[...] poi, non sarà che una ripresa infinita degli stessi temi teorici, e un approfondimento in senso sempre più moraleggiante dell'impianto tragico, con notevoli e rilevanti testi, tale però da non mutare nella sostanza i capisaldi del tragico così come erano stati posti nel primo cinquantennio.

(13)

La proposta è motivata dall'osservazione dei modelli prevalenti: il modello dell'*Antigone* è il più presente nella prima metà del secolo, mentre nella seconda si vede via via l'incremento e poi il sostanziale dominio del modello edipeo (31-32). Tale bipartizione, benché reale, è tuttavia da relativizzare: non mancano, anche nella seconda metà del Cinquecento, esempi di eroine in lotta per i propri ideali, né, nella prima metà, riferimenti alla tipologia dell'eroe in lotta contro un Fato inesorabile. È ad ogni modo significativo che a prendere il sopravvento, dopo la metà del secolo, sia proprio la tipologia dell'*Edipo* di Sofocle, che Aristotele aveva identificato come la migliore per il doppio meccanismo di peripezia e agnizione. Da un lato, infatti, questo è il periodo in cui abbondano i commenti alla *Poetica*, e conseguentemente i contributi teorici sul genere tragico, ed è quindi naturale che l'autorità di Aristotele si mostri con maggiore forza. Dall'altro, Edipo è il perfetto personaggio mezzano, che commette il proprio peccato non per malvagità, ma per errore, secondo una fenomenologia che ben si accorda con la morale dell'età della controriforma.

Il periodo centrale del secolo, che va dal 1545-50 al 1565, appare non privo di interesse proprio per la sua funzione di cerniera tra due momenti estremi. Esso si situa in un tempo successivo alla rifondazione del genere tragico, e proprio all'inizio delle discussioni teoriche sulla tragedia. Inoltre, sono gli anni del Concilio di Trento, della nascita dell'Indice dei libri proibiti e conseguentemente della censura libraria.[3] A questo periodo può essere riferita la pubblicazione di una ventina di testi tragici, ai quali si aggiunge un numero abbastanza cospicuo di tragedie oggi perdute, escluse dal circuito della stampa o pubblicate soltanto in seguito. Sugli autori di questi testi, fatte salve alcune eccezioni, possediamo scarse informazioni; le opere, spesso poco o per nulla studiate, rappresentano talvolta le uniche attestazioni della loro produzione

---

[3] Dell'intero repertorio tragico italiano a me noto, figurano all'*Indice* (che ho consultato nella versione cumulativa a c. di J. M. De Bujanda) soltanto l'*Orazia* di Pietro Aretino (del quale, dal 1559, è condannata l'*Opera omnia*), un'anonima *Tragedia d'un'altra sorte* e la *Tragedia intitolata Libero arbitrio* di Francesco Negri, colpite dall'interdetto già nel 1549. Inoltre, ho potuto costatare che gli *imprimatur* ecclesiastici sono apposti alle tragedie soltanto dal 1565, alla conclusione del Concilio tridentino; in quattro casi (l'*Edippo* di G.A. dell'Anguillara, di cui si è già detto; le tre tragedie di Aniello Paulilli, stampate nel 1566; la *Gismonda* di G. Razzi, del 1568; la *Merope* di P. Torelli, stampata nel 1589) è presente una nota inquisitoriale estesa, mentre, in particolare dalla metà degli anni Settanta, è frequente ma non scontata l'indicazione "Con licenza dei Superiori", apposta al frontespizio (e talvolta ripetuta nel *colophon*). La tragedia è evidentemente considerata come più "sicura", dal punto di vista della morale, rispetto alla commedia: nell'*Indice* promulgato a Parma nel 1580, per esempio, vengono bandite genericamente le "Comedie disoneste ò lascive".

letteraria. Tuttavia, pur non eccellendo sul piano linguistico, stilistico o drammaturgico, queste tragedie si fanno portavoce di idee e di prospettive degne di attenzione, anche perché rendono visibile la transizione verso il teatro di fine secolo. Da questo *corpus*, il presente contributo estrae quattro testi tragici che illustrano in modo esemplare queste evoluzioni.

Quattro tragedie paradigmatiche: trame e autori
a) *La "Cleopatra" di Alessandro Spinelli*
La prima tragedia in esame è pubblicata a Venezia nel 1550 da Pietro Nicolini da Sabbio. Come notato, tra gli altri, da Maria Pia Mussini Sacchi, la figura di Cleopatra è alla moda nel Cinquecento.[4] Spinelli nella sua tragedia narra però la triste e sanguinosa vicenda della meno nota Cleopatra II, vissuta nel II secolo a.C.[5] La tragedia è divisa in atti e in scene, non numerate ma distinte grazie all'annuncio dei personaggi (come l'*Ifigenia* e la *Marianna*, che riprendono una struttura molto diffusa all'epoca, mentre l'*Edippo* presenta scene numerate, come l'*Orbecche*), e si apre con il topico dialogo tra l'eroina e la balia (o nutrice) che ha la funzione di rendere noto l'antefatto. Il padre di Cleopatra, non trovando un marito degno della figlia, decide di darla in sposa al figlio maggiore, benché siano fratello e sorella. Dopo la morte del padre, il marito di Cleopatra è avvelenato dal fratello minore, Tolomeo, invaghitosi di lei e spinto dalla volontà di regnare. Costretta a sposarlo, la regina dà alla luce una bambina, Tebea, e un figlio, Menfi. Una volta cresciuta, Tebea risveglia tuttavia le brame del padre, che scaccia Cleopatra dal palazzo per potersi unire a lei. La tragedia prosegue con la descrizione del comportamento scellerato di Tolomeo, sordo a qualunque critica. In occasione di un banchetto, organizzato per festeggiare il compleanno del re, egli si dà a incredibili gozzoviglie insieme ai suoi "baroni" (con evidente anacronismo), dissoluti quanto il loro reggente.[6] Infastidito dalle lodi rivolte al figlio, più simile alla madre che a lui, e volendo trovare altri modi di infierire su Cleopatra, Tolomeo trucida orribilmente Menfi, e, fattone a pezzi

---

[4] Mi si permetta di rimandare anche al mio articolo *Tra mito e storia*.
[5] Nei repertori di Nicolò Toppi (8) e di Camillo Minieri Riccio (336), Spinelli è chiamato "cavaliere napoletano". La *Cleopatra* è l'unica opera a lui attribuita. Nella lettera di dedica (datata 10 marzo 1540; ma si tratterà verosimilmente di un errore di stampa da correggere in 1550) indirizzata a Ottaviano Raverta (1516-1564), vescovo di Terracina e legato apostolico del Papa presso Carlo V e Filippo II di Spagna, Spinelli offre un'importante indicazione sull'avvenuta messa in scena della tragedia. L'anno precedente, afferma Spinelli, era stata messa in scena una *Progne* (forse quella del Parabosco, edita nel 1548). Il Prologo, inoltre, è "a sodisfattione degli spettatori" (3v).
[6] Con le parole di Cleopatra, i sodali di Tolomeo "son tutti iniqui / adulatori rei, / che lo confortan sempre / a far opre crudeli, / senza rispetto alcuno / che 'l lodano del male; / onde 'l fanno venire / ogn'or più bestiale" (a. V, vv. 2125-32). I cattivi cortigiani, che spingono il principe ad agire contro l'onesto e il giusto, sono sanzionati dal *Libro del cortegiano* di Baldassarre Castiglione (IV VII). Esempi di cortigiani dissoluti nella tragedia del Cinquecento sono anche Tamule e Allocche nell'*Orbecche* di Giraldi Cinzio.

il corpo, l'invia alla regina sotto forma di macabre vivande. Dopo aver visto mani e capo del figlio e aver compreso di essersi cibata delle sue carni, Cleopatra organizza la propria vendetta, affidando al servo l'ordine di riunire coloro che le sono rimasti fedeli e di uccidere Tolomeo e tutti i suoi. La notizia della morte del tiranno giunge insieme a quella del suicidio della regina, che muore avvelenata sulla scena.[7] Cleopatra attua la propria vendetta, per interposta persona (come nella *Rosmunda* di Rucellai), contro il parere delle altre donne, che la esortano a lasciar agire la giustizia divina. Alla fine tuttavia anche il suo atto è ricondotto a una volontà superiore. Com'è noto, anche Clitennestra nel seguito del mito si vendicherà dell'uccisione della figlia ordinata dal marito Agamennone.

b) *L'"Ifigenia" e la "Marianna" di Ludovico Dolce*
La seconda e la terza tragedia investigate, l'*Ifigenia* e la *Marianna*, sono opera di Ludovico Dolce, autore, rifacitore e volgarizzatore, il quale ha conosciuto recentemente una nuova fortuna critica focalizzata sulla sua produzione tragica, grazie in particolare agli studi di Stefano Giazzon. Fra le sue tragedie, l'*Ifigenia* e la *Marianna* danno ampio spazio a considerazioni politiche, e offrono quindi lo spunto per indagare il rapporto dei personaggi con il potere. La prima, come nota Cremante (*Appunti sulla grammatica tragica* 284), fu pubblicata a Venezia nel 1551, presso Gabriele Giolito, mentre la seconda, per lo stesso stampatore, uscì nel 1565.[8]

---

[7] La vicenda narrata, che Spinelli poteva aver letto nell'opera del romano Giustino (XXXVIII 8. 2-4), si discosta un poco dalle fonti storiche. Cleopatra II Filometore, figlia di Tolomeo V Epifane e di Cleopatra I Sira, fu data in sposa al fratello Tolomeo VI Filometore. Alla morte del primo marito — della quale ignoriamo le cause — fu costretta a sposare il fratello minore, Tolomeo VIII Evergete II, che aveva in effetti precedentemente tentato di usurpare il potere di Tolomeo VI. I due ebbero almeno un figlio, Tolomeo Menfite. Tolomeo VIII sposò in seguito la figlia di Cleopatra II, Cleopatra III, e uccise il nipote, figlio di Tolomeo VI. Cleopatra II continuò a regnare insieme alla figlia e a Tolomeo VIII, finché costui non la costrinse a rifugiarsi in Siria. L'orrida tecnofagia, di derivazione senecana (*Thyestes*), è qui invenzione di Spinelli; in accordo con il mito narrato la utilizzerà invece Lodovico Domenichi nella *Progne* (1565). Il matrimonio tra consanguinei era una prassi comune tra i regnanti dell'Egitto antico. Questo non impedisce a Spinelli di criticare l'unione per bocca della balia di Cleopatra.

[8] Per entrambe le tragedie sono attestate rappresentazioni a ridosso della pubblicazione, e in occasione del carnevale; la lettera di dedica della *Marianna*, indirizzata all'attore Antonio Molino, detto il Burchiella, ricorda la realizzazione di due messe in scena. Le due tragedie hanno in comune anche un prologo, recitato dalla Tragedia stessa, in cui l'autore presenta una rassegna (adattata, a distanza di quasi quindici anni) di tragedie del Cinquecento, che vanno a formare un vero e proprio canone: *Sofonisba*, *Antigone*, *Canace*, *Orbecche*, *Rosmunda*; e poi la stessa *Ifigenia*, *Giocasta*, *Didone* (ricordate soltanto nella *Marianna*). La rinascita del genere è inoltre presentata come prolungamento naturale dell'esperienza antica. Per considerazioni sul canone qui delineato si rimanda a Cremante, *Appunti sulla grammatica tragica* 286-87.

L'*Ifigenia* è rifacimento dell'*Ifigenia in Aulide* di Euripide, grazie alla mediazione della versione latina di Erasmo. La trama è nota: la partenza dell'esercito greco per la guerra contro Troia, il cui principe Paride è reo di aver sottratto la moglie Elena a Menelao, re di Sparta, è impedita da venti contrari; soltanto il sacrificio di Ifigenia, figlia di Agamennone, fratello di Menelao e re di Creta, potrà placare gli dei. Dolce tuttavia esaspera una delle caratteristiche che erano già nel testo antico, la volubilità estrema delle *personae*, che agiscono in modo quasi del tutto privo di coerenza. Come nota Giazzon, egli "spinge sul versante dello smarrimento dell'identità dei vari personaggi coinvolti, secondo coordinate che appartengono alla cultura del Manierismo maturo e che sembrano quasi anticipare, *si parva licet*, amletici smarrimenti" (*Dante nel regno di Melpomene* 128-29). L'invenzione di alcuni personaggi, come l'indovino Calcante, e l'insistenza sull'inganno e sulla finzione permettono all'autore di inserire vari *coups de théâtre* e di presentare una vicenda in cui credere, celare e convincere assumono un'importanza primaria.

La *Marianna* è opera originale di Dolce, ed è anche l'unica delle quattro tragedie qui presentate a essere disponibile in edizione moderna, nel volume curato da Cremante per Ricciardi (731-877). La materia deriva dalle *Antiquitates iudaicae* di Giuseppe Flavio (XV 7). In questa tragedia s'incontrano l'interesse per le vicende legate al mondo biblico, diffusosi nel secondo Cinquecento, e il genere novellistico, qui sintetizzato nell'omicidio passionale dettato dalla gelosia. Erode, marito di Marianna, è infatti morbosamente geloso. Dovendo partire per Roma, egli ordina al capitano Soemo di uccidere la donna qualora egli non faccia ritorno. Soemo, in un impeto di umanità e fedeltà alla regina, confessa tutto a Marianna. Al ritorno di Erode, la moglie, incapace di fingere, gli si mostra ostile; le inquietudini del re, che è di natura portato al sospetto, sono fomentate dalle calunnie della sorella Salomè, che accusa Marianna di tramare con il coppiere per eliminarlo. Inquisito una prima volta, il servitore conferma le accuse, per poi ritrattarle, pentito, una volta confrontato alla regina. Erode è momentaneamente sollevato dai suoi crucci, rialimentati subitamente dall'eunuco Beniamino, che gli confida il tradimento di Soemo. Erode si convince che il coppiere, detto il vero la prima volta, non abbia poi osato confermarlo dinanzi a Marianna; messo ai tormenti, egli l'accuserà nuovamente prima di spirare. Il comportamento di Soemo, inoltre, è nella sua mente senza dubbio dettato dall'amore, e inizia quindi a immaginarsi una relazione clandestina tra i due. Erode ordina l'uccisione di Soemo, e mette davanti agli occhi di Marianna testa, mani e cuore della vittima, prima di gettarli in pasto ai cani. Ma la sua furia sfrenata si sfogherà in seguito anche su Alessandra, madre di Marianna, e sui propri figli, Alessandro e Aristobulo, che egli pensa nati dall'adulterio, prima di raggiungere la moglie. Abbandonato dal *raptus* omicida, Erode si pente di quanto fatto, piange la propria sorte e la morte dei suoi cari.

c) L'"Edippo" di Giovanni Andrea dell'Anguillara
Infine, la quarta tragedia che intendo esaminare è l'*Edippo*, che è stato a lungo considerato un semplice volgarizzamento. Tuttavia, come nota Paolo Bosisio, il fatto che i critici lo collegassero ora alle due tragedie di Sofocle, ora a quella di Seneca, mostra che il testo necessita di più attenta considerazione. Lo studioso offre una precisa e dettagliata analisi dell'opera, mostrando come "innegabilmente spunti sofoclei e senecani convivono nel testo che, tuttavia, sembra avere qualche ambizione di novità" (82-83). Richard Fabrizio osserva che "Anguillara tried to solve a problem, a problem that he and his contemporaries noticed in Sophocles' *Oedipus* and its Aristotelian interpretation: Oedipus did not act consistently" (180). La tragedia si apre con il dialogo tra Tiresia e la figlia Manto, che svela immediatamente agli spettatori l'identità di Edipo. Egli, sconfitta la Sfinge e sposata la regina Giocasta, è re e padre premuroso e rispettato. Il suo regno è tuttavia flagellato dalla peste, che, secondo l'oracolo, potrà essere allontanata soltanto quando sarà scoperto e punito l'omicida di Laio, precedente re di Tebe. La volontà di Edipo di scoprire a ogni costo il colpevole lo porterà a conoscere la verità: egli è l'assassino, Laio era suo padre e Giocasta sua madre, come era stato predetto dall'oracolo di Apollo. Edipo si acceca, Giocasta si uccide. Ma la tragedia non si conclude qui, e ingloba parte dell'*Edipo a Colono*, con le lotte immediate tra Eteocle e Polinice, figli di Edipo e Giocasta, per il governo di Tebe. Sarà Creonte, il fratello della regina, a sedare — almeno temporaneamente — il contenzioso tra i due, tra le lodi del coro.[9]

Come emerge dalle brevi descrizioni precedenti, le quattro tragedie offrono ciascuna spunti originali per trattare il problema dei rapporti tra il potere e la verità, e soprattutto tra chi detiene il potere e chi si trova nel dubbio se dire la verità o tacere. Le analisi che seguono sono volte a mettere in luce tali contrasti.

Verità molteplici: credere, dire e conoscere il vero
a) *La scelleratezza senza limiti del tiranno nella "Cleopatra"*
La *Cleopatra* di Spinelli è, fra quelle appena presentate, la tragedia meno studiata. Tolomeo è identificato immediatamente come tiranno perché usurpatore del regno del fratello. In seguito è sottolineata la sua lussuria, rivolta persino alla figlia, che egli costringe a divenire sua moglie. Cleopatra tenta di opporsi a questi "atti iniqui" con le parole: "io sovente 'l ripresi con bel modo" (a. I, v. 191); è inutile, anzi, egli si comporta "di male in peggio" (a. I, v. 193).[10]

---

[9] L'azione di Creonte esemplifica l'auspicio circa il comportamento del Principe nel *Cortegiano*: "Vorrei che avesse cura d'intendere le azioni ed esser censore de' suoi ministri; di levare ed abbreviar le liti tra i sudditi; di far far pace tra essi, e legargli insieme di parentati; di far che la città fosse tutta unita e concorde in amicizia, come una casa privata; populosa, non povera, quieta, piena di boni artífici" (IV XLI).

[10] Si cita dalle edizioni indicate in precedenza e in calce al contributo. La numerazione dei versi è mia, eccetto nel caso della *Marianna*.

La balia, con serafica saggezza popolare, non se ne stupisce: "Ah che non giova la riprensione / in un cor ostinato, e senza freno: / e chi fa questo se gli può ben dire, / nell'acqua solca, e nell'arena semina" (a. I, vv. 194-97). Tra i vizi di Tolomeo si annoverano anche l'ingordigia e la sfrenatezza nel bere, come dimostrano i festeggiamenti indetti per il suo compleanno, durante i quali egli è circondato da gente dissoluta e incline a "parole / men ch'oneste" (a. IV, vv. 1554-55); la moralità o l'immoralità dei personaggi passa anche dall'uso che essi fanno delle parole. L'insistenza sulla macabra scena dello smembramento del figlio Menfi è certamente finalizzata a dimostrare la crudeltà e la devianza di Tolomeo, che vi assiste con letizia: egli è intenzionato a infierire sulla regina fino a spingerla al suicidio. A nulla sono valsi i numerosi tentativi di temperare il comportamento di Tolomeo operati dal Sacerdote lungo tutta la tragedia. Una delle scene più interessanti, al fine dell'analisi dei rapporti dei vari personaggi con il potere, è la prima del secondo atto. Tolomeo si lamenta dei "molesti sacerdoti" che gli dicono "spiacevoli ed acre / parole", guastando la sua felicità di sovrano assoluto e dissoluto. Il Sacerdote esorta il re ad agire nel rispetto della giustizia e della religione, per evitare la nomea di tiranno; all'indignazione di Tolomeo, che lo minaccia di morte, il Sacerdote risponde di non temere l'ira del sovrano e di voler agire in accordo con il suo incarico e le leggi morali. L'ostinazione del tiranno è deprecata più volte anche in seguito dal ministro in lunghi monologhi. Il dialogo mette in scena l'incomunicabilità tra chi vuol mostrare il vero e chi, come Tolomeo, vede e sente soltanto ciò che vuole. L'elenco dei simboli del potere declamato dal re (lo scettro, il trono, le ricchezze, i servitori timorosi pronti a compiacerlo in tutto) è criticato dal Sacerdote, che vorrebbe insegnargli le qualità e le virtù necessarie al buon governo: "Ahi, che ti mancan le parti migliori, / che son giustizia, prudenza e fortezza, / religion e temperanza e fede. / Queste son quelle che fanno un Re vero, / e non l'altre apparenze esterne e false" (a. II, vv. 502-06). Ma Tolomeo riafferma la realtà oggettiva e materiale dei propri attributi regali, difendendo, machiavellianamente, le azioni in ragione del proprio utile.

I due personaggi difendono posizioni opposte sul fondamento della regalità: per Tolomeo il potere è espressione di una posizione sociale; per il sacerdote è invece inscindibile dalla realizzazione di determinate virtù. Il sacerdote, con la propria opposizione, delegittima il potere giustificato solamente dalla struttura sociale, e slegato dalla riflessione morale. Nel seguito della scena è introdotto un nuovo elemento che ricollega la tragedia ai dibattiti religiosi contemporanei. Le due idee che si scontrano ora sono la predestinazione e il libero arbitrio, di cui si fanno portavoce, rispettivamente, il tiranno e il Sacerdote:

> (To.) Però se aggrada a me quel ch'a te spiace,
> questo è 'l voler delle superne stelle:
> e come varie di qualità sono,
> così producon diversi desii
> nei nostri petti, contra i quali nulla

ci giova l'arte, né saper, né ingegno.
(Sac.) Ti veggio in molti errori preso e involto:
ma 'l saggio signoreggia l'alte stelle,
ed è dell'opre sue liber Signore.
Non stelle, non pianeta, o caso, o sorte,
ma la volontà sua libera, e a lui
solo conviensi onor e infamia in tutto.
(To.) Così creder io voglio fermamente,
ch'ogni nostro voler vien dalle stelle.

(*Cleopatra*, a. II, vv. 594-607)

Tolomeo difende la propria posizione sociale (*status quo*) riferendosi al Fato che non può essere e non va combattuto, mentre il sacerdote si richiama al libero arbitrio, mettendo in discussione la legittimità del potere basato solo sul diritto di nascita, difendendo così la ribellione al potere costituito qualora questo si riveli empio. Il tiranno, richiamandosi al destino, ha dunque un motivo in più per non ritenersi responsabile per le proprie azioni, ma soprattutto per poter credere alla propria finzione. Come nota Paola Mastrocola:

Fingere è costruirsi una propria verità: questo fa parte della libertà senza freni del Potere, che agisce [...] a dispetto di ogni verità o consiglio altrui: il Tiranno si finge quel che vuole e lo passa per l'unica verità. Ovviamente non tollera che vi siano altre visioni, ovvero opinioni, ovvero altre "verità": e quindi non può che circondarsi di servili adulatori che gli ripetono all'infinito, come tante immagini allo specchio, la sua unica verità.

(148)

Tolomeo non accetta le critiche: "ma se dicesti a me, quel che m'aggrada / t'ascolterei più volentieri ogn'ora" (a. II, vv. 613-14); il Sacerdote s'indigna: "Adulator non son falso o bugiardo, / ch'a te voglia narrar fole o menzogne, / ma voglio dirti il ver senza rispetto, / benché sappia da lui che l'odio nasce. / Perch'io t'amo d'Amor vero e sincero, / e però parlo a te liberamente, / senza speme o timor di cosa alcuna" (a. II, vv. 615-21). Benché inviso al tiranno, il comportamento del ministro in questa tragedia è sovrapponibile a quello preconizzato da Castiglione (IV v).

Il Sacerdote tenta nuovamente, nel quarto atto, di spiegare a Tolomeo quanto il suo regno manchi di doti essenziali, come la pace e la concordia. Ancora una volta, però, i due non possono intendersi: i loro discorsi si situano su due piani diversi. Il ministro rimane fermo nella sua volontà di "dire il vero" al tiranno, benché le sue siano parole gettate al vento. Un comportamento opposto assumerà invece il "Bailo"; al suo tentativo di avvertire Tolomeo che, uccidendo il figlio e facendone mangiare le carni a Cleopatra, si è attirato l'ira divina, il tiranno replica con minacce, alle quali egli cede immediatamente: "Io tacerò, ne più v'aprirò bocca: / fate pur tutto quel ch'aggrada a voi, / che troppo ho fatto in ciò l'ufficio mio" (a. IV, vv. 1787-89). Con il suo silenzio il servo cessa di opporsi al tiranno per evitare le possibili ritorsioni, e così facendo, tuttavia, ne avalla indirettamente l'operato.

b) *Il pericolo della gelosia e le accuse infondate della corte nella "Marianna"*
L'Erode della *Marianna* presenta caratteristiche simili a Tolomeo. È introdotto subito come empio tiranno (Prologo II, recitato da Plutone): il suo vizio principale, la gelosia, è appunto instillato dalle potenze infernali. Egli non esita a minacciare e sottoporre i servi alla tortura per estorcere confessioni ed è, come gli rimproverano i figli, "inver troppo soggetto all'ira, / troppo precipitoso e troppo fiero" (a. IV, vv. 2579-80). La regina conosce la natura sospettosa e quasi paranoica del marito: "send'ei pien di sospetto, / il vero crederà falso e il falso vero" (a. III, vv. 1459-60). Erode sembra non curarsi minimamente dell'opinione del popolo, dal quale è temuto e non amato (a. IV, vv. 2316-22).[11] Egli si fida inoltre delle persone sbagliate, come la furba sorella Salomè, che ha in odio Marianna; ne è cosciente Soemo: "Il Re facil è a creder ogni cosa, / ed ella è astuta e l'animo ha maligno" (a. I, vv. 626-27).[12] Salomè, qui figura del cattivo consigliere, insinua dubbi nella mente di Erode, già incline al sospetto, e sottolinea così la natura indipendente di Marianna:

> Quante volte s'è opposta a' saggi vostri
> giudicii? E della propria volontate
> ha fatto a molti ed a voi stesso legge? [...]
> O vergogna d'ognun che regge stati,
> ch'una femmina in man tenga la briglia
> e, come piace a lei, l'allenti e stringa!
>
> (*Marianna*, a. II, vv. 831-38)

A differenza di Cleopatra, che non incontra mai Tolomeo nel corso della vicenda rappresentata, Erode e Marianna sono protagonisti di più dialoghi. Una prima volta, la regina prende le proprie difese contro le accuse del coppiere; il marito è "geloso a torto / ed insieme crudel" (a. III, vv. 1554-55); "L'un veder non vi lascia quel che voi / veder dovreste, se non foste cieco, / e che conosce chiaramente ognuno, / cioè mia castità candida e pura / e la bontate e l'innocenza mia; / l'altro v'induce ad ogni strano effetto" (a. III, vv. 1556-61).

---

[11] L'attitudine di Erode sembra echeggiare il concetto che Machiavelli riassume nel titolo del diciassettesimo capitolo del *Principe*, "*De crudelitate et pietate; et an sit melius amari quam timeri, vel e contra*".
[12] La credulità del principe è uno dei problemi sollevati da Castiglione nel *Cortegiano*: "Però, se a me toccasse instituirlo, vorrei che egli [...] mai credesse tanto, né tanto si confidasse d'alcun suo ministro, che a quel solo rimettesse totalmente la briglia e lo arbitrio di tutto 'l governo; perché [...] molto maggior danno procede dalla credulità de' signori che dalla incredulità, la qual non solamente talor non nòce, ma spesso summamente giova; pur in questo è necessario il bon giudicio del principe, per conoscer chi merita esser creduto e chi no" (IV XLI).

La sua posizione è perentoria: "Io vi dico e dirò il ver senza spavento" (a. III, v. 1564). Erode, che non ha argomenti, taglia corto: "Io non contenderò teco in parole, / ch' i' sarei sciocco, sì come tu rea" (a. III, vv. 1567-68) e minaccia la tortura. L'opposizione di Marianna si attua, in primo luogo, tramite parole e discorsi eloquenti; al contrario, il tiranno non ha altri mezzi che la forza.

Subito dopo l'uscita di Marianna entra in scena il consigliere, che tenta di far ragionare Erode e lo esorta a ricorrere all'aiuto dei fedeli servitori prima di prendere decisioni, per non farsi guidare da odio o da affetto: "Re, per quel che tra me vo' discorrendo / (ed anco è openion de' dotti e saggi), / è felice quel Principe che prima / ch'ei faccia opera alcuna si consiglia / con suoi fedeli" (a. III, vv. 1574-78). Ancora una volta, l'importanza del confronto e del dialogo è posta in primo piano. Il tiranno è però certo di aver scoperto un delitto, e poco importa in realtà la sua natura, o l'assenza di prove: "Ma presupposto ch'ella del veneno / fosse innocente e sia l'accusa falsa, / esser falso non può già l'adultero" (a. III, vv. 1613-15). Erode è fermo nel suo intento di fare "degna e memorabile vendetta" di Marianna e Soemo, e rigetta tutte le considerazioni del Consigliere come "fievoli". Ancora una volta, l'autoinganno del tiranno soppianta la verità.

La terza controparte al tiranno è Soemo stesso, che Erode affronta alla presenza del Consigliere. Egli rimane muto, impallidisce davanti alle accuse del sovrano; poi cerca di giustificarsi, e dice di essere incorso in un "lieve errore commesso a caso" (a. III, v. 1815), non certo di aver tramato insieme alla regina, né tantomeno di aver commesso con lei adulterio. È stato, insomma, imprudente; ma ha commesso un errore perdonabile: "Or confesso, Signor, che sciocco io fui, / ma perfido non già" (a. III, vv. 1846-47). Erode tuttavia insiste con l'accusa di adulterio, prontamente negata; invano, perché il tiranno vede soltanto ciò che vuole: "Ma 'l peccato veggendosi palese, / quand'io ti perdonassi non sarei / quel giusto Re che tu mi di' ch'io sono" (a. III, vv. 1951-53).

Nella scena successiva, che conclude il terzo atto, il consigliere tenta nuovamente di far ragionare Erode. Il re sembra finalmente pronto a dare ascolto ai suoi consigli; ma all'apertura del quarto atto è annunciata la decapitazione di Soemo. Erode mostra trionfante a Marianna mani, testa e cuore del capitano, in una scena che ricorda da vicino quella dell'*Orbecche*. La regina difende l'operato della vittima, e nega ancora l'adulterio, criticando la credulità del re: "[...] tener il sospetto per certezza / è cosa da fierissimo Tiranno" (a. IV, vv. 2416-17). Il contrasto tra la fermezza di Marianna e la debole autodifesa di Soemo è reso qui evidente dal fatto che la regina non esita, non tace, ma risponde. Il terzo e ultimo intervento del consigliere è anche il più drammatico e accorato; quando Erode minaccia di uccidere non solo Marianna e sua madre, ma i suoi stessi figli, infatti, egli non trattiene le parole:

> Rivocate, per Dio, mentre potete,
> l'ingiusta, abominosa, aspra sentenza
> che contro a Marianna avete data,

Verità e potere, ubbidienza e menzogna nella tragedia italiana del Cinquecento

> contro a sua madre e contro a' figli vostri.
> Rivocatela, dico, e non v'incresca
> di consentir a chi vi porta amore
> e dell'utile vostro è desioso,
> e della pace e della vostra gioia. [...]
> Rivocatela, dico, immantenente. [...]
> Per Dio, rompete l'indurata mente,
> ed aprite quegli occhi che lo sdegno
> vi tien per vostro mal serrati e chiusi.
>
> (*Marianna*, a. IV, vv. 2706-29)

Erode, al pari di Tolomeo, è sordo alle critiche e privo di scrupoli. Ciò che lo distingue dal tiranno della *Cleopatra* è il suo finale e tardivo pentimento (fino a riconoscere che Soemo gli era fedele, e che i suoi ammonimenti erano veritieri), una caratteristica che lo avvicina invece a Eolo nella *Canace*. Il parallelo è rafforzato dalla patetica invocazione alla moglie morta alla quale egli chiede perdono, che ripete ossessivamente la singola domanda di Eolo: "Figliuol mio, ove sei?" (*Canace*, v. 1971).

c) *Credere, celare e convincere nell'"Ifigenia"*

A differenza di quanto accade nelle tragedie precedenti, nelle quali il tiranno è identificato in modo univoco, nell'*Ifigenia* comportamenti "tirannici" vengono assunti da due personaggi distinti: Agamennone e Menelao. Essi incarnano, a turno, due concezioni antitetiche del potere. È tuttavia al re di Creta che si contrappongono le due figure femminili, Clitennestra e Ifigenia, rispettivamente moglie e figlia di Agamennone, da lui attirate in Aulide con l'inganno: il re finge, infatti, di aver promesso in sposa Ifigenia ad Achille. Anche dopo che la moglie ha scoperto il tradimento egli si ostina a negarlo. Quando la Ragione di Stato si fa più pressante nella mente di Agamennone, egli cerca di imporre il proprio volere a una Clitennestra decisamente combattiva: "Clitennestra da te ricerco in questo / misterio obedientia più ch'amore" (a. III, vv. 1105-06); "Donna, questo / è il voler mio" (a. III, vv. 1119-20). Ma la moglie non è d'accordo:

> (Cl.) Sia detto senza offesa
> del vostro cuor: a ciò obedir non voglio.
> (Ag.) Dunque sarai contraria alle mie voglie?
> (Cl.) In cosa indegna e disonesta i' sono.
> (Ag.) Farai quanto t'ho detto immantenente.
> (Cl.) Anzi io men vado a ritrovar la figlia [...].
>
> (*Ifigenia*, a. III, vv. 1120-25)

Nota Giazzon: "[...] tutta e autenticamente politica è l'insistenza con cui Agamennone, indossata la maschera del re, continua a sostenere l'imminenza delle *nuptiae* con Achille di Ifigenia, ben sapendo che esse sono una fola" (*Il*

Manierismo a teatro 13).[13] La frattura tra comportamento paterno e agire da sovrano è percepita dal re stesso (sarà il caso anche nel *Filippo* di Alfieri): "però che l'esser padre fa, che m'esca / di mente l'esser Re; da cui s'aspetta / solo intrepido cuore, animo saldo, / e sempre armato agli accidenti umani / senza turbar giamai la fronte e 'l petto" (*Ifigenia*, a. III, vv. 1078-80). Anche Ifigenia ne è cosciente, e tenta di far leva sulla giustizia più che sugli affetti: acconsentendo alla sua uccisione, egli punirebbe un'innocente, comportandosi da re ingiusto.

A differenza dei tiranni visti in precedenza, Agamennone agisce in relazione al contrasto tra affetti e Ragione di Stato, che è però interno al suo animo; sa di mentire alla figlia e alla moglie, non sta mentendo a sé stesso. In un secondo tempo, tuttavia, finirà per credere alla verità che si è costruito, giustificando il proprio agire con l'imperativo della necessità. Il potere della parola, utilizzata in un primo tempo per ingannare gli altri, cresce fino a trasformare l'inganno in autoinganno.

Prima del suo improvviso ripensamento, il re è raggiunto da Calcante, che assume qui la funzione di consigliere (ma è in realtà una spia di Menelao, inviato per sondare l'animo del fratello). La seconda scena del primo atto (vv. 200-334) è così interamente occupata dal dialogo tra i due. L'indovino loda la capacità di Agamennone di anteporre il bene comune e la Ragione di Stato ai propri affetti, e di mostrarsi "servo ed amico" della religione, su cui si fonda la longevità dei regni. Il re, a questo punto, finge di essere convinto della necessità del sacrificio di Ifigenia e rassicura Calcante sulle proprie intenzioni. Nel monologo che segue, l'indovino tuttavia si dice dubbioso circa la veridicità delle parole del sovrano: "Quel ch'abbia Agamennon chiuso nel petto / sàsselo quei che solo intende e vede / ciò che non vede l'intelletto umano. / Certo è raro colui che ponga avanti / l'utilità comune al proprio bene" (a. I, vv. 321-25).

L'atto secondo si apre con Menelao, che ha scoperto il servo incaricato di trasmettere la seconda lettera di Agamennone a Clitennestra, nella quale egli la esortava a non raggiungerlo in Aulide insieme a Ifigenia. Il fedele servitore accusa il re di Micene di essere ingiusto: "Io pur dirò senza rispetto il vero: / disconviensi a Signor l'esser ingiusto; / disconviensi l'usar forza ad altrui, / e tanto più ad un servo, e in cosa tale / ch'offenderete il fratello e la ragione" (a. II, vv. 409-13). Menelao loda la fedeltà del servo, ma afferma che ciò di cui il fratello l'ha incaricato è "ufficio indegno e brutto", che sarà causa di vergogna per l'intera Grecia. Quando il servitore insiste, prendendo le difese del suo signore, Menelao lo minaccia, ma egli non cede e tenta comunque di opporre le proprie ragioni; alla fine, dovrà desistere, perché "poco val ragione incontro a

---

[13] Giazzon riconosce nel comportamento di Agamennone "la cosiddetta 'doppia morale' che Machiavelli aveva proposto nel *Principe* e che Hauser, per esempio, reputava essere uno dei tratti più pertinentemente rappresentativi della crisi del Rinascimento" (*Il Manierismo a teatro* 6).

forza" (a. II, v. 439).

Come precedentemente accennato, sono però il rapporto tra Agamennone e il fratello Menelao e i contrasti che nascono tra i due a essere particolarmente interessanti per il continuo rovesciamento nel comportamento dei personaggi. In un primo tempo, infatti, è Menelao, mosso dalla pura Ragione di Stato, a spingere perché il fratello permetta il sacrificio della figlia. Agamennone, che in prima istanza aveva accettato, è però padre e marito affettuoso, e tenta di evitare la morte di Ifigenia. All'inverso, in seguito è Menelao, afflitto dalla vista del fratello in lacrime, a non considerare più necessaria l'uccisione della nipote, mentre Agamennone è ormai convinto della sua ineluttabilità. I due momenti di confronto rispecchiano una situazione abbastanza singolare, poiché tra i personaggi non c'è un rapporto gerarchico, come si affretta ad affermare Menelao, cui Agamennone rinfaccia di non avere il diritto di intercettare la seconda lettera a Clitennestra: "Così di far mi piacque, e potì, e volli. / Voi signor non mi sete; io vostro servo" (a. II, vv. 471-72). Forse perché è il minore tra i fratelli, il re di Micene assume comunque un atteggiamento più cauto, e condanna la "peste degli adulatori".[14] Egli vorrebbe svelare ai Greci il comportamento di Agamennone, che considera indegno, fraudolento e superbo; il fratello giustifica il proprio operato e accusa Menelao di essere arrogante. Quest'ultimo tuttavia non esita a mostrarsi sorpreso per l'improvviso cambiamento avvenuto in Agamennone, che non esibisce più la sete di gloria che l'aveva caratterizzato prima di giungere in Aulide, quando aveva di buon grado accettato il sacrificio di Ifigenia. Egli ne ricerca le ragioni, chiedendosi se il fratello cerchi di proteggersi da accuse di crudeltà, oppure se si sia reso improvvisamente conto che l'impegno preso è troppo gravoso, o ancora, che sia mosso unicamente dal proprio "particulare".

Entrambi sembrano in realtà oscillare tra l'atteggiamento del sovrano assoluto e quello del consigliere politico. Agamennone offre massime morali: "Il savio spesso / muta voler: e quando è tempo ammenda / l'error commesso; e non indugia al fine" (a. II, vv. 484-86); "In anima gentil s'annida sempre / timor d'infamia, e bel desio d'onore" (a. II, vv. 554-55). Ma Menelao non è da meno: "E pur sapete, come / il buon, per acquistar gradi ed onori, / non suol mutar costume; e serba sempre / alla fortuna prospera, e all'avversa / un cuore istesso, e una medesma faccia" (a. II, vv. 522-26). Egli descrive in seguito il principe ideale:

> Ma quando fosse in poter mio concesso
> di dar il freno ed il governo in mano

---

[14] "E se non udirete ch'io vi lodi, / non vi turbate, acciocché non si dica / ch'a voi convenga quel proverbio antico, / che verità sovente odio produce. / Peste non è che più trafigga altrui, / di quel che fa l'adulator fallace. / Da me senza rispetto dire il vero / intenderete, purché d'ascoltarmi, / come amico e fratel, non vi sia noia" (a. II, vv. 495-503).

> di cittade, o d'esercito ad alcuno,
> contra l'uso che serbano gli sciocchi,
> a nobiltade io non avrei riguardo,
> né a merti di passati, né a ricchezze,
> ma solo eleggerei chi fosse adorno
> d'i tesori dell'animo; che questi
> è veramente nobile: e bisogna
> che sia ardito, sia astutto e d'alto cuore,
> sia discreto, prudente e forte e saggio
> chi di regger altrui cura si prende:
> e conchiudo che Principe è colui
> che di bontà, di cortesia, d'amore,
> di prudenza e virtù tutt'altri avanza.
>
> (*Ifigenia*, a. II, vv. 597-611)

Il catalogo delle virtù del regnante non si discosta di molto da quello presentato per bocca del Sacerdote nella *Cleopatra* e sistematizzato nelle opere dedicate all'*institutio principis*, da Pontano a Erasmo. Apparentemente, Menelao è quindi la figura positiva di questo dibattito. Tuttavia, alla fine Agamennone deflette sul fratello l'accusa di agire soltanto per il proprio "particulare", dimenticando il bene comune: è vero, egli vuole salvare la figlia, ma perché tocca a loro dover soffrire per la colpa della moglie fedifraga, Elena? È Menelao a spingere perché la Grecia faccia guerra a Troia, e lavare così la macchia sul proprio onore: "sciocco è ben chi se medesmo offende, / e nulla vede chi 'l suo bene non vede; / ma cieco essendo al beneficio suo, / ha nell'utile d'altri gli occhi d'Argo" (a. II, vv. 677-80).

Come detto in precedenza, Agamennone cambia improvvisamente idea: è ormai convinto di non poter più impedire il sacrificio della figlia, che è necessario: "Dura necessità lasso a quel giogo / piegar mi fai contra mia voglia il collo? / Ma la fortuna, che le cose umane / volge a suo modo, ha la mia astutia vinta" (a. II, vv. 746-49). A nulla valgono i discorsi di Menelao. Agamennone ringrazia il fratello per la pietà inaspettata; teme però che Calcante parli del vaticinio all'esercito, e di dover fronteggiare una rivolta. Al consiglio di Menelao, che vorrebbe uccidere l'indovino, il re di Creta risponde che i reggenti non devono agire ingiustamente. Egli però, machiavellicamente, ribatte: "È giusto tutto quel, ch'utile apporta" (a. II, v. 846).[15]

Il colpo di scena che avvia la tragedia al suo epilogo è però dovuto all'improvvisa decisione di Ifigenia di prestarsi come vittima volontaria al sacrificio, sentito ormai anche da lei come inevitabile e necessario; la giovane diviene così esempio di fortezza (a. IV, vv. 2288-300). L'opinione dell'autore sulla liceità o meno del sacrificio è resa esplicita dal commento del nunzio circa

---

[15] Anche Tolomeo nella *Cleopatra* pronuncia sentenze più machiavelliche che machiavelliane: "A Signori gli è lecita ogni cosa, / per aver un Dominio senza noia" (a. II, vv. 515-16).

le reazioni degli astanti:

> Altri della fortezza ragionava
> di sì tenera giovane e fanciulla,
> altri della bontà del padre, il quale,
> aspro alla figlia ed a se stesso, aveva
> l'onor di Grecia unicamente amato.
> Alcuno il biasimava, lui crudele
> chiamando, e ambitioso; e questo forse
> di tutt'altri giudicii era il più giusto.
>
> (*Ifigenia*, a. V, vv. 2786-98)

d) *La verità come arma a doppio taglio nell'"Edippo"*
La figura di Edipo descritta da Anguillara presenta, al pari di Agamennone e Menelao, caratteristiche ambivalenti. Nel racconto di Tiresia alla figlia Manto che apre la tragedia, ripercorrendo l'antefatto, viene sottolineato che l'omicidio di Laio è causato dalla "troppa ira" di Edipo, irritato dal tono sdegnoso del cocchiere della carrozza reale. Subito dopo, però, Edipo è identificato come padre e reggente esemplare; porta i figli al tempio e discute della propria successione perché preoccupato dall'epidemia di peste che affligge Tebe. Ha già iniziato a istruire i figli al governo, fatto testamento e contratto promesse matrimoniali illustri per le figlie. Per evitare future lotte di potere, ha previsto che Polinice regni su Corinto, Eteocle su Tebe. In seguito egli lascia loro una lunga serie di ammonimenti per guidarli nel buon governo: essere timorati di Dio, un esempio per i sudditi, non offendere l'onore altrui, e soprattutto avere rispetto per le donne, ed evitare di lasciarsi dominare dalla lussuria rischiando l'incesto. E ancora: prestare ascolto ai consigli, essere cortesi e liberali, perché l'avarizia e l'avidità sono fonte di ogni male. Tali "ricordi" hanno il sapore, per chi conosca il mito, di amara ironia, e si vedranno rovesciati nel seguito della tragedia.

Edipo è padre premuroso, non soltanto nei confronti dei figli: egli dice esplicitamente che colui che regna è *padre* dei suoi sudditi. Non solo; in seguito, quando è noto l'oracolo per cui soltanto la punizione dell'assassino di Laio potrà liberare la città dal morbo, Edipo afferma, ancora una volta con inconsapevole preveggenza: "Laio fu mio predecessor nel regno, / io suo fui successor, tanto che in loco / debbo averlo di padre; e come padre / mio proprio e debbo, e voglio vendicarlo" (*Edippo*, a. II, vv. 732-36). L'insistenza sul termine "padre" riporta qui in primo piano il parricidio; ma in definitiva, la pestilenza cesserà quando sarà punito il regicidio.[16]

---

[16] In un suo contributo Ossola sostiene che nel mito di Edipo il regicidio sia decisamente più importante di parricidio e incesto, e ripercorre la storia di questa teoria. Anche nell'*Ifigenia* è sottolineato come il sovrano sia padre dei sudditi: "che 'l Signor valoroso accorto e saggio / deve i sudditi amar come figliuoli, / e in giovar loro dimostrarsi padre" (a. I, vv. 203-08).

Il cambiamento nell'atteggiamento di Edipo avviene proprio quando il sovrano è spinto dal desiderio di salvare la città e vuole a tutti i costi scoprire chi abbia ucciso Laio. Quando Tiresia si rifiuta di dirgli apertamente ciò che sa, egli lo minaccia di tortura; in seguito, lo accusa di congiurare contro di lui insieme al cognato Creonte, che viene, al pari dell'indovino, fatto arrestare e gettato in prigione.[17] Edipo si trasforma in tiranno non quando gli altri tentano di dirgli la verità, ma quando si rifiutano di farlo. Giocasta, a questo punto, contesta il marito e tenta di difendere il fratello, di cui protesta la lealtà. Edipo risponde criticando la credulità delle donne: "Voi donne sete semplici, e credete / che sian semplici tutti; e non v'è noto / quel che può del regnar l'ingorda voglia" (a. III, vv. 1358-60).[18] La brama di regnare si affianca al timore di poter perdere, "in un volger di ciglia", il favore regale: basta "un minimo sospetto, un'empia lingua" (a. III, vv. 1389-93). Benché anche il coro prenda le difese di Creonte, Edipo si mostra inflessibile e pronto a punire il colpevole secondo giustizia, indipendentemente da chi sia, e senza farsi impietosire dai pianti delle donne. Alle rimostranze del coro, che gli rimproverano la poca prudenza nell'affrettare i propri giudizi e la mancanza di prove contro Creonte, il re oppone la necessità di agire tempestivamente contro i pericoli, per scongiurarli sul nascere.

Il tiranno e la verità: inganni e autoinganni, tra opportunismo e lealtà
Al pari di quanto accade nell'*Edippo*, l'agire sulla base di sospetti non sostenuti da prove certe è decisamente criticato come comportamento tirannico nella *Marianna*, e si lega al lamento che vede la corte luogo di inganni, invidie e calunnie (a. IV, vv. 2128-43). Nell'*Ifigenia* di Dolce è un vecchio che ha assistito ai preparativi per il sacrificio della giovane che si lancia in un'invettiva contro la vita di corte, dominata da lussuria e ambizione. Parallelamente, una critica feroce all'ambiente cortigiano, indifferente e votato unicamente all'ambizione personale, è mossa dal coro dell'*Edippo*, in seguito al racconto del "gentiluomo di corte"; dopo che il re si è accecato, chiede che qualcuno lo accompagni nell'esilio, ma tutti rifiutano ("E in un momento si sgombrò il palazzo / [...] / ciascuno al suo privato utile attese", vv. 2209-12):

    Miser colui, che di felice stato

---

[17] L'insistenza del re, la sua brama di *sapere* la verità, è un aspetto cui viene dato ampio risalto all'interno di questa tragedia. Per ben due volte Edipo ignora gli avvertimenti e le richieste da parte di altri personaggi (Tiresia e Giocasta) di non indagare oltre.

[18] Lo stesso rimprovero è mosso dagli uomini del coro nei confronti delle donne tebane nella seconda scena dell'atto quinto dell'*Edippo*, che si situa dopo che Creonte ha operato come mediatore tra Eteocle e Polinice, accordatisi sull'alternanza del potere su Tebe. Gli uomini temono che il primo fratello, una volta salito al trono, non vorrà state ai patti; le donne pensano che siano troppo sospettosi: "Noi vecchi abbiamo / visto per lunga esperientia quanto / l'ambitione e l'avaritia ponno / nell'uom. Voi donne sete troppo facili / a credere" (a. V, vv. 2867-72).

cade in miseria. Mentre il nostro Edippo
vivea felice, e non avea perduto
né 'l lume esterior né 'l lume interno,
ciascun dicea d'esser leale e fido;
come fu scorto poi stupido e cieco,
e caduto in miseria e 'n tristo stato,
tutti l'abbandonar.

(*Edippo*, a. IV, vv. 2213-20)

La difficoltà della vita dei potenti, *topos* già senecano e oraziano, e argomento di trattazione umanistica, è sottolineata anche nella *Cleopatra*, con il discorso del "Bailo" che occupa la scena seconda del primo atto (a. I, vv. 316-61).[19] Anche Erode è conscio dei pericoli del regnare; da vero tiranno, è guidato da timore e sospetto, soprattutto per quanto riguarda la fedeltà dei suoi servitori: "Si suol dir per proverbio antico e vero / che colui c'ha più servi, ha più nimici" (a. II, vv. 1314-15). In effetti, l'ubbidienza dovuta al sovrano si scontra talvolta con scrupoli di natura morale, o con un legame di fedeltà sentito come più forte.[20] Esemplare, in questo senso, proprio nella *Marianna*, è il caso del capitano Soemo.[21] Come la regina confida alla nutrice, egli "anteponendo in questo / all'obligo il dovere e la pietate, / a mia madre ed a me fece palese / quel ch'imposto gli avea l'aspro Tiranno" (a. I, 384-87), e cioè di uccidere le due donne qualora non avesse fatto ritorno ad Alessandria. Il capitano è cosciente del rischio corso svelando l'ordine; solo per la mancanza di ubbidienza Erode potrebbe condannarlo a "sanguinosa morte", "benché certo obedir è cosa indegna / a Signor che comanda offici ingiusti" (a. I, vv. 505-06). Questa riflessione ricorda indubbiamente il capitolo ventitreesimo del secondo libro del *Cortegiano*, in cui ci si chiede "se un gentilomo, mentre che serve a un principe, è obligato a ubidirgli in tutte le cose che gli commanda, ancor che fossero disoneste e vituperose." La risposta dei diversi interlocutori chiarisce che bisogna "ubidire al signor vostro in tutte le cose che a lui sono utili ed onorevoli, non in quelle che gli sono di danno e di vergogna" (225). L'opposizione di

---

[19] Simile l'avvertimento dato poco dopo: non bisogna credere a tutto ciò che si sente, soprattutto alle voci anonime. I signori devono essere ancora più attenti degli altri, perché "unque non mancan gl'animi volpini / che seminando van mille menzogne, / acciò sortisca effetto il loro pensiero" (a. II, vv. 645-47). Il luogo comune per cui una vita semplice è preferibile a quella dei potenti, ricca di insidie, è variamente presente nelle quattro tragedie qui esaminate, e si lega frequentemente al lamento per la precarietà dei disegni umani; si veda per esempio *Ifigenia*, a. I, vv. 26-36; a. II, coro; a. III, vv. 1143-50; *Marianna*, a. II, scena I.

[20] Il secondo è il caso, per esempio, del servo che confida a Clitennestra — al servizio della quale era già prima dell'unione con Agamennone — l'inganno del marito: "Quinci l'amore e 'l debito m'ha spinto / a romper fede al Re vostro marito, / per mantenerla e conservarla a voi" (*Ifigenia*, a. III, vv. 1317-20).

[21] Beatrice Alfonzetti e Ronnie Terpening hanno delineato con precisione le figure del capitano in alcune tragedie del Cinquecento, inclusa la *Marianna*.

Soemo, letta in quest'ottica, è dunque pienamente giustificabile; Erode, rifiutandosi di comprendere le ragioni del capitano, agisce nuovamente da tiranno.

Diversa, almeno inizialmente, è la reazione del servo di Tolomeo incaricato di portare a Cleopatra i resti del figlio. Le donne del coro tentano di avvisare, in modo piuttosto criptico, l'ignaro servitore, che tuttavia oppone alle loro parole una cieca ubbidienza al sovrano (a. IV, vv. 1761-62). Alla domanda se sappia cosa sta trasportando, egli risponde incurante: "Non so, né men di saperlo mi curo, / perché 'l Re sì m'ha imposto ch'io lo deggia / portar senza scoprir né pur vederlo / né io né altri, sotto pena grave / della vita, e però voglio obbedirlo" (a. IV, vv. 1766-70); e ancora, con spaventosa *naïveté*: "Sia pur quel che si voglia, io non mi curo; / farò l'ufficio mio, ch'io so pur troppo / che 'l Re non fece mai lodevol cosa, / ma forse che di questo v'ingannate" (a. IV, vv. 1774-77). Il sentimento di impotenza del servitore è evidente: "Fia pur di bene o mal, mezzo o cagione, / altro non posso far; ciò ben mi spiace: / ma patienza, così vuole il nostro / Signor e Re; ed io voglio obbedirlo, / perché ubbidir si deve i signor suoi, / così gli ingiusti, come i giusti e pii" (a. IV, vv. 1789-94).

Una volta scoperto ciò che Tolomeo gli ha ordinato di fare, il servo tuttavia si dispera, e accusa le donne di non avergli detto fino a che punto l'azione fosse scellerata. Il coro replica di aver agito per paura delle spie, che avrebbero potuto riferire tutto a Tolomeo:

> Io t'ho così parlato,
> senza più chiaro dirti,
> per tema del signor empio e Tiranno:
> perciò che delle cose dei signori
> non bisogna parlarne chiaramente,
> ma così in questa guisa
> che d'alcun non si possa esser ripresi:
> perché son sempre tesi
> gl'archi d'accusatori, in ogni parte
> per scoccar in color che senza tema
> parlano de' signori al modo loro:
> però buono è parlar poco ed oscuro;
> ma miglior è 'l tacer, e più sicuro.
>
> (*Cleopatra*, a. V, vv. 1882-94)[22]

Benché colmo di raccapriccio, il servitore ha la coscienza pulita: non sapeva, e ha agito unicamente su ordine del suo sovrano (a. V, vv. 1895-99).

---

[22] Nella *Cleopatra* un'altra scena di confronto tra cortigiani, che occupa tutta la terza scena dell'atto terzo, risulta particolarmente interessante, proprio perché, da un lato, viene mostrato ancora una volta il clima di diffidenza e sospetto che regna nelle corti, e dall'altro sono messe in opposizione due figure di servitori. Benché contrario all'operare di Tolomeo, il "Bailo" critica il sovrano soltanto in privato, quando è certo che nessuno lo senta. Il servo, invece, sembra incurante delle possibili spie.

L'inconsapevolezza sembra essere, in queste quattro tragedie, ciò che separa la colpa dal semplice errore. Come chiarisce Achille, "chi consente al mal pecca egli tanto, / quanto chi lo commette" (a. III, vv. 1526-27); la volontà di compiere il male è condizione necessaria perché si possa parlare di colpa. Naturalmente, l'*exemplum* di peccato compiuto inconsapevolmente è per antonomasia quello di Edipo. Nella tragedia di Anguillara questo è sottolineato più volte, e da diversi personaggi, al pari dell'inesorabilità del Fato, al quale "non si può contradir", nonostante tutti gli sforzi e le cautele messe in atto.

Conclusione: potere della parola e potere del silenzio
Spinelli, Dolce e Anguillara si muovono in contesti socio-culturali diversi, che solo marginalmente si sovrappongono, e tuttavia questo non sembra incidere sostanzialmente sulla loro prassi drammaturgica. Le opere qui prese in esame testimoniano infatti dell'emergenza, a metà Cinquecento, di un referente comune in ambito tragico. Questa koinè, che trova espressioni individuali nei singoli autori, può essere riconosciuta, sul piano generale, attraverso tre caratteristiche. In primo luogo, gli autori che a essa fanno ricorso rielaborano i *topoi* della trattatistica etico-politica classica e umanistica, codificate da ultimo dal *Cortegiano*. Inoltre, la componente macabra e orrida di stampo senecano viene enfatizzata sull'esempio del tragico giraldiano e speroniano. Da ultimo, il potere politico messo in scena è insensibile e perverso, e il tiranno è chiuso in un isolamento ai limiti della follia.

Le figure degli oppositori al potere tirannico qui messe in evidenza agiscono in nome di una morale più alta, ovviamente umana e cortigiana, ma nel senso migliore della parola (e cioè in accordo con i precetti esposti nel *Cortegiano*), che li spinge talvolta a sprezzare il pericolo della vita e a "dire la verità": consiglieri che sono quindi "perfetti cortigiani" e figure femminili combattive che tentano di instillare la ragione nelle menti distorte dei tiranni. Altri personaggi, come i servi nella *Cleopatra* e nella *Marianna*, si trovano tuttavia in posizione di sottomissione totale al potere, e decidono, per opportunismo o con rassegnazione, di mettere letteralmente a tacere i propri dubbi morali e ubbidire agli ordini ricevuti. Parlare e tacere diventano dunque sintomi, rispettivamente, dell'opposizione e della sottomissione. Fa eccezione il comportamento dell'indovino Tiresia, che, per il bene del sovrano e del regno, si oppone tacendo la verità. In due casi (Cleopatra e Clitennestra), l'eroina deciderà, a seguito del fallimento dei tentativi propri e altrui di contrastare a parole la follia del principe, di passare all'azione e vendicare l'uccisione dei figli.

La centralità della parola nella cultura rinascimentale, testimoniata anche dalla fortuna conosciuta dal genere dialogico nei secoli XV e XVI, si conferma dunque anche nella tragedia del Cinquecento, che è pure considerata da molti come il genere retorico per eccellenza, in cui la parola trionfa sull'azione. Alle parole è qui attribuito il potere di svelare o celare la verità, di ingannare sé e gli altri. Tuttavia, la loro forza ed efficacia si attuano soltanto se chi ascolta è pronto ad accoglierle. Il tiranno di queste tragedie, che crede rapidamente alle calunnie ma è sordo nei confronti di chi tenta di mostrargli un'altra verità rispetto a quella che egli stesso si è creato, non può far altro che opporre la violenza alle parole. Ecco quindi che, ricordando, insieme al servo di Agamennone, che "poco val ragione incontro a forza", la speranza di tutti è rivolta alla certezza della giustizia divina. Nelle quattro tragedie è infatti più volte auspicato, in particolare dal coro e dai personaggi cui viene attribuito un ruolo di guida e consiglio (balie, consiglieri, sacerdoti), che il tiranno sia punito per le proprie nefande azioni da Dio (e si è visto il caso della *Cleopatra*, in cui persino la vendetta della regina è letta, a posteriori, come azione guidata dalla giustizia soprannaturale). Tutti questi testi anticipano inoltre alcune caratteristiche riscontrate nelle tragedie di fine secolo da Scarpati:

[...] lentamente le coppie antitetiche del *Libro del cortegiano*, verità e menzogna, conoscenza di sé e presunzione, prudenza giusta e tracotanza del comando assumono le tinte del dibattito contemporaneo che mette in campo la contesa insolubile tra ragione di legge e ragione di stato.

(207)

Le quattro tragedie hanno funzione esplicitamente didattica; valga, per tutte, il coro che conclude l'atto quinto di ciascuna opera. Se nella *Cleopatra* l'ammonimento è rivolto ancora al tiranno, invitato al vivere virtuoso, nell'*Ifigenia* l'esortazione è a non confidare nella felicità e nei beni terreni, destinati a trasformarsi in "nebbia e polvere"; nella *Marianna* Dolce sanziona invece l'ira, e consiglia di non lasciarsi sfuggire di mano "il fren della ragione". Ma è l'*Edippo* che si fa portavoce del nuovo clima culturale:

> Quindi si può veder che 'l sommo Dio
> non sol dispon che i volontarii eccessi
> condannin l'uomo al debito castigo,
> ma quei peccati ancor ch'alcun commette
> per ignoranza e contra il suo volere
> vuol che condannin l'uomo a penitenza,
> e la debita pena ne riporti.
> Sicché preghiam la maiestà divina
> ch'apra talmente a noi l'interno lume,
> che non ne siano i nostri eccessi ascosi.

(*Edippo*, a. V, vv. 3235-44)

Con un finale che non lascia scampo e sanziona il peccato involontario come quello nato da malizia, Anguillara esplicita che l'unica speranza per i mortali è la misericordia divina.

Université de Fribourg

Opere citate

Alfonzetti Beatrice. *"Il traditor d'Oronte"*. *Consigliere e capitano: figure del tradimento*. In *I confini dell'umanesimo letterario: studi in onore di Francesco Tateo*. A c. di M. de Nichilo, G. Distaso, A. Iurilli. Roma: Roma nel Rinascimento, 2003. 1: 19-38.
Bertana Emilio. *La tragedia*. Milano: Vallardi [1906].
Bosisio Paolo. *Il tema di Edipo nella tradizione della tragedia italiana*. In AA.VV., *Edipo in Francia*. Firenze: Olschki, 1989. 78-122.
Castiglione Baldassarre. *Il libro del cortegiano*. A c. di B. Maier. Torino: UTET, 1969.
Clerc Sandra. *Tra mito e storia: le tragedie di Cesare de' Cesari*. "Aevum" 89.3 (2015), in stampa.
Cremante Renzo. *Appunti sulla grammatica tragica di Ludovico Dolce*. "Cuadernos de Filología Italiana" 5 (1998): 279-90.
_____. *Teatro del Cinquecento: La tragedia*. Milano: Ricciardi, 1988.
Dell'Anguillara Giovanni Andrea. *Edippo*. Padova: Lorenzo Pasquatto, 1565.
Dolce Lodovico. *Ifigenia*. Venezia: Gabriele Giolito, 1551.
_____. *Marianna*. In Cremante. *Teatro del Cinquecento* 731-877.
Fabrizio Richard. *The Two Oedipuses: Sophocles, Anguillara, and the Renaissance Treatment of Myth*. "MLN, Modern Language Notes" 110.1 (1995): 178-91.
Giazzon Stefano. *Dante nel regno di Melpomene: appunti sulla presenza dantesca nelle tragedie di Lodovico Dolce*. "Filologia e Critica" 36 (2011): 125-38.
_____. *Il Manierismo a teatro: l' 'Ifigenia' di Lodovico Dolce*. "Forum Italicum: A Journal of Italian Studies" 46.1 (2012): 53-81.
_____. *Venezia in coturno: Lodovico Dolce tragediografo (1543-1557)*. Roma: Aracne, 2011.
Giraldi Cinzio Giovan Battista. *Lettera sulla tragedia*. In *Trattati di poetica e retorica del Cinquecento*. 2 voll. A c. di B. Weinberg. Bari: Laterza, 1970. 1: 471-86.
Mastrocola, Paola. *Nimica fortuna: Edipo e Antigone nella tragedia italiana del Cinquecento*. Torino: Tirrenia Stampatori, 1996.
Mercuri Roberto. *Il teatro tragico*. In N. Borsellino e R. Mercuri. *Il teatro del Cinquecento. Il Cinquecento*. Letteratura italiana Laterza. Bari: Laterza, 1973. 72-107.
Minieri Riccio Camillo. *Memorie storiche degli scrittori nati nel Regno di Napoli*. Napoli: [s.n.], 1844.
Montorfani Pietro. *Uno specchio per i principi: le tragedie di Pomponio Torelli (1539-1608)*. Pisa: Edizioni ETS, 2010.
Mussini Sacchi Maria Pia. *Cleopatra* altera *Laura: la presenza di Petrarca in un personaggio del teatro tragico cinquecentesco*. In *I territori del petrarchismo: Frontiere e sconfinamenti*. A c. di C. Montagnani. Roma: Bulzoni, 2005. 209-29.
Neri Ferdinando. *La tragedia italiana del Cinquecento*. Firenze: Tipografia Galletti e Cocci, 1904.
Ossola Carlo. *'Edipo e ragion di Stato': mitologie comparate*. "Lettere Italiane" 34.4 (1982): 483-505.
Scarpati Claudio. *Dire la verità al principe: Ricerche sulla letteratura del Rinascimento*. Milano: Vita e Pensiero, 1987.
Spinelli Alessandro. *Cleopatra*. Venezia: Pietro de Nicolini da Sabbio, 1550.
Terpening Ronnie H. *'Topoi' tragici del Cinquecento: la figura del capitano nella 'Rosmunda' del Rucellai e nella 'Marianna' del Dolce*. In *Il Rinascimento: aspetti e problemi attuali*. Firenze: Olschki, 1982. 651-65.

Thesaurus de la littérature interdite au XVIe siècle: auteurs, ouvrages, éditions. A cura di J. M. De Bujanda. Sherbrooke: Centre d'Études de la Renaissance; Genève: Droz, 1996.

Toppi Nicolò. *Biblioteca napoletana.* Napoli: Bulifon, 1672.

Laura Benedetti

Le ragioni della poesia: Torquato Tasso e Silvio Antoniano

Sinossi: La vita e l'opera di Torquato Tasso sono profondamente e drammaticamente segnate da tensioni con le autorità politiche, religiose e artistiche. La decisione del padre Bernardo di seguire il principe di Salerno, Ferrante Sanseverino, che si era ribellato all'introduzione dell'Inquisizione nel regno di Napoli, avrà conseguenze drammatiche sul piccolo Torquato che, richiamato a Roma dal padre, dovrà abbandonare madre e sorella, facendo così precoce esperienza degli effetti devastanti dei contrasti religiosi sulla vita degli individui. Più tardi, le sue difficoltà di ritagliarsi uno spazio nell'ambito infido della corte, la reclusione, la ricerca di un impiego e una sede adeguati nonché la stessa, ossessiva revisione della *Gerusalemme liberata*, ne fanno esempio paradigmatico e quasi vittima sacrificale dei conflitti della sua epoca. Quello che rende la figura e l'opera del poeta così stimolanti è che questa tensione con il potere non si risolse né in una servile acquiescenza né in una radicale ribellione. Per anni Tasso cercò invece le occasioni per un dialogo che salvaguardasse al tempo stesso l'ossequio alle autorità, il prestigio degli interlocutori e la propria dignità di uomo e di poeta. In questo contesto, le lettere disposte lungo l'arco della sua intera esistenza costituiscono un prezioso documento dei dilemmi che gli si presentavano di volta in volta alla coscienza. L'obiettivo di questo saggio è quello di esaminare alcune delle strategie retoriche e delle argomentazioni elaborate dall'autore per cercare di preservare qualche libertà di azione personale ed artistica in contesti che tendevano invece a limitarla sempre di più. Data la vastità dell'argomento, sarà opportuno concentrarsi su un aspetto specifico, vale a dire il rapporto tra il poeta e il più temuto dei revisori della *Liberata*, Silvio Antoniano, così come emerge dall'unica, ricchissima lettera inviata direttamente al futuro cardinale, nonché da allusioni sparse in altri luoghi dell'epistolario.
Parole chiave: Silvio Antoniano, censura, Controriforma, Indice, *Gerusalemme liberata*, religione, revisione, Torquato Tasso.

1. La laboriosa revisione romana del "Goffredo"

Sottoporre i propri lavori a lettori influenti era prassi comune nel Rinascimento. Se Bernardo Tasso si era rivolto, per il suo *Amadigi*, a quello Sperone Speroni che finirà per giocare un ruolo significativo anche nella revisione della *Liberata*, lo stesso Torquato, rivolgendosi ai lettori nell'introduzione al *Rinaldo*, ricorda di aver interpellato diversi letterati. Danese Cattaneo e Cesare Pavesi, scrive l'esordiente scrittore, avevano incoraggiato la sua decisione di trascurare gli studi di giurisprudenza per assecondare la sua propensione per la poesia. Successivamente, Girolamo Molino e Domenico Venier avevano esaminato il poema e "esortato caldamente" l'autore a darlo alle stampe, vincendo così anche le resistenze del titubante Bernardo che, con paterna sollecitudine, fondato pessimismo e intuito divinatorio, dubitava che la letteratura potesse garantire al figlio una carriera prospera e una vita serena. È dunque "sotto lo scudo di tali auttorità" che il Tassino presenta il suo poema giovanile, ben protetto "da l'arme de le maledicenze altrui" (*Rinaldo* 45-46). Non è escluso che questa esperienza, in cui l'esame si era risolto in un benevolo *imprimatur*, avesse portato il poeta a sottovalutare la portata della revisione romana alla quale, tredici anni dopo, decise di sottoporre il *Goffredo*,[1] dando inizio ad un processo che sarebbe risultato paralizzante e avrebbe rischiato di privare la letteratura occidentale di uno dei suoi capolavori (Solerti I, 206).

Se è dunque possibile ipotizzare che l'iniziativa della revisione sia partita dallo stesso autore, non è chiaro invece se e in che misura sia dipesa da lui la scelta dei letterati preposti a tale funzione, e cioè Flaminio De Nobili, Pietro degli Angeli detto il Barga, Sperone Speroni e Silvio Antoniano. Si tratta di figure diverse per provenienza geografica (toscani i primi due, padovano lo Speroni, romano l'Antoniano), per età all'altezza dell'inizio della revisione (si va dai 35 anni di Silvio Antoniano ai 75 di Sperone Speroni, passando per i 42 di Flaminio De Nobili e i 58 di Pietro degli Angeli [Quondam 566]) e prestigio, concentrato in gran parte sul binomio Antoniano-Speroni.[2] La relazione con il De Nobili e il Barga, almeno per quanto ci è possibile ricostruire dalle lettere, si manterrà sempre entro i binari del reciproco rispetto. Quella con Speroni e Antoniano, invece, vissuta fin dall'inizio con maggiore apprensione, col trascorrere dei mesi susciterà nel poeta diffidenza e risentimento[3] e, cosa ben più grave, lo porterà a rimettere in discussione le sue scelte poetiche, con conseguenze che avrebbero potuto essere disastrose. Il giovane Antoniano e l'anziano Speroni, uniti tra l'altro dalla comune esperienza dell'Accademia delle Notti Vaticane, sembrano in effetti talmente lontani dalle posizioni tassiane, talmente insensibili alla novità della sua poesia, che viene spontaneo chiedersi se tutta la revisione non sia stata fin dall'inizio inficiata da un grave errore di valutazione relativo proprio alla scelta degli interlocutori. Indicativo dell'atteggiamento ambivalente del Tasso è la decisione di ritardare l'invio dei canti a Sperone Speroni, in modo da poter poi

---

[1] Così viene indicato nelle lettere il poema che sarebbe diventato famoso col titolo *Gerusalemme liberata*.

[2] Sui profili dei revisori vedere Molinari XVIII-XXIV e Quondam 565-68.

[3] Così commenta Ricci: "Anche se sin dall'inizio verso entrambi Sperone ed Antoniani l'atteggiamento di reverenza e stima è senza dubbio meno spontaneo e più calcolato, meno confidenziale e più distante, un crescendo della tensione operativa infiamma le ultime lettere degli anni presi in esame. A conclusione della corrispondenza romana i toni ossequiosi e fiduciosi cedono il passo ad impennate di esasperazione verso le resistenze pregiudiziali elaborate dai due interlocutori più ostici. Con il trascorrere del tempo il processo di revisione da fruttuosa collaborazione intellettuale viene drammaticamente percepito come strumento censorio della vena poetica [...]" (127).

ignorare eventuali commenti e critiche proprio a causa del poco tempo a disposizione.[4] Le obiezioni dello Speroni, tuttavia, si mantenevano nell'ambito di una diversa concezione del poema eroico; quelle dell'Antoniano sconfinavano invece nel campo della religione e della morale, risultando dunque insidiose e ineludibili. Ingenui espedienti come quello ideato per tenere a bada lo Speroni avrebbero difficilmente avuto successo col futuro cardinale. Unico "chierico" del gruppo (in quanto studioso di filosofia e teologia presso i Gesuiti del Collegio Romano), l'Antoniano era anche, come scrive Quondam, "un 'politico' [...] cioè un uomo di stato e di apparato istituzionale" (564). Come scrive Molinari, "[a] Roma, e questo doveva ben saperlo il Gonzaga, non si pubblicava opera di pregio senza il giudizio preliminare e il nullaosta dell'Antoniani" (XIX).

Le *Lettere poetiche*, vale a dire le lettere che Tasso scrisse a proposito della revisione del poema nel biennio 1575-1576, rimangono la testimonianza più significativa di questo processo, pur essendoci pervenute, al pari di altri lavori tassiani, solo in edizioni a stampa non avallate dall'autore.[5] La discussione si trascinò per due anni, tra difficoltà logistiche e incomprensioni. Già il ritardo con cui i canti venivano recapitati a Roma suscitava sospetti e preoccupazione nel poeta.[6] Le obiezioni sollevate da Speroni e Antoniano minacciavano le fondamenta stesse di un poema che mirava a conciliare, come argomentato nei *Discorsi dell'arte poetica*, unità e varietà, verosimile e meraviglioso, religione e amore. L'aperto confronto intellettuale si trasforma ben presto in una performance retorica in cui Tasso blandisce, concede il necessario, difende le sue posizioni e si afferma quale autorità nel campo della composizione epica. Nel frattempo la sua condizione psico-fisica comincia a deteriorarsi e il desiderio di lasciare Ferrara lo porta ad un'avventata trasferta romana in cui più tardi egli stesso riconoscerà la radice di tutti i suoi mali.[7]

---

[4] Così confida il poeta al fido Scipione Gonzaga il 13 aprile 1575 (*Lettere poetiche* 27).
[5] Per le *Lettere poetiche* possiamo ora avvalerci della splendida edizione di Carla Molinari, a cui si farà riferimento. L'unica edizione completa delle lettere del poeta rimane quella curata da Guasti alla metà dell''800.
[6] Così si esprime Tasso nella lettera del 18 marzo 1575: "Sono in grandissima ansietà d'animo, vedendo che Vostra Signoria non m'accusa la ricevuta de' quattro primi canti ch'io le mandai da Ferrara il 2 di quaresima, né meno la ricevuta del quinto ch'io le mandai da Padova quindici giorni sono; né risponde ad alcune mie lettere che vennero co i canti, di molta importanza, di maniera che stimo ch'ogni cosa sia mal capitata, almeno que' primi; nella perdita de' quali, oltre la fatica del trascrivere e 'l dispiacere ch'avrei che fossero in mano d'altri, vi sarebbe il danno di molte correzioni, delle quali non ritenni copia" (*Lettere poetiche* 3-4).
[7] Partito da Ferrara all'inizio di novembre del 1575, Tasso vi faceva ritorno alla metà di gennaio del 1576 (Solerti I, 215-17). Ai malumori che questo viaggio aveva suscitato nella corte estense sembra alludere una lettera di quindici anni dopo a Fabio Gonzaga: "[...] 'l principio e la cagione della mia infelicità fu la mia venuta a Roma ne l'anno santo" (*Lettere* IV, 296).

In tutto il processo, fondamentale risulta il ruolo di Scipione Gonzaga che per due anni riceve, smista e in parte copia i canti che Tasso invia da Ferrara, per discuterli con i revisori i cui commenti trasmette all'ansioso poeta. Proprio a Scipione Gonzaga sono infatti indirizzate ben trentacinque delle cinquanta lettere poetiche, mentre altre quattordici sono inviate a Luca Scalabrino.[8] Solo in un'occasione, infine, Tasso fa a meno del filtro di questi due corrispondenti per rivolgersi direttamente ad uno dei revisori. Si tratta della lunga, fondamentale lettera del 30 marzo 1576 a Silvio Antoniano.[9]

2. Da "Poetino" a Inquisitore: la parabola di Silvio Antoniano

L'inclusione del chierico romano nel numero dei revisori era stata probabilmente imposta, oltre che dal suo indiscutibile prestigio, anche dalla sua profonda conoscenza della corte ferrarese. La prodigiosa memoria e le grandi doti di improvvisazione del giovane Antoniano, che gli valsero l'appellativo di "Poetino" e la fama di "mostro" e "miracolo" tra i contemporanei[10], esercitarono una grande impressione anche sul duca Ercole II, che lo volle con sé a Ferrara. In quella città l'Antoniano trascorse quattro anni estremamente formativi, addottorandosi *in utroque iure* e stabilendo contatti con alcuni tra i più illustri rappresentanti della cultura ferrarese, quali Giovambattista Pigna e Bartolomeo Ricci. Tornato a Roma nel 1559, avrebbe tuttavia continuato ad intrattenere con la corte estense stretti rapporti[11]. L'uomo cui Tasso affida la revisione del suo poema, tuttavia, è

---

[8] Altra figura importante nella revisione, Luca Scalabrino era un gentiluomo ferrarese per cui Tasso nutriva affetto e stima, come si evince da una lettera a Scipione Gonzaga (18 marzo 1575) in cui ne illustra la cultura ("intendentissimo delle leggi e molto avanzatosi ne gli studi d'umanità e di buonissimo gusto nell'eloquenza così poetica come oratoria"), la personalità ("se v'è lealtà e nobiltà d'animo ne gli uomini, è in lui quanto in alcun altro") e il legame che lo lega al poeta ("è colui che più amo e da cui più sono amato") (*Lettere poetiche* 5-6).

[9] Sono andate purtroppo perdute tutte le lettere indirizzate al poeta durante la revisione, che non passavano sempre e necessariamente attraverso il filtro di Scipione Gonzaga. Scrivendo allo stesso Gonzaga il 24 aprile 1576, Tasso cita a più riprese una lettera inviatagli da Silvio Antoniano (*Lettere poetiche* 419 e 425-27). Esistevano evidentemente uno o più canali diretti tra Tasso e i revisori, e la corrispondenza era ancora più complessa di quanto possiamo ricostruire.

[10] Queste informazioni biografiche sono desunte dal primo volume di *Silvio Antoniano* di Elisabetta Patrizi. Ludovico Castelvetro parla di Antoniano come di un "miracoloso mostro di natura [...] il quale sprovedutamente in così tenera età fa versi molti in numero, et rari in bontà di qualunque materia gli sia proposta". Lusinghieri anche i giudizi di Benedetto Varchi ne *L'Hercolano* ("miracolo di natura") e Girolamo Ruscelli ("miracolo di questa età") (Patrizi 37).

[11] Per ironia della sorte, l'Antoniano sarebbe tornato a Ferrara solo nel maggio 1598, al seguito di Clemente VIII che, approfittando della morte senza eredi di Alfonso II, annetteva Ferrara ai territori pontifici (Patrizi, *Silvio Antoniano* 56). L'evento costituiva anche una clamorosa conferma della lungimiranza del Poetino, che quarant'anni prima aveva deciso di legare il suo destino alla corte papale piuttosto che a quella estense.

profondamente diverso dal giovane talentuoso che si era imposto grazie alla poesia. L'incontro con Carlo Borromeo, la partecipazione all'Accademia delle Notti Vaticane (cui entra a far parte con il nome significativo di Risoluto),[12] l'evoluzione in senso teologico e dottrinale dell'accademia stessa, la stesura a Milano degli atti del primo concilio provinciale dell'episcopato borromaico, sono tappe miliari di un percorso che porta l'intellettuale romano ad abbandonare gli studi letterari per abbracciare quelli filosofici e teologici sotto la guida dei Gesuiti del Collegio Romano, per diventare sacerdote nel 1568. Anche se i frutti più ricchi di questa conversione (l'ingresso nella Congregazione dell'Indice nel 1581, la pubblicazione dei *Tre libri dell'educatione christiana dei figliuoli* nel 1584, la nomina a cardinale nel 1599) verranno a maturazione solo più tardi, l'uomo a cui Tasso affida il suo poema nel 1575 ha comunque già priorità ben chiare. Ben presto, la sua figura austera si trasforma da consigliere in ostacolo. In una lettera dell'11 febbraio 1576 al fido Gonzaga, Tasso lamenta la lentezza e la severità delle risposte dell'Antoniano: "[...] io crederei che con minor severità fosse stato revisto il poema dal medesmo Inquisitore" (*Lettere poetiche* 309-10), protesta il poeta, esprimendo subito dopo che la preoccupazione che tanta inflessibilità si estenda dalla sfera morale a quella poetica, dove sarebbe stato più problematico fare concessioni.

Un momentaneo sollievo traspare da una lettera di un mese dopo (12 marzo 1576) a Luca Scalabrino: "la severità del Poetino" essendosi contenuta entro termini accettabili, Tasso si dichiara ben disposto a seguire i suoi consigli "in tutto e per tutto" (*Lettere poetiche* 329-330). La stessa lettera però contiene una decisione dalle conseguenze potenzialmente disastrose:

> La peste di Venezia cresce tuttavia, e omai ha cominciato ad entrare ne le case de' nobili con la morte di alcuni di loro; e qui si cominciano a far di grandissime guardie: sì che io non posso pensare a la stampa per tre o quattro mesi ancora [...]. Ma girino le cose del mondo come piace a chi le governa: io, poiché non vi posso rimediare, mi voglio sforzare di non pensarvi; e ingannando me stesso, voglio sperare che tutti questi impedimenti mi s'attraversino inanzi per mio bene, accioché io possa interamente sodisfarmi ne la revisione del libro, e mandarlo poi fuora con maggior mia riputazione.
>
> (*Lettere poetiche* 330-31)

Siamo ad uno snodo cruciale nella storia del poema. Accettando di rimandare la stampa a data da destinarsi, Tasso contestualmente modificava la natura della revisione da verifica condotta nell'imminenza della pubblicazione a radicale

---

[12] Introdotto come personaggio in *Filippo, ossia dialogo della letizia cristiana* di Agostino Valier, Silvio Antoniano così commenta il suo pseudonimo: "[...] presi il nome di Risoluto, perché mi protestava aver costante animo, niente maravigliando delle umane cose, anzi tutte spregiandole, e di niente curando, fuorché del servir Dio, e il suo Vicario Pontefice Romano, ed ogni pensier mio, e studio alla gloria di Dio e al ben pubblico rivolgendo" (67-68).

rimessa in gioco dei criteri fin lì seguiti, con conseguente condanna del poema ad uno statuto di *work in progress* cui solo la *Gerusalemme conquistata* avrebbe posto fine, e solo vent'anni dopo. Com'è noto, dobbiamo alla provvidenziale disonestà di editori senza scrupoli il salvataggio del sublime relitto della *Gerusalemme liberata* da questo naufragio della poesia tra i gorghi del dubbio.

Il 30 marzo 1576, dunque solo un paio di settimane dopo aver comunicato a Scalabrino questa decisione, Tasso scrive la sua unica lettera all'Antoniano, in un estremo tentativo di trovare dei compromessi ragionevoli. Circostanziato e preciso, questo documento permette di ricostruire le riserve avanzate dal religioso romano. La lettera si apre con una straordinaria *captatio benevolentiae* che ben illustra il triplice ruolo rivestito dall'Antoniano:

Negli avvertimenti di Vostra signoria dell'uno e dell'altro genere ho chiarissimamente conosciuto, o più tosto riconosciuto, il suo giudizio, la dottrina, la religione e la pietà; et insieme ho visto molta benevolenza verso me, molto zelo della mia reputazione e grandissima diligenza nelle cose mie. E poich'ella ha così pienamente adempiti tutti gli offici di cristiano, di revisore e d'amico, io (quel ch'a me si conviene) mi sforzarò di far sì che non abbia a parerle persona o incapace di ricevere i suoi benefici o ingrata nel riconoscerli.

(*Lettere poetiche* 342)

Il "giudizio", "la dottrina", "la religione e la pietà" riscontrati nei consigli dell'Antoniano corrispondono rispettivamente alle figure da lui incarnate dell'"amico", del "revisore" e del "cristiano", caratterizzato da "benevolenza", "diligenza" e "zelo". Ai suoi "avvertimenti" Tasso si dichiara pronto a corrispondere con una discussione che dimostri il suo apprezzamento e la sua gratitudine, come si addice al suo ruolo ("quel ch'a me si conviene"). Tasso cerca dunque elegantemente di presentare le proprie riserve e obiezioni alla linea severa dell'Antoniano non come recalcitrante resistenza ma, al contrario, come unico modo di mostrarsi degno dell'attenzione che gli viene riservata ("mi sforzarò di far sì che non abbia a parerle persona o incapace di ricevere i suoi benefici o ingrata nel riconoscerli"). Ai ringraziamenti fa seguito una concessione:

[…] de'suoi avvertimenti n'ho già accettati parte e sovra gli altri avrò diligente considerazione. Ho accettati quelli che appertengono alla mutazione d'alcune parole o d'alcuni versi, i quali potrebbono esser malamente interpretati, o in altro modo offender gli orecchi de' pii religiosi.

(*Lettere poetiche* 343)

La concessione viene dunque subito qualificata e limitata. Le non precisate espressioni ("alcune parole" e "alcuni versi") non vengono sacrificate per difetti intrinseci, ma solo perché possono essere "malamente interpretat[e]" o addirittura "offendere gli orecchi de' pii religiosi" (formulazione quest'ultima che, a lettori familiari con le frecciate riservate in altre lettere al "Poetino", non può non sembrare lievemente ironica). Dopo questa vaga concessione per quanto riguarda l'*elocutio*, Tasso passa ad affrontare le obiezioni più insidiose relative alla *dispositio* e soprattutto all'*inventio*, che minacciavano di alterare in maniera radicale la fisionomia del suo lavoro. Particolarmente disdicevole doveva essere risultata la profusione di incanti e meraviglie del poema tassiano a chi più tardi, nell'*Educatione*, tuonerà contro il "miserabile abuso" (1048), da parte dei Cristiani, di "superstizioni" e "vanità" (*L'educatione christiana* II, XXXIII). Tasso si affretta a rassicurare l'interlocutore che modificherà la mutazione dei cavalieri in pesci, il miracolo del sepolcro di Sveno, la metamorfosi dell'aquila, e "alcune altre particelle" che l'Antoniano "o condanna come Inquisitore o non approva come poeta" (*Lettere poetiche* 344).[13] Quasi per un lapsus rivelatore, al termine "revisore" si è sostituito quello di "Inquisitore", sintomatico non solo della portata simbolica che l'Antoniano aveva assunto agli occhi del poeta, ma anche del ruolo pratico che gli veniva attribuito ai fini di una possibile approvazione (o, viceversa, condanna) del poema.

3. *"Alcune [...] cosette" a proposito di Olindo e Sofronia*
Proseguendo nella lista dei passi incriminati, Tasso segnala "l'episodio di Sofronia, o almen quel suo fine che più le dispiace" (*Lettere poetiche* 344). Si tratta, anche in questo caso, di una concessione solo parziale, che mentre sacrifica la conclusione matrimoniale dell'episodio (il lambiccato "Va dal rogo a le nozze; ed è già sposo / fatto di reo, non pur d'amante amato. / Volse con lei morire: ella non schiva, / poi che seco non muor, che seco viva" di *Liberata* II, 55), sembra volerne salvare lo svolgimento e il disinvolto trattamento poetico di una delle questioni più accesamente dibattute di quegli anni, quella cioè del ruolo delle immagini e delle reliquie nella pratica cattolica. Si ricorderà che l'amore non corrisposto di Olindo per la casta Sofronia si inserisce nel contesto di una disputa sul potere miracoloso delle immagini. L'episodio prende infatti le mosse dalla decisione del mago Ismeno di trafugare da una chiesa di Gerusalemme un'icona della Vergine. Sottoposta ad incantesimi e collocata nella moschea, l'immagine, promette Ismeno, garantirà l'inespugnabilità di Gerusalemme. La successiva, misteriosa sparizione dell'icona dà adito a varie ipotesi tra cui spicca per chiarezza argomentativa ed efficacia retorica quella di Clorinda. La scomparsa dell'immagine, sostiene la guerriera, va attribuita ad un miracolo di "Macone", sdegnato per la contaminazione di pratiche religiose di cui Aladino e Ismeno si sono resi colpevoli. Clorinda conclude la sua perorazione riaffermando con decisione il rifiuto dell'adorazione delle immagini, precetto certamente in linea

---

[13] Come ricorda Rosa Giulio, le direttive tridentine erano chiare su questi aspetti: "In particolare, opere con episodi di incantesimi e magie ('divinationem seu superstitionem spectant') venivano condannate sulla base dell'ottava regola dei *Libri proibiti*, mentre la nona proibiva la geomanzia, l'idromanzia, la chiromanzia, la negromanzia e ogni forma di 'sortilegia, veneficia, auguria, auspicia, incantationes artis magicae'" (Giulio 25).

con la sua identità islamica nel contesto dell'azione del poema, ma che alle orecchie dei contemporanei non poteva non risuonare come un'eco della polemica protestante e soprattutto calvinista sullo stesso tema.[14] Ce n'era abbastanza per suscitare l'attenzione e i sospetti dell'Antoniano, che si avviava a diventare un'autorità in questo dibattito. Ne *L'educatione christiana*, difenderà fermamente l'uso "saluberrimo" e "antichissimo" dell'adorazione delle immagini che deve essere considerato come indirizzato non alle icone in sé, ma alle entità che queste rappresentano, "tal che adorando la imagine, et figura di Christo nostro Signore adoriamo Christo istesso, et così parimente veneriamo i santi che regnano con Christo, la similitudine de i quali le imagini loro ci rappresentano" (*L'educatione christiana* II, XXXVIII). L'Antoniano si situa dunque perfettamente in linea con la posizione emersa dal concilio di Trento e efficacemente illustrata nel 1582 da Gabriele Paleotti nel *De sacris et profanis imaginibus*. In seguito, tuttavia, l'Antoniano si dimostrerà più intransigente dello stesso Paleotti. Questi infatti, nel 1596, nel tentativo di contrastare il perdurante abuso di immagini sacre, stese il memoriale *De tollendibus imaginum abusibus*, in cui propugnava la necessità di chiare regole per quanto riguardava l'uso dell'iconografia sacra e la creazione di un "Indice delle immagini" da affiancare a quello per i libri. Nella sua replica, l'Antoniano esprimeva il timore che una pubblica ammissione degli abusi ancora frequenti in campo iconografico potesse alimentare la polemica protestante (Patrizi 120-23). Una conferma degli interessi dell'Antoniano in questo ambito è data dal suo ruolo nel programma decorativo del salone sistino della nuova Biblioteca Vaticana (Patrizi 118-19) nonché, secondo quanto attesta il suo biografo Castiglione, in quello di Santa Maria Maggiore e del Palazzo Laterano (Frajese 72). Anche se queste testimonianze risalgono ad un periodo successivo a quello della revisione, non c'è da stupirsi che l'Antoniano abbia avanzato delle riserve a proposito di un episodio in cui Tasso si avventura pericolosamente nel vivo di una questione tanto spinosa. Il poeta, come si è visto, promette di sacrificare la conclusione dell'episodio ma lascia aperta per il momento la possibilità di preservarne la sostanza.[15]

4. *Poesia, storia, amore*
Dopo queste concessioni, Tasso prende chiaramente posizione in difesa degli incanti più intimamente legati alla fisionomia del poema: impossibile alterare la

---

[14] Così si esprime Clorinda: "Fu de le nostre leggi irriverenza / quell'opra far che persuase il mago: / ché non convien ne' nostri tèmpi a nui / gl'idoli avere, e men gl'idoli altrui. / Dunque suso a Macon recar mi giova / il miracol de l'opra, ed ei la fece / per dimostrar ch'i tèmpi suoi con nova / religion contaminar non lece" (*Gerusalemme liberata* II, 50-51). Per una discussione più approfondita dell'episodio si veda Benedetti.

[15] Più tardi, illustrando a Luca Scalabrino le ragioni che l'avevano indotto ad eliminare l'episodio, Tasso ammetterà esplicitamente che il problema consisteva proprio nel trattamento delle immagini: "Io non vorrei dar occasione a i frati con quella imagine, o con alcune altre cosette che sono in quell'episodio, di proibire il libro" (*Lettere poetiche* 406).

natura del giardino di Armida e gli amori della stessa Armida, di Erminia, di Rinaldo e di Tancredi "senza manifesto mancamento del tutto". Tasso fa appello all'indulgenza dell'Antoniano, cui chiede di considerare la sua condizione cortigiana ("lo stato e la fortuna mia"), l'atmosfera della corte ferrarese ("il costume del paese nel quale io vivo") che l'Antoniano doveva ben conoscere e persino, in una compromettente ammissione, il suo stesso carattere ("quella che sin ora io giudico mia natural inclinazione" *Lettere poetiche* 344-46).

Prende qui il via una circostanziata difesa di quella che, con espressione che a noi moderni suona intimamente contraddittoria, potremmo definire "storicità degli incanti", vale a dire il riscontro di elementi soprannaturali nelle cronache delle crociate di cui Tasso si serviva. È la storia, protesta il poeta, a fornire "alcun seme, che, sparso poi ne' campi della poesia, produce quelli alberi che ad alcuni paion mostruosi" (*Lettere poetiche* 346). La precisazione ("ad alcuni"), spostando di nuovo il possibile difetto dal polo dell'emissione a quello della ricezione, ne limita drasticamente la portata. Come le espressioni segnalate dall'Antoniano potevano risultare offensive non agli orecchi del lettore medio ma solo a quelle dei "pii religiosi", così gli "alcuni" che troveranno non meravigliosi, ma "mostruosi", gli incanti del poema non corrispondono al pubblico cui il poeta vuole indirizzarsi. Più in là nella stessa lettera, infatti, Tasso non esiterà a dichiararsi "cupido molto dell'aura popolare, né contento di scrivere a i pochissimi, quando ancora tra quelli fosse Platone" (*Lettere poetiche* 359). Il poema, insomma, è pensato per un pubblico medio e ampio, certo più desideroso di "varietà e vaghezza di cose" di quanto potessero esserlo i "pii religiosi".

Ad un richiamo all'autorità dell'Antoniano, cui spetta di deliberare la liceità delle variazioni e degli abbellimenti apportati dal poeta al dato storico, fa seguito una sicura professione dei propri diritti di artista:

Questo solo a me pare di poter dire senza arroganza, ch'essendo l'istoria di questa guerra molto piena di miracoli, non conveniva che men mirabile fosse il poema.
(*Lettere poetiche* 348)

All'autorità della storia Tasso fa appello anche per giustificare l'altro elemento del poema che tanto disturbava l'Antoniano, e cioè l'amore. "È scritto" ricorda il poeta, che Tancredi, per quanto valoroso, "fu nondimeno molto incontinente et oltramodo vago degli abbracciamenti delle saracine", così come è scritto che Odoardo partecipò alla Crociata con la moglie, "et insieme vi morirono" (*Lettere poetiche* 348). Il problema, dunque, è lo stesso che si presentava a proposito degli incanti: accertato il "seme" della storia, resta da stabilire la liceità della misura dell'intervento poetico. Qui Tasso è ancora più sicuro nell'affermare le proprie ragioni: "l'accrescere, l'adornare e 'l fingere sono effetti che vengono necessariamente in conseguenza co 'l poetare" (*Lettere poetiche* 350).

Anche in questo caso, un'opera più tarda aiuta a comprendere come la posizione del Tasso e quella dell'Antoniano fossero inconciliabili. Si tratta del *Dialogo della Istoria*, opera incompiuta e tarda di Sperone Speroni, in cui Silvio Antoniano è introdotto come personaggio insieme al filosofo Girolamo Zabarella e all'editore Paolo Manuzio. In opposizione a quest'ultimo, che sostiene che la storia di per sé non sia arte, ma lo diventi solo "quando ella è fatta gramatica, o poesia, o oratoria locutione", l'Antoniano afferma:

> Delle forme della eloquenza, che varie sono in diversi istorici, sopra tutte io quella sola gli lodarei, che ci mostra la verità: non già quell'altra, che suole attendere a farla bella, ponendo mano alle favole per dilettare i lettori.
> (214)

Il fatto che proprio l'Antoniano fosse stato chiamato ad esprimere un parere sul dialogo di Speroni (Patrizi 209) conferisce autorità a questa sua controfigura e aiuta a capire le sue resistenze verso un poema che si proponeva proprio di abbellire la verità "per dilettare i lettori". Il suo atteggiamento intransigente finiva per minare le basi dell'arte tassiana, negando quella "licenza del fingere" (vale a dire, appunto, il diritto del poeta di elaborare il dato storico) che Tasso nei *Discorsi dell'arte poetica* aveva rivendicato come una delle componenti essenziali di un poema epico (14).

Dopo aver difeso con forza le ragioni della poesia, Tasso passa a rispondere ad una obiezione (non si sa se effettiva o solo ipotetica) riguardo il discredito che una tale strategia poetica di "accrescimento" potrebbe gettare sulla liberazione del sepolcro. Tasso sostiene di aver operato in maniera selettiva, concentrandosi non sulle "ingiustizie", "rapine", "frodi" e "tradimenti" operati dai Cristiani, ma su "gli amori e gli sdegni loro (colpe men gravi)", stabilendo una gerarchia del peccato che forse ottimisticamente presume condivisa dall'Antoniano[16] e proponendosi come complice nella divulgazione di una visione edulcorata dell'impresa crociata. Insomma, i lettori familiari con le cronache della Crociata non si stupiranno certo delle "imperfezioni" dei principi cristiani, con l'eccezione di Goffredo, "in tutto buono e pio". Sarebbe stato dunque ingiustificabile, scrive

---

[16] La benevola assoluzione dispensata da Tasso ai Crociati incontinenti difficilmente avrà riscosso l'approvazione di chi, ne *L'educatione*, scriverà: "[...] colui che vedendo alcuna donna si accenderà di concupiscenza, et di desiderio di peccare, già per la sola voluntà, et consenso, ha commesso, et consumato nel cuor suo l'adulterio, et la fornicatione, perilche è da stare in grande timore et custodia del cuore, pregando di continuo Iddio con grande humiltà che ci dia il dono della castità, sì che siamo mondi da ogni bruttezza di carne, et di spirito, et possiamo interamente adempire questo precetto, ilquale talmente prohibisce l'adulterio et ogni libidine, che insieme commanda la osservanza della castità, et pudicitia, laquale necessariamente si richiede non solo in coloro che ne hanno eletto l'alto, et sublime stato virginale, ma ne i vedovi, ne i maritati, et in quelli che hanno eletto di vivere sciolti, et liberi dal giogo matrimoniale, et finalmente è necessaria in ogni età, et in ogni stato, né potrà alcuno che non sia casto, et puro, haver parte con l'agnello purissimo, et immaculato" (II, LXXXV).

Tasso, attribuire ad altri la stessa perfezione morale di Goffredo, non solo perché così facendo sarebbe venuta meno la fedeltà alla storia, ma anche perché "nella poesia è altrettanto necessaria, quanto dilettevole, questa varietà di costumi" (*Lettere poetiche* 352). Forse incautamente, Tasso giustifica la lunga esposizione dei motivi che hanno ispirato la sua caratterizzazione dei principi cristiani sulla base delle presunte limitate conoscenze in materia dell'Antoniano. Conclude infatti il suo ragionamento esprimendo la speranza che "la notizia d'alcuni particolari, i quali peravventura non [...] erano così noti" al suo interlocutore, possa far sembrare la sua causa "assai più onesta, che non parrebbe se si presupponesse che tutti i principi che concorsero all'acquisto fosero in opinione di buoni e di santi" (*Lettere poetiche* 353). Non è difficile immaginare quanto gradita potesse risultare al Poetino tanto la divulgazione delle malefatte crociate quanto l'allusione ai limiti delle sue conoscenze in materia.

5. *Torquato Tasso e Silvio Antoniano: un dialogo impossibile*
Gli amori e gli incanti, insiste Tasso, sono perfettamente ammissibili da un punto di vista tanto politico quanto epico. Bisogna seguire Aristotele per quanto riguarda le leggi essenziali della poesia, non nella descrizione degli "accidenti" che variano secondo le epoche e le latitudini. Il meraviglioso, che nei poemi classici si manifestava attraverso gli dèi, sarà in un poema cristiano effetto delle opere di angeli, diavoli e maghi. Pretendere di adeguarsi in tutto al modello aristotelico sarebbe, scrive Tasso, "superstizione". Difficile, vedere, però, come tali spiegazioni potessero risultare accette al severo pedagogo della Controriforma che ne *L'Educatione*, nel delineare un programma di studi quanto mai restrittivo, tuonerà non solo contro "quei poeti, che à bello studio hanno scritto libri amatorij, et lascivi" (III, XXXVIII), ma anche, in generale, contro la poesia, che "è come un vischio che ritiene, et disvia molte volte da i studij più gravi, et troppo i giovani se ne invaghiscono, et si danno à scrivere amori, et cose vanissime" (III, XXXIX). Già in precedenza, discorrendo in maniera più generale sulla castità, aveva raccomandato:

Ma è ben da ricordare grandemente al nostro padre di famiglia che non permetta in casa sua libri d'amori, et di favole, et comedie, et romanzi, et altre cose tali, onde si trahe piccola utilità, et per il più son cagione di molto male, et sono occulti, et pernitiosi maestri di gravi peccati, et quanto più la dolcezza delle rime, et la varietà de gli avvenimenti che si raccontano, et la vaghezza del dire alletta et invita, tanto è maggiore il nocumento che apportano [...] e non parlo solo di quelli che a bello studio, et scopertamente trattano cose obscene, et impudiche [...] ma intendo anchor di quelli, che velati di apparente honestà, infondono più occultamente, ma non meno pernitiosamente il veneno della lussuria ne i petti giovanili.

(II,XCI)

"Varietà e vaghezza di cose", aveva dichiarato Tasso, sono necessarie in un poema. "Varietà de gli avvenimenti" e "vaghezza del dire", tuona adesso l'Antoniano, sono direttamente proporzionali al "nocumento" cagionato dalla letteratura. Chissà se, mentre scriveva queste righe, l'ex-Poetino ripensava al poema che aveva così aspramente censurato.[17] La giustificazione dell'esordio della *Liberata*, che presentava la poesia come un "soave licor" in grado di inculcare attraverso l'inganno insegnamenti storici e morali ad un pubblico altrimenti recalcitrante, doveva essere sembrata all'Antoniano un ingenuo tentativo di dissimulare un progetto di segno opposto, in cui un vago programma edificante veniva proposto come schermo per torbide storie di pulsioni inconfessabili.

A preoccupazioni di stampo aristotelico sembra rispondere Tasso nell'ultima questione sollevata nella lettera, vale a dire l'eccessiva rilevanza attribuita nel poema a Rinaldo. In questo aspetto, "giudiziosamente" segnalato dal revisore, Tasso teme di essersi "non [...] senza alcun pericolo dilungato dalle vestigie degli antichi" (*Lettere poetiche* 358). Tuttavia, invitando l'Antoniano all'esame del canto quattordicesimo, il poeta annuncia di aver schivato il pericolo unendo "in maniera la necessità di Rinaldo con la superiorità di Goffredo, che non solo l'attione ne resti una, ma uno ancora si possa dire il principio dal quale ella depende. E questo è Goffredo, il quale eletto da Dio per capitano, è fatto necessario all'impresa: e s'egli ha bisogno di Rinaldo, l'ha come il fabro del martello, o come il cuore delle mani" (*Lettere poetiche* 360). Di fatto, pur ammettendo in linea di principio l'obiezione, Tasso si dimostra poco intenzionato a modificare il suo poema.

Dopo questo strategico richiamo all'unità, il commiato riprende i toni ossequiosi iniziali. Tasso si congeda dal suo interlocutore formulando la speranza di averlo dalla sua parte in caso di critiche al poema:

E se pur d'alcuna riprensione io fossi meritevole, spero che Vostra Signoria altrimenti parlerà come avvocato, di quel ch'abbia parlato come consigliero; e che non meno sarà eloquente in difendere il mio errore che sia stata giudiziosa in conoscerlo.

(*Lettere poetiche* 361-62)

Deboli erano in realtà le basi per questa speranza, come dimostrano ampiamente le lettere successive. Il poeta si apprestò di malavoglia a correggere in "saggio" il nome di "mago" inizialmente attribuito al vecchio di Ascalona e a modificare altri particolari che potevano dar noia a "chi vuol esser vescovo o

---

[17] O forse, ed è questa ipotesi persino più sconfortante, non vi pensava affatto. Nessuna opera di Tasso è presente infatti nella sua biblioteca, o almeno nella ricca "libraria de libri stampati" che alla sua morte l'Antoniano lasciò ai "carissimi padri della Congregatione dell'Oratorio" e "nominatamente alla casa di S. Maria in Vallicella di Roma" (Patrizi, *"Del congiungere"* 3). Vi figurano tuttavia altre opere di genere epico e cavalleresco, quali *Dell'Hercole* di Giovambattista Giraldi Cinzio e *L'Italia liberata dai Goti* di Gian Giorgio Trissino (316 e 326).

Le ragioni della poesia: Torquato Tasso e Silvio Antoniano 255

cardinale" (*Lettere poetiche* 392-93). La lista dei cambiamenti annunciati a Scipione Gonzaga fa rabbrividire: già rimossi "il miracolo del sepolcro, la conversione de' cavalieri in pesci, la nave maravigliosa", e "moderata assai la lascivia dell'ultime stanze del vigesimo" (393). In via di rimozione "i miracoli del decimosettimo [...]; le stanze del papagallo, quella dei baci, et alcune dell'altre in questo e ne gli altri canti, che più dispiacciono a monsignor Silvio, oltre moltissimi versi e parole". Tutto questo, nella speranza di evitare "alcun impedimento da Roma" (*Lettere poetiche* 394). Rivolgendosi al Gonzaga, Tasso è ormai ridotto a pregarlo di "contener monsignor Silvio [...] e far ch'egli rimanga sodisfatto" (394-95). Ogni resistenza sembra travolta. Tasso cerca di limitare i danni chiedendo a Luca Scalabrino di non divulgare le obiezioni mosse dall'Antoniano, che evidentemente temeva potessero compromettere la pubblicazione del poema, e di attribuire i ritardi nella stampa alla peste. All'intransigenza dell'Antoniano si aggiungono le macchinazioni che Tasso attribuisce allo Speroni, altrove definito "maligno et ingrato" (*Lettere poetiche* 421). Questi, recentemente accusato di immoralità per i suoi *Dialoghi*, vorrebbe che la stessa sorte si abbattesse sul poema tassiano. "Mala deliberazione fu la mia quand'io mi risolvei a mostragli il poema!" esclama il poeta esasperato. Subito dopo, amarezza e rammarico investono non solo la sua relazione con Speroni, ma l'iniziativa stessa di sottoporre il poema a revisione: "E vorrei esser digiuno di cotesta revisione romana" (*Lettere poetiche* 410).

Se l'Antoniano era rimasto impressionato dall'abilità retorica e dalla profondità di riflessione esibite dal Tasso nella sua lettera, certo non ne fu tuttavia punto persuaso, come si evince chiaramente da una lettera a Luca Scalabrino in data 24 aprile 1576: "Male dimostra monsignor Silvio d'esser rimaso appagato della mia lettera, poiché continua ostinatamente in tutte le sue opinioni", lamenta il poeta, ormai timoroso di "qualche burla" che impedisca la pubblicazione del poema (*Lettere poetiche* 409). Simile scoramento traspare da una lettera del 4 maggio a Scipione Gonzaga. Il "lungo discorso" a Silvio Antoniano (cioè proprio la lettera del 30 marzo 1576) ha avuto come unico risultato quello di far acquisire al mittente la stima di "dotto", ma non quella di persuadere il destinatario. Il religioso romano "mostra di persistere a fatto nelle prime opinioni", che Tasso teme condivise da altri nel suo ambiente. Il poeta valuta la possibilità di far stampare il poema a Venezia e nell'Italia settentrionale "con licenza dell'Inquisitore", ma ne è dissuaso dall'esempio di Carlo Sigonio e Girolamo Muzio, che avevano percorso la stessa strada solo per vedere impedita la circolazione dei loro libri (*Lettere poetiche* 419-20). Ormai Tasso ne è certo: la revisione romana è stata un errore, ma è tardi per rimediare. Non resta che sacrificare la poesia agli scrupoli religiosi e eliminare dai canti quarto e sedicesimo (cioè i canti di Armida) le stanze che l'Antoniano considera "le più lascive, se ben son le più belle" (423). Tasso arriva persino a formulare un ingegnoso rimedio a tanta perdita, e cioè la stampa privata di una versione integrale di quei due canti da far circolare tra una quindicina di persone fidate, rassegnandosi a consegnare al pubblico quegli stessi canti "tutti così tronchi, come comanda la necessità dei tempi" (424). Non c'è dubbio che alla "necessità dei tempi" vada attribuito l'altro cambiamento qui annunciato da Tasso e fortunatamente mai messo in atto, e cioè la conversione di Erminia in "religiosa monaca".

6. La stagione del dubbio

La sfortunata stagione della revisione romana volgeva al termine. Il poeta appare ormai esasperato ("Quale sventura è la mia, che ciascuno mi voglia fare il tiranno addosso?" 429) e prostrato ("omai sono stanco e vorrei lasciar questa pratica di scrivere per ogni ordinario così lunghe lettere" 443). Irrimediabilmente compromessi i rapporti con lo Speroni, Tasso accoglieva con sollievo la partenza dell'Antoniano per la Germania (*Lettere* I, 173), che lo esonerava dall'obbligo di continuare un dialogo ormai frustrante.

Per una deleteria coincidenza, la revisione romana si era svolta in un periodo in cui la questione del rapporto tra autorità ecclesiastica e industria culturale era diventata ineludibile. Come segnala Ugo Rozzo, all'Indice universale di Paolo IV del 1559 (che già includeva Boccaccio, Aretino, Machiavelli, Della Casa, la *Monarchia* di Dante e sonetti e lettere antiavignonesi del Petrarca) si erano aggiunti altri elenchi tra cui quello del 1574, stilato dal Maestro del Sacro Palazzo Paolo Costabili, dove per la prima volta compaiono molte altre opere come i *Dialoghi* di Sperone Speroni e le *Rime* di Pietro Bembo (Rozzo 53-54). L'impressione che la provincia del censurabile si stesse allargando a vista d'occhio e rischiasse di inghiottire l'intera letteratura italiana non può essere imputata solo alla sensibilità esasperata del Tasso. Le condanne emanate da Roma, anche al di fuori dall'Indice, venivano in alcuni casi raccolte dalle singole diocesi che compilavano le loro proprie liste:[18] quella della zelantissima Parma, stampata nel 1580, includeva ben 544 voci, compreso *Il cortegiano* di Baldassar Castiglione (Rozzo 57). Poco rassicurante, poi, era la palese arbitrarietà di alcune condanne e il relativo sospetto che la sopravvivenza o meno di un'opera potesse dipendere dal momentaneo capriccio del censore (Rozzo 59).[19] Si aggiungano a queste considerazioni i danni che l'inclusione in un elenco, sia pur locale e

---

[18] Per l'importanza delle diocesi locali nell'esecuzione delle direttive romane si veda Fragnito, *"In questo vasto mare"* 4.

[19] Per Fragnito "[…] the censorial apparatus was not the well-oiled machinery that has often been depicted; rather, it frequently jammed, and changes of mind, reversals and dithering gave it a markedly erratic course. The plurality and conflicts of the bodies responsible for censorship, turnover in the Church executive and on the papal throne, and political pressures: these and other factors […] combined to determine the decisions taken by the coercive apparatus and to influence the directives issued by Rome — the contradictions, confusion and vagueness of which caused more damage than the Roman offices envisaged" ("Introduction" 4).

manoscritto, poteva arrecare alla reputazione di uno scrittore e alla circolazione delle altre sue opere, nonché la sorte incerta dei volumi ritirati dal mercato in attesa che ne venissero approntate delle edizioni espurgate.[20] Il mercato librario reagì ripiegando sulla letteratura religiosa. Gli studi di Paul Grendler documentano l'inversione di tendenza nell'editoria veneziana della seconda metà del Cinquecento, con una prevalenza sempre più spiccata di testi devozionali (Grendler 131-34). In particolare, la concessione di *imprimatur* relativa a nuove opere di carattere profano tocca il suo minimo storico proprio nel periodo della revisione della *Liberata*. Per un poeta che cercava di orientarsi nella selva di divieti veri o presunti, angosciato dal "benedetto romore della proibizione d'infiniti poeti" (*Lettere poetiche* 43), l'approvazione preventiva di Silvio Antoniano avrebbe potuto servire da lasciapassare e garanzia. L'evoluzione del rapporto tra i due finì però col mettere il poeta di fronte ad alternative opposte ma ugualmente impraticabili: o distruggere quanto di più sentito e vitale animava il poema, sterilizzandolo in modo da renderlo lettura idonea a "religiosi" e "monache", come esigeva l'Antoniano (427); oppure tirare dritto per la propria strada, col rischio di veder condannata la propria opera. La situazione si aggrava col manifestarsi dei primi segni di quella irrequietezza che condurrà alla terribile crisi del 1579 e alla reclusione in Sant'Anna, con la conseguente perdita di controllo sulle sorti del poema, pubblicato a partire dal 1580 sulla base dei vari manoscritti che il Tasso aveva avventatamente fatto circolare.[21] Mentre la *Gerusalemme liberata* si affermava come uno dei capolavori della letteratura occidentale, il suo autore languiva in una cella. Per il resto della sua vita avrebbe perseguito il sogno di dare al suo poema una forma corrispondente alle proprie intenzioni, giungendo finalmente, "già invecchiato, e vicino alla morte", a riconoscere nella *Gerusalemme conquistata* "l'idea della celeste Gerusalemme" (*Giudizio* 451). Nel poema riformato, Tasso fa suoi molti dei consigli dei revisori, formando un'opera che sarà stata magari ben accetta da "religiosi" e "monache", ma poco gradita ai più, e destinata a rimanere nel corso dei secoli una curiosità erudita.[22]

---

[20] "Stored in the inquisitorial archives while awaiting expurgation [...] many popular literary works disappeared until well into the eighteenth century" (Fragnito, "Introduction" 9).

[21] Enormi pertanto, e forse insolubili, sono i problemi relativi al testo della *Gerusalemme liberata*, di cui continua a mancare un'edizione critica. Fondamentali in questo campo gli studi di Luigi Poma (di cui si veda almeno *Studi sul testo*) e dei suoi allievi.

[22] La *Gerusalemme conquistata* fu ripubblicata tre volte durante la vita del poeta e sette volte nel diciassettesimo secolo. In seguito, sarebbe apparsa solo nell'ambito dell'edizione delle opere complete del Tasso, due volte nel '700, quattro nell'800 e solo una nel '900, per un totale di diciassette edizioni (si veda Oldcorn 25-46), in contrasto alle 508 accumulate dalla *Liberata* fino alla fine dell'800, secondo la stima di Quondam (590). In

Era il trionfo di Silvio Antoniano.[23]

Georgetown University

Opere citate

Antoniano, Silvio. *Tre libri dell'educatione christiana dei figliuoli*. In Patrizi. *Silvio Antoniano*.

Benedetti, Laura. La *"vis abdita" della* Liberata *e i suoi esiti nella* Conquistata." "Lingua e stile" 2 (1995): 465-78.

Fragnito, Gigliola. *"In questo vasto mare de libri prohibiti et sospesi tra tanti scogli di varietà et controversie": la censura ecclesiastica tra la fine del Cinquecento e i primi del Seicento*. A cura di Cristina Stango. *Censura ecclesiastica e cultura politica in Italia tra Cinquecento e Seicento. VI Giornata Luigi Firpo. Atti del convegno 5 marzo 1999*. Firenze: Olschki, 2001. 1-35.

―――. *Introduction*. Gigliola Fragnito (a c. di). *Church, Censorship and Culture in Early Modern Italy*, trad. Adrian Belton. Cambridge: Cambridge UP, 2001.

Frajese, Vittorio. *Il popolo fanciullo. Torquato Tasso e il sistema disciplinare della Controriforma*. Milano: Franco Angeli, 1987.

Giulio, Rosa. *Tempo dell'inquisizione tempo dell'ascesi. Spiritualità religiosa e forme letterarie dal Tasso al Settecento*. Salerno: Edisud, 2004.

Grendler, Paul F. *The Roman Inquisition and the Venetian Press, 1540-1605*. Princeton: Princeton UP, 1977.

Molinari, Carla. *Introduzione*. Torquato Tasso. *Lettere poetiche*. IX-XLIV.

Oldcorn, Anthony. *The Textual Problems of Tasso's "Gerusalemme Conquistata"*. Ravenna: Longo, 1976.

Patrizi, Elisabetta. *"Del congiungere le gemme de' gentili con la sapientia de'christiani." La biblioteca del card. Silvio Antoniano tra studia humanitatis e cultura ecclesiastica*. Firenze: Olschki, 2011.

―――. *Silvio Antoniano. Un umanista ed educatore nell'età del Rinnovamento cattolico (1540-1603)*. Vol. 1. *Vita e opere*. Vol. 2. *Documenti e lettere*. Vol. 3. *Edizione commentata*. A cura di Elisabetta Patrizi. Macerata: Edizioni Università di Macerata, 2010.

Poma, Luigi. *Studi sul testo della "Gerusalemme liberata"*. Bologna: Clueb, 2005.

Quondam, Amedeo. *"Sta notte mi sono svegliato con questo verso in bocca." Tasso, Controriforma e classicismo*. In *Torquato Tasso e la cultura estense* 2: 535-95.

Ricci, Roberta. *Scrittura, riscrittura, autoesegesi: voci autoriali intorno all'epica in volgare. Boccaccio, Tasso*. Pisa: ETS, 2010.

Rozzo, Ugo. *La letteratura italiana negli "Indici" del Cinquecento*. Udine: Forum, 2005.

Solerti, Angelo. *Vita di Torquato Tasso*. 2 voll. Torino: Loescher, 1895.

Speroni, Sperone. *Opere*. Venezia: Domenico Occhi, 1740.

Tasso, Torquato. *Rinaldo*. A c. di Matteo Navone. Alessandria: Edizioni dell'Orso, 2012.

---

tempi recenti va segnalata l'edizione critica di Claudio Gigante, basata sull'autografo mutilo del poema.

[23] Ringrazio Alberto Manai per la sua attenta lettura e i suoi commenti ad una prima versione di questo saggio.

———. *Gerusalemme conquistata. Ms. vind. lat. 72 della biblioteca nazionale di Napoli.* A c. di Claudio Gigante. Alessandria: Edizioni dell'Orso, 2010.
———. *Lettere poetiche.* A c. di Carla Molinari. Parma: Guanda, 1995.
———. *Gerusalemme Liberata.* A c. di Fredi Chiappelli. Milano: Rusconi, 1982.
———. *Discorsi dell'arte poetica e del poema eroico.* A c. di Luigi Poma. Bari: Laterza, 1964.
———. *Giudizio sopra la sua Gerusalemme da lui medesimo riformata.* A c. di Cesare Guasti. *Prose diverse.* Vol. I. Firenze: Le Monnier, 1875. 442-547.
———. *Lettere.* A c. di Cesare Guasti. 5 voll. Firenze: Le Monnier, 1852-55.
Torquato Tasso e la cultura estense. 3 voll. A c. di Gianni Venturi. Atti del Convegno Internazionale (Ferrara, 10-13 dicembre 1995. Biblioteca dell'"Archivum Romanicum". Ser. 1, Storia Letteratura Paleografia, vol. 280. Firenze: Olschki, 1999.

Francesco Sberlati

"Il buon poeta è il più bugiardo": adulazione e falsità nella letteratura barocca

Sinossi: Il saggio analizza il rapporto tra potere politico e produzione letteraria nel XVII secolo, e altresì la figura del letterato cortigiano, desideroso di affermarsi attraverso la composizione di opere encomiastiche, ossia destinate a celebrare e compiacere il detentore del potere. Si tratta di opere concepite all'interno di un preciso programma ideologico, il quale si serve anche della storiografia per sviluppare temi di carattere politico e sociale. In tale contesto, una particolare attenzione è dedicata alla trattatistica retorica e comportamentale, la cui conoscenza è indispensabile al letterato di corte. Questo studio dimostra la profonda unità che lega la letteratura alla vita civile nell'età dell'assolutismo.
Parole chiave: Barocco, letteratura encomiastica, retorica, politica, trattatistica cortigiana

1. *"Lo sfrenato amor di dir il vero"*

La trattatistica teorica del Seicento si è impegnata a dare ordinata sistemazione alle modalità con cui la letteratura deve rivolgersi al potere. Non ha inventato nulla, giacché essa si limita a riformulare pratiche già largamente diffuse tra Rinascimento e Controriforma, ma solo nella prima metà del XVII secolo gli intellettuali appaiono esperti nell'elaborare una strategia elocutiva inquadrata in un contesto di oratoria politica. Il letterato dunque interviene attivamente e in modo preciso nel dibattito circa il dominio della parola, con la chiara consapevolezza che il linguaggio della letteratura possa contribuire, attraverso la molteplicità dei generi in poesia e in prosa, a quel disciplinamento delle coscienze che costituisce una delle istanze essenziali della civiltà barocca.

Non sorprende perciò di ritrovare nei testi seicenteschi un ricco campionario di discorsi politici, i quali finiscono col funzionare come un modello di comunicazione nei confronti dei detentori del potere, siano essi i rappresentanti dell'assolutismo o gli "ottimati" delle istituzioni repubblicane. La sostanziale identità dei registri espressivi, nonostante le inevitabili contrapposizioni apologetiche o encomiastiche, consente di intravedere una certa uniformità dal punto di vista stilistico e topico: del resto la letteratura dell'età barocca si dimostra bene informata sulle vicende e le dinamiche politiche, sulle quali si riflette sempre ricorrendo al confronto o "paragone" con gli antichi. Tutto ciò impone, da parte del letterato, e specialmente del letterato cortigiano, ovvero quello stipendiato da un signore e impiegato presso uno dei tanti centri cortigiani dell'Italia di Antico Regime, un sistema di severo controllo sulla nozione di *veritas*, rifuggendo non solo da avventate dichiarazioni di onestà intellettuale, ma anche attenendosi alle aspettattive, spesso velleitarie, del mecenate.

Per meglio intendere la complessità del rapporto tra politica e letteratura è necessario non dimenticare che lo scopo dell'autore è ottenere il consenso (e il compenso) attraverso gli *elogia*: così la letteratura, al pari della storiografia, si fa strumento di elaborazione di una oratoria di consumo, talvolta prodotta anche per usi contingenti, fino a divenire il principale alimento della legittimazione ideologica o dell'istanza celebratoria. La concatenazione argomentativa dei *topoi*, nel grande laboratorio della letteratura barocca, in perenne attività dal punto di vista della discussione sulla liceità del potere, è pressoché obbligata, giacché dipende dall'opportunità di sostenere il principe — o il pontefice — nella *routine* quotidiana dello scontro tra fazioni.

Ben lo sa un genio della politica seicentesca come il marchese Virgilio Malvezzi, il quale si diffonde in continue meditazioni sulle forme con cui si esalta il potere, come se aspirasse a codificare, dentro la cornice teorica del tacitismo, un nuovo genere di oratoria politica, forgiata però nell'officina dello storico piuttosto che del retore. Così nelle pagine iniziali del suo *Romulo*, un romanzo storico la cui prima edizione è del 1626, Malvezzi avverte il lettore che "i fatti de' principi hanno ogn'altra faccia che la vera"; anch'essi infatti come "tutti gl'uomini fanno errori", ma pochi tra i principi "doppo avergli fatti gli vogliono udire": pertanto, aggiunge con disincantato realismo, "o bisogna adulargli, o tacere". Malvezzi è perfettamente consapevole che il potere ha bisogno degli intellettuali, e in particolare dei letterati, quali dispensatori di legittimazione e di prestigio, in veste insomma di propagandisti e panegiristi. Orbene, osserva Malvezzi, il colloquio tra potere e letteratura non sempre è disteso, e anzi spesso risulta improntato a un'accurata selezione strumentale delle *veritates* storico-politiche, per evitare il rischio di trapassare dall'epico al satirico: "Hanno anche gl'adulatori per così fatto modo aggrandite le azioni buone, che il dirle puramente è interpretato a biasimo, perché la verità della lode che si sente è diminuzione di quella che si crede".

Fondamento, e limite, del colloquio con il potere è dunque un pragmatico senso di soggezione di fronte al desiderio di "gloria" di colui che governa i sudditi: "[...] dedicare i sudori alla sola gloria è diabolico", ammonisce Malvezzi senza peraltro deplorare la puerile ostinazione di assicurarsi fama imperitura: "[...] aver solo pensiere all'utilità dei posteri è concetto o sovrumano o stolido" (*Romulo* 75). È inevitabile che alla letteratura barocca sia connaturata una forte dose di cortigianeria, ma nella prospettiva delineata da Malvezzi si scorge l'orgogliosa consapevolezza con cui la figura dell'intellettuale funzionario di corte esercita il proprio ruolo (Aricò 2007). Al di sotto di lui, nel corpo sociale, nessuno sa come rivolgersi al principe e come corrispondergli gradualmente la verità che questi vuole sentirsi dire. All'assolvimento di queste mansioni sono infatti rivolte in modo più diretto altre opere dello stesso Malvezzi, tra le quali i giovanili *Discorsi sopra Cornelio Tacito* (1622) occupano un posto di primissimo piano. Le potenzialità di sviluppo della letteratura nell'età della Controriforma si creano insomma con il favore della corte, e dunque con il sostegno e la mobilitazione di risorse non soltanto intellettuali, bensì anche e soprattutto politiche.

Certo il tiranno assoluto del Seicento è lontanissimo dall'ideale platonico del monarca filosofo. E anche quando tra potere e cultura s'instaura una convivenza (e convenienza) che dovrebbe alimentarsi di reciproca fiducia, le ragioni dello Stato, nel senso che il Botero dava al costrutto, non permettono che la letteratura resti soggetta alla verità. Per schivare il rischio di una eccessiva allusività, il potere richiede che le sue qualità siano presentate, e trasmesse ai secoli successivi, secondo un modello obbligato: ovvero un modello che impone di rispettare il marchio aulicamente sostenuto del *purpuratus*, "sempre intrepido, sempre magnanimo" (*Tarquinio superbo* 128), come auspica il Malvezzi nella dedica del suo secondo romanzo storico, *Tarquinio superbo* (1632).

Vi è qualcosa di paradossale in questa fiorentissima trattatistica storico-politica. La capacità di intuire le esigenze del potere resta talora offuscata dalla "nebbia della menzogna", poiché il sempre più perfezionato bagaglio di argomentazioni encomiastiche, fa notare Torquato Accetto nella *Dissimulazione onesta* (1641), "spesse volte" confligge con lo "sfrenato amor di dir il vero" (12-13). La letteratura insomma si inquadra in una tipologia retorica adatta, beninteso, a imbastire discorsi ambigui, poiché appunto "in questa vita non sempre si ha da esser di cuor trasparente" (Accetto 72). Passo illuminante, in quanto aiuta a comprendere la varietà di usi cui è suscettibile il vero, più o meno arbitrariamente considerato come la presunta autenticità di colui che compone il testo. Il prudente Accetto d'altronde sapeva quale terreno minato fosse la verità in letteratura, e perciò si impegnava a descrivere il penoso gravare della dissimulazione sull'attività intellettuale. Il cerimoniale delle lodi rientra del resto nelle incombenze del letterato, al fine sottinteso di controbilanciare la cruda realtà con l'esercizio dell'affabulazione, esaltando quando opportuno anche la stirpe del principe.

La riflessione sul "lume della verità" contenuta nella *Dissimulazione onesta* acquista pertanto sostanza politica e morale, giacché "il vero non si scompagna dal bene", sebbene Accetto si ingegni altresì a dimostrare che la verità "è variabile" o addirittura "multiplicata", si noti, "potendo questa passar dal vero nel falso, secondo il corso dell'opinioni". Il concetto di verità multipla sembra presupporre, in negativo come in positivo, la incessante mutevolezza dell'intelletto umano, distinto dal "divino intelletto", il quale invece è "immutabile". Né poi lo stesso Accetto, per quanto retoricamente dotato, appare in grado di rinunciare alla dimensione epidittica dell'argomentare, finendo con l'asserire che "la vera bellezza è nella verità stessa" (Accetto 14-16).

Impalcatura fondamentale di questo sistema è, come si è detto, la corte (Betti 280-90). La vita letteraria, naturalmente, non è chiusa nella corte, né la letteratura barocca coincide con un catalogo di ampollosi panegirici. Eppure anche quando si volge lo sguardo alla letteratura non illustre, la corte costituisce una categoria fondamentale del discorso. Il letterato cortigiano non può ovviamente non compiacersi dell'indubbio prestigio che gli deriva dall'essere parte di una *élite* da cui dipendono le sorti della collettività. In questo contesto non manca di esprimere le sue competenze un altro operoso trattatista, Matteo Peregrini, a lungo impiegato presso la cerchia del cardinale Antonio Barberini. Peregrini è un ecclesiastico, e sulla base della sua fede ragionata, fornisce all'aspirante letterato di corte un prontuario di precetti valido sia nell'ambito secolare sia nel controverso mondo della religiosità cattolica. Suggestione larga e durevole hanno nel corso del XVII secolo i suoi manuali di comportamento, il *Savio in corte* del 1625, e il più ambizioso *Difesa del savio in corte*, pubblicato nel 1636. Sotto la garanzia delle certezze neoaristoteliche, i fili dialettici dell'argomentazione sono riannodati in una sequenza ininterrotta di istanze con tutti i crismi dell'ufficialità. In fondo il letterato, dichiara il gesuita Daniello Bartoli nell'*Uomo di lettere difeso ed emendato* (1645), altro non è che "uno spettatore in un teatro di sempre nuove e tutte nobili maraviglie", al quale "l'uso delle lettere" ha "raffinata la mente e purgato il discorso" (326).

2. Il cuore nascosto

Mascherare idee e sentimenti è nel Seicento una forma elementare di autoprotezione. Lo riconosce persino l'appartato Fulgenzio Micanzio, allievo e biografo di Paolo Sarpi, anch'egli frate servita, attento osservatore dei *mores* della sua età e studioso degli ordinamenti pubblici: "Non è possibile conversar se non in mascara; chi palesasse realmente tutto che passa per mente, oh Dio! Ma ciascuno ha mascare infinite, le cava e mette, secondo con chi tratta, e muta ad ogni momento; se ragioniamo in dui, e viene un terzo, è necessario mutare. Ora, l'imprudente erra mettendo la mascara che non conviene con colui che tratta" (844).[1] L'idea che l'intera vita sociale debba svolgersi sotto il segno del travestimento si fa insistente proprio là dove essa assume il significato di una grande rappresentazione collettiva: "Chi nasce nella gran scena del mondo dovrebbe sapersi vestire di molti abiti, per potere in questa comedia rappresentare diversi personaggi" (241), osserva il Malvezzi nel *Davide perseguitato* del 1634. È vero d'altra parte che una tale impostazione mentale, avente il suo fulcro in un'esperienza retorico-letteraria, appare condizionata dalla simbiosi strettissima con il potere politico, simbiosi entro cui l'intellettuale si configura come un professionista postosi al servizio della comunità, la cui sopravvivenza dipende dallo zelo del principe. La crescente intimità e il condizionamento reciproco fra l'apparato politico-amministrativo e l'attività culturale favorisce così nell'Italia del XVII secolo — al tempo, non lo si dimentichi, colonia spagnola — lo sviluppo di istituti retorici e comportamentali da cui dipende la fortuna e il successo delle carriere. Quei medesimi trattatisti che tendono a unificare tutte le regole della condotta personale nella vita sociale, hanno assicurato la loro obbedienza ai detentori del potere, primo fra tutti il bolognese Malvezzi, asceso alla prestigiosissima carica di storiografo ufficiale (e diplomatico) di Filippo IV, e parimenti Tesauro e Accetto.

Nel ventunesimo capitolo della *Dissimulazione onesta* si percepisce, sotto la

---

[1] Per un profilo del Micanzio, vedere Guaragnella 2009: 141-75.

parvenza di una costruzione logica rigorosa, la malcelata diffidenza dell'autore per la sincerità (D'Ascenzi 471-76; Landolfi 9-19). I meccanismi argomentativi di Accetto si perfezionano proprio là dove riescono a codificare un atteggiamento ispirato al criterio della prudenza, la quale appare press'a poco una necessità nelle quotidiane vicende, e sempre più connessa alla virtù della discrezione. Meglio attenersi a un contegno artefatto piuttosto che acconsentire alla spontaneità, secondo un'impostazione rigoristica in qualche misura disposta a raccogliere l'eredità cinquecentesca della *sprezzatura*, ma ora — nell'età controriformistica — non scompagnata da una più precisa nozione di autodisciplina. Lecitamente dunque, in linea di principio, "può ogni uomo, ancorch'esposto alla vista di tutti, nasconder i suoi affari nella vasta ed insieme segreta casa del suo cuore" (Accetto 63-64).

È fondato pensare che Accetto si rendesse esattamente conto della portata di certi postulati sul piano comportamentale. A ribaltare gli iniziali rapporti di fiducia tra gli uomini del Seicento interviene nella *Dissimulazione onesta* la cospicua rilevanza assegnata alla "prudenza", che nelle proposizioni di Accetto si traduce essenzialmente in "diligenza del nascondere", dove il compiacimento per il "celarsi" interviene a completare una complessa pedagogia dell'apparire. Il ritornare degli stessi temi nel corso dell'intero secolo impone di inquadrare in questa prospettiva quel tipo di trattatistica che propone al "giudizioso lettore" gli strumenti con cui interpretare il denso paradigma della civiltà barocca. In forme variamente conceipte e articolate, la correlazione tra "prudenza" e "verità" costituisce un nucleo centrale anche nel più importante trattato retorico del secondo Seicento, il *Cannocchiale aristotelico* del conte torinese Emanuele Tesauro.[2] Sebbene lasci in secondo piano alcune delle matrici etico-culturali cui si ispira Accetto, è significativo che lo stesso Tesauro contribuisca alla riflessione su un argomento che ai contemporanei, stante il clima di inquietudine intellettuale, appariva decisamente preponderante: "Non piccola differenza", precisa il Tesauro, "passa fra la prudenza e l'ingegno. Però che l'ingegno è più perspicace, la prudenza è più sensata: quello è più veloce, questa è più salda; quello considera le apparenze, questa la verità" (Tesauro 32).

Un'immagine complessa della "verità", dunque, una sorta di compendio che documenta un ripensamento relativo al significato tutt'altro che univoco del "vero". Già l'energico Accetto aveva cercato di stabilire un ordine in questo accumulo di precetti, spesso effimeri, certo in una nuova prospettiva di cultura psicologica. Proprio su questo terreno l'antico segretario dei duchi Carafa sembra formulare la sua arguta teoria "della dissimulazione" a beneficio di coloro che, "amando come sempre la verità", cercano nondimeno di fuggire "il danno" o il "pericolo" derivante dal "dir il vero" (Accetto 12-13). Rispetto alla letteratura cinquecentesca c'è una variante importante: nel microcosmo delle piccole corti signorili italiane, fortemente condizionate dall'antagonismo tra le monarchie di Francia e Spagna, a partire dalla fine del Concilio di Trento

---

[2] Per una complessiva analisi critica dell'opera vedere Benassi 9-55; Bisi 57-87.

assume notevole incidenza la figura del letterato politicamente impegnato, ossia disposto a intraprendere una rischiosa carriera in cui la principale rimunerazione deriva dal servizio prestato entro la sfera di azione diplomatica e giurisdizionale (si pensi solo a personaggi come Fulvio Testi e Traiano Boccalini). È una svolta decisiva, che provoca un radicale cambiamento dello statuto sociale del letterato, fino a esasperare il contrasto con la figura del letterato-segretario tipica del XVI secolo.

Domina questa svolta la forte asseverazione con cui Accetto ribadisce l'impronta di decoro che egli assegna al "dissimulare", divenuto un'esigenza obbligata per ogni aspirante alla carriera cortigiana: "La dissimulazione è una industria di non far vedere le cose come sono. Si simula quello che non è, si dissimula quello che è" (Accetto 31). Il più incisivo elemento di novità introdotto dalla *Dissimulazione onesta* consiste nel fatto che Accetto si provi a impostare un piano di collaborazione tra l'uomo di cultura e le istituzioni entro una precisa distinzione di ruoli (Arnaudo 488-95). A conferma si può addurre che egli non si sottrae al confronto con la natura spesso crudele del potere, il quale talora fagocita proprio coloro che ne hanno assicurato il consolidamento: "Orrendi mostri son que' potenti, che divorano la sostanza di chi lor soggiace". La necessità del dissimulare alla "presenza de' tiranni" (Accetto 59) costituisce in effetti la trama di fondo del libello di Accetto, il quale si propone invero di istruire il lettore a valutare attentamente, in un'età tempestosa come il secolo XVII, la fisionomia della piramide sociale, con i suoi vistosi sussulti politico-dinastici e i suoi umbratili e instabili centri di potere: "Gran tormento è di chi ha valore, il veder il favor della fortuna in alcuni del tutto ignoranti; che senz'altra occupazione, che di attender a star disoccupati, e senza saper che cosa è la terra che han sotto i piedi, son talora padroni di non picciola parte di quella" (Accetto 57).

Non v'è dubbio che nell'algida testimonianza di Accetto si trovi una conferma di quella prontezza d'ingegno variamente modulata nel sodalizio cortigiano, fors'anche memore dei guai in cui si vanno a cacciare coloro i quali ingenuamente venerano la sincerità, poiché "in questa vita non sempre si ha da esser di cuor trasparente" (Accetto 72). È una impostazione utilitaria e forse opportunistica, che però si riscatta attraverso il rafforzamento delle attività ostentatamente retoriche, come pure asserisce il marchese (e cardinale dal 1659) Sforza Pallavicino nel suo *Trattato dello stile e del dialogo* (1662), consapevole anch'egli che "hanno cercato gli uomini di acquistarsi l'applauso con la falsità colorita di vero". Ebbene, "ove la falsità è ben coperta dalla sembianza del vero", prosegue Pallavicino nella sua pragmatica capacità di formulare utili insegnamenti, essa genera "nuova ammirazione". Anzi, "generalmente ogni professor" di siffatta "severa dottrina" che sia capace di allegare titoli di legittimazione alla sua "maniera di concettare", "tanto è più lodevole quanto più inganna", al punto che egli "divien maestro di verità" (Pallavicino 201-02).[3] Si comprende in tal modo la feroce polemica di Paolo Sarpi contro "le furberie dei

---

[3] Vedere Bellini 70-101.

gesuiti": in una lettera a Jacques Leschassier del settembre 1610, questi si dice scandalizzato per "il loro insegnamento", secondo cui "è lecito servirsi senza commettere peccato dell'ambiguità delle parole". Le conseguenze di questi "molti equivoci" sono a parere di Sarpi devastanti: è "dottrina questa che distrugge ogni relazione umana", mentre "l'arte di ingannare", propugnata dai gesuiti "per poter essere sicuri delle loro insidie", senza dubbio alcuno si rivela "la più perniciosa nei riguardi delle virtù" (Sarpi 267-78).[4]

3. *"Il linguaggio della corte è falso"*
In questa dimensione di raccoglimento disciplinare, il geloso mantenimento dei "segreti" appare la strategia più adatta a salvare la continuità della vita politica e intellettuale. E non sarà superfluo chiosare che anche la ragion di Stato, come insegna il Malvezzi nei *Discorsi sopra Cornelio Tacito*, impone che si mantengano dei segreti, riconoscimento concreto del delicato quadro al cui interno l'intellettuale di corte desidera palesare le proprie doti: "Hanno tutti gli Stati, o sieno republiche o sieno principati, alcuni fondamenti, o segreti vogliamo dire, per mezzo de' quali governandosi e si conservano e si augumentano, e perciò procurano sempre tenergli in maniera celati che solo sieno noti a' successori". Qui entra in gioco appunto il letterato che con il principe aspira a collaborare, il cui prestigio va di pari passo con le virtù della discrezione e della prudenza, in un'atmosfera di febbrile tensione segnata dalla rilevanza della sua affidabilità come servitore dei maggiorenti. Si spiega così il motivo per cui Malvezzi dedichi una parte consistente della sua teoria politica ai comportamenti cui devono attenersi coloro i quali ricoprono funzioni di consigliere e le cui funzioni fanno capo direttamente alla persona del principe o del sovrano: "Bisognerà dunque che i principi stiano avvertiti nel conferire i segreti, accioché non gli fidino a taluno che poi spontaneamente gli racconti, ed i ministri a' quali vengono conferiti dovranno stare vigilanti di non lasciarsi cavare da bocca i segreti con artificio", poiché "è facil cosa cavare il segreto di bocca ad uno, interrogandolo non con parole dubbiose ma affirmative, col mostrare di sapere quel che si vorria intendere". S'addensano nelle pagine del giovane Malvezzi le preoccupazioni per quella immaturità o inconsistenza culturale di certi vanitosi cortigiani facili alle lusinghe, perché come insegna la storia "molte volte gli uomini trascorrono a discoprire i segreti dell'animo loro", di fatto esponendo le istituzioni a rischiosi inconvenienti.

Insomma, nel commentare i costumi di corte, Malvezzi riserba singolare attenzione ai "segreti del cuore", i quali vanno accuratamente occultati entro quella specie di cenacolo, basato sulla comunanza di interessi e di *negotia*, costituito dalla corte: "[...] molte volte gli uomini da se medesimi e contro sua volontà scoprono i segreti con la voce, co' movimenti non usati o composti col motivo degli occhi, ne' quali appariscono i segreti del cuore, e finalmente con altri atti esteriori". È l'ideale di una dissimulazione costante e perpetua, che

---
[4] Sulle idee di Sarpi vedere Guaragnella 2009: 125-40; Guaragnella 2011; Vianello; Wottom.

corrisponde a una profonda fede nel valore politico della letteratura, il cui magistero fermamente ammonisce l'uomo di cultura a tenersi immune dai vizi dell'autocompiacimento e dell'ambizione insolente, e anzi lo sollecita ad accentuare la circospezione cui deve ispirarsi il suo comportamento in società. In caso contrario egli diverrà facile preda degli insidiosi avversari, pronti a mobilitarsi per sottrargli ruolo e dignità. La nervosa connotazione di Malvezzi non lascia adito a dubbi quando suggerisce al cortigiano di operare "con arte rettorica, per mezo della quale, movendo gli affetti ed eccitando l'umor peccante di colui i segreti del quale vorremo sapere, egli si lascierà trasportare senz'avvedersene ad aprire quanto rinchiude nel seno". Del pari in questo stesso ambiente, dominato dalla costante presenza di un deliberato mimetismo per il quale verità e menzogna si confondono reciprocamente, un singolare rilievo assume la strategia della disinformazione, con radicale scambio tra vero e falso, utile a depistare le ansiose curiosità di chi — misero credulo — anela a carpire o disvelare occulte trame: "[...] quando si volesse occultare qualche aviso, non è meglio che immediatamente por fuori una voce contraria alla verità" (Malvezzi *Discorsi* 302-08).

Quel che della dissimulazione più doveva interessare i letterati seicenteschi erano, comprensibilmente, gli aspetti applicativi entro l'orizzonte sociale della corte. È d'altronde attendibile il ritratto che di quella controversa realtà ci fornisce il gesuita Francesco Fulvio Frugoni nel sedicesimo dei suoi *Ritratti critici* (1669), una realtà nella quale tutte le manifestazioni dell'invidia e della maldicenza concorrono a consolidare le strutture gerarchiche, assicurando al dominatore un tranquillo appannaggio di consorterie clientelari:

Il linguaggio della corte è falso [...] et ha tutto il suo dialetto dalla simulazione. L'inganno lusinghiero, l'intrigo coperto, la frode palliata sono i caratterissimi di un cortigiano parlante con due cuori e con cento lingue. Apparisce ridente in faccia, irridente nell'intimo; sereno la fronte, e procelloso il pensiero. Ti fa un complimento di promesse abbondante, ma se ad uopo lo stringi ti diguizza di mano scarsi effetti. Tal è la natura della cerimonia cortigianesca, e ben dinotata dallo stesso termine *complimento*, che non vuol dir altro che *complo* e *mento*. [...] Tutti giuocano ad ingannarsi con iscambievole delusione. Il principe inganna perché si burla di ognuno, come quello che da niuno dipende, ma i cortigiani ingannano il principe [...] quando l'adulano [...]. Per questo non v'ha nella corte [...] una scintilla di compassione [...], non v'ha perciò amicizia in corte che vera sia, perché non fe' questa mai lega coll'interesse.

(Frugoni 3.132-33)

Non deve perciò stupire che ancora nella seconda metà del Seicento il caustico Frugoni si dimostri indignato per i comportamenti prevalenti nella corte, perlopiù ispirati alla menzogna e alla falsa esaltazione del principe: "[...] i principi, che godono di sentirsi adulare, amano l'adulazione et aborriscono l'adulatore [...]. L'ossequio al principe quando arriva ad idolatria è pernicioso all'idolatrato, ma molto più a colui che idolatra". Passo illuminante, perché l'impietoso *ritratto* della corte disegnato dal Frugoni evoca una educazione sociale che ha ormai smarrito le ideali matrici cinquecentesche per assumere posizioni di esplicito opportunismo, in un continuo contenzioso di rivalità personali: "[...] è ne' cortigiani un'infermità incurabile il falseggiare l'uno con l'altro, sì come nel principe è naturale il ridersi internamente di tutti loro" (Frugoni 3.108, 110). In questo ribollente groviglio di risentimenti e d'intrighi — si pensi solo all'avventura del Marino presso la corte sabauda e al feroce contrasto col Murtola, conclusosi con un colpo di pistola da questi sparato all'autore della *Lira* — i precetti di prudenza schematizzati dall'Accetto conservano intatte le loro prerogative morali, e anzi consentono lo stabilirsi tra i letterati di una solidarietà di classe tutt'altro che inutile in una comunità lacerata da tensioni intestine. Insomma, in un discorso sulla verità nel Seicento, punto di partenza obbligato è la corte, nella cui organizzazione interna s'inseriscono capillarmente i letterati, i quali a vario titolo occupano ruoli spesso di primo piano, con una precisa spartizione di compiti motivata in base alle esigenze del signore o del principe.

Da un punto di vista più propriamente letterario, l'adattamento della cultura cortigiana e dei suoi modelli di comportamento trova una coerente — benché ironica — ratifica persino in un testo in apparenza irregolare come *Le astuzie di Bertoldo* del bolognese Giulio Cesare Croce, nel quale è agevole cogliere una specifica intenzione sarcastica verso un mondo così compassato. Ed è significativo che sia proprio l'intemperante giulleria di un villano incolto e deforme a suscitare in re Alboino un autentico apprezzamento per questo "ribaldo", fino a rimpiargerne i motteggi provocatori. Non si tratta dunque dell'adulazione di un raffinato poeta cresciuto alla scuola delle lettere classiche, bensì delle bizzarrie di una allegorica figura carnevalesca che esce dai confini del convenzionale e che sta fuori dal galateo della discrezione.[5] Eppure alla parodia del sovrano, consapevole di essere al vertice di una grande costruzione gerarchica entro la quale si inquadrano rapporti di sottomissione, immancabilmente accompagnati da espressioni di dispotismo ("Io splendo in questa corte come propriamente splende il sole fra le minute stelle. [...] Mira quanti signori e baroni mi stanno attorno per ubidirmi e onorarmi" Croce 88-89), Croce associa la celebrazione delle "sottilissime astuzie" di un ingegno "accorto e astuto", come appunto insegna l'aristocratica trattatistica del Peregrini. Proprio dal manuale *Delle acutezze*, ancorché posteriore alla stesura del *Bertoldo*, nel capitolo dodicesimo, dove l'autore "propone venticinque cautele per l'uso delle acutezze", in corrispondenza del "diciasettesimo aviso", si apprende che le "acutezze" — il passo è emblematico nella prospettiva ricercata dal Croce — "non possono aver luogo [...] in tema che non sia per sua natura scherzevole, overo almeno per ischerzo dal dicitore dichiaratamente trattato" (Peregrini, *Delle acutezze* 143, 154). Ciò che precisamente avviene nel *Bertoldo*, poiché il protagonista, con "l'acutezza dell'ingegno" (Croce 85), si serve delle "acutezze ridevoli", le quali "non dilettano solamente, ma insegnano, muovono, in somma operano". In effetti, prosegue Peregrini, persino lo "scherzo", purché sensato,

---

[5] Sulle componenti della cultura di Croce e la peculiarità della sua produzione letteraria, vedere Anselmi 26-32; Rouch 145-78; per i *calembours* gergali Sardelli 43-64.

può essere utile: "La ragione è chiara, perché lo scherzo pungente non è contrario al parlar daddovero, poiché il serioso della puntura prevale e porta effetto assennato". Pertanto "tolerabile è l'abbondar d'acutezze pungenti" se queste — come appunto le sentenze pronunciate da Bertoldo — riescono a "palesare il dicitore per uomo d'ingegno (Peregrini, *Delle acutezze* 154-55). Così si spiega, in definitiva, la nostalgia del re per la mancanza di Bertoldo alla sua corte, e il rimpianto per la saggezza che quel villano "di sottilissimo ingegno" aveva condiviso con il detentore del potere:

Dopo la morte dell'astutissimo Bertoldo essendo restato il Re Alboino privo di così grand'uomo, dalla cui bocca scaturivano detti tanto sentenziosi e che con la prudenza sua aveva scampato molti strani pericoli nella sua corte, gli parea di non poter vivere senza qualcheduno il quale, oltre che gli desse consiglio e aviso nelle sue differenze, come facea già il detto Bertoldo, gli facesse ancora con qualche piacevolezza passar tal volta l'umore; e pur s'andava imaginando che della razza di esso Bertoldo vi fusse rimasto qualchedun altro, il quale, se bene non fusse stato così astuto e accorto come il detto, avesse almeno avuto alquanto di quel genio e di quella sembianza, per tenerlo appresso di sé, come faceva la buona memoria di esso Bertoldo.

(Croce 164)[6]

Troviamo qui il ritratto del perfetto cortigiano: astuto ma prudente, faceto ma accorto consigliere, capace di "detti" arguti e piacevoli, in grado persino di confortare il sovrano nei momenti di malumore, al punto da divenirne a tutti gli effetti un familiare con cui condivere la sfarzosa residenza. "Orsù, vuoi tu diventare uomo di corte?", aveva chiesto il re a Bertoldo dopo averne constatato la maliziosa intelligenza, tanto apprezzata da Alboino al punto da manifestare apertamente sentimenti di gratitudine nei confronti del suo prezioso consigliere: "Io non son tanto ingrato ch'io non conosca i tuoi meriti. [...] Io non ho mai veduto né praticato il più vivo intelletto del tuo; perciò serviti della mia corte in ogni tua occorrenza" (Croce 89, 120, 128). Emerge dalla satira di Croce, nelle forme allegoriche della corte longobarda, il ritratto di un ambiente animato da figure di diversa estrazione sociale e culturale,[7] le quali mirano ad affermarsi attraverso atti di omaggio all'autorità, riconosciuta in grado di dispensare favori e privilegi, sebbene sulla base di criteri interamente arbitrari, spesso capricciosi, ma sempre correlati ai modi dell'intrattenimento culturale e letterario. L'enigma consiste appunto nell'individuare ciò che sta a cuore al signore. È ancora il Malvezzi nel *Davide perseguitato* a interrogarsi se "vi sono ragioni da rendersi dell'affetto del principe verso un cortigiano, o sieno tratte dall'utile o dal diletto", salvo poi concludere che "è vanità il pensare di poter rendere ragioni degli amori affettuosissimi de' principi" (222).

---

[6] Il passo citato è tratto da *Le piacevoli e ridicolose simplicità di Bertoldino*, che costituisce la prosecuzione del *Bertoldo* dopo la scomparsa del protagonista. Per un'accurata analisi delle opere di Croce, vedere Camporesi.

[7] "Le corti non sono belle se non vi sono di tutti gli umori", precisa la Regina, consorte di Alboino, rivolta a Marcolfa, vedova di Bertoldo (Croce 189).

4. "L'essenza dell'adulazione"

Adulare significa perlopiù simulare. La simulazione, spiega Accetto, è "l'arte del fingere in cose che per necessità par che la ricerchino" (Accetto 23).[8] Il letterato di corte, intento a comporre versi di propaganda politica o ideologica, accetta una verità in parte falsata, assunta attraverso la mediazione dei più raffinati istituti retorici, a loro volta emblemi di una realtà inventata. Il contrappunto necessario alla convenzionalità degli *adulatoria verba* è la perfetta coincidenza tra la capacità di produrre testi encomiastici e l'abilità di circoscrivere il proprio campo di azione, dandosi necessariamente dei limiti: "[...] chi si stima più di quello che in effetto è, si riduce a parlar come maestro, e parendogli che ogni altri sia da men di lui, fa pompa del sapere, e dice molte cose che sarebbe sua buona sorte aver taciuto" (Accetto 53). Nel cenacolo letterario di corte ogni pronunciamento riesce difficile, non solo in forza dei legami personali di solidarietà all'interno di un organismo il cui impietoso ritratto ci è fornito dal Frugoni. L'aggancio alla lunga tradizione incentrata nella persona del principe o del signore, costringe il letterato a un permanente nascondimento degli insuccessi della dinastia: dunque meglio non ostentare né fare "pompa del sapere", attraverso una meditata rimozione delle "molte cose" che è preferibile tacere.

La letterarietà dei trattati storico-politici seicenteschi postula in prima istanza una riflessione sulla retorica, ovvero su quel repertorio di formule largamente impiegate per scopi celebrativi. I *Discorsi sopra Cornelio Tacito* di Malvezzi costituiscono da questo punto di vista una sorta di enciclopedia pedagogica (Aricò 2004), nella quale l'autore soggiunge, accanto agli elementi tradizionali, uno schema classificatorio delle varie "spezie" di adulazione nonché degli "adulatori". Sensatamente Malvezzi si attiene esplicitamente al valore politico dell'adulazione ("io, al mio solito, ne tratterò politicamente con brevità e forse anche con maniera non discorsa da alcuno"), cercando dapprima di spiegare quanto essa possa rivelarsi nociva a colui che detiene il potere. Vero è, osserva, "che i prìncipi fanno nascere gli adulatori", ma d'altra parte "è communemente approvato che gli adulatori siano la ruina de' prìncipi". L'aspetto essenziale della riflessione di Malvezzi è la responsabilità che egli imputa al potente: "essendo i prìncipi cagione essi dell'adulazione e non i sudditi, tutta la colpa si dee attribuire a loro" (Malvezzi, *Discorsi* 169-70).

Questa impostazione utilitaria non esclude un preciso disegno intellettuale, in grado di coesistere con la dialettica cerimoniale del panegirico aulico, dal quale prende alimento la plurisecolare continuità dell'egemonia aristocratica. Di là dalle ragioni prossime e remote delle ambizioni politiche, anzitutto importa cogliere la volontà irriducibile del dominatore di avere alle spalle una storia illustre, comparabile con quella degli eroi. Nella coscienza dei contemporanei, la storia è infatti prestigio e simbolo della regalità, ma il potente ha anche bisogno della poesia, con la sua drammatica impressività, per legittimare in un modello

---

[8] Per i richiami allusivi a certe immagini risalenti alla tradizione neoplatonica, si veda Vagnoni 92-116.

ideologico l'autorità che egli rivendica per sé e i suoi discendenti. Il letterato di corte deve essere perciò in grado di sostenere funzioni di assistenza alla complessiva mobilitazione delle strutture culturali, cui non può non rispondere un grado superiore di allestimento dei testi a carattere encomiastico.

In sostanza, l'attività richiesta al "savio in corte" consiste nella studiosa conservazione e adattamento di pratiche già introdotte nell'età delle signorie rinascimentali, ma ora, a circa un secolo di distanza, ricombinate entro una ricerca letteraria unilaterale, a carattere esclusivamente politico-celebratorio, e pertanto sempre caratterizzata da ingegnosi riferimenti alla tradizione storica e alle fonti epiche. Nel presupposto di un pubblico che abbia con tali forme retoriche tanta dimestichezza da poter cogliere richiami allusivi e riferimenti testuali, il modenese Alessandro Tassoni formula una precisa distinzione tra i generi letterari che si propongono di formulare un ritratto edificante del potere e delle sue azioni. Nel sesto "quisito" del nono libro dei *Pensieri diversi* (1612) Tassoni dichiara che "l'istoria e la poesia sono differenti", poiché "l'istoria narra le cose come furono e la poesia le narra come dovevano essere" (Tassoni 229). A redigere i due diversi statuti di storia e poesia, Tassoni vi è indotto in primo luogo da una prudente prospettiva politico-encomiastica, sotto una non disinteressata angolatura personale, e anzi professionale. La controversa nozione di verità senza dubbio influisce considerevolmente nel contesto qualificato e politicamente autorevole delle istituzioni signorili, delle quali Tassoni è un esperto conoscitore. Certe interferenze colpiscono l'attenzione del Tassoni, per il quale la separazione tra politica e cultura è inconcepibile, naturalmente assegnando alla cultura un valore strumentale, ma non accessorio, sullo sfondo di una più larga dimensione ideologica, indizio concreto d'una cosciente solidarietà tra i ceti superiori.

Il "quisito" ventesimo dell'ottavo libro dei *Pensieri diversi* è infatti dedicato alle relazioni tra "il principe" e i suoi "consiglieri". Difficilmente il principe presta attenzione a rimbrotti o esortazioni dei suoi collaboratori (tanto meno se poeti), giacché egli perlopiù si affida a una rigorosa concezione del proprio potere: "I principi vogliono il potere assoluto e libero: e non si lasciano correggere, se non in quelle cose, che non toccano il gusto loro". Non stupisce che Tassoni sottolinei, con disincantata amarezza, quanto possa rivelarsi politicamente deplorevole l'inclinazione alla superbia e alla presunzione, connaturata invece ai piccoli e grandi potenti che si contendono la scena pubblica nell'Italia spagnolizzata del primo Seicento. Vero è che "anche i principi buoni alle volte fanno di lor capriccio degli spropositi, per non dar adito a' consiglieri e ministri di pigliar loro piede addosso"; e per volere prima di tutto mantenere saldamente il proprio dominio sui subalterni "niuna cosa è più odiosa ad un principe, che l'avere a dipendere da altri, e d'essere in concetto d'aver bisogno di pedante". D'altronde, chiosa Tassoni, occorre non rovesciare i rapporti di forza, evitando che l'improntitudine di petulanti opportunisti condizioni le dinamiche dell'amministrazione dello Stato: "[...] i principi buoni tengono i consiglieri perché discorrano seco delle cose del governo, non perché governino essi" (Tassoni 210-11).

Sempre nel libro ottavo, dedicato in larga parte agli "interessi di Stato", per evitare di "mettere a maggior rischio la maestà dell'imperio", Tassoni consiglia al principe di "valersi di più consiglieri e ministri". Infatti, aggiunge, "i principi prudenti sogliono avere molte congregazioni e consulte, alle quali rimettono i negozi dello Stato più gravi" (Tassoni 222). Di là dalla prudenza, in un momento in cui per fare politica c'è bisogno di grandi mezzi, in un vivace sistema policentrico perennemente mutante, condizionato all'interno dalle indocili fazioni di una aristocrazia riottosa e riluttante a inquadrarsi in modo stabile sotto un potere superiore, Tassoni di fatto discute il problema del riconoscimento della verità da parte del reggitore dello Stato. Notevole è pertanto la sua convinzione che la politica sovrasti, con le sue concrete esigenze, i generi letterari più illustri: "Sotto la politica, come dipendenti da lei, vengono tre nobili arti, l'istorica, la poetica e l'oratoria; la prima delle quali riguarda l'ammaestramento de' principi e de' signori; la seconda l'ammaestramento del popolo; e la terza l'ammaestramento di coloro che consigliano sopra le cause publiche". Ancora più notevole l'opera di sistemazione qualitativa delle varie tipologie letterarie compiuta da Tassoni in questo libro dei *Pensieri diversi*, per rispondere a esigenze che egli stesso avverte mentre allestisce la sua opera enciclopedica secondo moduli socioculturali assai affini a quelli di Malvezzi, nonostante la profonda diversità delle opinioni politiche: "[...] se bene Aristotile nella *Poetica* disse che la poesia era cosa più ingegnosa, io stimo con tutto ciò, che l'istoria preceda, non tanto perché ha più nobil fine e oggetto, quanto perché tratta cose vere con gravità e decoro, e non finzioni come fa l'altra con vanità e leggerezza". Questo mobilitarsi in funzione delle "cose vere" e della storia, appunto analoga alle concezioni malvezziane esposte nei *Discorsi sopra Cornelio Tacito*, equivale insomma a una coraggiosa difesa della verità, poiché "l'istorie non si lasciano a' posteri per trattenimento, come i romanzi, ma per documento in esempio" (Tassoni 314). Turbato al pari di Malvezzi dalle drammatiche vicende della sua età, Tassoni deposita in ogni parola che affida alla pagina scritta i valori civili che la storia è tenuta a designare e difendere, allo scopo di tutelare quella civiltà di cui la poesia può al massimo celebrare i fasti e le icone.

Il processo di trasfigurazione per il quale la storia può essere idealizzata nella poesia rappresenta d'altronde la sostanza stessa della letteratura barocca. Dalla storia non è possibile staccarsi senza ricordare che proprio da essa discendono quelle *fabulae* venutesi ad aggregare nelle convenzioni poetiche — come appunto insegna il Tasso — né senza la storia la poesia potrebbe dissimulare sotto un leggero velo di finzione le vicende emblematiche che hanno rappresentato per secoli il livello più alto della cultura aulica e curiale, come appunto insegna il Marino. Proprio su questi controversi aspetti si diffonde l'opera che più di ogni altra ha approfondito la riflessione sul rapporto tra politica e letteratura nel primo Seicento, ovvero la *Poetica italiana* di Tommaso Campanella. Anch'egli consapevole del fatto che il letterato seicentesco agisce perlopiù nel composto formalismo delle liturgie cortigiane, Campanella, con una più accentuata sensibilità civile, mira a rivitalizzare la tradizione umanistica nella sua capacità di sintesi tra eloquenza e verità storica. Dopo aver sottolineato "quanto sia pernizioso il falsificar l'istorie", convinto che gli "istorici adulatori" siano "malevoli del genere umano", il frate calabrese afferma che per "esser buoni poeti" è imprescindibile "attender primieramente [...] all'istoria, più che ad ogni altra cosa" (Campanella 340).

Esponendo al lettore il suo ambizioso programma di illuminato antiaristotelico ("biasmar mi lece grandemente Aristotile" 341), Campanella esprime la sua insofferenza per un'estenuata convenzione secondo la quale "la poesia consiste in ingannar l'auditore" (343). Nel complesso emerge dalla *Poetica* il profilo di un filosofo che non risparmia uno sprezzante giudizio nei confronti del poeta che, per esigenze encomiastiche o politiche, si sente autorizzato a "falsificare l'istorie antiche e moderne", il quale così facendo "corrompe i buoni costumi" e anzi si rende còrreo di uno scellerato mercimonio "dove si comprano le bugie per fare ignorante il popolo" (340). Certo, qui ritornano i sanguigni umori anticuriali e anticlericali dell'incauto eversore che in gioventù organizzò la congiura antispagnola pagata con trent'anni di carcere. Eppure la diligenza morale con cui Campanella affida alla *Poetica* le sue idee letterarie, dimostra con quale fervore egli intenda rafforzare la missione civile di cui l'intellettuale è investito (Ernst 230-40). Instancabile propugnatore dell'autonomia del letterato nei confronti del potere, sorvegliando scrupolosamente la coerenza interna del suo sistema teorico, Campanella non può non rivolgere l'attenzione alla "favola" (intesa in senso tecnico come *fabula* sulla cui base si costruisce il testo letterario), utilizzata per colmare una carenza di verità: "[...] io dico che la favola si fa per la mancanza del vero", asserisce, "essendo le favole quelle che ammaestrano la vita" (Campanella 343-44). D'altronde il letterato esperto e avvertito è un maestro in operazioni di questo genere, capace di muoversi con sopraffina abilità tra le fonti classiche e moderne, dalle quali estrapolare contenuti ideologici ai limiti del più spregiudicato opportunismo.[9]

Non stupisce pertanto che una riflessione analoga, benché scaturita da motivazioni diverse, si trovi anche nei *Pensieri diversi* del Tassoni, certo all'insegna di un maggiore equilibrio di giudizio, ma sempre in funzione di una polemica verso il dilagante conformismo intellettuale della vita di corte. Tuttavia, pur nella somiglianza di certe analisi poetico-retoriche, Campanella e Tassoni hanno due diversi modi di intendere il ruolo sociale dell'uomo di cultura, e pertanto rivelano una radicale differenza circa i criteri di valutazione delle opere letterarie, specie quando la decifrabilità dei loro contenuti lascia intravedere o presumere una precisa intenzione encomiastica. Ovviamente un uomo come Tassoni, entrato al servizio del cardinale Colonna negli stessi anni in cui Campanella si adoperava per sovvertire il governo spagnolo, a lungo

---

[9] Prudentemente il Tesauro, che conosce bene lo scempio compiuto da certi disinvolti letterati adusi a ricorrere a generiche perifrasi pur di compiacere il mecenate di turno, osserva "che passa gran differenza tra l'insegnar favole e l'insegnar la verità con le favole" (Tesauro 104).

impiegato presso la corte sabauda in uffici di varia natura, era lontanissimo dai tormenti interiori di Campanella, angosciosamente oscillante tra l'irresolutezza moralistica e l'orgoglio per il proprio talento. Eppure se si scorrono le pagine che il Tassoni, da navigato cortigiano, dedica agli esiti della produzione letteraria, allora si scorge il medesimo rigore etico e anzi la medesima inquietudine per gli aspetti devianti di una professione in progressivo disfacimento morale, avviata verso una crisi penosa e un irreversibile processo involutivo.

Sempre di alta qualità, la prosa tassoniana attesta passo dopo passo una specifica identità culturale, alla quale è ricondotta l'intera dialettica con cui si discute il senso più autentico del testo letterario, inteso in prima istanza come veicolo di valori ideologici (Morando 71-86). Al fine di avviare nel giusto modo un processo analitico destinato a svilupparsi attraverso il confronto critico delle varie entità testuali, Tassoni trasferisce nella sua riflessione strumenti esegetici affini a quelli sperimentati dal Campanella, la cui principale implicazione consiste appunto nel significato da assegnarsi al vocabolo "vero". E nonostante talune sporadiche forzature esercitate sui precetti aristotelici, o meglio peripatetici, Tassoni ratifica il raffronto tra la matrice della "favola" e il testo definitivo, la cui *auctoritas* dipende appunto dal grado di *veritas* di cui esso è portatore. "La favola", asserisce il Tassoni, "è una falsa narrazione simile al vero", ove il discorso assume connotazioni e tonalità differenti in funzione del pubblico cui è destinato. Quindi sulla scorta di Aristotele specifica che essa è "una falsa narrazione di cose maravigliose simili al vero", sotto il cui *figmentum* si cela un preciso significato strettamente collegato alle intenzioni dell'autore e parimenti alle aspettative del lettore (o del committente). Il quale attende che gli si offra una raffigurazione complessiva di un determinato soggetto (epico, avventuroso, cavalleresco, amoroso, lirico, storico ecc.), sempre però adeguatamente formulata in un messaggio che risulti coerente rispetto a uno specifico paradigma politico (e pertanto religioso). Non a caso Tassoni inserisce certi spunti che lasciano intravedere orientamenti almeno in parte difformi da quelli di Campanella, ricordando che "la favola adunque ne diletta non come falsa, ma come maravigliosa e simile al vero, perciochè come maravigliosa produce una curiosa novità, che invaghisce la nostra mente, la qual sempre d'apprender cose insolite e nuove ha diletto". E qui d'altronde Tassoni non disdegna di riaprire l'irrisolto contrasto tra vero e falso, giacché "senza dubbio molto più diletta una cosa nuova e maravigliosa tenuta per vera sentendone favellare, che non farebbe sendo tenuta per falsa" (Tassoni 228-29).

Sullo sfondo di queste considerazioni si coglie una trama di riferimenti che sottolinea l'intrecciarsi della riflessione retorica con l'esigenza di assegnare alla narrazione storica uno statuto depurato dalle invenzioni favolose di cui si serve la letteratura encomiastica: "[...] l'istoria alcuni l'hanno diffinita narrazione di cose vere"; il che pone problemi di una certa rilevanza, poiché il vero suscita spesso scontento e irritazione. E lo stesso Tassoni non nasconde la sua indignazione per la facile irritabilità dei potenti difronte a improvvide evocazioni di verità: "[...] i principi moderni [...] non vogliano sofferire che si scriva la verità" (315), conclude sconfortato alla fine del lungo esame condotto su quel tipo di letteratura che autoassume, sotto una maschera di zelo ortodosso e con prudenti artifici, la missione ufficiale di costruzione del consenso e difesa dell'*establishment*. Un amareggiato Campanella, servendosi di formule meno allusive, ribadirà del resto lo stesso concetto: il "tiranno" infatti "riverisce quei poeti che adulano lui, e al popolo dànno utili documenti a mantenere la tirannide" (Campanella 355-56).

5. *"Saper ben mentire"*
"Non è maraviglia che si tenga da tutti che il buon poeta è il più bugiardo" (350-51), protesta Campanella nella sua *Poetica*. Una sorta di furente invettiva rivolta contro quei superbi letterati che senza avere nessun riguardo per la verità, e mentendo a se stessi, continuano a essere servi dei signori: "[...] hanno i nostri poeti tanto atteso alla bugia e vanità, che ognuno se n'accorge che sono mendaci" (376). Qui il contrasto tra politica e letteratura si fa sentire in maniera aspra, sebbene i penetranti e talora feroci giudizi campanelliani siano la diretta conseguenza della sua commossa e fallimentare partecipazione alla vita pubblica dell'epoca. Anche per questo Campanella ha incrementato il suo impegno sul versante filosofico-letterario, nella speranza che i traumatici contrasti degli anni precedenti sarebbero stati compensati da una più o meno esplicita gratificazione intellettuale. E infatti in certe sezioni della *Poetica* campanelliana è percepibile una tenace fedeltà per quella prospettiva di riforma delle istituzioni giuridiche su cui si basa l'utopia della *Città del Sole*, e che qui ritorna implicitamente anche nelle categorie letterarie, "perché il poeta deve essere istromento del legislatore" (345). La letteratura insomma può consentire e ispirare, nella sua stessa dimensione comunicativa, l'aggregazione dei principi fondamentali che regolano la vita sociale di una determinata collettività, a partire appunto dalla sfera legislativa, dalla quale dipendono la coesione dello Stato e le garanzie di giustizia: "[...] l'obbedire alle leggi si deve accendere con le parole e belle finzioni, sentenze e narrazioni" (358).

Per Campanella, a lungo detenuto nelle orrende prigioni napoletane e pontificie, la rigorosa amministrazione della giustizia, nel quadro di un sistema più equamente omogeneo e depurato da qualsivoglia arbitraria parzialità e sopraffazione, si può conseguire anche con il contributo della letteratura (in fondo è la stessa idea di Paolo Sarpi, un altro frate ostile al potere politico della Chiesa di Roma e strenuo oppositore dell'ingerenza del Tribunale dell'Inquisizione nelle vicende della *res publica*). Il miraggio di trovare una convergenza tra la verità delle leggi e la verità della filosofia avrebbe finito con l'assorbire tutte le energie di Campanella, come pure dimostrano certe sue composizioni poetiche in cui si celebrano "i gran dottor della legislatura" (198). A differenza della coeva trattatistica politica e comportamentale, alla cui origine c'è la volontà di prontamente tutelare la coscienza di una *élite* intellettuale, in Campanella si nota un ridimensionamento del peso e del ruolo del letterato impegnato negli ambienti di corte, per promuovere invece una nuova figura di "filosofo poetante", in grado di essere a un tempo "poeta e profeta, quando insegna il vero" (349). Il bersaglio polemico di Campanella è dunque l'adulatore, il quale soccorre i politici tacendo la verità nei suoi componimenti colmi di dottrina: "[...] queste orazioni [...] fatte in lode d'altrui, sono materie di puttane sfacciate, non da filosofi", poiché i loro autori non si "vergognano adulare e dire menzogne per aver mercede della bugiarda lode" (351-52).

Dalle pagine di Campanella sembra che il "fingere" sia parte essenziale del sistema cortigiano seicentesco, "laonde ogni savio principe, che ha fatto gran gesti e onorati, have a male esser posto in versi, perché tutti sospettano che siano cose finte per adulazione i suoi fatti immortali, e non veri" (376). La complessità di questo rapporto, che ha notevole rilievo per intendere la fisionomia di certe espressioni letterarie riconducibili al nome di illustri autori, neppure sfugge a uno studioso dei costumi come Emanuele Tesauro, il quale peraltro tratta certi argomenti proprio a beneficio di "que' della Corte", nella speranza di giovare ai "nobili 'ngegni" che aspirano a imparare "tutta l'arte rettorica". Il sempre più perfezionato bagaglio di elaborazione tecnico-retorica trova nel Tesauro un campo di applicazione nelle "cagioni strumentali delle argutezze", vale a dire in un surrogato barocco dell'oratoria politica, "richiedendosi" ragguardevole "sagacità nell'esporre" e altresì "nel comporre" qualsiasi opera che possa definirsi "arguta e ingegnosa" (Tesauro 20-21).

Nel *Cannocchiale aristotelico* il canone comportamentale si nutre dell'esperienza storica dell'autore — gesuita, *magister* di retorica, diplomatico, consigliere della corte sabauda — e dunque finisce con l'assumere una connotazione concreta, fino a configurarsi in uno sfondo sociale assai distinto, profondamente segnato dai rapporti assidui intrattenuti da Tesauro con il potere politico. E malgrado certi "paralogismi" cari all'autore, proprio dalla viva sensibilità per la tutela dell'autonomia del letterato nei confronti delle istituzioni, Tesauro trova il modo di insegnare al suo accorto lettore le puntuali corrispondenze tra l'enunciazione "de' veri concetti" e l'esercizio "del consigliare o sconsigliare", sulla base di un significato non soltanto retorico, ma anche ideologico: "[...] io conchiudo l'unica loda delle argutezze consistere nel saper ben mentire". Se si aggiunge poi "che le bugie de' poeti altro non son che paralogismi" (97-99), non v'è dubbio che il messaggio affidato al *Cannocchiale aristotelico*, in pagine fitte di implicazioni allusive e condotte sul filo di una sentenziosa precettistica (Santini 5-17; Zandrino 53-73), sia contrassegnato da una pervicace volontà di evitare il corrompersi della letteratura in un folto repertorio di falsi luoghi comuni.

I letterati del Seicento sanno quale terreno minato possa essere talora il mecenatismo, un *negotium* il quale in modo più o meno ricattatorio arbitrariamente si avvale e si impadronisce del testo per proprio tornaconto. Certo si tratta di un compromesso stipulato sotto il peso degli effettivi equilibri politici, anche se a prima vista può apparire agli occhi dell'osservatore sprovveduto un indulgente sussulto di generosità del patrono a favore dell'intellettuale. Al quale naturalmente si chiede di rispettare una rigorosa disciplina mentale, consistente innanzitutto nell'assegnare a se stesso una rassicurante posizione di obnubilata subalternità rispetto all'istituzione signorile.

Si tratta in fondo di una cautela a salvaguardia della propria professione (e della propria persona). Spesso il potere, sottolinea Accetto, "ha sospetto d'ogni capo dove abita la sapienza", e non è difficile immaginare, in simili circostanze, quante varie maschere occorra indossare per conservare un ruolo da protagonista sulla scena cortigiana: "[...] dura è la fatica di dover pigliare abito allegro nella presenza de'tiranni" (Accetto 59). Mediata attraverso il linguaggio della riflessione teorica, la precettistica di Tesauro e Accetto si risolve in una pedagogia dell'apparire, la cui espressione dipende da una approfondita conoscenza del carattere della vita pubblica seicentesca, nella quale, per avere successo, soccorre la "maravigliosa forza dell'intelletto, che comprende due naturali talenti: perspicacia e versabilità" (Tesauro 32).

Le astiose rivalità che percorrono l'asfittico mondo della corte non tardano a determinare — come del resto il Frugoni aveva rilevato nel corso delle sue indagini sulla società di Antico Regime — una cesura profonda tra cultura e politica, certo motivata dal desiderio di dar vita a una produzione letteraria credibilmente apologetica, vale a dire inserita in un'immagine diversa del principato, al tempo stesso solida e aperta alle innovazioni, esente da ogni velleità autocelebratoria e altresì capace di riassorbire l'eredità della storia recente. A quanto pare però, il principe continua a ricompensare soprattutto il letterato che professa la sua intenzione di ubbidire, certo determinato a lasciare un segno importante nella politica culturale della corte alla quale sente di appartenere, e dunque motivato a replicare una leale e paludata aulicità letteraria, così da ridare fiato a istanze encomiastiche ormai anacronistiche, eppure reiterate per perorare il cocciuto compiacimento del mecenate. "Oggi", scrive il Campanella nella *Poetica*, "il mondo è pieno di bugiardi adulatori venduti per patente" (349).

Invero quei medesimi principi che commissionano opere encomiastiche colme di "favole" e gesta tanto eroiche quanto fasulle sono mossi da motivazioni pressoché intrinseche alla ragion di Stato: "Così ingannato il volgo da una falsa apparenza di verità, ammira sempre più quello che meno intende", sentenzia il Bartoli nell'*Uomo di lettere* (333). Nelle società assolutistiche del XVII secolo, d'altronde, la sincerità ha un prezzo altissimo, e sovente si paga con la vita. "Per aver detto la verità ho da patir la morte? Deh, non esser così crudele contra di me, ti prego", implora Bertoldo al cospetto del sovrano che ha deliberato di condurlo al patibolo perché "troppo grave è stato l'oltraggio" (Croce 145) per aver dichiarato il vero.

Università di Bologna

Opere Citate

Accetto, Torquato. *Della dissimulazione onesta. Rime*. Ed. Edoardo Ripari. Milano: BUR, 2012.
Anselmi, Gian Mario. "Le voci della saggezza nel *Bertoldo*". *La festa del mondo rovesciato. Giulio Cesare Croce e il carnevalesco*. Ed. Elide Casali e Bruno Capaci. Bologna: il Mulino, 2002. 25-33.
Aricò, Denise. "Plutarco nei *Discorsi sopra Cornelio Tacito* di Virgilio Malvezzi." *Filologia e critica* 29.2 (2004): 201-43.
———. "'Vestire la persona de gl'altri'. Le orazioni immaginarie di Virgilio Malvezzi, fra Tito Livio, Guicciardini e Mascardi". *Studi secenteschi* 48 (2007): 3-37.
Arnaudo, Marco. "L'altra dissimulazione: Accetto, Pallavicino, Machiavelli." *Italica* 86.3 (2009): 488-99.
Bartoli, Daniello. *Dell'uomo di lettere difeso ed emendato. Trattatisti e narratori del Seicento*. Ed. Ezio Raimondi. Milano: Ricciardi, 1960. 323-61.
Bellini, Eraldo. "Linguistica barberiniana. Lingue e linguaggi nel *Trattato dello stile e del dialogo* di Sforza Pallavicino". *Studi secenteschi* 35 (1994): 57-104.
Benassi, Alessandro. "Lo 'scherzevole inganno'. Figure ingegnose e argutezza nel *Cannocchiale aristotelico* di Emanuele Tesauro." *Studi secenteschi* 47 (2006): 9-55.
Betti, Gian Luigi. "Trattatistica civile nel Seicento: la corte e il cortigiano". *Studi secenteschi* 42 (2001): 277-97.
Bisi, Monica. "Visione e invenzione. La conoscenza attraverso la metafora nel *Cannocchiale aristotelico*". *Studi secenteschi* 47 (2006): 57-87.
Campanella, Tommaso. *Opere letterarie*. Ed. Lina Bolzoni, Torino: Utet, 1977.
Camporesi, Piero. *Il palazzo e il cantimbanco Giulio Cesare Croce*. Milano: Garzanti, 1994.
Croce, Giulio Cesare. *Le astuzie di Bertoldo e le semplicità di Bertoldino*. Ed. Piero Camporesi. Milano: Garzanti, 2004.
D'Ascenzi, Damiano. "Il serpente e la colomba. Note sull'ambiguità della *Dissimulazione onesta* di Torquato Accetto". *Letteratura italiana antica* 13 (2012): 471-76.
Ernst, Germana. "'Bene e naturalmente domina solo la sapienza'. Natura e politica nel pensiero di Campanella." *Repubblica e virtù. Pensiero politico e monarchia cattolica fra XVI e XVII secolo*. Ed. Chiara Continisio - Cesare Mozzarelli. Roma: Bulzoni, 1995. 227-41.
Fiorani, Malvina. "Aristotelismo e innovazione barocca nel concetto di ingegno del *Cannocchiale aristotelico* di Tesauro". *Studi secenteschi* 46 (2005): 91-129.
Frugoni, Francesco Fulvio. *De' ritratti critici*. 3 voll. Venezia: Combi e La Noù, 1669.
Guaragnella, Pasquale. *Il servita melanconico. Paolo Sarpi e l' "arte dello scrittore"*. Milano: Franco Angeli, 2011.
———. *Teatri di comportamento. La "regola" e il "difforme" da Torquato Tasso a Paolo Sarpi*. Napoli: Liguori, 2009.
Landolfi, Mario. "La dissimulazione: ovvero il trionfo della prudenza nell'opera di Torquato Accetto". *Riscontri* 24.4 (2002): 9-19.
Malvezzi, Virgilio. *Discorsi sopra Cornelio Tacito*. Ed. Edoardo Ripari. Presentazione di Francesco Sberlati. Bologna: Persiani, 2014.
———. *Romulo. Opere*. Ed. Edoardo Ripari. Presentazione di Andrea Battistini. Bologna: Persiani, 2013. 74-120.
———. *Tarquinio Superbo. Opere*. Ed. Edoardo Ripari. Presentazione di Andrea Battistini. Bologna: Persiani, 2013. 128-89.

Micanzio, Fulgenzio. *Annotazioni e pensieri. Storici, politici e moralisti del Seicento.* Vol. 2. *Storici e politici veneti del Cinquecento e del Seicento.* Ed. Gino Benzoni e Tiziano Zanato. Milano: Ricciardi, 1982. 757-863.

Morando, Simona. *Il sogno di Chirone. Letteratura e potere nel primo Seicento.* Lecce: Argo, 2012.

Pallavicino, Sforza. *Trattato dello stile e del dialogo. Trattatisti e narratori del Seicento.* Ed. Ezio Raimondi. Milano: Ricciardi, 1960. 197-217.

Peregrini, Matteo. *Delle acutezze, che altrimenti spiriti, vivezze e concetti volgarmente si appellano. Trattatisti e narratori del Seicento.* Ed. Ezio Raimondi. Milano: Ricciardi, 1960. 113-68.

———. *Difesa del savio in corte.* Ed. Gian Luigi Betti e Sandra Saccone. Lecce: Argo, 2009.

———. *Il savio in corte distinto in quattro libri ove s'intendono e si disciolgono le ragioni che dissuadono dal corteggiare, e si mostra le necessità de' savi nelle corti, e perché sia a loro convenevole l'andarvi.* Bologna: Mascheroni, 1625.

Rouch, Monique. "Mondo agrario e letteratura popolare: Giulio Cesare Croce (1550-1609)". *Schede umanistiche* 21.1 (2007): 141-80.

Santini, Federica. "Argutezza e metafora. Considerazioni sul *Cannocchiale aristotelico* di Emanuele Tesauro." *Incontri* 17.1-2 (2002): 5-17.

Sardelli, Maria Antonietta. "El elemento paremiológico en *Le piacevoli e ridicolose semplicità di Bertoldino* (1608) de Giulio Cesare Croce". *Critica del testo* 11.1-2 (2008): 43-64.

Sarpi, Paolo. *Opere.* Ed. Gaetano e Luisa Cozzi. Milano: Ricciardi, 1969.

Tassoni, Alessandro. *Prose politiche e morali.* Ed. Giorgio Rossi. Bari: Laterza, 1930.

Tesauro, Emanuele. *Il cannocchiale aristotelico. Trattatisti e narratori del Seicento.* Ed. Ezio Raimondi. Milano: Ricciardi, 1960. 19-106.

Vagnoni, Debora. "Immagini neoplatoniche e teologia negativa nella dissimulazione di Torquato Accetto". *Linguistica e letteratura* 29.1-2 (2004): 89-118.

Vianello, Valerio. *La scrittura del rovesciamento e la metamorfosi del genere. Paolo Sarpi tra retorica e storiografia.* Fasano: Schena, 2005.

Wottom, David. *Paolo Sarpi between Renaissance and Enlightenment.* Cambridge: Cambridge University Press, 1983.

Zandrino, Barbara. "Emanuele Tesauro: letteratura e gioco." *Testo* 31/59 (2010): 53-73.

Elissa B. Weaver

"With Truthful Tongue and Faithful Pen": Arcangela Tarabotti Against Paternal Tyranny

Abstract: The prolific Venetian writer and Benedictine nun, Arcangela Tarabotti (1604-1652), dedicated her life to speaking out against the unfair treatment of women and especially the practice of forced monachization. In her writing she exposes the social, economic and political forces responsible for this practice and indicts fathers, the State, and the Church for their complicity in denying women the exercise of free will. Her most thorough treatment of the subject, and more broadly of the misogyny at its core, is found in her treatise *La semplicita ingannata* (*Innocence Deceived*), known in English as *Paternal Tyranny*, which was published posthumously and subsequently condemned by the Church.

Key Words: Arcangela Tarabotti, *La semplicita ingannata*, *Paternal Tyranny*, forced monichization, *Ragion di Stato*, Academy of the Incogniti, misogyny, *Querelle des femmes*.

In questo corrotto secolo pochi sono che non siano macchiati, almeno acconsentendo, di così enorme colpa, e per conseguenza appresso questi tali i detti miei faran poco o niun frutto, anzi rimarranno censurati, come nati da un animo non ben composto, sfornito di religione, e accusati di temerità, poiché sempre in questo fallace mondo *veritas odium parit*.

(Tarabotti, *Semplicità ingannata*, ed. Bartot 176-77)

In this corrupt age, alas, few are not tainted with the great fault I speak of, at least in giving their tacit approval. And so my words will bear little or no fruit and will remain unheeded, condemned as the offspring of a deranged mind stripped of religion and accused of imprudence, since in this false world, as the proverb goes, "Speaking the truth incurs hatred."

(*PT* 41)[1]

The Venetian writer Arcangela Tarabotti (1604-1652) spent most of her life in the Benedictine convent of Sant'Anna in the Castello district of Venice, a victim of coerced religious vocation. She had been hurt, unfairly treated by her father and her society, civil and religious, but she made the best of a sad situation, availing herself of the opportunity the cloister offered her to study and write. She was largely, if not entirely, self-taught, yet she became an eloquent and prolific writer; she used her talents to decry her fate, and that of many women like her, and to expose to all who would listen to her or read her prose the social,

---

[1] Hereafter I will refer to the *Semplicità ingannata* in the Italian edition by Simona Bortot as *SI* and the English translation, entitled *Paternal Tyranny*, by Letizia Panizza, as *PT*. Unless otherwise indicated I will cite from these editions.

Annali d'italianistica 34 (2016). *Speaking Truth to Power from Medieval to Modern Italy*

economic and political underpinnings of a system that, to preserve a family's patrimony and social standing, forced the children they could not or would not marry into religious life.[2] She did not spare fathers, nor the Venetian state that quietly supported the practice in order to limit the size of the aristocracy, nor the Church, which officially condemned it, but remained silently complicit, unwilling to uphold its principles and defend the exercise of free will. Tarabotti's complaint did not remain a personal one. She understood that misogyny was the source of her oppression and that all women were its victims, and she spent her life defending women and exposing the illogic of arguments for their inferiority and suppression. Through her writing and her forceful personality Arcangela Tarabotti made connections in the literary and publishing world of Venice and beyond, and despite being an enclosed nun she was able to publish her work. She could not let the misogynist behavior of men stand without response: she wrote that "he who stings must be stung" (*Letters* 152).[3] That she felt as she did is easy to understand, but that she was able to react publicly and accuse powerful men and institutions from within her convent walls, even in seventeenth-century Venice, is an astounding tale of conviction, courage, strong will, and exceptional intellect that made her then and now a voice to be reckoned with, that "spoke truth to power."

Since her rediscovery by Benedetto Croce, Giuseppe Portigliotti, and Emilio Zanette in 1929-30, Tarabotti's story has slowly entered the annals of Italian literary history. At the end of the 1970s Ginevra Conti Odorisio claimed an important place for Tarabotti in the history of feminism. Since that time there has been much new research into her life and we now have many modern editions, translations, and studies of her works. It is not my intention in this essay to survey that work. I will instead limit my discussion to characterizing Tarabotti's outspoken attack on the misogyny in her society and the responses she provoked.

Elena Cassandra Tarabotti was born in 1604 to Stefano Tarabotti, a chemist, and Maria Cadena dei Tolentini; she was one of ten children, the eldest of six daughters. So many girls presented the family with the serious problem of finding them marriage partners and the required dowry money. Of all the girls, Elena was the least likely marriage prospect, since she had a limp and was probably frail from an early age — her letters are filled with complaints of poor health — so her family destined her for the convent, where they would also pay

---

[2] The practice was not limited to female children, but male children had more options: a religious life without enclosure and military careers. Much has been written on forced monichization. See especially Medioli, Zarri, and the succinct summary of the practice of coerced religious vocations and of the unheeded Church regulations to prevent it in Schutte 3-5.

[3] "Se questi tali si degneranno, a me poco importa: chi punge debbe essere punto e chi ferisce altrui nella riputazione merita d'esser trafitto nell'onore" (*Lettere* 158).

a smaller dowry.[4] She was taken to Sant'Anna in Castello, not far from her family's home, when she was either eleven or perhaps thirteen years old; accounts are unclear. A convent document records her entry as a school girl ("educanda") on September 1, 1617 (Zanette, *Suor Arcangela* 26-27), and perhaps she was there earlier as a boarder, since she claims in a letter to have been taken to the convent when she was eleven: "I came to live in these cloisters when I was eleven years old without ever having basked in the light of learning" (*Letters* 152-53).[5] An unwilling nun, she, nevertheless, was clothed in 1620, becoming suor Arcangela, and she professed in 1623, a difficult time in her life that she describes in her *Soliloquy to God* (*Soliloquio a Dio* 8-9), and in a third person, yet passionate account in *Convent Hell* (*Inferno monacale*).[6]

In her short life Arcangela Tarabotti published six works and composed perhaps five others, though four, which she mentions, have not survived. In 1643 she published *Convent Paradise* (*Paradiso monacale*) and, together with it, *Soliloquy to God* (*Soliloquio a Dio*). *Convent Paradise* opened a trilogy that was to include *Convent Hell* (*Inferno monacale*), unpublished in her lifetime, though it circulated in manuscript, and the *Purgatory of Unhappily Married Women* (*Purgatorio delle malmaritate*), which Tarabotti mentions in two of her works, but which, if she indeed wrote it, is now lost. In 1644 she penned and published the *Antisatire* (*Antisatira*), a response to Francesco Buoninsegni's misogynist satire of women's dress and behavior, *Against the Luxuries of Women, a Menippean Satire* (*Contro 'l lusso donnesco satira menippea*) of 1638; and in 1647, with *That Women Are of the Same Species as Men* (*Che le donne siano della spezie degli uomini*), she responded to an even more outlandish misogynist tract that argued that women had no souls and did not belong to humankind. Originally published in Germany, it was translated into Italian by a fictitious Oratio Plata, who called it *A Most Delightful Disputation* (*Disputatio perjucunda*). Tarabotti found it offensive and heretical. In 1650 she

---

[4] The first and only thorough study of Tarabotti's life is that of Emilio Zanette (1960); it has been augmented and updated in the studies of Medioli, Ray and Westwater. According to Zanette 3-4, two of Arcangela's sisters married: Innocenza Elisabetta to Francesco Dario, the family doctor, and Lorenzina to the lawyer Giacomo Pighetti, a connection that proved important to Arcangela; it was probably through Pighetti that she made contact with men of the literary world. Three sisters, Camilla Angela, Angela Lorenza, and Lucia Caterina remained at home.

[5] "[...] d'undici anni sono venuta ad abitare nei chiostri senz'aver avuto lume alcuno di lettere" (*Lettere* 158).

[6] For Tarabotti's account of the clothing and profession rituals and the psychological suffering of young women, who, like herself, underwent them unwillingly, see her *Inferno monacale* (especially 40-42; on the clothing ceremony and on profession 65-67, 70). There is no English translation as yet of the *Soliloquio* or the *Inferno*, but they are in process, the first, *Soliloquy to God*, by Meredith K. Ray and Lynn Lara Westwater, and the latter, *Convent Hell*, by Francesca Medioli; they will be published in the Toronto University Press "Other Voice" series.

collected and published her letters, *Letters Familiar and Formal* (*Lettere familiari e di complimento*) and appended to them a lament entitled *Angela Tarabotti's Tears on the Death of the Most Illustrious Signora Regina Donati* (*Le lagrime d'Arcangela Tarabotti per la morte dell'illustrissima signora Regina Donati*). The letters provide information about her daily life in the convent, her precarious health and her contacts with the secular world. They document her attempts to publish her works and to defend her literary reputation from critics who argue that she could not have written them.

This is an impressive list of publications, and quite unusual for a nun, yet the work for which Tarabotti is best known, and justly so, is *Paternal Tyranny* (*Tirannia paterna*), which she probably began to write in the 1620s shortly after entering the convent. She claims to have composed it in a nine-month period of illness, but she may have chosen that number to conform to the birth metaphor she used, calling the work the offspring of her intellect (*Letters* 161; *Lettere* 168). She circulated it in manuscript and returned to it from time to time, while she sought for years unsuccessfully to publish it. She clearly made revisions after 1641, since she includes polemical references to *Il corriero svaligiato* by Ferrante Pallavicino and the *Adamo* of Giovanni Francesco Loredano, which were published in 1640-41, and to Angelico Aprosio's *Scudo di Rinaldo,* of 1642; and we know that sometime after 1644 she was still revising her work, since she mentions the death of Pallavicino, which occurred that year (Panizza, *PT* introduction 24-25; Bartot, *SI* introduction 153-54). Even in her correspondence with Ismaël Boulliau, who shepherded her treatise through its publishing in Holland, we find that she attempted to make a "last minute" change in the title (Westwater, "A Rediscovered Friendship" 92). She had decided to call it *Innocence Deceived* (*La semplicità ingannata*) rather than *Paternal Tyranny* (*Tirannia paterna*), its initial title, perhaps, as most scholars believe, arguably to appear less provocative to potential publishers and put the emphasis on the victim rather than the perpetrator of injustice (Panizza, *PT*, introduction 15). Yet in her last letter written to Boulliau she again changed her mind and asked him to inform the publisher that she wanted to call it *Paternal Tyranny, Or Rather, Innocence Deceived* (*La tirannia paterna overo semplicità ingannata*), to use the pseudonym Galerana Barcitotti, and to consecrate it to God, apparently removing an earlier sarcastic dedication to the Republic of Venice (Medioli 27-28; PT 37-38).[7] This request was not honored; either Boulliau neglected to forward it or, if he did, perhaps it did not get to the publisher in time. In 1654, two years after her death, *La semplicità ingannata* (*Innocence Deceived*) was published by the Elzevier Press in Leyden under a

---

[7] The former dedication to the Serenissima Repubblica di Venezia was discovered and published by Francesca Medioli in her edition of the *Inferno monacale* 27-28, and translated and published by Letizia Panizza together with the dedication to God in *PT* 37-38. See below an excerpt from the earlier dedication.

slightly different pseudonym, Galerana Baratotti.[8]

Three more texts, religious in nature, that are mentioned by Tarabotti and others, have been lost.[9] Her corpus, as most of her titles make clear, was a lifelong defense of women, a protest against their subjection and mistreatment by men, who consider women inferior, deny them an education, participation in public life, and the exercise of their free will, confining them in convents and in the home. Even her *Convent Paradise*, which extolls religious life for those who have a vocation, does not abandon the themes of her other works and contrasts the happiness of willing nuns with the misery of the unwilling.

In a letter to her friend Betta Polani, Tarabotti wrote: "[...] that I should not be writing is quite impossible. In this prison and in my illness nothing else will satisfy me [...] had I not this diversion, I would be dead by now [...]. Only a tempered pen can temper my suffering" (*Letters* 103-04).[10] Her writing was her salvation, and her obsession.

Arcagela Tarabotti had friends in circles of power in Venice, especially among the libertine literati of the Academy of the Incogniti. It was perhaps through her brother-in-law Giacomo Pighetti, a member of the Academy, that she met Giovanni Francesco Loredan, the Academy's founder, Girolamo Brusoni, Ferrante Pallavicino, Francesco Pona, Angelico Aprosio and others.[11] They were all at odds with religious authorities more often than not, and, even if they did not always sympathize with her protest against forced monichization, many of them wrote about it themselves. Clearly they were intrigued by such a talented and outspoken woman and unusual nun. They corresponded with her,

---

[8] According to Lynn Westwater, the pseudonym Baratotti (an anagram of Tarabotti) may be a misreading of Barcitotti, the form Tarabotti suggested in the version of the title page she sent to Ismaël Boulliau: the "ci" may have seemed to him an "a" ("A Rediscovered Friendship" 70n9 and figures 1 and 3, pp. 71, 74). There was a second edition bearing the same title, date and place of publication, but entirely reset and probably printed in Venice. For a description of the two editions, see Simona Bortot, *SI* 155-62.

[9] *Contemplations of the Loving Soul* (*Contemplazioni dell'anima amante*), *The Paved Road to Heaven* (*La via lastricata per andare al Cielo*), and *Convent Light* (*Luce monacale*), works Tarabotti cites in a letter to Betta Polani (*Letters* 82-83; *Lettere* 82-83). In that letter instead of "lastricata" Tarabotti (or her publisher) has written "lasciata" (abandoned), probably an error. Giovanni Dandolo, in his "Letter to the signori Guerigli" that introduces Tarabotti's letter collection, mentions *La via lastricata per andare al Cielo*, a more likely version of the title (*Letters* 49-50; *Lettere* 45). Giovanni Dandolo (1613-61) was a Venetian aristocrat and member of the Academy of the Incogniti, a friend of Tarabotti's and frequent correspondent.

[10] I have slightly altered the translation, substituting "not be" for "leave off": "[...] ch'io resti di scrivere m'è impossibile il farlo. In queste carceri, e ne' miei mali non ho altro di che contentarmi [...] se non avessi questo trattenimento, sarei di già morta [...] solo una penna temperata ha valore di temperar le mie pene" (*Lettere* 105).

[11] On the Accademia degli Incogniti, see Muir, especially 70-107, Maylander, Miato (but this study is not entirely reliable and includes errors regarding Tarabotti), and Cannizzaro.

visited her at the convent parlor, exchanged books; and she and they read one another's works. Brusoni and the librettist Giovanni Francesco Busenello modelled characters after her.[12] Loredan was responsible for the publication of her *Paradiso monacale* and of her letter collection, which she dedicated to him, and in which she includes twelve letters written to him; his published letters include four written to her. Yet her relations with Loredan, and with the others as well, were not always cordial, and their ups and downs are reported in her letters. In the words of a recent critic, their relationship was characterized by "a precarious equilibrium, in which sincere appreciation and demonstrations of esteem existed alongside an impossible divide that separated the fierce and unmitigated misogyny of the members of the academy and the feminist assertions of the nun" (Bufacchi 60-61; my translation).[13] Aprosio and Brusoni turned against Tarabotti following the publication of her *Antisatira*. She had gone too far and, at least in the case of Aprosio, she had not taken his advice to refrain from publishing it. They wrote angry responses: Brusoni's *Antisatira satirizzata* was never published and Tarabotti through her powerful connections was able to block the publication of Aprosio's *La maschera scoperta*.[14]

Tarabotti had friends too among the French diplomats in Venice and their families, who visited her often at the convent. The French ambassador to Venice between 1645 and 1647, Nicolas Bretel de Grémonville, and his wife Anne-Françoise de Loménie, entrusted their two daughters to her at Sant'Anna for their education, and it was ultimately through her French connections that Tarabotti made the acquaintances that led to the publication of *Paternal Tyranny* (as *La semplicità ingannata*) by the Elzevier Press in Leyden. Her Venetian supporters, who had read *Paternal Tyranny* in manuscript, were either unable to help her during the many years in which she sought a publisher in Italy, or they preferred not to, perhaps seeking to dissuade her, as they had in the case of her *Antisatire*. Yet they were almost certainly behind the clandestine publication of the second edition of her controversial treatise, which appeared in Venice,

---

[12] Girolamo Brusoni (1614-c.1686), apostate friar and author of several romances, erstwhile friend to Tarabotti. Characters modelled after Tarabotti appear in Brusoni's *Aborti dell'occasione*, and in his *Orestilla*. Tarabotti accused him of plagiarizing *Paternal Tyranny* in his *Degli amori tragici* (initially entitled *Turbolenze delle vestali*). Giovan Francesco Busenello (1598-1659) was a Venetian poet and librettist. On Busenello's allusions to Tarabotti in his libretti, see Heller, "'O delle donne miserabil sesso'" 5-46, and "La Forza d'Amore" 141-57. On the polemical relationship between Tarabotti and Brusoni, see Bufacchi.

[13] "[...] un precario equilibrio, in cui i sinceri apprezzamenti e le dimostrazioni di stima si affiancarono a un'incolmabile frattura tra la feroce ed esasperata misoginia degli accademici e le rivendicazioni femminili della monaca" (61).

[14] On the polemical reception to Tarabotti's *Antisatira*, see Biga, and for the positive reaction, instead, that it received from Francesco Buoninsegni, see Weaver, *Satira e Antisatira* 25-27.

masquerading as another Elzevier edition of 1654.[15]

Unlike the *Antisatire, That Women are of the Same Species as Men,* or even her letters, which respond to another text or person, *Paternal Tyranny* is a thorough, independent presentation of Tarabotti's thought. It is a defense of women and an indictment of men who enclose them, deprive them of their God-given free will, of an education, participation in public life, and, in general, it is a condemnation of misogyny and its deleterious effects on the lives of women. In this treatise Tarabotti presents her protest and defends women against the accusations of misogynists in three books, each with different emphasis and examples, and all characterized by recurring digressions. If there is one constant, it is a persistent refrain and cry of anguish in which with angry words she accuses men of being tyrants, persecutors, betrayers, and hypocrites in their treatment of innocent, loving, trusting, vulnerable women whom they imprison and condemn to permanent, irreversible solitude. Throughout *Paternal Tyranny* she accuses men in strong language, often speaking directly to them, primarily to fathers of forced nuns, but also to men generally: "You are tyrants from Hell," she writes, "monsters of nature, Christians in name, and devils in deeds" and "you are not men but beasts" (*PT* 59, 136).[16] Their daughters are their victims whom they have condemned to "a crushing unbearable torment," "buried alive," given life sentences in "harsh prisons" (*PT* 91, 95, 150).[17] Tarabotti occasionally reminds the reader that she is only directing her polemic to the tyrannical fathers, not to others, but it is hard to imagine who these others are, since she accuses all men of misogyny, and therefore of complicity. She is unrelenting in her attack on forced religious vocations, and she writes, in one of her strongest denunciations of this deplorable yet widespread practice, that it is abetted by the State and the Church:

For private individuals to commit such enormity through self-interest — cursed self-interest — is an abominable abuse of power, but for religious superiors and rulers to allow it makes one reel in horror at their insensitivity. The prince's eye, we know, guards not only the "interests of state" [*Ragion di Stato*] but the salvation of souls as well; he ought not to allow so many to perish wretchedly by thus subordinating their salvation to these same interests [*Ragion di Stato*][18] (*PT* 60)

---

[15] See note 8 above.

[16] "tiranni d'Averno, aborti di natura, cristiani di nome e diavoli d'operazioni"; "uomini, anzi non uomini ma fiere" (*SI* 210, 363).

[17] "supplizio affannoso e insoportabile;" "sepolte vive;" "crudo carcere [...] prigioni perpetue" (*SI* 270, 277, 389).

[18] "Che i privati per loro interesse benché (maledetto interesse) commettano tal enormità, è abuso detestabile; ma che i superiori e Prencipi il permettano, è cosa da far istupidir d'orrore la stessa insensibilità: quando l'occhio del Principe deve non solamente invigilare sopra la Raggion di Stato, ma eziandio sopra alla salute dell'anime, e non lasciarne perir tante miseramente, posponendo la salvezza dell'anime alla Raggion di Stato" (*SI* 214).

I include Tarabotti's term "Ragion di Stato" here to make clear that she is referring to and denouncing a political theory that argues that whatever is considered necessary for the good of the state is legitimate, independent of the effect it may have on the individual.[19] Her criticism in this passage and elsewhere of the State and the Church were certainly among the reasons she was unable to publish the treatise in Italy, though she tried to do so by appealing to powerful friends like Giovanni Dandolo in Venice and rulers in whom she hoped to find sympathy for it, such as the grand duchess of Tuscany Vittoria della Rovere. Yet members of the ruling class would have been stunned as they read the accusations and sarcasm of Tarabotti's original dedication, for instance where she writes:

This *Paternal Tyranny* is a gift that well suits a Republic that practices the abuse of forcing more young girls to take the veil than anywhere else in the world. My book does not deserve to be dedicated to other rulers, as it might cause them too much outrage. It is fair, however, to dedicate my book to your great Senate and its senators, who, by imprisoning their young maidens so they chant the Psalter, pray, and do penance in their stead, hope to make you eternal, most beautiful virgin Republic, Queen of the Adriatic.[20]

(*PT* 37-38)

By exposing their hypocrisy, she could hardly have expected them to promote her work. She must have already despaired of publishing it in Venice when she penned such words, though she may still have hoped to find a female ruler like the grand duchess sympathetic to her cause.

Paternal Tyranny is much more than the protest and accusations of a forced nun. While Tarabotti begins her treatise condemning the practice of coerced monichization, which will be a refrain throughout, she quickly moves to the misogyny that lay behind it. She demonstrates that the deplorable practice of which she was a victim and the many other ways that women were oppressed derive from the belief in women's inferiority, inconstancy, moral and intellectual weakness and the consequent need for male guidance, correction, suppression, and the confinement of women to protect them from others and

---

[19] Tarabotti employs the term "Ragion di Stato," which has specific resonances in the seventeenth century and should be noted. She demonstrates agreement here with Giovanni Botero's *Della ragion di stato* (1589) and its argument against a political theory of the state that justifies its actions in the name of the common good, independent of their morality: the policies of the state should be moral and promote the common good.

[20] "Ben si conviene in dono la *Tirannia paterna* a quella Republica nella quale, piú frequentamente che in qual altra si sia parte del mondo, viene abusato di monacar le figliole sforzatamente. Non merita d'esser presentata ad altri principi per non apportar loro scandoli eccessivi: proporcionata è la mia dedicatione al vostro gran Senato, che, con incarcerar le figliole vergini, acciò si maccerino, salmeggino et orino in cambio loro, spera d'etternar voi, Vergine belissima, Regina dell'Adria" (Medioli 27). See note 7 above.

from themselves. This is why, she argues, women are denied the exercise of free will, that gift of God to all human beings, and the course of their lives is decided by others. She finds fault with the reading of Genesis that gave men power over women, and declares that Adam, the first man, blaming Eve for the Fall, was the first misogynist of the plurimillenary tradition.[21] She disputes as well the justification for women's subservience deriving from the natural sciences and philosophy of the times, which, claiming the authority of Aristotle, held that man is a perfect animal, woman imperfect. Tarabotti demonstrates in her treatise that these invalid arguments are the underpinnings of the misogyny of her culture and are responsible for the unjust subjection of women to men. She adds her voice to those of the *Querelle des femmes*, the debate on the nature and social status of women that had produced by the early seventeenth century two centuries of pro- and anti-woman texts.[22]

Tarabotti presents her argument in three books, each restating the problem with different emphasis and examples. In the overall structure she charts a general progression from negative to positive, from Eve to Mary, from the Fall to Redemption. The first book centers on a reading of Genesis, the second on contemporary society, and the third provides a feminist reading of the Bible, especially of the New Testament. Throughout the treatise, and linking the whole, is a recurrent refrain of protest against the unjust enclosure of women in convents, the pain and suffering it costs, and the cruelty of men who perpetuate it.

The first words of *Paternal Tyranny* set the accusatory tone of the treatise: "Men's depravity could not have devised a more heinous crime" (*PT* 43).[23] The crime is that of defying God's laws, and pride of place goes to enclosing women in convents, depriving them of their free will and condemning them to imprisonment for life. To denounce this great wrong, Tarabotti turns to the Creation story. She explains that when God had created the heavens and the earth he then created the first man, Adam, so that he might enjoy the beauties and delights of creation. Tarabotti writes, he created Adam, "the proudest animal of all," but he did not consider Adam perfect; indeed God foresaw that without a companion Adam would remain a "compendium of imperfections," and his work would not be complete, so he gave Adam a "helpmate like unto himself"

---

[21] Tarabotti objects specifically to the reading of Genesis proposed by Giovan Francesco Loredan in his novella, *L'Adamo* (*The Life of Adam*). See the analysis by Panizza in her introduction to *Paternal Tyranny* 19-21, and in "Reader Over Arcangela's Shoulder" 110-13. Hers is also a polemical response to Angelico Aprosio's reading of Genesis in his *Maschera scoperta* and *Scudo di Rinaldo* (Bufacchi 72).

[22] For an overview and analysis of the *Querelle des Femmes*, see Kelly. Beginning with Christine de Pisan in France and Isotta Nogarola in Italy, women began to challenge the traditional reading of Genesis that blamed Eve for the Fall.

[23] "Non poteva la malizia degli uomini inventar la più enorme sceleratezza" (*SI* 178).

(*PT* 46; "*adiutorium simile sibi*" Gen 2.16).[24] Tarabotti calls woman a "compendium of all perfections," reporting that Eve existed in God's mind even before Creation (Sir. 24.3-5; Prov. 22-26), and states that her creation from the rib of Adam gave perfection to man (*PT* 45).[25] Much of this argument comes from Henricus Cornelius Agrippa's *Declamation on the Nobility and Preeminence of the Female Sex* (*De nobilitate et praecellentia foeminei sexus*, 1529), one of the most influential treatises of the *Querelle* tradition, but the careful logic with which Tarabotti tells her version of the Creation story and the obvious criticism of all men implied in the description of the first of their kind is a good demonstration of Tarabotti's rhetorical skills.

In the commentary which follows her account of the creation of Adam and Eve, Tarabotti reiterates that Eve perfected Adam and that the first woman is Adam's equal, endowed, like Adam, with free will. "What arrogant presumption is yours, then, you liars," she writes, "when you repeat time and again that woman serves man as a help only with respect to reproduction, and that for the rest, she is an imperfect animal meant, fittingly, to live in subjection to him as the unstable, weak and frail sex" (*PT* 50).[26] In this passage it is clear that Tarabotti is referring to those men, like the members of the Academy of the Incogniti, who claim, on the authority of Aristotle, that the male animal is perfect, the female imperfect.[27] When Tarabotti in *Paternal Tyranny* uses the terms perfect or imperfect animal, or simply applies the term animal, with whatever qualification, to persons, it is not accidental: she is referring to this theory that argues the inferiority of women.[28] In the passage cited above that

---

[24] "il più superbo animale fra tutti gl'altri," " l'epilogo di tutte l'imperfezzioni" (*SI* 183).
[25] "'l compendio di tutte le perfezzioni" (*SI* 182).
[26] "Che arrogante maniera di presumere è dunque la tua, o mendace, all'ora che milantando ti vai dicendo la donna ne serve d'aiuto in quanto alla generazione, del rimanente è animal imperfetto, e ci vive sogetta per debito, come di sesso infermo, debile e fragile?" (*SI* 192).
[27] Aristotle argues (in the *Generation of Animals* and elsewhere) that a female is produced when the generative act is not carried through to its final conclusion, and that, because a female animal is colder and moister in dominant humors, her sexual organs have remained internal, so she is less fully developed than a male animal. She is not a perfect animal (even though she is necessary for generation) also because in procreation a male animal is the more active: he generates in another, whereas a female generates in herself. Cesare Cremonini (1550-1630), an Aristotelian professor of philosophy and free thinker at the University of Padua, wrote a treatise on this subject entitled *De calido innato et semine* (1634); he was close to the members of the Venetian Academy of the Incogniti, many of whom had studied with him.
[28] A few examples: "the proudest animal of all" *PT* 46 ("il piú superbo animale" *SI* 183), "ungrateful animal" *PT* 52 ("ingrato animale" *SI* 197), "you perfect animals" *PT* 63 ("voi animali perfetti" *SI* 221), "ungrateful animal"(my translation; Panizza has "ungrateful creature" *PT* 96, "ingrato animale" *SI* 279), "you bestow on them the quality of 'imperfect'" *PT* 97 ("voi date attributo d'imperfette" *SI* 280), "insensitive animal" *PT* 148 ("indiscreto animale" *SI* 384).

begins "What arrogant presumption," she means to refute it with sarcasm. She uses such terms throughout the treatise, and in Book Three concludes her protestations with ridicule and with such rhetorical flourish that contemporary men, even if offended, will be amused by her cleverness and her opinion, in this case, of their facial hair. The sentence is also a good example of how adeptly Tarabotti wields extended metaphors:

> Oh how much more it is with envious spite than sincere truth that you call woman an imperfect animal, while you, who have hair on your face, and beastly behavior as well as unseemly visage, imitate brute animals, and, in order to become in every way an unreasoning creature like those to whom nature gave horns, you have worked hard to succeed in raising those hairs on your face, precisely in the form of horns, anxious to imprint above your mouth, if not on your head, a sign that distinguishes you as a perfect animal.[29]
>
> (*PT* 133)

Ridicule and satire in Tarabotti's writing often take the form of scorn, and, given her strong motivation to dismantle misogyny wherever she finds it, Tarabotti is more often serious than not in *Paternal Tyranny*.

When she takes up the subject of the Fall, Tarabotti insists on Eve's lesser and Adam's greater guilt. Eve sinned, she acknowledges, but she was naive and deceived ("ingannata") by the cunning of the serpent. Adam, instead, sinned knowingly, enticed to do so because he was taken with the charm of such an innocent and pure creature ("innocente e pura creatura") as Eve. Tarabotti calls him an "ungrateful animal" (*PT* 52),[30] because when God confronts him, he blames his wife. She must have had Loredan's account of the story in his *Life of Adam* before her or on her mind as she wrote. She adopts the language of his biblical novella, albeit to different effect. Loredan has a guilty Eve attempt to defend herself before God, saying, "My innocence has been deceived by the cunning of the serpent."[31] Tarabotti clearly sees Eve as the first in the long line of innocent women who, like Tarabotti herself, have been deceived by evil that disguises itself as good. It seems clear from this passage why she chose to use

---

[29] "O con quanto più di livore invidioso, che di verità sincera, dai titolo d'animal imperfetto alla femina, mentre tu col pelo sopra la faccia, apunto come nella ferità de' costumi, così anche nella ruvidezza del volto, imiti gli animali brutti, e per renderti in tutto e per tutto simile anche a quell'irragionevoli, cui la natura ha proveduto di corna, hai studiosamente mendicata invenzione d'inalzare, apunto in forma di corna, quei peli i quali tu hai ambizioso che sovra la bocca, se non sovra del capo, ti stampino un carrattere che ti contrasegni per un perfetto animale" (*SI* 357). I have translated it here myself, seeking to preserve the rhythm of the original. Panizza breaks the passage up into three sentences.

[30] "ingrato animale" (*SI* 197).

[31] "La mia semplicità [...] è stata ingannata dalla sagacità del serpente," cited in Panizza, introduction 15.

"innocence deceived" ("la semplicità ingannata") in the title of her work.

As critics, especially Letizia Panizza, have observed, *Paternal Tyranny* is characterized throughout by intertextuality ("Reader Over Arcangela's Shoulder" and *PT* 16-17). The author's discourse is constantly responding to anti-woman ideas and texts, especially to those of members of the Incogniti, and primarily to Giovanni Francesco Loredan's misogynist novella and Angelico Aprosio's *Maschera scoperta* and his *Scudo di Rinaldo* (Bufacchi 72-73). While Loredan's work is a subtext present throughout the treatise, in Book Three Tarabotti actually names him. In the last pages of *Paternal Tyranny* she also denounces the "indecent accusations [...] obscene, sarcastic, disgusting" of Giuseppe Passi's *The Defects of Women* (*I donneschi difetti*), which she has rejected earlier, especially in Book Two, and "the satirical viper's tongue" and "loathsome work" of Ferrante Pallavicino — lies and insults directed at women (*PT* 146-47).[32] Passi and Pallavicino were dead when she condemned their misogyny, but Loredan was a powerful man in Venice, who, beginning in the 1630s and 1640s, controlled the publishing industry there. He had supported her work, and brought her *Convent Paradise* and her collected letters to press. Tarabotti, nevertheless, does not hesitate to impugn his motives in his denigration of Eve and denounce his hostility to women:

[...] when a male writer composes to the detriment of women, he tells lies and nothing else. His warped mind produces envy's malformed offspring, not justice's whole ones. Let us hear Sir Giovan Francesco Loredan, the glory of modern letters, the wonder of the universe, the sun whose rays of virtue dazzle us. The world's eyes are turned towards him, gazing with pleasure. And what reason does he give in his novel, *The Life of Adam*, for not being able to find the death of Eve in Holy Scripture? He says one must not recall the death of a woman who should never have been born! [...] Men's bile, in short, is striving incessantly to employ sophistry with their lies against the female sex; they never stop blaming us for no other reason than envy, for since they cannot lord it over us by their merits, they must do so by their tongues [...].[33]   (*PT* 134)

---

[32] "Che sconci concetti, che aplicazioni oscene, mordaci e improprie" "satirica e viperea lingua [...] improperii" (*SI* 379-80); "con satirica e viperea lingua, in una sua detestabilissima opera va mendicando improperii e inventando ignominie contro il nostro sesso" (*SI* 380-81). On Giuseppe Passi's *I donneschi difetti* (1599) see Magnanini 143-94. Tarabotti refers to Ferrante Pallavicino's *Il corriero svaligiato* (1641) and probably also to *Il divorzio celeste* (1643). Letter 5 of *Il corriero svaligiato*, to which Tarabotti objects (*PT* 147; *SI* 381), is available in English, translated by Panizza in Appendix 2 of her edition of *Paternal Tyranny* 158-62.

[33] "[...] quando uno, sia oratore o poeta, scrive in pregiudizio delle donne, altro non sappia dire che bugie e l'ingegno di lui altro non sappia partorire che aborti d'invidie, non parti di giustizia. Odasi il signor Giovan Francesco Loredano, gloria delle moderne lettere, maraviglia dell'universo, e sole che ne' raggi delle sue chiare virtù gli occhi del mondo tutto stanno fissamente rivolti con diletto, qual mendicata ragione apporti nel suo *Adamo* del non trovarsi su le Sacre Scritture la morte d'Eva. Dice egli che non si deve ramentar la morte di colei che non meritò giamai di nascere. [...] In somma il livore degli

The time had no doubt passed when Tarabotti sought Loredan's help in publishing *Paternal Tyranny* in Venice, and she had criticized him before, without jeopardizing their friendship. Although it is not a very complete picture, we can learn something about their relationship from the little that remains of their correspondence. In a letter to her, Loredan responds to her strong objection to something he had written against women at the instance of the Academy: "So it is, my Lady Arcangela. You must learn patience, because *Dio fecit nos, non ipsi nos*. Yet I will not let your satire change my heart and keep me from declaring myself to be yours always" (my translation).[34]

In *Paternal Tyranny* Tarabotti takes a stand on many issues that were important to her. She argues for the education of women and for their access to public roles. She laments her own lack of learning; however, it is clear from the text itself that she has read widely and has learned to write extremely well.[35] She enlivens her prose with passages of poetry and is especially partial to Dante and Ariosto, and she is aware of a women's literary tradition in Italy. She treats many of the topics debated in the *Querelle* literature and adopts many of its features in her treatise, for instance, the catalogue of examples taken from literature, myth, history, and especially from the Bible, both Old and New Testament. She devotes Book Three to the positive role of women in the world and the special importance of one woman, the Virgin Mary, in the providential scheme of Redemption.

Given the controversial nature of *Paternal Tyranny* and its accusations of specific persons and institutions, of fathers, the Venetian state and the Church, Tarabotti could find no home for her treatise in Venice or anywhere else in Italy.[36] Her hopes to publish it in France were frustrated too. She had made two attempts and had even written to request the help of Cardinal Mazarin, but without success. Tarabotti never gave up. Despite the obstacles and the setbacks, she persisted until she found persons sympathetic to her cause and a publisher out of the reach of the Roman Church. In the last two years of her life Tarabotti

---

uomini va di continuo studiando di sofisticare con menzogne a pregiudizio del merito feminile, del quale non dice male con biasimi sì frequenti per altro che per un affetto invidioso, già che conoscendo di non poter sovrastar con le qualità vuol rimaner superiore con la lingua"(*SI* 358-59).

[34] "Così è, Signora Arcangela mia. Bisogna accomodarsi alla patienza, perché Dio fecit nos, non ipsi nos. Non voglio, però, che la sua satira alteri il mio cuore, onde non mi professi sempre di V[ostra] S[ignoria][...]" (Loredan, *Lettere* 272, 274). By satire, Loredan is referring to a satirical letter he received from Tarabotti in response to his misogynist satire, and not a literary work.

[35] Bortot provides an excellent, detailed analysis of Tarabotti's style in her Introduction to *La semplicità ingannata* 138-46.

[36] By 1650 relations between Venice and Rome had improved and the Venetian government had to give up some of its prerogatives in religious matters to the Church in exchange for aid in the war of Candia. Some of the freedoms enjoyed earlier were curtailed, among them the freedom to publish controversial texts. See Infelise 66-72.

had the satisfaction to learn that the printing was underway, but she died in 1652, two years before the book appeared.

Tarabotti did not enjoy the pleasure of seeing *Paternal Tyranny* in print, but she was spared the pain of learning that it was condemned by the Holy Office. In 1654, the book had scarcely appeared when the Congregation of the Index began to move against it, and in 1660 they banned the book. *Paternal Tyranny* (with the title *La semplicità ingannata*) was officially placed on the Index of Forbidden Books in 1661. The examiners considered many statements in *Paternal Tyranny* blasphemous, scandalous and offensive to the Church, and they feared reading the book would deter young women from entering the convent or from taking permanent vows. They found comparing the cloister with Hell, enclosure with prison, and exposing the economic incentives for coerced monichization offensive to the Church, a denial of the divine inspiration for religious vocations. They claimed that Tarabotti misunderstood doctrine and quoted erroneously from Scripture, and they deemed contrary to Catholic doctrine her interpretation of the Fall. They considered her appeal for liberty, for the equality of the sexes, and for a woman's right to choose freely her state in life to be a desire for license. They read her appeal for the freedom to marry and live in the world to smack of Lutheranism. The censors read many of Tarabotti's statements out of context and with no understanding of rhetorical conventions.[37]

As Tarabotti had written in her opening address to her reader, "my words will bear little or no fruit and will remain unheeded, condemned as the offspring of a deranged mind stripped of religion and accused of imprudence, since in this false world, as the proverb goes, 'Speaking the truth incurs hatred'" (*PT* 41).[38]

The University of Chicago

Works Cited

Agrippa, Henricus Cornelius. *Declamation on the Nobility and Preeminence of the Female Sex*. Ed. and trans. Albert Rabil, Jr. Chicago: U of Chicago P, 1996.

Biga, Emilia. *Una polemica antifemminista del '600: La"Mascherata scoperta" di Angelico Aprosio*. Ventimiglia: Civica Biblioteca Aprosiana, 1989.

---

[37] Costa-Zalessow, in "La condanna all'Indice," provides the full text of the *censura* in Latin with commentary in Italian; and in "Tarabotti's *La semplicità ingannata*" 320-21, she includes two lists of objections to the work made by examiners. Panizza, in her Introduction to *Paternal Tyranny* (27-29), provides a summary of the accusations and, in notes, direct quotations from some of the Latin documents; I have taken most of my summary from Panizza.

[38] "[...] i detti miei faran poco o niun frutto, anzi rimaranno censurati, come nati da un animo non ben composto, sfornito di religione, e accusati di temerità, poiché sempre in questo fallace mondo veritas odium parit" (*SI* 176-77).

Bufacchi, Emanuela. "'La mia semplicità è stata ingannata dalla sagacia del serpente.' Polemiche di Girolamo Brusoni con Arcangela Tarabotti." *Esperienze letterarie* 40.2 (2015): 55-77.
Buoninsegni, Francesco. *Contro il lusso donnesco, satira menippea con l'Antisatira di d. A. T. in risposta.* Venezia: F. Valvasense, 1644.
_____, and Arcangela Tarabotti. *Satira e Antisatira.* Ed. Elissa B. Weaver. Roma: Salerno Editrice, 1998.
Cannizzaro, Nina. "Studies on Guido Casoni, 1561-1642, and Venetian Academies." Diss. Harvard U, 2001.
Conti Odorisio, Ginevra. *Donne e società nel Seicento.* Roma: Bulzoni, 1979.
_____. *Storia dell'idea femminista in Italia.* Torino: ERI, 1980.
Costa-Zalessow, Natalia. "La condanna all'Indice della *Semplicità ingannata* di Arcangela Tarabotti alla luce di manoscritti inediti." *Nouvelles de la République des Lettres* 1 (2002): 97-113.
_____. "Tarabotti's *La semplicità ingannata* and its Twentieth-Century Interpreters, with Unpublished Documents Regarding its Condemnation to the Index." *Italica* 78 (2001): 314-25.
Croce, Benedetto. "Appunti di letteratura secentesca inedita o rara." *La Critica* 27 (1929): 468-80.
Heller, Wendy. "'La forza d'amore' and the 'Monaca sforzata': Opera, Tarabotti, and the Pleasures of Debate." *Arcangela Tarabotti: A Literary Nun.* Ed. Elissa B. Weaver. 141-57.
_____. "'O delle donne miserabil sesso': Tarabotti, Ottavia and *L'incoronazione di Poppea.*" *Il saggiatore musicale* 7 (2000): 5-46.
Infelise, Mario. "Books and Politics in Arcangela Tarabotti's Venice." *Arcangela Tarabotti: A Literary Nun.* Ed. Elissa B. Weaver. 57-72.
Kelly, Joan. "Early Feminist Theory and the *Querelle des Femmes.*" *Women, History and Theory.* Chicago: U of Chicago P, 1984. 65-109.
Loredan, Giovan Francesco. *L'Adamo.* Venezia: Sarzina, 1640.
_____. *Lettere divise in cinquantadue capi e raccolte da Henrico Giblet* [pseud. of Loredan]. Venezia: Guerigli, 1652.
Magnanini, Suzanne, with David Lamari. "Giuseppe Passi's Attacks on Women in *The Defects of Women.*" *Dialogue with the Other Voice in Sixteenth-Century Italy: Literary and Social Contexts for Women's Writing.* Toronto: CRRS, 2011. 143-94.
Maylander, Michele. *Storia delle accademie d'Italia.* 5 vols. Bologna: Licinio Cappelli, 1926-30. Vol. 3: 205-06.
Medioli, Francesca. "Monacazioni forzate: donne ribelli al proprio destino." *Clio. Rivista Trimestrale di studi storici* 30 (1994): 431-54.
Miato, Monica. *L'Accademia degli Incogniti di Giovan Francesco Loredan. Venezia, 1630-61.* Firenze: Olschki, 1998.
Muir, Edward. *The Culture Wars of the Late Renaissance: Skeptics, Libertines, and Opera.* Cambridge, MA: Harvard UP, 2007.
Pallavicino, Ferrante. *Il corriero svaligiato.* Venezia: Piacenini, 1541.
_____. *Il corriero svaligiato: con la lettera della prigionia.* Ed. Armando Marchi. Parma: Università di Parma, 1984.
_____. *Il divorzio celeste: cagionato dalle dissolutezze della sposa Romana* [...]. Villafranca: n. p., 1543.
Panizza, Letizia. "Reader Over Arcangela's Shoulder: Tarabotti at Work with her Sources." *Arcangela Tarabotti: A Literary Nun.* Ed. Elissa B. Weaver. 107-28.
Passi, Giuseppe. *I donneschi difetti.* Venezia: Somasco, 1599.

Portigliotti, Giuseppe. *Penombre claustrali.* Milano: Fratelli Treves Editori, 1930. 251-313.

Sesti, Lodovico. *Censura dell'Antisatira della signora Angelica* [sic] *Tarabotti fatta in risposta alla Satira menipea contro il lusso donnesco del sig. Franc. Buoninsegni. Scherzo geniale di Lucido Ossiteo* [pseud.]. Siena: Bonetti, 1656.

Tarabotti, Arcangela. *Antisatira.* Publ. anon. by d. A. T [donna Arcangela Tarabotti]. Buoninsegni 1998: 67-227.

_____. *Antisatira.* Sesti [29]-104.

_____. *Antisatira.* Buoninsegni and Tarabotti 56-105.

_____. *Che le donne siano della spezie degli huomini. Difesa delle donne di Galerana Barcitotti* [pseud.] *contro Horatio Plata.* Norimbergh: Iuvann Cherchenbergher, 1651.

_____. *Inferno monacale.* Ed. Francesca Medioli. Torino: Rosenberg & Sellier, 1990.

_____. *Le lagrime d'Arcangela Tarabotti per la morte dell'illustrissima signora Regina Donati. Lettere familiari e di complimento* 323-84.

_____. *Lettere familiari e di complimento.* Venezia: Guerigli, 1650.

_____. *Lettere familiari e di complimento.* Ed. Meredith K. Ray and Lynn Lara Westwater. Torino: Rosenberg & Sellier, 2005.

_____. *Letters Familiar and Formal.* Ed. and trans. Meredith K. Ray and Lynn Lara Westwater. Toronto: Iter, Centre for Reformation and Renaissance Studies, 2012.

_____. *Paradiso monacale.* Venezia: Guglielmo Oddoni, 1663 [but 1643].

_____. *Paternal Tyranny.* Ed. Letizia Panizza. Chicago: U of Chicago P, 2004.

_____. *La semplicità ingannata.* Ed. Simona Bortot. Padova: Il Poligrafo, 2007.

_____. *La semplicità ingannata di Galerana Baratotti* [pseud.]. Leida: Gio. Sambix [Elzevier], 1654.

_____. *Soliloquio a Dio. Paradiso monacale* 1-34.

_____. *Women Are Not Human: An Anonymous Treatise and Responses.* Ed. and trans. Theresa M Kenney. New York: Crossroad, 1998.

Schutte, Anne Jacobson. *By Force and Fear: Taking and Breaking Monastic Vows in Early Modern Europe.* Ithaca: Cornell UP, 2011.

Weaver, Elissa, ed. *Arcangela Tarabotti: A Literary Nun in Baroque Venice.* Ravenna: Longo Editore, 2006.

Westwater, Lynn Lara, "A Rediscovered Friendship in the Republic of Letters: The Unpublished Correspondence of Arcangela Tarabotti and Ismaël Boulliau." *Renaissance Quarterly* 65 (2012): 67-134.

Zanette, Emilio. "Elena Tarabotti e la sua *Semplicità ingannata.*"*Convivium* 2 (1930): 49-53.

_____. "Ancora di Elena Tarabotti." *Convivium* 3 (1931): 124-29.

_____. *Suor Arcangela, monaca del Seicento veneziano.* Venezia: Istituto per la Collaborazione Culturale, 1960.

Zarri, Gabriella. "Monasteri femminili e città." *Recinti. Donne, clausura e matrimonio nella prima età moderna.* Bologna: Il Mulino, 2000.

Nicla Riverso

Paolo Sarpi:
The Hunted Friar and his Popularity in England

Abstract: During the Council of Trent (1545-63), Protestants felt humiliated and excluded from the decisions made by the popes and had therefore been looking to redeem their position in Christendom. Because Sarpi was one of the most eminent Catholic theologians of the period, Protestants drew on his criticisms of the Church for support of their cause. Sarpi's work offered Protestant writers the means to demonstrate that their arguments against the pope and the Church of Rome were well founded. Moreover, Sarpi was considered a "hero" who had survived an assassination attempt and had defeated the pope during the Venetian interdict (1605-07). In this article, I explain how Sarpi's work gained a strong acceptance in England and how Sarpi tried to use his popularity to bring practical benefits to the Venetian Republic, which ultimately was left alone in its fight for "liberty" and in its attempt to reform the Church.
Key words: Sarpi, Venetian Republic, Protestants, Church of Rome, Council of Trent, Venetian interdict, James I, Church of England.

Introduction
Paolo Sarpi, whose life spanned the second half of the sixteenth century and the beginning of the seventeenth (1552-1623), lived and worked among a great number of learned men whose discoveries and theories irrevocably changed Western civilization. Even in this atmosphere of radical historical, political and religious ferment, Sarpi's intellectual contributions stood out, sometimes too starkly for the comfort of many of his cleric colleagues.[1] Sarpi's scholarship was

---

[1] Paolo Sarpi was born Pietro Sarpi in Venice (August 14, 1552) and was the son of a tradesman who had come to Venice from Friuli. Sarpi's father died when Sarpi was still a child. His mother, Isabella Morelli, was from a noble Venetian family. Sarpi's first teacher was his mother's brother, a priest and schoolmaster. Early in life, Sarpi showed prodigious scholarship, arousing the wonder of his contemporaries. At the age of thirteen, he excelled in Latin, Greek, Hebrew, philosophy, mathematics, theology in all its branches, and many of the sciences. At about this age, he joined the order of Servite friars and changed his name to Paolo. At eighteen, he became professor in the Cathedral of Bishop Boldrino in Mantua and the private theologian of Duke Gonzaga. In 1579, he was sent to Rome on matters connected with the reform of his order. He returned to Venice in

far more popular in the rest of Europe than in Italy during his era. Indeed, his political opposition to church authorities earned him many enemies, who tried to discredit him and devalue his works. However, at the same time that Sarpi's work was being condemned by the Inquisition in Italy, it was being received with great respect and acclaim throughout the rest of Europe. In the countries beyond the Alps, Sarpi was held in high esteem as one of the greatest eclectic scholars of his age and was likely the most frequently translated Italian writer of the era. He was also considered remarkable for the virtue and integrity with which he led his life, and was seen as a man who could bring concrete changes to the Christian religion by upholding the principles of the Reformation. His writings seemed to many to be an invitation to revive Christianity, purifying it of sin and corruption.

Sir Henry Wotton, the Ambassador to Venice, described Sarpi as "the most deep and general scholar of the world," and proclaimed the extent of Sarpi's philosophical and historical knowledge and his achievements in physics and science (Logan 1: 87).[2] In a letter to Adam Newton, William Bedell, Wotton's chaplain, describes Sarpi as a "miracle in all manner of knowledge divine and humane" (Clogie 231). Wotton and Bedell helped to increase Sarpi's popularity in England, writing letters to King James I and to a number of illustrious friends, describing not only Sarpi's intellectual achievements but also the active and courageous role that he played during the conflict between the Republic and Pope Paul V. Moreover, Wotton and Bedell sent the first pages of Sarpi's *History of the Council of Trent* to King James, who received it with enthusiasm and sponsored its publication in England (Walton 37).

The Interdict Controversy
Sarpi and the Venetian Republic received particular attention in seventeenth-century England because the "Interdict Controversy" between Venice and Rome moved the Venetian Republic away from Spain and brought it closer to England and France.[3] In 1606, the city of Venice tried Scipio Saraceni and Brandolino

---

1588, and spent the rest of his life in Venice. In 1606, Sarpi was appointed Theological Counselor by the Venetian Senate. This duty of this office, created in addition to three Counselors of Law, was to instruct the Doge and Senate in the law. After the other Counselors died, the Senate left their whole duties to Sarpi. The Servite friar held entire control of the legal and theological principles of Venice for many years. During this time Sarpi was very prolific and wrote his most important works, which were published only many years after his death. He died on January 15, 1623 in his cell in the convent of Santa Maria dei Servi in Venice.

[2] Henry Wotton served as ambassador to Venice intermittently from 1604 to 1625.
[3] Concerning the Interdict, see Bouwsma, "Venice, Spain, and the Papacy." On Sarpi and the British Protestants, see Bouwsma, *Venice and the Defense* 512-55; Wootton 93-117;

Valmarino, two ecclesiastics accused of several crimes, in a secular rather than an ecclesiastical court. Pope Paul V demanded the liberty of the two prisoners, claiming ecclesiastical immunity. Moreover, the Venetian Senate published two decrees, one of which forbade the founding of hospitals or monasteries, the institution of new religious orders, and the building of churches, without the permission of the Venetian Senate and the Council of Ten. The second decree outlawed throughout the whole republic the alienation by sale or by bequest of any Church real estate without the consent of the Senate (Cozzi, "Paolo Sarpi" 422). The pope was angered by these decrees and demanded their revocation. The Venetian Republic ignored the pope's demands.

On April 17, 1606, Paul V excommunicated the entire Republic and placed it under interdict. The Venetians, led by their Theological Counselor Paolo Sarpi, defied the pope: the bull of the interdict was despised and ignored. The pope invited Sarpi to Rome for discussions, but the Servite friar declined the invitation (Robertson 90-91). The relationship between Venice and Rome degenerated into intense hostility. During the interdict, Sarpi tried to ensure that people outside of Venice were aware of the tension and acrimony between the Republic and the pope, producing and distributing writings in defense of the Venetian cause (Cozzi, *Paolo Sarpi tra Venezia e l'Europa*). Sarpi's international network of friends and supporters helped publicize these strongly expressed writings, as well as a series of harsh responses from the papal curia's representative, Cardinal Roberto Bellarmino. These written exchanges became known as the "guerra delle scritture" (war of writings) in which Sarpi used his writing ability to condemn the supremacy of the Church of Rome and the injustices committed by the ecclesiastical authorities: "[...] non nelle sole armi sta la forza, ma nelle parole ancora" ("there is strength not only in arms but in words as well").[4]

English scholars, politicians and religious people felt affinity with and sympathy for the Venetian Republic and identified England with Venice, as both were involved in a strenuous struggle with the pope while attempting to confront

---

and Sarpi, *Lettere ai Protestanti*. On Sarpi and the French Gallicans, see the introduction by Ulianich in *Lettere ai Gallicani*.

[4] "Trattato intorno alla Scomunica" in Capasso XXXII. The term "war of writings" was coined by Sarpi: "[...] un'altra sorte di guerra, fatta con scritture, offensiva dal canto del pontefice, e difensiva dal canto della repubblica" ("another kind of war, made with writings, with the pontiff on the offensive and the Republic on the defensive") (*Istoria dell'Interdetto* 102). On Bellarmino and his role as a representative of the papal curia, see Frajese 139-52. On the Interdict, particularly in reference to *la guerra delle scritture*, see Burke and also de Vivo 157-248. On the clash between those who supported the *potestas absoluta* on behalf of the religious authorities and those who supported the *potentia ordinata* on behalf of the secular authorities during the interdict in Venice, see Belligni 272-74. On the question of religious and political authority, see also Oakley.

the supremacy of the Roman Curia. After Henry VIII broke with the Church of Rome, the relationship between the King of England and the pope became very strained indeed: the Catholic Church refused to recognize the Church of England as a separate Church ruled by the king.[5] During the era of the Venetian interdict, James I — survivor of the Gunpowder Plot in which a group of provincial English Catholics attempted to blow up him together with the Houses of Parliament on November 5, 1605 — offered military support to Venice, and threatened to intervene against the pope, likely hoping that the Venetian Republic would secede from the Church of Rome and establish a religion closer to the Protestant creed (Robertson 95). Nevertheless, James I had never explicitly shown his animosity towards the pope and claimed that he defended the Republic's cause only in order to accomplish a service for God, so as to keep the liberty that "sua Maestà divina" had given to Venice. In *Istoria dell'Interdetto* Sarpi writes:

Ma il re alla rappresentazione dell'ambasciator Giustiniano rispose che chiamava Dio in testimonio di non aver fatta risoluzione di difender la causa della republica per altro fine che per servizio di Dio, per conservare la libertà data da sua Maestà divina alli príncipi, e non per contesa propria che abbia col papa.
(But the King, in the presence of the ambassador Giustiniano, replied that he called upon God to testify that he had not resolved to defend the cause of the republic for any end other than service to God and the preservation of the liberty given by his Divine Majesty to the princes, and not for any dispute he might have with the pope.)[6]

(1: 124)

Sarpi played a central role in Pope Paul V's interdict. He entered the fray energetically, denying the pope's authority in secular matters and encouraging resistance to papal censure. Sarpi accused the pope of illegally exercising temporal power and illegitimately investing himself with absolute authority in political and governmental activities. He insisted that papal supremacy and authority should be limited:

La potestà del sommo pontefice di commandare alli cristiani non è illimitata, né si estende a tutte le materie e modi, ma è ristretta al fine della publica utilità della chiesa, ed ha per regola la legge divina.
(The power of the Supreme Pontiff to rule the Christians is not unlimited, nor does it extend to all matters and ways, but is limited to the purpose of the church's public utility, and is ruled by divine law.)

(*Istoria dell'Interdetto* 3:15)

Moreover, Sarpi attempted to persuade the Venetians to rebuff the pope's

---

[5] In fact, in 1538 Pope Paul III placed England under interdict and attempted to dethrone Henry VIII. Concerning this matter, see the collection of essays in McEachern.
[6] All translations are mine.

excommunication and disregard the pope's orders by explaining that the excommunication was not based on the pope's legitimate rights. Sarpi argued that these irregular and unlawful excommunications "non sono né da temere né da osservare" ("are neither to be feared nor to be observed") and that

[i] deboli di coscienza e scrupolosi [...] reputano che il papa sia un Dio che abbia ogni potestà in cielo e in terra. Ma si debbe liberare questi tali dalla sua sciocchezza con idonee e convenienti informazioni.
(The people who have a weak conscience and those who are scrupulous [...] consider that the pope is a God who has every power in heaven and on earth. But those people should be freed from this nonsense with appropriate and suitable information.)

(*Istoria dell'Interdetto* 2: 179)

But opposing the pope was a very dangerous deed and Bishop Bedell's letters to his British friends reveal his concern about the exposure of the Servite friar in his fight against the Roman Curia. In a letter to Adam Newton, preceptor to Prince Henry, Bedell describes a barbarous attack against Sarpi in Venice.[7] On October 5, 1607, Sarpi was stabbed in the head and neck and left for dead in the street by assassins from Rome, who were widely thought to have been sent by the pope (Bedell 31-32). In a letter to the Earl of Salisbury, Wotton also notes this attempted assassination and points out that suspicions of the Church of Rome's direct involvement in the criminal attack were well-founded (Logan 1: 404-06). The attempt on Sarpi's life caused a considerable stir throughout Europe, bringing even greater attention to the Servite friar and his actions. The episode was mentioned in various contemporary writings as an example of the cruelty and ruthlessness of the Church of Rome and its annihilation of anybody opposed to it.[8]

The "History of the Council of Trent" in England

After the assassination attempt Sarpi's popularity increased, in part because the Servite friar was seen as a helpless victim of an unscrupulous pope, who did not hesitate to use criminal methods to assert his supremacy. To many, Sarpi came to represent a Venetian Republic fighting boldly against the injustices and harassments of the Roman Curia. He wrote in defense of the Republic and won sympathy abroad, particularly in England, where his work interested many

---

[7] As evidence that Bishop Bedell was an intimate friend of Paolo Sarpi, Burnet writes that after Sarpi was wounded "much precaution was used before any were admitted to come to him, Bedell was excepted out of those rules, and had free access to him at all times" (7).

[8] For instance, Thomas Coryat, the British "walking tourist," recalls the attempt on Sarpi's life as part of his narration on Venice in his *Coryat's Cruditates*, a description of his experiences traveling through Europe (2: 8).

scholars, in large part because many of the points he raised allowed them to hone the arguments they used in their own fight against the Catholic Church. Because Sarpi was a Catholic friar writing against the supremacy of the pope, his *History of the Council of Trent* was considered an emblematic work.[9] The first edition of the *History* was published in London in 1619 from a copy of Sarpi's completed manuscript, smuggled into England by Marco Antonio de Dominis.[10] The work was published under the pen-name "Pietro Soave Polano," an anagram of Sarpi's own name, because of its strongly critical content.

During his stay in Venice, Sir Dudley Carleton, England's Ambassador to the Venetian Republic from 1610 to 1616 and an ardent Calvinist, encouraged Sarpi to write about the Council of Trent. Further, he convinced Sarpi to alter his original plan for the work, which was to have been a publication, with commentary, of some of the Council's documents (Cozzi, "Fra Paolo Sarpi" 573-75). Thus persuaded by Sir Dudley, Sarpi wrote a sharp, pungent interpretation of the Council of Trent's conclusions. To further this own goal, Sir Dudley sent the Servite friar a book about the Council written by his cousin George Carleton, Bishop of Chichester.[11] Just as Sir Dudley intended, Sarpi was consequently moved to write about the Council in order to correct some distortions and misunderstandings introduced by George Carleton and other British writers, such as Richard Field (*Of the Church*).[12] Sir Dudley achieved his aim: Sarpi's *History of the Council of Trent* became a colossal work about the Roman Curia and its efforts to derail the Protestant Reformation to confirm its

---

[9] On the *History* and its popularity in England see Yates.

[10] Marco Antonio de Dominis (1566-1624) was a Roman Catholic archbishop who, threatened by the Inquisition, left for England in 1616. On his way, he published a violent attack on Rome: *Scogli del naufragio cristiano* (*The Rocks of Christian Shipwreck*). He was received with great honors by James I. Three years later he returned to Rome, where he lived on a pension assigned him by Pope Gregory XV. But the pension ceased after the death of the Pope in 1623, and he was declared a heretic and confined to Castel Sant'Angelo. One year later he died in prison, probably poisoned, and his body was burned at Rome's Campo dei Fiori, along with all his manuscripts. On de Dominis and the doomed reaction to the Protestant Reform in the Catholic Church, see Cantimori 473-81.

[11] George Carleton (1559-1628) was an English churchman. He was a delegate to the Synod of Dort, in the Netherlands, and became Bishop of Llandaff in 1618, an office he held for a year. From 1619 to 1628, he was Bishop of Chichester. Among his many works on religious matters was *Consensus Ecclesiae contra tridentinos* published in 1613. On Sarpi and Dudley Carleton, see Lievsay 115-16.

[12] Carleton and Field argued that the Council of Trent drew the line between the pre-Reformation Latin Church and the corrupt, fraudulent and deceptive post-Reformation Church of Rome.

own power and greatness.[13]

English scholars and ecclesiastics were seeking support in the Catholic world to combat the Church of Rome's claim to universal catholicity and to prove that the Church of Rome was no longer the church of Christ.[14] They wished to show that the Council of Trent had not returned the Church of Rome to its original, authentic nature, nor had it united the Christian world. For these British divines, Sarpi's *History* was an inestimably valuable testimony of the true events at the Council of Trent, both "on the stage" and behind the scenes. Sarpi's inquiry aimed to unveil the intrigues of the Roman Curia which advertised the Council as a free and open synod of Christians whereas Protestants felt they lacked any true representation while Catholics dominated all the sessions.[15] The language of Sarpi's work is powerfully expressive and communicates in a direct, simple, striking way what he learned firsthand from friends and acquaintances.[16]

Even though Sarpi wished to give the impression of writing an impartial scholarly work, it is evident that his true commitment was to underlining the vices and immoralities that led the Council to fail in its purpose. When, for example, Sarpi writes about the lack of freedom during the Council, he explains very clearly how the Roman Curia was responsible for centralizing religious and

---

[13] On Sarpi and the achievement of his historical work in the European political and religious context, see Cozzi, *Paolo Sarpi tra Venezia e l'Europa* 264-81.

[14] Anti-papal polemics and arguments about whether Rome was the church of Christ were widespread among the English Reformation writers. See Bedell 257, Butterfield, Perkins and Carleton, *Directions to know the true Church*.

[15] The issue of the absence of Protestant reformers at the Council is very complex. Basically, they were invited, but, given the conditions imposed upon them, they refused to attend. Concerning the Catholic position on this matter, I refer to the entry on the Council of Trent: http://www.newadvent.org/cathen/15030c.htm.

[16] In Mantua, around 1574, Sarpi became a friend of Camillo Olivo, secretary of Cardinal Ercole Gonzaga, who took part in the last phase of the Council. Later, according to Vivanti, Sarpi, during his stay in Rome between 1585 and the end of 1588 or the beginning of 1589, had access to the letters written by the papal legates and to other documents that belonged to the Cervini's family until 1771 (609). During this stay in Rome, Sarpi met people who helped him gather information about the Council. In Rome, Sarpi became close to Giovan Battista Castagna, future cardinal, and, later, Pope Urban VII, who was president of the committee appointed for drawing up the decrees of the Council, and established friendly relations with Cardinal Roberto Bellarmino, who opened up to him the Cervini family archive that belonged to his uncle, Pope Marcello II (Asor Rosa 344). Later, in Venice, Sarpi was intimately acquainted with the French ambassador Arnaud du Ferrier, who had represented the king of France during the last stages of the Council of Trent (Wootton 9). "He was most intimate with those of France, with Ferrar, Demete and Fresnes, and particularly with Ferrier, who being present at the said Councell of Trent, had many great memorials (and letters which are the most secure and reall foundation of an History.)" (Micanzio 97).

secular power:

> [...] ogni cosa si consultava prima a Roma; l'altra, perché non era libero il proporre, avendo li legati soli assontisi questa libertà che doveva essere comune; la terza causa, per le pratiche che facevano alcuni prelati interessati nella grandezza della corte romana.
> ([...] everything was first consulted in Rome; there was no freedom in the proposals, because only the papal legates had this right, which should have been shared; the third cause [of Rome's centralizing power] depended on the practices of some prelates, who were interested [in maintaining] the greatness of the Roman court.)
> *(Istoria del Concilio Tridentino* 1:168)

Further, in his explanation of the unscrupulous means by which the pope arrogated more authority and power to himself, Sarpi notes that to amass temporal power is to ignore the divine injunction against exercising any authority over the bishops which might divert them from their main task, namely, the care of the believers:

> Perché se Dio ha comandato ai vescovi di reseder perpetuamente alla cura del gregge, per necessaria conseguenza li ha prescritto anco il carico, e dato loro la potestà per bene esercitarlo; adonque il papa non potrà né chiamarli né occuparli in altro, né dispensarli, né restringer l'autorità data da Dio.
> (Because, if God has commanded the bishops to take continuous care of their flock, as a necessary consequence He has also prescribed them these duties and has given them the power to exercise them well; therefore, the Pope is allowed neither to call them and give them another task, nor to exempt them and restrict the authority given them by God.)
> (1:370)

The accusations against the pope and the Roman Curia aroused the interest of those English Protestants who found important religious and political value in Sarpi's work. They used it quite openly to strengthen the position of the Church of England and to justify that church's separation from Rome, declaring on the strength of Sarpi's arguments that the Church of England alone had kept the original meaning of Catholicism intact. Moreover, James I and his supporters endorsed Sarpi's *History* because they saw in it a confirmation of the pope's arrogance towards other Churches, which constituted in their view a good reason to give religious power to the king.[17]

Sarpi's *History* makes no claim for the superiority of the Church of England, but does include many references to the arrogant and deceitful claims made by the Catholic Church during the Council of Trent. In Chapter I, Book I of the *History,* Sarpi declares that although the Council had been called for the purpose of reuniting the Christian world, it instead created deeper fractures between the Church of Rome and the Protestant Churches and increased the

---

[17] On James I and his religious ambitions see Butler, Figgis and Patterson.

pope's power, as a result of which the Council illegally affirmed the pope's authority; and by subduing even the bishops, the pope strengthened his position inside the Catholic Church:

Imperocché questo concilio, desiderato e procurato dagli uomini pii per riunire la Chiesa che principiava a dividersi, per contrario ha cosí stabilito lo scisma ed ostinate le parti, che ha fatto le discordie irreconciliabili; e maneggiato dai príncipi per riforma dell'ordine ecclesiastico, ha causato la maggiore disformazione che sia mai stata dopo che il nome cristiano si ode; e dalli vescovi adoperato per racquistar l'autorità episcopale, passata in gran parte nel solo pontefice romano, gliel'ha fatta perder tutta intieramente, ed interessati loro stessi nella propria servitú [...].
(For this Council, desired and organized by godly men to reunite the Church which was becoming divided, has so established the Schism and made the parties so obstinate that it has rendered disagreements irreconcilable, and, manipulated by princes to reform the ecclesiastical discipline, it has caused the greatest deformation ever to happen since the name of "Christian" was first heard; and, used by the bishops to regain episcopal authority, which has moved for the most part exclusively to the Pope, it has made them lose their authority altogether, bringing them into servitude [...].)

(1:4)

The pope's attitude during the Council caused anger and disappointment in Europe, and he became the object of a violent attack from the reformed churches across the Alps. In the *Direction to know the true Church*, Bishop George Carleton expresses bitterness towards the Church of Rome and argues that the true doctrines of the Roman Church had been wiped out because of the authority of the pope, not because of the authority of God. He claims that

the present Church of Rome, is not the church of Christ, but an assembly, I say, not of heretikes, but of farre worse, and more dangerous then any heretikes heretofore have bene: For the former heretikes, that have openly forsaken the Church, could neuer doe so much harme, as Antichrist with his creatures, who having secretly forsaken the Church, yet make open claime to the Church, and to all the rights thereof.

(65)

In his treatise Carleton meant to contrast the Roman corruption and degeneracy with the traditional values and ideals still in evidence in the only remaining "true" Catholic Church, which in his view was the Church of England.

In 1627, Rev. Thomas Jackson published *Two Treatises on the Church* defending the Anglican faith against the Roman, claiming that "the present visible Church of England retains the holy catholic faith, which the romish church hath defiled; and by defiling it hath lost that true union with the primitive and apostolic church which the visible church retaineth" (115).[18] In England, Carleton and Jackson were only two of many ecclesiastics focused on discerning which church was the "true church," and on identifying what truly pristine dogma would be. They were convinced that the Church of Rome had lost its purity and that it had become corrupt and its dogma erroneous.[19] Because the Church of Rome and the Church of England were different aspects of the same church, the latter had the right to pick up the mantle abandoned by the Church of Rome when it first began to stray from the path of truth.[20] Moreover, for the English divines, the pope's authority and arrogance was a deeply controversial problem that did not correspond to the principles of the "true church."

Sarpi: An Emblem among the British Anti-papal Writers
In many of his works, Sarpi points out the numerous deceits committed by the Church of Rome and describes his disappointment in the pope's unscrupulous handling of political and spiritual affairs and his use of religious means for political ends. In a *Consulto,* Sarpi writes:

Ma reputando parimenti li pontefici che ogni mezzo (se ben del resto iniquo ed empio) adoperato per conservare ed accrescere l'autorità temporale che pretendono, diventi giusto e legittimo, tentano tutti quelli che possono eccitare li sudditi a sollevazione e concitare li prencipi a muovere le arme usando a questi fini anco le indulgenze e altri tesori spirituali, ordinate dalla chiesa romana per salute delle anime.[21]
(But the popes, who believe that any means — even though wicked and impious — used to preserve and increase their secular power, become just and legitimate, try all possible means to incite the subjects to revolt and stimulate the princes to move their weapons for this purpose, even using indulgences and other spiritual treasures, intended by the Roman church for the salvation of souls.)

(Storia dell'Interdetto 2: 159)

When English authors accused the pope of usurping temporal powers, they often pointed to Sarpi's writings as strong testimony. For example, in his *A Treatise of the Holy Catholike Faith and Church,* Jackson mentions "Father Paul" as a

---

[18] Thomas Jackson (1579-1640) studied at Queen's College, Oxford, where Richard Crakanthorp was his tutor. He obtained a scholarship to Corpus Christi College in 1596-97. Later in life he became president of that same college, and in 1638 became dean of Peterborough. Jackson won a considerable reputation for his varied learning, but mainly devoted himself to theology.

[19] On the claims of the English Church against the Catholic Church, see Marshall.

[20] The idea of separating the true Church from the false one even though the two Churches had the same origin is expressed by English Protestant writers such as Sutcliffe, Hall, Carleton, Morton, Crakanthorp and Powels. On this topic, see Milton.

[21] The complete title of Sarpi's work is "Consulto sui rimedi da opporsi ad una eventuale aggravazione della scomunica," in *Storia dell'Interdetto e altri scritti.*

careful observer of the pope's inappropriate actions during the interdict against Venice (122), and refers to Sarpi's work, *The history of the quarrels of Pope Paul V with the state of Venice,* translated and printed in London in 1626.

We can find strong echoes of Sarpi's anti-papal line in the writings of Richard Crakanthorp as well.[22] Crakanthorp was an important Anglican divine and the author of a treatise entitled *Of the Popes Temporall Monarchy, and what important consequents doe ensue thereof* (London, 1621), in which he explains that the absolute and infinite power claimed by the pope is illegitimate because

> the Kingdome of Christ, is inomnicable [incommunicable] unto any mere creature whatsoever, for it is gronded on the Infinitie of Gods power, who as by his infinite power, he made all things of nothing, so by the same infinite power, he ruleth, ordereth, and disposeth of all things. And because no creature is capable of that Infinitie of Power neither is any, capable of that universall kingdome of excellencie, whith ariseth from the Infinitie of divine power. And as infinite of nature cannot be transferred unto any creature [...].
>
> (29)

In this passage, Crakanthorp refers to the pope's claim to be the most powerful person in the world and his self-investment with the absolute authority to subjugate all other Churches, princes and kings, as described in Sarpi's *History of the Interdict* (3, 5).

Even later, years after Sarpi's death, the Servite's work was kept alive and considered a strong reference. The scholar Isaac Barrow, in *A Treatise of the Pope's Supremacy*, refers to passages from Sarpi's *History of the Council of Trent* in describing the pope's illegitimate claims of authority with respect to temporal power (2).[23] Barrow explains that during the Council the pope could not be contradicted, and thus the legates of the pope had the task of warning that "nobody should for any cause whatever dispute the Pope's authority" (72). Here, Barrow introduces a quote from the *Historia del Concilio Tridentino*, the Italian edition published in London by Billio in 1619 (159).

The popularity of Sarpi's treatises in England was particularly driven by the desire to identify the pope as the "Antichrist" (Vester). The use of this expression in reference to the pope was widespread among divines and

---

[22] Richard Crakanthorp (1567-1624) was an English clergyman who wrote on religious controversies. Crakanthorp's most famous work is *Defensio,* where he extended the argument against transubstantiation and rejected de Dominis's assertion, claiming that the presence of Christ in the Eucharist was figurative, not literal.

[23] Isaac Barrow (1630-1677) was a classical scholar, mathematician and theologian. In 1673, Barrow was appointed master of Trinity College by King Charles II. He was regarded by his mathematical contemporaries in England as second only to Newton, but he was better known as a theologian. He gained high esteem for his sermons and other writings on behalf of the Church of England.

ecclesiastics; it has been estimated that over 100 pamphlets and treatises were written by British authors on the "Romish Antichrist" between 1588 and 1629 (Milton 93). Sir Henry Burton's *Truth's triumph over Trent* (1629) introduces claims for the pope's status as Antichrist that were related to Sarpi's exposition of the pope's corruption.[24] Burton compared the modesty of the ancient Fathers to the grasping ambition of the contemporary ecclesiastics who took part in the Council of Trent; he refers to them by the derogatory name "Pontificians," probably in order to highlight their similarity to the pope. Burton writes: "The Pontificians cast up their caps in triumph, as if the field were theirs" (83). In the margin, Burton notes his source to strengthen his argument: "Hist. Concil. Trid. p. 157 Latina editio."[25]

King James I also describes the pope as the Antichrist. In his *Apology for the Oath of Allegiance* (1609) and in his collected *Works* (1616), the king underlines the importance of bringing Protestants and Roman Catholics together and freeing them from the tyranny of the papal "Antichrist."[26] English divines and ecclesiastic writers were eager to find evidence in Sarpi's work that would endorse their arguments about the pope, but his work only aided them up to a certain point: he often portrayed the pope as a corrupt and venal person, but he never used the word "antichrist" in his treatises, and even less did he identify the pope with the antichrist.

In this aspect, we see one of the ways in which Sarpi's work was manipulated by English divines and ecclesiastical writers, who used the criticism of the papal office in his treatises as a fundamental element upon which to base their claims for the rights of the Anglican church against the religion of Rome, and to encourage a military conquest of the papal secular power.[27]

The Broad Use of Sarpi's Work in England
Sarpi's *History* was also an important source for English writers who sought to rebuild an understanding of events and situations as they had happened in Europe over a period of almost fifty years. Sarpi drew upon his knowledge of the political and religious aspects of European history from 1520 to 1565 to

---

[24] In this type of treatise, the Antichrist figure was usually introduced with an apocalyptic interpretation of Church history. Among the British authors who wrote about the pope as an Antichrist there are: Robert Abbot, George Downame, Nicolas Vignier and Gabriel Powel. Henry Burton (1578-1648) was an English puritan who in 1618 resolved to enter the ministry. He devoted himself to polemical religious controversy; his pulpit style was very effective and he had many followers.
[25] Burton mentions Sarpi's *History* as a source: 9, 44, 219, 232.
[26] On the *Apology*, see Patterson 75-123.
[27] On the use of military force against the papal power, the Essex clergyman Arthur Dent envisaged England taking part in the destruction of Rome with the help of Spain, Italy and France (250-51).

show the direct or indirect influence of political and historical events on the Council of Trent, and he was able to enliven and describe the history of the Catholic Reformation in its historical frame by reconstructing that historical period with numerous details and specifics.

In *An Historical Vindication of the Church of England in Point of Schism* (1663), Roger Twysden, a royalist pamphleteer and first baronet at the court of James I, drew on Sarpi's *History* as an important source (97, 150, 201, 202), and he references Sarpi's work directly.[28] Twysden extracted from Sarpi's *History* important historical and political information about the relationship between Mary Stuart and Paul IV, as well as that between Elizabeth Tudor and the Church of Rome (97, 150, 201). In particular, Twysden reports what he learned from Sarpi's work about Queen Elizabeth's invitation to the Council of Trent by the pope, how she was advised by Sir Edward Carne, and of the reaction of the Roman Curia, supported by France against England (202-03). Moreover, also drawing from Sarpi, Twysden describes the way in which the pope aggressively and audaciously declared himself the only person in Christendom to have absolute power, asserting "that he would have no prince his companion, but all subjects under his foot" (150).

England accepted Sarpi's pamphlets and other papers written during the interdict controversy with enthusiasm and excitement. Some of Sarpi's papers were even published together with English sermons in order to reinforce the Anglican Church's assertion that it, rather than Rome, was the true heir of the apostolic Church. For example, Christopher Potter published his *Sermon preached at the consecration of the right Reverend Father in God Barnaby Potter DD,* together with *An Advertisement touching the history of the quarrels of Pope Paul V with the Venetians,* written by Sarpi and translated into English.[29] Potter's sermon argued that the pope abused Scripture in order to assert his power (19). He wrote that the pope "pretends to be a king as well as a Bishop and says his temporal power is as wide and broad as his spiritual" (21). Potter then pointed out the pope's aggressiveness in asserting his omnipotence by arguing that the pope's dictums gave "him all power not only in heaven and earth but (where God hath nothing to doe) in Purgatorie" (22). Moreover, Potter

---

[28] Sir Roger Twysden (1597-1672) was an English historian and politician. He was knighted in 1620 and served in Parliament in 1625 and 1626, but later, in 1642, he opposed the Parliament and the ecclesiastical authorities. Accordingly, he was imprisoned for seven years. He is noted for his works on English law and constitutional government.

[29] The *Advertisement* is a translation from *Sarpi Historia particolare delle cose passate tra'l sommo pontefice Paolo V e la serenissima republica di Venetia.* Christopher Potter (1591-1646) was an English academic and clergyman. In 1636, he became Dean of Worcester and in 1642 he received the rectory of Great Haseley, Oxfordshire. In January 1646, King Charles I nominated him to the deanery of Durham, but he died before his installation.

wrote that "Scriptures and councils are needlesse: for the Pope claimes to be supreame judge off all controversies" (21). Potter added Sarpi's pamphlet to his published sermon because the Servite pointed out that both the pope and the other ecclesiastics bound to the Church of Rome gave themselves absolute authority in political as well as spiritual matters. In his pamphlet, Sarpi wrote, for example, about the Cardinal de Joyeuse, the French ambassador to Venice, who claimed that the pope gave him the "power to take away the censures" and prescribed for him "a form of absolving from the Excommunication, Protestation, Reservation, and other clauses [...]" (89). Moreover, Sarpi decried the forged authority of the Roman church and wrote: "It is a case evident out of the Word of God that the Church hath no authority to remit the sinners of any, or to grant absolution to any, save only to such as are penitent" (95). There is no doubt that Potter added Sarpi's pamphlet to his sermon in order to reinforce his assertion against the illegitimate power brought to bear by the Church of Rome and the pope.

At this point, we are led to ask who benefited more from the dissemination of Sarpi's work in England: was it of greater help to the English ecclesiastics in gaining support for the English Church, or did popularity in England bring Sarpi more benefit in his politicking against the pope and the Curia of Rome? Unquestionably, English writers and divines exploited Sarpi's work and used it to increase the popularity of the Anglican Church, claiming that the English Church was the only church whose liturgy, principles and doctrines remained untouched and, therefore, that it was the only church that hewed to the historic Catholic tradition of Christianity. Because Sarpi was one of the most eminent Catholic theologians of the period, Protestants gladly drew on his criticisms of the Roman church for support for their cause; his work offered Protestant writers the means to demonstrate that their arguments against the pope and the Church of Rome were echoed from within the Catholic Church as well as from without. Moreover, Sarpi was a "hero" who had survived an assassination attempt, had defeated the Pope during the interdict, and had defended Venetian liberty.[30]

Sarpi's Hopes and Disappointments
The effect of Sarpi's popularity in England because of his political and religious beliefs, on the other hand, was mixed. Sarpi was very unhappy at finding that Marco Antonio de Dominis had published his *History of the Council of Trent* in London without his knowledge or consent.[31] Though the treatise had been

---

[30] See Bouwsma, *Venice and the Defense* 339-623.
[31] Fra Fulgenzio Micanzio outlines Sarpi's dismay in a letter to de Dominis: "My padre maestro Paolo complains much of this excess; and even more because, having lent to your Most Reverend Lordship to read his manuscript of *The History of the Council of Trent*, which he guarded so jealously, you had a copy made of it and have abused him not

published under a pseudonym, the large audience who was interested in the book did not have difficulty working out the identity of the author (Cozzi, "Fra Paolo Sarpi" 561-63). Sarpi did not approve of the Archbishop's conduct because he understood that de Dominis had acted to achieve his own designs against the Roman Curia and had used the *History* (along with a flattering dedication) in order to receive the attention and benevolence of King James.

Sarpi was in all likelihood afraid that the publication of the *History* in England would stir up the Roman Curia's animosity toward him and increase problems for both himself and the Venetian Republic. The risk was that the pope's response would be bellicose enough to force Sarpi to leave Venice (this was in fact an option that Sarpi considered when King James offered him protection and greater safety in England after the attempt on his life).[32] Even though Sarpi contemplated taking asylum in England, he refused the offer because he believed that he could not help the Venetian Republic from England as well as he could from Venice. Sarpi was filled with and strengthened by a strong patriotic spirit and he served the Republic from "a sense of duty" (Robertson 123). As such, we can deduce that for Sarpi, leaving Venice would have meant betraying his motherland. And indeed, he spent almost all of his life in Venice except for the short periods of time in his youth that he passed in Mantua, Milan and Rome.

If Sarpi was worried about the publication of his *History of the Council of Trent*, why did he write this colossal work to begin with? Certainly, he wanted to leave his reading of the Council of Trent for posterity, and he hoped that his written testimony would influence later authors who might otherwise have approved of the Roman Church's actions. Sarpi intended to document papal absolutism and the corruption of the Roman Curia and to analyze the mistakes and abuses of the Church of Rome that caused (in his view) the reform movement at Trent to fail. To record the behavior of the Church of Rome towards the other churches during the Council would offer the Christian world a means by which to judge the decrees approved at Trent. His idea of writing for

---

only by causing it to be printed without his permission, but also by interposing that most improper title and the terrible and scandalous dedication and that, as we are well informed, out of motive of [self-] interest, not of honoring the modest author" (qtd. in Bianchi-Giovini 2: 308).

[32] King James offered Sarpi asylum in England on a number of occasions. Aside from being a supporter of victims of the Roman Curia's persecution, the king also played the role of protector. Among the people who were offered and accepted asylum in England were Doctor Gaspare Despotini, the Carmelitan friars Giulio Cesare Vanini and Giovan Battista Genochi, Isaac Casaubon and Marco Antonio de Dominis. On Sarpi and the offer of asylum from King James, see the letters from Dudley Carleton to Sarpi dated August 12, 1612 and September 9, 1612 and the letter from Sarpi to Carleton dated August 14, 1612 in Sarpi, *Opere* 643-48.

posterity rather than for the present is made clear in his September 4, 1607, letter to Jérôme Groslot De L'Isle:

Nessuno debbe scrivere, pensando d'aver lode o ringraziamento dalla sua età. Si scrive per la posterità sola, alla quale riguardando, egli si può consolare dell'ingratitudine che li viene usata.
(Nobody should write while thinking to receive praise and thanks from his age. You write only for posterity and looking at it, you can console yourself for the ingratitude that is being used against you.)

(Lettere ai Protestanti 1: 4)

Through his intense religious and political activity, Sarpi hoped to create an anti-papal alliance, wherein Venice would move closer to the Protestant powers in order to undermine the Church of Rome. Sarpi's correspondence with prominent people such as the English Ambassador Dudley Carlton, the British chaplain William Bedell, and French Gallican thinkers such as Jacques Gillot and Jacques Leschassier, served as a network of alliances to assure support and help for Venice during his fight against papal authority and power. Political motivations aside, Sarpi also sought to restore the beliefs of the early Church through the Protestant creed with the help of the Protestant powers.[33]

Sarpi's writings brought many British writers and ecclesiastics into sympathy with the Venetian cause, increasing La Serenissima's reputation and prestige in England and in the rest of Europe. Sarpi's popularity and the dissemination of his work did not, however, bring concrete, practical benefits to the Republic, which ultimately was left alone in its fight for "liberty" and in its attempt to achieve a reformed Church. No reformed Protestant power's army ever set foot in the Republic, for reasons beyond Sarpi's control: James I, despite misgivings, decided not to intervene and his backing was more moral than material. As a result, the king lost the opportunity to operate effectively in Venice and disappointed many of his supporters. Among them was Sarpi, who in his correspondence with Simone Contarini complained that James I contributed nothing to defend Venice but "books and words." He further deprecated the king by pointing out that "it is one thing to be a clever theologian, quite another to be a valorous King" (*Lettere inedite di Fra Paolo Sarpi a Simone Contarini* 49, 61). He also expresses his indignation in a letter written to Grosolt, wherein (referring to the king) he insists that "too much prudence ends in imprudence" (*Lettere ai Protestanti* 1: 48).

The weakness of James I's actions combined with the Venetian fear of an invasion by Philip II of Spain — who was backing the papacy and its cause —

---

[33] Sarpi believed in such Protestant tenets as the rejection of the Pope's temporal power, the acknowledgment of the faith as the only way to achieve salvation, and the recognition of the Scriptures as the sole way to receive guidance (Kainulainen 136).

resulted in the Venetians choosing to resolve the quarrel with the pope, to reinstate relations with Rome, and to restore a quiet and peaceful political and religious life to the Republic. By June 1607, the crisis had ended: the two imprisoned clerics were released and the interdict was withdrawn (Logan 1: 389).

Though the Venetians had shown enthusiasm for the Reformation, they were nonetheless content to return to their previous situation, continuing to venerate the Saints and observe the Church's feasts and ceremonies. Venetians were not ready for a radical change and were still much attached to their religious traditions and customs; after the interdict, the rise of a more pro-papal faction suggested that in Venice a sizeable group of patricians was in fact inclined to an alliance with Rome (Kainulainen 202).

After 1607, Sarpi became progressively more isolated from the Venetian government and excluded from political responsibility (Bouwsma, *Venice and the Defense* 514). From the other side, Rome successfully came between Sarpi and the Venetian theologians who had participated animatedly during the interdict, creating a vacuum around the Servite friar.[34]

After realizing that James I could not bring the hoped-for changes to the Republic, Sarpi made no real effort to continue working on behalf of reform.[35] Even though he won the conflict against Rome as a legal adviser, he lost his battle as theologian (Pin 350). But the English interest in Sarpi did not cease after his influence waned (Lievsay 196). Even after his death, when the Roman Church still offered a bitter opposition to Sarpi's writings, in England many of his works were translated and greeted with enthusiasm.[36] Likewise, many people

---

[34] In 1608, the jurist Menino who wrote in support of the Venetian Republic, moved to Rome. In the same year the Franciscan friar Fulgenzio Manfredi, who, during the interdict, preached against the Pope and the Jesuits, was lured to Rome. In 1610, he was captured and hanged for heresy, and his body was burnt in the Campo di Fiori by order of the Holy Office. Pietro Antonio Ribetti and Fra Marco Antonio Capello also moved to Rome (Bouwsma, *Venice and the Defense* 488-89). On the theologians of the Venetian republic, see Mayer 67-71; Benzoni 57-108.

[35] Sarpi was accused by his friends who believed in the Reformed Church of being inert and insensible. See the introduction to the correspondence with the English ambassador Sir Dudley Carleton in Sarpi, *Opere* 636-37.

[36] Sarpi's works were placed for centuries on the Church's index of banned books. The hostility against the Servite friar was so strong that, even after his death, the plan to erect a monument in his memory encountered fierce opposition from ecclesiastics. The project, which was decreed in 1623, was canceled, and the monument was finally erected only in 1892. For discussions about Sarpi's monument, see Robertson, *Fra Paolo Sarpi* 155-83 and AA.VV. *Fra Paolo Sarpi, il suo monumento e la storia.* Moreover, because Pope Urban VIII opposed the decision to bury Sarpi in a church, the Servite friars dug up Fra Paolo's body and kept it in a wall inside their monastery in order to secure it (Robertson

still admired Sarpi for his actions and his writing, for his courage in standing up to the Roman Curia, and for his ability to put Venice in the spotlight, making the city an emblem in the fight against the hegemony of the Roman Church.

Although we must admit that Sarpi and his writings were used by the Protestants, who presented him as a dissatisfied Catholic champion of Reform in Italy in order to discredit the Catholic Church and to help the English Church gain popularity, the publication and dissemination of Sarpi's works in England allowed the spread of his ideas, making him a most prominent representative of the political and religious thought of the early modern era, when the medieval papal-imperial debate on spiritual and temporal powers was still a pressing issue, and the boundaries between religion and politics were undefined.

University of Washington

Works Cited

AA.VV. *Fra Paolo Sarpi, il suo monumento e la storia.* Venezia: tip. ex Cordella, 1892.
Abbot, Robert. *Antichristi Demonstratio.* London: n.p.: 1603.
Asor Rosa, Alberto. *Genus Italicum: saggi sull'identità italiana nel corso del tempo.* Torino: Einaudi 1997.
Barrow, Isaac. *A Treatise of the Pope's Supremacy.* London: n.p.: 1683.
Bedell, William. *Some Original Letters of Bishop Bedell.* Dublin: printed by and for George Faulkner, 1742.
Belligni, Eleonora. "Marcantonio De Dominis, Paolo Sarpi e Roberto Bellarmino e il problema dell'autorità dopo il concilio tridentino." *Paolo Sarpi. Politique et religion en Europe.* Ed. Marie Viallon. Paris: Classiques Garnier, 2010. 257-307.
Benzoni, Gino. "I teologi minori dell'interdetto." *Archivio Veneto* 5.91 (1970): 31-108.
Bianchi-Giovini, Aurelio. *Biografia di Fra' Paolo, teologo e consultore di Stato della Repubblica Veneta.* Vol. 2. Zurich: n.p.: 1836.
Bouwsma, William. "Venice, Spain, and the Papacy: Paolo Sarpi and the Renaissance Tradition." *The Late Italian Renaissance.* Ed. Eric Cochrane. London: Macmillan, 1970. 353-76.
_____. *Venice and the Defense of Republican Liberty.* Berkeley: U of California P, 1968.
Burke, Peter. "Early Modern Venice as a Center of Information and Communication." *Venice Reconsidered: The History and Civilization of an Italian City-State, 1297-1797.* Ed. John Jeffries Martin and Dennis Romano. Baltimore: Johns Hopkins UP, 2000. 389-419.
Burnet, Gilbert. *The Life of William Bedell, D. D. Bishop of Kilmore in Ireland.* Dublin:

---

162). By contrast, after his death many works by Sarpi were translated into English and published in England.

Printed by M. Rhames, 1736.
Burton, Henry. *Truth's Triumph ouer Trent: or, the Great Gulfe betweene Sion and Babylon.* London: Robert Young, 1629.
Butler, John Anthony. *James I and Divine Right.* Tokyo: Renaissance Institute, Sophia University, 1999.
Butterfield, Robert. *Maschil, or Treatise to give instruction: touching the State of the Church of Rome since the Councell of Trent.* London: printed by Lownes and Young for N. Butter, 1629.
Cantimori, Delio. *Eretici italiani del Cinquecento.* Torino: Einaudi, 1992.
Capasso, Gaetano. *Fra Paolo Sarpi e l'interdetto di Venezia.* Firenze: Gazzetta d'Italia, 1879.
Carleton, George. *Consensus Ecclesiae contra tridentinos Demonstrans vnam ac perpetuam doctrinam è sacris scripturis excerptam ,...* Prostat Francofurti: Apud Rulandios, 1613.
_____. *Directions to know the true Church.* London: John Bill, 1615.
Clogie, Alexander. *Two Biographies of William Bedell.* Ed. E. S. Shuckburgh. Cambridge: Cambridge UP, 1902.
Collinson, Patrick, ed. *The Sixteenth Century, 1485-1603.* Oxford: Oxford UP, 2002.
Coryat, Thomas. *Coryat's Crudities.* 2 vols. London: printed for W. Cater, 1776.
Cozzi, Gaetano. "Fra Paolo Sarpi, l'anglicanesimo e la Historia del Concilio Tridentino." *Rivista storica italiana* 63 (1956): 559-619.
_____. "Paolo Sarpi." *Storia della letteratura italiana.* Ed. Emilio Cecchi and Natalino Sapegno. Vol. 5. Milano: Garzanti, 1967.
_____. *Paolo Sarpi tra Venezia e l'Europa.* Torino: Einaudi, 1978.
Crakanthorp, Richard. *Defensio Ecclesiae Anglicanae contra M. Antonii de Dominis, D. Archiepiscopi Spalatensis, Injurias.* London, 1625.
_____. *Of the Popes Temporall Monarchy, and what important consequents doe ensue thereof.* London: Bernard Alsop for John Teage, 1921.
de Dominis, Marco Antonio. *Scogli del naufragio cristiano quali va scoprendo la Santa Chiesa.* London: n.p. 1618.
Dent, Arthur. *Ruine of Rome.* London: n.p.: 1607.
de Vivo, Filippo. *Information and Communication in Venice: Rethinking Early Modern Politics.* Oxford: Oxford UP, 2007.
Downame, George. *Papa Antichristus.* London: n.p.: 1620.
_____. *A Treatise concerning Antichrist.* London: n.p.: 1603.
Field, Richard. *Of the Church.* 4 vols. Cambridge: n.p.: 1847.
Figgis, John Neville. *The Divine Right of Kings.* New York: Harper & Row, 1965.
Frajese, Vittorio. "Una teoria della censura: Bellarmino e il potere indiretto dei papi." *Studi Storici* 25. 1 (1984): 139-52.
Jackson, Thomas. *A Treatise of the Holy Catholike Faith and Church.* London: n.p.: 1627.
_____. *Two Treatises on the Church.* London: Elliot Stock, 1901.
Kainulainen, Jaska. *Paolo Sarpi: A Servant of God and State.* Leiden: Brill, 2014.
Lievsay, John. *Venetian Phoenix: Paolo Sarpi and Some of his English Friends.* Kansas: UP of Kansas, 1973.
Logan, Pearsall Smith. *The Life and Letters of Sir Henry Wotton.* 2 vols. Oxford: Clarendon Press, 1907.
Marshall, Peter, ed. *The Impact of the English Reformation 1500-1640.* New York: St

Martin's Press, 1997.
Mayer, Thomas F. *The Roman Inquisition on the Stage of Italy, c. 1590-1640.* Philadelphia: U of Pennsylvania P, 2014.
McEachern, Claire, and Debora Shuger, eds. *Religion and Culture in Renaissance England.* Cambridge, U.K.: Cambridge UP, 1997.
Micanzio, Fulgenzio. *The life of the most learned Father Paul.* London: Printed for Humphrey Moseley, and Richard Marriot, 1651.
Milton, Anthony. *Catholic and Reformed.* Cambridge: Cambridge UP, 1996.
Oakley, Francis. "Complexities of Context: Gerson, Bellarmine, Sarpi, Richer, and the Venetian Interdict of 1606-1607." *The Catholic Historical Review* 82. 3 (July 1996): 369-96.
Patterson, William B. *King James VI and I and the Reunion of Christendom.* Cambridge, U.K: Cambridge UP, 1997.
Perkins, William. *A reformed Catholike.* London: John Legatte, 1611.
Pin, Corrado. "'Qui si vive con esempi, non con ragione': Paolo Sarpi e la committenza di Stato nel dopo-Interdetto." *Ripensando Paolo Sarpi.* Ed. Corrado Pin. Venezia: Ateneo Veneto, 2006. 343-94.
Potter, Christopher. *A sermon preached at the consecration of the right Reverend Father in God Barnaby Potter DD. and L. Bishop of Carlisle. An advertisement touching the history of the quarrels of Pope Paul 5 with the Venetians....* London: John Clarke, 1629.
Powel, Gabriel. *Disputationum theologicarum et scholasticarum de Antichristo et eius ecclesia.* London: n.p.: 1605.
Robertson, Alexander. *Fra Paolo Sarpi: The Greatest of the Venetians.* London: Sampson Low, Marston & Company, 1894.
Sarpi, Paolo. *The Cruell Subtilty of Ambitioin.* London: printed for William Lee, 1650.
_____. *Discourse upon the Reasons of the Resolution taken in the Valteline.* London: printed for William Lee, 1628.
_____. *Free Schoole of Warre.* London: John Bill, 1625.
_____. *History of the Council of Trent.* London: printed by John Macock for Mearne, Martyn and Herrington, 1676.
_____. *History of the Inquisition.* London: printed by J. Okes for Humphrey Moseley, 1639.
_____. *History of the Quarrels of Pope Paul V.* London: John Bill, 1626.
_____. *The History of the quarrels of Pope Paul V with the State of Venice: in seven books...* London: John Bill, 1626.
_____. *Interdicti Veneti historia* de motu Italiae sub initia Pontificatus Pauli V commentarius. Cambridge: Bucke & Greene, 1626.
_____. *Istoria del Concilio Tridentino.* 3 vols. Ed. Giovanni Gambarin. Bari: Laterza e Figli, 1935.
_____. *Istoria dell'Interdetto e altri scritti editi ed inediti.* Ed. Manlio Duilio Busnelli and Giovanni Gambarin. 3 vols. Bari: Laterza, 1940.
_____. *Letter of Father Paul.* London: printed for Richard Chiswell, 1693.
_____. *Lettere ai Gallicani.* Ed. Boris Ulianich. Wiesbaden: Franz Steiner Verlag GMBH, 1961.
_____. *Lettere ai Protestanti.* Ed. Manlio Duilio Busnelli. 2 vols. Bari: Laterza, 1931.
_____. *Lettere inedite di Fra Paolo Sarpi a Simone Contarini, 1615.* Ed. C. Castellani. Venice: n.p.: 1892.

---. *Opere*. Ed. Gaetano Cozzi and Luisa Cozzi. Milano: Riccardo Ricciardi, 1969.

---. *The Opinion of Padre Paolo of the Order of the Servites, consultor of state given to the Lords the Inquisitors of state, in what manner the Republick of Venice ought to govern themselves both at home and abroad, to have perpetual dominion*. London: printed for Bentley, 1689.

---. *The Papacy of Paul the Forth. Or, the Restitution of Abby Lands and Impropriations*. London: printed for Richard Royston, 1673.

---. *A Treatise of Matters Beneficiary*. London: printed by Thomas Hodgkin for Crook and Bentley, 1680.

Shuckburgh, Evelyn, William Bedell, and Alexander Clogie. *Two biographies of William Bedell, Bishop of Kilmore*. Cambridge: UP, 1902.

Twysden, Roger. *An Historical Vindication of the Church of England in Point of Schism*. Cambridge: John W. Parker, 1847.

Vester, Matthew. "Paolo Sarpi and Early Stuart Debates over the Papal Antichrist." *Millenarianism and Messianism in Early Modern European Culture*. Dordrecht: Kluwer, 2001. 53-70.

Vignier, Nicolas. *Concerning the Excommunication*. London: n.p.: 1607.

Vivanti, Corrado. "Una fonte dell'*Istoria del Concilio Tridentino* di Paolo Sarpi." *Rivista storica italiana* 83 (1971): 608-32.

Walton, Izaac. *The lives of Sir Henry Wotton*. London: Printed by Thomas Newcomb for Richard Marriott, 1670.

Wootton, David. *Paolo Sarpi: Between Renaissance and Enlightenment*. Cambridge: Cambridge UP, 1983.

Yates, Frances. "Paolo Sarpi's 'History of the Council of Trent.'" *Journal of the Warburg and Courtauld Institutes* 7 (1944):123-43.

Paolo Sarpi: The Hunted Friar and his Popularity in England 318

Eighteenth-century engraving of the assassination attempt against Sarpi (Biblioteca Nazionale Marciana)

Marco Codebò

Potere, dissimulazione e verità nei *Promessi sposi* (1840) e nella *Storia della colonna infame*

A Manlio Calegari

Sinossi: Nei due testi che compongono la Quarantana, *I promessi sposi* e la *Storia della colonna infame*, il progetto manzoniano di racconto del vero si confronta con una società secentesca dove, nel dialogo fra alcuni parlanti, prevale la negazione della verità. Le forme di tale negazione comprendono la menzogna, la reticenza e la dissimulazione. Quest'ultima, che è tratto distintivo della vita di corte nell'Europa premoderna, si presenta nei *Promessi sposi* come pratica diffusa fra tutte le classi sociali, in quanto tecnica della sopravvivenza in un contesto dominato da un potere arbitrario e feroce. Ne risultano immuni solo figure sante come Lucia, padre Cristoforo e il cardinal Federigo. Nella *Storia della colonna infame* i giudici preposti all'accertamento della verità durante i processi contro gli untori falsificano invece la realtà effettuale attraverso una serie di confessioni menzognere estorte sotto tortura. Dopo aver tratteggiato i lineamenti che nella Quarantana caratterizzano la condotta del potere come esercizio sia del supplizio sia dell'autorità neofeudale, l'articolo descrive le varie modalità della pratica della dissimulazione. Il programma manzoniano di rappresentazione veridica di questo contesto si traduce nella narrazione dell'estrema rarità della parola vera, soprattutto nelle situazioni in cui siano gli inermi a rivolgerla a figure di potere. In questo caso, infatti, solo la fede permette l'esercizio del foucaultiano "coraggio della verità", evento che nella Quarantana ricorre nei due casi di Lucia, prigioniera dell'Innominato, e di Gaspare Migliavacca, imputato nelle mani dei suoi torturatori durante uno dei processi contro gli untori.
Parole chiave: Dissimulazione, martirio, potere, supplizio, verità

Questo saggio nasce da uno studio sul coraggio della verità nei due testi che Alessandro Manzoni ha pubblicato all'interno della Quarantana, *I promessi sposi* e la *Storia della colonna infame*.[1] Ho centrato l'indagine su contesti in cui i personaggi, storici o d'invenzione che siano, pronuncino la parola vera a partire da un dislivello di potere, in quanto parlanti inermi alle prese con interlocutori possenti. Tratto quindi, non delle manifestazioni del vero ontologico, che nella visione di Manzoni è leggibile nella Storia, perché lì si

---

[1] Di "coraggio della verità" parla Foucault nell'omonimo volume che ne raccoglie le lezioni al Collège de France durante l'anno accademico 1983-84. La verità si arma di coraggio nell'esercizio della *parrêsia*, il franco parlare che non è mai esente da rischi, a partire da quello di danneggiare la relazione fra il parresiasta e la persona a cui la verità è indirizzata (13).

invera il progetto della Provvidenza, ma dell'esperienza di quello dialogico, per come circola attraverso lo scambio linguistico fra i parlanti. È un vero di capitale importanza in testi narrativi, che della capacità di dare la parola ai personaggi fanno un punto di forza. È evidente che sul lungo periodo il secondo vero è sussunto nel primo: nel progetto provvidenziale, che è anche giustizia, le verità parziali, le omissioni o le menzogne degli esseri umani vengono giudicate e collocate nella posizione che loro compete in rapporto alla verità del disegno divino. Tuttavia sul breve periodo, quello dell'esperienza umana oggetto dei romanzi e delle narrazioni storiche, anche di largo respiro, i due veri corrono su linee che solo a tratti si sfiorano. La capacità del linguaggio di non dire, in varie forme, la verità, si colloca anzi al centro dell'esperienza che romanzieri e storici provano a narrare.

L'assunto di questo lavoro è che, nel caso specifico della Quarantana, a fronte di una verità ultima della Storia a cui tende il testo nel suo complesso, le aree, nelle sue varie forme, di non vero, che accedono alla rappresentazione siano particolarmente estese. Ne risulta che, proprio perché ambisce a creare rappresentazioni storiche veritiere, la scrittura manzoniana debba quasi sempre farsi portatrice del suo occultamento. Mentre nei *Promessi sposi*, il romanzo del vero, che è quello dei rapporti di forza dentro il corpo sociale, il discorrere dei personaggi è dominato dalla dissimulazione, nel racconto dell'errore, la *Storia della colonna infame*, i giudici che hanno l'obbligo di accertare la verità presiedono invece alla produzione sistematica del falso. Da qui discende la struttura di questo saggio, nella parte iniziale del quale tratto degli apparati di potere rappresentati nei *Promessi sposi* e nella *Storia della colonna infame*, nonché della dissimulazione come risposta del corpo sociale alla loro pressione, per riservare alla seconda parte la discussione dei casi, straordinari, in cui la parola vera ne sfida l'egemonia. Ho dato al mio argomento questa organizzazione perché, alle prese com'ero con manifestazioni del franco parlare così infrequenti, soprattutto se indirizzate al potere, tale rarità ne è diventata il primo tratto distintivo. Dare il giusto valore a tale caratteristica mi ha imposto di partire dal disegno dello scenario, quello del nascondimento del vero nel contesto storico del '600, su cui veniva a stagliarsi in primo piano lo scandalo della verità. A quest'ultimo ho potuto dedicarmi solo in un secondo tempo, quando si poteva apprezzarne in pieno lo stacco nei confronti dello sfondo: tutto questo allo scopo di misurare la sproporzione fra la norma e l'eccezione nei due testi manzoniani sotto esame e situare la seconda nel suo appropriato quadro di riferimento discorsivo. Se l'operazione non è riuscita, e il filo del discorso si è invece attorcigliato, "non s'è", naturalmente, "fatto apposta".

Corpi e potere nei "Promessi sposi" e nella "Storia della colonna infame"
Una riflessione sulle pratiche di potere descritte nei *Promessi sposi* e nella *Storia della colonna infame* non può che partire dall'osservazione di Angelo R. Pupino, secondo la quale il testo pubblicato a dispense da Manzoni fra il 1840 e

il 1842 va considerato come "un oggetto unitario e solidale ma tipologicamente articolato in romanzo e storiografia" (19). A sostegno di questa affermazione va portato anche l'inappuntabile argomento di Giuseppe Farinelli, che giudica le due componenti della Quarantana inseparabili perché ispirate da un'unica ragione storica, quella che presiede al racconto della vicenda degli untori tanto nel trentunesimo capitolo del romanzo quanto nella *Colonna,* e da un'unica ragione artistica: le pagine sulla peste nei *Promessi sposi* sono il proemio alla tragedia del processo, perché il "dagli, dagli all'untore" nei confronti di Renzo ci porta con inesorabile consequenzialità al momento in cui lo stesso grido è lanciato verso Piazza e Mora nella *Colonna* (56-57). A supporto delle tesi di Pupino e Farinelli, vorrei aggiungere un ultimo argomento, cruciale nella prospettiva di questo studio: *I promessi sposi* e la *Storia della colonna infame* sono articolazioni di un unico macroracconto, quello della dismisura esistente fra il potere e i suoi soggetti. Ognuno dei due testi narra specifiche maniere di questa sproporzione, in una complementarità che è necessaria per comprendere il senso dell'intera Quarantana, a partire dal perché della sua pubblicazione come ibrida combinazione di generi. Non si riuscirebbe, infatti, a capire con quali forze si confrontino per davvero Renzo e Lucia senza aver conoscenza della macchina mortifera all'opera nella narrazione storica. E, inversamente, senza aver visto nel romanzo il potere (nelle varie forme descritte nei *Promessi sposi,* legale, signorile, poliziesco, burocratico, religioso) mentre sottopone alla sua metodica pressione i gruppi e gli individui che compongono il corpo sociale, non ci si potrebbe spiegare il coordinato operare delle entità politico-giudiziarie (giudici, senato, governatorato), che decidono della sorte degli untori. Non si potrebbero neppure inserire le decisioni prese da questi organismi nel contesto della guerra europea, né situare le conoscenze scientifiche dei giudici all'interno dell'episteme del tempo, nel senso di sapere posseduto, con diversa consapevolezza, dai dotti come dalla moltitudine.

La Quarantana racconta come il Ducato di Milano sia scosso da due crisi, la carestia e la pestilenza, entrambe parte di uno sconvolgimento epocale, la Guerra dei Trent'anni, la cui gestione è competenza di lontani apparati, situati a Madrid, Parigi e Vienna. Il governo della carestia e della peste, invece, tocca interamente ad autorità con sede a Milano: il governatore, il senato, i decurioni, il vicario di provvisione e il tribunale della sanità. A queste autorità rispondono gli strumenti, magistratura e polizia, che agiscono sul campo. Si tratta di un potere che, dal punto di vista della gestione dell'illegalità, agisce secondo forme tipicamente premoderne: quando affronta il crimine individuale non mira alla trasformazione del colpevole ma alla sua punizione attraverso quell'automatismo che Foucault chiama "codice legale", ovvero "l'accoppiamento tra un tipo di azione proibita e un tipo di punizione" (*Sécurité* 7).[2] Davanti a commozioni dell'intero corpo sociale, come le carestie e le epidemie, lo strumento di governo è invece l'isolamento di chi, per via di tali fenomeni, si venga a trovare in condizione di anormalità, sia essa l'estrema indigenza o la malattia. Il lazzeretto si apre una prima volta per raccogliere mendicanti e sbandati durante la carestia, una seconda volta per rinchiudere gli appestati. È una pratica coerente con la spinta al "grand renfermement", l'internamento di accattoni, alienati e vagabondi, che si afferma in Europa fra la fine del Rinascimento e l'alba delle rivoluzioni borghesi (Foucault, *Histoire de la folie* 57-67).

La chiave di volta dei due strumenti, codice legale e internamento, con cui il potere premoderno investe il corpo dei suoi soggetti consiste nel supplizio, ovvero una maniera di amministrare la pena caratterizzata dal (1) produrre una certa quantità di sofferenza, (2) seguire un protocollo di regole e (3) far parte di un rituale (Foucault, *Surveiller* 43). Attraverso la rappresentazione visiva dello strapotere del sovrano, il supplizio traduce in spettacolo la sproporzione fra la potenza del potere premoderno e l'impotenza dei suoi soggetti; ne consegue che "negli 'eccessi' dei supplizi è investita tutta un'economia del potere" (44). Il supplizio, insomma, è esercizio smisurato del potere proprio perché la strapotenza di questi è fuori scala. Di tale asimmetrica relazione il supplizio è pratica e, nello stesso tempo, medium fra i più efficaci; da ciò la sua capacità di deterrenza in un'età così attenta alle forme dell'apparire. *La storia della colonna infame* è ovviamente il testo deputato al racconto della tecnologia del supplizio nella Quarantana. Si tratta di un terreno, tuttavia, che viene preparato con cura nel romanzo. Cosa si presenta allo sguardo di Renzo appena entrato a Milano durante la peste se non "l'abbominevole macchina della tortura", rizzata nella piazza di San Marco come "in tutte le piazze e nelle strade più spaziose"? L'ordigno sta lì a minacciare gli incauti che possano anche solo pensare di trasgredire le norme sull'internamento: i deputati del quartiere possono "farci applicare immediatamente chiunque paresse loro meritevole di pena: o sequestrati che uscissero di casa, o subalterni che non facessero il loro dovere, o chiunque altro" (655).[3]

Nei *Promessi sposi* la tecnologia del supplizio è al lavoro già prima dell'epidemia, durante la rivolta di San Martino contro il rincaro e la scarsità del pane. La ribellione, si sa, è sedata non solo imponendo ai fornai di abbassare i

---

[2] Se non altrimenti indicato le traduzioni dalle lingue straniere che compaiono in questo saggio sono mie.
[3] L'edizione dei *Promessi sposi* e della *Storia della colonna infame* che qui cito è quella curata da Salvatore Silvano Nigro nel 2002 per i Meridiani Mondadori. Il titolo dell'edizione Nigro è *Promessi sposi (1840). Storia della colonna infame.* Nell'edizione Nigro nessuna interruzione separa *I promessi sposi* (1-746) e la *Storia della colonna infame* (747-864), riproducendo così i criteri originali di pubblicazione della Quarantana. Nel resto del saggio farò riferimento a questo testo citandolo, quando sia necessario, come "Edizione Nigro".

prezzi e incrementare la panificazione, ma anche eseguendo quattro condanne a morte. Nelle parole del mercante fermatosi all'osteria di Gorgonzola durante la fuga di Renzo, i rivoltosi "'avranno quattro tristi, serviti con tutte le formalità, accompagnati da' cappuccini, e da' confratelli della buona morte'" (322).[4] A questo punto nel romanzo la macchina del supplizio ha già sfiorato Renzo, nella forma non tanto della forca su cui sarebbe finito se non fosse riuscito a fuggire, ma quanto dei manichini che gli vengono messi ai polsi la mattina dell'arresto. Quelle due cordicelle che circondano il polso del "paziente", e che i birri possono stringere a volontà per martirizzarlo, rappresentano solo il primo degli strumenti che, fosse Renzo rimasto in cattività, sarebbero stati chiamati a produrre sul suo corpo regolate quantità di sofferenza (303).

Il luogo dove si dispiega la capacità di intervento del potere, nelle due forme del supplizio e dell'internamento, è la città. Questo accade, da un parte per la capacità di questa di trasformarsi all'occorrenza in teatro e dall'altra per il fatto, notato da Foucault, che le aree urbane premoderne, racchiuse come sono da cinte murarie, già sottopongono i loro residenti all'internamento in uno "spazio murato e rinserrato" (*Sécurité* 14). Durante le due crisi narrate nei *Promessi sposi* Milano è infatti una città chiusa. Quando Renzo fuggiasco esce da porta orientale, il varco è presidiato da "un mucchio di gabellini, e, per rinforzo, anche de' micheletti spagnoli", che sbarrano l'ingresso ai potenziali rivoltosi provenienti dal contado (311). Quando compie il cammino inverso, al tempo della peste, "c'eran ordini severissimi di non lasciar entrar nessuno, senza bulletta di sanità" (649). Naturalmente ci si entra senza problemi, ma questo a causa dello sfaldarsi della pubblica amministrazione durante l'epidemia. Anche se il racconto delle torture, delle esecuzioni capitali e degli internamenti è centrato su Milano, la provincia rimane nondimeno interessata dalle ripercussioni a largo raggio di queste pratiche: le grida del governatore sono affisse anche nel Lecchese, l'ordine di cattura contro Renzo arriva in paese il giorno stesso della fuga, emissari del tribunale della sanità, infine, battono il contado nella prima fase della pestilenza per scoprire e isolare eventuali manifestazioni del morbo.

Retrovia delle pratiche di supplizio e internamento, la campagna è invece campo d'azione di un diverso tipo di potere, la cui presa sui subordinati è neofeudale, l'articolazione locale e lo strumento di dominio la sregolata violenza

---

[4] Il *Fermo e Lucia* anziché dare la semplice notizia del fatto racconta come vengono decise le esecuzioni capitali in sede politica. Nel *Fermo* si legge infatti di una riunione del Consiglio segreto, la sera della rivolta, nella quale viene adottata la strategia proposta da un "vecchio machiavellista": "'signori miei: ora il partito è chiaro: centomila pani e quattro capestri'" (562).

di bande di fuorilegge al soldo dei signori. È un potere che non applica ai corpi dei suoi soggetti la metodica sofferenza del supplizio, ma la forza bruta di spicci strumenti quali schioppettate, bastonate, pugnalate e sequestri di persona: nei *Promessi sposi* lo esercitano don Rodrigo, Egidio e, prima della conversione, l'Innominato. Elementi rituali — le passeggiate con scorta di bravi, i palazzotti in cima alle alture, le livree, lo sfoggio di disciplina militaresca — ne costituiscono lo spettacolo, mentre il suo fondamento è l'omertà. *I promessi sposi,* il testo della Quarantana dove il funzionamento di questo potere è raccontato, si concentrano esclusivamente su un'area del suo operare, la gestione dell'economia del piacere all'interno dei propri insediamenti. Tutto ciò che attiene alla sfera della produzione materiale — modi della proprietà agraria, regime dei fitti, privilegi signorili, servitù contadine — e a quella giuridica — le forme del diritto che quella proprietà, quei privilegi e quelle servitù regolano — rimane escluso dal racconto.[5] Si sa che don Rodrigo è un gran prepotente, ma non si capisce a cosa serva tutta quella prepotenza sotto l'aspetto economico, visto che non lo si vede esigere un tributo, vigilare sull'esecuzione di una corvée o far impiccare un bracconiere. Ben diverso, per esempio, è l'approccio a questa sfera nel *Gattopardo*, dove l'amministrazione dei propri beni crea non pochi problemi al principe di Salina. Ciò che *I promessi sposi* documentano, per mezzo di un esempio, quello dello scapolo don Rodrigo alle prese con gli oggetti del suo desiderio, giovani contadine e prostitute, è invece l'esercizio signorile della sessualità.[6] Si tratta di un documento redatto sul filo dell'allusione e della reticenza, come si addice a quel signore pieno di garbo che, come ha notato Nencioni, è diventato Manzoni nel passaggio dal *Fermo e Lucia* ai *Promessi sposi* (16).[7] Il *Fermo e Lucia* è infatti un testo più ricco di informazioni su questo terreno; narra, per citare l'episodio che fa scattare la trama, di come le visite di don Rodrigo fossero di routine alla filanda, riguardassero altre ragazze oltre a Lucia, incontrassero a volte debole resistenza e contassero sull'acquiescenza del padrone (55). Le puntate di don Rodrigo fra le giovani

---

[5] Calvino ha notato che Manzoni, sempre preciso nel delineare le gerarchie e la distribuzione dei poteri, "quando tocca il diritto feudale propriamente detto diventa d'un'insolita reticenza" (273). Poco oltre Calvino parla di un "meccanismo di autocensura", che scatterebbe nella coscienza di Manzoni al momento di trattare le istituzioni feudali.

[6] "Don Rodrigo entrò quel giorno [quello dell'incontro con padre Cristoforo] in una casa, dove andava, per il solito, molta gente, e dove fu ricevuto con quella cordialità affaccendata e rispettosa, ch'è riservata agli uomini che si fanno molto amare o molto temere" (127).

[7] Valesio considera Manzoni colpevole di *reticentia,* figura retorica assimilabile all' "interruzione di una frase già iniziata" e distinta dall'italiano *reticenza,* caratterizzata invece da "una connotazione negativa e furbesca" (148). Manzoni copre di *reticentia* l'Eros, con la disastrosa conseguenza di non riuscire né a narrare la passione di don Rodrigo né a dare una rappresentazione cristiana dell'amore fra Renzo e Lucia.

tessitrici sono in linea con quell'altra manifestazione della presa del potere neofeudale sul corpo femminile che è rappresentata dal comportamento dei soldati spagnoli di stanza a Lecco, i quali "insegnavan la modestia alle fanciulle e alle donne del paese, accarezzavan di tempo in tempo le spalle a qualche marito, a qualche padre" (Edizione Nigro10).

Per come la tratta Manzoni, la storia di Lucia è una sorta di *case study* accademico che spiega, per via di romanzo anziché di saggio critico, l'operare del potere neofeudale nella sfera del piacere. A questo proposito appare cruciale il racconto di come il problema individuale di don Rodrigo sia affrontato attraverso la mobilitazione delle varie autorità, ecclesiastica, giuridica, politica e criminale (da don Abbondio all'Innominato, passando per l'Azzeccagarbugli, il podestà di Lecco, Gertrude, il padre provinciale e il conte zio), operanti nella *polis* lombarda del '600. Risultano tutte solidali nel far sì che un membro dell'élite neofeudale possa esercitare il suo preteso diritto al godimento del corpo di una donna della classe contadina. Di questa mobilitazione va sottolineato il valore politico, perché è indizio di una compattezza spiegabile solo col fatto che non di una faccenda privata si tratta ma del rapporto di forza fra due gruppi sociali.

Come ha correttamente scritto Aldo Grasso, "il motore segreto della trama è Lucia in quanto paravento dietro cui si scatenano bramosie, desideri, attrazioni" (294). Nella struttura dei *Promessi sposi* Lucia viene ad occupare la posizione di un lacaniano *objet petit a*, la cui mancanza mette in moto una catena di significanti, nel nostro caso la storia innervata dall'intreccio di cui parla Grasso. Si tratta di un terreno scivoloso per Manzoni, che in un'apposita digressione all'inizio del secondo tomo del *Fermo e Lucia* aveva già dichiarato che d'amore ce n'era abbastanza nel mondo e non era necessario coltivarlo, anche per evitare di farne nascere dove non ce n'era bisogno (172). In presenza di tanto autocontrollo autoriale, al corpo di Lucia come primo mobile dell'universo del romanzo ci si potrà arrivare solo per induzione: e l'indizio sarà minimo. Del corpo dei due maschi impegnati nel triangolo di passioni rivali che scatena il romanzo non sappiamo niente: quant'era alto don Rodrigo, di che colore aveva i capelli Renzo? Erano, quei due, gracili, robusti, secchi, obesi? Nessuno lo può dire, Manzoni non ce li ha mai descritti.[8] Ma di Lucia, invece, qualche tratto del corpo ce l'ha mostrato: le sopracciglia e gli occhi neri, la modesta bellezza. È

---

[8] La rappresentazione del corpo desiderante non ha spazio nella Quarantana. Ne incontra invece molto quella del corpo sofferente, dei torturati della *Storia della colonna infame* come degli appestati dei *Promessi sposi*. Di questi fa anche parte don Rodrigo, di cui non è tanto il corpo, però, che è descritto, quanto la devastazione che vi ha portato la malattia.

pochissimo, ma è il segno che lo sguardo s'è fissato lì.[9] Che questo corpo sia il magnete della storia, in particolare l'oggetto su cui il potere neofeudale, di cui don Rodrigo è rappresentante, decide di affermare la propria autorità, lo si capisce dai primi ventuno capitoli dei *Promessi sposi*. Qui il movimento del romanzo segue quello dei potenti (don Rodrigo, Egidio e l'Innominato) lanciati alla cattura del corpo di Lucia, mentre le mosse degli antagonisti (Renzo, Agnese e padre Cristoforo) sono meri gesti di difesa. Alla fine, grazie ai bravi dell'Innominato che riescono una buona volta a mettergli le mani addosso e a chiuderlo in una stanza, quel corpo è conquistato. Perché il romanzo possa continuare è allora necessario il miracolo della conversione dell'Innominato, col suo passaggio dal gruppo degli oppositori a quello degli aiutanti di Renzo e la conseguente sconfitta dello schieramento che fa capo a don Rodrigo. Che di guadagnare il controllo del corpo di Lucia si trattasse, lo si comprende appieno da quel che segue la sua liberazione. Trasferita nel campo avverso, quello di Renzo e dei suoi alleati, Lucia viene posta in una sorta di libertà vigilata, o di arresti domiciliari, sotto l'attenta sorveglianza di Donna Prassede. Passa poi per l'internamento al lazzeretto e in sostanza riconquista la propria libertà soltanto come signora Tramaglino.

Una risposta: la fuga
I due poteri che ho descritto come separati — per brevità chiamiamoli suppliziale e neofeudale — nel romanzo appaiono in realtà compenetrati, e omogenee sono le risposte dei subalterni al solidale sistema di oppressione che li sovrasta. Così Renzo li confronta entrambi: prima sfugge alla possibile rappresaglia di don Rodrigo, dopo il fallito rapimento di Lucia, e poi evade il bando di cattura come uno dei capi della rivolta di San Martino. Entra a Milano durante la pestilenza per ritrovare la donna amata, cercando quindi di riparare al danno arrecato a entrambi dal potere neofeudale, ma è preso per untore e scampa per miracolo alla fine tragica di Piazza e Mora nella *Colonna*. Passando sul lato del potere, le voglie di don Rodrigo si giovano, attraverso la sapiente mediazione del cugino Attilio, dell'aiuto di un'alta autorità politica, il conte zio, membro del Consiglio segreto, che convince il padre provinciale dei cappuccini a spedire fra Cristoforo nella lontana Rimini. Lo stesso cardinal Federigo, l'uomo più potente del romanzo (è cardinale di Santa Romana Chiesa, dispone di un'immensa fortuna e sovrintende al più vasto accumulo di sapere del Ducato, la Biblioteca Ambrosiana), cerca di opporsi tanto al potere neofeudale, proteggendo Lucia e rimproverando don Abbondio, quanto a quello suppliziale, interessandosi al destino di Renzo colpito da mandato di arresto. Della solidarietà fra i due poteri ne ha un'idea chiara Renzo durante la rivolta di San

---
[9] L'area della passione è sottoposta a una censura più lieve nel *Fermo e Lucia*. Basti andare al "'Caro cugino, la cosa non è finita; costei la voglio...'", con cui don Rodrigo mette il conte Attilio al corrente delle sue brame (283).

Martino. La sua personale ribellione si nutre della voglia di raddrizzare il torto subito nella sfera privata così come dello scontento per il caropane: quando è ancora sobrio arringa la piazza sulla necessità di mettere in riga un ipotetico tiranno che sta "'un po' in campagna, un po' in Milano'", mentre poi, all'osteria, già inebriato, spiega come una giustizia incapace di proteggere due giovani onesti intenzionati a sposarsi non meriti di essere rispettata (272; 280).[10]

Di fronte alla presa totalitaria esercitata sulla società dall'associazione del potere neofeudale con quello suppliziale i poveri sono sempre in fuga. Renzo scappa dal paese fino a Milano e di lì a Bergamo, torna al paese, va e viene da Milano, abbandona per sempre i luoghi natii per sistemarsi insieme a Lucia e Agnese nella località del bergamasco dove vive suo cugino Bortolo. Ma anche da lì dovrà trasferirsi un'ultima volta, nel luogo dove diventerà imprenditore insieme al cugino. Lucia, pur se sempre accompagnata, si sposta a Monza, torna al paese dopo il rapimento, riparte per Milano e torna infine a casa passando prima per il lazzeretto. Agnese va e viene dal paese a Monza, compie due viaggi verso le montagne dove vive l'Innominato e si rifugia a Pasturo durante la peste. Gli spostamenti dei personaggi romanzeschi sono figura di quelli delle grandi masse, sospinte qua e là dalla carestia (con flussi e deflussi fra la campagna e la città a seconda dell'andamento del raccolto), dalla guerra e dalla pestilenza. Per quanto si tratti di movimenti forzati, motivati dal bisogno, e non certo di deleuziane "linee di fuga", il potere ne avverte la pericolosità, riapre il lazzeretto come luogo di internamento, chiude l'entrata in Milano nelle occasioni di crisi.[11] La fuga, il non stare mai fermi, è una delle due strategie con cui i sottoposti rispondono alle costrizioni indotte dal potere suppliziale e da quello neofeudale. L'altra attiene al livello discorsivo e si manifesta nella pratica della non verità sotto forma di dissimulazione.

Il romanzo della dissimulazione
C'è un gesto che si ripete più volte nei *Promessi sposi*, secondo modalità che ricalcano quelle seguite da don Abbondio al termine del primo capitolo: "Giunto su la soglia, si voltò indietro verso Perpetua, mise il dito sulla bocca, disse, con tono lento e solenne: 'per amor del cielo!' e disparve" (30). Sono le stesse

---

[10] Il conte Attilio ha un atteggiamento speculare a quello di Renzo: "[...] alle prime notizie del tumulto, e della canaglia che girava per le strade, in tutt'altra attitudine che di ricever bastonate, aveva creduto bene di trattenersi in campagna, fino a cose quiete" (Edizione Nigro 345).
[11] Nel *Fermo e Lucia* è la mobilità stessa di Renzo ad essere perseguita dalla legge. Su pressione di don Rodrigo, il podestà emana un ordine di cattura contro Renzo per contravvenzione alla grida che proibisce ai lavoratori della seta di lasciare il Ducato di Milano (289).

movenze usate da Lucia, nel terzo capitolo (59), per invitare al silenzio Agnese in occasione della raccolta delle noci, come anche dal vecchio servitore di don Rodrigo prima di parlare con padre Cristoforo (106), per due volte da Renzo per istruire Tonio sul matrimonio di sorpresa (114, 115) e infine dal pescatore che traghetta Renzo al di là dell'Adda (335). Anche i bravi che minacciano don Abbondio nel primo episodio del romanzo uniscono il gesto alle parole, "'non si lasci uscir parola su questo avviso'", con cui gli intimano di tacere (20). Non lo fanno nella componente verbale della Quarantana, tuttavia, ma nel disegno di Francesco Gonin, dove uno dei due scagnozzi è appunto ritratto mentre si porta il dito sulle labbra chiuse (18).

Il gesto del silenzio che serpeggia nel romanzo, non a caso finché l'eroe fuggiasco è ancora al di qua del confine, è lo stesso che il pittore piemontese Sebastiano Taricco (1641-1710) ha affrescato in varie forme sui muri della *Saletta del Silenzio*, nel Palazzo Salmatoris a Cherasco. Nell'analisi di Jon Snyder gli affreschi di Taricco rappresentano un "notevole documento visuale, non solo della resistenza del discorso della dissimulazione, ma della pressione a cui cominciava ad essere sottoposto verso la fine del Seicento" (163). Nei *Promessi sposi* il dito portato più volte alle labbra segnala come quel discorso sia presente nel romanzo, così da inserire i personaggi e il loro sistema di valori all'interno della più larga cultura della dissimulazione che s'impone in Europa fra il Rinascimento e le soglie della modernità. Contigua alla reticenza e al silenzio, ma di entrambi più sottilmente ambigua e capace, se del caso, di inglobarne le pratiche, la dissimulazione — sprezzatura nel lessico di Castiglione, secondo Snyder — crea un'accorta separazione, a livello del sé, fra l'essere e l'apparire.[12] Nata nella corte rinascimentale come sapere indispensabile nella competizione per i favori del principe, la dissimulazione, scrive Snyder, "era l'arte di produrre per gli altri, in assoluta consapevolezza, una certa immagine di sé (attraverso il linguaggio, i gesti e le azioni), anche se tale rappresentazione mirava a scoprire poco o niente delle vere intenzioni del cortigiano: la *sprezzatura* mirava espressamente a separare rappresentazione e intenzione" (75; corsivo nel testo).[13]

---

[12] Mancuso vede nella scrittura ironica di Manzoni uno strumento per dissimularne i pensieri intimi. Starebbe al lettore più scaltro andare al di là della dissimulazione e arrivare alla verità. Gli argomenti a sostegno di questa tesi mi sembrano fragili. Don Ferrante, ad esempio, sarebbe un intellettuale "libero, fraterno, preciso, [...] di piena umanità e di grande dignità" (66). Manzoni avrebbe coperto questa figura sotto una "divertente figura donchisciottesca" (66). Mancuso avanza anche l'ipotesi che Manzoni possa aver letto *Della dissimulazione onesta,* di Torquato Accetto (64). Questa supposizione è contraddetta da un critico dell'autorevolezza di Snyder, che ricorda come la scoperta del trattato di Accetto sia dovuta a Benedetto Croce, a quasi tre secoli dalla pubblicazione (59).
[13] Snyder considera sprezzatura e dissimulazione come sinonimi. Coniare il termine sprezzatura sarebbe anzi stata una suprema forma di dissimulazione da parte di

Spiega Castiglione come si abbia dissimulazione "quando si dice una cosa e tacitamente se ne intende un'altra" (220). Negli esempi presentati nel *Cortegiano*, chi si serve della dissimulazione capitalizza il doppio senso della parola ironica per inviare al proprio interlocutore una coperta critica che lo morda senza ferirlo. Così Alfonso I d'Aragona, davanti a un servo che non gli ha restituito per quasi un anno "molte preciose anella", che lui gli aveva affidato al momento di lavarsi le mani, e che ora gli si ripresenta davanti in occasione di un'altra abluzione, reagisce dicendo: "'Bastinti le prime, ché queste saran bone per un altro'" (221). Se confrontiamo questa maniera della dissimulazione con quella presente nei *Promessi sposi*, possiamo misurare la differenza fra le due, che corrisponde alla distanza fra la corte e la strada. Nel romanzo manzoniano dissimulatore stradaiolo è Renzo che, in fuga verso la Repubblica Veneta, chiede la via per Gorgonzola per coprire la sua vera destinazione, Bergamo.

Non si pensi però che nei *Promessi sposi* la dissimulazione cortigiana, quella consustanziale alle élite insediate nei centri di potere, non sia presente. Nel racconto entusiastico del podestà di Lecco, per esempio, il conte d'Olivares, ministro di Filippo IV di Spagna, "'è una volpe vecchia, parlando col dovuto rispetto, che farebbe perdere la traccia a chi si sia: e, quando accenna a destra, si può essere sicuri che batterà a sinistra: ond'è che nessuno può mai vantarsi di conoscere i suoi disegni'" (97). Nel romanzo si incontrano altri esercizi di dissimulazione d'élite, come quello eseguito dal padre provinciale dei cappuccini e dal conte zio quando si accordano per allontanare padre Cristoforo dal Lecchese, ma nella grande maggioranza dei casi la dissimulazione segue i modi di quella praticata da Renzo.[14] Si tratta di una tecnica di sopravvivenza, che ha in comune con la dissimulazione cortigiana la percezione dell'altro come potenziale nemico, dato inevitabile in un contesto di legalità assente o degenerata nell'arbitrio.[15] È l'identica situazione in cui, in un'altra società dominata dalla prepotenza, all'inizio del *Giorno della civetta,* davanti al

---

Castiglione, che così facendo avrebbe celato sotto un neologismo immune da critiche il termine dissimulazione, il cui status era controverso dal punto di vista della morale e della teologia (74).

[14] Nigro coglie un gioco di reticenza e dissimulazione nel rapporto fra il testo e le *Historiae Patriae* di Ripamonti. Quest'ultimo, che "nel romanzo aiuta il narratore a controllare il dettato dell'Anonimo, e a colmarne le reticenze", in quanto storico ufficiale della città, come riconosciuto da Manzoni, "era scrittore di secentesca dissimulazione onesta" (XXXVII).

[15] Caviglia ha notato come don Abbondio sia diventato sacerdote "per essere protetto, non per misurare il potere in rapporto alla Verità" (73). Don Abbondio vive la vita come una lunga dissimulazione, in cui la tonaca e la presunta vocazione nascondono la ricerca di protezione che sta alla base della scelta di prendere i voti.

maresciallo dei carabinieri che lo interroga su un omicidio che è stato appena commesso sotto i suoi occhi, il venditore di panelle in piazza Garibaldi risponde, "'Perché [...] hanno sparato?'" (Sciascia 394).

In tutto il ciclo romanzesco che impegna Manzoni dal 1821 al 1842, l'episodio in cui il testo riconosce nella maniera più esplicita la dissimulazione è raccontato nel *Fermo e Lucia,* quando il conte del Sagrato, ormai convertito, rientra al castello per liberare Lucia. Pensando a come affrontare i bravi con cui ha condiviso una vita da fuorilegge è tentato dall'idea di una confessione pubblica con cui rinnegare i passati delitti davanti ai vecchi complici. Consapevole del rischio che il coraggio della verità farebbe correre a Lucia, arriva alla conclusione che, in quel frangente, imboccare la strada del vero vorrebbe dire aiutare il male: "Facciamo il bene per l'unica via che è aperta. Bisogna dissimulare; si dissimuli" (411). È tutto il *Fermo e Lucia*, a ben vedere, che rappresenta la pratica della dissimulazione con un'apertura sconosciuta al testo pubblicato vent'anni dopo. Ma non si sia superficiali: di dissimulazione in realtà se ne fa di più nei *Promessi sposi,* solo che, nel passaggio dal *Fermo e Lucia,* non la si pratica nel narrato ma nella narrazione, con Manzoni che ne racconta ancora le manifestazioni, ma senza nominarla.[16] Lo conferma anche il dato quantitativo: termini appartenenti al campo semantico della dissimulazione ricorrono sedici volte nel *Fermo e Lucia* e sette nei *Promessi sposi* del 1840.[17] L'osservazione di Giovanni Nencioni, secondo cui la conversione del Manzoni del *Fermo e Lucia* a quello dei primi *Promessi sposi* corrisponde al passaggio "dalla profusione di sé alla dissimulazione onesta", si conferma corretta a partire proprio dal dissimulare, che rimane sì oggetto della rappresentazione, ma in maniera saviamente coperta.

I promessi sposi iniziano con un esercizio di dissimulazione, quello eseguito da don Abbondio nel suo approccio ai bravi in attesa: "Compose la faccia a tutta quella quiete e ilarità che poté, fece ogni sforzo per preparare un sorriso" (17); finiscono con la dissimulata dichiarazione d'amore di Lucia: "'Quando non voleste dire,' aggiunse, soavemente sorridendo, 'che il mio sproposito sia stato quello di volervi bene, e di promettermi a voi'" (745). La dissimulazione è stile di vita per don Abbondio, mentre è arte raffinata nel Conte Attilio, capace di coprire abilmente le proprie intenzioni nell'incontro col Conte Zio, così da ridurre quest'ultimo a pedina di un gioco condotto dal nipote. Povera dissimulazione è invece quella del notaio criminale che arresta Renzo. Prima si rivolge "con viso severo" ai birri che scortano Renzo intimando loro di non

---

[16] Brogi scrive che, a proposito dei *Promessi sposi*, "oltre che di 'romanzo dei rapporti di forza', è legittimo parlare di 'romanzo della dissimulazione dei rapporti di forza'" (112).

[17] Nel *Fermo e Lucia* il verbo dissimulare, diversamente coniugato, ricorre alle pagine 16, 115, 286, 297, 350, 380, 411 (2 volte), 447, 491, 560, 631, 652 e 691. Il sostantivo dissimulazione è invece presente alle pagine 201 e 449. Nei *Promessi sposi* le voci del verbo dissimulare appaiono alle pagine 23, 68, 124, 212, 222 e 423, mentre il sostantivo dissimulazione si incontra una sola volta, a pagina 139.

fargli del male e poi si volge al prigioniero "col viso divenuto a un tratto ridente, che pareva volesse dire: oh noi sì che siamo amici!" (304). Non funziona, come si sa, nonostante il notaio fosse "un furbo matricolato," tutt'altro che un novellino quindi: "[...] di tante belle parole, Renzo non ne credette una" (304). Perfido dissimulatore è il Griso, che riconosce i sintomi della peste in don Rodrigo, ma si dichiara d'accordo con il padrone, vittima lui di autodissimulazione, nell'attribuirli agli effetti inebrianti della vernaccia (626). Splendidi dissimulatori sono infine gli osti, che per necessità professionale possiedono anche un'acuta abilità di smascherare la dissimulazione altrui, come l'oste di Gorgonzola che risponde "'all'Adda per passare?'", a Renzo che con un "fare da addormentato" gli aveva chiesto a che distanza fosse il fiume (316).

Lontana per dato sociologico dalla sprezzatura cortigiana, la dissimulazione praticata dai personaggi dei *Promessi sposi* si avvicina piuttosto alla dissimulazione onesta che Snyder colloca nel territorio della civile conversazione teorizzata da Stefano Guazzo e Giordano Bruno. Si tratta della conversazione che si dipanava "nello spazio che si apriva fra la corte e la città, tra il *palazzo* e la *piazza,* tra i modelli del gusto cortigiano e chi da loro era influenzato; uno la poteva scoprire all'interno o nei paraggi di luoghi chiave della quotidiana interazione sociale, come la chiesa, la strada, la camera da letto e la tavola da pranzo" (31). Per chi operava in questo spazio, che corrisponde al *discretum* della vita di ogni giorno opposto al *continuum* della corte, ricorrere all'onesta dissimulazione significava riconoscere che "ad essere del tutto aperti nella maggioranza delle relazioni fra individui si correvano rischi intollerabili" (46). Nei *Promessi sposi* questa consapevolezza è parte fondante dei rapporti sociali, così da rendere la dissimulazione una pratica generalizzata. Se ne astengono solo le figure sante: Lucia, che come s'è visto ne fa sì pratica, ma un'unica volta e in versione "soave", padre Cristoforo e il cardinal Federigo, che ne ha meno bisogno di tutti in forza dell'alto potere di cui è investito. Ma per la restante umanità, da attento storico del Seicento e da romanziere capace di rappresentare la polifonia che vive nel sociale, Manzoni fa della dissimulazione uno stile di vita. La curva del suo esercizio taglia infatti trasversalmente i campi contrapposti del male e del bene: Don Rodrigo, gonfio com'è di superbia, non è un frequente dissimulatore, mentre Agnese e Renzo, personaggi positivi e amati, ricorrono senza problemi alla dissimulazione, pur con alterne fortune.

Lo spazio della dissimulazione nei *Promessi sposi* coincide con quello dove si parla la bachtiniana lingua del romanzo: la strada, l'osteria, il borgo e la piazza del mercato. La dissimulazione è una pratica che tracima al di là dei luoghi deputati alla civile conversazione per coinvolgere ogni componente del corpo sociale; è lo strumento, come osserva ancora Snyder, attraverso il quale gli individui possono "sopportare la pressione che su di loro fa pesare il mondo dell'assolutismo" (44). Narrandone l'utilizzo anche da parte di "gente meccaniche" Manzoni si mantiene coerente con la scelta di fare di due contadini semialfabeti gli eroi di un romanzo. Il guadagno cognitivo dell'operazione manzoniana è immenso; perché non potrebbe esserci strumento più adatto del racconto della dissimulazione per condurci dentro l'assolutismo, presentarcene gli snodi operativi, farcene toccare con mano, in tutte le sue articolazioni, la pressione che esercita su ogni gruppo sociale anziché sulle sole élite cortigiane o professionali. Ma se questo è ciò che il romanzo di Manzoni fa, allora non di assolutismo come forma astratta di governo ci parla, ma della sua capacità di esercitare potere a partire da un investimento politico e da una tecnologica politica del corpo (Foucault, *Surveiller* 34). E se quest'investimento e questa tecnologia operano secondo le linee che ho delineato nella prima sezione di questo articolo, allora lo spazio che rimane alla pratica della verità nel rapporto fra i sottoposti e il potere non potrà che essere ridotto al minimo e tale esercizio non potrà che radicarsi in comportamenti individuali al di fuori dalla norma.

Potere e parola vera nella Quarantana: due casi
Daniela Brogi ha scritto che "nessuno, prima dell'incontro con Lucia, ha mai tenuto testa all'Innominato" (131). Dei pochi esempi di parola vera che ho trovato nel romanzo quello di Lucia nelle mani del suo rapitore è l'unico nel quale l'evidente divario di potere fra due interlocutori venga superato di slancio, in realtà rovesciato, dal più debole.[18] In altri episodi in cui personaggi diversamente potenti si confrontano fra loro — don Abbondio fermato dai bravi, Renzo davanti all'Azzeccagarbugli, don Abbondio a colloquio con Federigo Borromeo e Agnese di fronte a Gertrude — gli inferiori rimangono al di sotto della capacità di articolare una regolare prestazione discorsiva. Un episodio a parte è rappresentato dall'invettiva di padre Cristoforo nei confronti di don Rodrigo, dopo che questi gli ha suggerito di far mettere Lucia sotto la propria protezione. Se esiste un esempio di franco parlare è sicuramente questo, ma due fattori mi convincono a una notevole cautela nel considerarlo un caso di verità pronunciata da un inferiore in consapevole sfida al potere. Prima di tutto, fra Cristoforo parla sotto l'impulso di uno sdegno così veemente da trasportarlo fin quasi al punto di mettersi al posto di Dio: "'Verrà un giorno...'" (104).[19] Qui si trattiene — "gli cadde ogni spirito d'ira e d'entusiasmo" — e passa alla più totale mansuetudine; ma prima di farlo ha perso il pieno controllo di sé (105).

---

[18] Un elenco dei pochi altri casi nei *Promessi sposi* in cui un personaggio dica la verità comprende i due propositi omicidi di Renzo nei confronti di don Rodrigo, l'invettiva di Padre Cristoforo davanti allo stesso don Rodrigo, il pianto dell'Innominato in presenza del cardinal Federigo, l'esclamazione "'Ah canaglia!'" del capitano di giustizia al balcone del forno delle grucce, il sollievo di don Abbondio alla notizia della morte di don Rodrigo.

[19] Devo l'osservazione su Padre Cristoforo e il suo trattenersi quand'è a un passo dal sostituirsi a Dio a un ponderato commento degli editori del volume, che qui ringrazio.

Ora, nei trattati rinascimentali e seicenteschi, l'ira del cui spirito è preda Padre Cristoforo è appunto uno di quegli elementi che impediscono la dissimulazione, come fa notare Rossi: "[...] non vi è affetto che più sciolga la lingua, dell'ira. L'amore ed il timore la legano. L'ira la scioglie, e vibra come spada" (139). Nel caso dell'ira, se non c'è dissimulazione è per l'impossibilità dell'adirato di simulare; non siamo quindi nel territorio della verità pronunciata con chiara coscienza. Per essere alternativa alla dissimulazione non basta che la parola corrisponda alla realtà dei fatti, deve anche essere emessa da un individuo in pieno controllo di se stesso, come non è chi è trasportato dai propri sentimenti. Padre Cristoforo, in secondo luogo, è privo di potere in quanto individuo, ma è parte di un gruppo sociale, l'ordine dei cappuccini, la cui potenza sovrasta quella di don Rodrigo, che ne è consapevole. In una società, come quella del Seicento lombardo, che l'illegalità ha frammentato in un arcipelago di corporazioni, l'appartenenza ad un aggregato più forte forniva appunto all'individuo quelle protezioni che la legge non sapeva dare: la vicenda umana di Don Abbondio ne è prova nei *Promessi sposi*. Così padre Cristoforo esce senza ricevere offesa dal palazzotto del tiranno e per allontanarlo da Pescarenico il conte Attilio dovrà risalire nella scala del potere politico e ricorrere ad un membro del consiglio segreto, il conte zio.

Lucia invece è del tutto inerme quando si trova nelle mani dell'Innominato, il più potente dei signori neofeudali rappresentati nel romanzo. Eppure a Lucia basta chiedergli "'Cosa le ho fatto io?'" per renderlo inoffensivo (Edizione Nigro 398). Il punto è che si tratta di una domanda inammissibile. Nel contesto del potere neofeudale, non è necessario che Lucia abbia fatto qualcosa per giustificare il suo ratto: il godimento del suo corpo è uno dei diritti signorili, a prestar fede al romanzo addirittura l'unico che al signore importi. Eppure la "sicurezza dell'indignazione disperata" di Lucia è sufficiente per mandare in pezzi la forza dell'Innominato (Brogi 131).[20] Con la sua domanda Lucia sovverte quei rapporti di potere che ogni altro personaggio dei *Promessi sposi* ha come introiettato dentro di sé. E il colpo di grazia, nel senso buono, non metaforico, lo porta poco dopo, con un'affermazione che pone il suo carceriere davanti a una scelta secca: "'Dio perdona tante cose per un'opera di misericordia'" (399). Ora è l'Innominato ad avere il problema di conquistarsi la libertà, e non dalle mura di un castello ma da una vita di sceleratezze, come la definisce Manzoni. Risolverà la questione il giorno dopo nel colloquio con Federigo Borromeo, ma sarà stata la frase di Lucia a risuonargli dentro durante la notte precedente, quella che porterà alla conversione.

---

[20] Vale la pena di ricordare, con Nigro, che Lucia è "il personaggio più 'forte' di tutti e tre i romanzi di Manzoni" ("Naufragi" XXIX).

Nella *Storia della colonna infame,* la dissimulazione che Lucia supera di netto, collocando l'autorità dell'Innominato in un contesto dove misura la propria debolezza, è un esercizio dal quale i sottoposti al potere suppliziale sono esclusi. Gli imputati processati come untori sono confrontati da una sola verità, quella dei loro giudici. Qui ci troviamo nel quadro giuridico descritto da Foucault, nel quale il giudice "costituiva da solo e in completo controllo una verità con la quale investiva l'imputato" (*Surveiller* 45). Nella sua lettura degli atti del processo del 1630 Manzoni spiega come la verità su cui i magistrati milanesi esercitavano un assoluto dominio fosse in realtà verosimiglianza, ossia un falso costruito come vero. Questa falsità, tuttavia, proprio per il suo essere distante dalle dichiarazioni, veritiere, degli imputati, bastava per qualificare queste ultime come menzognere. Passaggio questo indispensabile, perché una delle condizioni per la somministrazione dei tormenti era, appunto, che l'imputato fosse colto in fallo come bugiardo. Il confronto è quindi fra la falsità sotto veste di verosimiglianza dei giudici e la verità costretta a essere bugia degli imputati. Così, nell'interrogatorio di Piazza, ogni volta che il magistrato afferma che le dichiarazioni dell'imputato non sono verosimili, quest'ultimo risponde di aver detto la verità. Ma è un confronto impari perché una delle due parti, in quanto titolare del potere suppliziale, ha il diritto di mettere l'altra alla tortura. In un processo di tal fatta la confessione è l'elemento decisivo: unica vera fonte di prova, che trasforma il vero in falso e la falsa verosimiglianza in verità. Leggiamo: "'Signor no che non è vero; ma se mi date li tormenti perchè io neghi questa particolarità, sarò forzato a dire che è vero, benchè non sij'", come dichiara Girolamo Migliavacca al giudice che lo accusa di aver ricevuto "onto et danari" da Piazza e Mora (Edizione Nigro 842).[21]

Torturati, gli imputati si autoaccusano e s'incolpano l'un l'altro. Forniscono il materiale grezzo — in termini narratologici sarebbe la fabula — che i giudici modellano e combinano in una storia, confermata, un'ultima volta, sotto tortura. Ma c'è n'è uno con cui il metodo non funziona: Gaspare Migliavacca, figlio di Girolamo, di mestiere arrotino, condannato a morte sulla base delle accuse di Piazza e Mora. Viene sottoposto ai tormenti a sentenza già emessa, come volevano le regole di un sistema che aveva bisogno della confessione perché il processo diventasse "una vittoria davvero riportata sull'imputato" (Foucault, *Surveiller* 48). Farinelli, che ha pubblicato un ampio sunto dei verbali dell'interrogatorio, racconta come, nella seduta del 20 dicembre 1630, Gaspare Migliavacca sia stato torturato in cinque riprese, via via più dolorose (72-73). Manzoni dà di Migliavacca figlio un giudizio commosso e lo onora di un appellativo raro e impegnativo per un cristiano: "Ne' tormenti, in faccia alla

---

[21] Farinelli ritiene che Girolamo Migliavacca c'entrasse davvero con le unzioni. Queste furono un fatto reale, verificatosi in occasione di tutte le pesti del '600, anche se non furono certo la causa del contagio. Gli untori si comportarono come "gli sciacalli della peste del 1630" (64).

morte, le sue parole furon tutte meglio che da uom forte; furon da *martire*" (Edizione Nigro 843; corsivo mio). Che questo sia un passo cruciale della *Storia della colonna infame* lo si intende dal tono non "referenziale" ma "emozionale" che vibra nella parola di Manzoni. È quella voce che, secondo Renzo Negri, risuona nei "saggi d'inchiesta narrativa manzoniani", scritti non con l'oggettività dello storico professionale, ma "con uno stato d'animo di *indignation contenue* [...] e di fervore d'indagine" (324). Come la parola vera di Gaspare Migliavacca svetta nel contesto di dissimulazione in cui si dipana la conversazione del suo secolo, così la voce di Manzoni si stacca dall'oggettività della storiografia per modellarsi nel fuoco della partecipazione.

Gaspare Migliavacca sa di dover morire, sarà giustiziato tre giorni dopo, qualsiasi cosa dichiari ai giudici. Se accusare se stesso e gli altri imputati gli risparmierebbe ore di spietato dolore, negare le accuse non gli salverebbe la vita. Gli serve a qualcos'altro: "'[...] non dirò mai quello che non ho fatto, né mai condannerò l'anima mia; et è molto meglio che patisca tre o quattro hore de tormenti, che andar nell'inferno a patire eternamente'" (843). Conscio del peccato mortale che avrebbero rappresentato sia l'autocalunnia sia la calunnia di altri, fino all'ultimo ripete che quel che conta per lui è la salute dell'anima. Personaggio antifaustiano, per questa salvezza sopporta patimenti incredibili. Lo dovesse definire Foucault, egli sarebbe un parresiasta, colui che uniforma la sua vita ad un solo principio, quello secondo cui "bisogna dire la verità su se stessi" (*Courage* 6). La verità di Gaspare Migliavacca è quella della fede, di chi sa di essere una creatura in possesso di un'anima immortale e perciò responsabile delle proprie azioni; fattore, quest'ultimo, cruciale, è chiaro, nella *Storia della colonna infame,* il cui assunto è che alla responsabilità personale dei giudici, anziché all'arretratezza delle leggi, sia da addebitare la messa a morte di imputati innocenti. E quella di Gaspare Migliavacca è una fede assolutamente gratuita, che nessun premio si aspetta in questo mondo.

Davanti al potere la parola vera è rarissima. In ciò si apparenta al miracolo e al martirio come prodigio della fede. In coerenza con un testo che, come ha acutamente notato Pierantonio Frare, fa della "necessità e inevitabilità del giudizio" una sua conquista fondamentale, Gaspare Migliavacca fonda il coraggio della sua verità sulla fede nell'esistenza di un Dio che giudica (83). Come Lucia quando ricorda all'Innominato quali grandi braccia abbia la pietà divina, Migliavacca sposta su un livello più alto quei rapporti di forza che, secondo Calvino, sono il vero oggetto della rappresentazione nei *Promessi sposi* (271-75). A quell'altezza, per Manzoni, il potere terreno, neofeudale o suppliziale che sia, chiamato a confrontarsi con la giustizia divina, si rivela per quello che è: nient'altro che un breve sogno. Ma a quel confronto, nella *Storia della colonna infame*, lo convoca il più debole dei suoi soggetti, il condannato a morte non più padrone del suo stesso corpo, ormai preda della macchina della tortura.

Il martire, scrive Tertulliano, è "chi ha reso testimonianza ed è ucciso" ("confessus occiditur" 139). Facendosene, a sua volta, testimone, il testo porta al livello più alto la propria capacità di esprimere il vero, inteso questa volta nella sua pienezza ontologica.[22] Lo fa in due modi. In primo luogo attraverso il significato letterale delle parole di Migliavacca: è ontologicamente vero che esista l'inferno e che duri in eterno. In secondo luogo, lo fa per mezzo dell'insegnamento che dalla vicenda di Migliavacca si trae: il carattere insormontabile della responsabilità personale. Se è il personaggio con meno potere nell'intera *Quarantana*, cioè Magliavacca, a pronunciare la parola più coraggiosa, allora nessuna circostanza può essere invocata per esimerci dal dovere di schierarci sempre dalla parte del bene. Verità che è coerente con quella, in senso morale, della *Storia della colonna infame,* dall'individuazione della colpa personale dei giudici nella somministrazione della tortura fino all'affermazione della colpevolezza degli stessi Piazza e Mora, vittime innocenti, sì, ma anche colpevoli accusatori di altri nella loro stessa posizione.

Così la scoperta dell'insormontabile grumo di passioni perverse nascosto nel profondo dell'essere umano, che è poi il sugo della *Storia della colonna infame*, si accompagna in Manzoni al ritrovamento, nel luogo più buio e nel momento più disperato, di una scintilla di umanità che si slancia verso il divino. È in questo slancio che si manifesta la verità più alta del racconto manzoniano, quella affidata alla parola del martire. Di tutte le altre, in presenza degli insondabili abissi del cuore umano, nessuno può essere sicuro. Ma la certezza da opporre alla nostra ignoranza Manzoni la trova nel punto più basso dell'edificio sociale, nel fondo di un braccio della morte. Da quest'abisso il vero del testo si alza a sfiorare il senso della Provvidenza, quel mistero che nel suo sfrontato opporsi alle nostre convenzionali verità crea l'evento scandaloso — il condannato dalla giustizia umana testimone di quella divina — che non dovrebbe accadere eppure accade.

Long Island University

---

[22] Uso la parola "testimone" nel senso che assume in Agamben: essere testimone significa farsi carico di una lacuna, "provare ad ascoltarla" (9). Nella *Storia della colonna infame*, la lacuna non riguarda in sé le parole di Migliavacca, chiarissime e riportate su carta a differenza di quelle dei superstiti dei campi di sterminio di cui parla Agamben, ma il silenzio dell'archivio, nel quale sono rimaste sepolte e inascoltate per due secoli.

Work Cited

Agamben, Giorgio. *Il ricordo di Auschwitz. L'archivio e il testimone*. Torino: Bollati Boringhieri, 1998.
Brogi, Daniela. *Il genere proscritto. Manzoni e la scelta del romanzo*. Pisa: Giardini, 2005.
Calvino, Italo. *Una pietra sopra: discorsi di letteratura e società*. Torino: Einaudi, 1980.
Castiglione, Baldassar. *Il libro del cortegiano*. A cura di Amedeo Quondam. Milano: Garzanti, 2000.
Caviglia, Franco. "Sofocle in Manzoni? Il percorso di Padre Cristoforo." *Testo. Studi di teoria e storia della letteratura e della critica* 48 (2004): 69-78.
Farinelli, Giuseppe. "Per una rilettura critica della 'Storia della colonna infame'." *Manzoni/Grossi. Atti del XIV Congresso Nazionale di Studi Manzoniani, Lecco 10/14 ottobre 1990*. Milano: Centro Nazionale Studi Manzoniani, 1991. 55-121.
Frare, Pierantonio. *Scrittura dell'inquietudine. Saggio su Alessandro Manzoni*. Firenze: Olschki, 2006.
Foucault, Michel. *Histoire de la folie à l'âge classique*. Parigi: Plon, 1961.
———. *Le Courage de la vérité*. Paris: Gallimard Seuil, 2009.
———. *Sécurité, territoire, population*. Parigi: Gallimard, 2004.
———. *Surveiller et punir: naissance de la prison*. Parigi: Gallimard, 1975.
Grasso, Aldo. "Una lacrima sul Griso. Appunti in margine a una parodia televisiva." *Leggere I promessi sposi*. A c. di Giovanni Manetti. Milano: Bompiani, 1989. 293-97.
Mancuso, Giorgio. "Manzoni e la dissimulazione onesta tra storia e fede (linguaggio e inquietudini di un cattolico)." *Ermeneutica letteraria* 4 (2008): 63-80.
Manzoni, Alessandro. *Fermo e Lucia. Appendice storica sulla colonna infame*. Vol. 1 di *I romanzi*. A cura di Salvatore Silvano Nigro. Milano: Mondadori, 2002.
———. *I promessi sposi (1840). Storia della colonna infame*. Vol. 2, t. 2 di *I romanzi*. A c. di Salvatore Silvano Nigro. Milano: Mondadori, 2002.
Negri, Renzo. "Il discorso 'Del romanzo storico' nel trittico narrativo manzoniano." *Forum Italicum* 11 (1977): 307-29.
Nencioni, Giovanni. "Conversioni dei *Promessi sposi*." *Tra grammatica e retorica. Da Dante a Pirandello*. Torino: Einaudi, 1983. 3-27.
Nigro, Salvatore Silvano. "Naufragi di terraferma." Alessandro Manzoni. *Fermo e Lucia. Appendice storica sulla colonna infame*. Vol. 1 di *I romanzi*. A c. di Salvatore Silvano Nigro. Milano: Mondadori, 2002. IX-XXXIX.
Pupino, Angelo R. *Il vero solo è bello. Manzoni fra retorica e logica*. Bologna: il Mulino, 1982.
Rossi, Pio. *Un vocabolario per la menzogna*. In *Elogio della menzogna*. A c. di Salvatore Silvano Nigro. Palermo Sellerio, 1990. 85-151.
Sciascia, Leonardo. *Il giorno della civetta*. Vol. 1 di *Opere*. A c. di Claude Ambroise. Milano: Bompiani, 1987: 387-483.
Snyder, Jon R. *Dissimulation and Culture of Secrecy in Early Modern Europe*. Berkeley: University of California Press, 2009.
Tertulliano. *Scorpiace*. A c. di Giovanna Azzali Bernardelli. Firenze: Nardini, 1990.
Valesio, Paolo. "Lucia, ovvero la 'reticentia.'" *Leggere I promessi sposi*. A c. di Giovanni Manetti. Milano: Bompiani, 1989. 145-74.

Valentina Nocentini

L'Italia della guerra di Libia (1911-1912): un burattinaio contro il potere

Sinossi. Questo saggio presenta la Guerra di Libia del 1911-1912 come una costruzione retorico-letteraria originata dal primo legame moderno fra politica, economia e cultura con l'obiettivo di creare quella collettività nazionale che in Italia ancora mancava. La guerra divenne così uno strumento di controllo e regolamentazione delle masse, in modo da garantire il meccanismo della *governabilità* del giovane e frammentato Stato italiano, e per creare finalmente un popolo italiano unito e cosciente della propria identità e grandezza. L'analisi di un breve racconto di Arturo Rossato, pubblicato sulla *Terza Pagina* del quotidiano l'*Avanti* nel febbraio del 1912, serve, nella seconda parte del saggio, a mostrare un'accusa lanciata contro la manipolazione politica in atto.
Parole chiave. Guerra di Libia 1911-1912, governabilità, potere, popolo, Giovanni Giolitti, stampa, terza pagina, industrie siderurgiche, banche, costruzione mediatica, burattinaio

Introduzione e tesi
La conferenza di Berlino del 1884-85, durante la quale le grandi potenze coloniali europee si erano spartite l'Africa per assecondare i propri desideri di potenza, l'industrializzazione e il nuovo mercato economico-commerciale mondiale, non aveva preso in considerazione la Libia, rimasta fuori dai giochi politici internazionali in quanto parte dell'Impero Ottomano. Un giorno "doveva essere occupata da qualcuno," e "in Italia era un dogma quasi universalmente accettato che la occupazione per opera altrui sarebbe stata un disastro per noi, e che pertanto la Libia doveva essere occupata, o prima o poi, da noi" (xvii), scriveva lo storico Gaetano Salvemini nel 1914 nel suo saggio *Perché siamo andati in Libia*, dove per la prima volta si cercava di capire, "perché" nel 1911 "siamo andati in Libia" a fare una guerra, facendo "credere all'intero paese tutte le grossolane sciocchezze con cui l'impresa libica è stata giustificata e provocata" (x-xi). Il lavoro di Salvemini, prima collaboratore della rivista fiorentina *La Voce*, poi fondatore nel dicembre del 1911 dell'*Unità. Problemi di vita italiana*, dove affrontava senza vincoli ideologici i problemi del paese, fece da apripista ad una storiografia che avrebbe dovuto "ricostruire questo torbido periodo della nostra vita nazionale" (x-xi), la Guerra di Libia del 1911-1912 appunto, e dimostrare così che il colonialismo liberale italiano non era affatto straccione e improvvisato come da sempre veniva caratterizzato. Proprio in questi anni, infatti, l'Italia si dotò di quella che lo storico Silvio Lanaro chiama

"professionalità imperialista" (73), cioè di un'economia e di una politica coloniale che univano, in maniera armonica, potere e cultura, così da potere consolidare uno spirito nazionale italiano ed esprimere, ad oltre quarant'anni dal Risorgimento, un'idea concreta del "noi" cittadini dell'Italia unita. Se è vero che l'imperialismo è "il fenomeno psicosociale più pervasivo che la storia abbia conosciuto" (Lanaro 72) e il potere è invece quell'entità che forma un soggetto, "fornendo le condizioni necessarie alla sua esistenza e la traiettoria dei propri desideri", così che "il noi" formato diventa "fondamentalmente dipendente da un discorso che non abbiamo mai scelto, ma che paradossalmente inizia e sostiene il nostro agire",[1] la mobilitazione dell'opinione pubblica italiana intorno alla Libia generata dalla stampa nazionale e sostenuta dagli organi istituzionali, fu una precisa e coordinata tattica di governo allo scopo di creare un discorso retorico-letterario capace di legare politica, economia e cultura e di formare un *noi italiano nazionale*, ossia "una società di regole e discipline," uno "stato di governo" che con tale interconnessione poteva controllare e creare una "massa: la massa della popolazione" (Foucault, *1 February 1978* 110) specificatamente *italiana*. Grazie all'analisi di un breve racconto, *Il burattinaio*, scritto da uno sconosciuto Arturo Rossato[2] e pubblicato a guerra già iniziata sull'*Avanti*, questo saggio si propone di investigare proprio i meccanismi attraverso i quali la preparazione e la conseguente realizzazione della campagna di Libia del 1911-1912 vennero costruiti e usati da "un insieme formato da istituzioni, procedure, analisi e riflessioni, calcoli e tattiche" per permettere "l'esercizio di questo specifico, sebbene molto complesso, potere" della *governabilità*: il potere che ha "la popolazione come il suo obiettivo, l'economica politica come la sua maggiore forma di conoscenza, e gli apparati della sicurezza come il suo essenziale strumento tecnico" per far "sopravvivere lo stato" (Foucault, *1 February 1978* 108-109) subordinando a sé le persone.[3]

L'Italia del 1911: politica, industria e stampa
L'Italia del 1911 era un paese unificato, ma da tempo attraversato da numerose e spinose questioni sociali che animavano la società civile e premevano il governo di Giovanni Giolitti per una mediazione e soluzione rapida: le richieste di

---

[1] Butler, *The Psychic Life of Power* 1-2. Da questo momento, ogni traduzione in italiano appartiene all'autrice di questo saggio, se non diversamente segnalato.
[2] L'Enciclopedia Treccani online ha una breve nota su questo giornalista e commediografo di Vicenza che ha prodotto per il teatro numerose opere comiche, ma in dialetto veneto. Per maggiori informazioni, si veda la voce dell'enciclopedia, *Arturo Rossato*.
[3] Per ulteriori approfondimenti storici sugli inizi dell'avventura coloniale italiana in Africa, e soprattutto in Libia, si può fare riferimento alle pagine dei seguenti volumi: Labanca 18-94, 108-10; Segrè 3-6. Sugli inizi dell'*Unità* di Gaetano Salvemini, si veda Cantafio 193-95.

L'Italia della guerra di Libia (1911-1912): *burattini* subordinati al potere 341

aumenti salariali, di maggiori tutele lavorative, del diritto di voto alle donne e dell'estensione del suffragio universale maschile, fra le altre. Il paese era però da anni trainato da un non indifferente risveglio economico che aveva fatto dell'Italia una delle prime potenze europee a dotarsi di strutture capitalistiche e industriali nuove proprie di un "modo di produzione diverso e superiore — in quanto nato per liberare nuove risorse produttive e per soddisfare nuovi bisogni", scrive Silvio Lanaro (15). Il paese si muoveva verso la modernizzazione ed era tornato a crescere a livello economico su buoni ritmi, anche dopo la depressione che aveva colpito il vecchio continente tra il 1907 e il 1908. I settori trainanti erano quelli dell'industria siderurgica, della cantieristica navale, delle rotaie e dei motori, dell'industria tessile e chimica, la maggiorparte dei quali quasi totalmente sostenuti da ingenti investimenti pubblici. Come sostiene David Forgacs, in mancanza di una forte domanda interna che generasse profitti tali da potere essere reinvestiti per incrementare la produzione, ogni governo italiano post-unitario (da Depretis a Crispi e da Crispi a Giolitti) aveva forzatamente e autoritariamente imposto uno sviluppo industriale su base pubblica e posto i bisogni dell'industrializzazione al centro della politica di aggregazione del paese e di promozione all'esterno di un'idea manifatturiera-capitalistica forte, lontana dallo stereotipo di arretratezza notoriamente assegnato a livello internazionale al Bel Paese (43-44). Un'industrializzazione ancora precaria, comunque, appendice della società rurale, ed appunto povera di capitali freschi, che trovava di conseguenza nel credito bancario ulteriori (e necessari) finanziamenti per sostenersi. Lo strano e pericoloso intreccio fra istituti finanziari e capitali pubblici che si veniva così a creare, tendenza in generale comune a tutti i grandi paesi industriali ed imperialisti europei che si stavano allora spartendo il mondo, aveva però in Italia un'anomalia: quella delle strane interferenze della politica nell'industria e nella finanza. Qui, infatti, la classe dirigente italiana (composta ancora in maggioranza da membri di vecchie famiglie aristocratiche e benestanti) e i gruppi industriali nazionali cercavano di consolidare la propria autorevolezza e i propri interessi, perseguendo senza scrupoli le solite dinamiche clientelari proprie del *trasformismo*.[4] Non a caso, Richard Webster parla di una vera e propria comunità peninsulare di interessi economici che si era negli anni formata parallelamente alle maggioranze trasformiste del Parlamento, che mirava a rendersi più dinamica e competitiva e che, interessante, rappresentava allora l'unica vera forma di unità esistente in Italia. E Webster racconta anche che nell'agosto del 1911, cioè poco prima di un

---

[4] David Forgacs ci insegna che certe industrie italiane avevano nei consigli di amministrazione le banche, così come certi politici erano legati a queste ultime attraverso incarichi nei consigli di amministrazione. Lo stesso Giovanni Giolitti, per esempio, era in Banca Commerciale e a sua volta anche nel consiglio di amministrazione di industrie di rilevanza strategica quali la Terni, l'Ilva e la Falck (44).

mese dall'inizio delle ostilità in Libia, lo Stato avviò un'operazione di salvataggio del settore siderurgico italiano (Ilva, Elba, Piombino, Savona e Ferriere Italiane) agevolando un credito di oltre 96 milioni di lire[5] elargito dalla Banca d'Italia, alla testa di una cordata che includeva Banco di Roma, Banca Commerciale di Milano, Società Bancaria, Credito Italiano ed un certo numero di piccoli finanziatori privati. Il progetto che portava al coordinamento e all'unificazione di tutti i siti dell'acciaio italiano sotto il consorzio ILVA, mirava ad abbattere i costi, a essere più produttivi e a controllare meglio i prezzi in regime di totale autarchia. In più, si sanciva un importante matrimonio fra pubblico e privato grazie all'intervento di istituti finanziari nei cui consigli d'amministrazione sedevano molti manager delle stesse industrie siderurgiche salvate dallo stato.[6]

All'interno di questo quadro politico-industriale, si inserivano i produttori di informazione, i giornali *in primis*, che proprio in quegli anni godevano di una grande espansione grazie al forte calo dell'analfabetismo e, di nuovo, alla concentrazione di interessi politici, statali, bancari e industriali proprio su di essi. Dal primo decennio del 1900 era iniziata la costituzione di una vera e propria cultura industrializzata che cercava di legittimare la politica, organizzare il consenso ed assecondare gli interessi dei vari gruppi industriali esistenti. Nei casi più importanti, cruciali per la preparazione e realizzazione della guerra di Libia, notiamo che i maggiori finanziatori del *Corriere della Sera* (Milano), diretto da Luigi Albertini al 1900 al 1925, erano la Pirelli (industria della gomma) e la De Angeli (industria tessile); quelli della *Tribuna* (Roma), diretta da Olindo Malagodi dal 1910 al 1923, erano le industrie siderurgiche e la Banca Commerciale; de *La Stampa* (Torino) di Alfredo Frassati, liberale legatissimo a Giolitti, era lo stesso direttore, il quale ritenne in sé anche la carica di proprietario-editore dal 1900 al 1920; e dell'*Idea Nazionale*, fondata a Roma il primo marzo 1911, erano le industrie siderurgiche, meccaniche, zuccheriere, come anche gli armatori e le banche. L'esistenza già allora di un cosiddetto *quarto potere* trovava, dunque, riscontri evidenti proprio in questa conformazione dell'informazione. Due fatti, inoltre, meritano una certa attenzione. Prima di tutto, esattamente nel 1911, *La Tribuna*, di proprietà del senatore Luigi Roux, fedele sostenitore e seguace di Giovanni Giolitti, venne salvata dal fallimento attraverso un rifinanziamento operato dai gruppi siderurgici appartenenti all'Ilva, da alcune industrie manifatturiere di zucchero

---

[5] La linea di credito era largamente costituita da riduzione del debito e delle tasse, da concessioni e da estensioni di credito.
[6] Per maggiori e più dettagliate informazioni sull'Italia di Giovanni Giolitti, i legami fra politica e finanza, e sull'industria siderurgica, si rimanda alle pagine dei seguenti studi: Webster 14-19, 46-49, 58-71, 102-05; Gentile, *La Grande Italia* 9-16; Vivarelli 28-47, 62-72; Agnew 25, 28; Lanaro 2, 15-23, 28, 121; Labanca 23-26, 100-01.

del Nord Italia, dalla Banca Commerciale e Nazionale e dal Banco di Roma. Poi, la nascita dell'*Idea Nazionale*, ossia dell'organo ufficiale del movimento nazionalista di Enrico Corradini, cioè di un movimento politico aggressivo, imperialista e contrario a un sistema che, secondo la propaganda corradiniana, privilegiava solo gli interessi di certi settori della società, avvenne proprio a pochi mesi di distanza dall'inizio delle ostilità. Questo movimento rappresentava, infatti, quella corrispondenza ideologica, in gran parte demagogica, che Silvio Lanaro vede capace, in quello specifico momento storico, di fare concretamente il gioco del potere, attivandone le tecniche di controllo sulla massa in maniera autoritaria (21). Questa retorica imperialista dei Nazionalisti comunicava l'esistenza nel paese di un'organicità socio-nazionale da valorizzare e creava una coscienza collettiva intorno ad una struttura storico-culturale comune proiettata verso una logica da potenza estera. Un movimento, allora, anti-giolittiano, che però serviva proprio gli interessi del primo ministro italiano. Quando, nel marzo del 1911, nell'anniversario del cinquantenario di una data fondamentale del Risorgimento — la proclamazione del Regno d'Italia, il 17 marzo del 1861, in seguito alla Spedizione dei Mille —, il settimanale nazionalista pubblicò in prima pagina un editoriale nel quale sosteneva che "a un gran popolo non giova vivere se non crea continuamente nuove condizioni di vita più alte e più vaste" (*Cinquantenario* 1), Corradini anticipava le future mosse di un Giolitti sempre meno riformatore e sempre più interessato a mettere insieme i contrastanti interessi e bisogni di finanzieri, industriali, proletari, agrari e borghesi (Lanaro 16). Corradini spiegava, infatti, che per "tener congiunti gli elementi diversi" del paese "occorre un'idea-madre, che determini fra di essi una comunione spirituale superiore ad ogni influenza di interessi particolari e capace altresì di fornire l'energia necessaria ed il criterio giusto per soddisfare agli infiniti bisogni che continuamente mutano nella vita d'un grande organismo sociale" (*Cinquantenario* 1).[7]

E l'idea madre che in quel momento poteva legare insieme la molteplicità nazionale italiana in una individualità di paese era proprio l'impresa di Tripoli. Secondo alcuni concetti espressi da Michel Foucault in un suo seminario del 1978, "la sovranità" di uno Stato "è esercitata all'interno dei confini di un territorio, la disciplina è esercitata sui corpi degli individui, e la sicurezza è esercitata sull'intera popolazione" (*11 January 1978* 11) per il perfetto funzionamento di uno "stato capitalizzato" organizzato intorno ad una città capitale quale "sede della sovranità e fulcro della circolazione politica e commerciale" (15). La guerra di Libia, rappresentava, quindi, proprio

---

[7] È possibile approfondire le conoscenze sulla stampa italiana di inizio Novecento e sull'attività dei maggiori giornali italiani al tempo della guerra di Libia attraverso le pagine dei seguenti studi: Castronovo, Giacheri Fossati, Tranfaglia 67-68, 108-21, 172-81, 202-207; Tesoro 714-15; Forgacs 45-57.

un'occasione che, in maniera coercitiva, poteva finalmente unire le varie diversità italiane e garantire appunto questa perfetta sincronia dello Stato italiano, specialmente in un momento in cui lo stesso primo ministro Giolitti era bloccato dall'impasse delle mille voci del Parlamento. La campagna di Libia, iniziata il 29 settembre del 1911 e terminata il 18 ottobre del 1912 con la firma del trattato di Ouchy, fu un evento creato ad hoc per legare al meglio i tre elementi massa-politica-industria, organizzarli in maniera efficiente ed armonica, e creare così una solida Italia industriale unita.

La costruzione mediatica della Guerra di Libia e la creazione di un popolo
A sbloccare concretamente la politica estera italiana verso la Libia, non a caso, erano stati gli interessi del Banco di Roma, il quale già dal 1905 aveva avviato per conto del governo italiano "la penetrazione economica in Libia" (Salvemini xxii). L'istituto di credito della capitale, diretto dalla migliore aristocrazia del Vaticano nel cui consiglio d'amministrazione sedeva anche Romolo Tittoni, fratello dell'allora ministro degli esteri del governo Giolitti, Tommaso Tittoni, aveva investito in progetti agricoli, comprato proprietà ed aperto filiali in Libia ed avviato potenziali nuovi mercati capitali tanto che il cosiddetto "ricatto del Banco di Roma", così come lo definì Salvemini a posteriori, fu la minaccia della stessa banca di vendere le "concessioni economiche" acquisite in Libia "ad un gruppo di banchieri tedeschi" (xxii-xxiii) ed austriaci, se il governo italiano non avesse agito concretamente contro i turchi che stavano iniziando a frenare l'avanzata economica italiana in Nord Africa.[8]

I giornali iniziarono allora a raccontare della Libia, territorio dell'antica Roma, visto come complemento mediterraneo-coloniale della penisola italiana, come un paradiso, una terra fertile, un Eldorado dove gli abitanti del luogo non aspettavano altro che l'arrivo degli Italiani per essere liberati dall'oppressione turca. Quest'orchestrata costruzione mediatica, basata su palesi falsificazioni ed errate prospettive di ricchezza e benessere, era iniziata nel 1910 con "le corrispondenze su la 'Terra Promessa'" di Giuseppe Piazza su *La Tribuna* di Roma "e subito dopo" con "Giuseppe Bevione", il quale "iniziava la serie delle sue mirabolanti esplorazioni su *La Stampa*" di Torino (Salvemini xviii-xix). Fin da quel momento ed anche più tardi, in seguito ad operazioni militari già iniziate, c'erano state però testate come *La Voce*, *l'Avanti* e anche *L'Unità* di Salvemini che si erano impegnate nel denunciare queste mistificazioni del paese africano prima, e la spettacolarizzazione della guerra poi. *La Voce*, per esempio, riportava a fine 1911 un articolo di Giovanni Amendola, nel quale il politico

---

[8] Conferme e maggiori informazioni sugli affari del Banco di Roma in Libia e sul suo coinvolgimento nell'inizio della guerra possono essere trovate nelle seguenti opere: Mori 102-18; Del Boca 38-45; Mack Smith 274-75; Choate 173; Webster 152-60; Labanca 109-11.

affermava che la guerra di Libia serviva proprio per manipolare la prospettiva della normale divisione di una società e dell'inerzia improduttiva italiana "per un'opera di consolidamento interno", assicurando "il massimo di potenza nel momento del bisogno," che alla fine è aspirazione "a quella guerra più aspra e più dolorosa che si svolge nel fondo delle coscienze" (720). Un paio di mesi prima, invece, in una lettera di un soldato pubblicata su *L'Avanti*, quotidiano finanziato da fondi del partito socialista e da abbonamenti e donazioni di socialisti facoltosi, si parlava di un "artificioso entusiasmo tripolino" causato da "una assai ben condotta campagna giornalistica, favorita da una strana condiscendenza della parte che pur si mostra, o si mostrava, avversa" (*Controvapore* 4). In quel particolare momento storico lo spazio politico e sociale italiano si popolò di fratelli e sorelle che cominciarono a condividere un comune progetto nazionale, utilizzando proprio l'immagine della Libia e dei giovani soldati italiani che combattevano per la gloria dell'Italia, tanto che la strumentalizzazione pianificata dai giornali giolittiani finì per prevalere anche sull'obiettività di coloro che ne avevano inizialmente compreso la montatura. Il giornale di Salvemini, per esempio, ad operazioni militari ormai avviate, pubblicò in prima pagina: "[...] da questa guerra l'Italia già che c'è dentro, deve studiarsi di ricavare tutti i vantaggi possibili" (*Tripoli e i Socialisti* 1); e *La Voce* di Giuseppe Prezzolini, pochi mesi prima aveva annunciato addirittura, per il bene del paese, di essere "pronti a sacrificare le nostre personali vedute dinanzi all'interesse pubblico, oggi che le convinzioni altrui prevalgono" (*La Voce* 1). Lo stesso Giovanni Giolitti "sentì che i giornali lo avevano servito più che egli non desiderasse, e che l'opinione pubblica gli aveva preso la mano" (Salvemini xx). Il solo fatto di parlare della Libia, pro o contro che fosse, divenne un fenomeno inserito all'interno di uno spettacolo mediatico, ovvero di una "campagna di eccitamento dello spirito pubblico" (xix) che catalizzò l'attenzione delle masse italiane e che portò una folla estasiata e inebriata dal rumore dei giornali verso la conquista di Tripoli. La gente accettò la guerra perché incitata, con la retorica ed il linguaggio giornalistico, al sacrificio degli individui per il decantato bene della nazione.[9]

La stampa nazionale promosse gli eventi che portarono alla cosiddetta *fatalità storica* di Giolitti, creando sulla carta una guerra di conquista che avrebbe dovuto incrementare il fatturato industriale, aumentare le commesse, attivare i consumi interni e promuovere i commerci, unendo poi le masse allo

---

[9] Per maggiori informazioni sui dibattiti presenti sull'*Avanti*, l'*Unità* di Salvemini e *La Voce* in merito alla guerra in Libia, si vedano Gentile, *La Voce* 342-45; Cantafio 196-200; Forgacs 56-58; Adamson, *Avant-Garde* 143-52; Nardi e Gentili 25-29; Adamson, *Introduction* 6. Per avere, invece, un quadro più generale dei *reportages* dalla Libia e della strumentalizzazione che ne venne fatta, si può fare riferimento a Del Boca 54-60; Choate 170-72; Labanca 109-10, 114-15; Tesoro 719-23; Pincherle 461-62; Segrè 23-25; Vivarelli 68-72.

Stato facendole partecipare ad un evento unico di portata nazionale: un evento carico di valori civili e morali. Giuseppe Bevione, che, come abbiamo visto, era stato uno dei primi giornalisti ad operarsi per la diffusione in Italia del mito libico, riportava apertamente già a fine estate 1911 che "la questione di Tripoli è questione interna e non esterna" (1), ossia riguarda l'Italia nel suo essere paese e non "il coloniale", cioè il desiderio di conquistare e dominare territori, soprattutto in Africa. Per questo motivo è importante ricordare che un fondamentale contributo a questa operazione interna venne anche dall'attività della *Terza Pagina* dei giornali. Avviata tra il 1902 e il 1904 dal giolittiano *Giornale d'Italia* e concepita originariamente come punto di incontro della letteratura con l'attualità delle problematiche del paese, la *Terza Pagina* divenne con gli anni uno spazio per polemiche di interesse civico, etico e sociale mirate al consolidamento di un rituale nazionale-borghese proprio di una forte nazione industriale, come anche alla diffusione di una cultura militante capace di istruire appunto le masse. Con la guerra di Libia, anche la cultura umanistico-letteraria della *Terza Pagina* iniziò ad accreditarsi al grande pubblico e alla politica, promuovendo con la letteratura tale evento ed alterando il pensiero degli italiani suscitandone di conseguenza coinvolgimento, mobilitazione e conformità di pensiero. Per citare due esempi importanti, Gabriele D'Annunzio e le sue *Canzoni d'oltremare*, pubblicate in maniera seriale tra l'ottobre e il dicembre del 1911 sul *Corriere della Sera*, e Giovanni Pascoli e il suo discorso *La grande proletaria si è mossa*, pubblicato il 27 novembre del 1911 su *La Tribuna*, furono fra i tanti scrittori che si servirono della questione libica per ergersi ad educatori e creatori di un popolo italiano attraverso le proprie lettere.[10]

Se il consenso nazionale intorno a questa guerra venne costruito sulla stampa dell'epoca da "questa politica da letterati" (Salvemini ix) che, come fu poi confessato in un editoriale del marzo del 1912 su *Rivista coloniale*[11] dal sottosegretario alle finanze Vittorio Cottafavi, "era stat[a] una montatura" (187), i meccanismi di condivisione e disciplina qui creati riuscirono però ad impostare un'idea partecipativa della nazione basata sulla "consapevolezza di un'antica nobiltà e di un comune destino" che si erano in passato assopiti "nel particolarismo mediocre della vita ordinaria" (319), sosteneva l'esploratore ed allora direttore della rivista Renato Paoli. Il "Cinquantenario" del Risorgimento, scriveva sempre Paoli, veniva così "suggellato da un sì superbo atto di energia e di volontà" che permetteva all'Italia di chiudere "definitivamente un periodo di

---

[10] La guerra di Libia fu, quindi, anche una guerra che i maggiori letterati italiani combattevano con le parole, invece che con le armi, sulla *Terza Pagina* dei giornali nazionali. Per approfondire proprio la storia di questo spazio dei quotidiani riservato alla cultura e sull'attività di letterati come D'Annunzio e Pascoli, si possono consultare i seguenti lavori: Ajello 102-10; Re (online); Castronovo, Giacheri Fossati, Tranfaglia 146-47; Adamson, *Avant-Garde* 51; Segré 20-23.
[11] La *Rivista coloniale* era l'organo ufficiale dell'Istituto Coloniale Italiano di Roma.

L'Italia della guerra di Libia (1911-1912): *burattini* subordinati al potere   347

Storia" e di aprirne "un altro" (318). Una violenza, questa, geograficamente attuata al di fuori dell'Italia, ma perpetrata anche internamente contro la popolazione italiana, la quale accolse la notizia dell'inizio degli scontri con entusiasmo e sostegno unanime nei confronti dei soldati in guerra. Come suggerisce Michel Foucault, per attuare un tale programma di disciplina e regolamentazione del potere intorno alle masse sparse su tutto il territorio italiano, occorreva che i soggetti fossero "costruiti in modo da massimizzare e attrarre forze" verso il corpo dello stato ed "ottenere un completo stato di equilibrio e regolarità" (*17 March 1976* 246). Solo in questo modo, applicando questa forma di violenza, anche ogni singola individualità poteva diventare parte del popolo e trovare una sua collocazione ed efficiente funzionalità per assecondare inconsapevolmente la strategia del potere e programmare quella che Sigmund Freud in *Civilization and its Discontents* (*Das Unbehagen in der Kultur*) definisce "felicità dell'organismo". Lo psichiatra scriveva che l'inadeguatezza di certe relazioni di un essere è causa di infelicità, e questa è spesso causata dalla civiltà: "Solo l'abolizione o riduzione di queste [infelicità] potrebbe risultare nel ritorno alla possibilità della felicità" (23-24). Per Freud gli uomini tendono a trovare la felicità in tutto quello che "arriva dalla soddisfazione (preferibilmente improvvisa) di bisogni che sono stati arginati in maniera elevata" e non da una precisa "situazione che è desiderata dal principio di piacere" in maniera "prolungata" e che "produce solamente un lieve sentimento di contentezza". Per questo motivo, "si può trarre felicità intensa solamente da un contrasto e molto poco da uno stato di cose" (13).

Nell'Italia del 1911 questo cosiddetto "stato di felicità improvviso" generato da un opposto venne descritto in maniera emblematica sempre da Gaetano Salvemini: "[...] l'Italia nel 1911 si annoiava. Era disgustata di ogni cosa. I partiti democratici erano discesi all'ultimo gradino del pubblico disprezzo [...] qualunque cosa era meglio che questa stagnazione universale [...] e allora viva la guerra! In poco tempo i giornali furono sopraffatti dall'impazienza isterica dei lettori [...] ed allora bisognò che il Governo si decidesse alla guerra a un tratto" (xx) per evitare che dalla passività-infelicità della popolazione, il potere ottenesse soltanto insofferenza (agitazioni e sommosse erano allora frequenti) e richieste (equità sociale, voto). Olindo Malagodi, il direttore della *Tribuna*, affermò a tale proposito che "le classi inferiori avevano perduta l'abitudine della obbedienza passiva e presumevano di mettere in discussione continua la condotta delle classi dirigenti, e di insorgere politicamente contro di esse ad ogni occasione" (1). Per difendersi dalle masse, renderle efficienti al programma di strutturazione dello Stato e farle di conseguenza diventare popolo, venne ideata la Libia come sacrificio comune. In questo modo il popolo così costituito diventava partecipe ed utile ai meccanismi dello Stato, mentre contemporaneamente se ne placavano le sue "minacciose" pretese facendo presa sulle sue emozioni e sulla sua immaginazione. La massa venne intossicata dalla stampa attraverso uno spettacolo che riuscì — secondo quanto scriveva Freud a riguardo del comportamento degli uomini in relazione alla loro volontà di diventare membri di una comunità umana — ad "alterare le condizioni che governano la nostra sensibilità cosicché diventiamo incapaci di ricevere impulsi spiacevoli" (15) e gli Italiani iniziarono a vivere quella che Salvemini chiamava appunto un'illusione. L'intensa attività della stampa servì, per citare ancora la teoria della lotta per la felicità di Freud, a "diminuire la pressione esercitata dalla realtà e a trovare rifugio in un mondo a parte con migliori condizioni di sensibilità (15) fuori dal malessere quotidiano.[12]

Il "burattinaio" di Arturo Rossato: storia di un italiano libero
Le dinamiche di questa violenza perpetrata nel quadro della guerra di Libia sono rappresentate in una breve storia, *Il burattinaio*, apparsa sulla *Terza Pagina* dell'*Avanti*. Il racconto, scritto da Arturo Rossato, spiegava questo meccanismo di potere e, non a caso, si inseriva nella pagina culturale dell'unico quotidiano rimasto sempre anti-interventista. La vicenda narrata si svolge in una fredda e nevosa serata d'inverno, nell'osteria di uno sconosciuto paesino italiano, dove il sindaco, si reca per leggere il giornale, bere e brindare ai soldati della guerra con l'oste Togn. Il sindaco è "orgoglioso del coraggio degli altri" e degli "eroi", in quanto con questa dimostrazione di forza "non diranno più che gli italiani sono gente paurosa" (3). Il rappresentante della politica è raggiunto inaspettatamente da una sua vecchia conoscenza, il burattinaio, il quale gli confessa, fra un bicchiere e l'altro, che gli "avevan fatto avere la carta" per la Libia e che sarebbe dovuto partire. Il sindaco reagisce apparentemente in maniera entusiasta alla notizia, tanto che afferma: "Che eroe!...se l'Italia ne avesse tanti di uomini come te...." Questo fa vedere che l'anonima massa, diventa popolo e cittadina, cioè parte integrante di un organismo-paese solo se funzionale ad un progetto, in questo caso alla guerra, ed è utile solo se garantisce la positiva realizzazione di tale progetto. Non a caso, appena il burattinaio entra nel locale, nessuno lo riconosce e viene chiamato dal narratore "lo sconosciuto". Egli cerca di rendersi visibile agli altri: "non mi conoscete più Togn, non mi conosce più signor sindaco!" (3). Quando poi l'uomo si toglie sciarpa e cappotto, il sindaco e l'oste lo riconoscono come il burattinaio e lo invitano a bere vino insieme a loro al tavolo, ma egli rimane sempre distaccato e diverso rispetto agli altri due personaggi. Alla domanda "da dove vieni ora", il burattinaio risponde "senza muoversi, covando il vuoto con quei suoi occhi chiari" (3), completamente estraniato, quasi psicologicamente assente, frenato, come se fosse "con le mani impacciate nei fili. I piedi legati. Il collo irrigidito, come se fosse di legno" (3). Ancora non era infatti un cittadino modello, parte del popolo italiano al quale la

---

[12] Adamson presenta in maniera chiara e precisa la realtà storico-sociale delle masse in Italia al tempo di Giolitti (*Introduction* 12-14).

L'Italia della guerra di Libia (1911-1912): *burattini* subordinati al potere   349

"politica", come sostiene Giorgio Agamben, aveva dato "forma", perché con essa "si nazionalizza il corpo" (38). Ancora non era conformato agli altri membri dell'organismo-paese-Italia attraverso il meccanismo integrante della guerra, l'idea madre che univa, o doveva unire tutti. Alla domanda, "Da dove vieni ora?" il burattinaio risponde appunto di provenire "da un paese certo", ma non si sa quale; forse "da un cascinale. Dalla strada", perché lui è "un vagabondo" (3), e come tale rappresenta proprio tutte le individualità eterogenee che devono essere omologate in un luogo solido e certo, l'Italia.

L'entusiasmo del sindaco alla notizia della sua partenza per il fronte, tuttavia, nasconde una forte vena di sarcasmo ed umiliazione nei confronti del burattinaio. Quest'ultimo è estremamente addolorato e rammaricato, in quanto deve lasciare "qui ogni [suo] burattino" e deve andare "a farlo laggiù", mentre il sindaco reagisce a tale affermazione esclamando "Peuh!", ridendo "a denti stretti, serrando i pugni" e "brontolando" (3). Il sindaco, rappresentante della politica, la cui essenza è il potere e la violenza quali possibili strumenti per strutturarsi e legittimarsi (Arendt 50-53), apostrofa il burattinaio "con disprezzo" (3) perché con la sua mancanza di partecipazione emotiva all'impresa denotava un distaccamento dal progetto di ordine che lui rappresentava e promuoveva. Il sindaco etichetta quindi i presenti come "mosche bianche!", persone rare e da notare perché non partecipano attivamente alla nazione andando in Libia, ma se ne stanno invece protette al caldo dell'osteria. "Laggiù", al contrario, ci "sono mosche diverse" perché s'ammazzano e "ci volevano" (3) proprio per completare un percorso identitario di valore. Il sindaco è degno rappresentante degli intrighi di potere del tempo, simbolo dello spettacolo mediatico in scena allora in Italia, oltremodo stimolato da quei giornali che lui "si mise a leggere, certo per rintracciare gli altri eroi ... autentici," e sui quali, "piantando i gomiti e gli occhi" (3), si inebriava e si costruiva la sua stabilità identitaria.

Il burattinaio è sì un'individualità errante, ma lo è perché ha una sua consapevolezza e una propria coscienza storica, tanto che è pienamente conscio del fatto che l'autonomia individuale è limitata dal potere, dallo "spazio politico della sovranità" dello stato, che, secondo Agamben, costituisce una "sfera in cui si può uccidere senza commettere omicidio e senza celebrare un sacrificio" (92). Il burattinaio afferma infatti di dovere partire, ma di sapere anche che burattino era "se va" e burattino era "se riman[e]" (3). Il burattinaio, che per mestiere muove pupazzi di legno, li controlla e li lega a sé in quanto non autonomi, potrebbe apparentemente sembrare in una posizione di potere e controllo, ma invece esclama: "sulle mie spalle mi sembra di portare il campionario della nostra vita!" (3). Egli sa di esserne l'esempio ideale, il simbolo cioè dell'illusione dell'indipendenza delle persone, perché capisce che lo stato di cui fa parte si fonda sull'esercizio di una massa disciplinata, possibile solo grazie ad una "violenza sovrana" che si confonde con il "diritto" e "che mantiene la possibilità di deciderli nella misura stessa in cui li confonde" (Agamben 73).

Con l'immagine del lavoro del burattinaio, diritto e violenza si erano davvero perfettamente confusi, in quanto da padrone egli gestiva i fantocci, ma come padrone era anche lui stesso un fantoccio, in Italia come in Libia, di un'entità superiore: "Che granburattinaio deve essere chi ci fa vivere..." (3) in questa maniera così inerme, passiva e falsa, affermava al riguardo l'uomo. Lui, almeno, si differenzia dal resto della massa e dagli altri rappresentanti della politica, come lo stesso sindaco, in quanto è consapevole del fatto che, come scrive Agamben, si è "catturat[i]" all'interno di questo sistema, essendone contemporaneamente anche "esclus[i]", e che "la vita umana si politicizza", ossia diventa popolo "soltanto attraverso l'abbandono a un potere incondizionato di morte" (101), cioè di dipendenza. Non a caso il burattinaio continua le sue invettive contro il sistema dicendo che "attraversando i crinali e i paesi, trovo gente eguale... fantocci brutti e belli", ugualmente "tutti legati da un filo, mossi da una mano, buttati uno incontro all'altro senza neanche sapere il perché" (3). E rivolto allo stesso sindaco, esclama: "Beh, perché è sindaco,... crederà, certo, d'essere qualche cosa di più di me, povero ragazzo. Non pare: lei sbaglia" (3). Con tale lucidità e consapevolezza, il burattinaio risulta quindi vivo, padrone del proprio pensiero, di conseguenza "un burattino" sì, ma "vivo nelle mani della natura", "l'assoluto padrone di sé stesso" (3). Il sindaco, al contrario, "tirandosi dietro il fiasco di vino quasi vuoto, ed aprendo il giornale", continuava a nutrirsi e ad ubriacarsi di notizie artificiose, contribuendo lui stesso all'estasi generale di un popolo intero, ad uno spettacolo nel quale "gli altri eroi," quegli "autentici" (3), erano i soldati, non le persone "diverse ed indipendenti". Per questo motivo, a seguito dell'indifferenza con la quale il burattinaio aveva accolto la notizia della partenza, il sindaco esclamava sarcasticamente "Bravo", e continuava poi dicendo: "Bei pensieri. Se tutti fossero come te, si starebbe freschi laggiù" (3) perché la guerra perderebbe il suo senso, mentre la sua capacità costitutiva del popolo italiano, la *governabilità* del paese, verrebbe minacciata.

Il breve racconto di Rossato invita dunque il lettore a riflettere sulla possibilità di autonomia della massa e sul modo in cui le persone sono condizionate nell'essere cittadini modello. L'eccezionalità della vita del burattinaio termina proprio alla fine del racconto, alla vigilia della sua partenza per la Libia. L'uomo inizia lentamente ad immobilizzarsi fisicamente: "la sua faccia prese un'aria attonita e dura," raccontava Rossato, "come se fosse di legno, le sue braccia tonfarono lungo i fianchi come lasciate cadere da un filo, e gli occhi celesti, rimasero lì spalancati, quasi senza ciglia, stupiti", mentre lasciava l'osteria e se ne tornava "allo stallazzo", affondando "i piedi nella neve, curvo, le mani in tasca", pensando "ai suoi fantocci" e, "come altre volte", al fatto di essere "un fantoccio lui stesso" (3). La sera, solo con i suoi burattini, il burattinaio versò su di loro "tutta l'amarezza della sua anima" e "la mattina dopo lo trovarono appiccato per la gola, insieme alle sue marionette" (3). Con la

L'Italia della guerra di Libia (1911-1912): *burattini* subordinati al potere 351

chiamata al fronte, la sua coercizione fisica era diventata allora inevitabile. Se, come sostiene Judith Butler, "la guerra è precisamente uno sforzo per minimizzare la precarietà di alcuni e massimizzarla per altri" (*Frames* 54), l'arruolamento forzato del burattinaio come soldato in Libia rendeva la sua precarietà (cioè, l'essere condizionati) completa, in quanto diventava un "normale cittadino" dipendente dall'ambiente circostante al quale venivano sospese le primarie libertà personali (Butler, *Vite Precarie* 21, 61). La sua alterità veniva interrotta per conformarsi ad un NOI al quale, al contrario, doveva essere limitata ogni precarietà. Per questo motivo egli rifiuta drammaticamente di entrare a far parte di questo meccanismo di stabilizzazione del potere della *governabilità* attraverso la guerra e decide di morire. Prima di uccidersi davanti ai suoi burattini, però, egli "parlò a loro del suo dolore; recitò loro l'ultima improvvisa commedia; versò su quelle teste dure e buone tutta l'amarezza della sua anima..." (3). Con la morte, il burattinaio decide di rifiutare e rigettare la beffa, una commedia appunto, della sua stessa vita: quella di un burattinaio, di una persona rappresentante del potere, che di nascosto aveva manovrato ed amministrato "quel suo piccolo popolo obbediente, vivo di lui, gaio di lui" e "triste per lui" (3) e allo stesso tempo quella di un burattino-fantoccio in balia lui stesso di un potere che lo voleva subordinato alle proprie dinamiche di controllo. Per questo motivo egli decide di far morire i suoi pupazzi insieme a lui, anziché lasciarli da soli "a morire" e "dondolare da qualche affumicata trave di taverna, come suicida pel dolore dell'improvviso abbandono" (3). Non c'è via di scampo ad un'autonomia identitaria che è, sempre e comunque, condizionata dalla subordinazione e dalla dipendenza e che è di solito repressa. Quando emerge la realtà della sottomissione, come sostiene Judith Butler, emerge anche l'inconscio della persona (*The Psychic Life of Power* 7), come nel caso del burattinaio, il quale decide di portare via con sé anche le sue marionette nel suo ultimo viaggio. Il sindaco del paese concludeva tutta la vicenda affermando: "Bé, quello straccione lì però era un vigliacco... di coraggio!" (3). Il burattinaio per lui era stato solo un vile pauroso e in maniera semplicistica chiosava la sua vicenda umana come quella di un codardo che non aveva avuto coraggio fino in fondo e che aveva preferito il suicidio invece della guerra in Libia. In realtà, come ampiamente spiegato sopra, l'indipendenza e la consapevolezza che il burattinaio aveva sempre cercato di mantenere erano un qualcosa che il sindaco, così sicuro e certo della sua posizione di rappresentante politico, non aveva mai avuto. Anche il sindaco, del resto, non era altro che una pedina, un burattino a sua volta nelle mani del potere, ulteriore vittima di una sovranità indifferente capace di colpire indistintamente, senza riferimenti alle posizioni ricoperte.

A conferma di ciò, il racconto di Rossato si complementava con la vignetta di Giuseppe Scalarini,[13] riportata proprio in fondo alla pagina, come a concluderlo iconograficamente (si veda pagina 353 di questo volume). La vignetta ritrae un uomo gigante, ma dalla testa piccola, davanti ad una macchina automatica che spara palline al tocco di un pulsante e che assomiglia ad un essere vivente perché ha occhi e bocca. La scena ironizza sulla realtà sociopolitica del tempo, dove un Parlamento detto appunto "automatico", lavorava a comando, senza porre criticità, ma esprimendo soltanto il volere di ciò che gli veniva detto ed imposto: in maniera figurata, le palline sparate dentro il cassetto-bocca della macchinetta. I singoli membri politici dell'organo legislativo italiano erano robotizzati in quanto automi e frastornati dal rumore delle tante parole sulla Libia. Su di loro, in quel momento, era stata gettata "un po' di sabbia negli occhi" (3), la sabbia di Tripoli raffigurata ai piedi della macchinetta, e questo serviva a far uscire a richiesta le palle bianche, i voti, le decisioni necessarie al potere per consolidarsi e garantire la *governabilità*. Il sindaco del burattinaio è identico ai parlamentari italiani robotizzati, i quali approvavano e condividevano qualsiasi decisione parlamentare, abbagliati dall'euforia della guerra. Egli viveva la menzogna della sua vita come una virtù da salvaguardare in nome della grandezza dell'Italia, come anche una realtà da proteggere per fare scudo alla sua personale naturale vulnerabilità.

La storia di Rossato metteva in discussione proprio il senso della bugia come collante e forza di un'aggregazione politico-sociale che doveva risultare *governabile*. Inoltre, è ironico che la storia sia stata pubblicata sulla *Terza Pagina*, cioè su un simbolo dei meccanismi di controllo attuati in quegli anni per catturare le coscienze delle masse ed istituire un ideale culturale nazionale. Con le dinamiche sviluppate nel suo racconto, Arturo Rossato confermava sì la necessità di un'azione educativa delle masse, ma per svelare loro proprio come fossero ingabbiate e condizionate nel loro essere popolo solo se funzionali al potere. Gli intrusi come il burattinaio, ossia coloro che non seguono questa funzione normativa, dovevano essere espulsi o isolati per garantire la produttività della norma. Il burattinaio ne era stato, purtroppo, una triste conferma.

Pepperdine University, Malibu, California

---

[13] Antimilitarista convinto, collaboratore dell'*Avanti* per lungo tempo, Giuseppe Scalarini è considerato l'inventore della vignetta satirico-politica in Italia. Per maggiori informazioni, si veda *La Grande Guerra* su *l'Avanti!* online.

Il Burattinaio

Novella di Arturo Rossato

La pena di morte...

Per l'amnistia

Ciò che si scrive

Il parlamento automatico

Si getta un po' di sabbia negli occhi, si tira, e vengono fuori le palle bianche.

Due case svaligiate dai ladri

Un banchetto di sordo-muti a Londra

La grande manifestazione contro la guerra

Istantanee della Camera

Opere citate

Adamson, Walter L. *Avant-Garde Florence. From Modernism to Fascism*. Cambridge: Harvard University Press, 1993.
_____. "Introduction." *Avant-Garde Florence. From Modernism to Fascism*. Cambridge: Harvard U P, 1993. 1-14.
Agamben, Giorgio. *Homo Sacer. Il potere sovrano e la nuda vita*. Torino: Piccola Biblioteca Einaudi, 2005.
Agnew, John. *The Myth of Backward Italy in Modern Europe*. "Revisioning Italy: National Identity and Global Culture." A c. di Beverly Allen and Mary J. Russo. Minneapolis: U of Minnesota P, 1997. 23-42.
Ajello, Nello. *Storia della Terza Pagina*. "Nord e Sud" 9.32 (1962): 100-23.
Amendola, Giovanni. *La Guerra*. "La Voce" (28 dicembre 1911): 719-20.
Arendt, Hannah. *On Violence*. New York: Harcourt, Brace & World, 1969.
Bevione, Giuseppe. *Volontà d'agire*. "La Stampa" (21 agosto 1911): 1.
Butler, Judith. *Frames of War. When is Life Grievable?* New York: Verso, 2009.
_____, "Introduction." *The Psychic Life of Power. Theories in Subjection*. Stanford: Stanford UP, 1997. 1-30.
_____. *Vite precarie. Contro l'uso della violenza in risposta al lutto collettivo*. Trad. Laura Fantone e Florenzo Iuliano. Roma: Meltemi Editore, 2004.
Cantafio, Valerio. "L'Unità di Gaetano Salvemini e la battaglia antiprotezionista." *Rassegna storica toscana* 38.2 (1992): 193-216.
Castronovo, Valerio, Luciana Giacheri Fossati e Nicola Tranfaglia. *La stampa italiana nell'età liberale*. Bari: Laterza, 1979.
Choate, Mark. *Emigrant Nation. The Making of Italy Abroad*. Cambridge: Harvard UP, 2008.
Cinquantenario. Editoriale. "L'Idea nazionale" (29 marzo 1911): 1.
Controvapore all'artificioso entusiasmo tripolino. "L'Avanti" (14 ottobre 1911): 4.
Cottafavi, Vittorio. *Nella Libia: impressioni di un deputato*. "Rivista Coloniale" 6 (1912): 177-87.
Del Boca, Angelo. *Gli Italiani in Libia: dal fascismo a Gheddafi*. 2 voll. Roma: Laterza, 1988.
Forgacs, David. *L'industrializzazione della cultura italiana (1880-1990)*. Trad. Emanuela Alessandrini. Bologna: Il Mulino, 1992.
Foucault, Michel. *11 January 1978*. "Security, Territory, Population. Lectures at the Collège de France 1977-1978." A c. di Michel Senellart. New York: Palgrave, 2004. 1-27.
_____. *1 February 1978*. "Security, Territory, Population. Lectures at the Collège de France 1977-1978." A c. di Michel Senellart. New York: Palgrave, 2004. 87-114.
_____. *17 March 1976*. "Society Must Be Defended. Lectures at the Collège de France 1975-1976." A c. di Mauro Bertani e Alessandro Fontana. New York: Picador, 2003. 239-64.
Freud, Sigmund. *Civilization and Its Discontents*. Trad. Joan Rivere. London: The Hogarth Press, 1963.
Gentile, Emilio. *La Voce e l'età giolittiana*. Milano: Pan, 1972.
_____. *La Grande Italia. Ascesa e declino del mito della nazione nel ventesimo secolo*. Milano: Mondadori, 1999.
La Grande Guerra. L'Avanti con le vignette di Giuseppe Scalarini. "Avanti!" (31 ottobre 2014). Online. http://www.avantionline.it 28 dicembre 2015.

Labanca, Nicola. *Oltremare: storia dell'espansione coloniale italiana*. Bologna: Società Editrice Il Mulino, 2002.
Lanaro, Silvio. *Nazione e Lavoro. Saggio sulla cultura borghese in Italia, 1870-1925*. Padova: Marsilio Editori, 1979.
Mack Smith, Denis. *Italy. A Modern History*. Ann Arbor: The U of Michigan P, 1969.
Malagodi, Olindo. *Il popolo soldato*. "La Tribuna" (8 dicembre 1911): 1.
Mori, Renato. *La penetrazione pacifica italiana in Libia dal 1907 al 1911 e il Banco di Roma*. "Rivista di Studi Politici Internazionali" 24.1 (1957): 102-18.
Nardi, Isabella e Sandro Gentili. *Introduzione: L'"effetto" Libia nella letteratura e nel giornalismo del primo Novecento*. "La Grande Illusione: opinione pubblica e mass media al tempo della Guerra di Libia." A c. di Isabella Nardi e Sandro Gentili. Perugia: Morlacchi Editore, 2009. 11-36.
Paoli, Renato. *Tripoli Nostra*. "Rivista Coloniale" 2 (1911): 317-22.
Pincherle, Marcella. *La preparazione dell'opinione pubblica all'impresa di Libia*. "Rassegna storica del Risorgimento" 56.3 (1969): 450-82.
Re, Lucia. *Italians and the Invention of Race: The Poetics and Politics of Difference in the Struggle over Libya, 1890-1913*. "California Italian Studies" 1.1 (2010). Online.
Rossato, Arturo. *Il burattinaio*. "L'Avanti" (25 febbraio 1912): 3.
Rossato, Arturo. "Enciclopedia Treccani." www.treccani.it. Online. 28 dicembre 2015.
Salvemini, Gaetano. *Perché siamo andati in Libia*. "Come siamo andati in Libia." A c. di Gaetano Salvemini. Firenze: Libreria della Voce, 1914. ix-xxiv.
Segré, Claudio. *Fourth Shore. The Italian Colonization of Libya*. Chicago: U of Chicago P, 1974.
Tesoro, Marina. *Stampa e opinione pubblica in Italia al tempo della guerra con l'Impero Ottomano*. "Il Politico: Rivista italiana di scienze politiche" 55.4 (1990): 713-32.
Tripoli e i Socialisti. Editoriale. "L'Unità di Salvemini: problemi della vita italiana" (16 dicembre 1911): 1.
Vivarelli, Roberto. *Il fallimento del Liberalismo. Studi sulle origini del fascismo*. Bologna: Il Mulino, 1981.
La Voce. *A Tripoli*. Editoriale. "La Voce" (5 ottobre 1911): 1.
Webster, Richard. *Industrial Imperialism in Italy 1908-1915*. Berkeley: U of California P, 1975.

Quinto Antonelli

Una rivolta morale: lettere e diari di soldati dai fronti della Grande Guerra (1915-1918)

Sinossi: Dal 1915 al 1918 circolarono in Italia circa 4 miliardi di cartoline e di lettere. Un movimento postale enorme, tanto che la zona di guerra poteva essere considerata un vasto laboratorio di scrittura (soprattutto di scrittura popolare). In una situazione di estrema precarietà (i soldati si sentono confinati in un mondo dominato dalla paura), lo scambio epistolare con la famiglia rinsaldava i rapporti con la quotidianità del passato e gettava un ponte verso il futuro. Nel contempo le lettere dei soldati-contadini riaffermavano una dignità spesso negata e denunciavano le intollerabili condizioni di coercizione in cui erano tenuti.
Parole chiave: Prima guerra mondiale, Esercito italiano, Disciplina militare, Corrispondenza familiare, Dissenso popolare

1. Quattro miliardi di lettere
La Grande Guerra, la prima traumatica esperienza collettiva degli Italiani dopo l'Unificazione d'Italia, venne raccontata giorno per giorno non solo dagli inviati di una moderna stampa quotidiana (destinata a diventare lungo il corso del conflitto un'efficacissima macchina di propaganda), ma anche, in termini assai più drammatici e, oserei dire, palpitanti, da un flusso (da e per il fronte) di quasi quattro miliardi di lettere e di cartoline postali. "Questo immenso flusso di corrispondenza, che sembra quasi smentire e offuscare i dati sull'analfabetismo ancora consistente," — scrive Antonio Gibelli — "dipende da un bisogno inesausto di contatto che promana invariabilmente dai fronti quanto dall'interno" (2014: 11). I soldati che scrivevano dalle zone di guerra (dalle doline del Carso come dalle più impervie montagne trentine) cercavano dapprima di non preoccupare le loro famiglie, evitavano di raccontare i fatti più orribili, non rivelavano che la morte era sempre presente. Tuttavia nel corso della guerra, nei momenti di maggior difficoltà, era solo alla famiglia lontana che confidavano paure e angosce. Così, quando cadeva la barriera dell'autocensura, i soldati finivano per scrivere disperatamente cercando di spiegare quello che a casa non potevano sapere e neppure immaginare. Oltre alle lettere, alcuni registravano ancora in trincea in piccoli quaderni le date e i fatti più significativi della loro esperienza; altri, quand'erano nelle retrovie o ricoverati negli ospedali militari, a distanza di poco tempo dagli eventi, scrivevano in modo più ordinato i loro ricordi. Considerate tutte insieme, queste diverse scritture hanno creato un racconto collettivo in grado di illuminare la

"zona" di guerra e il popolo che l'abitava.[1]

Abbiamo accennato all'analfabetismo: più di un terzo degli Italiani nel 1914 ancora non era in grado di tracciare la propria firma (il 37,6 % secondo il censimento del 1911). Il differente livello di alfabetizzazione tra maschi (33%) e femmine (42%) suggerisce la percentuale di analfabeti che probabilmente veniva a interessare l'esercito. Ma il bisogno primario di scrivere per ricomporre la continuità della propria esistenza e tener stretti i legami familiari, era sentito dai soldati forse con maggior urgenza e disagio, poiché dovevano spesso delegare a un commilitone la stesura delle lettere. Ettore Travostino, uno dei soldati-scrivani, in una lettera ai familiari descrive con molta umanità questo suo servizio:

> Tutti i giorni, occupo le ore disponibili a leggere il giornale e scrivere. Ho molti amici militari, che mi mandano sovente cartoline, cui debbo pure rispondere. [...] Scrivono a me, anche quando salutano gli altri dell'86 e 87 che sono in questa Compagnia, ed io rispondo sempre per tutti. Ci sono poi di quelli che sanno scrivere così così. Se ricevono lettere di persone rispettabili, e desiderano ricambiare degnamente, vengono da me a farsi dettare la risposta. Infine vi è una vera moltitudine di analfabeti, che pare quasi incredibile. È già umiliante il far conoscere i propri interessi a persone estranee, e pregarle per la risposta; ma per essi sarebbe peggio ancora, se non trovassero chi li aiuta in simili contingenze. Ed io, quando posso non so rifiutarmi.[2]

Tuttavia nel corso della guerra molti soldati analfabeti, per opera di commilitoni più istruiti o di cappellani militari, impararono a leggere e a scrivere seppure in maniera elementare. Le retrovie delle prime linee si trasformarono così in un enorme laboratorio di scrittura: si scriveva e si imparava a scrivere nei luoghi di assistenza, nelle "case del soldato", negli ospedali militari, nei vastissimi accampamenti che, dietro le linee, erano destinati al riposo.

I soldati alfabetizzati quasi mai si esprimono in un italiano standard e le loro lettere poco assomigliano a quelle dei loro ufficiali che uscivano dalle scuole superiori, quando non dall'università, con ben altre competenze linguistiche. La diversa provenienza sociale e la differente formazione scolastica si riflettono dunque sulla qualità della scrittura epistolare: i soldati comuni danno vita a quello che è stato definito come un "italiano popolare", testi che si sottraggono in modo più o meno marcato alle norme dell'italiano letterario e presentano evidenti tracce del parlato regionale o più strettamente dialettale a livello grafico, lessicale, sintattico.[3]

---

[1] Ho tentato di restituire questo racconto collettivo in una mia storia "dal basso" della Grande Guerra (Antonelli 2014), alla quale si rimanda per ulteriori approfondimenti.
[2] Lettera del 12 ottobre 1916. Copia dell'intero epistolario di guerra di Ettore Travostino è depositato presso la Fondazione Museo storico del Trentino, Archivio della scrittura popolare.
[3] Come recentemente ha scritto Enrico Testa in una riflessione di sintesi, alla definizione di "italiano popolare" si è poi affiancata anche quella di "italiano dei semicolti". Che si

Le scritture di più faticosa realizzazione comunicano a chi ora le legge in tutt'altro contesto un senso di smarrimento dovuto, in primo luogo, alla tendenza a riprodurre graficamente la catena parlata e, viceversa, all'incapacità di scindere correttamente il continuum fonico. A questi fenomeni si accompagnano l'incerta distinzione tra maiuscole e minuscole, l'assenza o la casualità della punteggiatura e dell'accentazione, lo scambio di fonemi, lo scempiamento delle doppie e, per ipercorrettismo, raddoppiamenti incongrui. La costruzione sintattica è quasi sempre ardua e impacciata: concordanze logiche, ridondanza pronominale, accumulo di preposizioni. Il lascito dei dialetti, presente anche ad altri livelli, è più riconoscibile nel lessico.

Tuttavia, più che insistere sulle fragilità, per altro piuttosto note, ci sembra di dover sottolineare come la scrittura popolare sia il prodotto di una tensione, cioè dello sforzo di abbandonare il dialetto e il mondo dell'oralità per avvicinarsi alla scrittura dell'italiano e ai suoi modelli e generi (Antonelli 1996). Ovvio il carattere "anfibio". Ma l'immane fatica di questi nostri soldati per dare forma all'esperienza di se stessi nel "nuovo mondo" in cui si trovano scaraventati non può non suscitare ammirazione, rispetto e compassione. Tanto più se si considera che scrivere in zona di guerra è sempre un'impresa: si scrive di notte al lume di una candela, si scrive inginocchiati per terra, si scrive su un'asse appoggiata sulle ginocchia, dentro un ricovero, una caverna, una baracca, continuamente intralciati nei movimenti, spintonati dai compagni, privi di spazio e di intimità. Per farsi un'idea si leggano le vivacissime pagine del diario di Giuseppe Capacci:

> Io, che da cinque giorni che avevo ricevuto lettere da genitori e da Maria, mi misi subito a scrivere alla fidanzata; era quasi sera, mi misi nel mio pagliariccio vicino alla porticina scrivendo nelle ginocchia, mentre al difuori il tempo nevicava. Un soldato che si mise ritto nella porta, e io le chiesi se si levava che non potevo scrivere; lui mi rispose: "Vai fuori!"; io essendo agitato gli dissi quello che si meritava, e lui mi venne con le mani al viso, come se avesse avuto mille ragioni. Allora balsai in piedi incominciando la lotta; non vidi più niente: calci e cazzotti come se fosse stato un tedesco! La carta e l'inchiostro andiedero per terra, la penna la ruppi sopra di lui; la lotta luttò poco: me lo sentii strappare dalle mani, due soldati ci scompagnarono, così fù fenita; per quella sera dovetti cessare di scrivere.
>
> (Capacci 2014: 48)

---

adotti l'una o l'altra etichetta (che può comportare spostamenti d'accento o enfatizzazioni di aspetti particolari), ciò che rimane inalterato è il fatto che si tratta di "una realizzazione linguistica intermedia che, tenendo dell'uno e dell'altro, mette in contatto (e anche in attrito) i due mondi dell'oralità e della scrittura. Ovvero: la varietà multiforme delle parlate locali e la varietà standard dell'italiano normativo senza però sfociare in una trascrizione delle prime (anzi è opinione comune che i tratti dialettali siano minori di quanto ci si attenderebbe) e senza neppure coincidere tantomeno con la seconda" (Testa 2014: 20).

2. "La forza e la bellezza del sentimento familiare"

Leggendo le lettere dei soldati francesi prigionieri in Germania, Romain Rolland non può fare a meno di rilevare "la forza e la bellezza del sentimento familiare". Scrive nel suo diario: "Ne sono profondamente impressionato, leggendo in centinaia di lettere intrise dalla penosa e appassionata nostalgia del piccolo cerchio familiare. Queste povere anime non escono di là, fuori di là non vedono nulla, nessun motivo di interesse, nessuna ragione di vita, fuori di là si sentono perdute, non aspirano che a rientrarvi in gran fretta, a chiudersi dietro porta e finestre, per non sapere più nulla di quanto accade di fuori" (Rolland 1960: 172).

Roland si riferisce alle lettere dei prigionieri francesi, al mondo della famiglia e degli affetti che da esse traspare e che sembra all'Autore così particolare. Ma la sostanza del giudizio non muta se prendiamo in considerazione le lettere e i diari dei soldati italiani. "Reclusi", "carcerati" nel fondo paludoso delle trincee,[4] "legati alla catena", privati della libertà, confinati in un mondo dominato dalla paura, essi guardano alla famiglia e alla casa con sconfinata nostalgia non solo come al luogo degli affetti, ma anche dell'umanità e della civiltà.

Scrive nel suo diario Antonio Graziani, un fante romagnolo, dopo una licenza invernale:

Avicinandomi alla partenza cominciavo a pensare dove dovevo ritornare. Giunto alultimo giorno quello fù la rovina dei pasati. Pensando come stò bene qui e non ci posso stare. E cosa vado incontro non sapendo il perché. Sopra più dovevo las[c]iare la famiglia e compoca speranza di tornar più. Se in quel giorno mi fosse venuto vicino uno della clas[s]e dei macelanti [macellai] non saprei che cosa ci avrebbe fatto dalla rabbia.

(Graziani 1998: 41).

Antonio Graziani tiene un diario vibrante ed iroso e, come pochi, sa registrare il sentimento di una perdita complessiva: la famiglia, il paese, la libertà, la civiltà. Scrive l'11 febbraio 1917 in un giorno di riposo dietro le linee:

Oggi giorno 11, giorno di festa lo trascorso d[a] misero soldato, girando enon trovando pace, vedendo che catena mi toca subire, col pensiero sempre rivolto alla liberta che negodevo. Il barbero governerno mas trapato dalla civilta, per sequire questa infamia vita. [...] sono avilito avilito vedendo che questa vita non termina mai.

(Graziani 1998: 46).

Lo sguardo del soldato che scrive più che al teatro della guerra è rivolto al mondo familiare, evoca in modo struggente le immagini dei genitori, della moglie e dei figli.

---

[4] Scrive alla famiglia Giovanni Zanni l'8 marzo 1916: "Dal fondo da un Trincerone vi scrivo la mia misera vita. Io mi trovo in trincea, alla distanza del nemico a 30 metri. Stiamo qui come i carcerati, dal giorno non si può alsare un dito, la notte stiamo attenti, ai nostri buchi, per non essere presi allassalto" (Cavalli 1983: 218).

Filippo Guerrieri, giovane tenente di fanteria, scrive in una lettera indirizzata ai genitori il 29 giugno 1916:

> Su un blocco di calcestruzzo rimasto da una parte piano e liscio si è improvvisato un tavolino, dagli zaini, dai tascapani è uscito un foglio di carta, una penna stilografica ed ognuno scrive, e scrivendo si riposa, perché nel ricordare voialtri, nel narrare a voi la nostra vita sembra che la stanchezza si allontani, pare che ogni parola scritta si porti via uno dei nostri tanti dolori e quando la lettera è finita si prova realmente un dolce benessere, si respira più liberamente, direi quasi si comincia di nuovo a vivere. Per questo ogni minuto libero è dedicato a quelli che sono lontani e lo scrivere una cartolina e quando è possibile una lettera, non è un fastidio, ma una gioia; è il tempo meglio impiegato, l'unico che sia da noi benedetto. In quei momenti ci si astrae da tutto quello che ci circonda e che non è mai bello, non si è più sotto un sasso, nascosti in una roccia, non si è più al pericolo, no, no, si è accanto a voi nella casa tranquilla che non conosce che la pace e si parla di tante cose del tempo bello e del vino buono. È un'illusione lo sappiamo tutti, ma intanto anche quella è qualche cosa, ci aiuta a vivere in una certa allegria con sicura fede.

(Guerrieri 1969: 140)

I familiari ritornano nei sogni e di nuovo rivivono nei tempi della veglia e acquistano, per mezzo della fotografia, sostanza fisica. Più precisamente, come scrive Leo Spitzer, la fotografia è un "surrogato della presenza fisica", oggetto di investimento emotivo forse superiore a quello riservato alle lettere (Spitzer 1976: 104). Scrive Nello Lorenzi:

> "Ah, cara Ugenia, appena mi è giunto la tua fotografia, mi sono ritirato solo e mi sono divertito a baciarti, te e la nostra cara bambina! Credi che [in] qui' momento mi pareva di essere assieme e tutta la sera l'ho tenuta i[n] mano, e tanti baci ti ho dato e ti parlavo; ma te sempre zitta. Ma credi, Ugenia, quando mi metto a guardàlla io diventerei matto. Ora mi trovo più contento: almeno tengo u[n] ricordo di te e della nostra cara bambina, e mi posso divertire a baciarvi e abbracciarvi; già che no[n] vi posso abbracciare i[n] carne, vi abbraccerò i[n] carta. Ah, vigliacca di una guerra, come ci ha diseparato! No[n] ci voleva che la guerra per volere diseparare noi che tanto ci amiamo."

(Lorenzi 1996:183)

Anche i pacchi, con gli alimenti spediti da casa che assicurano in alcuni momenti la sopravvivenza al fronte, rinforzano il legame con la famiglia e riportano il combattente nel cerchio della quotidianità domestica e delle tradizioni familiari, forse irrimediabilmente perduto.

Le lettere dei soldati-contadini, in particolare, sono piene di domande sul clima, l'andamento delle stagioni, le coltivazioni, i vari lavori rurali, accompagnate da consigli e raccomandazioni. "Cara moglie", — scrive Augusto Tonetto il 13 giugno 1917 — "sepimi dire come va la vigna per conto della stagione se e resta pomi [mele] e se i fa[g]ioli e belli e la biava [biada] se la vien su bene come i altri ani e poi sepimi dire se le vi[gn]e e belle con le foglie e se e tanta uva come era prima" (Tonetto 2007).

Lo scambio epistolare rinsaldava i rapporti con la quotidianità del passato e serviva per progettare il futuro, senza lasciarsi travolgere dal presente. Scrive Antonio Gibelli a questo proposito: "Lo sguardo a casa, l'ancoraggio alle cose domestiche, ai sentimenti e ai legami familiari appaiono come l'unico rifugio in una situazione totalmente inospitale e precaria, quasi come l'unica fonte di identità in una condizione disorientante per i suoi stessi connotati di ambientazione percettiva [...]. Per certi aspetti dunque la lettera presenta il carattere di terapia, diventa un mezzo di autoconservazione: scrivere a casa e ricevere posta sono innanzitutto modi per alleviare il dolore della lontananza e l'orrore dello stato presente, ricomponendo in tal modo gli elementi di una identità fortemente minacciata" (1991: 55)

Se è così, comprendiamo meglio la sollecitudine con cui si scrive a casa, l'ansia con cui si aspetta la risposta, le tante espressioni di gioia e di commozione che accompagnano la lettura della lettera familiare (è come avessi ricevuto la "comunione", scrive un anonimo soldato con espressione carica di significato mistico). E si capiscono anche l'irritazione per la risposta che tarda a fronte delle lettere quotidiane che si scrivono e la delusione provocata da lettere troppo brevi o troppo evasive.

3. I "poveri soldati" e i "signori d'Italia"

Alle lettere colme di struggente nostalgia per la casa e il paese, piene di raccomandazioni e preghiere, di addii e testamenti, si affiancano, fin dall'inizio della guerra, lettere che esprimono, oltre lo sbigottimento e il terrore, anche un crescente rancore rivolto soprattutto contro due obiettivi: "uno, vicino: i propri superiori; l'altro più lontano: la classe dirigente che aveva voluto la guerra. Nei confronti degli uni come dell'altra, il rancore si accompagnò spesso alla disistima, sia riguardo alle loro capacità di dirigere, sia riguardo alla loro lealtà di comportamento" (Procacci 2000: 126).

Fino alla rotta di Caporetto, fino cioé all'autunno del 1917, la guerra italiana si era caratterizzata per una strategia aggressiva basata sull'attacco frontale alle posizioni nemiche, in sostanza sul binomio fuoco di artiglieria – assalto della fanteria. Scrivono Isnenghi e Rochat: "La fanteria italiana va all'attacco in formazioni compatte, subisce il fuoco delle mitragliatrici e dei cannoni, si arresta dinanzi ai reticolati, rifluisce indietro, ritorna all'attacco. Talora riesce a superare il reticolato e a raggiungere la trincea austriaca, dove però deve sostenere ripetuti contrattacchi; altre volte si aggrappa al terreno costituendo una linea precaria di mucchietti di pietre e sacchetti di terra sotto i reticolati come base per nuovi attacchi; oppure ripiega sulla trincea di partenza. L'azione prosegue fino all'esaurimento delle forze dei reparti, viene ripresa con nuove truppe e continuata con la rimozione dei comandanti che non mostrano sufficiente durezza" (2008: 177).

Ai soldati non era chiesto né consenso, né un particolare addestramento, ma obbedienza agli ordini, disciplina e una rassegnata passività: un "buon soldato" era colui che rispondeva in modo automatico agli ordini, che si mostrava indifferente alla morte dei compagni, che riusciva ad allontanare da sé la nostalgia per la famiglia lontana.

Questa coercizione psicologica, accompagnata dalle crudeli punizioni previste dal codice militare,[5] finiva per produrre tra i soldati una costante tensione, un sotterraneo malumore, un desiderio di fuga che pochi, a rischio della propria vita, riuscivano a mettere in pratica. La maggior parte esprimeva disgusto, sdegno, rancore e rabbia, per tutto quello che era costretta a subire, nelle lettere indirizzate ai familiari, ai commilitoni e agli amici rimasti in paese.

Non sempre la corrispondenza superava l'ostacolo della censura postale che aveva la pretesa (impossibile dato l'enorme traffico epistolare) di sottoporre a controllo ogni singola lettera e a incriminare gli autori di espressioni pessimistiche o di critiche nei confronti dei superiori o, peggio, di opinioni contrarie alla guerra. Tuttavia non per tutti gli scriventi la possibilità del controllo, con le durissime conseguenze giudiziarie previste, si trasformava in autocensura.

3.1. Le reazioni di sdegno più vistose si indirizzano verso la stampa: non date retta ai giornali, non credete alle loro bugie — scrivono coralmente i soldati ai parenti e agli amici, offesi per il drammatico contrasto tra la realtà del fronte e i racconti diffusi nel paese. Era questa una reazione rilevata da Adolfo Omodeo perfino nelle lettere degli ufficiali: "Ritorna frequente nelle lettere dei combattenti — scrive —— la nota amara e sprezzante per le corrispondenze di guerra. Sopra tutto inaspriva i soldati la falsificazione della loro psicologia, come di gente che in guerra si divertisse e ci pigliasse gusto, né più né meno che ad uno sport. Questo pareva un'offesa alle loro sofferenze e al loro dolore, e quasi un invito ai rimasti a dimenticarli" (Omodeo 1968, 4).[6] E riporta, fra le molte, una lettera indignata di Claudio Calandra del 23 ottobre 1916:

Quello che fa veramente schifo è quella loro ostinatezza a voler descrivere la guerra come

---

[5] Scrive un anonimo soldato il 7 aprile 1916: "Qui c'è una disciplina che è terribile, uno che sbaglia un po' lo portano subito davanti ai reticolati ovvero ad una pianta, e lo legano davanti ai reticolati e lo fanno stare lì magari 3 o 4 ore e magari tutta la notte, secondo quello che à fatto. Immaginati tu che crudeltà che adoperano dopo che uno è già esposto al pericolo della sua propria vita, adoperano ancora quella crudeltà lì, ti dico la verità che trattano più bene le bestie che noialtri poveri soldati" (2014: 51).

[6] Il riferimento che Omodeo fa allo "sport" è ripreso anche da altri soldati. Scrive "Bepi" da Santa Maria La Longa, il 21 febbraio 1916: "A furia di leggere sui giornali cose che riguardano la vita del soldato, chi da questa vita vive lontano, si forma la convinzione che la guerra sia una gran palestra ginnastica dove il soldato può sviluppare i suoi muscoli coi più svariati esercizi di acrobatismo! Ma purtroppo, nella guerra moderna ci si muove o eccessivamente, o niente! Quel ch'è vero, è l'umidità, è l'acqua che gonfia le gambe ai soldati e popola gli ospedali! Quel ch'è più certo ancora, è l'arrivo d'una pallottola, lo scoppiar d'una granata che tengono il soldato continuamente coi nervi tesi facendogli pensare alla morte mille volte in un giorno!" (Procacci 2000: 411).

cosa poetica, fatta di poesia e sentimento, anziché di sangue, d'orrore e di sofferenze inaudite. Io sono un disgraziatissimo pittore fallito, ma, nell'anima, artista quanto qualunque gazzettiere, e ti assicuro che nella guerra non ci ho trovato nulla di eccessivamente poetico: forse perché io sono sempre stato in trincea, e i signori *reporters* se ne stanno nei lontani osservatorii. Dipende dal punto di vista. Quando una granata scoppia in un cimitero, Barzini dice: 'che le croci s'inchinano al suo passaggio', ma non dice che i cadaveri in avanzatissima putrefazione volano per aria a brandelli e appestano col puzzo loro Dio sa quanti chilometri di trincea. Dov'era lui, il fetore non si sentiva; dov'eravamo noi, non si poteva respirare.

(Omodeo 1968: 4)

Luigi Barzini, inviato del "Corriere della Sera", era forse il più celebre corrispondente di guerra italiano per i suoi pezzi brillanti e una prosa molto visiva (*Il racconto italiano della Grande Guerra* 2015: 471-486). Le "barzinate", com'erano detti i suoi articoli da quei soldati che leggevano i giornali, erano esemplari per i pochi fatti descritti, ma enfatizzati con molta epica eroica. Come scrive Marco Mondini: "Le singole scaramucce divennero epocali battaglie, le modeste avanzate sfondamenti strategici, i massacri si tramutarono in sacrifici gloriosi, e anche le sconfitte, nonché i rovesci più temibili vennero dipinti nel modo più suggestivo e rassicurante attraverso formule di mascheramento verbale" (2014: 218).

Le lettere colpite dalla censura e trasmesse ai tribunali militari per provvedimenti disciplinari contengono innumerevoli espressioni di biasimo per i giornali che trasmettono al paese una visione edulcorata della guerra:

Chi sa con che ansia vi alzavate al mattino per prendere il giornale per vedere se cera delle buone nuove per gli Itagliani non combattenti, ebbene di tutto ciò che diceva il Corriere non è vero un bel niente, ve la sicuro io.

(Procacci 2000: 403)

In guerra stanno molto bene dice il Giornale I nostri soldati non ci manca niente. Invece di dire che ci manca tutto.

(Procacci 2000: 405)

Ha letto i giornali? Ha letto l'articolo di Barzini per la presa del Cucco? Quanto deve essere bello il leggierlo in Italia!"

(Procacci 2000: 458)

Non credere ai giornali specialmente agli articoli di Barzini, il traditore della patria; i soldati ce l'hanno a morte.

(Procacci 2000: 462)

Dunque se vuoi sapere qualche cosa prenderai il giornale nei primi di acosto vedrai che ci sara scritto le nuove vittorie italiane – Ma però tutto al contrario.

(Procacci 2000, 403)

Scrive P. G. al padre il 7 luglio 1916:

Siamo sani per miracolo. Secchi, magri senza far la barba e sporchi come le bestie. Altro che i giornali che parlano che i soldati al fronte stanno bene, mangiano e bevono. Vorrei farli provare un giorno o due ai Signori d'Italia che ridono al caffè quando leggono sul

giornale Vittorie dei soldati italiani... se provassero, se vedessero un minuto solo le cose che toccano ai poveri soldati, scapperebbero sotto terra.
(Forcella – Monticone 2014, 72)

3.2. Il risentimento dei soldati si rivolge genericamente anche contro i "signori", gli interventisti, gli studenti, gli industriali, i profittatori, che avevano voluto la guerra, ma che poi si erano "imboscati" negli uffici delle retrovie e al fronte c'era andato solo il "povero operaio": "Vo[g]liamo qui con noi" — scrive un soldato rimasto anonimo il 6 marzo 1916 — "quelli che un giorno dissero quella maledetta parola Eviva la Guerra ma che dal 24 Maggio sono sempre stati in Italia e ànno visto la guerra nei cinematografi quà bisogna vedere che cosa è la parola guerra" (Procacci 2000: 414-15).

Primo Farabegoli il 20 novembre 1915, un mese prima di morire per broncopolmonite, scrive ai genitori una lettera colma di affetto, ma in cui promette con inaudita lucidità di essere pronto a fare una seconda guerra contro gli interventisti:

[...] quelli di noi che avra la fortuna di rimanere salvi in questa guerra faremo unaltra guerra con li interventisti che volevano la guerra.
(*Verificato per censura* 2002: 288)

Anche Vitaliano Marchetti ricorda in una sua lettera le conferenze degli interventisti di Ancona:

Caro Attilio qua non si trova altro che gran montagne di sassi e niente altro. Queste era tutte le gran conferenze che facevano questi anconetani. Se avrò la fortuna sempre di poter ritornare fra voi tutti, che tutto al giorno il mio pensiero è sempre a voi tutti, parlerò con quei tali, e gli dirò qualche parolina, sottovoce.
Si fa la vita [...], la vita proprio di maiali. Si dorme sotto barache che noi quando si va, o in I linea o in II si deve costruire, che materiale non lo danno, alla meglio, mi pare di dormire dentro proprio, stale dei porchi, magari si potesse avere uno stanzino di quei in campagna che abbiamo.
(Marchetti 1988: 122)

A volte i soldati dovevano costatare con amarezza quanto era difficile comunicare ai familiari tutta la drammaticità della loro situazione e che spesso i genitori, la moglie o la fidanzata si lasciavano convincere più dalla propaganda che dalle testimonianze che provenivano direttamente dal fronte. A questo proposito le lettere indignate di Cesare Menghi sono particolarmente significative.

Il 15 agosto 1916, all'indomani della presa di Gorizia, primo autentico successo della guerra italiana, Menghi scrive alla sorella: "Capirai a noi qua si divora la rabbia nel sentire che in Italia fanno delle feste per la presa di Gorizzia e suonar le campane si dovrebbero vergognare" (*Verificato per censura* 312-14).

Tra coloro che dovrebbero vergognarsi forse c'è anche il padre, cui scrive il giorno successivo:

[...] vi debbo dire che a noi si [h]anno dato un grande dispiacere nel sentire che avete fatto delle feste e avete sonato tutte le campane perché [h]anno preso Gorizia pensate che dogni modo non sono mai contenti e che la guerra non finisse cosa vi fa a voi gorizia che un giorno non troverete più i vostri cari figli.

(*Verificato per censura* 312-14)

Quelli che "non sono mai contenti" sono coloro che hanno voluto la guerra, i militari e il governo, ma il padre dovrebbe essere di tutt'altro parere, scrive Menghi: che importa a lui di Gorizia se poi i suoi figli non torneranno a casa. In dieci giorni, dal 6 al 16 agosto, l'esercito italiano aveva perso, infatti, tra caduti, feriti e dispersi, 51.200 uomini.

Il 19 settembre, dopo aver partecipato alla settima battaglia dell'Isonzo (14-17 settembre 1916), Cesare Menghi scrive al padre una lettera drammatica, in cui se la prende con la fidanzata Esterina che probabilmente aveva fatto sfoggio di patriottismo:

Carissimo Padre [h]o ricevuto vostra cartolina la quale godo nel sentire che vi trovate in ottima salute e come al presente di me. Appunto alla esterina non ci scrivo sapete che io era tre notte che combatevo che si siamo ameschiati [t]ante volte e non so come sia stata a salvarmi e lei mi viene a parlarmi di vittorie lo so che in Italia bona parte siete contenti e a noi si chrepa il cuore a vedere una cosa simile e ora [h]anno inventato le bombarde[7] che fanno un macello non pensate che ritorna acasa che sara dificile ramatismo mal di ossa e gli animali che si mangiano[8] e cadde la neve io mi dispiace adirvi tutto questo ma mi viene dimpazirmi.

(*Verificato per censura* 312-14)

Cesare Menghi morirà per malattia il 23 aprile 1917 all'ospedale militare di Pavia.

3.3. Ma il "Potere" contro cui i soldati vorrebbero ribellarsi e dal cui controllo tentano di sfuggire è quello militare, che si ramificava dall'ufficiale subalterno fino ai gradi superiori, dagli addetti della censura ai giudici dei tribunali militari.

La disciplina poteva avvalersi di un Codice militare vecchio di mezzo secolo, ma che il Capo di stato maggiore Luigi Cadorna aveva irrigidito

---

[7] "La bombarda era un'arma nuova, caratteristica della guerra di trincea. Consisteva in un tubo metallico di diametro da 30 a 200 e più mm, che poggiava su una piastra metallica per i pezzi più piccoli, su una base di travi di legno per quelli più grossi. Era più facile da costruire dei cannoni, perché impiegava cariche di lancio ridotte [...]; e sparava grosse bombe con una traiettoria molto curva e una portata limitata, anche poche centinaia di metri. In sostanza era un'arma economica e rustica, non troppo precisa, ma molto efficace contro trincee e reticolati, perché le sue bombe contenevano più esplosivo dei proietti d'artiglieria" (Isnenghi – Rochat 2008: 197-98).
[8] Si intenda: non pensate che possa ritornare a casa, sarà difficile: ho dolori reumatici, le ossa mi fanno male, ci sono animali (pidocchi) che *ci* mangiano....

ulteriormente, moltiplicando le figure di reato e aggravando le pene. "L'aspra pedagogia dell'intervento esemplare, che si espanderà sino alla dottrina e alla prassi spietata della decimazione, — scrivono Isnenghi e Rochat — si ispira al criterio che in guerra l'essenziale non sia individuare e colpire, in un singolo, il colpevole effettivo e provato, ma sanzionare immediatamente agli occhi dei responsabili e di tutti un crimine sociale" (Isnenghi – Rochat 2007: 255).

Nelle lettere e nelle note diaristiche i soldati registrano l'insensatezza di gran parte delle punizioni, comminate solo per poter rimarcare le gerarchie. Giuseppe Ruberti, addetto all'ospedaletto da campo, nota come "ricordevole per sempre" la giornata del 9 settembre 1916

perché punito ingiustamente con 2 ore di ferri legato ad un albero mentre il bombardamento infuriava. Il fatto è così. Qui in questa ambulanza non c'è barbiere, e siccome avevamo bisogno di tosarci, fu chiamato il barbiere della centuria, il quale venuto, incominciò a tagliarmi i capelli. Mentre finivo e mi pulivo, vistomi il Colonnello Cannas, perché li facevo in un ora di lavoro, mi ha punito. Eppure il permesso lo tenevo di tagliarmeli in quel momento. Questo fatto mi ha disturbato moltissimo e mi ha abbattuto moralmente. I ferri non l'ho portati perché mancavano e sono stato 2 ore sotto un albero dalle 4 alle 6 mentre le granate passavano sulle nostre teste. Mi veniva da piangere ed avrei certamente pianto in altre circostanze. Quest'altro mancava. Nel tempo di permanenza sotto le armi e in 15 mesi di guerra non sono stato mai punito. Dovevo venire qui per essere punito di ferri.[9]

Altri soldati annotano, a futura memoria, anche i modi arroganti e spregevoli di molti ufficiali. Pietro Ferrari, sceso dalla prima linea con i i piedi gonfi e semicongelati, tenta inutilmente di marcare visita. Scrive sotto la data dell'8 dicembre 1915:

Un giorno facendomi male tanto i piedi, andai alla visita, ed il medico villanamente mi disse: via, via, bastonate. La compagnia qui faceva tutti i giorni la corvée, andava a prendere le tavole o altro a Ronchino, ma io non ero mai andato. Una volta andai, ma appena aviatomi, non potendo camminare che a stento, mi venne dietro a cavallo il Mag. Cav. Porta Giuseppe, mi prese per il colletto della giubba, mi diede due scapaccioni gettandomi a terra e mi disse! — avanti fannullone per Dio. Io sottovoce gli dissi che non era la maniera di fare, che ci voleva più educazione. Ritornai tosto non visto indietro, perche era nell'impossibilita di andare con loro.

(Ferrari 2004: 35).

Provoca lo sdegno dei soldati anche il fatto che gli ufficiali impartiscano gli ordini di assalto con la pistola in pugno, minacciando di usarla. Antonio Graziani, che già abbiamo citato, descrive la dinamica di un caotico assalto (uno dei tanti che la guerra di Cadorna prevede) in questi termini:

Alle 14 arriva lordine che alle 16 comincia il sbalzo. per mè èstato come abbia detto

---

[9] Ruberti Giuseppe, *Note e appunti militari*, dattiloscritto (nota del 9 settembre 1916), in Fondazione Museo storico del Trentino, Archivio della scrittura popolare.

m[u]ori. Che due ore penose furono quelle sono cose di diventar pazzo, come tanti diventano. Arriviamo alle ore 16 gliufficiali con rivoltella in mano, E con unsol grido fuori, Io nulla più capivo trovarmi nell'inferno, canonate che piovevano atutte le parte fucilate, e metragliatrice che falciava, Esendo un sol grido di disgraziati caduti sul tereno e bentanti si vedevano sfrantumati era unscompiglio incredibile, Io fortunatamente rimasi ferito alla mano sinistra, Lasia[i] tutto presi la corsa per quanto potevo, scavalcando tereno rovesiato dalle canonate fucilate mi fischiavano alle orecchie i canoni palpavano tutto il tereno, Doppo aun chilometro di strada arivai al posto di socorso.

(Graziani 1998: 53-54).

Inoltre sembra offensiva la differenza di trattamento cui erano soggette le truppe rispetto agli ufficiali superiori, sia in prima linea che nelle retrovie. Scrive dal fronte Virginio in una lettera del 5 aprile 1916 intercettata dalla censura:

Poveri nostri fratelli parevano stritolati come se fossero carne di belve feroci, come possiamo avere più il coraggio di andare avanti vedendo queste barbarie contro la nostra cara ed amata gioventù! I nostri bravi ufficiali se ne stanno sotto le grotte come niente fosse per il nostro disagio... mandano bigliettini per iniziare le operazioni e loro belli tranquilli se ne stanno sotto sensa ricorrere alcun pericolo e noi con alcuni Aspiranti o sotto Tenenti antiamo affrontare la morte.

(Procacci 2000: 425)

Nel corso del conflitto i sentimenti di avversità non si attenuano, anzi, afferma Bruna Bianchi, "sono proprio le lettere scritte nell'ultimo anno di guerra ad avere i toni più esasperati, le espressioni di rancore più violente: 'Porco Dio, fanno bene a dare il pane ammuffito così finirà presto la guerra! Ed io ho piacere, popolo cornuto e bastonato, vuoi continuare a fare la guerra? Ma ribellatevi, uccidete tutti gli ufficiali e che sia finita!'" (Bianchi 2001: 476).

Affermò un aspirante di 20 anni: "Io sono un ufficiale per forza, e non ho voluto la guerra e ho quasi fatto a cazzotti prima della guerra con gli studenti che facevano le manifestazioni interventiste. La guerra è stata voluta da due o tre gruppi di mascalzoni" (Bianchi 2001: 476). Talvolta il rancore trova modo di trasformarsi in una riflessione più ampia, sulla natura della guerra, sul militarismo, la pace, il modo di realizzarla. Riflessioni di questo genere, che naturalmente non passano la censura, sono opera di militanti socialisti capaci, meglio di altri, di dar forma ai diffusi sentimenti di ostilità. B. E. di Udine, 28 anni, soldato del 54° Reggimento di Fanteria, condannato a 4 mesi per lettera denigratoria, il 27 agosto 1916 scrive al padre:

Come si può rassegnarsi a questa orrida vita dal momento che si ha abbracciato una santa idea di giustizia? Come si può approvare questa guerra che più che barbara è stupida, di una stupidità grottesca, colossale, e vogliono farla credere civile, e come una lotta pel diritto, mentre invece è un cumulo di ingordigie e di interessi di pochi a danno del popolo che soffre e che paga col miglior sangue?

(Forcella – Monticone 2014: 83)

Francesco Giuliani, un pastore abruzzese, ma autodidatta e lettore appassionato della *Divina commedia* e dei poemi cavallereschi, oppone al Potere militare un'integrità e una condotta di "non-combattente". Scrive alla moglie il 10 marzo 1916:

Di guerra mia cara non te ne dovrei parlare per non tener vivo il tuo dolore; ma che vuoi questa è come quando uno ha una malattia, non dice e non pensa altro che se ne vuol liberare.
Io ho cercato sempre di non farmi vincere dalla paura, perchè quando si è nel pericolo può riuscire dannosa che fa perdere il lume della ragione. Io posso dire che non sono un vile ne un coraggioso, il coraggio tante volte non mi è mancato ma non ne ho fatto abuso inutilmente. Io non ho l'ambizione di salire in alto con atti di valore, mi contento di restare nel primo gradino, basta che mi riuscisse di salvare la pelle. Io non ho stima, né simpatia per quelli che sono i coraggiosi eroi; in guerra tutti quelli che vi sono distinti come eroi sono assassini, il vero eroe è quello che mette in pericolo la propria vita per salvare quella degli altri.
Nell'austriaco io non vedo un nemico come mi si vuol far credere, che devo dargli la caccia ed ammazzarlo ad ogni costo; penso che nel suo villaggio ha lasciato i suoi cari dai quali fu strappato come io lo fui da te. Nel mio cuore non c'è la frenesia omicida, rifletto che la vita di tutti è cara, ad ogni soldato morto o amico o nemico resta una madre senza figlio, o una sposa senza sposo o dei figli senza padre.
L'uomo non deve essere come il cane che aizzato si avventa; dalla natura ha avuto il dono del cervello, deve cercare di capire tutto, pensare e riflettere, e quando è spinto a fare il male, si deve guardare di non farlo.
Forse mia cara dirai che mi sono troppo divagato in queste cose che tu credi inutili; vuoi forse che mi interesso degli affari di casa, ma questi da tanto tempo li ho messi da parte che non posso averne più cura.

(Giuliani 2001: 355-356)

4. Uomini in fuga
"Quali erano le possibilità di fuga che si offrivano ai soldati?" — si chiede Antonio Gibelli, il quale poi commenta:

La renitenza, cioè evitare l'arruolamento, sottrarsi prima dell'arruolamento; la diserzione, che significa fuggire quando si è già arruolati o andando verso il nemico o rendendosi irreperibili nelle retrovie, la malattia, intesa specialmente come malattia mentale (la malattia mentale è una forma di fuga, è un modo di sottrarsi là dove le risorse pratiche, intellettuali, psicologiche del soldato non offrono altre vie); infine la malattia fisica come malattia autoprovocata, simulata, quella che si chiama autolesionismo o automutilazione. Queste sono quattro possibilità di fuga, di sottrazione alla logica totalizzante della guerra, all'imperativo del massacro su scala industriale. Sono modi diversi che hanno avuto peso quantitativo diverso ma che indicano tutti questa linea di tendenza.

(Gibelli 1994: 27)

Dal 24 maggio 1915 al 2 settembre 1919, coloro che si sottrassero all'arruolamento nell'esercito italiano furono 470.000; di questi, 370.000 erano italiani emigrati all'estero che decisero di non tornare. La diserzione fu invece fenomeno più complesso e sfaccettato. Intanto i numeri: "[...] le denunce per diserzione furono 189.425; nel corso del conflitto si conclusero 162.563 processi e furono emesse 101.685 condanne. Se quindi nell'arco di 4 anni di guerra 1 soldato su 12 subì un processo penale, 1 soldato su 26 comparve di fronte ai giudici militari per rispondere del reato di diserzione e 1 su 41 subì una condanna" (Bianchi 2001: 160-61). Pochissime le diserzioni che conducono i militari verso le file del nemico (circa 3.000), mentre la gran parte dei disertori si indirizza semplicemente verso casa. Ma sono considerati tali anche coloro che ritardano di qualche giorno il rientro da una licenza o si allontanano temporaneamente dal reparto o che, dopo un'azione, si sbandano e vagano privi di riferimenti.

Le condanne erano severissime: la diserzione "in faccia al nemico" era punita con la fucilazione, la diserzione all'interno con pene variabili da tre a quindici anni a seconda delle circostanze aggravanti. Oltre alle condanne dei tribunali, si procedeva anche ad esecuzioni sommarie in caso di rifiuto ad avanzare, ammutinamento, sbandamento involontario. Approvate dal Comando supremo, le fucilazioni sul campo riaffermavano la subordinazione della truppa, ristabilivano i rapporti gerarchici, imponevano un clima di terrore.

Scrive un soldato anonimo il 5 giugno 1917 in una lettera intercettata dalla censura e mai giunta a destinazione:

Tutti siamo qui, soggetti minutamente alla barbara morte (uccisione) come tante bestie da macello, giornalmente vi è un enorme numero di feriti e di morti, la medesima granata ne uccise tre del 159° fant., uno del Genio e parecchi altri feriti — ieri solo una granata ne ferì 17 della mia compagnia e parecchi gravissimi. Siamo qui addiacciati nel bosco, non c'è più un buco per ripararsi, demoralizzati in modo straordinario, che gli ufficiali stessi pazzescano, non è la morte che demoralizza perché già sappiamo che dobbiamo morire, ma sono i casi straordinari che s'affacciano i macelli — le strage — i patimenti e poi i maltrattamenti — la crudeltà che purtroppo è stata pagata cara verso il colonnello brigadiere F. cav. Temistocle, ucciso pure lui, il due corrente da una granata nemica, facendo fucilare in presenza di noi tutti 4 soldati, due di questi perché assetati si erano permessi di allontanarsi due ore dal reparto andando all'Isonzo a prendere una borraccia d'acqua. Torno a dire che io, noi, siamo stati la parte di 3 giorni senza avere nemmeno una goccia d'acqua. Dunque speriamo ad una buona ferita o ad una maledetta morte. Ah Se ci riesco venire a casa quale teppista vorrò diventare, altro che la civiltà e il progresso.

(Bianchi 2001: 179-80)

Oltre alle diserzioni consapevoli, ci sono anche quelle inconsapevoli: sono soldati che vagano senza meta, confusi, regrediti ad uno stato infantile; uomini in fuga senza sapere dove nascondersi, obbedendo ad un impulso profondo che li spinge lontano dal fronte. Entrano negli ospedaletti da campo, spesso dopo azioni lunghe e sanguinose, attoniti, paralizzati, privi dell'uso della voce e dell'udito, smemorati. Altri, eccitati, sembrano ossessionati dal ricordo della famiglia, sicuramente in rovina come tutto a causa della guerra. Altri colpiti da *shock* da bombardamento (*shell shock*) sono squassati da tic nervosi e si rifugiano in una totale estraneità. Il fenomeno dei soldati traumatizzati investì tutti gli eserciti. I soldati italiani che passarono per i manicomi furono circa 40.000: cifra ufficiale sottostimata da accogliere con grande cautela (Bianchi 2001: 63-64).

Ma la casistica dell'uomo in fuga dal quotidiano rischio di morte è ancora lunga e comprende tutte le forme atroci e ripugnanti di autolesionismo, come apprendiamo da questa citazione:

> Il tribunale di guerra ha recentemente condannato a cinque anni di reclusione militare un soldato che è andato per le spiccie — scrive Attilio Frescura: si è forato senz'altro il timpano dell'orecchio destro con un chiodo di ferro da cavallo; ed a venti anni ha condannato un altro che si è spalmato in un occhio la secrezione blenorragica di un compagno".

(Frescura 1966: 184)

L'ampiezza dei comportamenti autolesionistici è inesauribile: ascessi ottenuti con iniezioni sottocutanee di benzina, petrolio, piscio; dermatiti prodotte con preparati di ranuncolacee; congiuntiviti provocate da affumicazioni o da solfato di rame o da polvere di tabacco; otiti ottenute con l'applicazioni di sostanze irritanti; bronchiti provocate con protratte inalazioni di fumo. I più disperati si mozzavano le mani con colpi di vanghetta o se le stritolavano sotto grossi massi; altri si sparavano a bruciapelo alle mani o ai piedi.

Sono numerosi i diari che registrano i modi con cui i soldati tentano, quasi sempre inutilmente, di sottrarsi alla prima linea, alla vita di trincea, all'ordine di avanzare, al Potere assoluto della gerarchia militare (vie tortuose, a volte inconsapevoli, quasi sempre disperate). E contemporaneamente mostrano, attraverso l'efficienza di ufficiali, giudici, medici e psichiatri, la forza repressiva della macchina militare.

Fondazione Museo Storico del Trentino

Bibliografia

Antonelli, Quinto. *"Io ò comperato questo libro...". Lingua e stile nei testi autobiografici popolari*. In *Pagine di scuola, di famiglia, di memorie. per un'indagine sul multilinguismo nel Trentino austriaco*. A c. di Emanuele Banfi e Patrizia Cordin. Trento: Museo storico in Trento, 1996. 209-63.

_____. *Storia intima della Grande Guerra. Lettere, diari e memorie dei soldati dal fronte*. Roma: Donzelli, 2014.

Bianchi, Bruna. *La follia e la fuga. Nevrosi di guerra, diserzione e disobbedienza nell'esercito italiano (1915-1918)*. Roma: Bulzoni, 2001.

Capacci, Giuseppe. *Diario di un contadino alla "Grande Guerra"*. A c. di Dante Priore. Firenze: Aska Edizioni, 2014.

Cavalli, Tullio. *Isonzo infame. Soldati bresciani nella guerra '15-'18*. Brescia: Edizioni del Moretto, 1983.

Ferrari, Pietro. *Vita di guerra e di prigionia. Dall'Isonzo al Carso. Diario 1915-1918*. A

c. di Maria Teresa Aiolfi. Milano: Mursia, 2004.
Forcella, Enzo e Monticone, Alberto. *Plotone di esecuzione. I processi della prima guerra mondiale*. Roma: Laterza, 2014.
Frescura, Attilio. *Diario di un imboscato*. In *Tre romanzi della Grande Guerra*. A c. di Mario Schettini. Milano: Longanesi, 1966. 41-292.
Gibelli, Antonio. *La fuga impossibile. Autolesionismo, simulazione, follia*. In *1914-1918 Scampare la guerra. Renitenza, autolesionismo, comportamenti individuali e collettivi di fuga e la giustizia militare nella Grande Guerra*. A c. di Lucio Fabi. Ronchi dei Legionari: Centro Culturale Pubblico Polivalente, 1994. 27-34.
———. *La guerra grande. Storie di gente comune*. Roma: Laterza, 2014.
———. *L'officina della guerra. La Grande Guerra e le trasformazioni del mondo mentale*. Torino: Bollati Boringhieri, 1991.
Giuliani, Francesco. *Diario della guerra 1915-18. Lettere dal fronte*. A c. di Paolo Muzi. L'Aquila: Japadre Editore, 2001.
Graziani, Antonio. "Cera Cadorna...". *Diario (1915-1917) della Grande Guerra del soldato Antonio Graziani*. A c. di Leardo Mascanzoni. "I quaderni del Cardello" 8 (1998): 23-55.
Guerrieri, Filippo. *Lettere dalla trincea (Libia – Carso – Trentino – Macedonia)*. A c. di Enrico Guerrieri. Calliano (Trento): Manfrini, 1969.
Isnenghi, Mario e Rochat, Giorgio. *La Grande Guerra 1914-1918*. Bologna: il Mulino, 2008.
Lorenzi, Nello. *Lettere ai familiari (1913-1917). Epistolario di un giovane soldato valdarnese*. A c. di Dante Priore e Carlo Fabbri. San Giovanni Valdarno: Biblioteca comunale di Terranova Bracciolini, 1996.
Marchetti, Vitaliano. *"Se avrò la fortuna sempre di poter ritornare fra voi tutti..."*. A c. di Ruggero Giacomini. "Storia e problemi contemporanei" 1-2 (1988): 115-33.
Mondini, Marco. *La guerra italiana. Partire, raccontare, tornare 1914-18*. Bologna: il Mulino, 2014.
Omodeo, Adolfo. *Momenti della vita di guerra. Dai diari e dalle lettere dei caduti 1915-1918*. Torino: Einaudi 1968.
Procacci, Giovanna. *Soldati e prigionieri italiani nella Grande Guerra. Con una raccolta di lettere inedite*. Torino: Bollati Boringhieri, 2000.
Il racconto italiano della Grande guerra. Narrazioni, corrispondenze, prose morali (1914-1921). A c. di Emma Giammattei e Gianluca Genovese. Vol. 4 di *La letteratura italiana: storia e testi*. A. c. di Carlo Maria Ossola. Milano: Ricciardi, 2015. 471-658.
Rolland, Romain. *Diario degli anni di guerra 1914-1919. Note e documenti per lo studio della storia morale dell'Europa odierna*. A c. di Marie Romain Rolland. Vol. I. Milano: Parenti, 1960.
Spitzer, Leo. *Lettere di prigionieri di guerra italiani, 1915-1918*. A c. di Lorenzo Renzi. Torino: Boringhieri, 1976.
Testa, Enrico. *L'italiano nascosto. Una storia linguistica e culturale*. Torino: Einaudi, 2014
Tonetto, Augusto. *Carissima moglie. Lettere dal fronte della Grande Guerra da Ca' Savio a Caporetto 1916-1917*. A c. di Lisa Bregantin. Padova: NovaCharta, 2007.
Verificato per censura. Lettere e cartoline di soldati romagnoli nella prima guerra mondiale. A c. di Giuseppe Bellosi e Marcello Savini. Cesena: Il Ponte Vecchio, 2002.

Diana Garvin

Singing Truth to Power: Melodic Resistance and Bodily Revolt in Italy's Rice Fields

Abstract: This article investigates how the *mondine* negotiated state demands for female bodies to both feed and populate the nation during Italy's Fascist period. Using testimonials and work songs, I rely on the *mondine*'s own words to chronicle their lived experience of field work and the resulting spirit of rebellion that echoed across the rice paddies. I then frame these narratives against the propaganda that attempted to cast the *mondina* as a symbol of productive Fascist womanhood. By emphasizing women workers' accounts of their bodily revolt from labor strikes to inducing abortion, I reveal how the *mondine* sang truth to Fascist power.
Keywords: Fascism, propaganda, women, *mondine*, rice fields, labor, work, agriculture.

Alla mattina, appena alzata
(coro) O bella ciao, bella ciao, bella ciao, ciao, ciao
alla mattina appena alzata
in risaia mi tocca andar.

E tra gli insetti e le zanzare
(coro) O bella ciao, bella ciao, bella ciao, ciao, ciao
un duro lavoro mi tocca a far.
O mamma mia! o che tormento!
(coro) O bella ciao, bella ciao, bella ciao, ciao, ciao
È così ogni doman!

Il caposquadra col suo bastone
(coro) O bella ciao, bella ciao, bella ciao, ciao, ciao
e noi curve a lavorar.
Ma verrà un giorno che tutte quante
lavoreremo in libertà!
(coro e voce principale, insieme) Ma verrà un giorno che tutte quante
lavoreremo in libertà!

[In the morning just got up
(chorus) Oh bye beautiful, bye beautiful, bye beautiful, bye, bye,
In the morning just awakened
in the rice fields I must go.

And among the insects and the mosquitoes
(chorus) Oh bye beautiful, bye beautiful, bye beautiful, bye, bye,
A difficult work I must do.

Oh mamma mia! Oh what torment!
(chorus) Oh bye beautiful, bye beautiful, bye beautiful, bye, bye,
And it goes on like this every day.

The overseer with his rod
(chorus) Oh bye beautiful, bye beautiful, bye beautiful, bye, bye,
And us bent over at work.
But a day will come when all of us
will work in liberty![1]
(chorus and lead, together) But a day will come when all of us
will work in liberty!

"Bella ciao" sings the story of one day and every day in the life of the *mondine*, the female rice weeders[2] annually contracted for forty days of migrant agricultural work in Northern Italy during the 1930s. These song lyrics use an impressionistic, nonlinear temporal framework to highlight the emotionally salient moments of this gendered form of labor. At dawn, the *mondina*, the *bella* of "Bella ciao," absorbs her family's anguished goodbye as she departs for the rice fields..By day, she is at work in the field with the other *mondine*, bent over in front of the overseer with his stick (almost a phallic symbol of power and even violence) at their backs. But her emotive focus remains on her faraway family, whose presence pulses through every chorus. Time telescopes, collapsing the emotional wrench of departure into the physical torment of rice weeding, an interminable present of curved spines and hands deep in the water and mud. But in a final push, time shoots forward: the final, collective female "we" cloaks the lead and the chorus, the *mondina* and her family, under a new vision for the future, where the *mondine* will work together in liberty. "Bella ciao" thus condenses three governing themes

---

[1] Vasco Scansani, *Bella ciao* (Vercellese, written as part of a song competition [*concorso sonoro*] for the Festa della Mondina a San Germano Vercellese, 1952), Italian lyrics cited in Manicardi, *Il coro delle mondine* 37. Although Manicardi cites Scansani, the *bracciante* (laborer) turned songwriter as the author of this text, earlier versions of this song demonstrate that Scansani was by no means the sole author of this song. Manicardi notes, for instance, that Giovanna Daffini added the last section of lyrics to *Bella ciao* in the 1930s. As such, it would be more accurate to say that Scansani was not the author of the song, but rather the first person to transcribe the lyrics for a public forum. CGIL Milan's digital audio collections possess multiple recorded versions of "Bella ciao." Similarly, various transcriptions can be found in ethnographic histories such as *La fatica delle donne* and *Senti le rane che cantano*. All of the songs analyzed in this article come from the CGIL and Ente Nazionale Risi repositories. Unless otherwise specified, all translations are my own.

[2] *Mondina* derives from the verb *mondare*, to clean, or to weed, in an agricultural context. This umbrella term encompassed different forms of field labor related to rice production, such as transplanting the tender young shoots at the beginning of the growing season (Cortelazzo 772).

of women's agricultural labor in the context of Italy's Fascist period: the mutually constitutive formation of women's personal and political identities at collective work sites, the harmonic profusion and diversity of women's voices and concerns, and the primacy of the corporeal in shaping social roles and relations in spaces of food production (the field) and consumption (the home) — three of the interlaced motifs of this article. Specifically, I examine the interplay of working conditions, music creation, and the gendered body within the context of rice production at the national level to demonstrate how state attempts to control gendered work and the goods it produced resulted in numerous points of negotiation between women and the government. Under the Fascist regime, a new emphasis on domestic economy and production required a double sense of women's work, both on and in the body.

But "Bella ciao" also reveals a paradox, borne out by the *mondine*'s own words in written and oral testimonials.[3] The *risaia* (rice field) constituted a key site for the formation of female identity. Absence of normal social contexts (the family, the parish) and presence of unique social contexts (a near-exclusively female space) pushed working class women to consider their roles at the level of the individual and the group. This exceptional environment provides a case study to examine one specific relationship between the female individual and the Fascist state. Through songs, jokes, dances, and pranks, returning *mondine* instructed new arrivals in a dense local culture of class relations and politics. As such, analyzing the productions of the *risaia* underscores the personal and political significance of women's collectivity in terms of the body and the body politic. The diversity of viewpoints inherent in the choral form of these social productions points to the idea that identity is relational, multivalent, and ever-shifting. And yet a common note rings through each testimony: the *mondine* claimed that labor not only shaped individuals' physical bodies, but also organized the social body into identifiable classes with specific political goals.

The *mondina* song corps taught women to sing truth to power by providing the means to catalogue their difficult labor conditions and to rehearse for political resistance. In the first section of this article, I investigate how the *mondine* successfully used these songs as both collective expressions of culture and as social tools: culture, in that the songs' popularity, persistence, and pervasiveness suggests that they captured common and deeply felt aspects of the *mondine*'s work and life; tools in that the *mondine* used them to accomplish a specific goal,

---

[3] These testimonials largely come from the Archivio dei Diari in Pieve Santo Stefano, outside of Arezzo in Tuscany. Because testimonials constitute memories of the past composed in the present, their interpretation requires consideration of the context in which these women recorded their stories. To interpret these materials, I draw on Luisa Passerini's approach: "All memory is valid, the guiding principle should be that all autobiographical memory is true; it is up to the interpreter to discover in what sense, where, how, and for which purpose" (Thomson, Frisch, and Hamilton 34). In the context of the testimonials, I take this historiographic approach to mean that every *mondina*'s history blends objective and subjective information. These forms of evidence have different but equal value.

to keep their spirits up even as their bodies flagged. Because these songs derive their creative power from the intersection of the body and the mind, this particular subset of popular Italian music demonstrates how the material conditions of women's labor and the lived experience of the female body affected and reflected women's cultural creations under Fascism.

But what of the relationship between the *mondine* and the regime? In particular, how did the *mondine* negotiate pronatalism (the bearing of numerous children) and autarchy (Italian economic self-sufficiency) through music and metaphor? In this second section, I move from individual *mondine*'s first-hand accounts of physical and emotional work to their collectively authored songs and their symbolic renderings of women's labor.[4] Testimonial analysis provides specific and concrete examples of the formidable themes intimated through the song corps. Themes of gendered body at work link rhyme to reason: both the songs and testimonials suggest that decisions regarding menstruation, abortion, miscarriage, birth, and breastfeeding emerged as key points of contention between individual women and the regime. The historical specificity of these solos thus underwrites the credibility of the chorus, providing a powerful counter-narrative to the Fascist conceit that the *mondine* happily produced rice and children in service to the nation. Ultimately, the *mondine*'s binary framing of these choices reveals the flaw in the Fascist dream: women could work in the fields or they could have children, but they could not do both at the same time.

Alimentary Autarchy and Pronatalism in Everyday Life

Fascist propaganda rarely addressed the *mondine* directly.[5] More commonly, the regime spoke to countrywomen (*massaie*) in general, as though women hailing from the northern extremes of Lombardy to the southern reaches of the Mezzogiorno comprised one homogenous group by dint of their common social class.[6] In an attempt to inspire the *massaie* to support autarchy and pronatalism

---

[4] Former *mondine* wrote these testimonials late in life, often in their eighties or nineties. While they recorded their memories for a number of reasons, the vast majority explicitly stated their desire to share their past with their grandchildren. Oftentimes, it is these grandchildren who deemed these personal works "historical" as well as "familial" documents, and donated copies to the Archivio Santo Stefano.

[5] In line with Forgacs and Gundle, I take propaganda to mean "any communication designed to express the opinions, beliefs, or values of an organized collective group and to persuade others of its truth, or at least of its ideological force" (214).

[6] Specifically, Benito Mussolini referred to the *mondine* under the broader heading of the *massaie* (countrywomen) or *donne dei campi* (women of the fields). Although the *massaia* can be a countrywoman, the term itself does not indicate geography. Rather, it means every woman (typically a mother or grandmother) in charge of managing household chores. For further information regarding the regime's treatment of rural working-class women and their sociopolitical responses, see Willson.

through food consumption and production, the covers of cooking magazines like *La cucina italiana* regularly featured photos of women breastfeeding beside quotations from Mussolini's pronatalist speeches.[7] Inside printed propaganda materials, recipes provided instructions for autarchic cookery.[8] Recipes prominently featured domestic products and decried foreign imports. They also advocated Italian preparations as patriotic, eschewing French and British preparations. Similarly, *L'almanacco della donna* (a home reference guide) featured photocollages combining images of infants, farm work, nuns, and the Duce with daily work plans to rationalize childcare, animal raising, and home gardening.[9] As the ideological collisions in these gendered forms of propaganda

---

[7] To combat infant mortality among working-class women, the Senate established the National Bureau for the Protection of Maternity and Infancy, known by the Italian acronym O.N.M.I. Originally titled Opera Nazionale Fascista per la Protezione della Maternità e dell'Infanzia, a subsection of law #2277 created this group on December 10, 1925. *La cucina italiana* featured images of breastfeeding both on the cover and throughout the magazine during the Fascist period. This tendency peaked in the late 1930s. See covers of *La cucina italiana,* "Verso la Vita" (August 1937), "La Donna e La Razza" (October 1938), and November 1938 (untitled).

[8] Delia Notari and Umberto Notari, the co-founders and editors of *La cucina italiana*, enthusiastically supported Fascism, and used the magazine to promote autarchic cooking among middle-class Italian women. Umberto Notari's adherence to Fascist political doctrine appears to have developed in his early 20s, during his collaboration with F. T. Marinetti on the magazine *Poesia.* His enthusiasm for social conservatism in general and Fascist racial policy in particular manifested in many of his publications, from *La donna 'Tipo Tre'* to his signature on *Manifesto della razza* and *Panegirico della razza italiana.*

[9] Bemporad, a Florence-based publishing company, in connection with *La donna*, a Rome-based women's magazine, released a total of 24 almanacs from 1920 to 1944. Silvia Bemporad, wife of founding publisher Enrico Bemporad, served as the editor from 1920 to 1936. During this time, her husband regularly sent sample books to the regime, including Italian almanacs. He also sought commercial relations with the Fascist government: in a January 13, 1932 letter, Bemporad offers to supply textbooks to elementary schools in the colonies. Three years hence, Enrico sought protection from the regime as well. A memo from the State Polygraph Institute (Istituto Poligrafo dello Stato), dated April 9, 1935, from the Undersecretariat of the Press (Sottosegretariato Stampa) to Mussolini summarizes his letter. The memo notes that Bemporad's partners (soci) "lo hanno cacciato dall'Azienda" ("chased him out of the business") and that he "invoca un posto di lavoro nel suo campo d'azione dove possa ancora rendersi utile" ("requests a work position in his field where he might still make himself useful"). These behind-the-scenes machinations suggest Enrico Bemporad's increasing dependence on state intervention regarding commercial concerns. Almanac content also replicates this tendency. The 1938 race laws further complicated Bemporad's relationship to the regime. Negative publicity campaigns led by the government denigrated the publishing house for their Jewish leadership, a move that contributed to the firm's pre-existing financial woes and ultimately silencing their editors for the remainder of the Fascist period. See annual memos from Enrico Bemporad to Mussolini (ACS, SPD, CO, b. 509, f. 230). For almanac photo collages referenced here,

suggest, Fascist boards like the National Rice Board (Ente Nazionale Risi) and the Board for the Protection of Motherhood and Childhood (O.N.M.I.) expected women to participate in these projects through the habits of everyday life. In theory, the regime's conservative social politics sought to keep women in the private sphere. But in practice, the success of domestic policies like autarchy and pronatalism depended on women's active participation in public political projects across different social spaces; home, field, factory, and clinic thus provided a series of sites for the daily negotiation of politics between individual women and the regime.

Autarchy took edible form in The (so-called) Battle for Grain, a 10-year propaganda campaign promoting Italy's economic self-sufficiency by convincing women to increase their families' consumption of non-standard grains, such as rice, and to decrease their consumption of pasta and bread.[10] To push rice as a substitute for pasta, the regime established the National Rice Board in January 1928, and established the National Day for Rice Propaganda one month later. Pronatalism, or the increased production of Italian children, might be read as a parallel form of autarchic push. O.N.M.I. produced didactic films, magazines, and pamphlets instructing women in hygienic breastfeeding practices and rational childcare at government obstetric clinics.[11] Like autarchy, pronatalism emerged as a guiding principle of domestic policy due to the regime's intense preoccupation with Italy's declining birthrate and its potential implications for Fascism's political dominance at the international level.[12] Both projects thus shared a common goal: to increase different forms of domestic production to increase the nation's autonomy on a global stage. And both identified working-class women's (re)production and field labor as the means to this end.

---

see Bemporad's *Almanacco della donna italiana 1936*, pp. 5-6 and *Almanacco della donna italiana 1941*, pp. 2-4 (Wolfsoniana Collection, Genoa, Italy).

[10] Italy's grain production could not keep pace with domestic consumption. During the early twentieth century, the vast majority of wheat was imported from Turkey (Helstosky 88).

[11] Pietro Francisci's didactic films for the Istituto Nazionale LUCE, *La protezione della stirpe* (*The Protection of the Race*, 1933) and *Alle madri d'Italia* (*To the Mothers of Italy*, 1935), exemplify this genre. O.N.M.I.'s monthly periodical *Maternità e infanzia* and pamphlets like Pietro Corsi's *La tutela della maternità e dell'infanzia in Italia* and Attilio Lo Monaco-Aprile's *Protezione della maternità e dell'infanzia* are characteristic of O.N.M.I.'s textual media in their tendency towards paternalistic prescriptions for childcare.

[12] Mussolini's 1927 Ascension Day address emphasized the "'alarming' national decline in rates of marriage and fertility" (Horn 95). Demographic statistics verified regime fears: ISTAT data cited by Carl Ipsen indicates that 35% of all *comuni* experienced a decline in population between the 1911 and 1921 censuses and that "the overall trend was one of decline" (Ipsen 174).

Women's Agricultural Work under Fascism

Migrant agricultural labor implicates questions of social class, as economic necessity typically compels workers to accept the difficult conditions inherent to field work. In the context of the *mondine* working in Fascist Italy, the classed dimensions of rice transplanting and weeding evoked a gendered context as well. Although rural working-class Italian women had historically taken on agricultural work outside the home, they generally did so on a piecemeal basis to augment household income. Rice transplanting and weeding traditions departed from these general working norms in that women planned to participate in the year's *monda* (40-day weeding season) in advance to generate what was often the only liquid capital their families possessed. But convenience alone cannot account for the duration and exclusivity of this peculiar gender breakdown. By the time Mussolini marched on Rome, 80 to 95% of all weeders were women (Zappi 10). National Rice Board propaganda and women's testimonials alike demonstrate that economic concerns account for the predominance of women in the field, but they also suggest that this concern came from the male employers as well as the female workers. Predominant attitudes towards the low relative value of women meant that employers could pay them half or two-thirds as much as they would pay male laborers (*braccianti*) for the same work. The *braccianti* earned 1038 *lire* per year in 1938, at a time when 1 kilogram of rice cost nearly 2 *lire* (ISTAT 1939). For forty days of work at the *monda*, Erminia Confortini recalled being paid 220 *lire*, plus "a few kilograms" of rice (Minardi 29). Ermanna Chiozzi recalled being paid 16 *lire* per day in 1927 (Chiozzi 8). National Rice Board publications offered ad hoc biological arguments for employing women to obscure these economic reasons: they argued that only women had the patience for weeding, that their bodies were lighter and more agile, and the fingers were more delicate, and thus less likely to damage the tender plants. Francesco Pezza, the public health officer of Mortara, went so far as to note that women's flexible backbones naturally suited them for this arduous labor (Zappi 13). Put more broadly, officials like Pezza drew on gendered stereotypes to naturalize occupational gender segregation. Many women bent these arguments to their own purposes, taking pride in their ability to perform work that men could not endure. And yet these same women also seem to recognize the latent justificatory edge of such statements. As Milena Scalabrini recalled, "Nella risaia erano occupate solo le donne perché più brave, svelte, precise, pazienti nel togliere le erbacce e perché venivano pagate meno degli uomini" ("In the rice fields there were only women because [they were] better, faster, precise, patient in pulling the weeds and because they were paid less than men" 1). In the broader context of Italian agricultural labor, the economic necessity of the female presence in the rice fields implicitly contradicted state narratives dictating that a woman's place was in the home. Scalabrini's account speaks to the *mondine*'s awareness of their standing within this larger socioeconomic framework and points to the historical importance of integrating first-person testimonials with state-published accounts.

Cut-and-Paste Consent: The mondine *in Fascist Propaganda*
In propaganda (Figs. 1-4), the regime celebrated the rice workers as symbols of ideal Italian femininity: robust, florid, rustic, maternal, and working class. Engaged in the twin occupations of producing autarchic staple foods and Italian bodies, they constituted a symbol of gendered hyper-productivity based on and in the female body. But despite the regime's enthusiasm for this particular group of female workers as emblems of a socially conservative national past projected into a hyper-productive future,[13] the *mondine* rarely reflected a similar admiration for the regime. The vast majority voted Communist: many women recalled carrying red voting cards in their wallets, a colorful if hidden mark of dissent in an era dominated by black, the Fascist voting card color.[14] They did not see Fascism as responsive to their interests, and, indeed, letters and memos between town-level representatives of the National Rice Board and the regime reveal a near-constant state of politicized revolt catalyzed by socioeconomic concerns.[15] Most of these *mondine*'s protests contested the length of the workday, and agitated for better pay. For these women, Leftist politics went hand in hand with their precarious economic status. Many former *mondine* recalled that the older women taught the younger women about politics through songs, explicitly instructing them in international politics and Communist history.[16] Many *mondine* recalled using

---

[13] To curry favor with the *mondine*, Mussolini sent regular financial infusions to the Ente Nazionale Risi, earmarked for direct aid to the rice workers. The memo reads, "On the order of the DUCE I send you 10,000 *lire* for the workers engaged in the next campaign for the weeding and harvest of rice. I would be grateful to you if you would give me the receipt for the sum so that I can order my accounts." This memo, written in the informal *tu* form of address, traveled between two of the highest ranking officials in the Fascist party, from Osvaldo Sebastiani to Achille Starace, indicating the importance that the regime assigned to rice promotion, and to the *mondine* as the means to increase autarchic food production, and ultimately forge new, autarchic foodways based on domestic staple foods. No record exists of how these funds were used, or if they even reached the *mondine* at all. See financial promemorium and record of 10,000 *lire* deposit, Rome, Italy, 1939, in folder *Milano: Ente Nationale del Riso, Contributi del Duce per l'assistenza alle Mondariso* (ACS, PCM, 1934-1936, b. 509.488, f. 2).

[14] The image of the red versus black card seems to have resonated with many former *mondine*: Antonietta Chierici and Laura Scalabrini repeat this phrasing throughout their testimonies, as do two unnamed *mondine* interviewed in Manicardi.

[15] For a characteristic example, see the 1935-1936 letter and memo exchange between Novarese prefect Aldo Rossini and Benito Mussolini (ACS, PCM, 1934-1936, b. 509.488, f. 2).

[16] The 1909 and 1917 Russian Revolutions appear in many popular *mondine* songs, as do political figures ranging from militant Socialists to the royal House of Savoy, often in the space of a single song. The lyrics of "Giuriam giuriam" "We Swear, We Swear," allude to local political leaders such as the Mayor of Ronsecco and Socialist agitator Camillo Cerrati, a former *bracciante* and rare *mondariso*, as well as to Queen Margherita, King Umberto I,

Fascist song structures and replacing the lyrics with pro-Socialist, Communist, and Anarchist messages. The Fascist hymn *Giovinezza* seems to have been particularly prone to this type of refashioning, often popping up as laments for Socialist politician Giacomo Matteotti, who was assassinated by members of the Fascist secret police in 1924 (Castelli 65). Sometimes, women changed the words of the song to better reflect their personal beliefs. Chierici's mother appears to have done so, as Antonietta recalls the opening to "La Lega" as beginning with the words, "E noi che siamo donne, paura non abbiamo" ("And we who are women, fear we do not have" 16). The common openings contrast women against courage by using a concessive conjunction, typically "sebben che" or "benché," both of which translate to "although." This single word or phrase change serve to reflect Chierici's feminist (in her own words) stance that bravery is constitutive of femininity rather than exceptional or situationally dependent. Other diaries and testimonials from the *mondine* also reveal a gendered dimension to this state of unrest. Writing in retrospect, many characterized their stance against the regime as an intersectional form of feminism deriving from their class-based status as agricultural workers.[17] Chierici's mother, like many other *mondine*, conflated the figure of the *padrone*, and upper-class employers in general, with the Duce. Both bore blame for lauding women's work while paying them half of what male *braccianti* received.

In these visceral terms, the *mondine* seem to have understood how their rice-weeding work fed the Fascist economy. Their words indicate awareness that the regime controlled and regulated the market from the top down.[18] In the specific context of the rural economy, Fascist policies consistently favored landowners over migrant workers, and the land itself over those who labored on it. Political and economic motives meshed: the Fascist party was indebted to the landlords and rich farmers who had provided the money and the arms that cleared their way for victory over left-wing movements in the Italian countryside.[19] As a result of this history, the *mondine* would have felt the heavy hand of the Fascist economy

---

and their children Vittorio Emanuele and Amedeo of Savoy, and his second wife Maria Letizia Napoleone (Castelli 377-78).

[17] Because many of the *mondine* use and refashion feminist terms dating from later periods to describe these earlier protests, one cannot say with certainty that they envisioned their actions as feminist in the 1930s. But despite the possibility of anachronism, former *mondine* writing in the 1990s and 2000s heavily rely on feminist concepts like "the problem with no name" to make sense of their personal motives during the Fascist period, ultimately underlining the centrality of gender in the construction of political identity.

[18] For an investigation of the Fascist manipulation of the national economy and its effects, see Celli.

[19] See Squeri's study of rural voting records and political payments.

through the regime's suppression of peasant landholding[20] and land use (*usi civici*) as well as through the higher taxes that they paid in proportion to their take-home income [21] and loan-fixing schemes. [22] New policies of market standardization and hygiene favored large estates over small farms, as only wealthy landowners could afford to meet the new regime policies for spraying, sorting, and packing agricultural goods. Further, regime policies targeted the products themselves on a classed basis: the purchasing power of commodities produced by Northern commercial farms and the great Southern estates (rice, wheat, tobacco, sugar beets) increased or remained stable during the 1930s thanks to Fascist tariff protection, direct subsidies, organization of markets, and wage cutting. By contrast, the purchasing power of products that provided the livelihood for peasants (vineyard, orchard, and garden crops) enjoyed no such government protections. Their purchasing value dropped precipitously. Taken in sum, Fascist agricultural economics disproportionately benefited wealthy landowners. The effects were striking: ISTAT data show a major reduction in peasant ownership

---

[20] Fascist labor organizations worked through legislation to quash peasant landholding both at the level of the township and at the level of the family. Prior to this period, *usi civici*, a legacy of feudal land policy, allowed inhabitants of rural communities to use nominally private lands for pasturage, wood cutting, watering stock, and in some cases even cultivation and habitation. The Fascist policy of enclosing common lands, begun with the decree of May 22, 1924, abolished this tradition. For the effects of this decree on subsequent land use, see *Annuario statistico* 1936, p. 62. Further, the Charter of Share Tenancy (May 13, 1933) revoked many of the rights gained by Socialist protests in the previous two decades, including guarantee of a minimum income, maximum working hours, pay for overtime, and insurance benefits. See Schmidt 334.

[21] In theory, the productivist concept (*concetto produttivistico*), the advocation for capital rather than capitalism, guided Fascist taxation policy. But in practice, farm proprietors rather than farm workers saw the benefits of these policies. For example, on January 4, 1923, the new tax on agricultural income stipulated that, for large farm owners, tax would be based on income remaining after payment of *braccianti* wages or crop shares, but in the case of small farm owners, tax would be based on income before any such payments. This distinction doubled the income tax burden on the peasantry in relation to the gentry (Marabini 219).

[22] The borrowing ability of peasants sharply decreased under Fascism due to government consolidation of control over rural banks. When the government centralized the management of far-flung branches, it changed the social dynamic of local borrowing: loan officers were less likely to know the borrower personally and began to insist on property as security instead of reputation. This dynamic once again benefited the landed class and diminished financial options for the peasantry, who lacked the land to access bank loans. Increasingly, small farmers and *braccianti* sought loans not from banks but from large landowners, who charged usurious rates of 50 to 100% per year. For outlines of Fascist agricultural credit reforms, see Costanzo, U.S. Department of Agriculture, Bureau of Agricultural Economics, *Foreign Crops and Markets,* September 3, 1936, cited in Schmidt 344.

of small farms and homesteads, and a rise in tenant farming. Between 1921 and 1931, the number of operating owners declined by nearly half a million, while the number of cash-tenants rose by nearly 400,000.[23] The *mondine* were not working in a free labor market, and they knew it. How then could they respond to the economic injustice of the dictatorial state?

Because the figure of the *mondina* held a central place in the regime's propagandistic push for agricultural autarchy, graphic designers had to rely on artistic techniques to reconcile the state's reliance on the *mondina* as a symbol of ideal Fascist womanhood with the reality that many, if not most *mondine*, despised the regime. Figures 1-4 speak to the successive stages involved in creating a propagandistic photo collage, and demonstrate how the regime relied on the artistic process to construct false images of consent. Graphic designers working for the regime used photography to evoke the veracity then popularly associated with the medium. But they also heavily mediated these images by discarding those parts that did not support their message, and combining images taken in different times and places. In Figures 2 and 3, the contrastive scale of the two photographs used for the foreground and background highlights the extensive editing involved in the construction of photocollage. This juxtaposition miniaturizes the agricultural workers even as it aggrandizes the shafts of wheat, suggesting that the two are bound together in a relationship of patriotic production to support the regime's goal of autarchy. Rather than hiding the cut and paste approach, this form of propaganda highlights the extensive editing involved in its construction, casting revision as an artistic move rather than a political one.

This series of images reveals the artistic techniques used by the regime to obscure the *mondine*'s general distaste for the Fascist regime in general, and the Duce in particular. Figures 2 through 4 show a spectrum of obeisance in their finished or near-finished collages. Distant shots (Fig. 3), side profiles (Fig. 4), and turned heads (Fig. 2) all served to hide the *mondine*'s facial expressions, which often evoked unacceptable emotions ranging from neutrality to incredulity to distaste. By contrast, Figure 1, a single piece destined for a larger collage, reveals an almost comical level of contrast between Mussolini's enthusiasm and that of the male and female rice workers present. As Mussolini poses with his hand on his hip in full military regalia, his mouth open in a grin, the *mondina* stares down the audience, poker-faced, as the *mondino* warily glances at the Duce, and continues to work. This frozen scene vividly recalls the menacing warning of "La Lega": "E voi altri signoroni, che ci avete tant'orgoglio, abbassate la superbia e aprite il portafoglio" ("And you other big shots, who are so proud, lower the arrogance and open the wallet"). The rice workers' facial expressions communicate their distaste for the leader of the regime and his transparent bid for

---

[23] See Istituto Centrale di Statistica, Censimento della popolazione del Regno d'Italia, 1 dicembre 1921 (Rome 1928) and VI Censimento generale della popolazione, 21 aprile 1931 (Rome 1934) IV, part 2.

positive publicity as a hero of workers. Wisely, the regime decided to discard this image, electing to use other, more mediated images for propagandistic purposes instead.

In calling for hyper-productive female bodies to meet the new economic goals of increased domestic production, the regime inadvertently set two of its key goals against one another.[24] Implementing pronatalism and autarchy as gendered forms of labor points to the biological limit of increasing the productivity of the female body. In the particular case of rice weeding, the latter absorbed the former. Rice weeding resulted in more productive fields and a higher yield of rice at harvest time, but it directly undermined women's fertility while they worked the fields. To the regime, on the contrary, women's bodily labor had the unique capacity to simultaneously create both Italian food and new Italians.

(Re)production: Managing Menstruation, Birth, and Abortion in the Fields

During the *monda*, female bodily processes became public, political, and economic issues as well as private, social, and personal ones. Because of the hard labor and rough living conditions involved, the *mondine* had to confront politically charged questions of the fertile female body in public or semi-public. The *mondine* knew from the start that the hyper-productive female body was a biological impossibility: the intense labor of rice weeding often stopped women's menstrual cycles for the duration of the *monda*. And since poverty tended to be a pre-condition of working the rice fields, women could not afford to take time off while menstruating, a then-common practice among the middle and upper classes even though their daily physical labor was less taxing.[25] On the rare occasions when menstruation did occur in the fields, Laura Scalabrini[26] notes that the *mondine* typically attached an elastic or a scrap of cloth around their waists and, using two safety pins (*spille da balia*) one in the front and one in the back, attached a piece of white fabric taken from old bed sheets. This diaper (*pannolino*) would be washed and reused the following month (12). In contrast to other *mondine* accounts, Scalabrini contends that countrywomen did not wear underwear, only an undershirt, often a hand-me-down from the woman's husband or a wool shirt

---

[24] On the regime's legislative and financial support of O.N.M.I. outreach to the *mondine*, see Cioccetti.

[25] According to Antonietta Chierici, Silvana Mangano, star of the 1949 neorealist film *Riso amaro* (*Bitter Rice*), discussed menstruation and working conditions with Chierici's mother and other *mondine* while filming. Chierici states that the topic arose when the cast suspended filming for the week of Mangano's menses, on the assumption that working in the water would risk her health. She notes Mangano's surprise that the *mondine* continued to work throughout the month, and her admiration for their ability to do so (5).

[26] Scalabrini's account is rare in its detailed descriptions of menstruation, miscarriage, and abortion. As such, I use it as a key to unlock other accounts that use more coded language to describe these processes and events. In terms of inducing abortion, many other *mondine* refer to taking parsley tisanes and "helping things along."

when it was cold. She points to underwear as a semi-visible marker of social status: "I grandi mutandoni legati in vita, ricamati e di mussola di lino leggero, erano riservati a categorie di donne che non avevano bisogno di andare nei campi" ("The big underwear tied at the waist, embroidered and of light muslin linen, was reserved for categories of women who didn't need to go to the fields" 12). Regardless of whether women's periods stopped or continued during the *monda*, in their writings former *mondine* cast menstruation as an economic concern, and its cessation as a direct consequence of their physical labors.

For the *mondine*, each birth was embedded in local systems of politics, economics, and social class that stood metonymically for national frameworks of power and control. Women negotiated these systems by making use of the gendered tools at their disposal, namely, their employers' lack of knowledge of the female body and their friendship with the other *mondine*. As Scalabrini recalled her mother's situation and her own birth, she writes,

[…] stavo per nascere ma lei testarda non avendo dolori continua a lavorare, tanto che il sior Padron dalle braghe bianche per paura che partorisse in risaia la mandò a casa, appena il tempo di lavarsi e mettersi a letto, io senza levatrice sono nata, quando le sue amiche mondine finito il lavoro passando per la finesta, 'cosa hai fatto? … mamma orgogliosa alle amiche dicendo, è femmina … *negra come un topon*! [Mantuan dialect]... E per tutti sono sempre stata la negra perché molto scura di pelle, come sono nata velocemente la mia vita è sempre stata di corsa …

(4)

([…] I was about to be born, but she, stubborn, not having pains continued to work, up to the point where the landowner, wearing white shorts [this appellation comes from a popular *mondina* song], fearing that she would give birth in the rice field, sent her home, just in time to wash and get into bed, I was born without a midwife, when her rice worker friends having finished work passed below the window, 'What did you have?' … mamma, proud, said to her friends, it's a girl … black as a mouse [dialect].' And to everyone I have always been the black one because [I am] very dark of skin; just as I was born quickly, my life has always been in a hurry.)

Scalabrini's testimonial speaks to three themes that characterize numerous *mondine*'s first-hand accounts of their and others' pregnancies and births. First, female workers and male overseers negotiate the timing and conditions of birth, the former by withholding information about the duration of the pregnancy and the latter by early termination of the work without pay.[27] Second, the narrative casts the circumstances of the birth as formative of personal identity. In Scalabrini's case, she uses the speed of her birth to account for her life's frenetic pace, using material conditions to account for characteristics and tendencies, all anchored within her family mythology. And finally, the collective nature of

---

[27] Later, a law was established barring women from working the fields while pregnant. See "Stralcio contratto monda," Article 5, "Iscrizione della mano d'opera," p. 3 in Minardi, index.

female friendship among the *mondine* reaches beyond the fields. Those bonds provide a traveling version of the state of local culture forged in the *risaia*, allowing women to invert the social value of traditional dichotomies. When Scalabrini's mother celebrates her dark-skinned female child using the local dialect, she inverts the associated value of gender, class, and racial categories. In a small way, she uses the advent of her daughter's birth to rewrite pervasive social values at the level of the country village.

As the story of Scalabrini's birth suggests, many women wanted to restrict their fertility for economic reasons, citing the importance of practicality in the face of emotional distress. For the *mondine*, an ill-timed pregnancy could imperil their work opportunities. When women did abort, they often went to the fields to do so, adding another inflection to the question of women's fertility and production in the rice fields. Further, poverty and lack of access to birth control often trumped legislation, for many came to work in the fields even while pregnant, sometimes resulting in spontaneous miscarriages in the fields. Scalabrini recalled that a neighbor who worked as a *mondina* had given birth to seventeen children, seven of whom survived; compared to the thirty-seven pregnancies she had had, the seven survivors "non erano un gran numero ... Abortiva silenziosamente nei campi dove andava a giornata a zappare la terra" ("wasn't a large number ... she miscarried silently in the fields where she went to hoe the earth according to her daily contract") (12). Scalabrini's neighbor may have chosen to miscarry in the field at night both for reasons of privacy and to avoid the inevitable cleanup. Along these lines, she also draws out the connection between countrywomen's clothing and their practices regarding miscarriages: "Senza mutande era facile, in caso di aborto spontaneo, far cadere i piccoli feti sulla terra nuda dove erano nascoste tra le zolle con un pietoso colpo di zappa e, spesso, con un profondo sospiro di sollievo per quella gravidanza spontaneamente interrotta" ("Without underwear it was easy, in the case of a natural miscarriage, to let the little fetuses fall on the naked earth where they were hidden among dirt clumps with a piteous turn of the hoe, and, often, with a profound sigh of relief for that suddenly interrupted pregnancy" 12). After all, each birth for a *mondina* extracted a double burden, another mouth to feed plus wages lost from missing the *monda*. But Scalabrini's vocabulary points to the angst threaded through the relief of miscarriage. Although the setting of a darkened, vacant field allows her the option of ignoring the infants' bodies, Scalabrini focuses in on the "little fetuses." This two-word characterization shuns euphemistic darkness in favor of description of the body size and stage of development. This directness illuminates this sentence as an amphiboly: a listener with any knowledge of miscarriage would recognize it as anything but "easy." By dividing her audience between those knowledgeable and those ignorant of the physical strain of miscarriage, Scalabrini creates solidarity with the first group by conveying shared knowledge of the female body in doubled language that only this group will understand. In this way, Scalabrini's account exemplifies the complex verbal coding that many *mondine* use to critique those who view the female, working-class bodies as inherently robust and insensate by signaling the physical, emotional, and economic tolls of fertility to an audience capable of hearing such a message.

Along these lines, some women considered a pause in their cycle to be a welcome relief from frequent pregnancies. Laura Scalabrini recalled her mother's reaction to her fifth pregnancy: "Sperò con tutte le forze in un aborto spontaneo e per [...] agevolarlo saltò dalla sedia, faticò nei campi e come era d'uso bevve anche un infuso di prezzemolo" ("She hoped with all her might for a miscarriage, and to [...] help it along she jumped from the chair, worked in the fields and, as was the custom, drank an infusion of parsley" 24). The child was eventually born, only to die days later. For years after, Scalabrini's mother dreamt of carrying the live child to a cemetery, leaving her there alone and ignoring the girl's tiny arms as they flailed in silent protest against the closed gates. It is important to note that Scalabrini's tisane is not unique to the *mondine*; the beverage makes shadow appearances across a number of women's accounts of the Fascist period, regardless of social class. This suggests that a common body of folk wisdom concerning abortion existed, and that women responded to unwanted pregnancies in their own kitchens by drinking tea to prepare for abortion in the fields. And indeed, the space of the kitchen served as a key site of regime intervention in the home and daily practices.[28] The fact that women induced abortion in this room, either by drinking tea or jumping from the kitchen chair suggests that women made use of this space not only for cooking for, and eating with their families, but also for the most private and personal engagements in questions of consumption, both of tea to induce abortion, and more largely, to end the potential for a life.

Rehearsing for Revolt
While a diverse network of workers' groups and cultural historians has documented the oral history of the *mondine*, few scholars have studied the trove of songs, testimonials, and interview transcripts. In the second section of this article, I hope to contribute a feminist cultural history perspective to the seminal anthropological accounts and ethnomusicological studies of Franco Castelli, Emilio Jona, Alberto Lovatto, and Nunzia Manicardi. In the *mondine*'s songs, the issue of blended authorship, in terms of both lyrics and melody, speaks to the broader issues of women's cultural production, individual voice within a choral collectivity, and the contested definitions regarding the origins and ownership of nationally valued goods. Many of the *mondine*'s songs predate the 1930s; some can be traced back as far as pre-Unification Italy. Their provenance is similarly diverse: some songs derive from tavern songs ("Sul ponte di Verona" "On Verona's Bridge" [Ente Nazionale Risi, Milan]); others from Socialist hymns ("Sebben che siamo donne" "Although We Are Women" [Ente Nazionale Risi, Milan]); still others from work song traditions ("Mondarisi" "Rice Weeders"

---

[28] See Helstosky's *Garlic and Oil*; "Fascist Food Politics"; and "Recipe for the Nation."

[Ente Nazionale Risi, Milan]). But women did not simply repeat those songs. Instead, they consciously and actively changed the lyrics, adapting them to privilege female perspectives and themes. Often, the *mondine* used an older piece of music as a frame on which to hang new words. Finding a new use for old melodies is a typical mode of song (re)creation in the popular Italian tradition. In the words of ethnomusicologist Placida Staro, "L'aria melodica [...] rappresenta un'armatura interna metrico-ritmica per la costruzione di 'nuovi' testi" ("The melodic aria [...] represents an internal metric-rhythmic scaffolding for the construction of 'new' texts," Staro 43). As such, one cannot claim that the *mondine*'s songs were exclusively authored or composed by the *mondine*. Rather, the *mondine* made use of pre-existing song structures and shaped them to fit their own needs, evoking a specifically rural, female, working-class genre of cultural production. Over a period that could range from hours to years, and over distances that encompassed the whole of Northern Italy, the *mondine* edited old songs to the point of creating new ones. Traditional notions of authorship simply did not apply.

Because of the difficult conditions in the fields, women were physically uncomfortable and thus very aware of their bodies as they worked. In other words, the physical labor of rice weeding made the female body loud. It is unsurprising then that the place and type of labor shaped, and were in turn shaped by, the musical tradition. Song lyrics describe the environment in the fields and their toll on the *mondine*, as noted in the references to insects and tormented vocatives of "mamma mia" in "Bella ciao." This focus on the interplay of place and person characterizes the *mondine*'s songs as a group. They render connections of place and body as a minute and specific catalogue of the associations of rice weeding work, like bent backs and repetitive movements, as well as the effects of environmental factors like dampness, cold, strain, glare, insects, and water snakes. Frequently used musical keys and percussive elements reflect the conditions under which the songs were sung. Because the *mondine* sang while bent over the the rice fields, choruses are generally sung in the *ambito di una quinta* (Sib4-Fa4), and more rarely in the eighth (Lab3-Sol4). These keys allow for singing despite prolonged diaphragm constriction (Staro 46). Percussive elements originated from the repeated slapping of mosquitoes on the women's legs which the women incorporated into the songs at regular intervals. Smacks, claps, and slaps converted the environmental hazards of the rice fields into some of the characteristic features of *mondine* music. Sting transformed into song.

Unlike other song traditions based on the male experience of agricultural work, the *mondine*'s musical tradition emphasizes the trials of gendered labor, such as cooking with few resources, and sexual labor, encompassing both childbirth within marriage and the travails of prostitution.[29] Songs refer to sexually transmitted diseases ("Quando avevo quindic'anni" "When I was Fifteen" [Castelli 315]); infanticide ("Cara Adele" "Dear Adele" [250]; "L'infanticida," "Infanticide" [279]); and violence against prostitutes ("Il ventinove luglio" "July 29th" [338]) as well as common themes such as seduction and abandonment, the domestic cage ("Bell'uccialin dal bosc," "Beautiful bird of the woods" [Staro 94]) and the frustrated sexual desires of women at or past middle age ("Ho quarant'anni compiuti "I have lived forty years" [276]). Although some ethnomusicologists and folklorists have attempted to organize the *mondine*'s song corps by dividing songs into typologies based on predominant song themes (love, politics, work), genres (comic, heroic, tragic), and antecedents (tavern song, political rally song), such typologies mischaracterize the songs by imposing the categories that they mean to describe.[30] *Mondine* testimonies suggest that such categorization inserts anachronistic concepts of theme that reflect academics' conceptions of the *mondine,* but ignores the *mondine*'s opinions. Further, theme and genre do not exist in isolation: gender, class, and politics typically collide in a single song, rendering ad hoc separations illusory. And finally, the boundaries of the musical tradition, and the songs themselves, are porous and flexible, because the *mondine* shaped these songs over time and place.

"Son la mondina" exemplifies the *mondine*'s creative use of temporal drift in its alternating invocations of past political events and possible visions of the future. In the case of "Son la mondina," the reverberations of the famous *mondine* strike of 1909 for the eight-hour workday resound throughout the song. The lyric "with our bodies under the wheels" refers to the *mondine*'s effective protest tactics in shutting down the Northern Italian railway system "from Vercellese to Molinella," as memorably captured by illustrator Achille Beltrame for the cover of the popular newspaper *Domenica del Corriere* (Fig. 5).

Son la mondina, son la sfruttata	*I am the rice-weeder, I am the exploited*
Son la mondina, son la sfruttata,	I am the rice-weeder, I am the exploited,
son la proletaria che giammai tremò:	I am the proletariat that never trembled;
mi hanno uccisa, incatenata,	they killed me and chained me.
carcere e violenza, nulla mi fermò,	prison and violence, nothing stopped me.
Coi nostri corpi sulle rotaie,	With our bodies on the train tracks,

---

[29] The economic disadvantages that pushed women into the rice fields required them to assume what was, for both local townsfolk and for the *mondine* themselves, a symbolic position of female sexual submission and abandon as well. Although very few *mondine* engaged in prostitution themselves, the group nonetheless explored these themes in their songs. Like prostitutes, the *mondine* bore a stereotype for promiscuity. Living outside of the family house away from male supervision likely contributed to this label (Castelli 488).
[30] Both Jona and Castelli rely heavily on categorization to organize their song catalogues and analysis. For foundational examples of these typologies, see Jona, *Le canzonette che fecero l'Italia* and "Sul cantare in risaia." See also Castelli, Jona, and Lovatto.

noi abbiam fermato i nostri sfruttator;	we have stopped our exploiters,
c'è molto fango sulle risaie,	there is so much mud in the rice fields,
ma non porta macchie il simbol del lavor,	but the symbol of our work carries no stain.
E lotteremo per il lavoro,	And we will fight for our work,
per la pace, il pane e per la libertà,	for peace, bread, and liberty,
e creeremo un mondo nuovo	and we will build a new world
di giustizia e di nuova civiltà.	of justice and true civilization.
Questa bandiera gloriosa e bella	This flag glorious and beautiful,
noi l'abbiam raccolta e la portiam più in su	we have picked it up and carried it higher,
dal Vercellese a Molinella,	from the Vercelli region to Molinella,
alla testa della nostra gioventù.	ahead of all our youth.
E se qualcuno vuol far la guerra,	And if anyone wants to make war,
tutti uniti insieme noi lo fermerem:	all united together we will stop him:
vogliam la pace sulla terra	we want peace on earth
e più forti dei cannoni noi sarem.	and stronger than cannons we will be.
(Ultima strofa di un'altra versione)	(Final verse of an alternate version)
Ed ai padroni farem la guerra.	And we will make war on landowners.
Tutti uniti insieme noi vincerem.	All united together we will win.
Non più sfruttati sulla terra,	No longer exploited on the earth
ma più forti dei cannoni noi sarem.	But stronger than cannons we will be.

Recurrent references to this early strike point to its enduring significance for the *mondine*. The emotional relevance of this event stemmed in part from its physical manifestation of female political collectivity created with the body. As Beltrame's rendering and "Son la mondina"'s invocation of this dramatic episode suggest, the *mondine*'s decision to make their voices heard by using their bodies to obstruct the machinery of production presented a heightened moment when the singularity of the individual's body melded into the collective body politic. The steam-powered train — a single, powerful entity — suggests the ramrod approach of the landowner, dehumanized in his machine-like approach to labor. By contrast, the women appear as discrete individuals with unique facial expressions, collectively engaged in a group effort. The train also evokes the larger system of rice distribution and consumption in which the *mondine*'s productive labor was inscribed. As discussed in the next section, the regime's propagandistic rice trains carried this foodstuff to Southern Italy as an economic inducement to change regional food ways for the benefit of the national autarchic project. Women objected to riding to and from the rice fields in the *carri bestiame* because riding the stock cars inherently associated the *mondine* with the farm animals normally transported in these wagons. Put more broadly, women contested this mode of transport not only for reasons of physical comfort, but also because of their sense of dignity and human value. This protest's potent blend of the concrete and the symbolic gained further intensity in its reversal of traditional dichotomies: the old-fashioned over the modern, the rural over the urban, the lower class over the upper, and, most significantly, the female over the male, as Beltrame hints with the imaginative addition of the *capo*'s phallic *bastone* in the hands of the *mondine*. In general, such upendings suggest a David and Goliath parable, with the relatively less powerful party ultimately triumphant in halting the local Northern Italian train schedule and gaining the eight-hour workday.

"Son la mondina" provides a case study for the relationship between the individual and the group in its exploration of the relationship between the singer and the chorus through personal and vocal doubling. In the first two verses of the song "Son la mondina, son la sfruttata" ("I am the rice weeder, I am the exploited") the repetition of "son" ("I am") casts the narrative as a personal story stemming from the first-hand work experience. But it also casts the song content as a larger issue of class and labor struggles, as in the charged word *sfruttata*, "exploited." The first person voice, that of a *proletaria*, includes all the women in a similar condition. The "us" contrasts against the plural: *i nostri sfruttator*, our exploiters: the anonymous group who "killed" and "chained" the *mondine*. While these two violent verbs appear in the *passato prossimo* form, indicating recent past actions, the *mondina* or *mondine*'s refusal to stop (*fermò*) or even tremble (*tremò*) occur in the *passato remoto*, indicating a more distant, perhaps even historic, temporal phase. The *sfruttator*'s actions and the *sfruttata*'s reactions are, as these nominal forms suggest, intimately connected as forms of cause and effect. But by differentiating these past actions into additional chronological forms, the lyrics assign different historical values to the actors' actions based on the role they played in this event. The *passato remoto* consecrates the *mondine*'s actions as historic and thus significant, even as they relegate their catalyst, the killing and chaining by their exploiters, to the sphere of the recent everyday, which still affects all the *mondine*.[31] By filtering events from the same temporal period through two different verb forms, the song elevates female protest to the realm of the heroic, neatly overturning gendered historical traditions that emphasize the importance of national events and the names of great men at the expense of lived history and its daily struggles.

And yet, when narrating the events of the strike itself, the collective "we" of the *mondine* shifts to the *passato prossimo*: "Coi nostri corpi sulle rotaie, / noi abbiam fermato i nostri sfruttator." The reference to this bodily action must have resonated with the *mondine* as they sang this song under a great deal of physical stress in the rice fields. But, furthermore, they speak to the broader value of these labors and to the ever-present possibility of revolt by pointing to a successful past strike.[32] These temporal shifts underscore the idea that the past creates the present, and the future too. In a cohesive temporal progression from past to present to

---

[31] The song also relies on two verbs in the *passato prossimo* to describe the *mondine*.
[32] Zappi, "The First Results of Mobilization" and "Years of Progress, Years of Action, 1903-1906," in *If Eight Hours Seem too Few* (100-66).

future, the Socialist utopia of the final stanza appears built on the struggles of the common historical past established by the first two stanzas of the song. This oral history lesson also provides a course in civics by instructing the young *mondine* in the history of this particular social group, igniting intergenerational solidarity among the newly arrived and more experienced *mondine*.

This song plays out that progression in miniature. Having established the common historical past of the *mondina*, the collective "we" reemerges in more strident terms. Whereas the first stanza uses the first person pronoun "we" once and the second uses the possessive adjective "our" twice, a single line in the fifth stanza emphasizes the collective in each word choice, "Tutti uniti insieme noi lo fermerem" ("All united together we will stop him")." With five out of six words in this verse indicating collectivity, the *sfruttator* are completely surrounded. As such, this song exemplifies the metonymic collectivity common to both the *mondine*'s songs and first-person testimonials wherein the singer is at once a real individual and the archetypal *mondina*, a general or typical character exemplifying all the female workers' toils and aspirations.

In addition to the song's lyrical content, the history of the song also reflects the contested nature of origins and authorship. At stake is the question of the nature of production: is it an isolated moment or a continual process of negotiation and renewal? Castelli's account of the song's origins and reworkings suggests the latter. In his history of "Son la mondina," Castelli notes that Pietro Besate wrote the lyrics in the 1950s for the Federbraccianti workers' meeting, fitting them to the music of "E la rondinella la va per aria" ("And the swallow goes up into the air"), an older popular song (Castelli 417). However, many *mondine* incorporate snatches of this song in direct quotations of jokes and laments in their memories of the 1920s and 1930s, which suggests that either antecedents of the song could be found by those dates, or that the song already existed in its entirety and that Besate simply transcribed the song, as many male political organizers and folk song writers of the 1950s and 1960s also did. As Castelli himself notes, this song enjoyed a particularly widespread popularity across Northern Italy (417). And the authorship of popular songs, associated with the *mondine* or with other groups, is extremely difficult to determine because of their oral rather than written origins, a fact which also plays a role in the continual nature of their revisions.

The act of rewriting was not simply tacitly permitted but actively welcomed by the other *mondine*, for whom lyric borrowing was equated to invention rather than plagiarism. Many *mondine* make jokes and asides by lightly changing the lyrics, even in spoken and written conversation. Ermanna Chiozzi, for instance, makes a joke that turns on the reader's knowledge of the standard opening of "Son la mondina" to speak to her experience of being exploited. She recounts a personally significant episode in which the wind blew her straw hat off her head while at work in the rice paddies. She left the weeding line to chase after it, and for this infraction the *padrone* fired her immediately. She wryly sums up the episode with a twist in the song lyrics, "Son la mondina, son la licenziata," ("I am the rice weeder. I am the fired one" 19). In addition to tiny but intentional changes that dramatically shifted song meaning, unintentional changes also occurred naturally because of the way that these songs were used in the fields. On this microscopic scale, musical recycling evolved to cultural creation.

Singing Truth to Power
Through song and story, the *mondine* bore witness to the physical and emotional toll of rice weeding, a central form of autarchic food production and thus a key plank in the Fascist platform of economic self-sufficiency. In defiance of state demands for increased production of rice and infants, the *mondine* made use of the cloaking and amplifying properties of choruses and solos to assert their bodily autonomy. By recording their counter-history to the Fascist party line through the gestures and sayings of daily work, the *mondine* voiced resistance and rehearsed revolt, speaking truth to Fascist power. Because many historians of the Fascist period have focused on women's role as consumers, this article has endeavored to address the question of how women's role as producers of food fits into national questions of female agency and political identity.

There are many different ways to feed the nation: directly, by cooking and serving food, and indirectly, by producing the raw ingredients. When the *mondine* provided food sanctioned by the regime for the nation through agricultural production, they held a symbolic role as nurturers. In the realm of rice weeding, the *mondine* not only provided the rice necessary to feed a nation but they also earned several kilograms of it to bring home to their families as part of their payment. This form of doubled feeding of nation and family revealed several awkward contradictions within the Fascist party. First, the social conservatism of the Italian Fascist party claimed that a woman's place was in the home, but strongly supported using a predominantly female labor force in the fields for economic reasons. In this particular case, economics overturned ideology. The cheapest labor force won the contracts to produce a crucial foodstuff. Second, pronatalist rhetoric celebrated the high fertility of the Italian country women but working in the fields temporarily suspended women's fertility. Not only were they away from men for this period, but the difficult labor conditions suppressed menstruation. And finally, the Fascist party celebrated the *mondine* as a positive symbol for rurality, tradition, and sacrifice, even though the majority of *mondine* voted Socialist or Communist because of their identification with the international working class. This last point is particularly relevant to the study of the *mondine* within the larger political context of the day.[33] What does it mean to be celebrated by the state as a human symbol of ideas that you reject?

---

[33] During the early 1920s, Fascist interference with Italian electoral law diminished the power of proportional representation, allowing Mussolini to consolidate his hold on the government. The Acerbo Law, passed in November 1923, assigned two thirds of parliamentary seats to the party with the largest share, rather than total number, of votes.

"Singing Truth to Power" looks at this question from the point of view of the workers themselves in order to avoid taking the regime's symbolism at its word. Contrary to the fulsome images of National Rice Board propaganda, the *mondine* did not, in fact, celebrate their iconographic designation as the bearers of an idealized national past, refreshed for the future with a lick of make-up on National Rice Day. Their resistance to this designation played out in both symbolic and literal terms. In the 1930s, as a chorus, the *mondine* sang work songs to condemn the working conditions of the rice fields and their devastating effects on the female body. Using these tactics, women practiced rebellion in collaboration, out in the fields away from normal pressures to conform to state dictates. Later, as individuals, many *mondine* wrote first-hand accounts of their time in the rice fields, recording individual counter-narratives that, collectively, provide a dictionary of specifics to support the generalities of the songs. And in doing so, they brought their wrenching reproductive choices, born of poverty, into the light.

Cornell University

Works Cited

Borgatti, Mario. *Canti popolari emiliani: raccolti a cento*. Firenze: L. S. Olschki, 1962.

Castelli, Franco, Emilio Jona, and Alberto Lovatto. *Senti le rane che cantano: canzoni e vissuti popolari della risaia*. Roma: Donzelli, 2005.

Celli, Carlo. *Economic Fascism: Primary Sources on Mussolini's Crony Capitalism*. New York: Axios Press, 2013.

Chierici, Antonietta. "Mia madre: una donna dell'Emilia," 1920-1960. Transcript of manuscript MP/Adn2 05024, Archivio dei Diari, Pieve Santo Stefano, 1960.

Cinotto, Simone. "Memories of the Italian Rice Belt, 1945-65: Work, Class Conflict and Intimacy during the 'Great Transformation.'" *Journal of Modern Italian Studies* 16.4 (2011): 531-52.

Cioccetti, Urbano. "Il finanziamento," *Esperienze e prospettive dell'O. N. M. I.* Roma: Opera Nazionale Maternità e Infanzia, 1956. 38-60.

Corsi, Pietro. *La tutela della maternità e dell'infanzia in Italia*. Roma: Società Editrice di novissima, 1936.

Cortelazzo, Manilio and Paolo Zolli. "Mondina," *l'Etimologico della lingua Italiana* Bologna: Zanichelli editore, 2004.

Forgacs, David, and Stephen Gundle. *Mass Culture and Italian Society From Fascism to the Cold War*. Bloomington: Indiana UP, 2007.

Helstosky, Carol. "Fascist Food Politics: Mussolini's Policy of Alimentary Sovereignty." *Journal of Modern Italian Studies* 9.1 (2004): 1-26.

_____. *Garlic and Oil: Politics and Food in Italy*. Oxford: Berg, 2004.

_____. "Recipe for the Nation: Reading Italian History through *La scienza in cucina* and *La cucina futurista*." *Food and Foodways* 11.2 (2013): 113-40.

Horn, David G. *Social Bodies: Science, Reproduction, and Italian Modernity*. Princeton: Princeton UP, 1994.

Ipsen, Carl. *Dictating Demography: The problem of population in Fascist Italy*. New York: Cambridge UP, 1996.

Jona, Emilio. *Le canzonette che fecero l'Italia*. Milano: Longanesi, 1963.

_____. "Sul cantare in risaia." *Colture e culture del riso: una prospettiva storica.* Ed. Simone Cinotto. Vercellese: Edizioni Mercurio, 2002.

Lo Monaco-Aprile, Attilio. *Protezione della maternità e dell'infanzia.* Roma: Istituto nazionale fascista di cultura, 1934.

Manicardi, Nunzia. *Il coro delle mondine: immagini e canti dalle risaie padane.* Modena: Il Fiorino, 1998.

Marabini, A. "La mezzadria in Italia." *Lo stato operiao.* March 1936. 219.

Marcus, Millicent. "Miss Mondina, Miss Sirena, Miss Farina: The Feminized Body-Politic from *Bitter Rice* to *La voce della luna*." *RLA: Romance Languages Annual* 4 (1992): 296-300.

Minardi, Marco. *La fatica delle donne: storie di mondine.* Roma: Ediesse, 2005.

Passerini, Luisa. *Fascism in Popular Memory: The Cultural Experience of the Turin Working Class.* Cambridge, UK: Cambridge UP, 1987.

Ruberto, Laura E. *Gramsci, Migration, and the Representation of Women's Work in Italy and the U.S.* Blue Ridge Summit, PA: Lexington Books, 2007.

Scalabrini, Laura. "Sette pater ave e gloria," 1927-1990. Transcript of manuscript MP/10 06139, Archivio dei Diari, Pieve Santo Stefano, 2010.

Schmidt, Carl T. "Agricultural Property and Enterprise Under Italian Fascism." *Science & Society* 1.3 (1937): 326–49.

Squeri, Lawrence. "Who Benefited from Italian Fascism: A Look at Parma's Landowners." *Agricultural History* 64.1 (1990): 18-38.

Staro, Placida. *Lasciateci passare siamo le donne: il canto delle mondine di Bentivoglio.* Udine: Nota, 2009.

Thompson, Alistair, Michael Frisch, and Paula Hamilton. "The Memory and History Debates: Some International Perspectives." *Oral History* 22.2 (1994): 33-43.

Thompson, Edward Palmer. "History from Below." *The Times Literary Supplement* April 7, 1966): 279-80.

Willson, Perry. *Peasant Women and Politics in Fascist Italy: The Massaie Rurali.* London: Routledge, 2002.

Zappi, Elda Gentili. *If Eight Hours Seem too Few: Mobilization of Women Workers in the Italian Rice Fields.* Albany: State University of New York Press, 1991.

Fig. 1 Photo cutout for propagandistic collages, Crescentino, Italy, 1932, in folder *Milano: Ente Nationale del Riso, Contributi del Duce per l'assistenza alle Mondariso* (ACS, PCM, 1934-1936, b. 509.488, f. 2).

Singing Truth to Power: Melodic Resistance & Bodily Revolt in Italy's Rice Fields 397

Fig. 2 Partially completed propagandistic collage, Crescentino, Italy, 1932, in folder *Milano: Ente Nationale del Riso, Contributi del Duce per l'assistenza alle Mondariso* (ACS, PCM, 1934-1936, b. 509.488, f. 2).

Fig. 3 "Il Duce Trebbia il Riso," "The Duce Threshes Rice" completed propagandistic collage, Melegnano, Italy, 1934, in folder *Milano: Ente Nationale del Riso, Contributi del Duce per l'assistenza alle Mondariso* (ACS, PCM, 1934-1936, b. 509.488, f. 2).

Singing Truth to Power: Melodic Resistance & Bodily Revolt in Italy's Rice Fields 399

Fig. 4 "Il Duce Trebbia il Riso," "The Duce Threshes Rice" completed propagandistic collage, Melegnano, Italy, 1934, in folder *Milano: Ente Nationale del Riso, Contributi del Duce per l'assistenza alle Mondariso* (ACS, PCM, 1934-1936, b. 509.488, f. 2).

Fig. 5 Newspaper illustration of the Rice Weeders' May 26, 1909 protest, drawn by Achille Beltrame, caption reads, "Dal Vercellese a Molinella," "From Vercellese to Molinella," a reference to the train line running through the heart of Italy's rice belt, successfully blocked by the *mondine* protesting for the 8-hour work day. (*Domenica del Corriere* [June 6, 1909])

Alan Perry

Giovannino's "Libertà":
Guareschi's Personal Freedom in Opposition to Power

Abstract: Through personal testament, written word, and illustration, Giovannino Guareschi successfully resisted Nazi brutality as a prisoner of war, opposed the Communist party in the Italian *dopoguerra*, and denounced the high-handed Christian Democratic leadership of Alcide DeGasperi. His primary *Novecento* legacy centers on his consistent non-violent call for the dictates of personal conscience to triumph the abuses of those who wielded power.

Key Words: Italian Resistance; storytelling; conscience; Nazi-fascists; *dopoguerra*; Communists; political cartoons; humor; 1948 Italian general election; short story; Don Camillo; Peppone; Talking Crucifix; libel; De Gasperi; imprisonment.

"Libertà è dovunque vive un uomo che si sente libero" avevo scritto su un cartoncino appeso al muro della mia cella. Adesso, nella mia stanza delle Roncole, ho appeso al muro lo stesso cartoncino aggiornato: "Libertà è soltanto là dove vive un uomo che si sente libero."

(Giovannino Guareschi)[1]

Guareschi Speaks up to Power: The Experience of the Lager
Most scholars and the general public know of Giovannino Guareschi through the immense success of his *Mondo piccolo* anthologies that have sold millions of copies worldwide.[2] But more than his accomplishments as a journalist of popular literature, he deserves greater recognition as an unfaltering proponent of speaking truth to power. Indeed, we can view so much of his personal actions and life's work, especially during World War II and the *dopoguerra*, from this perspective. Guareschi was a superb storyteller who saw humor as a weapon of reason used to champion the primacy of conscience and individual freedom. In crafting entertaining tales, vignettes, and newspaper editorials, he sought to awaken readers to appreciate their ability to think for themselves as a way to counter potential abuses of power. In this study, beyond discussing this point,

---

[1] I am thankful for this opportunity to write about Guareschi as a stalwart advocate for speaking truth to power, and in this study I integrate several paragraphs from my previous works undertaken during these last fifteen years, which are listed under Works Cited.

[2] Indeed, according to a few sources, Guareschi is Italy's most translated author of the Novecento (Bocca 34; Dossena 25), and the cinematic lore of *Mondo piccolo* screen adaptations further bolster Guareschi's fame. Italian television stations frequently broadcast Don Camillo movies, and the cantankerous priest remains an endearing character in Italian popular culture (Romano 439).

Annali d'italianistica 34 (2016). *Speaking Truth to Power from Medieval to Modern Italy*

we will specifically explore his non-violent opposition to Nazi tyranny, Communist politics, and Christian Democratic leadership in the figure of Alcide De Gasperi. Guareschi's most important legacy as a Novecento writer and public figure finds its deepest root in this resistance.

On 9 September 1943, after Italy's Armistice with the Allies, German forces captured Guareschi, who was serving on active duty in Piedmont as a Lieutenant of Artillery. He had been forced to return to military duty several months prior in order to avoid serving jail time: in a drunken stupor upon finding out in October 1942 that his brother had been killed in Russia — an erroneous report as it turned out — he caused a ruckus and cursed Mussolini's regime. Angelo Rizzoli, who employed Guareschi as an editor of his humorous weekly *Bertoldo*, convinced fascist authorities to be lenient on him by recalling him to arms in lieu of incarceration.[3] With the Armistice, Guareschi honored his military oath made to Vittorio Emmanuele III, but he refused to swear allegiance to the Third Reich. Shortly thereafter he was shipped by train, along with more than five thousand other former Italian soldiers, first to Poland and then to Germany. Since Italy had not declared war on its former ally (a decision the Badoglio government takes on October 13, 1943), the Germans classified Guareschi and the other Italians they captured as Internati Militari Italiani (IMI) instead of Prisoners of War, rendering void their 1929 Geneva Convention rights. As internees, therefore, the International Red Cross could not provide Italian soldiers adequate assistance, and the rules governing imprisonment did not apply (Nello, "La resistenza clandestina" 147).

To cope with the tribulations of prison life, Guareschi maintained a diary and several notebooks in which he captured his daily activities, psychological state, and musings on the meaning of his captivity that he then would share with fellow inmates in the form of public lectures, going from barrack to barrack to raise morale.[4] Guareschi gravitated seamlessly to this activity because of his

---

[3] Guareschi donned his Alpino uniform and was posted to Alessandria where he received news of the Armistice. As Guareschi shared in a 1946 letter in *Candido*: "Si tratta di un episodio poco onorevole in quanto accade che io, la notte del 14 ottobre 1942 — riempitomi di grappa fino agli occhi in casa di amici — per tornare alla mia casa di via Ciro Menotti che è lontana non più di ottocento metri, impieghi due ore. E in quelle due ore (dall'una alle tre) urlo delle cose che poi l'indomani trovo registrate diligentemente in quattro pagine di protocollo che un importante personaggio di certa U.P.I. mi mostra nel suo ufficio di via Pagano" ("Lettere al Postero" 3).

[4] In one of his prison notebooks ("Quaderni del lager"), Guareschi gave full expression to his sense of isolation and frustration upon capture, deportation, and internment. Mussolini's government chose not to help them, and the International Red Cross did not have the right to provide assistance: "Tutti si dimenticarono di noi. Nessuno ci rivolse mai una parola, nessuno dimostrò d'accorgersi della nostra cupa situazione. Avevamo bisogno di qualcosa per coprirci, avevamo fame, eravamo senza notizie di casa nostra, molti soffrivano né potevano curarsi per completa mancanza di medicinali: nessuno si

extensive experience in journalism and radio broadcasting. After the war, he published many of his reflections of this experience in his *Diario clandestino* (1949). Forty years later his children published more of his writings in *Ritorno alla base* (1989), and then in 2008 they released *Il grande diario*, a thorough integration of their father's IMI diary and notebooks.

In his lectures to his IMI companions, Guareschi spoke of everything, from hunger and longing to see his children to his conception of humor, holding in all eighty-three of these encounters, an average of one a week (Bertellini 8). Together with other enterprising prisoners, he helped to form a culture of resistance that aimed to protect human dignity and stiffen the resolve to persevere. These interventions represent a full-fledged example of how Guareschi spoke truth to power and urged others to do the same. Indeed, the minute and dwindling numbers of surviving Italian ex-prisoners, now in their mid-nineties, often recall Guareschi as the "cantore collettivo" of their travails (Nello 44).

As Guareschi later reflected in his preface to the *Diario clandestino*, in prison the inmates were worse than abandoned: "[...] si ritrovò soltanto con le cose che aveva dentro. Con la sua effettiva ricchezza o con la sua effettiva povertà" (XV). Out of meager means, they built a democratic existence:

Non abbiamo vissuto come i bruti. [...] Sorsero i giornali parlati, le conferenze, la chiesa, l'università, il teatro, i concerti, le mostre d'arte, lo sport, l'artigianato, le assemblee regionali, i servizi, la borsa, gli annunci economici, la biblioteca, il centro radio, il commercio, l'industria.

(XV)

Nevertheless, as his diary entries attest, he suffered terrible bouts of homesickness and boredom. And yet, in spite of the loneliness, deprivations, and deplorable conditions in the *lager*, he began to comprehend that humor was not a literary genre "ma un modo particolare d'intendere la vita" (64). Although imprisoned, he thought that if he and his fellow prisoners could assign positive meaning to events in the present, they would not be subjected to interpretations shaped by others in the future (64).

Through humor, Guareschi began to fathom that he wielded a reasoning power that could allow him to remain free even if he was held prisoner. In a lecture entitled "Finalmente libero," for example, Guareschi conveyed how the Germans may have entrapped his physical body but that his "other self," his conscience or soul, was ultimately free (164-65), and in "Signora Germania," he leveled a diatribe against his captors, brazenly vaunting this freedom. For Guareschi, the hardships his German guards imposed on him did not mean subjection. Rather, they helped him to undergo a conversion of self and to

---

sentì di mandarci un pezzettino di pane, una pasticca per la tosse, che significassero un qualsiasi interessamento. Abbandonati da tutti" (90-91).

discover the priceless gift of his own ability to think and reason for himself, a gift he saw as divine:

> Signora Germania, tu mi hai messo tra i reticolati, e fai la guardia perché io non esca.
> È inutile, signora Germania: io non esco, ma entra chi vuole. Entrano i miei affetti, entrano i miei ricordi.
> E questo è niente ancora, signora Germania: perché entra anche il buon Dio e mi insegna tutte le cose proibite dai tuoi regolamenti.
> Signor Germania, tu ti inquieti con me, ma è inutile. Perché il giorno in cui, presa dall'ira, farai baccano con qualcuna delle tue mille macchine e mi distenderai sulla terra, vedrai che dal mio corpo immobile si alzerà un altro me stesso, più bello del primo. E non potrai mettergli un piastrino al collo perché volerà via, oltre il reticolato, e chi s'è visto s'è visto. L'uomo è fatto così, signora Germania: di fuori è una faccenda molto facile da comandare, ma dentro ce n'è un altro e lo comanda soltanto il Padre Eterno.
> E questa è la fregatura per te, signora Germania.
>
> (41)

Guareschi's realized that the one inviolate freedom the Nazis could never take away from him was his own ability to decide what life's events meant and how he thus chose his own reaction to them.[5]

Infused with this same emotional charge for his supreme freedom, Guareschi implored his fellow inmates in "Ricerca" to refrain from blindly following the whims of the masses when they returned to Italy after the war:

> La verità non si insegna; bisogna scoprirla, conquistarla. Pensare, farsi una coscienza. Non cercare uno che pensi per voi, che vi insegni come dovete essere liberi. [...] Strapparsi dalla massa, dal pensiero collettivo [...] ritrovare in se stessi l'individuo, la coscienza personale.
>
> (182)

In prison, Guareschi came to grasp that personal conscience should always trump any value, cultural movement, or dictates guided by the masses.[6]

---

[5] The spirit expressed in "Signora Germania" provides a nice parallel to Holocaust survivor and psychotherapist Viktor Frankl's words in *Man's Search for Meaning* (1962): "We who lived in the concentration camps can remember the men who walked through the huts comforting others, giving away their last piece of bread. They may have been few in number, but they offer sufficient proof that everything can be taken from a man but one thing: the last of human freedoms — to choose one's attitude in any given circumstances, to choose one's own way" (86).

[6] Guareschi describes the fundamental impact the *lager* had upon him as a journalist in these terms: "La mia scuola di *giornalismo politico* io l'ho fatta in un *Lager*: e migliaia di degni galantuomini che hanno vissuto quei dolorosi giorni assieme a me possono testimoniare come il tenente Guareschi signor Giovannino abbia onorevolmente svolto la sua attività di *giornalista libero, onesto e sereno* dal primo all'ultimo giorno della sua permanenza nel *Lager*. Ho imparato, in quella dura scuola, come sia bello, come sia virile, come sia civile dire pubblicamente ciò che si pensa, specialmente quando ciò comporti un grave rischio. [...] Io ho fatto una severa scuola di *giornalismo politico* e

Imprisonment taught Guareschi about the tremendous power he actually possessed: faithfulness to follow his conscience formed by the reasoning process ultimately guaranteed his personal liberty.

The basis of this awareness authorized him to oppose those in power, and during the war, that meant his German guards. One of the more common forms of storytelling that Guareschi adopted in his lectures was the fairy tale with the incipit "C'era una volta." Most of these stories, however, are not magical or supernatural, nor do they reflect the classical structures, motifs, and elements that many folklorists have identified. Instead, as their titles indicate — "La domenica," "La strada," "Il grammofono," "La ragazza," "Il panettone Motta" and "Il letto" published in *Ritorno alla base* — these tales, nostalgic in tone, describe events, themes, and objects belonging to a world that prisoners could no longer access.[7]

Quite often, these talks played upon hidden meanings and double entendre that even Italian-speaking German guards in attendance could not understand. One former inmate, for example, recalled listening to a lecture:

In fondo allo stanzone, c'era un "Sonderführer", un ufficiale amministrativo della Wehrmacht. Sapeva l'italiano meglio di molti di noi poiché era cresciuto a Firenze, dove, da civile, era insegnante di musica. Giovannino "sfotteva" Hitler, Göbbels, il nazismo, la superiorità degli Ariani biondi. Era una sparatoria di doppi sensi, tutti li capivamo e ridevamo fragorosamente. L'Ufficiale tedesco si guardava attorno un po' seccato, domandandosi tra sé e sé cosa ci fosse da ridere.

(Biscossa 41)

Thus, Guareschi was able to lambaste his captors and let his companions in on the derision.

As he chided his guards, he constantly stressed the point that he and his comrades at all costs had to keep from aiding the Germans. Guareschi wrote two important discourses, "Macchie indelibili" and "La ragione per cui," about the moral stain Italians would incur even by simply helping the Germans to pick ripened cherries (*Ritorno alla base* 40; 59). If they did choose to fight for Mussolini, or even serve the Reich by working in German industries, they would be aiding an enemy who ravished the Italian countryside and terrorized Italians, both partisans and civilians alike. A former internee recalled that Guareschi

---

sono ben convinto che un giornalista veramente libero come io sono deve sempre sostenere la causa che egli, in *piena coscienza*, ritenga giusta, *costi quel che costi*" (*Se ciascun* 20).

[7] As Giovanni Mosca, Guareschi's co-founder of *Candido*, explained: "Le chiamava, queste rievocazioni, favole, tanto erano lontane nel tempo e nello spazio, sì da sembrare irreali o vissute in un'altra vita. [...] Guareschi leggeva, e quasi sempre lo accompagnava una fisarmonica. [...] alla fine, si piangeva nella baracca, si piangeva per la tovaglia, per il calamaio, per i fiammiferi: sì, perché c'erano una volta, in quel paese tanto lontano forse sparito, che si chiamava Italia, anche i fiammiferi ("La lettera" 4).

buoyed their resistance to keep from cooperating with the Germans by once saying, "Non farlo, perché per i tedeschi non bisogna attaccare neanche un francobollo" (Ascari 22). Guareschi himself twice refused to help the Nazis, once with the offer to become a journalist in Berlin and again with the chance to return to Milan and resume his editorial duties with *Bertoldo*, the satirical newspaper he directed before the war.[8] As he wrote several years later, his choice cost him dearly in physical terms — "Allora il mio peso era di chilogrammi 46: peso lordo, compresi i miei stracci, i miei pidocchi, le mie pulci, i miei zoccoli di legno e un magone grosso così" ("La coda di Riccardo" 248) — but, along with his fellow prisoners who opted to remain in prison, they came back "tarati nel corpo ma integri nello spirito" (249).

Guareschi's most inspiring model of denouncing power as a prisoner comes with his 1944 Christmas show, *Favola di Natale*, written and produced in the Sandbostel *lager*. The work, performed as a musical production and later published with illustrations after the war, specifically aimed to mock his German guards and impugn the morally impoverished Nazi regime.[9] With the *Favola*, Guareschi obtained clearance from the censors and conducted a few rehearsals. Opening night took place in the camp's theater on Christmas Eve and

> la sera della vigilia, nella squallida baracca del "teatro", zeppa di gente malinconica, io lessi la favola e l'orchestra, il coro e i cantanti la commentarono egregiamente, e il "rumorista" diede vita ai passaggi più movimentati.
>
> (6)

The narrative action is a dream in which Guareschi's son, Albertino, his pet dog Flick, and Albertino's grandmother, all journey north from Italy, striving to see Giovannino. Along the way they encounter magical animals, trees, and other vegetation that all provide information on how to proceed to the *lager*. At a certain point the crew meets a family of three Sparrows that skips along and sings cheerfully as they carry knapsacks on their shoulders. At the same

---

[8] For an insightful study of Italian internees who chose to swear allegiance to Mussolini or the Reich, see Ferioli.

[9] Guareschi told fables simply because his fellow prisoners liked them. For instance, after he had written and performed, in December 1943, his first Christmas tale, also entitled "Favola di Natale," a story about the Holy Family who comes to the *lager* and manages to enter to give birth to the Savior, a compatriot sent him a hand-written note, letting him know how much the narrative had meant to him: "[...] sono tornato proprio ora dal teatro, dove ti ho ascoltato a occhi chiusi! Non meravigliarti di questa lettera, entusiasta come quella di una ragazzetta. E non te ne meraviglierai certamente quando ti dirò che le due 'piccole, semplici parole' e le tue 'piccole, semplici cose' mi hanno riportato per un'ora nella mia casetta di Roma, dove vivo ogni ora con la fantasia, nella sottile, dolorante nostalgia di ogni giorno" (Vietri n.p.). Guareschi carried the letter back to Italy with him from the *lager*, and the fact that he kept it shows that he knew his storytelling had a special effect on other internees.

moment, descending from the north comes a group of three Crows that orders the Sparrows to halt:

"Altolà: documenta!" ordinarono con malgarbo le tre Cornacchie ai Passerotti: e vollero sapere dove andassero e cosa facessero. E i Passerotti spiegarono che andavano alla ventura e vivevano alla giornata nell'attesa che tornasse il bel tempo.
"Pessima vita!" borbottarono le Cornacchie. "Perché non venite con noi, invece? Vi daremo prima di tutto miglio e orzo a volontà per rimettervi in carne . . . ."
"E poi?" chiesero i Passerotti.
"E poi vi infilzeremo in uno spiedo nuovissimo, sterilizzato, d'acciaio inossidabile, e vi cuoceremo con fuoco di legna di primissima scelta. Sentirete che bel calduccio!"
"Preferiamo rimanere al freddo!", risposero i tre Passerotti.
Ma le Cornacchie insistettero. "Non vi piace forse l'arrosto? Possiamo accontentarvi col bollito! Vi cuoceremo in una splendida pentola in duralluminio cromato . . . No? Vi dà forse noia il fumo? Noi abbiamo ogni riguardo per i nostri amici! Se vi dà noia il fumo vi cuoceremo su un potente fornello elettrico di 200 watt. Anzi, facciamo 300: non badiamo a spese, noi! . . .".
Ma i Passerotti dissero ancora di no.
"Magri ma crudi!" esclamarono.
Allora le Cornacchie se ne andarono indignate borbottando con disprezzo: "Fannulloni!" [...]

(32-33)

This encounter conveys the tale's most crucially significant allegory. As earlier discussed, one of the most effective ways that the prisoners undermined the Nazi war effort was to refuse to serve the Reich by working for the Germans in any capacity. The Sparrows, refusing to be bullied, would rather remain skinny and uncooked than fall into a trap.

When the Crows walk away, Albertino, Grandma and Flick receive the surprise of their lives: Babbo, who has himself left the *lager* in a dream, comes to greet them. The reunited family sits quietly together, sharing a few morsels of food, when they hear a plaintive, eerie chant of those people who wait for their loved ones. When the song fades, midnight arrives, and the family hears the cry of the Christ Child. Far to the north, however, another baby cries in his bunker; he is the God of War who already has small claws and is warmed by the fires of a flamethrower. Then silent shadows catch Albertino's eye: they prowl through the woods to stand near infinite numbers of tombstone crosses. As Babbo explains, they are the spirits of the living who come in search of the dead. When a mother finds the tomb of her son, she sits and speaks with him about treasured days that will never return. Dawn arrives, and thus the family's reunion, Albertino's dream, and the actual show come to a close.

Several prisoners who saw the recital testified how the *Favola* convincingly moved them to thunderous applause and the unabashed shedding of tears (Tira, "Ricordi" n.p.; Fantasia, *I raconti* 124). Ironically, however, both Guareschi's own journal entries of the time and a letter to his wife Ennia specify how the writing and production of the *Favola* made him feel all the more acutely and terribly alone:

[...] ed ecco un altro Natale è passato. Un altro tristissimo Natale. Pensavo a voi nella squallida casa di Maore. [...] Ho anche mangiato perché mi hanno invitato. Sempre senza notizie, senza pacchi, senza niente. Forse il Natale del '45? Non lo spero. Coraggio. Nino.
("Postkarte," n.p.)

His diary entry a week later at the turn of the New Year is even more somber: "Anche quest'anno è finito. Anno maledetto. Ne comincia un altro — che sarà forse peggio. Non ho più speranza che la guerra finisca. [...] Vedrò la mia bambina a due anni? ("Diario Quotidiano," 31 December 1944, n.p.). Deprivations in the *lager* caused him to lose close to sixty pounds, but as stated earlier, longing for home gave Guareschi his toughest challenge. These words in intimate correspondence with both himself and his wife help us fathom the emotional price he paid at the hands of the Third Reich as he spoke truth to its power.

After the war in the fall of 1945 Guareschi published the *Favola* with Edizioni Riunite, and for the book Guareschi provided seventy-four cartoons, sketched by himself, to accompany the narrative. Three of them shed important light on the fable's satirical function that motivated Guareschi when he first composed the work as a prisoner. As he explains in the preface:

[...] la banalissima vicenda interessava i prigionieri forse più ancora del contenuto polemico della fiaba stessa.
Perché *La favola di Natale* ha anche un contenuto polemico che le illustrazioni rendono oggi evidente anche al meno avvertito dei lettori, sì che io potrei premettere alla fiaba: "I personaggi di questo racconto sono tutti veri e i fatti in esso accennati hanno tutti un preciso riferimento con la realtà". La "realtà" era tutt'attorno a noi, e io la vedevo seduta a tre metri da me, in prima fila, vestita da Dolmetscher: e quando il "rumorista-imitatore" cantava con voce roca la canzoncina delle tre Cornacchie e il poliziotto di servizio sghignazzava divertito, io morivo dalla voglia di dirgli che non c'era niente da ridere: "Guardi, signore, che quella cornacchia è lei."
(*Favola* 6-7)

The Crows, crafted as German guards that have been shot out of the air, appear much like Stuka dive bombers that have smashed to earth. Another image suggests how Guareschi saw his captors as pigs: German warriors that march to greet their newborn King of War appear swine-like with their stumpy legs and fat hocks, even without curly little tails. Finally, a sketch of three Toadstools portrays the likeness of Hitler, Hindenburg, and Mussolini (Visentin 234-38). But, perhaps more than mushrooms, Guareschi depicted a more vulgar representation of three phalli.

These cartoons evince the bitterness he still felt more than seven months after his liberation. It naturally took him time to work through the pain and anger over captivity so that by 1949 he was able to write in *Diario clandestino* how his greatest accomplishment in surviving the war was having returned to Italy without hate in his heart: "[...] io esco senza medaglie ma vittorioso perché, nonostante tutto e tutti, io sono riuscito a passare attraverso questo cataclisma senza odiare nessuno" (XI). The publication of the *Favola* thus also gives testament to his private journey of exorcising harsh and bitter feelings. But, as a show in a German prisoner-of-war camp, the work eloquently reads as Guareschi's spiritual capstone where he brilliantly synthesized all that he had come to learn in the *lager* about the capabilities of humor and the inviolability of the conscience to bend to the abuses of power. It provides a striking example of Resistance literature: in opposing Nazi might, he could indeed retain his dignity and remain ultimately free, and his efforts of storytelling helped others to resist in much the same measure. As he wrote after the war:

Nel '43 ho rifiutato di servire i tedeschi e fascisti e mi hanno portato in un Lager dove ho usato tutta la mia intelligenza e la mia abilità per impedire che i tedeschi riuscissero a prendere per fame i disgraziati che erano con me. Ho fatto un buon lavoro.

(*Chi sogna* 273)

Guareschi Speaks up to Power after the War
After the English liberated Guareschi in April 1945 and he returned to Italy in September, Angelo Rizzoli hired him once again to found a new satirical weekly called *Candido*. With this forum, Guareschi immediately set about defending the Italian monarchy on the occasion of the national referendum to decide what institutional form of government Italy would follow and, in time, he became a true post-war champion of conscience, both through his political opposition to communism and his sensational libel trial that Alcide De Gasperi brought against him.

We do well to study this aspect of Guareschi in detail.

After the Italians decided upon instituting a republic in 1946, Guareschi hurled himself fervently against the powerful Communist Party. As we have gathered, the experience of the *lager* greatly sharpened Guareschi's stake in championing individual human freedom, and he detested Communism because in his opinion Communists blindly followed the wishes of their superiors and the masses, negating their own, and everybody else's, ability to think for themselves, a God-given right imprinted upon the human conscience. Having lived under Fascism, Guareschi had come to know firsthand the disastrous effects of totalitarian doctrine; he did not want Italy to plunge into that peril again. Indeed, any political movement of the masses concerned him immensely (Gualazzini 129).

In *Candido's* first year of publication, Guareschi created a cartoon figure that left a lasting impression. Since Communists inhaled so much false propaganda that they did not scrutinize, they obviously needed a third nostril to exhale the extra quantity of smoke. The *trinariciuto* (the one with three nostrils) became one of Guareschi's signature vignettes, especially present in "Obbedienza cieca, pronta e assoluta" cartoons, where a Communist party official shouting "Contrordine, compagni!" perpetually hastens to tell his companions that they should read a directive in *L'Unità* in a completely different way.[10] Guareschi also created two extremely effective and popular political posters that helped to ensure the Popular Front's defeat in 1948. In one poster, a man stands alone in an election booth ready to vote, the curtains pulled. The caption reads: "Dio ti vede, Stalin no." In the other, the skeleton of an Italian prisoner of war left to die in Russia, entrapped behind barbed wire, points his bony finger to the Popular Front symbol of Garibaldi imposed over a star. The caption reads: "Mamma, votagli contro anche per me." So effective was Guareschi's political censure that *Life* magazine hailed him as Europe's most effective anti-Communist spokesperson, who together with De Gasperi had effectively won the elections (Sargeant 115). In 1948 the *Democrazia Cristiana* (*DC*) had a powerful ally in Guareschi.

In all of his writings, Guareschi continued to accentuate his central message — that readers steadfastly needed to heed their individual conscience in order to protect themselves against the power of mass political movements. In doing so, he continued to refine his understanding of humor and what its use meant for him. Guareschi held that although collective demonstrations and group philosophies fostered hate and discord, Italians could defeat them through humor. For example, with "Signore e signori" in *Italia provvisoria* — an album of his own political musings interspersed with newspaper clippings and photos — he drove home the notion that humor's primary function is to undermine rhetoric with its capacity to break "la spirale della retorica" (20). Humor, as a practical and ethical construct of the spirit, combatted the pompous rhetoric of the "partiti di mandria" (24): "L'umorismo è il nemico dichiarato della retorica perché, mentre la retorica gonfia e impennacchia ogni vicenda, l'umorismo la sgonfia e la disadorna riducendola con una critica spietata all'osso" (26). Therefore, for Guareschi, humorous words must be ruthlessly simple, trenchant, quick, and potent: "L'umorismo è semplificazione, e, costretto a ridurre ogni cosa all'osso, riesce (più o meno bene) a fare lunghi discorsi con pochissime parole. E dice senza dire. E per dire si serve della forma più facile: la storiella" (31).

---

[10] As a stickler for proper spelling and grammar, Guareschi often lambasted *L'Unità* for the quantity of its typographical errors. For example, in one cartoon a group of Communist *trinariciuti* is in a classroom instructing a bunch of bugs. The caption reads: "Contrordine compagni! La frase pubblicata sull'*Unità*: 'Bisogna fare opera di rieducazione dei compagni insetti', contiene un errore di stampa e pertanto va letta: 'Bisogna fare opera di rieducazione dei compagni inetti'" ("Contrordine compagni!" 32). As a simple "Google" search will verify, the term has fully entered the Italian political lexicon and remains current.

Since Guareschi thought that Italians for centuries had been imbued with rhetoric, he presently challenged them to learn how to laugh, to see the incongruous and thus paradoxically to become, through reason, more serious (44). He then exhorted Italians to rediscover the best part of themselves in order to defeat the post-war rhetoric prone to foster hate and discord:

Cominciamo col distruggere la parte peggiore di noi stessi: quella che pascola nei prati della retorica e si ubriaca di frasi fatte, di aggettivi altisonanti, di fedi inconcusse, di dogmi politici, di imprescindibili destini.

(44)

As with several of his discourses in the *lager*, here too Guareschi issues the call to follow one's inner voice rather than political dogma.

From a reading of "Signore e signori," we can further grasp how Guareschi conceives of humor as a serious endeavor whose function is well beyond mere laughter. For him, humor rejects presumptuousness and self-importance, abrading all that is superfluous. Ethically, it calls one to be honest about faults and shortcomings, and it asks one to live life without hatred. For Guareschi, once this internal operation takes place, one may use humor to observe the incongruities of life, to penetrate political platforms and incongruities, and to check ruthlessly the *prepotenza* of alleged leaders and the masses, exalting one's own individual conscience in the face of social pressure. Through his reflections, Guareschi tells us that since humor has the power to expose extremist rhetoric used to foment social friction and strife, he does not take lightly the critical essence and role of his own craft.

Guareschi returned again to discuss his use of humor when he delivered a 1951 speech, "Conferenza a Lugano," in Lugano, Switzerland. At this occasion, Guareschi stated his belief that humor was a weapon born out of the human capacity to reason that protects personal freedom and meaning and defends against the intrusion of vulgar thought and culture. Humor, as a capacity of reason, unveils the comical and illogical in any situation.[11] It defends us from being swept away by the spiteful rhetoric of those in power (6). Short stories that are humorous, in other words, have a most serious function since humor leads to honesty and rigor and dictates what we should reject or embrace:

L'umorismo è l'acido col quale si prova se il metallo che voi presentate come oro è veramente oro. L'umorismo non distrugge. L'umorismo rivela ciò che deve essere

---

[11] Guareschi's concept of humor is Pirandellian inasmuch as humor, defined as the "sentimento del contrario," is predominantly a function of critical and analytical reflection. As Dante Della Terza explains in "On Pirandello's Humorism," the "feeling" of which Pirandello speaks is really something much more. It "is not really a kind of seismograph limiting itself to measuring the waves of an emotional earthquake, in spite of the qualifications attributed to it by Pirandello; it is not a sentiment at all since its activity is overwhelmingly critical, analytical, and rational" (20-21).

distrutto perché cattivo. L'umorismo risana. L'umorismo distrugge soltanto l'equivoco. Rafforza ciò che è sostanzialmente buono.

(30)

Humor in storytelling triggers the capacity for human reflection and thought, calling readers ultimately to affirm what their conscience knows is good and to reject what it knows as evil.

Guareschi, a Champion for all Times
Both "Signore e signori" and the "Conferenza a Lugano" detail how Guareschi championed a profound reverence for individual conscience, and for him, a practicing Catholic, this stance had deep theological rooting. In light of Christian faith, the Church from the earliest times has always recognized the central role conscience has for helping humans open up to grace.[12] Since humans, through the presence of the Holy Spirit, carry God's divine light within them, each person must follow the dictates of his or her heart in making moral decisions. At the same time, of course, the Church calls its faithful to have an informed mind and conscience based on two thousand years of its own wealth of wisdom expressed through the scriptures, moral argument, official teaching, sermons, and traditions. In the end, however, personal conscience, in the words of John Henry Cardinal Newman, "is the messenger of him, who, both in nature and in grace, speaks to us behind a veil, and teaches and rules by his representatives. Conscience is the aboriginal Vicar of Christ" (129). An informed conscience opens the faithful to receive the gifts of the Holy Spirit and to move closer to God (*Catechism* 438-42).

In the *Mondo piccolo* series, the best example of humor's close link to reason and the call to heed individual conscience comes with the voice of Jesus as the talking crucifix.[13] In his introduction to the first collection of *Mondo*

---

[12] One of the more interesting Gospel reflections on an intimate aspect of conscience occurs in Matt. 16: 13-18 and Mark 8: 27-30, when Jesus of Nazareth, having come to Caesarea Philippi, asks his followers to explain who people say that he is. They respond by telling Jesus that some say John the Baptist, others Elijah, and still others one of the prophets. Then Jesus addresses them directly: "But who do YOU say that I am?" (my emphasis). Simon Peter then responds: "You are the Christ, Son of the Living God," and Jesus rewards him by telling him that He will build his Church upon him. For the faithful, each person responds to that same question only by searching the reasons of the heart teased through the reflections of his or her own inviolate and divine conscience. All biblical citations are taken from *The Jerusalem Bible*.

[13] The *Mondo piccolo* short-story series has Don Camillo, Peppone and the Talking Crucifix as its main characters. Over the next twenty years, Guareschi wrote 366 tales anthologized in three compilations beginning in 1948 with *Don Camillo*, followed by *Don Camillo e il suo gregge* in 1953 and *Il compagno Don Camillo* in 1963. Together with the five films made of the *Mondo piccolo* — *Don Camillo* (1952), *Il ritorno di don Camillo* (1953), *Don Camillo e l'onorevole Peppone* (1955), *Don Camillo, Monsignore*

piccolo stories, Guareschi explicitly states that Christ's voice represents his own conscience:

Ebbene, qui occorre spiegarsi: se i preti si sentono offesi per via di don Camillo, padronissimi di rompermi un candelotto in testa; se i comunisti si sentono offesi per via di Peppone, padronissimi di rompermi una stanga sulla schiena. Ma se qualcun altro si sente offeso per via dei discorsi del Cristo, niente da fare; perché chi parla nelle mie storie non è il Cristo, ma *il mio Cristo*: cioè la voce della mia coscienza.

(*Don Camillo* 33)

As a protagonist along with Peppone and Don Camillo, this voice is present in 154 of the 346 tales (*Tutto don Camillo* 576), issuing the call to readers to think for themselves. That example, Guareschi hoped, would induce others to oppose any person or movement that could abuse its power.

Guareschi himself did just that through his column "Giro d'Italia," bravely reporting politically motivated vendetta murders in the *dopoguerra*, conducted ostensibly by Communist thugs in his home region of Emilia-Romagna. As the journalist Giovannino Lugaresi wrote, the column

in sintesi dava notizie, attraverso i ritagli dei giornali locali inviati dai lettori, di quel che accadeva nella Penisola. E nel testo di tale rubrica, i fattacci della rossa Emilia erano di gran lunga i più numerosi e più efficaci rispetto al resto della nazione, al punto che parlò della sua regione come del "Messico d'Italia" [...].

(8)

This horrific brutality captivated Guareschi. In the tales of *Mondo piccolo* of 1947 and 1948 he fictionalized the sense of collective fear in "Notturno con campane," "Paura," "La paura continua," and "Il cerchio si ruppe." Indeed, well into the 1950s, he returned to this theme often with stories like, "Due mani benedette" and "Il sangue non è acqua," when Don Camillo, Peppone, and the town folk have to solve a haunting mystery surrounding an "eliminato." Guareschi did not hide from recounting this post-war viciousness, even fearing that he might be personally harmed as a journalist for discussing them.[14]

Christ's voice of conscience often has a didactical function, serving to call Don Camillo (and readers more generally) to refrain from using violence. For instance, in "Uomini 2 — Mucche 100," Peppone has called an agricultural strike, and workers have abandoned a farm, letting its animals go hungry and

---

ma non troppo (1961) and *Il compagno don Camillo* (1965) — these works have ensured that Don Camillo is one of the most recognizable literary figures in all of Italian culture.

[14] Apart from his children telling me personally in an interview that their father feared a reprisal because he reported the murders in the Triangolo Rosso, I have not found any personal note from Guareschi detailing the same. But, it is interesting that in "Revolverata" Jesus (Guareschi's conscience) replies to Don Camillo, who has revealed his fears to the Talking Crucifix in light of the assassinations: "'[...] se tu non avessi paura, che valore avrebbe il tuo coraggio?'" (4).

sick. Don Camillo cannot stand this mistreatment, especially since an unattended cow is about to give birth, and he does his best to repress his rage. The following exchange demonstrates well Guareschi's capacity to illustrate the reasoning process of one person struggling to honor the true voice of conscience:

> "Gesù," disse al Cristo Crocifisso "tenetemi o faccio la marcia su Roma!"
> "Calmati, Don Camillo" lo ammonì dolcemente il Cristo. "Con la violenza non si può ottenere niente. Bisogna calmare la gente col ragionamento, non esasperarla con atti di violenza."
> "Giusto" sospirò don Camillo. "Bisogna indurre la gente a ragionare. Peccato però che, mentre si induce la gente a ragionare, le vacche crepino di fame."
> Il Cristo sorrise.
> "Se, usando la violenza la quale chiama la violenza, riusciamo a salvare cento bestie, ma perdiamo un uomo: e se, usando la persuasione, perdiamo cento bestie ma evitiamo la perdita di quell'uomo, secondo te cosa è meglio? La violenza o la persuasione?"
> Don Camillo, che non riusciva a rinunciare all'idea di fare la marcia su Roma tanto era indignato, scosse il capo.
> "Voi, Gesù, mi spostate i termini: qui non è questione di cento bestie! Qui si tratta di patrimonio pubblico. E la morte di cento bestie non rappresenta semplicemente un danno per quella testa di ghisa del Pasotti [the owner of the farm who refused to bargain with Peppone], rappresenta un danno per tutti, buoni e cattivi. E può avere ripercussioni tali da inasprire ancor più dissidi esistenti e creare un conflitto nel quale invece di uno scappano fuori venti morti."
> Il Cristo non era d'accordo:
> "Se col ragionamento eviti il morto oggi, perché col ragionamento non potresti evitare i morti domani? Don Camillo, hai perso la tua fede?"
>
> (85)

Later, Don Camillo convinces Peppone to rescue the dying cows, and he puts an end to the strike. In the end, therefore, Don Camillo has listened to that divine voice which calls him to reason, and he helps them terminate the strike with peaceful means.

Our understanding of Guareschi's thoughts on humor and his self-reflections helps us better to grasp the ideological underpinnings that his *Mondo piccolo* articulated masterfully through Jesus's discourse with Don Camillo. At a spiritual level, the humor inherent in the series speaks directly to the lesson he learned in the *lager* about his inviolate conscience, while the tales embody his fervent desire that his readers heed their own conscience through reason in order to do the same.

As Guareschi continued to elaborate his Don Camillo series in *Candido*, he began to distance himself more and more from the Christian Democrats that he had helped elect to power in 1948. The growing might of that political party began to worry Guareschi, who saw its power as potentially capable of unduly commanding the will of the Italian people (Rossini 862; Chiesa 165). He firmly disliked how the DC took advantage of its favored status with the Church, and he often exhorted the party not to foment confusion among the electorate concerning the distinction between the two ("Se a ciascun" 1).[15] Guareschi never shied away from attacking any political party, personality, movement or ideology that he saw as dangerously invasive of conscience. He particularly disdained anyone who saw himself or herself above the law, and he at times (one could argue) went too far in his censure.

One such moment occurred in 1951 through a cartoon in *Candido* that satirized Luigi Einaudi for promoting his personal business interests as a producer of Nebbiolo wine while using his public and political clout as President of the Republic. The Undersecretary of Justice authorized proceedings against Guareschi for libel, and he was absolved. But upon appeal brought by the Procuratore Generale della Repubblica he was subsequently found guilty and given a suspended sentence of eight months in jail. Three years later a Milan tribunal would activate this suspended sentence upon the conclusion of one of the most sensational Italian trials of the twentieth century. For Guareschi the experience from start to finish proved, after the *lager*, to be the most spiritually and physically taxing in his life.

In the pages of *Candido* in January 1954, Guareschi published two facsimiles of letters dated March 1944, during the Nazi occupation, written on Vatican letterhead and signed by Alcide De Gasperi, at that time in self-exile in the Vatican. The letters requested that the Allies bomb the periphery of Rome. Guareschi felt incensed not so much by De Gasperi's action as loathsome in terms of inviting destruction upon the Italian people, but by how De Gasperi had supposedly passed himself off as a Vatican representative in order to make the request to the Allies ("Il Ta-pum" 21). He held the statesman's political integrity as suspect.

De Gasperi took Guareschi to court for defamation of character. The trial, itself a fascinating study in Italian jurisprudence, lasted two months. In the end, De Gasperi won, and the court sentenced Guareschi to serve time in prison, adding the time for the suspended sentence of the Einaudi affair.[16] Incensed by what he experienced as a lack of justice, Guareschi refused to appeal. Since the

---

[15] In early 1952, he expressed his concerns in these terms: "Il 18 aprile, la gente aveva sfiducia nei comunisti e fiducia in De Gasperi. Oggi la sfiducia nei comunisti è la stessa, se non aumentata. E la fiducia in De Gasperi è, sì, ancora grande; ma la sfiducia negli uomini che lo attorniano aumenta: questo è il guaio. De Gasperi è un uomo che cammina con un sacco in spalla: dentro il sacco ci sono le fesserie che commettono i suoi. Bisogna stare attenti perché, se il sacco diventa troppo pesante, De Gasperi o mollerà il sacco, o finirà assieme a esso per le terre" ("Il caso Vanoni" 2).

[16] Both Gnocchi and Tritto provide excellent studies of the case, accusations, proceedings and sentencing. Giuliani-Balestrino contextualizes the case while considering the broader mystery of a secret correspondence between the British and Italian prime ministers. Finally, Franzinelli's 2014 study makes a very strong case that the letters were indeed forgeries in spite of Guareschi's belief to the contrary. My own analysis of the case was published in *The Italianist*.

tribunal had never allowed Guareschi to submit his letters to a scientific examination, he had no effective way to prove that the letters were authentic. At the same time, even though the court never proved that the letters were false, it had charged Guareschi with defaming De Gasperi's character through the editorial commentary that had publicized the letters. To this day, legal scholars still study the reasoning the court used in reaching its verdict.

In any event, Guareschi accepted the sentence, honorably respecting Italian law, but he vehemently rejected the unfair process that in his opinion led to the guilty verdict. Thus, in an impassioned article, he explained to his readers that he would refuse to appeal:

No, niente Appello.
Qui non si tratta di riformare una sentenza ma un costume. La sentenza è regolare, ha il crisma della legalità. Il costume è sbagliato, e non è una questione che riguardi la Magistratura: è una questione di carattere generale, che riguarda l'Italia intera. [...]
Hanno negato tutta la mia vita, tutto quello che io ho fatto nella mia vita. Non si può accettare un sopruso di questo genere. [...]
Vado in prigione. Accetto la condanna come accetterei un pugno in faccia: non mi interessa dimostrare che m'è stato dato ingiustamente. Il pugno l'ho già preso e nessuno potrà far sì che io non l'abbia preso.
Non mi pesa la condanna in sé, ma il modo.
E il modo ancor m'offende.

("No, niente appello" 16)

Guareschi then said he would gladly take up his old rucksack and enter prison: "Niente di teatrale, niente di drammatico. Tutto semplice e naturale. Per rimanere liberi bisogna, a un bel momento, prendere senza esitare la via della prigione" (16).[17] Guareschi spent 409 days in Parma's San Francesco Prison, at the time the only Italian journalist since the founding of the Republic ever to

---

[17] Guareschi crafted a Don Camillo tale to vent his frustration. In it, Alcibiade, a landowner, sues his renter Bazzigà for having fabricated a letter with Alicibiade's signature that invalidated his contract. Alcibiade had in reality signed the letter but later thought it best not to get out of the contract. The court decides in favor of Alcibiade, who then triumphantly returns to town and brings a candle to Don Camillo, inviting him to light it on the altar in front of the Madonna. Don Camillo lights the candle. It flickers and then goes out. He whittles the wax and tries once more, but again the light falters. He brings the candle to the rectory, lights it, and sure enough, the candle burns brightly. As soon as he brings it to the altar in front of the Blessed Mother, the candlelight continues no more. Don Camillo begins to think that something diabolical is at work. He takes the candle, leaves the chapel and walks along the bank of a canal. Just as he stops to toss the candle in the water, it squirts from his hand and slithers away into the darkness: "'Meno male che non mi ha morsicato' sussurra don Camillo che ormai non capisce più niente" ("Il cero" 10-11).

have spent actual jail time for libel (Zincone 2).[18] He spent another six months on probation, confined to his home in Roncole.

Misconstrued appraisals of Guareschi's sentence and refusal to appeal began immediately. The day after the trial, as Guareschi reported in *Candido*, the official newspaper of the Christian Democrats, *Il Popolo*, proclaimed in its broad head: "Le lettere attribuite a De Gasperi sono false! Un anno di reclusione al diffamatore Guareschi" ("Un anno" 1). Over the years, many journalists and historians have repeated this same claim (Franchi 33; Battista 3; Montanelli 43; Biagi 31).[19] But to his dying days, Guareschi continually stated that he still considered the letters to be authentic. Guareschi had obtained the documents from Enrico De Toma, a former soldier and aide to Mussolini; in 1959 when a journalist reported that Guareschi was the person "che sposò la causa dei documenti falsi di Enrico De Toma," Guareschi retorted:

Ciò è inesatto: io sposai la causa di due lettere autentiche a me affidate — perché ne disponessi gratuitamente come meglio credevo — dal De Toma. Non sposai la causa dei "documenti falsi" di Enrico De Toma".

("Rispetta almen" 12)

A few years earlier, he had answered the notion that he wanted to serve jail time in order to expiate his sins and undertake penance with these words:

Dopo il Referendum, salutando il mio Re che partiva per l'esilio, ho dichiarato che, pure non accettandola, mi impegnavo a subire la Repubblica così come, più avanti, pur non accettando una condanna da me ritenuta ingiusta, ho subito il carcere rifiutando sdegnosamente di appellarmi.

("25,000 trinariciuti" 8)[20]

---

[18] To the best of my knowledge, this claim is still true: no other Italian journalist has ever served actual behind-bars jail time for libel.

[19] Montanelli and Biagi claimed that, after he had served his time, Guareschi later admitted to them that he had made a mistake and wanted to atone for his error by serving out his sentence. Giulio Andreotti also suggested something similar. Writing in a letter to a lawyer who in 1996 attempted to help Guareschi's children have the sentence officially overturned, the senator stated: "'Uno dei miei collaboratori aveva ottime relazioni con Guareschi [...]. Mi disse dopo aver parlato più volte con Giovannino di avere la certezza che il carattere fiero del personaggio lo avesse indotto a subire il carcere, pur essendosi convinto di essere stato tratto in inganno'" ("Letter to Ubaldo Giuliani-Balestrino" 7). Here Andreotti implies that his confidant had somehow gathered directly from Guareschi that he knew that he had been tricked, and that Guareschi thus knew that the letters were forgeries.

[20] A year before he had stated: "[...] quella stampa governativa [...] si arrabattò per cambiare le carte in tavola presentando una condanna per diffamazione a mezzo stampa come una condanna per pubblicazione di documento falso. [. . .] le lettere ispiratrici di quel commento che mi fruttò ospitalità al San Francesco esistevano, erano autentiche e ne possedevo io stesso gli originali" ("Lettera al puerpero" 2).

While behind bars, Guareschi relied upon both his faith and ribald sense of humor to cope, a point best understood in his defiantly passive-aggressive way to pillory Mario Scelba, the prime minister who he believed had counseled De Gasperi to bring suit against him. He taped Scelba's picture to the bottom of the lid that covered his chamber pot, as Guareschi illuminated his readers:

Il "merdometro" consisteva nella foto di Scelba che avevo incollato sotto il coperchio del bojolo e, osservando la mattina la particolare colorazione e il particolare grado di umidità assunti dal viso spirituale dell'allora Presidente del Consiglio, formulavo l'oroscopo politico della giornata.

("Lettere dal carcere" 2 Oct. 1955 6)

As soon as his cell was renovated with a flushing toilet, he jokingly wrote to Ennia:

Adesso ho l'acqua corrente, ma sento tanto la mancanza del mio caro 'merdometro'. Tu mi capisci: per quanto rustico, io sono un sentimentale! E, stando così le cose, vorrei che Alberto incollasse quella cosa sotto il coperchio del W.C. del primo piano. Credi, mi farebbe tanto piacere.

(15 March 1955)

Guareschi left prison and returned home to a triumphant family celebration; however, he remained on probationary parole. This experience, as Guareschi would explain to his readers, truly vexed him emotionally. Although he was no longer in prison, he had really not regained his freedom. He expressed his displeasure by creating a new column for *Candido* called "Lettere dal carcere," and introduced it with a cartoon of himself wearing a collar and leashed to his house on a run-line next to a shorter one upon which he kept his dog Amletto, similarly constricted. These letters, somewhat tongue-in-cheek, were addressed to Margherita, the fictional name he used in his writings for Ennia:

"Libertà è dovunque vive un uomo che si sente libero" avevo scritto su un cartoncino appeso al muro della mia cella. Adesso, nella mia stanza delle Roncole, ho appeso al muro lo stesso cartoncino aggiornato: "Libertà è soltanto là dove vive un uomo che si sente libero".
Margherita, questa è la prima lettera che io ti scrivo dal carcere: le lettere che hai ricevuto da San Francesco non contano, perché io, allora, non mi sentivo prigioniero.
Io non mi sento libero, Margherita; il collare della "vigilanza" mi pesa mille volte più dell'inferriata e dei catenacci del carcere. Anche se la catena è lunga e mi permette di fare viaggi in automobile, è sempre una catena.
Ho ritrovato il mio mal di stomaco. In questi lunghi mesi di riposo si è irrobustito e mi sveglia tre volte ogni notte. Ha preso il posto delle tre ronde notturne di San Francesco.

("Lettere dal carcere" 2 Oct. 1955 7)

The humiliating experience of prison and the subsequent period of parole finally took their emotional toll on Guareschi. As his "Lettere dal carcere" indicate, he was tired, disillusioned with Italian society, spiritually drained, and aware that he struggled to recover his creative spark.[21] Luckily, in December 1955, a medical doctor declared to authorities that, for the good of his health, Guareschi needed to travel far away from home.

Guareschi and Ennia first went to Naples for a brief stay, and then, seeking true solitude, they went to Assisi. It was there on 26 January 1956 when he received news that his parole had expired. His children sent a short telegram that simply said: "Viva babbo libero. Bacioni." Later that year he would return to *Candido* and take up the Hungarian cause, decrying the barbarity of the Soviet invasion. His long ordeal had come to an end.

Guareschi's detention, however, had left a permanent scar upon him. In an interview, his daughter Carlotta recalled how her father appeared more deflated, spiritually less vibrant, and his physical movements seemed labored (Author's Interview 2006). In total, Guareschi had spent fourteen months behind bars, and another five confined on parole. He had lived among common thieves and had been treated as such. Unlike his *lager* experience ten years earlier, he had not been swept up by the events of war, nor had he seen his confinement as a way to redeem Italy; and, although he had received his wife and other visitors regularly, he had not found true culture of camaraderie with others.[22]

Perhaps the best-written evidence of the considerable stress Guareschi had endured in prison — a steep consequence of his opposition to power — comes in his 1961 letter to Andrea Rizzoli, in which Guareschi provided reasons for ending his sixteen-year collaboration with *Candido*. He needed to resign, he said, as a measure of protest over the production of the fourth Don Camillo film,

---

[21] Note, for example, how he explains a pervasive lethargy that consumes him: "Faccio fatica a ingranare marcia. [...] L'orologio mi dice che ho vegliato una notte invano e che oggi è un altro inutile giorno. [...] Oramai è mezzogiorno e il mio secchio è ancora vuoto. [...] Le ore scivolano via rapide come minuti secondi, ed è inutile cercar d'inseguirle. [...] Probabilmente sarebbe meglio se cambiassi mestiere: il mio povero vocabolario forse non ce la fa più. Le mie duecento parole forse sono consumate dall'uso e non riescono più a dire niente di preciso. Non riescono a fermare un concetto e la pagina è slavata" (1956, 6-7). Furthermore, here is how he voiced his frustration with Italian life: "Purtroppo questi sono i giorni dei falliti, degli uomini senza idee; è l'era dei demagoghi, dei politicanti, degli ipocriti che, nel nome della Giustizia sociale, stanno perpetrando la più orrenda ingiustizia: spersonalizzare l'individuo, ucciderlo per creare quel cretino medio alla cui mentalità la radio, la televisione e l'altra propaganda governativa vanno ogni giorno di più adeguando i programmi" ("Lettere dal carcere" 28 Aug. 1955 6).

[22] In his memoirs of POW life, *Diario clandestino*, Guareschi often stresses the communal experience of imprisonment as a way to resist Germans and Fascists. The IMIs had to rely on each other as a matter of life and death. In Parma, Guareschi was truly alone, and it is no coincidence that in order to recapture a sense of belonging to a wider community, he traveled back to his former POW camps in Poland and Germany in 1957, an experience that he related serially in *Candido* and that his children later published, together with other World War II writings, in *Ritorno alla base*.

Don Camillo, monsignore ...ma non troppo, since it had made his literary creation into a farce, and Rizzoli, the owner of the film company producing the film — the same owner of Guareschi's newspaper — had done nothing to help curtail the abuses of interpretation. In balancing all the positives and negatives that the editor had experienced with Andrea and his father Angelo, Guareschi explained:

> Il sopruso del processo, la feroce campagna diffamatoria condotta contro di me dalla stampa e l'aver dovuto vivere, per tredici mesi, tra delinquenti della più spregevole specie, trattato alla loro stregua, l'aver dovuto subire per tredici mesi i piccoli e grandi soprusi, le piccole e grandi viltà [...] tutto questo ha inciso profondamente sul mio spirito. [...] io, uscendo dal carcere, non ero più Giovannino Guareschi. Né più riuscii a ridiventare il Guareschi che ero.
>
> (3-4)

Far from living a springtime in his cell, as he often led his family, and even himself, to believe, this important passage shows how he detested his detention and all the deprivations that it brought. Quite simply, prison had fundamentally shaken Guareschi. He was never afterwards fully the same in spirit.

Guareschi's Ultimate Legacy

As this study has shown, Giovannino Guareschi spoke truth to power and advocated for individual freedom throughout his literary life. He saw humor as a weapon to curtail those in power who used threats to impede others from thinking for themselves. He resisted the Nazi juggernaut in World War II. *La favola di Natale*, together with his other POW writings that were replete with double meanings, continues to illustrate how he told stories that shrewdly inspired others to persevere in an unarmed struggle against injustices. Even though his stories may entertain us today, back then, to the IMIs, those tales were crucially important in bolstering their will to oppose their captors as best they could. We should note that in sustaining this resistance, Guareschi never espoused physical violence, and not because he knew that his captors, with possible reprisals, could severely injure, torture, or kill him and other IMIs. Guareschi detested violence as a means to speaking up to power since, as a victim himself of Nazi tyranny, he knew it degraded human dignity. He relied upon humor as much more efficient expedient in advocating for justice since he saw its power to awaken the human conscience and grasp what was right.

After the war, Guareschi always honored this tenant. He engaged Italian society in *Candido* with the oppositional acumen and humor that he had gained as a prisoner, and, beyond his Don Camillo stories, his vignettes bolstered the force of his sardonic reporting that aimed to lay bare any political situation, person, or movement that undermined justice and liberty. For more than twenty years, during the Cold War, Guareschi generated influential cartoons, posters, and tales that cautioned his fellow citizens against the sway of Europe's most powerful Communist Party. More importantly, his overriding concern as a political journalist focused on getting his readers to think as individuals for themselves — to jar them into considering what they really held as important values as functioning members of a postwar Italian society. In many ways, with a much simpler literary style, Guareschi's message recalls how a generation earlier G. K. Chesterton had attempted to debunk the tenets of modernism, atheism, and existentialism through brilliant apologetic essays and paradoxical witticisms. Indeed, both writers convey a prophetic voice that cautions against blindly following cultural and intellectual trends simply because they are in vogue.[23]

For his part, Guareschi's stance against the abuses of power was so strident that he even denounced one of Italy's greatest postwar heroes, Alcide De Gasperi, an act that landed him in prison. Fourteen months later, he left his second captivity haggard in body and sapped in spirit. He paid the price for having stubbornly championed the truth as he knew it, but his personal actions and words used to check those people and movements in power truly deserve our recognition.

Gettysburg College

Works Cited

Primary Sources
Andreotti, Giulio. "Letter to Ubaldo Giuliani-Balestrino." n.d. Giovannino Guareschi Archives, Roncole Verdi (PR).
Guareschi, Alberto and Carlotta. Telegram. 26 January 1956. Giovannino Guareschi Archives, Roncole Verdi (PR).
_____, Giovannino. "Conferenza a Lugano." Typed script (ts), 1951. Giovannino Guareschi Archives, Roncole Verdi (PR).
_____. "Diario Quotidiano." Written script (ws), 31 Dec. 1944, n.p. Giovannino Guareschi Archives, Roncole Verdi (PR).
_____. "Lettera a Dott. Andrea Rizzoli," ts, 17 Oct. 1961. Giovannino Guareschi Archives, Roncole Verdi (PR).

---

[23] Quite strikingly, I have yet to come across scholarly research that compares the Chesterton and Guareschi in the full breadth of their literary production. In very general terms, both were journalists who gained tremendous popularity as writers through the invention of two Catholic priests — Father Brown and Don Camillo — and who have side-kicks —Flambeau and Peppone — that helped them to underline their human goodness in spite of the errors they commit. Both Chesterton and Guareschi were also illustrators and cartoonists. Chesterton graduated from the Slade School of Art in London, and Guareschi, although not formally trained, drew thousands of images for *Bertoldo* and *Candido*. Finally, and most importantly, both writers were devout Catholics who conserved a strong sense of Christian optimism found especially in *Orthodoxy* and *Diario clandestino*.

———. "Lettera a Ennia," ws, 15 March 1955. Giovannino Guareschi Archives, Roncole Verdi (PR).
———. "Postkarte (Kriegsgefangenenpost) to Ennia," ws, 25 Dec. 1944. Giovannino Guareschi Archives, Roncole Verdi (PR).
———. "Quaderni di lager," ws, 10 Oct. 1944. Giovannino Guareschi Archives, Roncole Verdi (PR).
Tira, Alberto. "Ricordi di prigionia: La 'Favola di Natale di Giovanni Guareschi'," ts, No date. Giovannino Guareschi Archives, Roncole Verdi (PR).
Vietri, Luigi. "Letter to Guareschi at Beniamino, STALAG 333," ws, 26 December 1943. Giovannino Guareschi Archives, Roncole Verdi (PR)

Secondary Sources
Ascari, Odoardo. "Quei giorni a Sandbostel con Guareschi." *Il Giornale* (30 July 2002): 22.
Battista, Pierluigi. "E adesso spuntano le lettere di De Gasperi." *La Stampa* (8 Feb. 1992): 3.
Bertellini, Mario. "Patto d'acciaio con la libertà." *Bacherontius* 4 (Apr. 1990): 8-9.
Biagi, Enzo. *Mille camere*. Milano: Mondadori, 1984.
Biscossa, G. "Faceva nascere il sorriso entro i cupi 'verboten' dei reticolati." *Corriere del Ticino* (21 Oct. 1988): 41.
Bocca, Giorgio. "Trapezisti e mentitori." *La Repubblica* (6 Mar. 1991): 34.
Catechism of the Catholic Church. United States Catholic Conference. Vatican City: Libreria Editrice Vaticana, 1994.
Chesterton, G. K. *Orthodoxy*. London: John Lane, 1909.
Chiesa, Adolfo. *La satira politica in Italia*. Roma: Laterza, 1990.
Della Terza, Dante. "On Pirandello's Humorism." *Veins of Humor*. Ed. Henry Levin. Cambridge, MA: Harvard UP, 1972. 17-33.
Dossena, Giorgio. "Oggi sono i giovani a scoprire Guareschi e Mosca." *La Stampa* (22 Mar. 1986): 25.
Fantasia, Matteo. *I racconti della prigionia.* Bari: Levante Editori, 1999.
Ferioli, Antonio. "Dai Lager all'esercito di Mussolini: gli internati militari italiani che aderirono alla Repubblica Sociale Italiana." *Nuova storia contemporanea,* n. IX, 5 (Sept.-Oct. 2005): 46–67.
Franchi, Stefania. *"Tango" e il PCI*. Catanzaro: Rubettino Editore, 2000.
Frankl, Viktor. *Man's Search for Meaning*. Baltimore: Washington Square Press, 1984.
Franzinelli, Mimmo. *Bombardate Roma! Guareschi contro De Gasperi: uno scandalo della storia repubblicana*. Milano: Mondadori, 2014.
Giuliani-Balestrino, Ubaldo. *Il carteggio Churchill-Mussolini alla luce del processo Guareschi*. Roma: Edizioni Settimo Sigillo, 2010.
Gnocchi, Alessandro. *Una storia italiana*. Milano: Rizzoli, 1998.
Guareschi, Giovannino. "25.000 Trinariciuti bianchi" *Candido* 24 (15 June 1958): 8.
———. *Chi sogna nuovi gerani*. Ed. Alberto and Carolotta Guareschi. Milano: Rizzoli, 1993.
———. "Controrordine compagni!" *Candido* 5 (31 Jan. 1954): 32.
———. *Diario clandestino*. Milano: Rizzoli, 1947.
———. *Don Camillo*. Milano: Rizzoli, 1948.
———. *Favola di Natale*. Milano: Rizzoli, 1998.
———. "Finalmente Libero." *Diario clandestino*. Milano: Rizzoli, 1949. 164-65.
———. "Il caso Vanoni." *Candido* 6 (10 Feb. 1952): 2.
———. "Il cerchio si ruppe." *Tutto don Camillo* 226-31.

———. "Il cero." *Candido* 17 (25 Apr. 1954): 10 – 11.
———. *Il grande diario: Giovannino cronista del Lager, 1943-1945*. Ed. Alberto and Carlotta Guareschi. Milano: Rizzoli, 2008.
———. "Il Tam-pum del cecchino." *Candido* 4 (24 Jan. 1954): 1+, 17-21.
———. "Il Tam-pum del cecchino: No, niente appello!" *Candido* 17 (25 Apr. 1954):18-22.
———. "La coda di Riccardo." *Vita con Giò*. Milano: Rizzoli, 1995: 245-51.
———. "La paura continua." *Tutto don Camillo* 214-18.
———. "Lettere dal carcere." *Candido* 35 (28 Aug. 1955): 6-7.
———. "Lettere dal carcere." *Candido* 40 (2 Oct. 1955): 6-7.
———. "Lettere dal carcere." *Candido* 1 (6 Jan 1956): 6-7.
———. "Lettere al postero." *Candido* 21 (25 May 1946): 3.
———. "Lettera al puerpero." *Candido* 32 (11 Aug. 1957): 2.
———. "Mondo piccolo: La paura continua." *Candido* 49 (7 Dec. 1947): 4
———. "Notturno con campane." *Tutto don Camillo* 81-84.
———. "Paura." *Tutto don Camillo* 202-07.
———. "Rispetta almen le ceneri!" *Candido* 3 (18 Jan. 1959): 11-12.
———. *Ritorno alla base*. Milano: Rizzoli, 1989.
———. "Se a ciascun l'interno affanno...." *Candido* 10 (11 Mar. 1951): 1.
———. "Signore e signori." *Italia provvisoria*. 2nd ed. Milano: Rizzoli, 1984: 11-45.
———. "Uomini 2 – Mucche 100." *Tutto don Camillo* 84-90.
———. *Tutto don Camillo*. Milano: Rizzoli, 1998.
Gualazzini, Beppe. *Guareschi*. Milano: Editoriale Nuova, 1981.
The Jerusalem Bible. Ed. Alexander Jones. Garden City, NY: Doubleday, 1966.
Lugaresi, Giovanni. "Guareschi: 'Il Messico d'Italia'." *Il Gazzettino* (22 Sept. 1990): 8.
Montanelli, Indro. "La stanza di Montanelli." *Corriere della sera* (29 Apr. 1998): 43.
Mosca, Giovanni. "La lettera." *Candido* 1 (16 Dec. 1945): 4.
Nello, Paolo. "Guareschi, gli Internati Militari Italiani e il *Diario clandestino*." *Un Candido nell'Italia provvisoria: Giovannino Guareschi e l'Italia del "mondo piccolo."* Ed. Giuseppe Parlato. Roma: Fondazione Ugo Spirito, 2002. 39-58.
Newman, John Henry Cardinal. "Letter to His Grace the Duke of Norfolk." Vol. 5. "Conscience." *Newman and Gladstone: The Vatican Decrees*. Part 2. Notre Dame: Notre Dame P, 1962. 127-38.
Romano, Giuseppe. "Giovannino Guareschi, nostro padre." *Studi cattolici* (June 1999): 438-41.
Perry, Alan R. "'C'era una volta la prigionia': Guareschi's Resistance in the *Favola di Natale*." *Italica* 86.4 (2009): 623-50.
———. "Freedom of Imprisonment: Giovannino Guareschi and the Primacy of Conscience". *Italian Culture* 20. 1-2 (2001-2002): 67-78.
———. "Giovannino's Secret Weapon: The German Lager and Guareschi's Use of Reason as Humor." *Italian Quarterly* 153-54, (Summer-Fall 2002): 39-53.
———. "Guareschi's *Mondo piccolo* and the Sacrality of Conscience." *Annali d'Italianistica* 25 (2007): 337-60.
———. "'Io sono qui muto e solitario': Giovannino Guareschi's Prison Writing 1954-1955." *Modern Italy* 17.1 (2012): 85-102.
———. "'No, niente appello!': How De Gasperi Sent Guareschi to Prison." *The Italianist* 25 (2005, ii): 239-59.
———. *The Don Camillo Stories of Giovannino Guareschi: A Humorist Portrays the Sacred*. Toronto: U of Toronto P, 2008.

———. "Oral Interview with Carlotta Guareschi." 29 May 2006. Giovannino Guareschi Archives, Roncole Verdi (PR).
Il Popolo (Milano). "Un anno di reclusione al diffamatore Guareschi." (16 Apr. 1954):1.
Rossini, Mariella. "Umoristi e stravaganti del novecento." *Letteratura italiana contemporanea*. Vol. 2. Ed. Gaetano Mariani and Mario Petrucciani. Roma: L. Lucarini, 1980. 845-62.
Sargeant, Winthrop. "Anti-Communist Funnyman." *Life* (10 Nov. 1952): 115.
Tritto, Paolo. *Il destino di Giovannino Guareschi*. Matera: AltreMuse Editrice, 2003.
Visentin, Tiziana. "La favola di Guareschi." *La voce scritta: laboratorio sulle strutture della fiaba e della lettura infantile fra tradizione e modernità*. Ed. Matilde Dillon Wanke. Bergamo: Bergamo UP, 2002. 191-241.
Zincone, Vittorio. "Giovannino va in galera." *Il Resto del carlino* (6 May 1954): 2.

Filmography
Comencini, Luigi. *Il compagno don Camillo*. 1965.
Duvivier, Julien. *Don Camillo*. 1952
———. *Il ritorno di don Camillo*. 1953.
Gallone, Carmine. *Don Camillo e l'onorevole Peppone*. 1955.
———. *Don Camillo, Monsignore… ma non troppo*. 1961.

Maria Giménez Cavallo

Elsa Morante's *La storia:*
A Posthumanist, Feminist, Anarchist Response to Power

Synopsis: Elsa Morante introduces *La storia: romanzo* as an attempt to rewrite history by shifting the reader's attention from the major political figures of the 1940s to the personal vicissitudes of those typically excluded from political power. Rather than signaling a retreat from the political arena, this change of perspective purposefully allows the author to more clearly articulate her political vision. Using insights drawn from posthumanism, feminism, and anarchism, this essay aims to show how the novel's principal characters give bodily form to Morante's passionate denunciation of all institutionalized systems of control.
Key words: Elsa Morante, *La storia*, posthumanism, feminism, anarchism, animals in literature.

Following the publication of *La storia* in 1974, Morante was attacked by representatives of all political persuasions who took issue with those parts of her message that did not coincide with their own ideology.[1] A group of leftist intellectuals went so far as to write an article for *Il Manifesto,* "Contro il romanzone della Morante," and even her close friend Pier Paolo Pasolini publicly denounced her novel, claiming that she wrote "senza tuttavia (a mio parere) aver meditato abbastanza su tale ideologizzazione e di conseguenza sul proprio progetto narrativo" 77 ("without having [in my view] sufficiently meditated on such an ideologization and consequently on her own narrative project"). It would be more accurate to say, however, that Morante's meditation led her to distrust the prevailing ideologies of the period.[2] Her political vision cannot be understood by applying the narrow, horizontal categories of Left vs. Right since it tends to move in a different spatial direction altogether, a vertical axis in which state power is opposed to freedom. As she states in her 1970 letter

---

[1] Anticipating their criticism, Morante presents a metaphor of those contemporary intellectuals not in revolt against all current systems as being only nourished by pills of propaganda and thus assimilated into a prevailing ideology (*Pro o contra* 113). The essay, published posthumously, was originally a talk that Morante gave in Turin in 1965. For a discussion of this piece, see Lyons.
[2] Lucamante blames the critics of the time for their blindspot due to misplaced political priorities, finding that most of them misinterpreted her "deliberate transgressions against the subgenre of the historical novel" and failed to see how Morante "challenges the classic Aristotelian opposition between *poiesis* and praxis, between political and ethical spheres" (168).

Annali d'italianistica 34 (2016). *Speaking Truth to Power from Medieval to Modern Italy*

"Piccolo manifesto dei comunisti (senza classe né partito)," the true struggle of humanity is that of liberty against power — "il disonore dell'uomo è il *Potere*" ("the dishonor of mankind is *Power*") — whereas "l'onore dell'uomo è la libertà dello spirito" (7-8; "the honor of mankind is liberty of the spirit"; emphasis in the original). The title of this brief work clarifies right from the start that although Morante employs the term *communist* — whether to engage head-on with the Left or simply for her lack of a more appropriate term — she empties it of its conventional meaning by rejecting the two basic tenets of Italian communism: class opposition and political party affiliation.[3] The academy has only recently begun to seriously consider the political aspects of Morante's work. Most notably, the 2014 volume *Elsa Morante's Politics of Writing: Rethinking Subjectivity, History, and the Power of Art* offers various essays devoted to *La storia*'s political dimension. Sharon Wood, for example, reads the novel as "an effort at restoration, a philosophical rather than party political refusal of official history that negates individual experience in favor of the political narrative" (76); Stefania Lucamante similarly interprets Morante's message as acting against "politics intended as freedom but understood, rather, in terms of an administrative machine whose only tasks are bureaucracy and exercise of force against the Other" (94).[4] In another recent volume, Lorenza Rocco Carbone finds that the novel reveals that "il crollo delle ideologie può indurre a considerare *sine ira* che nazismo e comunismo, aspetti di una stessa ideologia — il totalitarismo, padre di tutte le illusioni —, sono entrambi colpevoli contro l'Uomo" 103-04 ("the fall of ideologies can induce one to consider *sine ira* that nazism and communism, two sides of the same ideology — totalitarianism, father of all illusions — are both guilty against Humanity"). Yet the novel does more than simply denounce the system: it presents the possibility of a completely different paradigm. As this essay argues, *La storia* imagines an alternative world in which a series of hierarchical binary relations are reversed: Morante privileges not only personal stories over institutional History, and female nurturing over male aggression, but also animals over humans, children over adults, individual spirituality over established religion, and, most relevant from a political standpoint, anarchism over statism. By flipping these key relations, Morante not only critiques the traditional structures

---

[3] Morante's continued use of Marxist terminology despite her stated idea of pitting liberty against power outside established political parties may also indicate that she had not broken completely free from the prevailing comunist framework. She later employs such Marxist categories as proletariat and bourgeois even as she argues against the communist goal of the working class seizing political power ("chiunque desidera il Potere, per sé e per chiunque altro, è un reazionario; e, pure se nasce proletario, è un borghese!") "whoever desires Power, for himself or for anyone else, is a reactionary; and, even if he's born a proletariat, he's a bourgeois" 9).

[4] Lucamante reads the novel primarily through the lens of Hannah Arendt (see especially 191-97).

of power but offers an antidote to counteract the effects of a diseased world on several fronts. The theoretical lens of seemingly different movements — posthumanism, feminism, and anarchism — helps to uncover a fundamental ethical engagement at the core of Morante's novel: the condemnation of any form of oppression or aggression against sentient beings by those wielding power.

Reconfiguring "History"
According to Morante's collection of critical essays *Pro o contro la bomba atomica*, *La storia* itself should be read as a manifesto. In an atomic age of destruction in which art represents the only hope for salvation, novels become ideological weapons with the capacity to subvert the system. Thus "il romanziere, [è] al pari di un filosofo-psicologo" ("the novelist [is] on the level of a philosopher-psychologist") and every *romanzo* should be "tradotto in termini di saggio, e di 'opera di pensiero'" ("translated in terms of an essay, and of a 'work of thought'") since its main purpose is to "interrogare sinceramente la vita reale, affinché essa ci renda, in risposta, la sua verità" ("sincerely interrogate real life, so that it can render to us, in reply, its truth" 46-48). More than just a novel, then, *La storia* acts as a philosophical treatise to present Morante's vision of the world, in which even the style of writing makes a political statement. In explaining why the power elite fear poetic truths, Morante links the novelist-poet to heroes of chivalric myth:

L'apparizione, nel mondo, di una nuova verità poetica, è sempre inquietante, e sempre, nei suoi effetti, sovversiva: giacché il suo intervento significa sempre, in qualche modo, un rinnovamento del mondo reale [...]. E per questo certi dittatori, armati di eserciti e di bombe atomiche, hanno paura al cospetto di una inerme poesia, feroce solo della sua bellezza, e le vietano l'ingresso nei loro confini [...]. [P]aragonavo la funzione del romanziere-poeta a quella del protagonista solare, che nei miti affronta il drago notturno, per liberare la città atterrita [...]. La qualità dell'arte è liberatoria, e quindi, nei suoi effetti, sempre rivoluzionaria.

(72-73; 107-08)

The appearance in the world of a new poetic truth is always anxiety-provoking and always, in its results, subversive: given that its intervention always means, in some fashion, a renovation of the real world [...]. And for this reason certain dictators, armed with military forces and atomic bombs, are afraid in front of an unarmed poem, ferocious only in its beauty, and they prohibit its entry within their borders [...]. I was comparing the function of the novelist-poet to that solar protagonist who in the myths confronts the nocturnal dragon, to free the terrified city [...]. The nature of art is liberatory, and therefore, in its consequences, always revolutionary.

In what way, then, is Morante herself a revolutionary who wields her art in *La storia* in order to liberate others?

Right from the title, Morante challenges the authority of standard *history* whose narrative is produced by those in power. The physical dimension of the novel, with dates and statistics provided in a dry factual style at the beginning of each chronologically arranged chapter, recalls a conventional textbook form. Morante further mimics the accepted mode of writing history by opening the novel with a summary of relevant events from World War II in a very neutral manner, as if purposefully beckoning the reader to view the fictionalized story of the *romanzo,* announced by the subtitle, on the same level as a historical account. In contrast to these peripheral elements of the book, however, the plot is a complete reversal of the expectations associated with historical writing. In this alternative form of history, Morante also reframes the perspective from a textbook-like claim of absolute truth to the subjective narrator, who accepts her limited capacity for knowledge. The narrator does not place herself in a God-like position, watching over and describing the characters from a distance, but rather puts herself on par with them as she poses as a researcher making use of photographs, documents, testimony, and oral accounts in her search for truth.[5] This method of narration thus reframes the point of view to that of the individual investigator, against the presumption of complete knowledge in conventional "historical" writing. Siriana Sgavicchia notes the quantity of archives which Morante cites in her notebooks in preparation for her novel, confirming that she took news articles from the war and actual events that had been somewhat fictionalized (106). The author thus anticipates the narrator's stance in her quest to uncover the truth beyond the emotionlessly conveyed headlines, inserting testimonials into her story.[6]

In keeping with her reverse perspective, Morante focuses on quotidian events experienced by those who suffer the consequences of political decisions but have no voice in the matter. Writing in the wake of World War I, Randolph

---

[5] Carbone maintains that *La storia* resembles the "romanzo ottocentesco, con la presenza del narratore onnisciente che guarda dall'alto la materia" ("eighteenth-century novel, with the presence of the omniscient narrator who sees his subject matter from above" 99) as opposed to the contemporary style of writing in the first person. However, I would argue that *La storia* is written in the first person in order to produce a communal archive. As Lucamante reminds us, Morante was "a woman artist scarred by the Shoah; she thusly considered herself a victim/survivor akin to her characters" (159).

[6] Sgavicchia cites in particular the events of "sabato nero" 110 ("black Saturday") as related by the historical account, *16 ottobre 1943* by Debenedetti. Sgavicchia notes that Morante "esclude dalla narrazione il racconto dell'azione di polizia delle SS nelle case dell'ex ghetto [...]. La scrittrice focalizza, invece, l'attenzione sulla partenza degli ebrei dalla Stazione Tiburtina, completando e integrando il racconto di Debenedetti, il quale non si sofferma su questa scena" 111 ("excludes from the narration the action story of the SS police in the ex-ghetto houses [...]. The writer, instead, focuses her attention on the departure of the Jews from the Tiburtina Station, completing and integrating Debenedetti's telling, which does not linger on this scene"). Thus, according to Morante's stated intentions for writing the novel, we see that she indeed "dà forma a ciò che rimane taciuto nel racconto" 112 ("gives form to that which remains silenced in the news article").

Bourne had expressed this dichotomy by distinguishing the State from the people living in a territory, which he referred to as the Country: "Our idea of Country concerns itself with the nonpolitical aspects of a people, its way of living, its personal traits, its literature and art, its characteristic attitudes toward life" whereas the State is "armed power, culminating in a single head, bent on one primary object, the reducing to subjection, to unconditional and unqualified loyalty of all the people of a certain territory" (41, 28). Although official history was generally regarded as a grand narrative focusing on the armed power of the State, Morante directs her attention instead to interconnected private lives, representative of the disenfranchised Country as a whole. The privileging of *storia* (story) over *Storia* (History), then, accords with one of the novel's stated objectives: to give voice to those whose stories are silenced in conventional historical narratives.[7] Our discussion of these stories begins with those who communicate outside the structures of human language.

Political Posthumanism
The Australian posthumanist scholar Dinesh Wadiwel makes the case that mistreatment of animals is tied to mistreatment of human beings:

The humanist will say "Stop treating humans like animals: respect the human and violence will not be possible. But there is [an] alternative line of thinking that responds in an apparently oblique way to the humanist: "Stop treating animals like we treat animals; then it will not be possible to treat humans like animals." Understood in this fashion, human violence represents not only a capacity for dehumanization alone, but is tied closely to the justification of violence against the non-human.
("Animal by Any Other Name?" 2)

Similarly, Cary Wolfe argues that the oppression of animals has actually served to justify and normalize the oppression of humans:

One might well observe that it is crucial to pay critical attention to the discourse of animality quite irrespective of the issue of how nonhuman animals are treated. This is so, as a number of scholars have observed, because the discourse of animality has

---

[7] Carbone notes that the individual stories "singolarmente [...] non lasciano traccia, pedine insignificanti sullo scacchiere della Storia, ma le microstorie si intrecciano tra loro, diventano tasselli della grande Storia, fotogrammi di un puzzle figurato, rientrano in un disegno di trascendenza storica [...]. È persino epopea, per la struttura, per la grandiosità delle scene, che si allargano fino ad occupare tutto il mondo, tutto il secolo: per il numero dei personaggi, degli episodi" 95 ("alone, do not leave a trail, insignificant pawns on the chessboard of History, but the micro-histories are weaved together, becoming tassels of the great History, photograms of a puzzle, they create a design of historical transcendence [...]. It is even epic, for the structure, the grandiosity of the scenes, which are extended until they take up all the world, the whole century: for the number of characters and episodes"). Thus, Morante "trasforma il vero storico in vero poetico" 98 ("transforms the true historic into the true poetic").

historically served as a crucial strategy in the oppression of *humans* by other humans — a strategy whose legitimacy and force depend, however, on the prior taking for granted of the traditional ontological distinction, and consequent ethical divide, between human and nonhuman animals.

(Zoontologies: The Question of the Animal xx)

This valorization of animals as sentient beings much like humans, in line with the non-speciest theories of Morante's friend Giorgio Agamben, can be found in Morante's non-fictional writing.[8] *Pro o contro la bomba atomica* grants animals a soul and imagines them participating in a prelapsarian world: "E chi negò che i nostri compagni animali possiedano un'anima? [...] Lodiamo tutta la multiforme nazione dei nostri compagni animali, questo circo angelico in cui l'uomo può riconoscere, a testimonianza del suo rango perduto, la nobile infanzia dell'Eden" 20-21 ("And who denied that our animal companions possess a soul? [...] Let us praise the multiform nation of our animal companions, this angelic circle in which man can recognize, as a testimony of his lost rank, the noble infancy of Eden"). These posthumanist reflections help shed light on scenes within the novel that, on the one hand, depict the "human" quality of animals and, on the other, show the dire consequences that stem from treating them inhumanely.

In addition to explicitly dedicating her novel to the *analfabeto*,[9] i.e., literally one who is without the (written) alphabet, Morante devotes substantial attention in the course of the narrative to creatures who communicate (to those capable of understanding them) without the use of human language.[10] For example, the child prodigy Useppe decodes the meaning of the songs of the birds and even the silence of the forest. Tellingly, the boy's foster mother is the non-human Bella, a shepherd dog ("pastorella maremmana") who takes care of him while his biological mother is out working. Morante not only conveys the canine's thoughts, but demonstrates the perfect understanding between Bella and Useppe despite their difference of species. By highlighting the intrinsically natural and instinctive qualities of Bella's motherhood as the most important aspect of her identity, Morante treats her as a mother figure on the same level as his biological

---

[8] For more information on the influential posthumanist ideas in Morante's entourage, see Mecchia, "Elsa Morante at the Biopolitical Turn."

[9] The dedication in Spanish reads: "Por el analfabeto a quien escribo."

[10] Morante makes her non-speciest view explicit in the following passage: "E Davide, frattanto, rincorreva le sue proprie meditazioni a voce alta, quasi ragionasse in sogno con qualche gran Dottore, senza più accorgersi di parlare a due poveri analfabeti. Quasi non rammentava più, anzi, chi fra i tre, là dentro, fosse lo studente colto, e chi il pischelletto e chi il cane" 524 ("And Davide, meanwhile, pursued his own meditations aloud, as if he were disputing in a dream with some great Doctor, no longer realizing he was speaking to two poor illiterates. As if, indeed, he no longer remembered who, among the three there in the room, was the cultivated student, and who the kid and who the dog" 589).

one ("al pari dell'altra madre" 649).[11]

At the end of the novel, Bella is killed for trying to protect her family from the police officers who storm into Ida's home. Morante first presents the scene by purportedly summarizing the chronicle section of newspapers, whose official wording employs an impersonal infinitive verb without a subject: "si è reso necessario abbattere la bestia" 647 ("it was necessary to destroy the [beast]" 547). This phrasing not only depersonalizes Bella as a generic and even beastly creature ("bestia"), but implies that her murder was necessary for the common good. Yet the falseness of this official story is immediately exposed as Morante's subjective narrator reclaims Bella's identity as their shepherd dog ("la nostra pastora" 647). She goes on, moreover, to rewrite the scene with Bella as protagonist and pays tribute to her heroic "guerra [...] contro i nuovi intrusi ("war [...] against the new intruders") in defense of her family: "Da sola, essa riuscì a far paura a una squadra di nemici, fra i quali almeno un paio erano muniti delle armi di ordinanza" 648 ("Alone, she managed to frighten a squad of enemies, at least two of whom were armed with ordnance weapons" 547). Thus the novel's action comes to a close with the maternal female dog ("cagna") executed by a squadron of enemies representing the State's legal system ("i loro compiti legali"). Recalling Wadiwel's argument, one is compelled by this scene to ask: when animals are treated in such a way, how is it possible for human beings to be treated humanely?

Morante also makes ample use of animal metaphors throughout the text, linking humans in various ways to other species. Concetta D'Angeli finds that in these metaphors "l'animalità [...] non è un'alternativa paradisiaca, ma la metafora del desiderio di cancellare la storia e, della storia, l'immagine più traumatica per la memoria contemporanea, i carri bestiame che portano gli ebrei allo sterminio" 67 ("animality [...] is not a paradisiacal alternative, but the metaphor of the desire to cancel history — and, from history, the most traumatic image in contemporary memory, the cattle cars that bring the Jews to their extermination"). Morante's use of animal metaphors goes beyond the anthropomorphization of her characters, as it extends a political metaphor throughout the novel in line with the theorist John Simons's redefinition of history in posthumanist terms: "The history of all hitherto existing society is the history of the struggle between humans and non-humans" where the so-called non-humans refer to the marginalized citizens viewed as such by systems of power (7). More than just a debate about animals in and of themselves, this form of posthumanism also denounces the systematic oppression of human groups, allowed to be ostracized and even murdered legally with the excuse of their animality. Through her animal metaphors, then, Morante not only advocates for animals to be considered on par with her characters, thus eradicating the

---

[11] Notably, after Useppe's death, even Ida "non voleva più appartenere alla specie umana" 647 ("no longer wanted to belong to the human race" 547).

difference between "humans" and "non-humans," but again she also attempts to change the way History is related by levelling the prevailing hierarchical system of order and giving voice to those previously marginalized.

Morante provides a chilling morality tale on the symbolic importance of animals for human wellbeing — and, conversely, on the connection between the mistreatment of animals and both criminal activity and political power — in a secondary episode involving Nello D'Angeli, lover and protector of the aging prostitute Santina. Nello, growing up an orphan, had nothing and no one except for the teddy bears the nuns would give the children on Christmas, though these were later taken away. Once Nello had been "preso da una nostalgia dell'orso" 425 ("seized by a longing for the bear" 361) but was subsequently beaten by the nuns and deprived of the bear the following Christmas when they found that he had taken it. This seemingly minor anecdote is revealed to be the traumatic experience that triggered his propensity for murder. As a symbol of unconditional love, the teddy bear was a replacement for the mother he never knew. As an adolescent, Nello tried again to fill this void when he nursed a dying dog back to life ("rimesso in vita" 426) but the dog was confiscated from him and sent to the slaughterhouse (362). As a result, in a perverse sort of substitutional revenge, when Nello would find a stray animal on the street, "si prendeva il gusto di torturarlo, finché non lo vedeva crepare" (427; "he took pleasure in torturing it, until he saw it kick the bucket" 363). Through these affective stories, Morante points out how social institutions taught Nello to hate and to inflict pain, contrary to his natural yearning for love during his childhood. He later looks to Santina to fill his longing for maternal care, but then ends up murdering her even though she was the only person who could have saved him from himself. The narrator then pointedly remarks that his excessively large signature resembled those of Benito Mussolini and Gabriele D'Annunzio, purposefully creating a comparison with two notorious historical figures. Mussolini's infamy was universally acknowledged, but the inclusion of D'Annunzio reminds readers that the literary *Duce*, an interventionist and war agitator during the First World War, influenced Italian fascism. Through Nello's background story, Morante connects the mistreatment of children to that of animals, and then links both to political totalitarianism and warmongering.

Politicizing Gender Roles: The Symbolic Mother
Morante's privileging of female over male is the hierarchical reversal that has received the most extensive critical attention. Cristina della Colletta, for example, writes that "*La Storia* rejects the rigid binary opposition between fiction and history and demonstrates that the contribution of fiction is essential for the resurrection of women's voices from the depths of historical oblivion" (119). Maria Ornella Marotti refers to Morante's "objection to power as exerted by the patriarchy, and her embracing of maternal love as the only antidote to the

male violence of history" (63). It is important to keep in mind, however, that Morante's opposition of maternity to patriarchy is not the privileging of one biological gender over the other, but rather a contrast between life-takers, those who seek power and domination over others, and life-bearers, those who on the contrary nurture and sustain others.

According to the feminist critic Carla Lonzi's *Manifesto di rivolta femminile,* "liberarsi per la donna non vuol dire accettare la stessa vita dell'uomo perché è invivibile, ma esprimere il suo senso dell'esistenza" ("liberation for woman does not mean accepting the life man leads, because it is unlivable; rather, it means expressing her own sense of existence"). Applying this concept to *La storia,* we can see that Morante might have written Ida as a strong and powerful woman of action, to be admired and respected as the equivalent of a strong male protagonist. Instead, Ida is misshapen, mediocre, and frightened; yet precisely her unexceptionality reveals the true courage and strength that comes from motherhood. Morante compares her to a tiger who rips her own flesh so that she can feed her child,[12] an image set up in direct opposition to the male world in which her older son would almost be capable of devouring her: "[L]e fami di Nino lo inferocivano al punto da trasformarlo quasi in un cannibale, pronto a mangiarsi la madre" (127; "Nino's hunger so ravaged him that he was almost transformed into a cannibal, ready to eat his mother" 109). Rather than biological strength or physical violence, it is the supernatural force of maternal love that merits our awe.

Morante's novel essentially centers around a mother figure as the origin and means of life. The wholeheartedness with which Ida loves her child, despite the way he was forced upon her unwillingly through a rape, shows the true power of motherhood. In this light, maternal love thus becomes paradoxically the cure for the male violence inflicted on women's bodies. The crucial importance of love and nurturing represented by the mother is even brought home in moments of utter despair on the part of the male characters who participate in destructive warfare. For example, a German soldier calls out for his *Mutti* as he is being killed by Davide Segre. In this yearning for the mother, he reveals his humanity and his wish for salvation through love. Through this reminder of his genealogy, he is no longer considered merely as part of the almost mechanical German military, but is suddenly seen as an individual capable of love. Even Ida's rapist, Gunther, longs for his mother during his moments of loneliness.[13] The narrator

---

[12] Benedetti argues that Morante's metaphor "elevates [Ida] to a majestic status: maternal love turns Ida into a tigress, self-regenerating in her sacrifice [...] a symbol of Christ, who gives his body to redeem humanity" (79).

[13] Sgavicchia provides a comparison of Gunther with Eichmann, the protagonist from Arendt's *Banality of Evil,* described as an "individuo obbediente alla legge ma incapace di pensare" (115; "an individual who obeys the laws but is incapable of thinking"). However, Morante ultimately humanizes even this character through his search for maternal love.

emphasizes this aspect of their short-lived relation by stating that "si arrestava per aspettarla, uguale a un figlio" (64; "he stopped to wait for her, like a son" 54). Morante portrays these men as instinctively searching for maternal love to save them from the systematic violence of the world, while at the same time showing that it is too late for them to return to the loving female realm after having participated in the brutal male one.

The Child
Given Morante's assertion in *Pro o contro la bomba atomica* that "in ogni poeta c'è rimasto sempre un bambino" (116; "within every poet there has always remained a child"), it is not surprising that many of her protagonists are actually children.[14] Morante had previously introduced a subversive and symbolic child character in *Il mondo salvato dai ragazzini* (1968).[15] Like Useppe, Pazzariello is presented as a child who rejects the conventional world of institutions, preferring the company of animals.[16] The government officials who try to collect his information for the archives declare his civil state ("stato civile" 167) as "ragazzo" ("child") and his nationality as "apolide" ("stateless"). Under gender, Pazzariello defines himself as "felice e magico" ("happy and magical"), not conforming to the biological division of the sexes nor what that may symbolize. He wanders the city, turning objects previously thrown away as garbage into clothes, and street leftovers into meals which he shares with stray cats. Accused of being "anarchico" ("anarchist") and "astorico" ("ahistorical"), he is shunned by the community since he "disonora la Patria" ("dishonors the Fatherland"), "oltraggia la Pubblica Moralità" ("outrages Public Morality"), and "non rispetta l'Autorità" (170; "does not respect Authority"). No government institution could control him: he was so dangerous as to be expelled from the prisons for creating chaos and driven out of the mental ward for laughing. The State, however, eventually manages to annihilate him: "A séguito della Nuova Riforma Sociale s'è trovata una soluzione moderna e razionale in merito all'individuo in questione eliminandolo scientificamente nella camera a pressione [...]. E così l'affare 'Pazzariello' è stato, infine, liquidato" (179-80; "A modern and rational

---

[14] Regarding specifically *La storia*, Zlobnicki finds that the radical and symbolic "choice of the humble subject of a preschool child as a protagonist of an 'historical' novel is unique within the context of Italian literature [...]. For the first time, a baby dominates a vast novel of over 600 pages" (79).
[15] Notably, Morante chose to print his story horizontally on the page, thus physically manifesting her own rebellion from the norm. She does not respect the line and rather presents the story as a poem, including a few musical notes and hand-made drawings.
[16] One might further note the similarity in the poem's final sentence — "In sostanza e *verità* tutto questo non è nient'altro che un *gioco*" ("In substance and *truth* all of this is nothing other than a *game*"; emphasis in the original) — and Useppe's translation of the birds' song as, "È uno scherzo uno scherzo tutto uno scherzo!" (269; "It's a joke a joke all a joke" 534).

solution following the New Social Reform has been found in regard to the individual in question, eliminating him scientifically in a gas chamber [...]. And thus the 'Pazzariello' case has been, finally, liquidated").[17] Pazzariello had effectively — and legally — been exterminated by the State, with clear reference to the Holocaust and its possible recurrence. After he is murdered, the radio spews out statist propaganda in its press announcement: "Sacrosanto dovere e diritto d'ogni individuo è l'inquadramento nella perfetta compàgine dello Stato fuori della quale la persona umana si riduce a un quid inqualificabile e superfluo" (187; "It is a sacrosant duty and right of every individual to be squared into the State as a whole, outside of which a human being is reduced to an unqualifiable and superflous entity"). The story of Pazzariello's life and death is thus a fable about how the political system attempts to kill the individual spirit personified as an innocent child.

Pazzariello's story can offer added insight into the ideological foundation for Useppe's character.[18] Within the novel, Useppe must remain a child who will never reach adulthood since, as we are repeatedly told, he is too good for this world.[19] Morante emphasizes this aspect not only because he acts as the metaphoric *fanciullo divino*, but because he is the antithesis of the violence and aggression that characterize the male-dominated world of the novel. Susanna Scarparo notes that Useppe opposes "integration into the symbolic order, preferring a world of dreams, poetry and silence to that of the oppressive fascist body politic" (62). Indeed, Morante expressly includes anecdotes that reveal his inherently anti-authoritarian spirit. For example, he vehemently refuses to sit behind benches in school as "tutte le norme della scuola: la clausura, il banco, la disciplina, parevano prove impossibili per lui; e lo spettacolo della scolaresca

---

[17] The emperor then declares that the problems of the world are to be blamed on women over the age of forty, and then on canary birds, ordering their immediate deaths – again showing Morante's proximity to women and animals, in addition to children.
[18] Sgavicchia considers *La storia* to be in opposition to Morante's previous novel, *L'isola di Arturo*, in which "il protagonista esce dall'infanzia ed entra nella storia" (100; "the protagonist leaves his childhood and enters history") by enlisting in the army. Although Arturo's caretaker warns him that modern war is "tutta un macchinario di macelleria, e un orrendo formicaio di sfaceli, senza nessun merito di valore autentico" (1357; "nothing but mechanized butchery, a loathsome ant heap of destruction and not a matter of courage" 340-41), Arturo innocently mistakes the fictional tales of heroism in chivalric epics for his contemporary reality. Sgavicchio relates this character to Useppe, as "nel finale del romanzo, il fanciullo sacro, rammemorato platonicamente il proprio paradiso, chiude il cerchio del 'mito' aperto da Arturo nell'*Isola*: dopo aver attraversato la storia [...] incontra la visione della poesia" (121; "at the end of the novel, the sacred child, platonically calling to mind his own paradise, closes the circle of the 'myth' opened by Arturo in *Arturo's Island*: after crossing history [...] he finds the vision of poetry"). It is also worth noting that, in the opening pages, Arturo mentions that his dog is his only friend, having even invented a language to communicate between them (3).
[19] Tellingly, his full name is Giuseppe Felice Angiolino (i.e., Joseph Happy Little Angel).

seduta in fila doveva sembrargli un fenomeno incredibile" (446; "all the regulations, the confinement, the bench, the discipline were impossible trials; and the sight of the pupils seated in rows must have seemed an incredible phenomenon to him" 379).[20] He does not put his faith in a fiat money system either, as he considers that "i soldi" (money) "in mano sua, non avevano altro valore che di carta qualunque" (368; "had no more value than ordinary paper" 313).[21] Morante's empathic portrayal of Useppe's plight encourages readers to cheer his rejection of a statist world with its systematic attempts to exact conformity through control.

Morante gives particular importance not only to Useppe's actions, but also to his very method of expression since he speaks an alternative language, not confined by the strict regulations imposed by grammar. As he learns to speak, his use of semantics reflects the essential unity of his worldview, for example his referring to everything that shines — even a gob of spit — as a star. Yet he also creates his own definitions to express distinctions where others see only sameness: he becomes offended when told that snow is white, insisting instead that it is made up of many colors. He spontaneously creates mystical poems about the harmony of nature, poems that a fascist mentality would consider to be nonsense but that, according to his adult friend Davide, reveal "DIO" (523; "GOD" 444).[22] In his innocence, Useppe perceives a different world than the one accepted as reality, one in which there are no horrors but only eternal delight. His older brother Nino tries to integrate him into the order of language by correcting his pronunciation, but Useppe insists that his anomalous way of speaking is intentional. He even maintains that his name should be Useppe instead of Giuseppe, thus expressing his unique personal identity against a

---

[20] According to Chappell, public schools are frequently referred to as "holding tanks" by libertarians (365).

[21] Fiat money is decreed legal tender by a government even though it has no inherent worth. This statement further proves that Useppe's perspective lies outside the state system and that he refuses to play by their rules.

[22] "Le stelle come gli alberi e fruscolano come gli alberi. / Il sole per terra come una manata di catenelle e anelli. / Il sole tutto come tante piume cento piume mila piume. / Il sole su per l'aria come tante scale di palazzi. / La luna come una scala e su in cima s'affaccia Bella che s'annisconne. / Dormite canarini arinchiusi come due rose. / Le 'ttelle come tante rondini che si salutano. E negli alberi. / Il fiume come i belli capelli. E i belli capelli. / I pesci come canarini. E volano via. / E le foie come ali. E volano via. / E il cavallo come una bandiera. / E vola via" (523 ; "Stars like trees and rustle like trees. / The sun on the ground like a handful of little chains and rings. / The sun all like lots of feathers a hundred a thousand feathers. / The sun up in the air like lots of steps of buildings. / The moon like a stairway and at the top Bella looks out and hides. / Sleep canaries folded up like two roses. / The ttars like swallows saying hello to each other. And in the trees. / The river like pretty hair. And the pretty hair. / The fish like canaries. And they fly away. / And the leaves like wings. And they fly away. / And the horse like a flag. And he flies away" 443).

standardized system in which children are given pre-existing names. Morante leads us to believe that only Useppe can grasp the world in all its marvelous harmony and richness, whereas the rest of society perceives it merely through preordained categories prescribed by others. Sharon Wood points to the transcendence of duality expressed in Useppe's final poem before his death: "Il sole è come un albero grande / che dentro tiene i nidi. / E suona come una cicala maschio e come il mare / e con l'ombra ci scherza come una gatta piccola" 632 ("The sun is like a big tree / that has nests inside. / And it sounds like a male cicada and like the sea / and it plays with the shadow like a little cat" 697). According to Wood, the poem "transforms the syntagms of Davide's own poetry through simile and metaphor to create a linguistic universe of light that is whole and undivided, which heals the split between signifier and signified, masculine and feminine, heaven and earth. [...] Useppe's understanding of his world is affective, inclusive, an implicit rejection of the fractures that inhabit Davide's discourse" (83). Analyzed thus, even the poem's use of language becomes political, keeping with Morante's understanding of the poet as revolutionary and of the novel as manifesto.

In pointed contrast to the negative connotations of manhood as violent, the child Useppe is incapable of harming others — not only because he is weak and small when confronted, but more so because he relates to others through benevolence. Displaying the non-aggression principle as well as a posthumanist perspective, Useppe even refuses to eat meat because of the inherent violence in the act of murdering and then consuming another living being. Nor can he bear to see violence perpetrated upon other humans. Whereas images of war atrocities had become mainstream and quotidien, Useppe is so horrified by pictures of Holocaust victims in the newspaper that he is haunted by those images in his nightmares. Scarparo points to this reaction as the moment when he "learned that the symbolic order is hurtful and brutal" (65). Only once does Nino take Useppe into the outside world; and while he is initially exhilarated by his brother as paternal substitute, he is repulsed by the violence of the partisans and again demonstrates a refusal of this brutal world. After a while, Useppe stops even mentioning Nino and wholly recoils into the domestic space. Otherwise, Useppe is allowed to wander on adventures, but he only dares to do so when accompanied by Bella, meaning that he never truly leaves the female sphere since he is still being guided by one of his mothers.

Useppe, therefore, holds a special place in the symbolic realm of the novel, since he is portrayed in a way that blurs the distinctions between male and female, human and animal. Indeed, the choice of a child protagonist may already be a posthumanist move, since children themselves are often, and legally, considered less than human adults. As Concetta D'Angeli remarks, "se un personaggio come Useppe fa il suo ingresso da protagonista in un romanzo, allora l'universo narrativo può essere aperto anche agli animali, assunti con dignità di personaggi" (66-67; "if a character like Useppe can become the protagonist of a novel, then the narrative universe is open also to animals, to be considered with dignity as characters"). Morante initiates Useppe's ties to the animal kingdom by comparing him to a kid, or baby goat, at the moment of his birth: "Si annunciò con un vagito così leggero che pareva un caprettino nato ultimo e scordato fra la paglia" (95; "He announced his presence with a whimper so faint he seemed a little lamb [literally, baby goat], born last and forgotten in the straw" 82). Acting as a bridge between animals and humans, Useppe is even mistaken for a pup (by other dogs) given his proximity to Bella: "Anzi, questa sua puzza s'era attaccata pure a Useppe; tanto che a volte diversi cani gli giravano intorno annusandolo, forse nell'incertezza che lui pure fosse una specie di cucciolo canino. Costoro (i cani) erano si può dire i soli frequentatori di Useppe" (494; "Indeed, this stink of hers had been communicated also to Useppe; so at times various dogs circled around him, sniffing him, perhaps wondering if he too wasn't some kind of puppy. They (the dogs) were, you might say, Useppe's only companions" 419).[23] Thus, the comparison of Useppe to animals does not belittle him, as if he were a non-human, but rather elevates him for his capacity to transcend biological categories and almost become unified with nature.

Anti-Authoritarian Spirituality and Religion
The main characters of the novel do not adhere to any religious doctrine or conventional practice, as they each have their own individual belief and way of expressing their spirituality. Useppe, for example, finds God in the silence of nature. He explains to his friend Scimò that God is present in the surrounding trees even though the latter, unable to think outside institutional sanction, insists that God can only be found inside a church building. The anarchist Davide Segre (as I will illustrate below) writes about God in his poems — not as an omnipotent ruler over a divine kingdom, but rather as a spiritual energy only

---

[23] D'Angeli makes the point that animals are not idealized by Morante, citing the cat Rossella as an example: "Sottolineo i tratti di cattiveria e violenza di Rossella perché mi sembra importante non cadere in un luogo comune che verrebbe spontaneo — ma sarebbe inesatto — adottare interpretando il ruolo degli animali nella narrativa di Elsa Morante: che essi cioè siano la parte buona del mondo in opposizione alla crudeltà umana" (67 ; "I underline Rossella's moments of cruelty and violence because it seems important not to fall in the stereotypical dichotomy, which would be easy — but would be incorrect — in interpreting the role of animals in Elsa Morante's narrative: that they are the good part of the world in opposition to human cruelty"). However, Morante uses this feline character to criticize a refusal to the call of motherhood, further treating humans and animals as equals in the novel. Rossella leaves her kittens to fend for themselves while she wanders and mingles with the human population.

found where there is beauty, whether in nature or in art.[24]

Morante focuses most extensively on non-authoritarian spirituality through the character Santina, whose name, which could be translated as "little saint," might initially evoke Catholicism. Instead, this fortune-teller is the embodiment of an unconventional, and even pagan, spirituality. Eschewing both imposed regulations and violence, she forbids the male members of society from entering during readings. Her room is decorated with religious relics pertaining to the Madonna, celebrating motherhood and maternal love as the means through which salvation entered the world. The women who visit her lend greater credence to her fortunetelling than they would to the words of a preacher or a priest. They truly believe that she can communicate with the dead, putting her in the position of mediating between the realms of life and death. Morante further subverts the rigidly established hierarchy of Catholicism by ignoring religious doctrine and re-appropriating the symbolic value of the Madonna and Baby Jesus. Morante presents Ida as a metaphorical reincarnation of the Holy Mother, having conceived a child out of wedlock while still being chaste. At the end of the novel, Useppe's death suggests the imagery of Jesus in the way he falls with his arms outstretched as if he were on a cross (646), thus reinforcing the idea of Ida as the Savior's mother. This symbolism represents the hope of redemption, even though the novel ends in absolute death as no resurrection is possible.[25]

Despite Ida's suggestive Christian symbolism, when she is about to become a mother it is her Jewish origin which is highlighted. She seeks the assistance and support of midwives in the marginalized Jewish ghetto as she prepares to give birth. This community of women, independent of the authoritative and male-dominated institutions of both Christianity and Judaism, illustrates the solidarity that is possible between individuals in their time of need, and which can only exist outside of the dominant system. Here Ida also learns of current events from the women, as they describe their own form of history, and relate a personal truth rather than national propaganda. Morante emphasizes the maternal domestic quality of this space, saying that Ida was drawn there by "un richiamo di dolcezza, quasi come l'odore di una stalla per un vitello" (93; "a summons of sweetness, like the stable's smell for a calf" 81). The fact that the Jewish ancestry is transmitted through matrilineal descendency may further support the importance of female genealogy in the novel. Morante thus

---

[24] Morante possessed Eastern esoteric works in her library, including *Milarepa* (1955), *Bhagavad Gita* (1958), and *Trois Upanishads* (1955), which, according to Sgavicchia, likely influenced the author in developing Useppe's vision of God (118).

[25] Cazalé Bérard points out that the plot contains various elements from Morante's unfinished novel titled *Senza i conforti della religione,* which ends in the disillusionment and loss of faith in both God and poetry on the part of the young child Giuseppe. The fact that the new version of the character retains his innocence in death, rather than losing his faith in life, suggest a much less pessimistic outcome in the novel than was previously intended, and thus a more hopeful overall message.

introduces a vision of religion which valorizes supportive female communities and personal spirituality against a background of imposed hierarchical masculine structures.

Anarchism

Studies that interpret *La storia* through a strictly feminist lens fail to account for the prominence of Davide Segre, the self-proclaimed anarchist and pacifist.[26] His character demonstrates that men, in the world of the novel, are eminently capable of acting against predominantly masculine codes that encourage violence. His rational speech, in particular his defense of anarchism, also allows Morante to expressly condemn political power through spoken words as well as narrative actions: "l'idea anarchica è la negazione del potere. E il potere e la violenza sono tutt'uno..." (225 ; "The anarchist ideal is the negation of power. And power and violence are the same thing..." 193). Segre is also an outlier through his ethnicity since, although an atheist, he is culturally Jewish and thus forced to hide outside the political system which aims to destroy him. He is overcome with the urge for violence only once, when he mercilessly murders a German soldier. This act, so contrary to his nature, haunts him for the rest of his life and fills him with regret. Davide escapes the mandates of an imposed political structure by physically confining himself inside the female realm, first at the shelter and then in Santina's room. Yet this affinity with the feminine realm is not a choice about gender, but a facet of his anarchist philosophy, expressed in a series of speeches that constitute a political manifesto at the heart of the novel.

Near the novel's climax, Morante gives Davide twenty pages to explain his anarchist vision to drunken onlookers at a bar. This scene creates an extradiagetic parallel, for Morante's own political position seems to have been as poorly understood as Davide's speech, by those of her peers programmed to think within a given political ideology.[27] Davide echoes Morante's own

---

[26] As Carbone points out, in fact, Morante's vision is embodied by the two male characters of the novel: "Se Useppe rappresenta la favola, Davide riveste il ruolo intellettuale [e] nel romanzo rappresenta l'ideologia. [...] La Morante è tutta in queste due figure: se da un canto presta a Davide gran parte della sua vita, delle sue letture, della sua personalità, del dono del narratore; d'altro canto, barbara e selvaggia, si sente vicina a Useppe, cercando la salvezza nella verità primordiale, nell'innocenza, nella poesia, nella bellezza" (90 ; "If Useppe represents the fairy tale, Davide incarnates the role of the intellectual [and] he represents ideology in the novel. [...] Morante is complete in these two figures: if on the one hand she gives a large part of her life to Davide, her readings, her personality, the gift of narration; on the other hand, uncivilized and wild, she feels close to Useppe, searching for salvation in primordial truth, in innocence, in poetry, in beauty").

[27] This insertion of a political manifesto in the form of a character's speech is reminiscent of John Galt's public announcement in Ayn Rand's *Atlas Shrugged* from 1957.

Elsa Morante's *La storia*: A Posthumanist, Feminist, Anarchist Response to Power   441

ideological rejection of History when he states:

"[I]nsomma *tuta* la Storia *l'è* una storia di fascismi più o meno larvati [...]. Il quale centro di gravità, sempre lo stesso, qua è: il Potere. Sempre uno: il POTERE [...]. [R]azze, classi, cittadinanze, sono balle: spettacoli d'illusionismo montati dal Potere. È il Potere che ha bisogno della Colonna Infame [...]. E la sola rivoluzione autentica è l'ANARCHIA! A-NAR-CHIA, che significa: NESSUN potere, di NESSUN tipo, a NESSUNO, su NESSUNO! Chiunque parla di rivoluzione e, insieme, di Potere, è un baro! e un falsario! E chiunque desidera il Potere, per sé e per chiunque altro, è un reazionario; e, pure se nasce proletario, è un borghese! [...] I loro Stati sono delle banche di strozzinaggio, che investono il prezzo del lavoro e della coscienza altrui nei loro sporchi affari: fabbriche d'armi e di immondizia, intrallazzi rapine guerre omicide!"

(566-76)

"All through the course of human History, there has existed no other system but [fascism] [...]. Which center of gravity, always the same, is: Power. Always one: POWER [...]. Races, classes, citizenships, are all balls, tricks performed by Power. It's Power that needs the gallows [...]. And the only genuine revolution is ANARCHY! AN-ARCHY, which means: NO power, of NO sort, for NO one, over NO one! Anybody who talks about revolution and, at the same time, about Power, is a liar! He's a cheat! And anyone who wants Power, for himself or for anybody else, is a reactionary; and even if he was born a proletarian, he's a bourgeois! [...] Their States are banks, usurers, who invest the price of others' labor and consciousness in their own dirty dealings: factories of weapons and garbage, intrigues, robberies, wars, murders!"

(478-88)

Strikingly, Davide defines all forms of government as *fascism*, regardless of the political structure, since they claim power in order to exert violence through an industry of extermination ("*Industria dello sterminio*" 566; emphasis in the original).

In addition to denouncing governments as all inherently fascist because they are sustained by power, Davide describes the paradigms that need to be changed in order for humanity to be set on the right path. Unsurprisingly, these themes again tie in closely with the world Morante envisions within the novel. Davide is equally disgusted by the imposed marginalization of people by national powers through propaganda, stating:

"E i sensi, guariti del *delirio de pestilensia* del Potere, ritornano alla comunione con la natura [...]. [D]entro a ciascuno di noi c'è un Cristo. [...] [B]asterebbe riconoscere il Cristo in tutti quanti: io, te, gli altri [...]. Insieme: né tedeschi né italiani, né pagani né ebrei, né borghesi né proletari: tutti uguali, tutti cristi nudi."

(573, 591-93)

"And the senses, healed from the pestilential raving of Power, return to communion with nature [...]. [T]here's a Christ inside each one of us. [...] It would be enough to recognize the Christ in everybody: me, you, the others. [...] Together, not Germans or Italians, not pagans or Jews, not bourgeois or proletariat: all the same, all naked christs."

(486, 501-02)

A declared atheist, Davide espouses an alternative conception of religion in which he reclaims the essential figure of Jesus Christ apart from the institutionalized Church. He asserts that Jesus's preachings of love in a State based on war and oppression is the anarchy that all should embrace: "E quel cristo là storicamente fu un vero Cristo: ossia un uomo (ANARCHICO!) che non ha mai rinnegato la coscienza totale" 593 ("And that Christ, historically speaking, was a real Christ: that is, a man (ANARCHIST!) who never denied total consciousness" 499).[28]

Anyone doubting that Davide speaks for the author may go back to the first page of the novel in which Morante, through the narrator's voice, denotes the division in society between the power elite and the rest of humanity: "[N]oto principio immobile della dinamica storica: *agli uni il potere, e agli alti la servitù*" (7; "[I]mmobile principle of historical dynamics: *power to some, servitude to others*" 3; emphasis in the original). She also exposes the fact that industry under state power gives rise to the military industrial complex: "E siccome il lavoro dell'industria è sempre al servizio di Poteri e Potenze, fra i suoi prodotti il primo posto, necessariamente, spetta alle armi (*corsa agli armamenti*) le quali, in base all'economia dei consumi di massa, trovano il loro sbocco nella guerra di massa" ("And since labor in industry is always at the service of the Powerful and the Powers, among its products prime importance is naturally given to arms (the armament race), which in a mass-consumption economy, find their outlet in mass warfare"). Her definition of *Potenze* (*Powers*) is "alcuni Stati [that] praticamente si dividono l'intera superficie terrestre in rispettive proprietà, o Imperi" ("certain Nations [...] which have virtually divided the entire surface of the globe into their respective properties, or Empires") while *Poteri* would correspond to those who hold the capital. Therefore, her designation of *Poteri* (the *Powerful*) as *capitalistici* (*capitalistic*) is not a reference to free market capitalism, but on the contrary, the depiction of a situation in which industry and capital are at the service of State power. In this regard she remains independent of the communist ideology fashionable in Italy at the time since her division is not between "bourgeois" capitalists and proletariat workers, but between those who hold political power and those who suffer the consequences. While the *Potenze* (*Powers*) are bent exclusively on advancing their own interests, those subjected to servitude are made to further the interests of Power through political propaganda: "Agli altri, i soggetti alla servitù, che non partecipano agli utili ma che tuttavia servono, tali interessi vengono presentati in termini di astrazioni ideali, varianti col variare della pratica pubblicitaria" (7; "For the others, those in servitude, who have no share of the gain but still must serve, such interests are presented in terms of ideal abstractions, varying with the variations of advertising methods" 3). Thus the

---

[28] Cinquegrani views Davide Segre as a representation of the Antichrist (via Nietzsche's Zarathustra), meant to overturn the Christian God and illuminate a new anarchic consciousness.

only solution for the world, as she has Davide explain, are societies in which the State would not hold Power over individuals.

Morante appears to have formulated her vision of anarchism, as espoused by her character Davide, without the systematic treatment of a specific political theory, nor does she undertake elsewhere a sustained effort to elucidate the outlines of her particular conception of it. Nonetheless, she insists upon the basic premise that anarchism is the antithesis of *Power* and therefore cannot be arrived at through the use of violence or state power in any form. This approach is fundamentally opposed to the general formulation of anarchism within communist circles in which it was deemed necessary to first institute a coercive regime before imagining that the state itself would somehow dissolve into statelessness. This refusal to align anarchism with Leftist paradigms might seem at first glance to bring her vision in line with that of the American libertarian philosopher, economist, and activist Murray Rothbard, who articulated a comprehensive and coherent conception of anarchism in his writings beginning in the 1950s and 1960s. Rothbard opens his treatise *Anatomy of the State* (1965) with the absolute separation of society and state — "'we' are *not* the government; the government is *not* 'us'" (10) — defining the latter along with Max Weber as "that organization in society which attempts to maintain a monopoly of the use of force and violence in a given territorial area" (11). Accusing establishment intellectuals as "opinion-molders" who spew propaganda to the masses (20), Rothbard critiqued nationalism as an ideological weapon through which "a war between *rulers* [is] converted into a war between *peoples*, with each people coming to the defense of its rulers in the erroneous belief that the rulers [are] defending *them*" (24).[29] These statements have affinities with those made by both the character Davide Segre and the author Elsa Morante. Where they split company, however, is on the issue of property rights. Whereas Rothbard, in Lockean fashion, grounds human rights in the self-ownership of one's body and one's rightfully acquired property, advocating free market capitalism, Morante includes private property in the list of evils to combat in order to arrive at a collectivist anarchic society.

An anarchist whose political theories may resonate more consistently with the anarchic ideas expressed in the novel is the nineteenth-century Russian philosopher and activist Mikhail Bakunin, who had gathered a following in Italy in the 1860s, where he entertained relations with Giuseppe Garibaldi. Distrusting political power of any sort and referring to governments as "systematic poisoners" (1), Bakunin distanced himself from the Marxist goal of a

---

[29] Bourne had famously declared: "War is the health of the State" (9, 21). Rothbard's manifesto of libertarianism, *For a New Liberty* (1973), following in the wake of nineteenth-century anti-statists the likes of Gustave de Molinari, Lysander Spooner, and Benjamin Tucker, outlines his vision of a functioning rights-based anarchist society meeting all social needs.

dictatorship of the proletariat: "In a word, we reject all legislation, all authority, and all privileged, licensed, official, and legal influence, even though arising from universal suffrage, convinced that it can turn only to the advantage of a dominant minority of exploiters against the interests of the immense majority in subjection to them. This is the sense in which we are really Anarchists" (II). Given Morante's insistence on the evils of Power, we might imagine that Morante would have a similar definition of her political ideology. Bakunin's main work, *God and the State*, argues against both the political power of the State and the manipulative power of organized religion: "Christianity is precisely the religion *par excellence,* because it exhibits and manifests, to the fullest extent, the very nature and essence of every religious system, which is *the impoverishment, enslavement, and annihilation of humanity for the benefit of divinity* [...]. God being master, man is the slave [...]. *The idea of God implies the abdication of human reason and justice; it is the most decisive negation of human liberty, and necessarily ends in the enslavement of mankind, both in theory and practice*" (II; emphasis in the original). Although Morante does not explicitly speak out against the idea of God, her emphasis on a non-institutional spirituality linked to maternity accords well with Bakunin's rejection of a supreme authority held over people by a deity. The correspondence, nonetheless, is not absolute: while Morante shared Bakunin's rejection of statist and hierarchical systems of power, her writings do not advocate a Bakuninian-style revolt on the part of workers to collectivize the means of production.

Morante not only invites her readers to imagine an alternative system through the novel's various anti-authoritarian characters, but in one instance she actually envisions the workings of an alternative anarchist society in action, even within the larger frame of government control outside their walls. When the victims of the air raids move into a shelter, they create a community ad hoc with a new system of order. In fear of being arrested by the police, the able-bodied men must hide whenever there is a knock on the door. They cannot — nor do they have the will to — exert violence on others as they are in hiding. The women therefore command and organize society by their own rules, feeding and protecting the others. Morante shows that such an alternative system, where the nurturing mother is the center of the community, is possible and even successful. Useppe refers to this period as one of the happiest times of his short life, as he was not aware of the hardships but only of the safety he felt. Through this example, Morante is again putting the emphasis on mothers above all other members of society — a society in which lust for Power is unimaginable and maternal love is the guiding principle.

Death and Failure
Despite these glimpses of an alternative world, the narrative of *La storia* ends in tragedy: the deaths of Useppe, Davide, Bella, and eventually Ida, who in her madness undergoes a symbolic death even before her physical demise. The final

epileptic fit which leads to Useppe's death unsurprisingly occurs in the oppressive and violent outside world. Useppe falls as he is being harassed by a gang of older boys who expose him to the world of force which he ardently refuses. The gang uses real physical brutality, as they "per punirlo l'abbiano un po' sbatacchiato, dandogli magari qualche botta" 635 ("slammed him around a bit to punish him, maybe hitting him a couple of times" 536). This violent death encapsulates the underlying problem of society, for if every member practiced the non-aggression principle, then neither gangs nor Fascists would ever be able to rise to power. Useppe is, we may say, not so much killed by a natural disease as by the external physical assault and the trauma of senseless violence inflicted on his tiny body.[30] Davide, on the other hand, is found dead from a drug overdose, having been too weak to face the world or fight the system.

Morante ends the novel with the statement, "... e la Storia continua ..." (656 ; "... and History continues..." 554), signalling that the political forces of domination controlling the official record go unabated outside the boundaries of her fictional world. The end of her *storia* with the return of the official form of *Storia* is the most tragic outcome possible within the ideological framework of the novel and seems to confirm Davide's assertion that "la felicità non è di questo mondo" (520 ; "happiness is not of this world" 441). Nevertheless, while Morante's refusal of a facile and optimistic ending within the novel acknowledges the difficulty of such an occurrence, the novel itself is a political act that aims to actualize its program in the real world though a widespread rejection of Power on the part of her readership.[31] As Etienne de la Boétie had reasoned in sixteenth-century France, political systems can only be dissolved when subjects begin to withhold their obedience: "It is therefore the inhabitants themselves who permit, or, rather, bring about, their own objection, since by ceasing to submit they would put an end to their servitude. [...] Resolve to serve no more, and you are at once freed" (46-48).

Morante warns of the world's destruction into nothingness if History continues to be ruled by the unchanging politic of power and violence rather than the non-speciest, feminine, spiritual and especially anarchist world suggested in the novel. As she argues elsewhere, "l'arte è il contrario della disintegrazione" ("art is the opposite of disintegration"), and thus her novel itself can be seen to serve as a possible antidote which will "impedire la disintegrazione della coscienza umana" ("prevent the disintegration of human

---

[30] Wood refers to Morante's long description just before Useppe dies as "a moment of witness, a rejection of the solitude of violent death, and through description, a simultaneous holding of the character within the gaze of the narrator and therefore the reader; we experience a halting of narrative time, a moment of contemplation before the character is returned to the maelstrom of 'history'" (77).

[31] Morante insisted on releasing the paperback edition at the affordable price of only 2,000 lire. Lucamante notes that also for this reason, the "violent critique" by intellectuals "did not stain *La storia*'s positive reception by the general public" (156).

consciousness" *Pro o contra* 101-05). Using the form of a novel, Morante thus aims to expose the horrific effects of Power, condemning established institutions and ideologies and portraying her own truth against political manipulation and propaganda.

Columbia University (alumna)

Works Cited

Amberson, Deborah, and Elena Past. "Editors' Introduction." Amberson and Past, eds. 1-21.

———, eds. *Thinking Italian Animals: Human and Posthuman in Modern Italian Literature and Film*. New York: Palgrave Macmillan, 2014.

Bakunin, Michail Aleksandrovič. *God and the State*. New York, NY: Mother Earth Publ. Assoc., 1905. https://www.marxists.org/reference/archive/bakunin/works/godstate/

Balestrini, Nanni, Elisabetta Rasy, Letizia Paolozzi, and Umberto Silva. "Contro il romanzone della Morante." *Il Manifesto* (18 July 1974): 3.

Benedetti, Laura. *The Tigress in the Snow: Motherhood and Literature in Twentieth-century Italy*. Toronto: U of Toronto P, 2007.

Boétie, Etienne de la. *The Politics of Obedience: The Discourse of Voluntary Servitude*. Intro. Murray N. Rothbard. Trans. Harry Kurz. Auburn, AL: The Ludwig von Mises Institute, 1975.

Bourne, Randolph S. *The State*. Tucson, AZ: See Sharp Press, 1998.

Cazalé Bérard, Claude. "Il romanzo in-finito." *Testo e senso* 13 (2012): 2-32.

Chappell, Robert H. "Anarchy Revisited: An Inquiry into the Public Education Dilemma." *Journal of Libertarian Studies* 2.4 (1978): 357-72.

Cinquegrani, Alessandro. "Davide Segre e l'Anticristo." *La storia di Elsa Morante*. Ed. Siriana Sgavicchia. Pisa: ETS, 2012. 173-82.

D'Angeli, Concetta. "Soltanto l'animale è veramente innocente. Gli animali ne *La Storia*." *Letture di Elsa Morante*. Ed. Gruppo la Luna. Torino: Rosenberg & Sellier, 1987. 66-73.

Debenedetti, Giacomo. "16 ottobre 1943. " Milano: il Saggiatore, 1959.

Della Coletta, Cristina. *Plotting the Past. Metamorphoses of Historical Narrative in Modern Italian Fiction.* West Lafayette, Indiana: Purdue UP, 1996.

Kalay Zlobnicki, Grace. *The Theme of Childhood in Elsa Morante*. Mississippi: Romance Monographs, 1996.

Lonzi, Carla. *Manifesto di rivolta femminile.* 1970. http://www.columbia.ed/itc/ architecture/ ockman/pdfs/ feminism/manifesto.pdf. Web.

Lucamante, Stefania, ed. *Elsa Morante's Politics of Writing: Rethinking Subjectivity, History, and the Power of Art*. Madison, NJ: Fairleigh Dickinson UP, 2014.

———. *Forging Shoah Memories: Italian Women Writers, Jewish Identity, and the Holocaust*. New York, NY: Palgrave Macmillan, 2014.

Lyons, Kenise. "Pro o contro la rabbia: Elsa Morante, Pier Paolo Pasolini, and the Work of Art in the Atomic Age." Lucamante, ed. 247-57.

Marotti, Maria Ornella. *Gendering Italian Fiction: Feminist Revisions of Italian History.* Madison, NJ: Fairleigh Dickinson UP, 1999.

Mecchia, Giuseppina. "Elsa Morante at the Biopolitical Turn." Amberson and Elena Past,

eds. 129-45.
Morante, Elsa. *Arturo's Island*. London: Collins, 1962.
_____. *La canzone degli F. P. e degli I. M. in tre parti: The Song of the H. F. and of the U. M. in Three Parts*. Trans. Mariangela Palladino and Patrick Hart. Novi Ligure: Joker, 2007.
_____. *History: A Novel*. Trans. William Weaver. New York: Alfred A. Knopf, 1977.
_____. *L'isola di Arturo; Romanzo*. Torino: Einaudi, 1957.
_____. *Il mondo salvato dai ragazzini e altri poemi*. Torino : Einaudi, 1968.
_____. *Piccolo manifesto dei comunisti: (senza classe né partito)*. Roma: Nottetempo, 2004.
_____. *La storia: romanzo*. Torino: Einaudi, 2014.
_____, and Cesare Garboli. *Pro o contro la bomba atomica: e altri scritti*. Milano: Adelphi, 1987.
Pasolini, Pier Paolo. "La gioia della vita: la violenza della storia." Editorial. *Tempo* (July 1974).
Rand, Ayn. *Atlas Shrugged*. New York: Random House, 1957.
Rocco Carbone, Lorenza. *Il mondo salvato dai ragazzini: nel centenario di Elsa Morante, 1912-2012*. Napoli: Kairós, 2013.
Rothbard, Murray N. "The Anatomy of the State." *Rampart Journal* (summer 1965): 1-24. Rpt. T. R. Machan, ed. *The Libertarian Alternative*. Chicago: Nelson-Hall Co., 1974. 69-93.
_____. *For a New Liberty*. New York: Macmillan, 1973.
Scarparo, Susanna. *Across Genres, Generations and Borders: Italian Women Writing Lives*. Newark, Del.: University of Delaware, 2004.
Sgavicchia, Siriana. "Fonti storiche e filosofiche nell'invenzione narrativa della storia." Sgavicchia, ed. 99-122.
_____, ed. *La storia di Elsa Morante*. Pisa: ETS, 2012.
Simons, John. *Animal Rights and the Politics of Literary Representation*. Houndmills, Basingstoke, Hampshire: Palgrave, 2002.
Wadiwel, Dinesh. "Animal by Any Other Name? Patterson and Agamben Discuss Animal (and Human) Life." *Borderlands* 3.1 (2004): *Borderlands e-journal*. Web.
Wolfe, Cary. *Zoontologies: The Question of the Animal*. Minneapolis: U of Minnesota P, 2003.
Wood, Sharon. "Excursus as Narrative Technique in *La storia*." Stefania Lucamante, ed. 75-86.

Romance Notes

Romance Notes is published three times a year. The journal accepts articles on any literary, cultural, or linguistic topic dealing with Romance studies. Articles may be written in any Romance language and in English. The articles should be no longer than 3,000 words in length and should consist of original material not published nor under publication elsewhere.

Submissions:

Romance Notes strictly adheres to *MLA* style and citation format, including a "Works Cited" at the end of the essay. Electronic submissions are preferred. Please send Microsoft Word-compatible attachments to romlpub@unc.edu, preferably in .doc or .docx format.

The Editors have a policy of "double blind submissions" for readers. Therefore, authors should send their name and university affiliation on a separate cover sheet. Once your work is submitted, we will acknowledge receipt via email. An evaluator will be assigned at the earliest possible moment. Evaluations are typically completed within 1-2 months. At that time, we will contact you regarding the decision of our reader, providing you with any available comments, recommendations, and edits.

Subscriptions:

Upon acceptance for publication, each author must subscribe to *Romance Notes* for at least one volume year (3 issues). The individual subscription price is $40.00 and the student subscription cost is $25.00.

Institutions interested in subscribing to the journal may do so at $50.00 per volume year. Back issues and single copies of the journal are also available for purchase at $25.00 + shipping.

Online Access:

Current issues may be accessed electronically on Project MUSE through subscribing libraries.

Journals past and present are also available to participating institutions from EBSCO.

Hispanófila

Hispanófila appears three times a year. The journal accepts essays on any literary, linguistic, or cultural topic dealing with the Spanish and Portuguese-speaking worlds. Articles may be written in English, Spanish, or Portuguese but cannot exceed 8,500 words, including notes and works cited. Previously published work and work under consideration by other journals should not be submitted.

Submissions:

All submissions must conform to the current *MLA Style Manual*. Articles written in Spanish or Portuguese may use traditional punctuation that does not necessarily reflect *MLA* standards. Electronic submissions are preferred. Please send Microsoft Word-compatible attachments to romlpub@unc.edu, preferably in .doc or .docx format.

Once your work is submitted, we will acknowledge receipt via email. An evaluator will be assigned at the earliest possible moment. Evaluations are typically completed within 1-2 months. At that time, we will contact you regarding the decision of our reader, providing you with any available comments, recommendations, and edits.

Subscriptions:

Upon acceptance for publication, each author must subscribe to *Hispanófila* for at least one volume year (3 issues). The individual subscription price is $40.00 and the student subscription cost is $25.00.

Institutions interested in subscribing to the journal may do so at $50.00 per volume year. Back issues and single copies of the journal are also available for purchase at $25.00 + shipping.

Online Access:

Current issues may be accessed electronically on Project MUSE through subscribing libraries. Back issues will be launched in Fall 2012.

Journals past and present are also available to participating institutions from EBSCO.

Online Blog:

Visit Hispanofila.org for the online blog and article discussions.

Consider

ARACNE

FOR YOUR NEXT PUBLICATION

ARACNE
is an independent publisher founded in Rome, Italy, in 1993. Its mission is to advance research in the sciences, humanities, and arts through publishing works by scientists, scholars, novelists, poets, and journalists as well as through disseminating their works throughout the scientific and academic world and society at large.

ARACNE welcomes proposals of publications, ranging from monographs to miscellaneous volumes, annotated editions, conference proceedings, and didactic materials.

ARACNE's rapidly expanding catalogue already includes more than 2,500 titles, some of which are winners of prestigious awards.

ARACNE has adopted a system of peer reviewing, and its staff collaborates with all contributors in order to publish works of the highest scholarly quality.

ARACNE
allows its authors to maintain copy-wrights of their works. ARACNE avails itself of the most advanced methods of publishing, printing books expeditiously and on demand so that updated editions can be easily made and volumes are never sold out. For further information, catalogue, and series, please visit Aracne's website: http://www. aracneeditrice.it

ADDRESS ALL YOUR INQUERIES TO:

info@aracneeditrice.it

STUDI E TESTI

A Collection of Monographs sponsored
by
Annali d'Italianistica, Inc.

ALL VOLUMES ARE AVAILABLE ON PRINT
ALL VOLUMES ARE AVAILABLE ELECTRONICALLY EXCEPT
VOLS. 1, 2, 4

Carmine Di Biase, ed. *"Oh! Mio vecchio William!" Italo Svevo and His Shakespeare.* Studi & Testi 10. Chapel Hill, NC: Annali d'Italianistica, 2015. Pp. X+118.
Editions:
1. Kindle.Amazon.com: E-book
2. CreateSpace.com - Books on Demand:
    ISBN-13: 978-0692545522 (Annali d'italianistica, Inc.)
    ISBN-10: 0692545522
3. PDF E-book: Email annali@unc.edu ($6.99)

Email annali@unc.edu to order the following volumes:
North America: Print copy $35; Print and digital $40; Digital only $ 25
Outside North America: Print copy $50; Print and digital $55; Digital only $25

Rosetta D'Angelo and Barbara Zaczek, editors and translators. *Resisting Bodies: Narratives of Italian Partisan Women.* Studi & Testi 9. Chapel Hill, NC: Annali d'Italianistica, 2008. Pp. 33 + 224. ISBN 0-9657956-8-3.

Thomas C. Stillinger and F. Regina Psaki, eds. *Boccaccio and Feminist Criticism.* Studi & Testi 8. Chapel Hill, NC: Annali d'Italianistica, 2006. Pp. vii + 273. ISBN 0-9657956-7-5

Robert C. Melzi. *The Conquering Monk. The Story of El Mansur, An Eighteenth-Century Italian Cleric who Conquered Chechnya and Daghestan.* With the translation of Boetti's *Relazione* (Turin, Archivio di Stato) and the *Biografia manoscritta* (Turin, Biblioteca Reale). Pp. vii + 95. Library of Congress Control No.: 2004106764. ISBN 0-9657956-6-7

Maria Domitilla Galluzzi. *Vita da lei narrata* (1624). Edition, introduction, and notes by Olimpia Pelosi. Studi & Testi 6. Chapel Hill, NC: Annali d'Italianistica, 2003. Pp. xxxiv + 273. Library of Congress Control No.: 2003114534. ISBN 0-9657956-5-9

Daria Valentini & Paola Carù, eds. *Beyond Artemisia: Female Subjectivity, History, and Culture in Anna Banti.* Studi & Testi 5. Chapel Hill, NC: Annali d'Italianistica, 2003. Pp. vi + 196. Library of Congress Cont. No.: 2003110677. ISBN 0-9657956-4-0

Giuseppe Conte. *Le stagioni / The Seasons.* Studi & Testi 4. Chapel Hill, NC: Annali d'italianistica, 2001. Pp. xvi + 136. Library of Congress Control No.: 2001086991. ISBN 0-9657956-3-2

Massimo Maggiari, ed. *The Waters of Hermes / Le acque di Ermes.* Studi & Testi 3. Chapel Hill, NC: Annali d'italianistica, 2000. Pp. 208. Library of Congress Catalog Card No.: 00-131648. ISBN 0-9657956-2-4

Rosamaria Lavalva. *The Eternal Child: The Poetry and Poetics of Giovanni Pascoli.* Studi & Testi 2. Chapel Hill, NC: Annali d'italianistica, 1999. Pp. 226. Library of Congress Catalog Card No.: 99-072079. ISBN 0-9657956-1-6

Augustus Mastri, ed. *The Flight of Ulysses: Essays in Memory of Emmanuel Hatzantonis.* Studi & Testi 1. Chapel Hill, NC: Annali d'italianistica, 1997. Pp. 360. Library of Congress Catal. Card No.: 97-72098. ISBN 0-9657956-0-8

Annali d'italianistica, Inc., Dey 141, UNC-CH,
Chapel Hill, NC 27599-3170 USA
Fax: (919) 962 5457; Web site: www.ibiblio.unc.edu/annali
Email: annali@unc.edu

Annali d'italianistica: AN INVITATION TO SUBSCRIBE

Volume 1 (1983), Pulci & Boiardo; 2 (1984), Guicciardini; 3 (1985), Manzoni; 4 (1986), Autobiography; 5 (1987), D'Annunzio; 6 (1988), Film & Literature; 7 (1989), Women's Voices in Italian Literature; 8 (1990), Dante and Modern American Criticism; 9 (1991), The Modern and the Postmodern; 10 (1992), Images of America & Columbus in Italian Literature; 11 (1993), Goldoni 1993; 12 (1994), The Italian Epic and Its International Context; 13 (1995), Italian Women Mystics; 14 (1996), Travel Literature; 15 (1997), Anthropology and Italian Literature; 17 (1999), New Landscapes in Contemporary Italian Cinema;

>   volume 18 (2000), Beginnings/Endings/Beginnings
>   volume 19 (2001), Literature, Criticism, and Ethics
>   volume 20 (2002), The Literature of Exile
>   volume 21 (2003), Hodoeporics Revisited
>   volume 22 (2004), Petrarch and the European Lyric Tradition
>   volume 23 (2005), Literature and Science
>   volume 25 (2006), Negotiating Italian Identities
>   volume 25 (2007), Literature, Religion, and the Sacred
>   volume 26 (2008), Humanisms, Posthumanisms, Neohumanisms
>   volume 27 (2009), A Century of Futurism: 1909-2009
>   volume 28 (2010), Capital City: Rome 1870-2010
>   volume 29 (2011), Italian Critical Theory
>   volume 30 (2012), Cinema italiano contemporaneo
>   volume 31 (2013), Boccaccio's *Decameron*:
>   Rewriting the ChristianMiddle Ages
>   Volume 32 (2014), From *Otium* & *Occupatio* to Work & Labor in Italian Culture

INDIVIDUALS
North America:
Subscription for print copy: $30; back issue: $41; Subscription for digital copy: $25
  Subscription for print copy and digital copy: $35; back issue $41
Outside North America:
Subscription for print copy: $45; back issue: $58; Subscription for print copy & digital copy: $50; back issue: $63
  Subscription for digital copy: $25

INSTITUTIONS
North America: Subscription for print copy: $45; back issue: $51
Outside North America: Subscription for print copy: $60; back issue: $73

AGENCIES
North America: Subscription for print copy: $40; back issue, $46
Outside North America: Subscription for print copy: $55; back issue: $68

PLEASE SEND YOUR SUBSCRIPTION, CHECK OR INTERNATIONAL MONEY order, payable to *Annali d'italianistica,* to:

Annali d'italianistica
Department of Romance Studies
The University of North Carolina at Chapel Hill
Chapel Hill, NC 27599-3170

Annali d'italianistica
Subscription Rates
2015

INDIVIDUALS

North America:

Subscription for print copy: $30; back issue: $41

Subscription for digital copy: $25

Subscription for print copy and digital copy: $35; back issue $41

Outside North America:

Subscription for print copy: $45; back issue: $58

Subscription for print copy & digital copy: $50; back issue: $63

Subscription for digital copy: $25

INSTITUTIONS

North America:

Subscription for print copy: $45; back issue: $51

Outside North America:

Subscription for print copy: $60; back issue: $73

AGENCIES

North America:

Subscription for print copy: $40; back issue, $46

Outside North America:

Subscription for print copy: $55; back issue: $68

PLEASE SEND YOUR SUBSCRIPTION, CHECK OR INTERNATIONAL MONEY ORDER, PAYABLE TO

ANNALI D'ITALIANISTICA
UNC-CH, CB# 3170, Dey Hall 141
Chapel Hill, NC 27599-3170, USA